Jesus and the Remains of His Day

Jesus and the Remains of His Day

Studies in Jesus and the Evidence of Material Culture

CRAIG A. EVANS

HENDRICKSON PUBLISHERS

Jesus and the Remains of His Day:
Studies in Jesus and the Evidence of Material Culture

P. O. Box 3473
Peabody, Massachusetts 01961-3473
www.hendrickson.com

ISBN 978-1-61970-705-4

Printed in the United States of America

First Printing—December 2015

Library of Congress Cataloging-in-Publication Data

Evans, Craig A.
Jesus and the remains of his day : studies in Jesus and the evidence of material culture / Craig A. Evans.
pages cm
Includes bibliographical references and index.
ISBN 978-1-61970-705-4 (alk. paper)
1. Bible. Gospels—Antiquities. 2. Jesus Christ—Historicity. I. Title.
BS621.E8855 2012
225.9'3—dc23

2015031660

For my daughter Jill

Contents

List of Figures

Foreword

The scholarly work of Craig A. Evans is well known. His books deal with the text of the Bible and biblical archaeology. He has published widely in these areas of study and his work is immensely important to scholars and informed readers with a professional or personal interest in Jesus and his times. Professor Evans' publications are always meticulously argued, vast in scope, rooted in scientific sources, and easy to read. *Jesus and the Remains of His Day* is the latest of his gifts to us, and it illustrates all these virtues of his sturdy scholarship.

It is crucial to biblical scholarship that researchers and writers are well versed in a number of different though related fields. To be a wise and honest interpreter of the Bible, one must be a master of the study of the biblical text itself. That text is the carrier of the messages that the sacred writings wish to express. Whether one is a devotee of biblical religion or an objective observer of biblical content and style, it is crucial to have the skill and training necessary to treat the text honestly and thoroughly, as with any literary material. The authors' intended messages and meanings must be set forth accurately, in their cultural contexts, as would be the case with the literary material of Shakespeare, Chaucer, Whitman, or Nietzsche, for example. That means that a biblical scholar must have years of study and experience in the areas of exegesis (exposition), hermeneutics (interpretation), the history of interpretation, and different standard methods of critical evaluation of the text of the Bible, which number from at least ten to fifteen. One must also understand the many points of view from which the Bible can be and has been studied.

Moreover, it is important that scholars engaged in biblical interpretation in the present day have not only mastered the text of the Bible but also have a rich knowledge of a number of fields that bear on the meaning of the words of the Jewish and Christian Scriptures. These numerous fields include ancient history, archaeology, literature, ancient languages related to or used in the Bible, the relationship of Qur'anic Studies to the Bible, and other domains that deal with a wide range of information about ancient cultures. *Jesus and the Remains of His Day* is the work of such a scholar. Professor Evans has published a great variety of studies that attest his signal ability to critique, comment upon, and lay out for our profit texts from nearly the entire Old and New Testaments in terms of the rich cultural context from which they arose and in which they were celebrated and preserved by the early church and rabbinic Judaism. The study offered in the present book is focused upon the way in which archaeology illumines, amplifies, and corrects the biblical writings—and makes them come alive.

A decade ago, an Israeli archaeologist from the Hebrew University in Jerusalem dug up a clay seal (*bulla*) in Jerusalem. Three years later, she discovered another, and the two were surprisingly related. The import of the two seals is that they spell out in detail that these two artifacts belonged to two men mentioned in the book of Jeremiah. These men were prophets who, according to Jeremiah 37, opposed Jeremiah's prophecy. This conflict between a true prophet and false prophets came at a critical time in Israelite history. Suddenly the narrative of Jeremiah came alive with "you are there" vividness. There has indeed been much scholarly controversy concerning the historical reliability of the book of Jeremiah over the years, but in my view this was largely laid to rest when the specific names and lineages of Gedaliah and Jehukal were found on the respective seals of these two men. This illustrates the exciting way in which archaeology can clarify the meaning or validate the historical reliability of a biblical text.

The field of biblical archaeology has developed over a number of centuries, but only in the past 150 to 200 years has it become a really scientific discipline. The field deals, of course, mostly with research in the lands of the Bible. *Jesus and the Remains of His Day* is a creative and appropriate title for a book that brings the biblical text and the material remains of the cultures of the biblical world into an illuminating interface. Professor Evans has spent a great deal of time in Israel, Palestine, Jordon, Syria, and Turkey mastering the world of archaeology and the published reports about it, as thoroughly as he has mastered the biblical text. This book is about the material remains of the cultures of Jesus' day that have been uncovered by archaeology. It centers on the region around the Sea of Galilee but ranges widely, including not only the sites of Bethsaida, Capernaum, and Migdal, but also Jerusalem, Qumran, and the Judean Desert, as well as other sites familiar from the Bible and the writings of Josephus, Philo, and Roman authors. Evans cites nearly all the relevant studies in archaeology and biblical interpretation of the last forty years related to the subjects with which he deals.

As a result, in *Jesus and the Remains of His Day* we have in hand a highly informed, carefully reasoned, extremely helpful, and enjoyably illumined and illuminating volume. We are greatly indebted to the author for his careful scholarship and his hearty enthusiasm for the integrity of biblical interpretation.

I am honored to have been asked to introduce this important volume, which will undoubtedly have a sustained life of service to professors, students, and laypersons for the next quarter century.

J. Harold Ellens
Professor, Ecumenical Theological Seminary
Detroit, Michigan

Preface

Jesus and the Remains of His Day is made up of ten studies that investigate recent advances and discoveries in archaeology in the land of Israel. In these studies, I am especially concerned to consider how the remains of material culture clarify aspects of the world of Jesus and his first followers. Houses, synagogues, a boat from Galilee, faunal remains, inscriptions, epitaphs, ossuaries, tombs, and the evidence of literacy are the principal material remains treated here.

The studies assembled in this book were made possible because of the opportunities I have had in recent years to visit Israel and a number of museums many times. Writing these studies was also made possible because of the collegial support of several archaeologists and experts in related fields, who generously gave of their time and knowledge. Among these are Rami Arav of the University of Nebraska at Omaha and Director of Excavations and Research for the Bethsaida Excavations Project. In 2013, Rami spent an entire day showing me and my graduate student Greg Monette the Bethsaida site and many recovered artifacts. He has been prompt and courteous in answering my queries. I deeply appreciate this. Richard Freund of the University of Hartford and Project Director and Corresponding Secretary of the Bethsaida Excavations Project has also been very helpful. Richard spent an afternoon showing us hundreds of artifacts recovered from the Bethsaida excavations now in storage in the basement of the Yigal Allon Museum in Ginosar. I am very grateful to Rami and Richard.

I extend thanks to Arfan Najar of the Israel Antiquities Authority, who, along with Dina Avshalom-Gorni and Marcela Zapata Meza of Mexico, has given supervision to the archaeological excavation at Magdala. In the summers of 2013 and 2014, I and my students were able to explore and observe the work at this important site. The explanations provided by Arfan and some of the members of the team from Mexico were very illuminating, including discussion of the remarkable ornamented stone found in the midst of the synagogue. In 2014, Byron McCane showed me and my students the excavation at Horvat Kur, also in Galilee and only a few minutes from Magdala. At Horvat Kur a fourth-century synagogue has been uncovered and a second ornamented stone, probably dating to the first century, has been found.

Thanks also go to Shimon Gibson of the University of North Carolina at Charlotte and the University of the Holy Land, who is the director of the Mount Zion archaeological excavation in Jerusalem. It has been a privilege for me and my graduate students to work alongside Shimon, his graduate students, and several volunteers at this important site. What has been uncovered in the 2013, 2014, and 2015 seasons is truly remarkable. On the same subject, thanks go to Thomas Davis of Southwestern

Baptist Theological Seminary, in Texas, who directs the Kourion excavation on the island of Cyprus. Besides having the pleasure of working with his team in a setting very different from that in Israel, in 2014 I was treated to several informative tours, including ones of Paphos and Kyrennia and of various Hellenistic tombs.

In 2013 and 2015, Israel Hershkovitz of the Department of Anatomy and Anthropology in the Sackler Faculty of Medicine of Tel Aviv University gave generously of his time and expertise, showing and discussing with us several artifacts relating to crucifixion. In 2013, Michael ("Miki") Sebanne, head of the Israel Antiquities Authority's Beth Shemesh Storage and Research Facility, permitted me and Greg Monette to spend several hours among the ossuaries and other archaeological treasures housed there. In 2013, Jerome Hall of the University of San Diego, in California, and curator of the Kinneret Boat, conserved and exhibited at the Yigal Allon Museum in Ginosar, pointed out several interesting features of the boat and took several photographs for us that otherwise would have been impossible. We are very grateful to him.

In 2014, Rachel Hachlili of the University of Haifa invited my graduate students and me into her home in Jerusalem and discussed with us her work on synagogues and Jewish burial traditions. We appreciate our time with her and her husband, Gad. In 2015, we also had the opportunity to visit the excavation at el-Maqatir, a few miles north of Jerusalem. Scott Stripling and his team were most accommodating. I extend a word of thanks to Jodi Magness and her team at Huqoq, who in 2015 showed us the synagogue that they are uncovering, along with its remarkable mosaics. I thank Itzhaq Shai and his team at Tel Burna, whose work at a difficult site is progressing well. Our visit in 2015 was very productive. I would be remiss if I did not also thank Seth Postell of the Israel College of the Bible in Natanya, whose hospitality in the summers of 2013, 2014, and 2015 has been very refreshing and who has helped defray some of the costs of these visits to Israel.

I have also benefited from the work of a number of scholars through correspondence. I am especially grateful to Ken Dark of the University of Reading, in the United Kingdom, for providing me with information relating to the excavations of the house beneath the Sisters of Nazareth Convent. I am grateful also to Jane Evans of the British Geological Survey for supplying me with very helpful information relating to decapitation and burial in antiquity. On matters concerning texts and artifacts relating to criminal trials, executions, and burial, I have received help through communications with John Granger Cook, Gunnar Samuelsson, and Eckhard Schnabel. Their recently published books on crucifixion in the Roman Empire in late antiquity have been enormously helpful.

I thank too my graduate students—especially Greg Monette (PhD candidate, Radboud University in Nijmegen)—for their assistance, including hauling around equipment and baggage and taking hundreds of high-quality photographs. And, finally, I extend my thanks to my Acadia TA Dwight Crowell, also one of the veterans of the Israel campaigns, for assisting with the indexes.

Craig A. Evans
Acadia Divinity College

Acknowledgments

The author acknowledges with gratitude permission received to republish all or portions of the following studies:

"A Fishing Boat, a House, and an Ossuary: What Can We Learn from the Artifacts?," in *The Missions of James, Peter, and Paul: Tensions in Early Christianity*, ed. Bruce D. Chilton and Craig A. Evans, NovTSup 115 (Leiden: Brill, 2005), 211–31, which appears, in revised form, as chapter 2.

"Excavating Caiaphas, Pilate, and Simon of Cyrene: Assessing the Literary and Archaeological Evidence," in *Jesus and Archaeology*, ed. James H. Charlesworth (Grand Rapids: Eerdmans, 2006), 323–40, which appears, in revised form, as chapter 3.

"Jewish Scripture and the Literacy of Jesus," in *From Biblical Criticism to Biblical Faith: Essays in Honor of Lee Martin McDonald*, ed. William H. Brackney and Craig A. Evans (Macon, GA: Mercer University Press, 2007), 41–54, which appears, in revised form, as chapter 4.

"Jesus and Psalm 91 in the Light of the Exorcism Scrolls," in *Celebrating the Dead Sea Scrolls: A Canadian Collection*, ed. Peter W. Flint, Jean Duhaime, and Kyung S. Baek, SBL Early Judaism and Its Literature 30 (Atlanta: Society of Biblical Literature, 2011), 541–55, which appears, in revised form, as chapter 5.

"Hanging and Crucifixion in Second Temple Israel: Deuteronomy 21:22–23 in the Light of Archaeology and the Dead Sea Scrolls," in *Qumran und die Archäologie: Texte und Kontexte*, ed. Jörg Frey, Carsten Claussen, and Nadine Kessler, WUNT 278 (Tübingen: Mohr Siebeck, 2011), 481–501, which appears, in revised form, as chapter 6.

"The Family Buried Together Stays Together: On the Burial of the Executed in Family Tombs," in *The World of Jesus and the Early Church: Identity and Interpretation in the Early Communities of Faith*, ed. Craig A. Evans (Peabody, MA: Hendrickson, 2011), 87–96, which appears, in revised form, as chapter 7.

"The Shout of Death," in C. A. Evans and N. T. Wright, *Jesus, the Final Days: What Really Happened*, ed. T. Miller (Louisville: Westminster John Knox, 2009; London: SPCK, 2008), 1–38, which appears, in revised form, as chapter 8.

Chapters 5 and 9 each reuse a small amount of material, with permission, from my book *Jesus and His World* (Louisville: Westminster John Knox, 2012).

In this book, translations of the biblical text are, unless otherwise marked, either the author's own or taken from, or based on, the RSV.

Quotations from the Dead Sea Scrolls are normally taken (sometimes with minor modifications) from M. Wise, M. Abegg, and E. Cook, *The Dead Sea Scrolls: A New Translation* (San Francisco: HarperSanFrancisco, 1996).

Quotations from Philo and Josephus are normally taken from the Loeb editions of these authors' works, though occasionally the author has used the translations of Whiston (Peabody, MA: Hendrickson, 1987), for Josephus, and Yonge (Peabody, MA: Hendrickson, 1993), for Philo. On still other occasions, the author has made his own translations of these authors' works.

Abbreviations

General Abbreviations

ad loc.	*ad locum,* at the place
BCE	before the Common Era
ca.	circa
CE	Common Era
cf.	compare
ch(s).	chapter(s)
col.	column
d.	died
ed(s).	edited by; editor(s); edition
Eng.	English
esp.	especially
et al.	*et alii*, and others
fig(s).	figure(s)
frag(s).	fragment(s)
Heb.	Hebrew
ibid.	*ibidem*, in the same place
idem	the same
LXX	Septuagint
no(s).	number(s)
OG	Old Greek
pace	contrary to the opinion of
repr.	reprinted
Targ.	Targum
trans.	translated by; translator
v(v).	verse(s)

Ancient Sources

Deuterocanonical Works

Tob	Tobit
Jdt	Judith
Wis	Wisdom of Solomon
Sir	Sirach

Bel	Bel and the Dragon
1 Macc	1 Maccabees
2 Macc	2 Maccabees
1 Esd	1 Esdras
4 Macc	4 Maccabees

Old Testament Pseudepigrapha

2 Bar.	*2 Baruch*
3 Bar.	*3 Baruch*
4 Bar.	*4 Baruch*
1 En.	*1 Enoch*
Jub.	*Jubilees*
Liv. Pro.	*Lives of the Prophets*
Rechabites	*History of the Rechabites*
T. Abr. A	*Testament of Abraham A*
T. Dan	*Testament of Dan*
T. Levi	*Testament of Levi*
T. Mos.	*Testament of Moses*
T. Sim.	*Testament of Simeon*
T. Sol.	*Testament of Solomon*
T. Zeb.	*Testament of Zebulun*

Josephus

Ag. Ap.	*Against Apion*
Ant.	*Jewish Antiquities*
J.W.	*Jewish War*
Life	*The Life*

Philo

Agriculture	*On Agriculture*
Dreams	*On Dreams*
Embassy	*On the Embassy to Gaius*
Flaccus	*Against Flaccus*
Flight	*On Flight and Finding*
Good Person	*That Every Good Person Is Free*
Joseph	*On the Life of Joseph*
Moses	*On the Life of Moses*
Posterity	*On the Posterity of Cain*
Spec. Laws	*On the Special Laws*

Dead Sea Scrolls

1QapGen	Genesis Apocryphon
1QH^{a}	Hodayot
1QpHab	Pesher Habakkuk

4QpNah (4Q169)	Pesher Nahum
4Q242	Prayer of Nabonidus
4Q243–4Q245	Vision of Daniel
4Q246	Apocryphon of Daniel
4Q282i	Unidentified fragment i
4Q285	Sefer Hemilh.amah
4Q385	Pseudo-Ezekiel[a]
4Q386	Pseudo-Ezekiel[b]
4Q521	Messianic Apocalypse
4Q552	Four Kingdoms[a]
4Q553	Four Kingdoms[b]
11Q5 (11QPs[a])	Psalms Scroll[a]
11Q11 (11QapocrPs, 11QPsAp[a])	Apocryphal Psalms[a]
11QT[a]	Temple Scroll[a]
CD	Cairo Genizah copy of the Damascus Document

Babylonian Talmud

b. Giṭ.	*Giṭṭin*
b. Ḥag.	*Ḥagigah*
b. Ḥul.	*Ḥullin*
b. Ketub.	*Ketubbot*
b. Meg.	*Megillah*
b. Moʿed Qaṭ.	*Moʿed Qaṭan*
b. Pesaḥ.	*Pesaḥim*
b. Qidd.	*Qiddušin*
b. Šabb.	*Šabbat*
b. Sanh.	*Sanhedrin*
b. Šebu.	*Šebuʿit*
b. Yebam.	*Yebamot*

Mishnah

m. B. Bat.	*Baba Batra*
m. Meg.	*Megillah*
m. Mid.	*Middot*
m. Moʿed Qaṭ.	*Moʿed Qaṭan*
m. Pesaḥ.	*Pesaḥim*
m. Taʿan.	*Taʿan*
m. Šabb.	*Šabbat*
m. Sanh.	*Sanhedrin*

Tosefta

t. B. Bat.	*Baba Batra*
t. Menaḥ.	*Menaḥot*

t. Qidd.	*Qiddušin*
t. Šabb.	*Šabbat*
t. Ter.	*Terumot*
t. Yebam.	*Yebamot*

Jerusalem Talmud

y. ʿErub.	*ʿErubin*
y. Ḥag.	*Ḥagigah*
y. Ketub.	*Ketubbot*
y. Meg.	*Megillah*
y. Moʿed Qaṭ.	*Moʿed Qaṭan*
y. Šabb.	*Šabbat*
y. Maʿaś.	*Maʿaśer Šeni*

Other Rabbinic Works

ʾAbot R. Nat.	*ʾAbot de Rabbi Nathan*
ʾAg. Ber.	*ʾAggadat Berešit*
Gen. Rab.	*Genesis Rabbah*
Exod. Rab.	*Exodus Rabbah*
Mek.	*Mekilta*
Midr. Jonah	*Midrash I Jonah*
Midr. Pss.	*Midrash I Psalms*
Midr. Tanḥ.	*Midrash I Tanḥuma*
Num. Rab.	*Numbers Rabbah*
Pesiq. Rab.	*Pesiqta Rabbati*
Pesiq. Rab Kah.	*Pesiqta de Rab Kahana*
Pirqe R. El.	*Pirqe Rabbi Eliezer*
Sem.	*Semaḥot*
Sipre Deut.	*Sipre Deuteronomy*
Sipre Num.	*Sipre Numbers*
Song Rab.	*Song of Songs Rabbah*
Sop.	*Soperim*
Tg. Neof.	*Targum Neofiti*

Apostolic Writings

1 Clem.	*1 Clement*
Barn.	*Barnabas*
Did.	*Didache*
Justin Martyr, *1 Apol.*	*First Apology*
Polycarp, *Phil.*	*To the Philippians*

Journals, Series, and Reference Works

AB	Anchor Bible (Commentary)
ABD	*Anchor Bible Dictionary*. Edited by D. N. Freedman. 6 vols. New York: Doubleday, 1992
ABRL	Anchor Bible Reference Library
ABW	*Archaeology in the Biblical World*
AE	*Année épigraphique*
Aev	*Aevum: Rassegna de scienze, storiche, linguistiche, e filologiche*
AGJU	Arbeiten zur Geschichte des antiken Judentums und des Urchristentums
AJ	*Antiquaries Journal*
AJA	*American Journal of Archaeology*
AJEC	Ancient Judaism and Early Christianity
ANRW	*Aufstieg und Niedergang der römischen Welt: Geschichte und Kultur Roms im Spiegel der neueren Forschung*. Part 2, *Principat*. Edited by W. Haase and H. Temporini. Berlin: de Gruyter, 1972–
ANTF	Arbeiten zur neutestamentlichen Textforschung
AOS	American Oriental Series
ArBib	The Aramaic Bible
ArOr	*Archív orientální*
ASOR	American Schools of Oriental Research
BA	*Biblical Archaeologist*
BAG	Bauer, W., W. F. Arndt, and F. W. Gingrich. *Greek-English Lexicon of the New Testament*. 2nd ed. Chicago: University of Chicago Press, 1957
BAIAS	*Bulletin of the Anglo-Israel Archeological Society*
BAR	*Biblical Archaeology Review*
BASOR	*Bulletin of the American Schools of Oriental Research*
BBR	*Bulletin for Biblical Research*
BCH	*Bulletin de correspondance hellénique*
BDB	Brown, F., S. R. Driver, and C. A. Briggs. *A Hebrew and English Lexicon of the Old Testament*
BE	*Bulletin épigraphique*
Bib	*Biblica*
BibInt	Biblical Interpretation Series
BK	*Bibel und Kirche*
BibOr	Biblica et Orientalia
BibSem	The Biblical Seminar
BMAP	*Brooklyn Museum Aramaic Papyri: New Documents of the Fifth Century B.C. from the Jewish Colony at Elephantine*. Edited by E. G. Kraeling. New Haven: Yale University Press, 1953
BN	*Biblische Notizen*
BRev	*Bible Review*

BZAW	Beihefte zur Zeitschrift für die alttestamentliche Wissenschaft
CahRB	Cahiers de la Revue biblique
CB	*Cultura Bíblica*
CBC	Cambridge Bible Commentary
CBQ	*Catholic Biblical Quarterly*
CBQMS	Catholic Biblical Quarterly Monograph Series
CEJL	Commentaries on Early Jewish Literature
CH	Calwer Hefte
CH	*Church History*
CIG	*Corpus Incriptionum Graecarum*. Edited by August Boeckh. 4 vols. Berlin, 1828–1877
CIIP	*Corpus Inscriptionum Iudaeae/Palaestinae. Volume 1, Jerusalem, Part 1: 1–704*. Edited by H. M. Cotton et al. Berlin: de Gruyter, 2010; *Volume 1, Jerusalem, Part 2: 705–1120*. Edited by H. M. Cotton et al. Berlin: de Gruyter, 2012; *Volume 2, Caesarea and the Middle Coast: 1121–2160*. Edited by W. Ameling et al. Berlin: de Gruyter, 2011
CIJ	*Corpus Inscriptionum Judaicarum*. Edited by J.-B. Frey. 2 vols. Rome: Pontifical Biblical Institute, 1936–1952
CIL	*Corpus Inscriptionum Latinarum*. Berlin, 1862–
CIS	Copenhagen International Studies
CLE	*Carmina Latina Epigraphica*. Edited by F. Bücheler. 2 vols. Leipzig: Teubner, 1895–1897
Corinth	*Corinth: Results of Excavations Conducted by the American School of Classical Studies at Athens*. Edited by B. D. Merritt. Vol. 8, part 1, *Greek Inscriptions*. Cambridge: Harvard University Press, 1931
CPJ	*Corpus Papyrorum Judaicarum*. Edited by V. A. Tcherikover. 3 vols. Cambridge: Harvard University Press, 1957–1964
CPL	*Corpus Papyrorum Latinarum*
CRINT	Compendia Rerum Iudaicarum ad Novum Testamentum
DDD	*Dictionary of Deities and Demons in the Bible*. Edited by K. van der Toorn, B. Becking, and P. W. van der Horst. 2nd rev. ed. Grand Rapids: Eerdmans, 1999
DJD	Discoveries in the Judaean Desert
DJG	*Dictionary of Jesus and the Gospels*. Edited by Joel B. Green, Jeannine K. Brown, and Nicholas Perrin. 2nd ed. Downers Grove, IL: InterVarsity Press, 2013
DMOA	Documenta et Monumenta Orientis Antiqui
DSD	*Dead Sea Discoveries*
ECL	Early Christianity and Its Literature
Ebib	*Études bibliques*
EDSS	*Encyclopedia of the Dead Sea Scrolls*. Edited by L. H. Schiffman and J. C. VanderKam. 2 vols. Oxford: Oxford University Press, 2000
EG	*Epigrammata Graeca*. Edited by G. Kaibel. Berlin: G. Reimer, 1878

ErIsr	*Eretz-Israel*
EstBib	*Estudios Bíblicos*
FBBS	Facet Books, Biblical Series
GD	Gorgias Dissertations
GNS	*Good News Studies*
Greg	*Gregorianum*
HNT	Handbuch zum Neuen Testament
HOS	Handbook of Oriental Studies
HTR	*Harvard Theological Review*
HTS	Harvard Theological Studies
HUCA	*Hebrew Union College Annual*
IAA	Israel Antiquities Authority
ICC	International Critical Commentary
IEJ	*Israel Exploration Journal*
IG	*Inscriptiones Graecae. Editio minor.* Berlin: de Gruyter, 1924–
JA	*Journal Asiatique*
JAOS	*Journal of the American Oriental Society*
JBL	*Journal of Biblical Literature*
JEH	*Journal of Ecclesiastical History*
JJS	*Journal of Jewish Studies*
JPOS	*Journal of the Palestinian Oriental Society*
JRA	*Journal of Roman Archaeology*
JRS	*Journal of Roman Studies*
JSHJ	*Journal for the Study of the Historical Jesus*
JSHRZ	Jüdische Schriften aus hellenistisch-römischer Zeit
JSJ	*Journal for the Study of Judaism in the Persian, Hellenistic and Roman Periods*
JSJSup	*Journal for the Study of Judaism in the Persian, Hellenistic and Roman Periods*, Supplements
JSNT	*Journal for the Study of the New Testament*
JSNTSup	Journal for the Study of the New Testament Supplement Series
JSOT	*Journal for the Study of the Old Testament*
JSOTSup	Journal for the Study of the Old Testament Supplement Series
JSPSup	Journal for the Study of the Pseudepigrapha Supplement Series
JSS	*Journal of Semitic Studies*
JTSA	*Journal of Theology for South Africa*
LASBF	*Liber Annuus Studii Biblici Franciscani*
LCL	Loeb Classical Library
LSJ	Liddell, H. G., R. Scott, H. S. Jones. *A Greek-English Lexicon.* 9th ed. with revised supplement. Oxford: Clarendon, 1996
LSTS	The Library of Second Temple Studies
MAMA	*Monumenta Asiae Minoris Antiqua.* Manchester and London, 1928–1993
MdB	*Le Monde de la Bible*
NEA	*Near Eastern Archaeology*

NEAEHL	*The New Encyclopedia of Archaeological Excavations in the Holy Land*. Edited by E. Stern. 4 vols. Jerusalem: Israel Exploration Society, 1993; vol. 5, *Supplementary Volume*. Jerusalem: Israel Exploration Society, 2008
NEB	New English Bible
Neot	*Neotestamentica*
NETS	New English Translation of the Septuagint
NewDocs	*New Documents Illustrating Early Christianity*. Edited by G. H. R. Horsley and S. Llewelyn. North Ryde, NSW: The Ancient History Documentary Research Centre, Macquarie University, 1981–
NICNT	New International Commentary on the New Testament
NICOT	New International Commentary on the Old Testament
NIGTC	New International Greek Testament Commentary
NovT	*Novum Testamentum*
NovTSup	Supplements to Novum Testamentum
NRSV	*New Revised Standard Version*
NTL	New Testament Library
NTM	New Testament Message
NTOA	Novum Testamentum et Orbis Antiquus
NTS	*New Testament Studies*
NTTS	New Testament Tools and Studies
OCP	*Orientalia Christiana Periodica*
OGIS	*Orientis Graeci Inscriptiones Selectae*. Edited by W. Dittenberger. 2 vols. Leipzig: Hirzel, 1903–1905
OIS	Oriental Institute Seminars
OP	Oxyrhynchus Papyri. London: Egypt Exploration Society, 1898–
Or	*Orientalia* (NS)
OTL	Old Testament Library
PEFQS	Palestine Exploration Fund Quarterly Statement
PEQ	*Palestine Exploration Quarterly*
PG	Patrologia graeca. Edited by J.-P. Migne. 162 vols. Paris, 1857–1886
PGM	*Papyri Graecae Magicae: Die griechischen Zauberpapyri*. Edited by K. Preisendanz. 2nd ed. Stuttgart: Teubner, 1973–1974
PNTC	The Pillar New Testament Commentary
PSBF	Publications of the Studium Biblicum Franciscanum
PSI	*Pubblicazioni della Società italiana per la ricerca dei papiri greci e latini in Egitto*. Edited by G. Vitelli et al. 15 vols. Florence: E. Ariani, 1912–1979
PTSDSSP	Princeton Theological Seminary Dead Sea Scrolls Project
QDAP	*Quarterly of the Department of Antiquities in Palestine*
RAr	*Revue archéologique*
RB	*Revue biblique*
REA	*Revue des études anciennes*
REG	*Revue des études grecques*
RevQ	*Revue de Qumran*

RGM	*Wissenschaftliche Kataloge des Römisch-Germanischen Museums Köln.* Cologne: Römisch-Germanischen Museum, 1975
RILP	Roehampton Institute London Papers
RSN	*Religious Studies News*
SAIS	Studies in the Aramaic Interpretation of Scripture
SBA	Studies in Biblical Archaeology
SBFCMa	Studium Biblicum Franciscanum, Collectio major
SBFCMi	Studium Biblicum Francescanum, Collectio minor
SBL	Society of Biblical Literature
SBLDS	Society of Biblical Literature Dissertation Series
SBLRBS	Society of Biblical Literature Resources for Biblical Study
SBLSBS	Society of Biblical Literature Sources for Biblical Study
SBLSP	Society of Biblical Literature Seminar Papers
SEG	Supplementum epigraphicum graecum
SFSHJ	South Florida Studies in the History of Judaism
SJLA	Studies in Judaism in Late Antiquity
SNTSMS	Society for New Testament Studies Monograph Series
SP	*Studia Pontica.* 3 vols. Brussels: Lamertin, 1910
SSEJC	Studies in Scripture in Early Judaism and Christianity
STAC	Studien und Texte zu Antike und Christentum
STDJ	Studies on the Texts of the Desert of Judah
StPB	Studia Post-biblica
Syr	*Syria*
TAM	*Tituli Asiae Minoris.* Vienna: Hoelderi, 1920–
TDNT	*Theological Dictionary of the New Testament.* Edited by G. Kittel and G. Friedrich. Translated by G. W. Bromiley. 10 vols. Grand Rapids: Eerdmans, 1964–1974
TENTS	Texts and Editions for New Testament Study
TS	Texts and Studies
TS	*Theological Studies*
TSAJ	Texte und Studien zum antiken Judentum
TWOT	*Theological Wordbook of the Old Testament.* Edited by R. L. Harris, G. L. Archer Jr., and B. K. Waltke. 2 vols. Chicago: Moody Press, 1980
USFSHJ	University of South Florida Studies in the History of Judaism
VTSup	Supplements to Vetus Testamentum
WBC	Word Biblical Commentary
WUB	*Welt und Umwelt der Bibel*
WUNT	Wissenschaftliche Untersuchungen zum Neuen Testament
YJS	Yale Judaica Series
ZDPV	*Zeitschrift des deutschen Palästina-Vereins*
ZTK	*Zeitschrift für Theologie und Kirche*

Introduction

The principal concern of archaeology is the recovery and interpretation of the remains of material culture. Of course, the interpretation of these remains is greatly facilitated by the writings that have survived from antiquity. The physical remains and the literary texts clarify one another. The authors of a book on archaeology, one a biblical scholar and one an archaeologist, expressed this mutuality well:

> Words talk. Stones talk too. Neither talks from the past without interpretive dialogue with the present. But each talks and each demands to be heard in its own way. Only after archaeology and exegesis each get their own full voice should they come together in doubled chorus and common report.[1]

Less poetically, perhaps, but every bit as incisively, Ronald Hendel has stated: "Biblical archaeology involves the rigorous correlation of textual data from the Bible and material evidence from archaeology."[2] Hendel is quite correct. If there were no correlation, then there would be no discipline called "biblical archaeology." The studies in this book are very much concerned with this correlation of textual data and material evidence.

Archaeology has matured much in the last half century or so. Part of this is due to the great advances in technology that permit archaeologists to acquire and record data that their predecessors could not have imagined. But part of this maturation is due to changes in thinking and method. Today archaeologists are much more concerned with the bigger picture, the fuller context. Knowing well the lay of the land, the routes of travel, the way the ancients built, the food they ate, the clothes and shoes they wore, the records they kept, how they worshipped, how they viewed one another, and the like are the kinds of things with which archaeologists are now concerned. We don't ask if we can find this or prove that.

Of course, along the way archaeologists ask how certain finds might clarify certain texts. But not too many any more undertake archaeology to "prove" something. The discipline frowns on this approach. The intent instead is to collect and record the data, to do as little damage as possible to the site and to the artifacts that are recovered, and to be as fair as possible to the interpretation of what is exposed and recovered. The goal is to be open, to present findings to the public (expert and non-expert alike), and to receive criticism and make revisions accordingly. The

1. J. D. Crossan and J. L. Reed, *Excavating Jesus: Beneath the Stones, Behind the Texts* (San Francisco: HarperSanFrancisco, 2001), xv.

2. R. S. Hendel, "Giants at Jericho," *BAR* 35, no. 2 (2009): 20, 66 (quotation from p. 20).

task of archaeology is a collegial one, with scholars assisting one another, and with student volunteers (and seniors too!) making much of the actual work of excavation possible. It is also important not to overinterpret the finds. Oftentimes we just don't know how old something is or who made it or what it signifies.

A number of the studies published in this book have appeared in briefer form in other venues in the last decade or so. I have taken the opportunity to revise and expand. In a few cases, I have changed my mind (as in reference to the Caiaphas ossuary) or made corrections in light of clarifications and updates (as in reference to the remains recovered from the Abba Tomb). Three of the studies make their first appearance in this volume.

Chapter 1 focuses on the recent archaeological work at Bethsaida and Magdala. The first is located two kilometers north of the north shore of the Sea of Galilee. The second is located on the northwest shore of the lake. The identifications of both sites are disputed, but their antiquity is not. The light that the work at Bethsaida may shed on Peter, Andrew, and Philip, three disciples who came from the city, is potentially quite significant. What light "Magdala" may shed on Mary Magdalene is much in question, but the debate does open up a very interesting line of inquiry.

Chapter 2 looks at two specific artifacts—a boat and an ossuary—and a house. The boat helps us understand aspects of maritime life in Galilee, while the ossuary, which bears the inscription "James, son of Joseph, brother of Jesus," may have relevance for understanding the context of the leader of the Christian church in Jerusalem by this name. The house, which is located in Capernaum, may tell us something about the activities of Jesus and Peter in the city that apparently served as the headquarters of the Jesus movement. Discussion of the Capernaum house provides the occasion for considering the first-century houses in Nazareth some think may be related to Jesus.

Chapter 3 looks at three specific artifacts: one relates to the high priest Caiaphas, another to the Roman prefect Pontius Pilate (almost certainly), and the third may relate to Simon of Cyrene, who helped Jesus carry his cross. All three figures played roles in the death of Jesus. Comparison of these artifacts (two ossuaries and a dedication inscription on stone) illustrates what often is involved in making direct links between archaeological discoveries and persons mentioned in ancient literature.

Chapter 4 considers the question of the literacy of Jesus. By itself, the question is very difficult to address, for there is simply very little evidence—perhaps none—that directly bears on the question. The approach I take is to consider all of the evidence for literacy in the Roman Empire of late antiquity, ranging from Vindolanda, in Roman Britain, in the northwest, to Mons Claudianus, in Roman Egypt, in the southeast, and everything between. What we shall find is that the evidence for literacy is quite substantial. What will surprise some is the extent of the evidence that suggests that many of the uneducated were also literate.

Chapter 5 looks at a specific text, Ps 91, and explores how this psalm was understood in Jewish and Christian late antiquity. The text is important not only because it makes its appearance in the temptation narratives of Matthew and Luke but also because Jesus himself alludes to it in his teaching. In the New Testament Gospels,

Ps 91 is clearly understood as having something to do with Satan and evil spirits. We shall find that this interpretation was widespread, being attested not only in surviving literature (such as a scroll of psalms found at Qumran) but in a number of artifacts as well.

Chapter 6 investigates the archaeology of crucifixion as it was practiced in the Hasmonean and Roman periods. Of special importance is Deut 21:22–23. Not only did this text influence judicial practice in Israel in late antiquity but its interpretation was itself influenced by the practice of crucifixion. We shall take special interest in art, including crude graffiti, that depicts crucifixion. We shall also take into account the physical remains of archaeology. Readers may find aspects of some of this evidence somewhat gruesome. Here I have in mind the evidence of the iron nails and spikes that were used in crucifixion and their strange later usage.

Chapter 7 explores further the archaeological evidence relating to crucifixion and execution by other means. Of special interest here are the laws and customs relating to the burial of the executed and the expectation that eventually their remains would be interred in the family tomb. Like the previous chapter, this one will touch on macabre beliefs and practices relating to crucifixion nails and skeletal remains.

Chapter 8 narrows the discussion to the death and burial of Jesus of Nazareth. The two previous chapters provide the background and context for this one, which deals with some of the specific questions that arise in interpreting the New Testament Gospels' respective passion narratives. We shall consider aspects of the mockery of Jesus and the much debated "Passover pardon," including the potential relevance of Roman law as preserved in Justinian's *Digesta*.

Chapter 9 speaks to an overlooked feature in the debate surrounding the tomb in East Talpiot, Jerusalem, that a maker of documentaries in recent years has claimed is probably the tomb of Jesus and his family. The chapter focuses on tomb art and architecture and shows that the Talpiot tomb's façade strongly argues against any identification with Jesus, his family, and his movement. The study will also take into account the second Talpiot tomb and the extravagant claims regarding the inscription and artwork on two of the ossuaries found in it.

Chapter 10, this book's last study, reviews pagan, Jewish, and Christian epitaphs and burial art and considers what these artifacts tell us about beliefs and fears in late antiquity. What we shall find is that it was believed that, in a sense, the dead could talk, offering advice, warnings, and consolation to the living. The differing views concerning the afterlife are fascinating. The concern with memory provides a context for understanding an important nuance in the Words of Institution. This chapter will also look at beliefs concerning the spirits of the departed and the importance of placating them in order to avoid hauntings and harm.

In the Preface, I expressed gratitude to a number of people who provided me with assistance, in correspondence and in person. Here I would like to mention several important publications that I found especially helpful in writing this book. First and foremost are Rachel Hachlili's *Jewish Funerary Customs, Practices, and Rites in the Second Temple Period* (2005) and *Ancient Synagogues—Archaeology and Art: New Discoveries and Current Research* (2013). These magisterial volumes are indispensable, providing texts, descriptions, plates (some of them in color), and very current bibliography. The sourcebook compiled by Anders Runesson, Donald Binder, and Birger Olsson, *The Ancient Synagogue from Its Origins to 200 C.E.* (2010), is very concise and goes hand in hand with Hachlili's work. Tal Ilan's *Lexicon of Jewish Names in Late Antiquity* (2002) is another resource that is enormously helpful. Tracking down various names, in various languages, and their various spellings and contexts is greatly facilitated by this work.

Another resource of great value is the *Corpus Inscriptionum Iudaeae/Palaestinae* (*CIIP*), whose two volumes, edited by Hannah Cotton and her colleagues, appeared (in three parts) in 2010–12. These volumes provide texts, bibliography, and images. Related is Levi Rahmani's indispensable *A Catalogue of Jewish Ossuaries in the Collections of the State of Israel* (1994). Although dated, the work remains very valuable. One hopes that it will be updated in the not-too-distant future.

Three general reference works that I found very helpful in my research are *The Oxford Encyclopedia of Archaeology in the Near East* (5 vols., 1997), edited by Eric Meyers; *Alexander to Constantine: Archaeology of the Land of the Bible*, volume 3 (2012), edited by Eric Meyers and Mark Chancey; and *The New Encyclopedia of Archaeological Excavations in the Holy Land* (4 vols., 1993, plus supplement volume, 2008), edited by Ephraim Stern.

And finally, I need to mention two more very useful books. *Jesus and Archaeology* (2006), edited by James Charlesworth, is a rich collection of learned and stimulating studies. Shimon Gibson's *The Final Days of Jesus: The Archaeological Evidence* (2009) is a fine example of how to bring the textual and archaeological evidence together. Without works such as these, it would not have been possible to write the studies in the present book.

CHAPTER ONE

A Tale of Two Cities: What We Have Learned from Bethsaida and Magdala

When, a quarter century ago, Sherman Johnson (1908–1993) published his popular book *Jesus and His Towns*, he had little to say about Bethsaida and Magdala.[1] Were he able to revise his book today, he would have a great deal more to say. This is so thanks to some very productive archaeological work, some of it quite recent.

The present chapter evaluates the recent discoveries at Bethsaida and Magdala. Both cities were important in the public activities of Jesus, and some of the most prominent followers of Jesus came from these two cities. New and important data continue to emerge from the ongoing archaeological excavations at these Galilean sites. Excavation has been underway at Bethsaida for just over a quarter of a century, and at Magdala for about five years.[2] The excavations at both sites are still in progress, so one cannot speak of final results. Nevertheless, the finds in recent years are quite suggestive and do advance the field of New Testament studies, even if only in a preliminary way.

Bethsaida: The Village of Peter, Andrew, and Philip

In a study published a decade ago, New Testament scholar Markus Bockmuehl drew attention to Oscar Cullmann's sweeping conclusion regarding the significance of Bethsaida, Simon Peter's hometown, for understanding the most prominent member of Jesus' closest disciples and followers.[3] Cullmann had suggested that,

1. S. E. Johnson, *Jesus and His Towns* (GNS 29, Wilmington, DE: Glazier, 1989). Johnson devotes four pages to Magdala (pp. 47–51) and three to Bethsaida (pp. 74–77). Much of what he says is out of date and in some cases it is contradicted by the new data.

2. In the summers of 2013, 2014, and 2015, I and a few of my graduate students were able to visit these sites and were favored by onsite tours and explanations given by the respective archaeologists, Rami Arav of Bethsaida and Arfan Najar of Magdala. We owe a debt of gratitude to these colleagues and take the opportunity here to express our thanks.

3. M. N. A. Bockmuehl, "Simon Peter and Bethsaida," in *The Missions of James, Peter, and Paul: Tensions in Early Christianity* (ed. B. D. Chilton and C. A. Evans; NovTSup 115; Leiden: Brill, 2005), 53–90.

by growing up in Bethsaida, a cosmopolitan city where many Gentiles lived, Peter would have been prepared for his later ministry, which eventually would take him to Rome, the capital city of the empire.[4] Growing up in Bethsaida, says Cullman, explains why "Peter champions a universalistic point of view and . . . is not too far removed from Paul in his theology."[5] It is this claim that serves as Bockmuehl's point of departure in what I think is to date the most insightful application of the archaeological work at Bethsaida to Simon Peter. To a great extent, Bockmuehl's fine study, along with the more up-to-date archaeological assessment by Heinz-Wolfgang Kuhn,[6] will serve as this chapter's point of departure.

Thanks to the work that was launched in the late 1980s by Rami Arav and his colleagues, scholarly literature concerned with Bethsaida has grown exponentially. Pride of place goes to the four volumes edited by Arav and Richard Freund, which appeared between 1995 and 2009.[7] In addition to these volumes, a number of other important studies and collections of studies have been produced by scholars and archaeologists who have participated in the excavations at Bethsaida.[8] Not surprisingly, several studies have focused primarily on the implications of the archaeological findings for understanding Jesus and his movement.[9]

---

4. O. Cullmann, *Peter: Disciple, Apostle, Martyr. A Historical and Theological Study* (trans. F. V. Filson; 2nd ed.; London: SCM, 1962). The original German edition appeared in 1952.

5. Cullmann, *Peter: Disciple, Apostle, Martyr*, 24; cited by Bockmuehl, "Simon Peter and Bethsaida," 53.

6. H.-W. Kuhn, "Did Jesus Stay at Bethsaida? Arguments from Ancient Texts and Archaeology for Bethsaida and Et-Tell," in *Handbook for the Study of the Historical Jesus* (ed. T. Holmén and S. E. Porter; Leiden: Brill, 2011), 4:2973–3021.

7. R. Arav and R. A. Freund, eds., *Bethsaida: A City by the North Shore of the Sea of Galilee* (4 vols.; Kirksville, MO: Truman State University Press, 1995–2009). Additional studies by Arav include H.-W. Kuhn and R. Arav, "The Bethsaida Excavations: Historical and Archaeological Approaches," in *The Future of Early Christianity: Essays in Honor of Helmut Koester* (ed. B. A. Pearson; Minneapolis: Fortress, 1991), 77–106; R. Arav, "New Testament Archaeology and the Case of Bethsaida," in *Das Ende der Tage und die Gegenwart des Heils: Begegnungen mit dem Neuen Testament und seiner Umwelt. Festschrift für Heinz-Wolfgang Kuhn zum 65. Geburtstag* (ed. M. Becker and W. Fenske; AGJU 44; Leiden: Brill, 1999), 75–99; idem, "Bethsaida, 2000," *IEJ* 51 (2001): 239–46; idem, "Betsaida—Geschichte und materielle Kultur einer Stadt im Königreich Geschirr," in *Leben am See Gennesaret: Kulturgeschichtliche Entdeckungen in einer biblischen Region* (ed. G. Fassbeck; Mainz: von Zabern, 2003), 52–65; idem, "Bethsaida," in *Jesus and Archaeology* (ed. J. H. Charlesworth; Grand Rapids: Eerdmans, 2006), 145–66; and idem, "The Archaeology of Bethsaida and the Historical Jesus Quest," in *The Archaeology of Difference: Gender, Ethnicity, Class and the "Other" in Antiquity. Studies in Honor of Eric M. Meyers* (ed. D. R. Edwards and C. T. McCollough; Boston: ASOR, 2007), 317–31.

8. C. E. Savage, *Biblical Bethsaida: An Archaeological Study of the First Century* (Lanham, MD: Lexington Books, 2011); J. H. Ellens, ed., *Bethsaida in Archaeology, History and Ancient Culture: A Festschrift in Honor of John T. Greene* (Newcastle upon Tyne: Cambridge Scholars, 2014); and H.-W. Kuhn, ed., *Betsaida/Bethsaida – Julias (et-Tell): Die ersten 25 Jahre der Ausgrabung (1987–2011)—The First Twenty-Five Years of Excavation (1987–2011)* (NTOA, Series Archaeologica 4; Göttingen: Vandenhoeck & Ruprecht, 2014).

9. J. J. Rousseau, "The Impact of the Bethsaida Finds on Our Knowledge of the Historical Jesus," in *Society of Biblical Literature 1995 Seminar Papers* (ed. E. H. Lovering Jr.;

The importance of Bethsaida for Jesus research lies in the fact that three of the twelve disciples are said to be from Bethsaida, that Jesus alludes to a number of mighty works performed in that city, and that two noteworthy miracles (the feeding of the five thousand and the healing of a blind man) are remembered to have taken place in Bethsaida. Of these three elements, the first two have good claim to authenticity, the third less so.

First, the claim that Peter, his brother Andrew, and Philip were in fact from Bethsaida has a reasonable claim to authenticity, even though the evidence for this comes not from the earlier Synoptic Gospels but from the Fourth Gospel: "Now Philip was from Bethsaida, the city of Andrew and Peter" (John 1:44; cf. 12:21). There really are no compelling grounds for regarding this tradition as fictive, for it is hard to see why the city of Bethsaida would have been picked out of the hat, so to speak. For one thing, there was nothing special about this city (which is sometimes called a village) and, for another, the villages and cities from which the other disciples come seem to be of little interest in the tradition. So, what makes Bethsaida important?

There is a third reason for suspecting that the Bethsaida tradition is authentic. The headquarters of the Jesus movement apparently was at Capernaum, and it is there that Peter's mother-in-law lived, and it was in her house that Peter and Jesus apparently resided. If early Christians had no idea where Peter was from, then surely Capernaum, not Bethsaida, would have been the city of choice. Indeed, the archaeology of Capernaum's "House of Peter" shows that in the first century this private residence was transformed into a gathering place or church, which indicates that first-century followers of Jesus believed this was the very house mentioned in the Gospels (e.g., Mark 1:29–31); and it may well have been.[10] One would think a first-century focus on a house believed to have been the very one in which Jesus and Peter lived would have encouraged early Christians to speak of Peter and Andrew as from *Capernaum*, not Bethsaida, had their hometown not been known. That early Christians spoke of Bethsaida rather than the more prominently featured Capernaum speaks in favor of the Bethsaida origins of these disciples. Moreover, Bethsaida was not actually in Galilee but in Gaulanitis (just to the east of the Jordan River), so why identify Galilean disciples with a non-Galilean city?

The second tradition that has good claim to authenticity is seen in the woes that Jesus pronounced against Bethsaida and other cities:

> Woe to you, Chorazin! Woe to you, Bethsaida! For if the mighty works done in you had been done in Tyre and Sidon, they would have repented long ago, sitting in sackcloth and ashes. But it shall be more tolerable in the judgment for Tyre and Sidon than for you. And you, Capernaum, will you be exalted to heaven? You shall be brought down to Hades. (Luke 10:13–15)

SBLSP 34; Atlanta: Scholars Press, 1995), 187–207; and J. J. Rousseau and R. Arav, *Jesus and His World: An Archaeological and Cultural Dictionary* (Minneapolis: Fortress, 1995), 19–24.

10. For discussion of the archaeological evidence, see V. C. Corbo, *The House of St. Peter at Capharnaum: A Preliminary Report of the First Two Campaigns of Excavations, April 16–June 19, Sept. 12–Nov. 26, 1968* (trans. S. Saller; SBFCMi 5; Jerusalem: Franciscan Printing Press, 1969); J. F. Strange and H. Shanks, "Has the House Where Jesus Stayed in Capernaum Been Found?," *BAR* 8, no. 6 (1982), 26–37. The matter is pursued in ch. 2 below.

Given how the evangelists emphasize the success of Jesus' ministry of healing and exorcism, including the responses of the large crowds that react in enthusiasm and follow him (e.g., Matt 4:23–25; 8:1; Mark 1:32–33; 4:1; 5:14, 24; Luke 4:42–44), it is hard to see how these woes would have been invented had Jesus said nothing like them. Would early tradents invent such words of judgment directed against Bethsaida, the hometown of three prominent disciples, or against Capernaum, the very headquarters of Jesus and his movement? This seems unlikely. The woes are best understood as authentic utterances.

Another reason scholars are inclined to accept the authenticity of these woes is that there appears to be a Hebrew/Aramaic wordplay involving Bethsaida (בית ציידאן) and Sidon (צידון) based on the fact that the word "catching (fish)" is pronounced almost the same way as "Sidon." In other words, Bethsaida, the "house of catching [*ṣêdāʾ*] (fish)," has more in common, Jesus implies, with *Sidon*, the well-known wicked city against which the prophets of old often spoke (e.g., Isa 23:2–12; Jer 25:12–31; 27:1–11; 47:1–7; Ezek 28:20–24). A play on words such as this does not prove that the woe derives from Jesus, but it does speak in favor of its antiquity, and it is consistent with the style of Jesus, in which we find alliteration and plays on words.[11]

In addition, Bethsaida appears three times loosely linked to miracles, two of them quite notable. The first time is in the context of the feeding of the five thousand (Mark 6:35–44). After the miracle, according to Mark, Jesus sends his disciples away in their boat to Bethsaida, while he dismisses the crowd and then ascends a hill to pray (Mark 6:45–46). Matthew retains the sending away but omits reference to Bethsaida (Matt 14:22–23), while Luke omits the dismissal altogether (Luke 9:18). Bethsaida appears again in Mark, this time as the place where Jesus heals the blind man in two stages (Mark 8:22–26). Both Matthew and Luke omit the story. And finally, Bethsaida appears in Luke 9:10, after the disciples have returned from their preaching tour (Luke 9:1–6) and after the brief report of Herod Antipas fearing that Jesus could be John the Baptist raised from the dead (Luke 9:7–9). It is there, at Bethsaida, that Jesus is said to have "cured those who had need of healing" (Luke 9:11).

Mark Appold defends the authenticity of the Bethsaida linkage to these stories. He believes they are part of an old Bethsaida tradition. The miracles are examples of the "mighty works" (αἱ δυνάμεις) that Jesus performed in and around Bethsaida, which, in the opinion of Jesus, should have led to repentance but did not.[12] Kuhn, on the other hand, believes these references to Bethsaida are late and secondary.[13]

11. Perhaps one of the best-known examples is the word of criticism directed against the hypocrisy of the Pharisees, who are in the habit of "straining out a gnat [*qalmāʾ*] and swallowing a camel [*gamlāʾ*]!" (Matt 23:24). I should mention that Jesus' summons of Peter and Andrew to become "fishers of men" (Mark 1:17; Matt 4:19; cf. Luke 5:10, "you will be catching men") could allude to their hometown, Bethsaida ("house of catching [fish]"), as well as to their actual profession.

12. M. Appold, "The Mighty Works of Bethsaida: Witness of the New Testament and Related Traditions," in *Bethsaida: A City by the North Shore of the Sea of Galilee* (ed. R. Arav and R. A. Freund; 4 vols.; Kirksville, MO: Truman State University Press, 1995–2009), 1:229–42.

13. H.-W. Kuhn, "Bethsaida in the Gospel of Mark," in *Bethsaida: A City by the North Shore of the Sea of Galilee* (ed. R. Arav and R. A. Freund; 4 vols.; Kirksville, MO: Truman State University Press, 1995–2009), 3:115–31.

He does, however, accept the authenticity of the woe sayings, including the woe uttered against Bethsaida.[14] Whichever position we take, the woe pronounced against Bethsaida clearly implies that Jesus performed mighty works in that city, works that should have occasioned repentance.[15] Shortly, we shall inquire into the lack of faith on the part of the people of Bethsaida, despite their witnessing these works of power.

As has been noted, the Gospel of John explicitly states that Peter, Andrew, and Philip were from Bethsaida. One of the first things we notice is their names—all three of them are Greek. This fact may say something about the cultural and linguistic complexity of Bethsaida and at the same time something about Jewish life in that city. It will be helpful to review what we know of these names from late antiquity, as well as the tradition that Peter received his name from Jesus.

(1) *Simon Peter* (Σίμων Πέτρος). Simon is a biblical name, deriving from שִׁמְעוֹן (*šimʿôn*, though usually transliterated into English as Simeon; cf. Gen 29:33), the name of one of the patriarchs and a name popular in the Hasmonean period (160–40 BCE). Tal Ilan identifies more than 250 Jewish men in late antiquity who bore this name.[16] It is sometimes written שמון (*šmwn*) or סמון (*smwn*), probably under the influence of the shorter, simpler Greek transliteration Σίμων (*Simōn*), which was also written Συμεών (*Symeōn*). The Greek form Simon (Σίμων) occurs on several ossuaries.[17] Greek examples from ossuaries include "Sarah, (daughter) of Simon of Ptolemais,"[18] "Mathia and Simon, brothers, sons of Yaʿir; masters of the tomb,"[19] "(Ossuary) of Simon, age 41,"[20] and "Alexa Mara, mother of Judas Simon, her son."[21]

The Greek form Συμεών appears many times in the LXX (e.g., Gen 29:33; 34:14; Exod 1:2; 6:15), Josephus (e.g., *J.W.* 4.159: "Symeon, son of Gamaliel"; cf. *Life* 190: "Simon, son of Gamaliel"), and the New Testament (e.g., Luke 2:25; 3:30; Acts 13:1; 15:14; 2 Pet 1:1; Rev 7:7). The shortened Hebrew forms סמון and שמון occur once each

---

14. Kuhn, "Did Jesus Stay at Bethsaida?," 2979–87.

15. Bockmuehl ("Simon Peter and Bethsaida," 57) calls our attention to fragment 27 credited to the *Gospel of the Nazarenes*, in which it is asserted that Jesus performed some fifty-three miracles in the cities of Chorazin and Bethsaida. This tradition, however, is quite late.

16. T. Ilan, *Lexicon of Jewish Names in Late Antiquity*, part 1, *Palestine 330 BCE–200 CE* (TSAJ 91; Tübingen: Mohr Siebeck, 2002), 218–35. See also G. Hölscher, "Zur jüdischen Namenkunde," in *Vom Alten Testament: Karl Marti zum siebzigsten Geburtstage gewidmet* (ed. K. Budde; BZAW 41; Giessen: Töpelmann, 1925), 148–57; J. A. Fitzmyer, "The Name Simon," *HTR* 56 (1963): 1–5 (reprinted in idem, *Essays on the Semitic Background of the New Testament* [London: Geoffrey Chapman, 1971; repr. SBLSBS 5; Missoula, MT: Scholars Press, 1974], 105–10).

17. See L. Y. Rahmani, *A Catalogue of Jewish Ossuaries in the Collections of the State of Israel* (Jerusalem: Israel Antiquities Authority, 1994), nos. 332 (where the spelling is Σίμων), 794, and 795; B. Bagatti and J. T. Milik, *Gli scavi del "Dominus Flevit": Monte Oliveto-Gerusalemme*, vol. 1, *La necropoli del periodo Romano* (PSBFMa 13; Jerusalem: Franciscan Printing Press, 1958), no. 37d.

18. Rahmani, *Catalogue of Jewish Ossuaries*, no. 99.

19. Ibid., no. 560.

20. Ibid., no. 778.

21. Ibid., no. 868.

on ossuaries.[22] The example on which the first one appears is interesting: "Simon, builder of the temple." The temple that Simon helped to build was, of course, the Herodian temple, a project not fully completed until 64 CE. I will remark on this example shortly.

The longer, conventional spelling שמעון (*šmʿwn*) occurs many times on ossuaries: "Our father, Shimʿon the elder, Yehosef his son,"[23] "Yehosef, son of Shimʿon,"[24] "Shimʿon, son of Alexa,"[25] "Shlamzion, daughter of Shimʿon,"[26] "Hoshea, son of Shimuʿon,"[27] "Shimʿon, son of Yannai,"[28] "Shimʿon and his wife,"[29] "Eli, son of Shimʿon, Yehoʿezer,"[30] "Qyria Shimʿon,"[31] "Hanania, son of Shimʿon,"[32] "—m, son of Shimʿon,"[33] "Ashuni, son of Shimʿon, son of Ashuni,"[34] and "Maris and Shimʿon, sons of Shaʿul."[35] The Hebrew name also occurs on several Masada ostraca.[36] The Greek form of the name is found on epitaphs in Rome[37] and on a Greek marble epitaph from Jaffa.[38]

The name "Peter" presents a number of difficulties. All four Gospels agree that Jesus gave Simon the nickname Peter. According to Mark 3:16, Jesus "gave to Simon the name 'Peter'" (ἐπέθηκεν ὄνομα τῷ Σίμωνι Πέτρον). Mark is followed by Matt (10:2) and Luke (6:14). To this testimony the fourth evangelist adds σὺ εἶ Σίμων ὁ υἱὸς Ἰωάννου, σὺ κληθήσῃ Κηφᾶς, ὃ ἑρμηνεύεται Πέτρος, "You are Simon son of John? You shall be called Cephas, which means 'Peter'" (John 1:42). The Markan evangelist (as well as the fourth evangelist?) is apparently referring to the story in which Peter confesses Jesus as Messiah (Mark 8:27–30). But in Mark's (and Luke's)

22. Ibid., nos. 200 and 651.
23. Ibid., no. 12.
24. Ibid., no. 16.
25. Ibid., no. 18.
26. Ibid., no. 26.
27. Ibid., no. 38 (note the spelling variation).
28. Ibid., no. 61.
29. Ibid., no. 150.
30. Ibid., no. 151; Ilan, *Lexicon of Jewish Names*, 168.
31. Rahmani, *Catalogue of Jewish Ossuaries*, no. 428 (the name *šmʿwn* is crossed out).
32. Ibid., no. 488.
33. Ibid., no. 501.
34. Ibid., no. 520 (the deceased was named after his grandfather).
35. Ibid., no. 820 (Shaʿul is also Saul). For additional Hebrew examples, see Bagatti and Milik, *Gli scavi del "Dominus Flevit,"* 76–77 (no. 5).
36. For examples of ostraca, see Masada Ostraca nos. 415, 416, 421, 423, 693, and 694; for examples of jars, see Masada Ostraca nos. 462, 463, 464, 465, 466, 467, 478, 479, 514, 898, and 899.
37. See H. J. Leon, *The Jews of Ancient Rome* (Morris Loeb Series; Philadelphia: Jewish Publication Society of America, 1960; rev., with Introduction by C. Osiek; Peabody, MA: Hendrickson, 1995), 289 (nos. 163 and 165), 326 (no. 403: "Here lies Simon. May his sleep be in peace").
38. *CIJ* 2.920; cf. S. Klein, *Jüdisch-Palästinisches Corpus Inscriptionum (Ossuar-, Grab- und Synagogeninschriften)* (Vienna: Löwit, 1920), no. 155; W. Horbury and D. Noy, *Jewish Inscriptions of Graeco-Roman Egypt* (Cambridge: Cambridge University Press, 1992), 239–40 (no. 147: "Thanoum, son of Simon, grandson of Benjamin the centenarius of Parembole. Peace"). The last word of this Greek inscription is written in Hebrew.

version of the story, the naming of Simon as Peter is not found; it appears only in Matthew's longer version: κἀγὼ δέ σοι λέγω ὅτι σὺ εἶ Πέτρος, καὶ ἐπὶ ταύτῃ τῇ πέτρᾳ οἰκοδομήσω μου τὴν ἐκκλησίαν, "But I tell you, you are Peter, and on this rock I will build my church" (Matt 16:18). Because the tradition that Jesus called Simon "Peter" is old (as seen in Mark and Paul, who prefers the name Κηφᾶς), interpreters of Matthew are very much open to seeing Matthew's longer version of this statement as original and the shorter version in Mark (followed by Luke) as an abbreviation.[39]

In Matthew, we not only have the nickname, we also have the well-known play on words: "You are Peter and on this *rock* I shall build my church" (Matt 16:18, emphasis added). "Peter" (Πέτρος), of course, means "rock," which facilitates the play on words with πέτρα, the "rock" on which Jesus intended to build his community. In Aramaic, the nickname is כפא, which in the New Testament is transliterated Κηφᾶς—for example, in John 1:42b, cited above.[40] The apostle Paul refers several times to Cephas, who is almost certainly Simon Peter (cf. 1 Cor 1:12 [and *1 Clem.* 47.3]; 3:22; 9:5; 15:5; Gal 1:18; 2:9, 11, 14).[41]

It has been suggested that the renaming of Simon may deliberately parallel the change of Abram's name to Abraham (Gen 17:1–8), "to signify that he would be the father of a multitude."[42] What may have encouraged the parallel is the oracle in Isa 51:1–2, in which Abraham and Sarah are likened "to the rock [צור/πέτρα] from which" the people of Israel sprang. Perhaps Jesus has applied the concept to Peter, who now becomes the rock on which Jesus will build his congregation of people.

Some have contended that כפא was not used as a proper name in the time of Jesus or before. Accordingly, it has been argued that Jesus did not give Simon the name "Rock" but simply designated him as a rock. (The Aramaic word "rock" is found in pre-Christian sources, e.g., 11QtgJob XXXII, 1; XXXIII, 9; 4QEnoch[e] 4 III, 19.) This explanation is not convincing, for several times Paul calls the apostle Κηφᾶς (Cephas, i.e., כפא) as though it is a proper name (see the references two paragraphs above). In my view, the issue has been settled by Joseph Fitzmyer, who has called our attention to an Aramaic papyrus in which כפא appears as a name.[43]

39. See the discussion in B. F. Meyer, *The Aims of Jesus* (London: SCM, 1979), 185–97; R. T. France, *The Gospel of Matthew* (NICNT; Grand Rapids: Eerdmans, 2007), 613–14; and, with some hesitation, D. C. Allison Jr. and W. D. Davies, *A Critical and Exegetical Commentary on the Gospel according to Saint Matthew*, vol. 2, *Commentary on Matthew VIII–XVIII* (ICC; Edinburgh: T&T Clark, 1991), 602–15.

40. For further discussion of linguistic and related issues, see *TDNT* 6:100–112; J. A. Fitzmyer, "Aramaic *Kepha'* and Peter's Name in the New Testament," in *Text and Interpretation: Studies in the New Testament Presented to Matthew Black* (ed. E. Best and R. M. Wilson; Cambridge: Cambridge University Press, 1979), 121–32 (reprinted in idem, *To Advance the Gospel: New Testament Studies* [New York: Crossroad, 1981], 112–24); M. Casey, *Aramaic Sources of Mark's Gospel* (SNTSMS 102; Cambridge: Cambridge University Press, 1998), 84.

41. Bart Ehrman recently resurrected the idea that Peter and Cephas refer to two men. See B. D. Ehrman, "Cephas and Peter," *JBL* 109 (1990): 463–74. There are difficulties with this suggestion, not least that it creates more problems than it solves. In any event, very few have followed this suggestion.

42. Allison and Davies, *Critical and Exegetical Commentary*, 624.

43. Fitzmyer, "Aramaic *Kepha'* and Peter's Name," 116–18.

According to one of the papyri from the island of Elephantine, Egypt (*BMAP* no. 8, line 10), which dates to ca. 416 BCE, a witness to the transfer of a slave from one owner to another is one "ʿAqab, son of Kephaʾ" (עקב בר כפא).[44] If we have one attested Jewish man named Kephaʾ, we should assume that there were other men with this name. Simon's nickname was not, therefore, unique, even if it was somewhat rare in Aramaic.

Although it is true that no examples of the Greek name Peter have been found dating to the middle of the first century CE or earlier, there is some evidence that this name was in use in the second half of the first century CE and in the second century. Some have suggested that the name Peter (Πέτρος) is attested in Josephus: "Marsyas thereupon bade Peter, a freedman of Agrippa's mother Berenice . . ." (*Ant.* 18.156). But most manuscripts read Πρῶτον (i.e., Protos), not Πέτρον. The reading of the name "Peter" probably owes its origin to a Christian scribe. The Greek name does appear, in Aramaic transliteration, in rabbinic literature as פיטרס (*y. Moʿed Qaṭ.* 3:6, 82d: רבי יוסי בר פיטרס, "Rabbi Jose, son of Petros").[45] But this person, Jose, son of Petros (or Peter), cannot be earlier than the second century. We also have a "Petron [פטרון], son of Joseph" in P.Yadin 46 and a "Petrine [פטרין], son of Istomachus" among the ostraca found at Masada (Masada Ostracon no. 413).[46] The papyrus dates to the Bar Kokhba era, and the ostracon to the fall of Masada in 73 CE.[47] Another relevant text is Masada Ostracon no. 668, which seems to read "(belonging?) to the 'Stones,' son of 'Rocks'" (לאבניא בר צונמין).[48] The name Petrus (פתרוס) appears in a magic bowl, but this artifact dates to the fourth or fifth century CE and, in any case, whether the bowl is Jewish or not, the name probably refers to Peter the disciple of Jesus.[49]

There is a striking point of comparison between Simon Peter and the individual mentioned in one of the many ossuary inscriptions that bear the name Simon—namely, the one that reads "Simon, builder of the temple."[50] We again think of Matt 16:18, where Jesus tells Simon, "I will build my church." I am not suggesting that either Jesus or the Matthean evangelist alluded to the person mentioned on this ossuary. Rather, it may well be that the occupational description "builder of the temple" was as much metaphorical as it was literal. This Simon and many others were involved in building the temple of Jerusalem, a project that commenced be-

---

44. For facsimile, text, and notes, see B. Porten and A. Yardeni, *Textbook of Aramaic Documents from Ancient Egypt*, vol. 1, *Letters* (Winona Lake: Eisenbrauns, 1986), 84–85. The name ʿAqab (עקב) may, in fact, be a shortened form of Jacob (יעקב).

45. See also *Gen. Rab.* 62.2 (on Gen 25:8); *Exod. Rab.* 52.3 (on Exod 39:33).

46. Y. Yadin, J. Naveh, and Y. Meshorer, *Masada I: The Yigael Yadin Excavations 1963–1965, Final Reports. The Aramaic and Hebrew Ostraca and Jar Inscriptions / The Coins of Masada* (Jerusalem: Israel Exploration Society, 1989), 22 + plate 23.

47. Ilan, *Lexicon of Jewish Names*, 303.

48. Yadin, Naveh, and Meshorer, *Masada I*, 66 (no. 668) + plate 55.

49. C. Isbell, *Corpus of the Aramaic Incantation Bowls* (SBLDS 17; Missoula, MT: Scholars Press, 1975), 118–19 (bowl no. 52). This magic bowl will be discussed in more detail in ch. 5 below.

50. Rahmani, *Catalogue of Jewish Ossuaries*, no. 200; cf. Masada Ostracon no. 561: "Simo [*sic*] the builder."

fore Jesus was born and that finally concluded some thirty years after Jesus' death. Building the temple, therefore, was a constant throughout the lifetime of the Simon mentioned on the ossuary. While literally building the temple, this Simon was also building Israel's faith. Perhaps mimicking this way of speaking, as reflected in the Simon ossuary inscription, Jesus declares that his Simon Peter will become the builder of Jesus' church, something parallel to and perhaps over against the temple.

But there might be another reason for the nickname "Rock." In 30 CE, Philip the tetrarch, who, so far as we know, was not a practicing Jew, refounded and renamed Bethsaida "Julias" in honor of Augustus' daughter and Tiberius' mother, Livia Julia, who had died in 29 CE. In doing this, Philip elevated Bethsaida from a village (κώμη) to a city (πόλις).[51] Whether Philip was able to expand and enhance the new city to the degree he planned is hard to say, for he died in 34 CE (and was buried in the refounded city).[52] *(See fig. 1.1.)*

The heights of Bethsaida rest on a rocky ridge of volcanic basalt. The earliest phase of the city reaches back to the Bronze Age. The site was chosen because it is the highest ground along the north shore of the Sea of Galilee, the ridge provides plenty of rock for building and defensive purposes, there is ready access to fresh water (such as the Jordan and Meshosim Rivers, as well as the Sea of Galilee), and there is also abundant arable land surrounding the ridge.[53] Indeed, the original name of Bethsaida may have been Zer ("rocks").[54] It was on this "rock" that Philip the tetrarch refounded Bethsaida and began building the new city of Julias in honor of a Roman matriarch, now divinized in death (by order of the will of Augustus).[55]

51. "Philip . . . raised the village of Bethsaida to the status of city by adding residents and strengthening the fortifications. He also named it after Julia, the emperor's daughter" (Josephus, *Ant.* 18.28; cf. *J.W.* 2.168).

52. There is very little evidence that Bethsaida was enhanced in honor of Julia, as Philip had apparently intended. Arav and others believe they have exposed a temple built in her honor, but the evidence is ambiguous. For a summary of evidence in support of the identification, see Arav, "Bethsaida," in *Jesus and Archaeology*, 162–65 + figs. 38 and 39. The principal objections are that the temple-like structure that has been unearthed does not fit the pattern of Roman temples and that the structure may be too early. On the latter problem, see H.-W. Kuhn, "Jesu Hinwendung zu den Heiden im Markusevangelium im Verhältnis zu Jesu historischen Wiren in Betsaida, mit einem Zwischenbericht zur Ausgrabung eines vermuteten heidnischen Tempels auf et-Tell (Betsaida)," in *Die Weite des Mysteriums: Christliche Identität im Dialog. Für Horst Buerkle* (ed. K. Kraemer and A. Paus; Freiburg im Breisgau: Herder, 2000), 222–29. Mark Chancey finds the evidence thus far presented unconvincing: see M. A. Chancey, *The Myth of a Gentile Galilee* (SNTSMS 118; Cambridge: Cambridge University Press, 2002), 106–8; idem, *Greco-Roman Culture and the Galilee of Jesus* (SNTSMS 134; Cambridge: Cambridge University Press, 2005), 91–94.

53. J. F. Shroder Jr. and M. Inbar, "Geological and Geographic Background to the Bethsaida Excavations," in *Bethsaida: A City by the North Shore of the Sea of Galilee* (ed. R. Arav and R. A. Freund; 4 vols.; Kirksville, MO: Truman State University Press, 1995–2009), 1:65–98, esp. p. 76, in reference to the rocky ridge providing advantages of defense. See also ibid., figs. 3 and 4.

54. As seen in the old geographical list in Josh 19:35, which lists "the fortified cities . . . Ziddim, Zer [צֵר], Hammath, Rakkath, Kinneret," cities that encircle the Sea of Galilee.

55. A provision with which emperor Tiberius did not comply. However, Livia Julia was divinized when Claudius became emperor.

Simon the disciple of Jesus was named the "Rock," for Jesus planned to build his new community on rock. Jews annoyed at Philip's move to transform Bethsaida into a Roman city would have appreciated Jesus' act of nicknaming Simon.[56]

The Matthean tradition also has Jesus address Simon Peter as "bar Jonah" (Βὰρ Ἰωνᾶ), or "son of Jonah" (Matt 16:17). Was Jonah the name of Simon's father, or is it one more nickname, i.e., Simon, the son of Jonah the prophet, who called upon wicked Nineveh to repent? According to John 1:42a, the name of Simon's father was John: "So you are Simon, the son of John [Σίμων ὁ υἱὸς Ἰωάννου]?" John's Greek implies an underlying *bar yōḥānān*, though *Iōna* could be an abbreviation of this fuller form of the name;[57] the names do seem interchangeable, at least in the manuscripts, in a few places in the Old Greek (cf. LXX 1 Chr 26:3; 1 Esd 9:1, 23).

Ilan identifies three other persons named Jonah, besides (possibly) Simon Peter's father.[58] One occurrence of the name is found in the *Mekilta de Rabbi Ishmael*. The other two are found inscribed on ossuaries; one of these reads, for example, "Mariame, wife of Jonah [Ἰωνᾶ]."[59] There are at least three examples of "Yoḥanan, son of Simon."[60] We have a "Simon, son of Yoḥanan" in early rabbinic literature (cf. *Sipra* §160, *Zabim* 1.1 [on Lev 15:2]).[61] The name and filiation also occur on an ossuary from the Kidron Valley: שמעון בר יוחנן, "Simon, son of Yoḥanan," though at points the reading is uncertain.[62]

(2) *Andrew* (Ἀνδρέας). This name (Andreas, though in English usually Andrew) is Greek and probably means "manly" (from ἀνδρός, the genitive of ἀνήρ, "man"); it appears inscribed on at least two Jewish ossuaries.[63] The second inscription was found on an ossuary in the Tomb of Jason. It reads: Σάολος [Ἰο]ύδου Ἀνδροῦς, "of Saul, of [Jo]udah, (son) of Andreas (or Andrew)."[64]

(3) *Philip* (Φίλιππος). This name is also Greek, meaning "horse lover"; it appears transliterated in Hebrew as פלפס.[65] Besides the apostle Philip (named after the tetrarch?), there is Philip the deacon and evangelist (Acts 6:5; 8:5–13; 21:8). It is interesting to observe that the deacon and evangelist Philip left a far bigger imprint on the memory of the early church than did Philip the apostle. It might also be noted

56. On the politics of the refounding and renaming of Bethsaida, see E. McNamer, "Philip, Julia, and the Imperial Cult," in *Bethsaida in Archaeology, History and Ancient Culture: A Festschrift in Honor of John T. Greene* (ed. J. H. Ellens; Newcastle upon Tyne: Cambridge Scholars, 2014), 242–51.

57. See *TDNT* 3:406–10.

58. Ilan, *Lexicon of Jewish Names*, 143–44.

59. Rahmani, *Catalogue of Jewish Ossuaries*, no. 233.

60. J. T. Milik, "Trois tombeaux juifs récemment découverts au Sud-Est de Jérusalem," *LASBF* 7 (1956–57): 232–67.

61. Ilan, *Lexicon of Jewish Names*, 221.

62. Milik, "Trois tombeaux juifs," 243.

63. *CIJ* 2.1272 (Ἀνδροῦς); see E. Puech, "Inscriptions funéraires palestiniennes: Tombeau de Jason et ossuaires," *RB* 90 (1983): 481–583, at 528 (Ἀνδροῦς).

64. Ilan, *Lexicon of Jewish Names*, 262–63.

65. Ibid., 310.

that Philip the deacon and evangelist seems to have been every much as Hellenized, if not more, than Philip the apostle.

The name Philip has not yet turned up on an ossuary of late antiquity from Palestine. The name does appear on an epitaph from Leontopolis (Tell el-Yehoudieh), dating perhaps to 23 BCE. It reads: "Hilarion, daughter of Philip [Φιλίππου], untimely dead, friend of all, who caused pain to none, excellent girl, farewell. About 6 years old. In year 7, Epeiph 5."[66] The name also appears on an epitaph from Rome, which reads: "Here lies Eutychis, daughter of Philip [Φιλίππου]. May her sleep be in peace."[67]

We turn now to the city itself. Arav and his team have worked at et-Tell for more than twenty-five years. They are convinced that it is the site of New Testament Bethsaida. Not everyone agrees. Not long ago, Steven Notley flatly rejected the identification, with Arav responding.[68] Others, however, have argued in support of the identification.[69] Probably the biggest reason for challenging the identification of et-Tell with Bethsaida is that the site is almost two kilometers north of the shoreline. For this reason, some think El-Araj, which is south of et-Tell and is quite close to the shore, is the more likely candidate.[70] However, geological tests and archaeological work have found that El-Araj did not exist prior to the Byzantine era and that pottery fragments found at the site that date earlier had washed down from the hill on which et-Tell sits. Geological analysis shows that due to erosion and massive mudslides in the third and fourth centuries (the latter probably as a result of the earthquake in 363 CE) the shoreline at the north end of the Sea of Galilee was pushed south and the lagoon to the west of Bethsaida was filled in. This is why et-Tell today is so far from the shoreline. It was close to the shoreline in the time of Jesus.

Further evidence that et-Tell is the site of ancient Bethsaida, the "house of catching (fish)," is seen in the number of stone anchors, lead weights for nets, fishhooks, and other tools used for fishing that have been recovered.[71] Much of the

66. *CIJ* 2.1494; see Horbury and Noy, *Jewish Inscriptions of Graeco-Roman Egypt*, 140–41 (no. 70).

67. *CIJ* 2.334; see Leon, *Jews of Ancient Rome*, 314. The epitaph includes a menorah.

68. For the exchange between Notley and Arav, see R. S. Notley, "Et-Tell is not Bethsaida," *NEA* 70 (2007): 220–30; R. Arav, "Bethsaida—A Response to Steven Notley," *NEA* 74 (2011): 92–100; R. S. Notley, "Reply to Arav," *NEA* 74 (2011): 101–3; R. Arav, "A Response to Notley's Reply," *NEA* 74 (2011): 103–4.

69. Among others, see Shroder and Inbar, "Geological and Geographic Background," 65–66; J. F. Shroder Jr., M. P. Bishop, K. J. Cornwell, and M. Inbar, "Catastrophic Geomorphic Process and Bethsaida Archaeology, Israel," in *Bethsaida: A City by the North Shore of the Sea of Galilee* (ed. R. Arav and R. A. Freund; 4 vols., Kirksville, MO: Truman State University Press, 1995–2009), 2:115–73.

70. J. F. Strange, "Beth-Saida," *ABD* 1:692–93.

71. S. Fortner, "The Fishing Implements and Maritime Activities of Bethsaida-Julias (et-Tell)," in *Bethsaida: A City by the North Shore of the Sea of Galilee* (ed. R. Arav and R. A. Freund; 4 vols.; Kirksville, MO: Truman State University Press, 1995–2009), 2:269–82. I thank Rami Arav and Richard Freund for showing me and my student Greg Monette hundreds of artifacts, including anchors, lead weights, and fishhooks, recovered from Bethsaida.

evidence of this nature remains buried under the debris from the slides and floods mentioned already. *(See fig. 1.2.)*

The faunal remains that have been recovered tell an interesting story. The lead investigator has been Toni Fisher. In the strata and loci of Bethsaida that concern us (Hasmonean, Herodian, and early Roman), she has found some, but not many, non-kosher faunal remains. The non-kosher remains include pig, which is mostly wild boar, for a total of 3 percent of all faunal remains, and catfish.[72]

Fisher's finds are consistent with what has been learned about the demographics of Bethsaida. Although we cannot be sure what the percentages of Jews and non-Jews living in this place were, we have reason to believe that most of the population was Jewish. This would account for the small percentage of non-kosher faunal remains. It would also account for the presence of artifacts that are normally associated with Jewish populations. These artifacts include Galilean coarse ware, Hasmonean coins, stone vessels, and pottery from Kefar Hananya. The evidence suggests that the population of Bethsaida was mostly Jewish.[73] But how zealous this population was for the practices of the Jewish faith is another matter.

I raise this question because no *miqwāʾôt* (ritual immersion pools), no synagogue, and no ossuaries have been recovered from Bethsaida. Of course, one or more of these things may be found in future digs, but for now their absence, after more than twenty-five seasons of excavation, is remarkable. On the other hand, the use of stone vessels, the preference for earthenware from Hananya, and the avoidance of non-kosher meat suggest that the Jewish population avoided obvious transgressions, particularly with respect to food.

The ambiguities of the religious adherence of the Jewish population of Bethsaida may shed some light on two passages in the New Testament that concern Simon Peter and food. In one, Peter is criticized for withdrawing from Gentiles and no longer eating with him. In the other, Peter insists that he has never eaten non-kosher food. The findings at Bethsaida may help us to understand these somewhat discrepant passages.

Prior to his visit to the Roman centurion Cornelius, Peter, the recognized leader of the infant church, receives a vision in which he is bidden to kill and eat foods described as "all kinds of animals and reptiles and birds of the air" (Acts 10:12). The implication is that at least some of these fauna are not kosher. Peter protests: "No, Lord; for I have never eaten anything that is common or unclean [κοινὸν καὶ ἀκάθαρτον]" (Acts 10:14). Peter's refusal is remarkable, given that he has seen heaven open and the sheet filled with the animals descend. Surely he suspects that his vision is from God. Even so, he refuses to comply with the heavenly instructions. At the very least, Peter's response implies that he has observed kashrut faithfully

72. T. Fisher, "Faunal Analysis: Zooarchaeology in Syro-Palestinian/Israeli Archaeology," in *Bethsaida in Archaeology, History and Ancient Culture: A Festschrift in Honor of John T. Greene* (ed. J. H. Ellens; Newcastle upon Tyne: Cambridge Scholars, 2014), 84–121; idem, "A Zooarchaeological Analysis of Change in Animal Utilization at Bethsaida from Iron Age II through the Early Roman Period" (PhD diss., The University of Tennessee, Knoxville, 2005). I thank Dr. Fisher for making her dissertation available to me.

73. Savage, *Biblical Bethsaida*, 91–123.

throughout his life. He is then instructed, "What God has cleansed, you must not call common" (Acts 10:15). The vision makes it possible for Peter to visit Cornelius in Caesarea Maritima and remain with him for several days (Acts 10:48), which would have meant—given the context—eating non-kosher food.[74]

Years later, in Antioch, Peter seems to be guided by the heavenly vision he received in Joppa; he eats with Gentiles, whose food, we should assume, was not necessarily kosher (Gal 2:11–12). This is not to say, of course, that Jewish Christians who dined with Gentile Christians ate pork. But the Gentile food, nevertheless, would likely not be kosher, at least not by the strict standards of some Jewish groups. However, when "men from James" arrive in Antioch (Gal 2:12), Peter withdraws from the Gentiles and no longer eats with them (μετὰ τῶν ἐθνῶν συνήσθιεν).

When Paul learns of this, he reacts angrily. In his letter to the churches of Galatia, Paul describes the scene: "But when I saw that they were not straightforward about the truth of the gospel, I said to Cephas before them all, 'If you, though a Jew, live like a Gentile and not like a Jew, how can you compel the Gentiles to live like Jews?'" (Gal 2:14).

It is not hard to understand Paul's criticism of Peter for his inconsistency and hypocrisy. But what of Paul's stinging irony to the effect that Peter, though ethnically Jewish, did not live like a Jew but rather like a Gentile? The irony may be based on the fact that Peter was from Bethsaida—a town east of the boundary separating Galilee from Gaulanitis and therefore in closer proximity to Gentile populations, a town whose refuse has been discovered to contain some non-kosher animal remains and that perhaps had no synagogue and no *miqwāʾôt*. Growing up in Bethsaida was not the same as growing up in Galilee, in most Galilean villages, including cities. After all, no non-kosher bones have been found in pre–70 CE Sepphoris, a large, prosperous city just seven kilometers from Nazareth. From Paul's former Pharisaical point of view, the "Jewishness" of Peter was minimal. How ironic that Peter threw in his lot with those who wished to Judaize the Gentile converts.

Magdala: The Village of Mary

In a series of eccentric studies published between twenty-five and twenty years ago, Howard Clark Kee argued that there really is no evidence of synagogues prior to the destruction of the temple in 70 CE. To maintain this thesis, it was necessary for Kee to ignore or discredit a considerable amount of evidence, including statements by Philo, Josephus, the four New Testament Gospels, the book of Acts, the Theodotus Inscription, the Cyrenaica Inscription, and the ruins of four or five first-century structures that archaeologists at that time had identified as synagogues. Kee argued that prior to 70 CE the word synagogue (συναγωγή) only referred to assemblies of

74. D. G. Peterson, *The Acts of the Apostles* (PNTC; Grand Rapids: Eerdmans, 2009), 341: "Staying with these Gentiles involved eating with them" and experiencing "the novelty of table fellowship."

people and not to dedicated *buildings* where Jews met for prayer, singing, reading Scripture, socializing, and, in some cases, study.[75]

Historians and biblical scholars have not followed Kee; neither have archaeologists. Kee's arguments have been challenged in a number of critical responses.[76] Probably the most devastating study has been published by John Kloppenborg.[77] Ongoing archaeological work has confirmed these buildings as synagogues, and a number of new candidates have been uncovered more recently.

In her recently published, magisterial study of synagogues, Rachel Hachlili identifies ten synagogues that were probably or certainly in use prior to 70 CE.[78] They are found at Capernaum, et-Tuwani, Gamla (or Gamala), Herodium (or Herodion), Jericho, Masada, Magdala (or Migdal I), Modiʿin (Hurvat Umm el-Umdan),

---

75. H. C. Kee, "The Transformation of the Synagogue after 70 C.E.: Its Import for Early Christianity," *NTS* 36 (1990): 481–500; idem, "The Changing Meaning of Synagogue: A Response to Richard Oster," *NTS* 40 (1994): 281–83; idem, "Defining the First-Century CE Synagogue: Problems and Progress," *NTS* 41 (1995): 481–500 (reprinted in H. C. Kee and L. H. Cohick, eds., *The Evolution of the Synagogue: Problems and Progress* [Harrisburg, PA: Trinity Press International, 1999], 7–26). In the second study, Kee is responding to Richard Oster, whose study is cited in the following footnote. Richard Horsley, with some qualifications, supports Kee's position: see R. A. Horsley, "Synagogues in Galilee and the Gospels," in *The Evolution of the Synagogue: Problems and Progress* (ed. H. C. Kee and L. H. Cohick; Harrisburg, PA: Trinity Press International, 1999), 46–69.

76. See R. E. Oster Jr., "Supposed Anachronism in Luke–Acts' Use of ΣΥΝΑΓΩΓΗ: A Rejoinder to H. C. Kee," *NTS* 39 (1993): 178–208; R. Riesner, "Synagogues in Jerusalem," in *The Book of Acts in Its Palestinian Setting* (ed. R. Bauckham; Grand Rapids: Eerdmans, 1995), 179–211; L. I. Levine, "The Nature and Origin of the Palestine Synagogue Reconsidered," *JBL* 115 (1996): 425–48, esp. 428n4; K. Atkinson, "On Further Defining the First-Century C.E. Synagogue: Fact or Fiction? A Rejoinder to H. C. Kee," *NTS* 43 (1997): 491–502; L. I. Levine, *The Ancient Synagogue: The First Thousand Years* (2nd ed.; New Haven: Yale University Press, 2005), 47–48; and L. L. Grabbe, "Synagogue and Sanhedrin in the First Century," in *Handbook for the Study of the Historical Jesus* (ed. T. Holmén and S. E. Porter; Leiden: Brill, 2011), 2:1723–45, esp. 1723–29. Grabbe rightly remarks that virtually no one (Horsley, cited in the previous footnote, being a rare exception) has followed Kee. The evidence shows that by the middle of the first century CE the word συναγωγή could refer to either the *building* or the *people* who met together, not only the latter.

77. J. S. Kloppenborg Verbin, "Dating Theodotos (*CIJ* 1404)," *JJS* 51 (2000): 243–80; J. S. Kloppenborg, "The Theodotos Synagogue Inscription and the Problem of First-Century Synagogue Buildings," in *Jesus and Archaeology* (ed. J. H. Charlesworth; Grand Rapids: Eerdmans, 2006), 236–82.

78. R. Hachlili, *Ancient Synagogues—Archaeology and Art: New Discoveries and Current Research* (HOS, Section 1: Ancient Near East 105; Leiden: Brill, 2013), 22–54 + figs. To illustrate how much progress has been made in the last twenty years, one should see D. E. Groh, "The Stratigraphic Chronology of the Galilean Synagogue from the Early Roman Period through the Early Byzantine Period (ca. 420 C.E.)," in *Ancient Synagogues: Historical Analysis and Archaeological Discovery* (ed. D. Urman and P. V. M. Flesher; StPB 47; Leiden: Brill, 1995), 1:51–69, esp. 57–60, where "First-Century Synagogues" are discussed. Groh believes that of "the list of candidates, only two probably prove to be Jewish public structures . . . Migdal and Gamala" (p. 57). Writing at about the same time, E. P. Sanders accepted that "synagogues were common wherever Jews lived," but that, nevertheless, only a "total of three have been found that can be dated to the period before the destruction of Jerusalem in 70 C.E." (E. P. Sanders, *The Historical Figure of Jesus* [New York: Penguin, 1993], 99–100).

Qiryat Sefer, and Qumran. In addition to these ten, Korazin (or Chorazim) and Horvat Burnat are two more possible sites. Three other sites, Horvat ʿEthri, Migdal II, and Shuafat, are either very doubtful or have been excluded. These candidates will be briefly surveyed.

Capernaum, on the northwest shore of the Sea of Galilee, presents the greatest challenge, for the fourth-century limestone synagogue rests upon a much older black basalt foundation that is neither level nor square. How much of this foundation supported an older synagogue is debated. Most now agree that the original basalt pavement and perhaps part of the foundation reach back to the first century.[79] If so, these very probably belong to the synagogue that the Capernaum centurion funded (Luke 7:1–5) and in which Jesus healed and preached (Mark 1:21–29; Luke 4:31–38; John 6:35–59).[80]

Little has been published about the ruins identified as a synagogue at *et-Tuwani*, located in the south Hebron hills. Stepped bench seating along the north, west, and south walls confirms identification as a synagogue. It is dated to the first century BCE.[81]

The synagogue excavated at *Gamla* (or Gamala), in the southwest of the Golan Heights, is a beautiful example of a well-preserved early synagogue. The synagogue dates to the first century BCE. It was destroyed by the Romans during the Jewish revolt. Stepped bench seating runs along the interior of the walls. Archaeologists debate how many columns were originally present. A *miqwê* is located next to the synagogue. Coins discovered at the site have led to speculation that the synagogue rests upon the foundation of an even older one.[82]

The makeshift synagogue built by zealots in the dining hall of the *Herodium* (or Herodion) dates to the Jewish rebellion. The layout closely corresponds to the common synagogue footprint.[83] During the rebellion, zealots also built a synagogue

---

79. A. Runesson, "Architecture, Conflict, and Identity Formation: Jews and Christians in Capernaum from the First to the Sixth Century," in *Religion, Ethnicity, and Identity in Ancient Galilee: A Region in Transition* (ed. J. K. Zangenberg, H. W. Attridge, D. B. Martin; WUNT 210; Tübingen: Mohr Siebeck, 2007), 231–57 + tables. For a brief summary of scholarly discussion, see Hachlili, *Ancient Synagogues*, 23–26 + fig. II-2.

80. For all relevant data, see A. Runesson, D. D. Binder, and B. Olsson, *The Ancient Synagogue from Its Origins to 200 C.E.: A Source Book* (Leiden: Brill, 2010), 25–32 + figs. 2 and 3. The authors conclude that the "black basalt platform underneath the main hall of the limestone synagogue constitutes the ruins of a first-century synagogue" (p. 32).

81. For a brief report, see Hachlili, *Ancient Synagogues*, 26.

82. For a full report, see Z. Yavor, "The Synagogue and Miqveh Complex," in *Gamla II: The Architecture. The Shmarya Gutmann Excavations, 1976–1989* (ed. D. Syon and Z. Yavor; IAA Reports 44; Jerusalem: Israel Antiquities Authority, 2010), 40–61. For brief reports, see Groh, "Stratigraphic Chronology of the Galilean Synagogue," 59–60; Levine, *Ancient Synagogue*, 54–55 + fig. 4; Runesson, Binder, and Olsson, *Ancient Synagogue from Its Origins to 200 C.E.*, 33–35 + figs. 4 and 5; Hachlili, *Ancient Synagogues*, 26–28 + fig. II-3.

83. G. Foerster, "The Synagogues at Masada and Herodium," in *Ancient Synagogues Revealed* (ed. L. I. Levine; Jerusalem: Israel Exploration Society, 1981), 24–29 (this is an abridged English translation of a Hebrew study that appeared in *ErIsr* 11 [1973]: 224–28). For brief reports, see Levine, *Ancient Synagogue*, 54–55; Runesson, Binder, and Olsson, *Ancient Synagogue from Its Origins to 200 C.E.*, 35–36 + fig. 6; Hachlili, *Ancient Synagogues*, 28 + fig. II-4.

by renovating a room in Herod's mountaintop fortress at *Masada*. There are stepped benches of four tiers on the east, south, and west sides. On the north side there is only one tier. The floor and benches are plastered. Fragments of Deuteronomy and Ezekiel were found in a concealed pit beneath the floor, which perhaps served as a genizah.[84]

One of the rooms that was part of the Hasmonean palace complex at *Jericho* has been identified as a synagogue. Some contend that this room was part of a private villa and therefore was not a synagogue. But the architectural typology and the presence of a *miqwê* support the synagogue interpretation. It has also been suggested that the room was a private synagogue, restricted to those who lived or served in the palace complex itself.[85] *(See fig. 1.3.)*

A first-century synagogue has recently been exposed at a location that currently is identified as *Magdala*, on the northwest shore of the Sea of Galilee, about two kilometers south of Ginosar. If the identification is correct, then we may also have identified the hometown of Mary Magdalene, one of the followers of Jesus. In September 2009, during a survey conducted prior to construction of a retreat center on property owned by the Notre Dame Pontifical Institute, a synagogue and other buildings were discovered. The site has been partially excavated by Dina Avshalom-Gorni and Arfan Najar of the Israel Antiquities Authority. The first phase of the work was completed in the spring of 2014, and there are plans to resume at a future date.

The footprint of the synagogue is almost square (comprising some 120 square meters), with interior pillars and stepped benches along the walls. Mosaic of simple pattern covers portions of the floor. About seventy meters south of the synagogue, three *miqwāʾôt* were exposed.[86] The most unusual find was the decorated stone near the center of the synagogue. It is believed that the synagogue, along with the city, was destroyed by the Romans during the first Jewish rebellion.[87] The problems regarding the identification of this site will be treated in more detail below.

---

84. Y. Yadin, "Synagogue at Masada," in *Ancient Synagogues Revealed* (ed. L. I. Levine; Jerusalem: Israel Exploration Society, 1981), 19–23. For brief reports, see Levine, *Ancient Synagogue*, 61–63 + fig. 7; Runesson, Binder, and Olsson, *Ancient Synagogue from Its Origins to 200 C.E.*, 55–57 + fig. 10; Hachlili, *Ancient Synagogues*, 30–33 + figs. II-6 and II-7.

85. E. Netzer, "A Synagogue from the Hasmonean Period Recently Exposed in the Western Plain of Jericho," *IEJ* 49 (1999), 203–21; Y. Rapuano, "The Hasmonean Period 'Synagogue' at Jericho and the 'Council Chamber' Building at Qumran," *IEJ* 51 (2001): 48–56. For brief reports, see Runesson, Binder, and Olsson, *Ancient Synagogue from Its Origins to 200 C.E.*, 40–42 + figs. 8 and 9; Hachlili, *Ancient Synagogues*, 28–30 + figs. II-1a and II-5.

86. R. Reich and M. Zapata Meza, "A Preliminary Report on the *Miqwaʾot* of Migdal," *IEJ* 64 (2014): 63–71 + figs. 1–6. The *miqwāʾôt* are fed by spring water. In this they are unique.

87. For preliminary reports concerning the "Magdala" synagogue, see J. K. Zangenberg, "Archaeological News from the Galilee: Tiberias, Magdala and Rural Galilee," *Early Christianity* 1 (2010): 471–84, at 476–77 (includes photograph); idem, "Magdala—Auferstehung aus Ruinen," in *Judäa und Jerusalem: Leben in römischer Zeit* (ed. J. Schefzyk and W. Zwickel; Stuttgart: Katholisches Bibelwerk, 2010), 182–83; R. Wenning, "Israel, Magdala: Die wirkliche Synagoge? Und die älteste?," *WUB* 55 (2010): 65; J. Corbett, "New Synagogue Excavations in Israel and Beyond," *BAR* 37, no. 4 (2011): 52–59, esp. 52–56; Hachlili, *Ancient Synagogues*, 33–34 + figs. II-8 and II-13.

At *Modiʿin* (Hurvat Umm el-Umdan), hometown of the Hasmonean family, archaeologists have uncovered a synagogue that was founded during the Hasmonean period (ca. 100 BCE), built over during the Herodian period, and then built over again at the end of the first century or beginning of the second century CE. Foundations for benches were found lining three of the four walls of the rectangular structure. The walls were plastered and painted. In the Herodian-era synagogue, benches rested along all four walls. West of the synagogue a *miqwê* was found.[88]

A small, square-shaped synagogue was uncovered at *Qiryat Sefer*, an ancient village not far from Modiʿin. The Herodian-style structure boasted four pillars with Doric capitals. The northern and southern walls were adorned with pilasters. The entrance faced north. The building and village were abandoned during or after the Bar Kokhba revolt (132–135 CE).[89]

It has been suggested that locus 77 of the ruins at *Qumran* functioned as a synagogue. It is the largest room found at the site, measuring 22 x 4.5 meters. This room probably also served as a dining room. The evidence in support of the identification of this renovated room as a synagogue is circumstantial. The Damascus Document states that "everyone who enters a house of prostration should not enter with impurity requiring washing . . . it is a holy house [בית קודש]" (CD XI, 22–XII, 1). Elsewhere, the Damascus Document speaks of the "house of the law" (CD XX, 10, 13), which may be a way of referring to a synagogue, a place where Scripture was read and studied.

Locus 77 is the only room at Qumran that could have accommodated the whole community. The War Scroll also speaks of a "meeting house" where the leaders of the congregation gather. "Meeting house" (בית מועד) may be the earliest designation for the synagogue. Philo claims that on the Sabbath the Essenes abstain from work and "proceed to sacred spots that they call synagogues [συναγωγαί]," where they sit in rows and hear Scripture read (*Good Person* 81–82). Josephus says the Essenes purify themselves and then "repair to the refectory as to some sacred shrine [εἰς ἅγιόν τι τέμενος]" (*J.W.* 2.129). These descriptions fit well Qumran's locus 77. Nevertheless, the "synagogue" of Qumran is somewhat anomalous in that it was not, so far as we know, a readily recognized synagogue building. Yet the statements in Philo, Josephus, and the Scrolls themselves about meeting and the presence of a large hall that would have accommodated the whole community suggest that it is probably correct to identify locus 77 as the community's synagogue.[90]

88. For brief reports, see Levine, *Ancient Synagogue*, 70 + fig. 10; Runesson, Binder, and Olsson, *Ancient Synagogue from Its Origins to 200 C.E.*, 57–58 + fig. 11; Hachlili, *Ancient Synagogues*, 34 + fig. II-9.

89. For brief reports, see Levine, *Ancient Synagogue*, 69 + fig. 9; Runesson, Binder, and Olsson, *Ancient Synagogue from Its Origins to 200 C.E.*, 65–66 + fig. 13; Hachlili, *Ancient Synagogues*, 34–36.

90. A. Steudel, "The Houses of Prostration CD XI, 21–XII, 1—Duplicates of the Temple," *RevQ* 16 (1993): 49–68. For brief reports, see Levine, *Ancient Synagogue*, 63–66 + fig. 8; Runesson, Binder, and Olsson, *Ancient Synagogue from Its Origins to 200 C.E.*, 66–75 + figs. 14 and 15; Hachlili, *Ancient Synagogues*, 37.

As mentioned above, there are two other structures that could be pre–70 CE synagogues. The first is found at *Chorazin* (or Korazim). Visitors to Chorazin see a striking fourth-century synagogue, built mostly of black basalt stone. In this synagogue was found an inscribed "Seat of Moses," which is now on display in the Israel Museum. In an unpublished excavation report dating to 1926, archaeologist J. Ory stated that he located the ruins of a synagogue about two hundred meters west of the fourth-century synagogue. He described a "square colonnaded building of small dimensions" with three columns on each side and tiers of stone benches running along three of the walls.[91] In the 1970s, Gideon Foerster visited the site and could not find a trace of these ruins (and others have made attempts as well). It is surmised that the ruins were destroyed by modern building activities. Foerster believes, on the basis of Ory's description, that the lost synagogue should be dated to the first century CE.[92] Unfortunately, it is no longer possible to confirm this.

The second possibility is the rectangular room in a residential building at *Horvat Burnat*. It is dated to the late Second Temple period. However, there are no stone benches along the walls, nor is there any feature that requires us to identify the room as a synagogue. It may have been a dining hall.[93]

Other sites that have been thought to preserve ruins of Second Temple synagogues include Horvat ʿEthri, Migdal II, and Shuafat. There are, however, problems with all of them. The large room at *Horvat ʿEthri*, in close proximity to two *miqwāʾôt*, may well be a synagogue, but it is now dated no earlier than the end of the first century CE.[94] The function of the building (i.e., D1) identified as a synagogue at *Migdal II*, a site thought by some to be Magdala, is much disputed. Some think it was a spring house that perhaps later was used as a synagogue.[95] Some date the building to the first century. Following Ehud Netzer, Anders Runesson and his colleagues do not think the building ever served as a synagogue.[96] A new excavation at this site, closer to the Sea of Galilee, has been initiated by Dina Avshalom-Gorni. And,

---

91. Ory's 1926 report is discussed in Foerster, "Synagogues at Masada and Herodium," 26, and Groh, "Stratigraphic Chronology of the Galilean Synagogue," 57–58nn34–35. The unpublished report, according to Groh, is in file 120 for 1926 (p. 227) of the Department of Antiquities of Palestine (now the Israel Antiquities Authority).

92. Foerster, "Synagogues at Masada and Herodium," 26. For brief reports, see Levine, *Ancient Synagogue*, 72; Runesson, Binder, and Olsson, *Ancient Synagogue from Its Origins to 200 C.E.*, 32–33; Hachlili, *Ancient Synagogues*, 30.

93. For a brief report, see Hachlili, *Ancient Synagogues*, 36.

94. For a brief report, see ibid. + fig. II-10.

95. As in V. C. Corbo, "Scavi archeologici a Magdala," *LASBF* 24 (1974): 5–37; idem, "La città romana di Magdala: Rapporto preliminare dopo la quarta campagna di scavo, 1975," in *Studia Hierosolymitana in onore del P. Bellarmino Bagatti* (ed. E. Testa, I. Mancini, and M. Piccirillo; 2 vols.; Collectio maior 22–23; Jerusalem: Franciscan Printing Press, 1976), 1:355–78, at 365–68; Groh, "Stratigraphic Chronology of the Galilean Synagogue," 58–59.

96. For brief reports, see Levine, *Ancient Synagogue*, 71–72; Runesson, Binder, and Olsson, *Ancient Synagogue from Its Origins to 200 C.E.*, 55; Hachlili, *Ancient Synagogues*, 37–38 + fig. II-11. A recent study lends additional support to the interpretation that the building was not a synagogue but was rather a fountain house (as Ehud Netzer proposed in 1987): R. Bonnie and J. Richard, "Building D1 at Magdala Revisited in the Light of Public Fountain Architecture in the Late-Hellenistic East," *IEJ* 62 (2012): 71–88.

finally, in 1991 ruins at *Shuafat* were uncovered and dated to the first century BCE. The remains of at least one *miqwê* encouraged the identification of one of the rooms as a synagogue. However, most archaeologists no longer accept this identification.[97]

I return now to the recently discovered synagogue at a location that many assume is first-century Magdala, the probable city of Mary Magdalene. That this synagogue was constructed prior to 70 CE does not seem to be disputed. At the present time, archaeologists are suggesting, on the basis of pottery, architectural features, and coins, that the synagogue was built in the 20s (perhaps atop an even older structure), that it was expanded in the 40s, and that it was destroyed by General Titus as the Roman army, under the command of Vespasian, overpowered the rebellion in Galilee in 66–67 CE. Future excavations and study should clarify and perhaps modify this proposed history.[98]

Scholars are fascinated with the discovery because of the possible linkage with Mary Magdalene, a woman who is mentioned some dozen times in the four Gospels of the New Testament. But this is where a number of questions arise. In a recent learned study, Joan Taylor has addressed these questions.[99] She points out that although the name Magdalene (Μαγδαληνή) could mean that Mary is from a city called Magdala (Μαγδαλά)—just as "Jesus the Nazarene" (Ναζαρηνός) implies that Jesus is from Nazareth (Ναζαρά or Ναζαρέτ)[100]—there is no city or village anywhere in Israel that we know of with the name "the Tower," either in Hebrew (המגדל, *ha-Migdal*) or Aramaic (מגדלא, *Magdala*). The Hebrew and Aramaic words simply mean "the tower," without specifying a particular place or city. Taylor discusses several sites in Galilee and Judea whose names include the word "tower" (e.g., in Galilee: Migdal El, Migdal Nuniya, Migdal Malha; in Judea: Migdal Senna, Migdal Tsebaya, Migdal Eder, Migdal Gad, and Migdal Thauatha).[101]

Taylor's point is that the only place known to us as "Tower" in the vicinity of Capernaum (to the north) and Magadan Dalmanutha (to the south) is Migdal Nuniya ("Tower of Fish" or "Fish Tower"), located about one mile north of Tiberias and mentioned in rabbinic literature (cf. *b. Pes.* 46a: "as long as it takes a man to walk from Migdal Nuniya [מגדל נוניא] to Tiberias, which is a mile").[102] If Mary

97. For brief reports, see Levine, *Ancient Synagogue*, 72; Runesson, Binder, and Olsson, *Ancient Synagogue from Its Origins to 200 C.E.*, 75–76; Hachlili, *Ancient Synagogues*, 39.

98. For a very current description and assessment of the findings at Magdala, see R. Bauckham and S. De Luca, "Magdala as We Now Know It," *Early Christianity* 6 (2015): 91–118. See also M. Aviam, R. Bauckham, and S. De Luca, eds., *Magdala, Jewish City of Fish* (Waco, TX: Baylor University Press, forthcoming); M. Zapata Meza, "Magdala Archaeological Project (2010–12): Preliminary Report," *'Atiqot* (forthcoming).

99. J. E. Taylor, "Missing Magdala and the Name of Mary 'Magdalene,'" *PEQ* 146 (2014): 205–23.

100. Or, similarly, the Gadarenes (Γαδαρηνοί) of Matt 8:28, who are from Gadara (Γάδαρα).

101. Taylor, "Missing Magdala," 207–12 + fig. 1 (a map of Israel showing the locations of the various places with the name "tower"). Migdal Tsebaya is not shown on the map, because its location is unknown. It seems to have been in the vicinity of Jerusalem.

102. Ibid., 218–21 + fig. 8 (which shows the locations of Capernaum, Magadan Dalmanutha, and Migdal Nuniya, among others). Dalmanutha (Δαλμανουθά) is mentioned in

Magdalene was from this city, then referring to her, in Aramaic, simply as Mary "of the Tower" (מגדלא, *Magdala*) would be meaningful to locals but not to anyone outside of the region surrounding the Sea of Galilee.

Calling Mary "of the Tower" might also mean more than a mere reference to Mary's city. Taylor suggests that "Magdalene" was as much a nickname as those given to some of the other disciples: Simon was "called 'Zealot' [τὸν καλούμενον ζηλωτήν]" (Luke 6:15; Acts 1:12), Judas was "called 'Iscariot'[103] [τὸν καλούμενον Ἰσκαριώτην]" (Luke 22:3), Simon (Peter) was "called 'Rock' [ὁ ἐπικαλούμενος Πέτρος]" (Acts 10:5, 18), John and James, sons of Zebedee, were dubbed "'Boan Erges,' that is, the 'Sons of Thunder' [βοανηργές, ὅ ἐστιν υἱοὶ βροντῆς]" (Mark 3:17), and Joseph was "called 'Barsabbas'[104] [τὸν καλούμενον Βαρσαββᾶν]" (Acts 1:23)—and, in similar fashion, Mary was "called 'of the Tower' [καλουμένη Μαγδαληνή]" (Luke 8:2).[105]

Taylor further suggests that Mary's nickname conveyed status, implying that she was no ordinary female follower of Jesus. This possibility receives support from the prominence of this woman in the Gospel stories. Not only is she an eyewitness of the empty tomb and apparently the first to see the risen Jesus (Matt 28:1; Mark 16:1; Luke 24:10; John 20:1, 18; cf. Mark 16:9), she is placed alongside the very notable "Joanna, the wife of Chuza, Herod's steward" (Luke 8:2–3). Taylor wonders if the status Jesus conferred on Mary through her nickname approximated that conferred on Simon Peter: as Simon was the "Rock" of the Jesus movement, so Mary was its "Tower."[106]

Consideration of Mary's designation (or nickname) as "Magdalene" could cast doubt on the identification of the site currently being excavated as Magdala. If Mary's sobriquet Magdalene refers to a place (and it probably does) and is not purely metaphorical, then the only relevant place with the name "tower" in it seems to be Migdal Nuniya. The site that is currently being excavated is located 250 meters from the shore of the Sea of Galilee, about two kilometers southeast of modern Migdal, including "Mount Migdal," and about the same distance south of the Yigal Allon Museum (which houses the ancient boat) in Ginosar, on the shore.

Mark 8:10. In the parallel at Matt 15:39 it is called Magadan (Μαγαδάν). Taylor (pp. 217–18) rejects, with justification, the identification of Migdal Nuniya with Tarichaea, as seen in S. De Luca, "La città ellenistico-romana di Magdala/Taricheae: Gli scavi del Magdala Project 2007 e 2008. Relazione preliminare e prospettive di indagine," *LASBF* 59 (2009): 343–62.

103. Perhaps from the Aramaic *ʾiskaryûtāʾ*, meaning "choked up" (Taylor, "Missing Magdala," 206). If this was the meaning of Judas' nickname (perhaps originally a reflection of his emotions or some other mannerism), at a later time the meaning may have taken on a darker significance in the minds of some, who perhaps understood it as an adumbration of his suicide by hanging.

104. Perhaps from the Aramaic *bar šabbāʾ*, meaning "Son of the Sabbath," or *bar sābāʾ*, meaning "Son of the Scholar [or Elder]," as suggested by Taylor, "Missing Magdala," 207.

105. Taylor, "Missing Magdala," 206–8. Taylor feminizes "Tower" as "Tower-ess." Her interpretation is supported by the Syriac versions of the Gospels, where Mary is not referred to as *mrym dmgdlʾ* ("Mariam of Magdala"); rather, she is regularly referred to as *mrym mgdlytʾ*, "Mariam the Tower-ess."

106. Taylor, "Missing Magdala," 222.

Given finds in recent years in and around modern Migdal that date to the late Hellenistic period and on into the Roman period, it may be that the place currently called Magdala was part of a harbor-front, perhaps linked with or part of the city situated to the immediate west in the hills. The "Magdala" of Mary's time may have been Migdal Nuniya, to the south. The "Magdala" site currently being excavated, where yet another pre–70 CE synagogue has been exposed, may have been linked with or been part of a major city whose name at this time is not known.[107]

Nevertheless, in a recent study Richard Bauckham and Stefano De Luca vigorously maintain the identification of the site as Magdala, notwithstanding Taylor's arguments.[108] We are told that additional evidence for the Magdala identification is forthcoming.[109] For now, I cautiously accept the Magdala identification. Taylor's point about Mary's nickname could still be correct, even if the Magdala interpretation is accepted.

Perhaps the most important discovery at the "Magdala" site has been the decorated stone, referred to above, found more or less in the center of the synagogue. The stone, made of limestone, has four short feet and a sloping top, which makes some think it was a reading stand of some sort. The top and all four sides are decorated with religious symbols, most if not all of which relate to the Jerusalem temple. Mordechai Aviam, Richard Bauckham, and Donald Binder have published the most detailed descriptions and interpretations of the stone's ornamentation.[110] I offer a summary of their analyses. *(See fig. 1.4.)*

In situ, the "front" side of the stone was facing south, that is, toward Jerusalem. At the center of the façade is a menorah (with seven branches) resting on a square object; both of these are flanked by two amphorae, which in turn are enclosed by two fluted pillars that rest on pediments, are topped with capitals, and support an arch. The two long sides of the ornamented stone are identical. They present an

---

107. K. R. Dark, "Archaeological Evidence for a Previously Unrecognized Roman Town near the Sea of Galilee," *PEQ* 145 (2013): 185–202. I shall make a few more comments about Dark's study in ch. 2 below. Dark wonders if the harbor town currently being excavated grew up the banks and hills westward to become a major city.

108. Bauckham and De Luca, "Magdala as We Now Know It," 91–92.

109. For support of the identification of the current site of excavation as New Testament Magdala, Bauckham and De Luca refer to S. De Luca and A. Lena, "Magdala," in *Galilee in the Late Second Temple and Mishnaic Periods, 100 BCE–200 CE*, vol. 2, *The Archaeological Record of Galilean Cities, Towns, and Villages* (ed. D. Fiensy and J. R. Strange; Minneapolis: Fortress, forthcoming). Also, for the rabbinic literature they refer to R. Bauckham, "Magdala in Rabbinic Literaure," and for Taricheae they refer to M. H. Jensen, "Magdala/Taricheae and the Jewish Revolt," both in *Magdala, Jewish City of Fish* (ed. M. Aviam, R. Bauckham, and S. De Luca; Waco, TX: Baylor University Press, forthcoming).

110. M. Aviam, "The Decorated Stone from the Synagogue at Migdal," *NovT* 55 (2013): 205–20; R. Bauckham, "Further Thoughts on the Migdal Synagogue Stone," *NovT* 57 (2015): 113–35; D. D. Binder, "The Mystery of the Magdala Stone," in *A City Set on a Hill: Essays in Honor of James F. Strange* (ed. D. A. Warner and D. D. Binder; Fayetteville, AR: BorderStone Press, 2014), 17–48. For brief descriptions, see Corbett, "New Synagogue Excavations," 52–54, with excellent photo; Hachlili, *Ancient Synagogues*, 40–41 + fig. II-13. Archaeologists Najar and Avshalom-Gorni have published a brief report on the Israel Antiquities Authority's website (2009) and have presented preliminary results in Hebrew (2010).

arcade of four arches, within three of which are either stylized depictions of the menorah or perhaps sheaves of corn. Within the fourth arch is a lamp. The "back" side of the stone presents three fluted pillars supporting a decorated lintel. Between the pillars are two rosettes. In the center of the top of the stone is a large rosette flanked by what could be palm trees. "The rest of the space is taken by twelve other motifs, both floral and geometric."[111]

Much of the description in the preceding paragraph reflects the interpretation of the archaeologists. Aviam accepts some of it but disagrees with most of it. He believes all of the symbolism is a reflection of the Jerusalem temple. In his view, the front of the stone depicts the temple, with the menorah at the center. Its tripod legs match the depiction of the temple's menorah in the relief on the Arch of Titus in the Roman Forum. The square object on which the menorah seems to rest is the golden altar, which is depicted *in front* of the menorah, not beneath it.[112] The two amphorae represent the "sons of oil" (Zech 4:10–14), which contain oil for the menorah.[113] On the sides of the stone are not sheaves of corn but a series of arches, creating a three-dimensional effect. Bauckham plausibly suggests that the decorated stone actually symbolizes the showbread table itself.[114] In the fourth arch is not a lamp but a censer. Between the pillars on the back of the stone are not rosettes but the "spoked wheels" of the *merkabah*, God's chariot throne (Ezek 1:18; Dan 7:9).[115] (One immediately thinks of the decorated stone from the fourth-century Capernaum synagogue.[116]) The large, centered rosette on the top side of the stone represents, Aviam believes, the zodiac, with its six inner petals and six outer petals representing the zodiac's twelve signs. For support of his zodiac interpretation, Aviam cites Josephus, who, speaking of the showbread table, refers to "the loaves on the table, twelve in number, the circle of the zodiac and the year" (*J.W.* 5.217).[117] Zodiacs, of course, became commonplace in synagogues (in Israel and in the Diaspora). Like others, Aviam believes the ornamented stone was part of a stand for reading Scripture.[118]

All of this leads Aviam to conclude that the ornamented stone found in the synagogue in what right now most call Magdala testifies to the devotion the Galileans who lived in this place had for the temple in Jerusalem. Worshipping in this synagogue, with the rich temple symbolism in plain view and undergirding the very place where Scripture was read, provided a link with those who worshipped in the

111. Aviam, "Decorated Stone," 208–9, with quotation from p. 209.

112. This interpretation is questioned in Bauckham, "Migdal Synagogue Stone," 115.

113. Again, the interpretation is questioned by Bauckham, in ibid., 116. He thinks the amphorae represent the golden flagons of wine that were associated with the table of showbread (as in Exod 25:29; 37:16; Num 4:7; Josephus, *Ant.* 14.72).

114. Bauckham, "Migdal Synagogue Stone," 121–22, 126–28.

115. This same thought occurred to me the first time I saw the stone. Bauckham agrees with Aviam, adding that greater stress should be placed on the depiction of the chariot throne in Ezekiel (ibid., 118). See also Binder, "Mystery of the Magdala Stone," 29–30.

116. Aviam, "Decorated Stone," 217–18 + fig. 6.

117. Ibid., 211–16.

118. Ibid., 217, fig. 5. Hachlili agrees (*Ancient Synagogues*, 41).

temple in Jerusalem. The menorah was more than a general Jewish symbol; it was a symbol specifically of the temple, God's house.[119] Bauckham adds that if the stone itself represented the showbread table, which symbolized the very presence of God, then the stone was meant to show that God was as present in the synagogue as he was in the temple in Jerusalem. People seated along the inner sides of the four walls of the "Magdala" synagogue would gaze upon the stone in the center of this place of worship and think of the showbread table in the temple.[120]

Without necessarily accepting every detail in Aviam's interpretation, I think he, Bauckham, and Binder have made a compelling case for the meaning of the ornamented stone.[121] This stone, which reflects temple themes, underscores the strong link between the Galilean synagogue where the stone was found and the temple cultus in Jerusalem, to which the stone's ornamentation apparently refers.

That the stone found in the "Magdala" synagogue is not "one of a kind" has been shown by the even more recent discovery, in 2010, a year after the discovery of the "Magdala" stone, of another stone in the synagogue at Horvat Kur, a few miles northwest of "Magdala." Jürgen Zangenberg, Byron McCane, and others have been working on and off at Horvat Kur since 2008. In 2010, a synagogue was discovered that has been dated to the fourth century CE. What was especially intriguing was the discovery in it of a stone similar to the ornamented stone found in the "Magdala" synagogue.[122]

The Horvat Kur synagogue stone, however, does not date to the fourth century; it dates to the first century. It was found embedded in one of the walls of the Horvat Kur synagogue and is similar in size and dimensions to the stone from "Magdala." This newly discovered stone is decorated with symbols and geometric patterns, such as pillars and amphorae, on all four sides. The only major difference between the Horvat Kur stone and the "Magdala" stone is that the former is made from black basalt. The Horvat Kur stone was evidently salvaged from an earlier synagogue, one

119. Aviam's conclusions seem fully justified, for almost all of the artistic themes on the stone are approximated in decorations on ossuaries found in Jerusalem. A frequent theme in these ossuaries is temple art—pillars, blocks, foundations, and gates being the most common elements (see ch. 9 below). Not only have my graduate students and I examined the replicas of this stone housed on site at the Magdala excavation and in the Notre Dame Centre in Jerusalem, but my student Greg Monette and I were able to view the stone itself in the Israel Antiquities Authority storage facility in Beth Shemesh (and for this we express our gratitude to the very accommodating staff).

120. Bauckham, "Migdal Synagogue Stone," 129–32. See also Binder, "Mystery of the Magdala Stone," 41, 44.

121. Hachlili (*Ancient Synagogues*, 41) summarizes Aviam's interpretation from what seems to be a sympathetic perspective.

122. For preliminary reports, see J. K. Zangenberg, "Israel, Horvat Kur: Erneut antike Synagoge am See Gennesaret entdeckt," *WUB* 58 (2010): 62–63; idem, "Ein Dorf auf dem Hügel: Neue Entdeckungen des Kinneret Regional Project in der Synagoge von Horvat Kur," in *Bauern, Fischer und Propheten: Galiläer zur Zeit Jesu* (ed. J. K. Zangenberg and J. Schröter; Darmstadt: von Zabern, 2012), 131–44, at 140–43; idem, "Israel, Horvat Kur: Antike jüdische Synagoge weiter ausgegraben," *WUB* 67 (2013): 58–69; Corbett, "New Synagogue Excavations," 59; P. Wyssmann, "Israel, Horvat Kur: Ein Münzdeposit aus einer spätantiken Synagoge in Galiläa," *WUB* 68 (2013): 60–61.

that dates to the first century CE, if not earlier. We should assume that this stone, like the "Magdala" stone, reflected the synagogue congregation's sense of connection to the temple in Jerusalem.[123]

Summing Up

The two sites that may be linked to two of Jesus' most famous followers, Simon Peter and Mary Magdalene, raise a number of important questions. The demographics of Bethsaida remain uncertain. Some still question the identification of et-Tell with Bethsaida/Julias, though in my opinion that matter has been resolved. The location of Bethsaida, the people of Bethsaida and their habits, and the political orientation of Bethsaida could potentially shed light on Simon Peter and the other two men from that place who became disciples of Jesus. What we know about Bethsaida may even shed light on the sobriquet that Jesus gave Peter.

The synagogue at "Magdala" and its remarkable stone are of great importance, but is this site really Magdala/Migdal, after which Mary Magdalene received her name? This question remains very much open. Even if we cannot posit a link with this woman, the site itself is pre–70 CE and could tell us important things about life near the northwest shore of the Sea of Galilee in the time of Jesus and his disciples.

In the chapter that follows, we shall look at a number of finds that may shed light on persons who figured prominently in the life and activities of Jesus. These findings will help us better understand life and business in first-century Israel.

123. I express my gratitude to Byron McCane for showing me and my graduate students the Horvat Kur synagogue in June 2014 and answering many questions.

CHAPTER TWO

A Boat, a House, and an Ossuary: What Can We Learn from the Artifacts?

The correlation between the biblical narratives and the findings of archaeology and the study of late antique topography gives rise to the discipline called "biblical archaeology." Without such correlation, the discipline would not exist. The discoveries of archaeology often shed light on the biblical narrative, while the biblical narrative often provides a contextual thread by which the archaeologist may more fully understand his or her discoveries.

The correlation is usually quite general, but sometimes it can be quite specific. In some cases, archaeology may uncover artifacts that have a direct bearing on figures mentioned in the biblical narrative. In this chapter we shall consider a few examples that seem to refer to figures in the New Testament Gospels and Acts.

Texts, Artifacts, and New Testament Historiography

In 2002, the discovery of an ossuary that may have contained the remains of James the brother of Jesus was made public. The uproar that ensued was predictable, but the amount of thought given to the value and relevance of artifacts in the tasks of archaeology, historiography, and interpretation has been interesting and on the whole quite useful.

There have been several other archaeological finds that have had direct bearing on the world in which early rabbinic Judaism and Christianity emerged. In 1871, Charles S. Clermont-Ganneau found a limestone block on which was inscribed a warning to Gentiles to stay out of the perimeter surrounding the Jewish sanctuary.[1] The warning coincides with statements made by Josephus (*J.W.* 5.193–194; cf.

1. Initially announced in the *Palestine Exploration Fund Quarterly* (1871): 132; cf. C. S. Clermont-Ganneau, "Une stèle du temple de Jérusalem," *RAr* 28 (1872): 214–34 (esp. 220), 290–96 + plate X. See also J. Derenbourg, "Une stèle du temple d'Hérode," *JA* 20 (1872): 178–95. A fragment of a second inscription was found in Jerusalem in 1935; see J. H. Iliffe, "The θάνατος Inscription from Herod's Temple: Fragment of a Second Copy," *QDAP* 6 (1936): 1–3 + plates I–II; J. Finegan, *Light from the Ancient Past: The Archaeological Background of*

6.124–128; *Ant.* 12.145; 15.417; *Ag. Ap.* 2.103) and Philo (*Embassy* 212) and provides a clarifying backdrop to the story of Paul's trouble in the temple precincts (cf. Acts 21:27–36), to the Pauline assertion that in Christ the dividing wall has been broken down (see Eph 2:14–15), and probably also to the story of Jesus' demonstration years earlier in these same precincts (see Mark 11:15–18 and parallels).

In 1878, a marble slab surfaced in Nazareth on which was inscribed Caesar's edict forbidding tampering with tombs and burials. In 1925, it was sent to Paris, and a few years later Franz Cumont published and commented on its text.[2] Most think the inscription dates to the reign of Augustus (though this is not certain).[3] Because the edict specifically forbids transferring bodies from one grave to another, some scholars think it may have relevance for the Gospel story of Jesus' burial and the discovery of the empty tomb, especially with regard to the story that circulated (whatever its origin) that the disciples may have illegally removed the body of Jesus (Matt 27:62–66; 28:11–15).[4]

In 1956, Józef T. Milik published an ossuary inscription in which the word *qorbān* ("gift") appears: "Everything that a man will find to his profit in this ossuary (is) an offering [קרבן] to God from the one within it."[5] A few years later, Joseph Fitzmyer published a study in which he rightly perceived the relevance of this inscription for Jesus' debate with some Pharisees over the authority of oral traditions (Mark 7:9–13, esp. v. 11).[6]

In 1968, an ossuary was discovered that contained the bones of a man, one Yehoḥanan, who had been crucified. Amazingly, an iron spike with fragments of

---

Judaism and Christianity (2nd ed.; Princeton: Princeton University Press, 1969), 119–20. For other editions of the inscription(s) and additional comments, see *OGIS* no. 598; *CIJ* no. 1400; *SEG* VIII no. 169; C. A. Evans, *Jesus and the Ossuaries: What Jewish Burial Practices Reveal about the Beginning of Christianity* (Waco, TX: Baylor University Press, 2003), 31–35; *CIIP* no. 2.

2. F. Cumont, "Un rescrit impérial sur la violation de sépulture," *Revue historique* 163 (1930): 241–66. See *SEG* VIII no. 13.

3. See Cumont, "Un rescrit impérial," 265; F. de Zulueta, "Violation of Sepulture in Palestine at the Beginning of the Christian Era," *JRS* 22 (1932): 184–97, esp. 186–87.

4. For further discussion, see B. M. Metzger, "The Nazareth Inscription Once Again," in *New Testament Studies: Philological, Versional, and Patristic* (NTTS 10; Leiden: Brill, 1980), 75–92; P. W. van der Horst, *Ancient Jewish Epitaphs: An Introductory Survey of a Millennium of Jewish Funerary Epigraphy (300 BCE–700 CE)* (Kampen: Kok Pharos, 1991), 159–60; L. Boffo, "L'ordine imperiale di Nazaret (?) sulla violazione dei sepolcri," in *Iscrizioni greche e latine per lo studio della Bibbia* (Brescia: Paideia, 1994), 319–33 (for additional bibliography, see pp. 319–20); R. E. Brown, *The Death of the Messiah: From Gethsemane to the Grave. A Commentary on the Passion Narratives in the Four Gospels* (2 vols.; ABRL; New York: Doubleday, 1994), 2:1293–94; Evans, *Jesus and the Ossuaries*, 35–37.

5. Milik, "Trois tombeaux juifs," 232–39.

6. J. A. Fitzmyer, "The Aramaic Qorbân Inscription from Jebel Hallet et-Tûrî and Mk 7:11/Mt 15:5," *JBL* 78 (1959): 60–65 (repr. in idem, *Essays on the Semitic Background of the New Testament* [London: Geoffrey Chapman, 1971; repr. as SBLSBS 5; Missoula: Scholars Press, 1974], 93–100). See now the updated reports in Evans, *Jesus and the Ossuaries*, 96–98; *CIIP* no. 287. For two more ossuary inscriptions that mention *qorbān*, see M.-J. Lagrange, "Epigraphie sémitique," *RB* 2 (1893): 220–22 ("for the fire, a gift [*qorbān*]—Martha"). For additional examples, see *CIIP* nos. 466, 528, and 605.

wood still attached was found in the right heel bone (or *calcaneum*).[7] The ossuary and its contents have been dated to the administration of Pontius Pilate. At the very least, the ossuary provides evidence that during peacetime proper Jewish burial, followed by ossilegium (i.e., the placement of the bones of the deceased into an ossuary), was permitted in the case of a crucified criminal.[8]

In 1971, Amos Kloner discovered the words של בית דוד ("belonging to the house of David") inscribed on an ossuary.[9] This inscription provides significant artifactual support of literary evidence that seems to refer to Jews in late antiquity who believed that they were descendants of Israel's great king (cf. Eusebius, *Ecclesiastical History* 3.12–13, 19–20; *m. Taᶜan.* 4:5).

Other finds may relate directly to figures mentioned in the New Testament. These include one ossuary that refers to Alexander, son of Simon, who apparently hails from Cyrene. The lid of the ossuary reads אלכסנדרוס קרנית ("Alexander, the Cyrenite") and the side of the ossuary reads Αλέξανδρος Σίμωνος ("Simon (son) of Alexander").[10] If these readings (which are disputed) are correct, this person may well be the son of the man who carried Jesus' cross (Mark 15:21: "they compelled a passer-by, Simon of Cyrene . . . the father of Alexander and Rufus").[11] Another

7. See N. Haas, "Anthropological Observations on the Skeletal Remains from Givᶜat ha-Mivtar," *IEJ* 20 (1970): 38–59; J. Naveh, "The Ossuary Inscriptions from Givᶜat ha-Mivtar, Jerusalem," *IEJ* 20 (1970): 33–37; V. Tzaferis, "Jewish Tombs at and near Givᶜat ha-Mivtar," *IEJ* 20 (1970): 18–32, esp. 20–27; Y. Yadin, "Epigraphy and Crucifixion," *IEJ* 23 (1973): 18–22 + plate; H.-W. Kuhn, "Der Gekreuzigte von Givᶜat ha-Mivtar: Bilanz einer Entdeckung," in *Theologia Crucis–Signum Crucis: Festschrift für Erich Dinkler zum 70. Geburtstag* (ed. C. Andresen and G. Klein; Tübingen: Mohr, 1979), 303–34; V. Tzaferis, "Crucifixion: The Archaeological Evidence," *BAR* 11, no. 1 (1985): 44–53; J. Zias and E. Sekeles, "The Crucified Man from Givᶜat ha-Mivtar: A Reappraisal," *IEJ* 35 (1985): 22–27; J. Zias and J. H. Charlesworth, "Crucifixion: Archaeology, Jesus, and the Dead Sea Scrolls," in *Jesus and the Dead Sea Scrolls* (ed. J. H. Charlesworth; ABRL; New York: Doubleday, 1992), 273–89 + plates following p. 184; Rahmani, *Catalogue of Jewish Ossuaries,* no. 218 + plate; *CIIP* no. 50.

8. Evans, *Jesus and the Ossuaries,* 98–103. The proper Jewish burial of Yehoḥanan militates against the speculation that the bodies of Jesus and the men crucified with him were not buried but either were left hanging on the cross or were cast into a ditch and eaten by animals. The remains of other individuals who suffered execution and were properly buried have been recovered, showing that the burial of Yehohanan was not exceptional.

9. A. Kloner, "A Burial Cave of the Second Temple Period at Givᶜat ha-Mivtar, Jerusalem," *Qadmoniot* 19–20 (1972): 108–9 (in Hebrew); idem, "A Burial Cave of the Second Temple Period at Givᶜat ha-Mivtar," in *Jerusalem in the Second Temple Period: Abraham Schalit Memorial Volume* (ed. A. Oppenheimer, U. Rappaport, and M. Stern; Jerusalem: Yad Izhak Ben-Zvi, 1980), 191–224 (in Hebrew), with English abstract on pp. xii–xiii; D. Flusser, *Jesus* (rev. ed., in collaboration with R. S. Notley; Jerusalem: Magnes, 1997), 180–86; Evans, *Jesus and the Ossuaries,* 103–4; *CIIP* no. 45.

10. The name is inscribed on an ossuary discovered by E. L. Sukenik in the Kidron Valley in 1941. Sukenik announced the discovery in *BASOR* 88 (1942): 38, but the inscriptions and ossuary descriptions were not fully published for another twenty years. See N. Avigad, "A Depository of Inscribed Ossuaries in the Kidron Valley," *IEJ* 12 (1962): 1–12 + plates I–IV. See also "Tomb South of the Village of Silwan," in N. Avigad, "Tombs," *NEAEHL* 2:750–53, at 753.

11. See M. Hengel, *The "Hellenization" of Judaea in the First Century after Christ* (Philadelphia: Trinity Press International, 1989), 11, 67n39. More will be said about this ossuary and its inscriptions in ch. 3 below.

Gospel personage reflected in the archaeological record is Pontius Pilate, whose name and rank as prefect were found, in 1961, inscribed on a stone in Caesarea Maritima: "The Tiberieum of Pontius Pilate, prefect of Judaea, restored(?)."[12] The inscription is part of a dedication that may have had something to do with the refurbishing and expansion of the harbor.

Of even greater interest was the discovery, in 1990, of a crypt containing ossuaries on which may be inscribed the name Caiaphas. The inscription found on the left end of one of the ossuaries appears to read יהוסף בר קיפא,[13] "Joseph, son of Caiaphas," the latter of whom most would now identify with "Caiaphas" the high priest mentioned in the Gospels and Acts (Matt 26:3, 57; Luke 3:2; John 11:49; 18:13–14, 24, 28; Acts 4:6) and with "Joseph Caiaphas" and "Joseph called Caiaphas" mentioned in Josephus (*Ant.* 18.35, 95).[14] Some scholars, including myself, at one time expressed reservations about the Caiaphas identification,[15] but the recent discovery of an ossuary on which reference is made to one Miriam (perhaps better vocalized as "Mariam"), the daughter of "Yeshua son of Caiaphas, priests" (ישוע בר קיפא כהנם),[16] has removed most if not all of these doubts. (More will be said about Caiaphas and his ossuary in chs. 3 and 7 below.)

The crypt of the family of Annas the high priest, father-in-law of Caiaphas, may also have been found in Akeldama. In describing Roman siege works encircling Jerusalem, Josephus states that the wall ascended from Siloam "over against the tomb of the high priest Ananus" (*J.W.* 5.506). This tomb may well have been discovered among the tombs and monuments found in Akeldama.[17] It is palatial in

12. For the text and an attempted restoration of this Latin inscription, see A. Frova, "L'iscrizione di Ponzio Pilato a Cesarea," *Rendiconti dell'Istituto Lombardo* 95 (1961): 419–34, esp. 424, with frag. 3 on p. 424; and, more recently, G. Alföldy, "Pontius Pilatus und das Tiberieum von Caesarea Maritima," *Scripta Classica Israelica* 18 (1999): 85–108, who thinks the building may have been the "seamen's [*nautis*] Tiberieum." One year before the discovery of the inscription, A. H. M. Jones ("Procurators and Prefects in the Early Principate," in *Studies in Roman Government and Law* [Oxford: Blackwell, 1960], 117–25) had correctly deduced that Pilate's rank was not procurator (*pace* Tacitus, *Annals* 15.44) but prefect (Latin: *praefectus*). For more on this inscription and its interpretation, see ch. 3 below.

13. The last word may be קופא.

14. Z. Greenhut, "Burial Cave of the Caiaphas Family," *BAR* 18, no. 5 (1992): 28–36, 76; idem, "The 'Caiaphas' Tomb in North Talpiyot, Jerusalem," *'Atiqot* 21 (1992): 63–71; R. Reich, "Caiaphas Name Inscribed on Bone Boxes," *BAR* 18, no. 5 (1992): 38–44, 76; idem, "Ossuary Inscriptions from the 'Caiaphas' Tomb," *'Atiqot* 21 (1992): 72–77; W. R. Domeris and S. M. Long, "The Recently Excavated Tomb of Joseph Bar Caipha and the Biblical Caiaphas," *JTSA* 89 (1994): 50–58; Flusser, *Jesus*, 195–206; Crossan and Reed, *Excavating Jesus*, 242.

15. For studies that questioned the Caiaphas identification, see E. Puech, "A-t-on redécouvert le tombeau du grand-prêtre Caïphe?," *MdB* 80 (1993): 42–47; idem, *La croyance des Esséniens en la vie future: Immortalité, résurrection, vie éternelle? Histoire d'une croyance dans le judaïsme ancien* (2 vols.; EBib 21–22; Paris: Gabalda, 1993), 1:193–95; W. Horbury, "The 'Caiaphas' Ossuaries and Joseph Caiaphas," *PEQ* 126 (1994): 32–48; Evans, *Jesus and the Ossuaries*, 107–8.

16. B. Zissu and Y. Goren, "The Ossuary of 'Miriam Daughter of Yeshua Son of Caiaphas, Priests [of] Maʿaziah from Beth ʾImri,'" *IEJ* 61 (2011): 74–95. One will also want to see R. Bauckham, "The Caiaphas Family," *JSHJ* 10 (2012): 3–31.

17. G. Avni, Z. Greenhut, et al., *The Akeldama Tombs: Three Burial Caves in the Kidron Valley, Jerusalem* (IAA Reports 1; Jerusalem: Israel Antiquities Authority, 1996); G. Avni,

size, design, and ornamentation, and at one time was adorned with an impressive superstructure. The quality of this tomb complex and its location (remnants of the siege wall mentioned by Josephus are nearby) support the identification. Indeed, the very resting place of the former high priest (known in the New Testament as Annas, but Ananus elsewhere) may also have been discovered.

We have archaeological and inscriptional evidence of other high priests from this period, including members of the family of Annas. An ossuary appeared in the antiquities market in 1983 that almost certainly had been looted from a crypt either in Jerusalem or in nearby Hizma. The ossuary's inscription, found on its decorated side within the middle arch of three arches, identifies the occupant as "Yehoḥanah, daughter of Yehoḥanan, son of Theophilus the high priest [בר תפלוס הכהן הגדל]." It is probable that this Theophilus—appointed to the office of high priest in 37 CE by Vitellius, after the recall of Pontius Pilate (Josephus, *Ant.* 18.123–124; 19.297)—was the son of Annas and the brother-in-law of Caiaphas.[18]

We find the words ה[נני] כהנא רבא עקביא בריה ("A[nanias] the high priest, 'Aqavia his son") inked on an ostracon found at Masada (Masada Ostracon no. 461).[19] The inscription may refer to Ananias, son of Nedebaeus, who served as high priest from 47 to 59 CE (cf. Josephus, *Ant.* 20.103). This may be the man mentioned in the New Testament who orders a guard to strike Paul (Acts 23:2–5).

We may have the name of another high priest attested. On a circular stone weight found in the ruins of the "Burnt House" (70 CE) in the old city of Jerusalem (not too far from the southwest corner of the Temple Mount), we find inscribed: [ד]בר קתרס ("[of] the son of Qatros").[20] This may be the family name of one of the ruling priests recalled by later rabbis: "Violent men of the priesthood came and took away (the tithes) by force. . . . Concerning these and people like them. . . . 'Woe is me because of the House of Boethos [ביתוס]. Woe is me because of their clubs. Woe is me because of the house of Qadros [קדרס]. Woe is me because of their pen. Woe is me because of the house of Hanan [i.e., Annas]. Woe is me because of their whispering. Woe is me because of the house of Ishmael ben Phiabi' " (*t. Menaḥ.* 13:19, 21). This activity of violence and theft is also described by Josephus (*Ant.* 20.206).

We may also have the name of Boethos, whose name appears above in the passage cited from the Tosefta. On an ossuary found on the western slope of Mount Scopus, Jerusalem, we find inscribed: בוטון שמעון בוטון ("Boethos. Shim'on, of [the

Z. Greenhut, and T. Ilan, "Three New Burial Caves of the Second Temple Period in Aceldama (Kidron Valley)," in *Ancient Jerusalem Revealed* (ed. H. Geva; Jerusalem: Israel Exploration Society, 1994), 206–18; L. Ritmeyer and K. Ritmeyer, "Akeldama: Potter's Field or High Priest's Tomb?," *BAR* 20, no. 6 (1994): 22–35, 76, 78.

18. D. Barag and D. Flusser, "The Ossuary of Yehoḥanah Granddaughter of the High Priest Theophilus," *IEJ* 36 (1986): 39–44; Rahmani, *Catalogue of Jewish Ossuaries*, no. 871; Evans, *Jesus and the Ossuaries*, 108–9; *CIIP* no. 534.

19. Yadin, Naveh, and Meshorer, *Masada I*, 37 + plate 30; Evans, *Jesus and the Ossuaries*, 109–10.

20. N. Avigad, "Excavations in the Jewish Quarter of the Old City of Jerusalem," *IEJ* 20 (1970): 1–8, at 7; Evans, *Jesus and the Ossuaries*, 110–11; *CIIP* no. 674.

family of] Boethos").[21] Eleazar Sukenik links this inscription and ossuary to the family of Simon, son of Boethos of Alexandria, whom Herod appointed to the high priesthood (Josephus, *Ant.* 15.320–322). The Qatros mentioned above may have been his son.

We may have inscriptional evidence of yet another member of the Boethos family. On an ossuary we have "Yoezer, son of Simon" (*CIJ* no. 1354: יועזר בן שמון), and on ostraca from Masada we have "Yoezer" (Masada Ostracon no. 383: יועזר) and "Simeon, son of Yoezer" (Masada Ostracon no. 466: שמעון בן יועזר).[22] The affiliation of Yoezer and Simeon is significant in light of what Josephus relates: "Jozar [Γόζορος = Yoezer], also a Pharisee, came of a priestly family; the youngest, Simon [Σίμων], was descended from high priests" (*Life* 197). This "Jozar" may be the same person as Joazar, son of Boethos (cf. Josephus, *Ant.* 17.164; 18.3: τοῦ ἀρχιερέως Ἰωαζάρου Βοηθοῦ δὲ οὗτος υἱὸς ἦν), who himself served as high priest briefly in 4 BCE.

Finally, two interesting inscriptions bearing the name Simon may be mentioned. The first is סמון בנא הכלה ("Simon, builder of the temple");[23] the second is הב לסמו בניא ("give to Simo [*sic*] the builder").[24] *(See fig. 2.1.)*

The value of these artifacts is not apologetic (as so often is claimed); it is contextual and exegetical. For example, the *qorbān* inscription clarifies the meaning of the use of this word in Mark 7 and provides an important attestation of the practice in Jesus' time of dedicating one's property to divine service. The temple warning lends precision to the warnings, customs, and specific events found in literary sources, while the skeletal remains of the crucified man clarify aspects of this fearful form of execution and the possibility of proper Jewish burial for its victim. The inscription mentioning the house of David does not prove Jesus' Davidic descent, but it does document the reasonableness and intelligibility of such a claim, while the edict against tampering with sepulture sharpens our understanding of burial customs and sensitivities. The Petrine and Jacobean artifacts that are discussed below fit within the general context of the artifacts that have just been surveyed.

Two Petrine Artifacts

There are two Galilean "Petrine" artifacts that deserve mention. The first is the so-called house of Peter and the other is the Sea of Galilee boat. The first—the house,

21. E. L. Sukenik, "A Jewish Tomb Cave on the Slope of Mount Scopus," *Qovetz* 3 (1934): 62–73, at 67 (in Hebrew); Rahmani, *Catalogue of Jewish Ossuaries*, no. 41; Evans, *Jesus and the Ossuaries*, 111–12; *CIIP* no. 76. The form בוטון may correspond with the genitive plural βοηθῶν, meaning "of the Boethians."

22. Y. Yadin, *Masada: Herod's Fortress and the Zealots' Last Stand* (New York: Random House, 1966), 96; Yadin, Naveh, and Meshorer, *Masada I*, 40 + plate 31.

23. Rahmani, *Catalogue of Jewish Ossuaries*, no. 200; P. Figueras, *Decorated Jewish Ossuaries* (DMOA 20; Leiden: Brill, 1983), 13–14; Evans, *Jesus and the Ossuaries*, 92–93; *CIIP* no. 54. The ossuary was found at Givʿat ha-Mivtar in 1968. The inscription occurs a second time on this ossuary, in Hebrew: סמון בנה הכלה.

24. Yadin, Naveh, and Meshorer, *Masada I*, 53 + plate 46. For the relevance of these inscriptions for our understanding of Jesus' giving Simon the nickname Peter, see p. 13 above.

in Capernaum—may actually have belonged to Peter, or to his family. The second—the boat, found near Ginosar—almost certainly had no connection to Peter, but it may well represent a type of fishing boat that Peter and his colleagues employed.

The Capernaum Synagogue and the House of Peter

Modern study of ancient Capernaum commenced in 1838 with Edward Robinson's survey. He was the first to identify the remains of the synagogue, though he did not realize that the site was ancient Capernaum. In 1866, Charles Wilson identified the site as Capernaum and linked the synagogue to the one mentioned in Luke 7:5, the synagogue built by the Roman centurion (τὴν συναγωγὴν αὐτὸς ᾠκοδόμησεν ἡμῖν).

Regrettably, with the exposure of artifacts and architecture, the site was looted and vandalized. In 1894, the site was secured by the Franciscan Fathers, and new excavations were undertaken in 1905. The synagogue, built of limestone and measuring just over 24 meters in length and 18.5 meters in width, was partly reconstructed and eventually was dated to the fourth or fifth century CE. However, the underlying black basalt foundation, damaged and no longer level or square (perhaps due to an earthquake), is probably a much older foundation, whose footings reach back to the time of Jesus, if not earlier.[25] *(See fig. 2.2.)*

In 1968, the Franciscan excavations, extending into the area surrounding the synagogue, uncovered the remains of a building complex at the approximate center of which may have been the house of Peter.[26] This complex seems to have had three major manifestations. The first was as a private house, probably originally built in the first century BCE. The house, including its floors, was built of round, black basalt wadi stones. Only the stones of the thresholds and doorjambs were dressed. This structure could not have supported a second story, but had a thatched roof

---

25. The basalt foundation descends slightly as one moves toward the Sea of Galilee, which required the builders of the limestone synagogue to go to a great deal of trouble to level the floor of the new synagogue. Indeed, the basalt foundation in places actually extends beyond the limestone structure. The preservation of the old basalt foundation, despite its flaws, attests to its antiquity and the sacredness with which it was regarded, something in step with Jewish tradition (see 1 Cor 3:10–14, where Paul speaks of the need to build on the foundation already laid). Initially, the Franciscans dated the synagogue to the first century, claiming that it was the very synagogue in which Jesus ministered (see V. C. Corbo, S. Loffreda, and A. Spijkerman, *La Sinagoga de Cafarnao, dopo gli scavi del 1969* [SBFCMi 9, Jerusalem: Franciscan Printing Press, 1970]). This early date is now almost universally rejected. Some Israeli archaeologists contend that the limestone synagogue dates to the second or third century CE, but most date it to the fourth century (see Runesson, Binder, and Olsson, *Ancient Synagogue from Its Origins to 200 C.E.*, 29–32). Runesson, Binder, and Olsson conclude that the "black basalt platform underneath the main hall of the limestone synagogue constitutes the ruins of a first-century synagogue" (p. 32). Pottery found in and under this floor confirms the ancient date of the older, basalt foundation. For further discussion, see J. F. Strange and H. Shanks, "Synagogue Where Jesus Preached Found at Capernaum," *BAR* 9, no. 6 (1983): 24–31, esp. 28–31.

26. Corbo, *House of St. Peter at Capharnaum*. For a popular presentation of the data, see J. F. Strange and H. Shanks, "Has the House . . . Been Found?," 26–37.

supported by beams. At the center of the structure was a courtyard surrounded by a series of rooms. Sometime in the middle of the first century CE, the floor and walls of the largest room were plastered. Evidence of cooking and domestic life ends. The plaster and a large number of lamp fragments suggest that the room had been converted into a public meeting place, some eight meters by nine meters.

It is speculated that the Capernaum house had become a gathering place for early Christians. Evidently, it continued to serve this function for centuries, with a wall in the fourth century being built around the aging house. The complex had been converted into a "house-church," its second manifestation. Graffiti suggest that this interpretation is correct.[27]

The complex was updated again in the fifth century with an octagonal structure superimposed over the old house but within the boundaries of the fourth-century "house-church" walls. This new complex was complete with apse and baptistry. The house-church was destroyed in the early seventh century.

Was the original domestic structure the house of Peter and his brother Andrew (cf. Mark 1:29)?[28] Fishhooks found beneath the paving of the later house-church are not of much probative value. We should assume that generations of inhabitants in Capernaum before and after Peter's time were fishermen. The name of Peter himself is said to be inscribed on a dislodged stone (i.e., "Peter, the helper of Rome"), but this reading is very doubtful.[29]

The Gospels' frequent mention of Capernaum and the evident fact that Peter, whose wife was from Capernaum, was the leader of the disciples constitute reasonable circumstantial evidence for concluding that Capernaum did in fact serve as Jesus' base of operations and that it was specifically the house of Peter's mother-in-law in which he stayed. Accordingly, we may justly suppose that early Christian interest in this site was due to the belief that this was indeed the very house in which Jesus frequently stayed and taught (Mark 1:21, "they went into Capernaum; and immediately on the sabbath he entered the synagogue and taught"; 1:29, "he left the synagogue, and entered the house of Simon and Andrew"; 1:32–33, "at sundown, they brought to him all who were sick . . . the whole city was gathered at the door"; 2:1, "when he returned to Capernaum after some days, it was reported that he was at home"; 9:33, "they came to Capernaum, and when he was in the house . . ."; cf. Luke 4:23; 7:1).[30]

---

27. One graffito reads, "Lord Jesus Christ, help your servant," and another, "Christ have mercy" (Strange and Shanks, "Has the House . . . Been Found?," 33). Some 111 Greek inscriptions have been identified, as well as nine in Aramaic, nine in Syriac, two in Latin, and one in Hebrew. There are also pictures, including forms of crosses and a boat.

28. See the discussion in C. Breytenbach, "Mark and Galilee: Text World and Historical World," in *Galilee through the Centuries: Confluence of Cultures* (ed. E. M. Meyers; Duke Judaic Studies 1; Winona Lake, IN: Eisenbrauns, 1999), 75–85, esp. 80–84.

29. Strange and Shanks, "Has the House . . . Been Found?," 35–36; J. F. Strange, "The Capernaum and Herodium Publications, Part 2," *BASOR* 233 (1979): 68–69. For a summary of work in Capernaum, see S. Loffreda and V. Tzaferis, "Capernaum," *NEAEHL* 1:291–96.

30. For additional reports of archaeological work at Capernaum, which take into account more fully the Greek Orthodox section of the site, see V. Tzaferis et al., *Excavations at Capernaum 1, 1978–1982* (Winona Lake, IN: Eisenbrauns, 1989).

The Gospels also tell us that Peter, his brother Andrew, and James and John, the sons of Zebedee, were fishermen (Mark 1:16–20). The location and archaeology of Capernaum support this tradition. A spectacular find some thirty years ago provides additional insights.

The Kinneret Boat

In 1986, after several years of less-than-average rainfall, the level of the Sea of Galilee (Kinneret Lake) was several meters lower than normal. Two brothers, Moshe and Yuval Lufan, wandering along the shore near Ginosar noticed the outline of what appeared to be a boat. They reported their find and the boat was recovered. The ingenuity and technology required to salvage this boat constitute a remarkable story in its own right.[31]

The boat, which Israelis call the "Kinneret Boat," is 8.27 meters long, 2.3 meters wide, and 1.3 meters deep. When discovered, it was mostly submerged in mud. Because the wood had become almost completely waterlogged and oxygen-free, it was not consumed by the bacteria that normally feed on wood. Carbon 14 tests have dated the boat to the second half of the first century BCE and the first half of the first century CE.[32] This range of dates is consistent with the pottery finds. The boat is now conserved and on display in the Yigal Allon Museum in Kibbutz Ginosar, on the northwest shore of the Sea of Galilee. *(See fig. 2.3.)*

The recovery and preservation of the Kinneret Boat may be compared to the recovery and study of the Kyrenia Ship of Cyprus. The latter boat was first observed by diver Andreas Cariolou in 1965, just over one mile northeast of the harbor of Kyrenia, at a depth of thirty-three meters. The wreck was salvaged from 1967 to 1969. Preservation of the timbers and study of the finds, with some interruptions, have continued to the present. Most of the hull and a selection of the artifacts found with the boat are on display in the Ancient Shipwreck Museum in the Kyrenia Castle.[33]

---

31. This story is well told in S. Wachsmann, *The Sea of Galilee Boat: A 2000 Year Old Discovery from the Sea of Legends* (Cambridge, MA: Perseus, 2000); cf. S. Wachsmann and K. Raveh, "The Discovery," and O. Cohen, "Conservation of the Boat," in S. Wachsmann, J. R. Steffy, et al., *The Excavations of an Ancient Boat in the Sea of Galilee (Lake Kinneret)* (*'Atiqot* 19; Jerusalem: Israel Antiquities Authority, 1990), 1–7 and 15–22, respectively.

32. See R. Riesner, "Das Boot vom See Gennesaret," *BK* 41 (1986): 135–38; D. Adan-Bayewitz, "Dating the Pottery from the Galilee Boat Excavation," *BAR* 14, no. 5 (1988): 24–29; I. Carmi, "How Old Is the Galilee Boat?," *BAR* 14, no. 5 (1988): 30–33; idem, "Radiocarbon Dating of the Boat," in S. Wachsmann, J. R. Steffy, et al., *The Excavations of an Ancient Boat in the Sea of Galilee (Lake Kinneret)* (*'Atiqot* 19; Jerusalem: Israel Antiquities Authority, 1990), 127–28; S. Wachsmann, "The Date of the Boat," in Wachsmann, Steffy, et al., *Excavations of an Ancient Boat*, 129–30; A. Raban, "The Boat from Migdal Nunia and the Anchorages of the Sea of Galilee from the Time of Jesus," *International Journal of Nautical Archaeology and Underwater Exploration* 17 (1988): 311–29; S. Wachsmann, "The Excavation of the Kinneret Boat," *BAIAS* 6 (1986–87): 50–52; idem, "The Galilee Boat: 2,000-Year-Old Hull Recovered Intact," *BAR* 14, no. 5 (1988): 18–23; C. Peachey, "Model Building in Nautical Archaeology: The Kinneret Boat," *BA* 53 (1990): 46–53.

33. No complete report of the discovery, recovery, and restoration of the Kyrenia Boat has been published. For now, one must consult J. R. Steffy, "The Kyrenia Ship: An Interim

The Kyrenia Ship is 14.7 meters long, 4.42 meters wide, and about 1.5 meters deep (with reference only to the hull), and was originally fitted with a single square sail. Accordingly, it is almost twice the size of the Kinneret Boat. Found within the Kyrenia wreck were four complete sets of eating utensils and a large common cooking pot, which suggests that there were four crew members. Damage to the stern, including what look like spear and javelin thrusts, gives rise to the speculation that the ship and crew came under attack, probably by pirates. Whether the ship was intentionally scuttled is difficult to determine. In any event, it appears that most if not all of the cargo went down with the ship. No human traces have been recovered. It is estimated that the Kyrenia Ship sank sometime around 300 BCE. It is further estimated that it may have been in service for almost one century.

Like the Kinneret Boat, the remains of the Kyrenia Ship survived thanks to anoxic conditions on the ocean floor. But the recovery of the Kyrenia Ship was nothing like the later recovery of the Kinneret Boat. Whereas the Kinneret Boat was refloated in one piece and towed to a shelter where it would be cleaned and preserved, the Kyrenia Ship was salvaged one timber at a time. These timbers, mostly pine, were preserved and eventually reassembled, with the result that approximately three-quarters of the original hull has been restored. A great many planks and timbers today remain in storage. The hull was protected, probably late in the life of the boat, with lead sheathing. It is theorized that the hull had been weakened by woodworm, a common problem for wooden vessels in the Mediterranean.

The cargo in this modest transport was immense. The ship contained about four hundred wine amphorae of standard size and several jars containing some nine thousand almonds. The latter are remarkably well preserved. Only a small sample of these items are on display in the museum. The Kyrenia Ship also contained twenty-nine millstones, whose arrangement in the hull suggests they served as ballast. The bulk of the cargo is today undergoing further analysis and preservation.[34]

It is estimated that the Kinneret Boat—which, again, is about half the size of the Kyrenia Ship—could have accommodated as many as fifteen people.[35] This is interesting and is probably the single most important datum when one thinks of references to Jesus and his disciples together in a boat (e.g., Mark 8:10), for it indicates that it is possible that Jesus and the twelve could have sailed together in a single boat. The size is also consistent with the comment in Mark 1:20 that Zebedee, the father of James and John, employed hired hands to help in the fishing. Boats of the size of the one found at Ginosar were manned by more than the members of a

---

Report on Its Hull Construction," *AJA* 38 (1985): 71–101; S. W. Katzev, "The Ancient Ship of Kyrenia, Beneath Cyprus Seas," in *Great Moments in Greek Archaeology* (ed. P. Valavanis and D. Hardy; Los Angeles: J. Paul Getty Museum, 2007), 286–99. To date, three replicas of the Kyrenia Ship have been built.

34. I wish to record my thanks to Dr. Tom Davis and the technicians and volunteers currently at work on the timbers and cargo of the Kyrenia Ship. They answered my questions and allowed me to observe their work and examine many of the artifacts.

35. See the discussion in Wachsmann, *Sea of Galilee Boat*, 309–12. On the basis of the boat depicted in the Migdal Mosaic, the Kinneret Boat, and references in Josephus (cf. *J.W.* 2.635), Wachsmann estimates that these fishing boats had crews of five to seven men and could accommodate up to fifteen crew and passengers in total.

single family. And finally, the design of the boat's stern is consistent with the story of Jesus asleep on a cushion in the stern (Mark 4:38).

The Kinneret Boat is often talked about as though it had served as a fishing boat and that it at one time had been equipped with a mast and sail. However, there is no indication that this boat ever had a mast. Although it may have served as a fishing boat, the Kinneret Boat may well have been used for transportation of goods (or people).[36]

Well designed and well made, the Kinneret Boat was constructed from no fewer than ten species of wood (cedar and oak being the most common). The planks and supporting beams are small; they are joined and fastened with wooden pegs and iron nails. The boat had been repaired frequently and had probably been retired at shore (and not sunk), where it was later cannibalized for parts. It eventually sank beneath the water and became partially submerged in the mud, whose anoxic environment, as already mentioned, made the boat's preservation possible.

Archaeologist Ken Dark of the University of Reading has surveyed the recent work at Magdala (see ch. 1 above) and surrounding areas, including the modern city of Migdal, situated in the nearby hills to the west.[37] While field-walking "in the area between Migdal and the coast, south of Ginosar," he and his team found hundreds of sherds from the Roman period and even some specimens from the Hellenistic period.[38] In Migdal itself, Dark and his team observed fragments of architectural stonework from the Roman and Byzantine periods.[39] Because of the presence of many sherds and pieces of stonework, Dark suspects that the decorated stonework is local and that it was not brought in from other regions in recent times. Dark suggests that these materials provide evidence of an as-yet-unidentified city situated where modern Migdal sits today, a city that existed from the late Hellenistic period to the Byzantine period. This unidentified city, Dark surmises, was supported by the harbor town of what archaeologists today identify, rightly or wrongly, as Magdala. He further surmises that the harbor at "Magdala," whose stone quay has been exposed, may have been the home berth of the Kinneret Boat.[40]

One Jacobean Artifact

The announcement in the fall of 2002 of the discovery of an ossuary on which are inscribed the words "James, son of Joseph, brother of Jesus" stunned the public and

36. I am grateful to Dr. Jerome Hall of the University of San Diego for permitting a private examination of the Kinneret Boat in 2013. Careful viewing of the interior of the hull (which is not possible from the floor of the exhibit room) clearly shows that there had never been the fittings necessary for support of a mast. The condition of the boat is truly remarkable. At the bottom of the hull, at the stern, one can still see traces of red paint. (Again, this part of the boat cannot be viewed from the floor of the exhibit.)

37. K. R. Dark, "Archaeological Evidence," 185–202.

38. Ibid., 187–88.

39. Ibid., 188–94 + figs. 4–14.

40. Ibid., 194–96. For a photo of Magdala's stone quay, see J. Corbett, "New Synagogue Excavations," 52–59, at 54.

the academic world like no other find since the discovery of the Dead Sea Scrolls. As a single artifact, the "James Ossuary"—if authentic and if indeed belonging to James of Nazareth, brother of Jesus—will surely be ranked as one of the most important artifacts ever to come to light.

Because the ossuary was not uncovered in situ by qualified archaeologists,[41] the question of authenticity was hotly debated for several years. Worse yet, because we do not know precisely where it was found and what it contained, we have lost the most important data with which the ossuary might have been able to provide us. Nevertheless, the ossuary and its inscription are not without value.

The ossuary is some fifty centimeters long at the base, widening to fifty-six centimeters at the top, some thirty centimeters wide at one end, about twenty-six centimeters wide at the other end, and about thirty centimeters high. (Thus, the ossuary is not perfectly rectangular in form.) The inscription, which is made up of five words, is nineteen centimeters long. The lid is flat and rests on a ledge inside the rim. Badly weathered, the ossuary reveals faint traces of rosettes on one side. It is also reported that tiny bone fragments were present in the dust and debris at the bottom of the ossuary.

The ossuary is quite shabby in comparison to most. It is badly weathered, with the decorated side having suffered the worst of it. The inscription is for the most part deeply incised and is quite legible. Even to the naked eye, it is clear that the inscription has been retraced in more recent times, which, along with weathering and cleaning in modern times, has seriously compromised the forensic evidence on which geologists and archaeologists depend in order to ascertain dating and authenticity.

The workmanship of the ossuary is poor to average, as the sloppy measurements indicate. However, the inscription itself compares favorably to those of the other 895 ossuaries that have been catalogued by Levi Rahmani. I would rate it above average (and much better than the inscriptions on the "Caiaphas" ossuary).[42]

The inscription is quite legible and reads as follows:

> יעקוב בר יוסף אחוי דישוע
> Jacob, son of Joseph, brother of Yeshuʿa
> (*or:* James, son of Joseph, brother of Jesus)

There are no spaces between the words, and the letters are deeply etched into the limestone. André Lemaire, who published the first scholarly study of the ossuary, concluded that the style of writing points to the last two decades prior to the destruction of Jerusalem and that in all probability the inscription is authentic and refers to early Christianity's James the brother of Jesus.[43]

---

41. It was discovered quite by accident in April 2002 by French paleographer and Hebrew scholar André Lemaire, while viewing artifacts owned by private collector Oded Golan of Tel Aviv.

42. I was able to view the ossuary when it was displayed in the Royal Ontario Museum in Toronto during the annual meeting of the American Academy of Religion and the Society of Biblical Literature in November 2002.

43. A. Lemaire, "Burial Box of James the Brother of Jesus," *BAR* 28, no. 6 (2002): 24–33, 70, esp. 28, 33; idem, "L'ossuaire de 'Jacques fils de Joseph, le frère de Jésus," *Polish Journal of Biblical Research* 2, no. 2 (2003): 81–87.

This conclusion has been disputed, with some claiming either that the Aramaic is faulty or that it is Aramaic of a later date, and that in either case the inscription, or at least the last two words ("brother of Jesus"), is a forgery.[44] The two linguistic objections are without foundation, however, and the ongoing scientific study of the ossuary has in fact confirmed the antiquity of the whole inscription.

First, it is not true that the Aramaic is faulty (as one or two have claimed). The exact construction is attested in one of the targumim: for example, *Targum Neofiti* translates the Hebrew אֲחִי אֶשְׁכֹּל וַאֲחִי עָנֵר ("brother of Eshcol and brother of Aner") in Gen 14:13 as אחוי דאשכל ואחוי דענר, which employs precisely the same construction we find in the latter half of the inscription on the James ossuary.[45] The אחוי form is also attested in a synagogue inscription: ושמעון אחוי, "and Simeon his brother."[46] More importantly, the form is attested in 1QapGen XXI, 34: לות בר אחוי, "Lot, son of his (Abram's) brother."[47]

Second, it is not true that the second part of the inscription reflects an Aramaic that was not in use in the first century. The exact construction is found on another ossuary inscription dating from the same period:

> שימי בר עשיה אחוי דחנין
> Shimi, son of ʿAsaiah, brother of Ḥanin

Note the use of אחוי ד, "brother of." Admittedly, the *dalet* before the name Ḥanin must be partly restored (the horizontal stroke is effaced), but no other reading will work.[48] The construction matches the one found in the James Ossuary exactly.

It has been suggested that mention of the deceased's brother probably implies that the brother was well known, probably much better known than either the deceased or his father. In the case of the James Ossuary, this would certainly be true. Josephus himself identifies James as the brother of Jesus (*Ant.* 20.200–203). So why is Ḥanin mentioned in the inscription that identifies Shimi? Could this Ḥanin be none other than the well-known Ḥanin whose sons were known for supplying Jerusalem with sacrificial animals (cf. *y. Peʾah* 1:5; *b. Sanh.* 41a)?

There are no compelling linguistic or epigraphic reasons to regard the James Ossuary inscription as inauthentic. Even the claim that the last two words (i.e., אחוי

---

44. Several publications appeared in 2002 and 2003 discussing issues surrounding this ossuary and its controversial inscription. A few of these include E. Puech, "À propos de l'ossuaire de Jacques le frère de Jésus," *Polish Journal of Biblical Research* 2, no. 1 (2002): 7–23; H. Shanks and B. Witherington III, *The Brother of Jesus* (San Francisco: HarperCollins, 2003); M. M. Mitchell, "Does the 'James Ossuary' Bring Us Closer to Jesus?," *RSN: SBL Edition* 1, no. 2 (2003): 9–10. Several essays have appeared in recent issues of the *Polish Journal of Biblical Research*, including a surprisingly lengthy bibliography in 2, no. 2 (2003): 91–96.

45. For more examples, see *Tg. Neof.* Gen 10:21; 28:5; 43:29. (At Gen 14:13, *Onqelos* reads אחוהי דאשכל ואחוהי דענר.)

46. J. A. Fitzmyer and D. J. Harrington, *A Manual of Palestinian Aramaic Texts (Second Century B.C.–Second Century A.D.)* (BibOr 34; Rome: Pontifical Biblical Institute, 1978), 268–69 (no. A42) and 298 (for notes).

47. Ibid., 122. 1QapGen probably dates to the end of the first century BCE or the beginning of the first century CE.

48. See Rahmani, *Catalogue of Jewish Ossuaries*, no. 570.

דישוע) were inscribed later, perhaps by a second hand, proves little. In the case of the ossuary of the crucified man, the name Yehoḥanan occurs twice, clearly written by two different hands. After a lengthy trial in which several witnesses, including geochemists, gave testimony, the court ruled that there is no convincing evidence of forgery.[49] Even one of the scientists who had originally claimed that the James Ossuary inscription was modern recanted, acknowledging the presence of traces of ancient, authentic patina in the disputed words. There are no longer legitimate grounds for calling into question the authenticity of this ossuary or any part of its inscription.[50] The only remaining question centers on the identification of the persons whose names appear in the inscription.

All three names of the James Ossuary (James [or Jacob], Joseph, and Jesus) were common in the late Second Temple period and are well represented in ossuary and crypt inscriptions. We may review the evidence briefly.

James (or Jacob). Tal Ilan identifies forty-five individuals in the corpus she surveys in her study *Lexicon of Jewish Names* who bore the name Jacob.[51] In the James Ossuary, Jacob is spelled with the *waw*: יעקוב (as in Jer 30:18: יַעֲקוֹב). It appears in this form on at least three other ossuaries: two of these simply have the name "Jacob" and the other has "Aha and Jacob, his son."[52] Jacob also appears without the *waw* on two ossuaries (i.e., יעקב, as in Gen 25:26 and passim: יַעֲקֹב): "Martha, daughter of Joseph, son of Jacob, wife of Joseph, from Hin" and "Jacob Birebbi" (or "Jacob, son of the great").[53] Jacob appears in Greek inscriptions as well, spelled variously ιακω,[54] ιακωβ,[55] ιακωβω,[56] ιακωβος,[57] ιακκωβος,[58] ιακως,[59] ιακουβος,[60] and

49. In June 2003, the Israel Antiquities Authority issued a report declaring the inscription to be a forgery. But the geological aspects of this report were severely criticized. Questions of bias were also raised. Besides Lemaire, "Burial Box of James," 29 (for a copy of the geologists' report), see also H. Shanks, "Between Authenticity and Forgery," *RSN: SBL Edition* 4, no. 2 (2003): 6–8; idem, "Cracks in James Bone Box Repaired," *BAR* 29, no. 1 (2003): 20–25; E. J. Keall, "Brother of Jesus Ossuary: New Tests Bolster Case for Authenticity," *BAR* 29, no. 4 (2003): 52–55, 70; A. Lemaire, "Critical Evaluation of the IAA Committee Reports Regarding the Ossuary Inscription," *Polish Journal of Biblical Research* 2, no. 2 (2003): 29–60; J. A. Harrell, "Final Blow to IAA Report: Flawed Geochemistry Used to Condemn James Inscription," *BAR* 30, no. 1 (2004): 38–41.

50. For a report on the trial and the evidence presented, see H. Shanks, *James Brother of Jesus: The Forgery Trial of the Century* (Washington, DC: Biblical Archaeology Society, 2012). One will also want to see idem, *Jerusalem Forgery Conference: Biblical Archaeology Society Special Report* (Washington, DC: Biblical Archaeology Society, 2007).

51. Ilan, *Lexicon of Jewish Names*, 171–74.

52. Rahmani, *Catalogue of Jewish Ossuaries*, nos. 104, 678, and 396, respectively.

53. Ibid., nos. 290 and 865, respectively.

54. *CIJ* no. 956; M. Schwabe and B. Lifshitz, *Beth Sheʿarim*, vol. 2, *The Greek Inscriptions* (New Brunswick, NJ: Rutgers University Press, 1974), nos. 83, 126, and 130, respectively.

55. Schwabe and Lifshitz, *Beth Sheʿarim*, no. 75.

56. *CIJ* no. 1482.

57. Schwabe and Lifshitz, *Beth Sheʿarim*, no. 125.

58. Ibid., no. 6.

59. Ibid., no. 203.

60. *CIJ* nos. 1467 and 1505.

ικουβος.[61] In the LXX, the name regularly appears as Ιακωβ, while in the New Testament manuscripts it appears as ιακωβ or ιακωβος. The latter form is an accommodation to Greek inflection.

In the early Jesus movement, James became known as "the Just" (cf. Eusebius, *Ecclesiastical History* 2.23.12–14). Evidently he was not unique in this respect. One of the men nominated to replace Judas Iscariot was "Joseph called Barsabbas, who was called Justus" (Acts 1:23). "Justus" (Ιοῦστος) is Latin (*justus*) and means "the just one."

From an earlier time, we know of the much-respected high priest Simon the Just, who succeeded Onias (Sir 50:1; Josephus, *Ant.* 12.43; *m. Parah* 3:5). We are told that Simon was called "the Just" (ὁ δίκαιος) because of his piety toward God and his kindness to his people. The sobriquet also parallels the title given the Teacher of Righteousness mentioned in the Dead Sea Scrolls (CD I, 1; 1QpHab I, 13).

Joseph. Ilan identifies 232 individuals who bore the name Joseph.[62] In the James Ossuary, Joseph is spelled יוסף (*ywsp*), which is the standard spelling of the name in the Hebrew Bible (e.g., Gen 30:24: יֹסֵף). There is one other example of this spelling in an ossuary inscription: "Pinhas, son of Joseph."[63] The most common spelling of this name on ossuaries is יהוסף (*yhwsp*), which only occurs once in the Hebrew Bible (Ps 81:6 [Eng. 81:5]: יְהוֹסֵף). Indeed, there are numerous examples of this spelling in ossuary inscriptions: "Our father, Simeon the elder, Joseph his son," "Master Joseph, son of Benaia, son of Judah," "Joseph, son of Haggai," and many others.[64] Other Semitic forms include יוסי, יהסף, יהוסיף, and יוסה. Greek forms include ιωσε, ιοσε, ιοση,[65] ιωσηφ,[66] ιωσηφος,[67] ιωασαφ,[68] ιωσεφος,[69] ιωσηπος,[70] and ιωσης.[71] The most common biblical Greek form is Ιωσήφ, though Ιώσηπος is attested a few times in the Apocrypha (1 Esd 9:34; 1 Macc 5:18, 60; 8:22; 10:19).

Jesus. Ilan identifies 104 individuals who bore the name Jesus or its older form Joshua.[72] There is a similar range of diversity in the forms of the name Jesus as we have seen in the names Jacob and Joseph. In the James Ossuary, the name is spelled ישוע (*yšwʿ*). This is the late biblical form of the name (occurring several times in Ezra, Nehemiah, and Chronicles) and is vocalized יֵשׁוּעַ. The older, fuller form is יְהוֹשֻׁעַ (*yĕhôšūaʿ*), "Joshua." In postbiblical Hebrew, ישוע was sometimes abbreviated יֵשׁוּ (*yēšû*). ישוע, the form found on the James Ossuary, is attested on at least another four or five ossuaries: "Jesus, son of Dostas," "Jesus," "Judah, son of Jesus,"

61. Schwabe and Lifshitz, *Beth Sheʿarim*, nos. 94 and 96, respectively.
62. Ilan, *Lexicon of Jewish Names*, 150–68, 449.
63. Rahmani, *Catalogue of Jewish Ossuaries*, no. 573.
64. Ibid., nos. 12, 327, and 603.
65. Schwabe and Lifshitz, *Beth Sheʿarim*, nos. 19, 41, 43, 48, 93, 124, and 221.
66. Ibid., nos. 23, 26, 32, 33, 44, and 178.
67. *CIJ* no. 1485; Horbury and Noy, *Jewish Inscriptions of Graeco-Roman Egypt*, no. 132.
68. Schwabe and Lifshitz, *Beth Sheʿarim*, no. 45.
69. Horbury and Noy, *Jewish Inscriptions*, no. 143.
70. *CIJ* no. 1427.
71. Horbury and Noy, *Jewish Inscriptions*, no. 12.
72. Ilan, *Lexicon of Jewish Names*, 126–33, 449.

and "Jesus, son of Joseph."[73] In one example, the longer form ישוע and its abbreviation ישו occur together: "Yeshu . . . Yeshuʿa, son of Joseph."[74] In rabbinic literature, the abbreviated form is used in reference to Jesus of Nazareth (cf. *b. Sanh.* 43a, 103a: "Yeshu ha-Noṣri," or "Jesus the Nazarene"). Greek forms of the name Jesus include Ιησοῦς (the most common form in the LXX and New Testament, as well as in the Greek ossuary inscriptions),[75] ιησιος,[76] ιεσους,[77] ιεσουος,[78] and ισουος.[79]

Like the Petrine artifacts, the James Ossuary—if indeed it is the ossuary that at one time contained the remains of the brother of Jesus—clarifies and may even confirm important details about the background of the New Testament narratives.[80] Scientific study has determined that the inscription in its entirety is ancient and authentic. The identifications of the named individuals remain uncertain. If the names in the James Ossuary inscription do refer to the well-known New Testament figures of the same names, we learn at least four things:

(1) James and his family probably spoke Aramaic. Scholars have long considered Aramaic to have been Jesus' first language, and the James Ossuary lends an important measure of support to this hypothesis. Of course, one could object and say that all we know is that the inscriber of the ossuary, but not necessarily James, spoke Aramaic. However, given the personal, family-oriented reality of ossilegium, it is prudent to assume that the language used in the inscription is the language of the family and, therefore, of the deceased.

(2) James, originally from Galilee, later lived in or near Jerusalem. We are left with this impression in the New Testament (particularly in the book of Acts and in Paul's letter to the churches of Galatia). After all, if James' family and home were still in Galilee, then we should not have expected his ossuary to be found in Jerusalem. Its discovery in Jerusalem shows that in all probability his home had become Jerusalem. Therefore, when his bones were gathered and placed in an ossuary, the ossuary remained in Jerusalem, in the family tomb.

(3) The James Ossuary may also suggest that James died in or near Jerusalem, as early church traditions maintain (Eusebius, *Ecclesiastical History* 2.23.4–18; cf. Josephus, *Ant.* 20.200–203). If the ossuary was discovered in a burial vault near the Temple Mount, perhaps in the Kidron Valley, as has been conjectured,[81] this may offer a measure of support to the tradition that James was closely associated with

---

73. Rahmani, *Catalogue of Jewish Ossuaries*, nos. 121, 140, 702, and 704; the "Joshua" form is attested in no. 63.

74. Ibid., no. 9.

75. *CIJ* nos. 1476 and 1511; Schwabe and Lifshitz, *Beth Sheʿarim*, no. 51; Rahmani, *Catalogue of Jewish Ossuaries*, nos. 56, 113, 114, and 751.

76. Rahmani, *Catalogue of Jewish Ossuaries*, no. 89.

77. Klein, *Jüdisch-Palästinisches Corpus Inscriptionum*, no. 46.

78. Schwabe and Lifshitz, *Beth Sheʿarim*, nos. 138, 139, and 140.

79. B. Lifshitz, *Donateurs et fondateurs dans les synagogues juives: Répertoire des dédicaces grecques relatives à la construction et à la réfection des synagogues* (CahRB 7; Paris: Gabalda, 1967), 58.

80. I make this point in C. A. Evans, "Jesus and the Ossuaries," *BBR* 13 (2003): 21–46; idem, "On the Recently Discovered James Ossuary," *DavarLogos* 2 (2003): 65–72.

81. J. Murphy-O'Connor, "Where Was James Buried?," *BRev* 19, no. 3 (2003): 34–42.

the temple, even if he was at odds with the powerful priestly family of Annas. Of course, this suggestion is at best tenuous, but the discovery of the ossuary of James in the general vicinity of the Temple Mount does lend a small measure of support to Christian tradition and to the brief report of James' death found in Josephus.

(4) And finally, secondary burial according to Jewish burial custom implies that James, though a follower of Jesus and a part of a movement that was beginning to drift away from its Jewish heritage, continued to live as a Jew, and so was buried as a Jew. The Christianity of James, we may infer, was not understood as something separate from or opposed to Jewish faith. This observation is completely in step with a critical reading of the traditions about James found in the New Testament, especially in the unvarnished account we have in Paul's letter to the churches of Galatia. There we are told that even a major figure like Peter was cowed by the arrival in Antioch of "men from James," with the result that the apostle no longer ate with Gentiles (Gal 2:11–14). It is clear from the context that Peter withdrew from the Gentiles because the men from James were Torah-observant and evidently expected Peter and other Jewish believers (such as Barnabas) to be Torah-observant also.

Thus, we may have the ossuary of a man who was interred without ostentation, in accordance with proper Jewish burial custom, and in the vicinity of Jerusalem, perhaps in close proximity to the Temple Mount itself. All of these details are consistent with what we are told in our literary sources, namely, that James lived in Jerusalem, frequented the temple, did not waver in his adherence to the Jewish faith, and was known as a man of modest and humble means. In short, the James Ossuary is consistent with the Judaic character of James and the community that he guided and defended. If the ossuary is authentic, this is probably the most important detail that it can tell us.[82]

Postscript: Two Houses in Nazareth

I should also mention briefly the remains in Nazareth of two houses that from Byzantine times, if not earlier, Christians believed were the homes in which Mary and her son Jesus were raised. Review of these two sites and the archaeological evidence provides a helpful perspective in evaluating the claims in support of the Petrine identification of the house in Capernaum that was considered above.

In the lowest level of the Basilica of the Annunciation in Nazareth are the remains of a domestic dwelling that most are willing to date to the first century BCE. The modern Basilica of the Annunciation, built in 1969, stands over the remains

82. See J. Magness, "Ossuaries and the Burials of Jesus and James," *JBL* 124 (2005): 121–54. Magness doubts that the remains of James, after primary burial, would have been reburied in an ossuary. She thinks instead that his body would have been placed in a trench-cut grave without later reburial. Magness could be correct, of course, but the assumption that James, the leader of the Jerusalem church, would have received a poor man's burial (whatever the economic circumstances of his prior life in Nazareth) is questionable.

of three older churches. The oldest dates to the Byzantine era, perhaps as early as the fourth century.[83] Pottery recovered from the site ranges in date from the beginning of the First Temple period on into the Byzantine period. Twenty-three tombs, dating from the Seleucid and Roman periods, have been uncovered, lying a few hundred meters to the north, south, and west; these tombs provide us with an approximation of the boundaries and size of the city.

Bellarmino Bagatti, who excavated the site in the 1950s and then again, briefly, in the 1960s, before the construction of the new church, believes a Jewish-Christian synagogue/church lies beneath the oldest Byzantine church. He dates it to the third century and wonders if this synagogue stands where the first-century synagogue stood, in which Jesus himself preached (Mark 6:1–6; Luke 4:16–30).[84]

In 2009, the Israel Antiquities Authority uncovered, across the street from the Basilica of the Annunciation, the remains of another house believed to date to the same time as the proposed house of Mary.[85] According to Yardenna Alexandre, who directed the excavation, the house was part of the small village that included the house beneath the Basilica of the Annunciation. She describes the house as small and typical of the houses in villages like Nazareth. Finds included a cistern, sherds of pottery, and pieces of chalk lamps.[86] The house excavated by Alexandre provides some additional context for study of the house beneath the church but does nothing to confirm the house as having belonged to the family of Mary.

The second potentially significant first-century Nazareth house is located beneath the Sisters of Nazareth convent. The convent stands above the Byzantine "Church of the Nutrition," that is, the place where, according to tradition, it is believed Jesus grew up and was nurtured. The ruins of this house, part of which cuts into the limestone hill, were discovered in the 1880s and were excavated by the nuns of the convent. In 1936, Henri Senès, a Jesuit priest and scholar, examined the site and did some additional excavation work. *(See fig. 2.4.)*

In 2006, Ken Dark initiated a new excavation of this house. He and his team were able to date the house to the first century. Besides pottery, they also recovered stone vessels, which reflect Jewish views of purity and impurity (cf. John 2:6).[87] Dark has concluded that the house was abandoned in the first century and subsequently two tombs were hewn adjacent to it. A few centuries later, Byzantine Christians erected a church over the house and the tombs.[88] The early veneration of the site

83. B. Bagatti, *Gli scavi di Nazaret*, vol. 1, *Dalle origini al secolo XII* (SBFCMa 17; Jerusalem: Franciscan Printing Press, 1967), 26–212; ET: *Excavations in Nazareth*, vol. 1, *From the Beginning till the XII Century* (trans. E. Hoade; SBFCMa 17; Jerusalem: Franciscan Printing Press, 1969), 27–218. See also the helpful summary in J. McRay, *Archaeology and the New Testament* (Grand Rapids: Baker, 1991), 157–58.

84. Bagatti, *Gli scavi di Nazaret*, 24–25, 226–27 (ET: *Excavations in Nazareth*, 25–26, 233–34); idem, *The Church from the Circumcision* (Jerusalem: Franciscan Printing Press, 1971), 126.

85. The excavation took place before the construction of the International Marian Center of Nazareth.

86. A brief report is posted on the IAA website.

87. Unlike earthenware, stoneware resists impurity.

88. One of these tombs became known as the Tomb of Joseph.

leads Dark to conclude that it is possible, but not proven, that the house was that of Jesus and his family.[89]

How do the supposed houses of Mary and Jesus in Nazareth compare to the house of Peter in Capernaum? What evidence there is lends some support to the identification of these houses as the house in which Mary grew up and the house in which Jesus grew up. Both Nazareth houses were identified in the early Byzantine era as the houses of Mary and Jesus. Archaeological excavations have established that both houses date to the right period. Perhaps the continuity of "village memory" was in play and was accurate (as it seems to have been in Capernaum and perhaps in Jerusalem also, with respect to the locations of the crucifixion and burial of Jesus). The house alleged to have been the house of Jesus was abandoned in the first century, which is consistent with the tradition that Mary and her son James (and perhaps other members of her family) relocated to Jerusalem (cf. Acts 1:14; 12:17; 15:13; 21:18; Gal 2:9, 12). No other locations rival these two houses.

This evidence, as supportive as it is for these identifications, falls short, in my opinion, primarily because of the absence of a convincing link between the first-century houses and their later Byzantine veneration. In the case of the house in Capernaum believed to have belonged to Peter's family, there is archaeological evidence that in the first century the house was transformed into a place for meeting, with indications that those who met in this house were Christians. No evidence of this nature has been found in the case of the two Nazareth houses some think should be linked to Mary and Jesus. If evidence of Christian presence in or contact with the two Nazareth houses should come to light, this could change our judgment from possible to probable.

The house beneath the Basilica of the Annunciation may have been the house in which Mary grew up, and the house beneath the Sisters of Nazareth convent may have been the house in which Mary raised Jesus and her other children. But the evidence at hand only allows us to speak of possibility. Again, however, that may change, should new evidence come to light.

Concluding Comments

The principal value of artifacts and of the archaeology that uncovers, contextualizes, and interprets them lies in their supplying us with the details of material culture that are presupposed in literary texts but are rarely mentioned and even more rarely explained. The excavations of Capernaum have uncovered homes, one of which Peter and his wife and family may have lived in, and a synagogue foundation that

89. Dark has published a series of reports under the title *Nazareth Archaeological Project* (London: Late Antiquity Research Group, 2008–12). One should also consult K. R. Dark, "The Roman-Period and Byzantine Landscape between Sepphoris and Nazareth," *PEQ* 140 (2008): 87–107; idem, "Early Roman-Period Nazareth and the Sisters of Nazareth Convent," *AJ* 92 (2012): 1–28 (see the summarizing comments on pp. 25–26). See the popular presentation of the evidence in idem, "Has Jesus' Nazareth House Been Found?," *BAR* 41, no. 2 (2015): 54–63, 72.

probably reaches back to the time of Jesus and Peter. When the Gospels speak of Jesus in the home of Peter or preaching and healing in the local synagogue, we can actually visualize these edifices. Indeed, we now know what a fishing boat from this period of time actually looks like and that it could in fact accommodate Jesus and his disciples.

Thanks to archaeological discoveries, we have attestations of the name Cephas, or Peter (ch. 1), and even a sobriquet—"Simon, builder of the temple"—that may provide relevant background for the nickname that Jesus gave to Simon Peter, especially in the context of the solemn declaration that the church would be built upon the rock (again, see ch. 1).

Much of what we have learned regarding the world of Peter probably applies to James the brother of Jesus, who grew up in another Galilean village not too far away. Ongoing excavations at Nazareth will no doubt shed light on day-to-day life there. Should one or both of the Nazareth houses that some think should be linked to Mary and Jesus be confirmed as such, then no doubt our knowledge of the living context of Jesus and his movement will be further increased.

But the artifact that is potentially the most important—the ossuary that bears Jesus' name and that of his famous brother—remains hotly debated. Although geochemical analysis supports the inscription's authenticity, scholars remain uncertain of the identities of the named persons. If at some point we conclude that the named individuals are those who feature so prominently in the New Testament narratives, we will finally be in a position to assess the value of this ossuary for understanding better the world of James and his community, especially as it existed in first-century Jerusalem, thus potentially shedding important light on the Judaic nature of the early messianic movement that at a later time and in another place became Christianity.

In the following chapter, we shall examine the archaeological materials that relate to three key figures involved in the death of Jesus. We shall see that, compared with what was discussed in the present chapter, the linkages between the artifacts and known persons is in most cases firmer.

CHAPTER THREE

Excavating Caiaphas, Pilate, and Simon of Cyrene: Assessing the Literary and Archaeological Evidence

Almost all historians and interpreters of the New Testament agree that the arrest, examination, and execution of Jesus of Nazareth constitute the most important series of events in the Gospel narratives. Who killed Jesus, why he was killed, and the juridical factors involved have been hotly debated for centuries. The two most prominent figures in this drama are Caiaphas the Jewish high priest and Pontius Pilate the Roman governor. As fortune would have it, we are in possession of significant literary and archaeological materials that relate to these two men. A third figure in the drama was Simon of Cyrene, the man who carried Jesus' cross to the place of crucifixion. Although this man did not possess the authority of Caiaphas and Pilate, his place in the crucifixion narrative is quite conspicuous. Fortune may have smiled on us once again, for we may be in possession of archaeological materials relating to him as well.

It is the purpose of this chapter to review these materials and to offer a somewhat revised assessment of the administrative functions and dispositions of Caiaphas and Pilate. The role played by Simon of Cyrene in the crucifixion of Jesus will be taken into account, along with the archaeological evidence.

Caiaphas in Literature and Archaeology

Caiaphas appears in the Gospels and the book of Acts.[1] In the earliest account of passion week, the Markan evangelist states that the "ruling priests [οἱ ἀρχιερεῖς] and scribes were seeking how to arrest (Jesus) by stealth, and kill him" (Mark 14:1). The Matthean evangelist expands this statement, adding Caiaphas: "Then the ruling

1. For a very helpful and still current interpretation of Caiaphas in history and in the New Testament and Josephus, see B. D. Chilton, "Caiaphas," *ABD* 1:803–6; H. K. Bond, *Caiaphas: Friend of Rome and Judge of Jesus?* (Louisville: Westminster John Knox, 2004); R. Metzner, *Kaiaphas, der Hohepriester jenes Jahres: Geschichte und Deutung* (AJEC 75; Leiden: Brill, 2010).

priests and the elders of the people gathered in the palace of the high priest [τοῦ ἀρχιερέως], who was called Caiaphas [τοῦ λεγομένου Καϊάφα]" (Matt 26:3). Likewise, while Mark says simply that Jesus was led to the high priest (Mark 14:53), the Matthean parallel identifies this high priest as "Caiaphas" (Καϊάφα; Matt 26:57). The Lukan evangelist links Caiaphas with Annas (Luke 3:2, "in the high-priesthood of Annas and Caiaphas [ἐπὶ ἀρχιερέως Ἄννα καὶ Καϊάφα]"; Acts 4:6, "with Annas the high priest [Ἄννας ὁ ἀρχιερεύς] and Caiaphas and John and Alexander, and all who were of the high-priestly family [ἐκ γένους ἀρχιερατικοῦ]"), perhaps because Caiaphas was the son-in-law of Annas (according to John 18:13). The close association of the two high priests is seen in the Fourth Gospel (John 18:13–28). Caiaphas also appears in the Fourth Gospel and is remembered for his "prophecy" that it is more expedient for one man to die than for the nation as a whole to perish (John 11:49–51; 18:13; Caiaphas was high priest "that year," that is, the year that Jesus was executed). In the Synoptic Gospels, Jesus is taken to the house of Caiaphas, while in the Fourth Gospel he is taken "first" to Annas (John 18:13), before being sent to Caiaphas (John 18:24). Although it is possible that two separate households are in play, given the size of some of the mansions southwest of the Temple Mount, the area in which some of the ruling priests lived, it might be better to think of Annas and his son-in-law Caiaphas living in separate portions of a very large compound.[2]

The Gospels tell us very little about Caiaphas the high priest. Mark says that Jesus was led to the high priest (and we should assume, along with Matthew, that Caiaphas is meant). But it is the other ruling priests who are said to seek testimony against Jesus, at least initially (Mark 14:55). Caiaphas becomes involved in verses 60–64, when he asks Jesus to reply to the accusations and then asks him directly if he is the Messiah, the Son of God (Mark 14:61). When Jesus says he is, and that as "son of man" he will be seated at the right hand of God and will come with the clouds of heaven (Mark 14:62)—implying that he will be seated next to God on the chariot throne (alluding to Ps 110:1 and Dan 7:9–14), thereby further implying that he will at that time judge the high priest and his associates—Caiaphas "tore his garments" and accused Jesus of blasphemy (Mark 14:63–64). The other ruling priests condemn Jesus as deserving death (Mark 14:65). The following morning, the ruling priests convene and decide to hand Jesus over to the Roman authorities (Mark 15:1). What role, if any, Caiaphas played in this deliberation is not said.

In the Matthean Gospel, Caiaphas plays only a slightly more active role. He accommodates the ruling priests, who plot against Jesus, by allowing them to gather in the courtyard (εἰς τὴν αὐλήν) of his home (Matt 26:3). And, as already noted,

2. I have in mind the palatial compound in the Jewish Quarter of Jerusalem, now housed in the Wohl Museum of Archaeology. Although it is too early to tell, the lower portion of the first-century house currently being excavated at Mount Zion under the direction of Shimon Gibson may be another example. Thus far, a number of important parallel features have been uncovered, including a large kitchen that had been equipped with three ceramic cookstoves, a stepped and plastered *miqwê*, and a luxurious bathroom with tiled floor, plastered walls, and a large plastered bathtub. All of these features are seen in the well-appointed compound in the Wohl Museum. For an archaeological report of the Herodian-era mansion, see N. Avigad, "Palatial Mansion," *NEAEHL* 2:733–35.

Caiaphas is mentioned by name when the arrested Jesus is brought to the ruling priests (Matt 26:57). In Luke, as in Mark, the name of Caiaphas is not mentioned during Jesus' hearing before the ruling priests and elders. He is mentioned by name when the apostles are brought before the Council and are ordered to cease their proclamation (Acts 4:1–6). In the Fourth Gospel, Caiaphas utters his *ex cathedra* pronouncement (John 11:49–50), which is recalled at the time of Jesus' arrest (John 18:14). Later colorful portraits of Caiaphas in Christian apocryphal literature, some of which were passed on uncritically by ecclesiastical authorities (such as Justin Martyr and Eusebius), have no historical value.

All in all, the role played by Caiaphas is essentially what one should expect of the high priest, as we may surmise from the evidence from Josephus and other sources. The ruling priests have taken offense at Jesus' teaching and conduct in the temple precincts, have contrived to effect a quiet arrest, and have presented him before members of the Council, with Caiaphas the high priest presiding. What personal interest in or antipathy toward Jesus that Caiaphas may have had is a matter of pure speculation. Even the action of tearing his robe has more to do with Jesus' remarkable assertion than with his views of Jesus and his movement. Tearing his clothes was the appropriate response of the judge who hears what may be regarded as blasphemy (cf. *m. Sanh.* 6:5).

Another important first-century witness to the life and career of Caiaphas is Josephus. The Jewish historian tells us that Tiberius appointed Valerius Gratus as governor over Judea. The latter then

> deposed Ananus from his sacred office, and proclaimed Ishmael, the son of Phabi, high priest. Not long afterwards he removed him also and appointed in his stead Eleazar, the son of the high priest Ananus. A year later he deposed him also and entrusted the office of high priest to Simon, the son of Camith. The last-mentioned held this position for not more than a year and was succeeded by Joseph, who was called Caiaphas ['Ιώσηπος ὁ καὶ Καϊάφας]. After these acts Gratus retired to Rome. (*Ant.* 18.34–35)

Later in his narrative, Josephus explains that the Syrian legate Vitellius, having sent Pilate to Rome to explain his conduct toward the Samaritans, returned the high-priestly vestments to Jewish custody. He goes on to relate that after Vitellius "had bestowed these benefits upon the nation, he removed from his office the high priest Joseph surnamed Caiaphas [τὸν ἀρχιερέα 'Ιώσηπον τὸν Καϊάφαν ἐπικαλούμενον], and appointed in his stead Jonathan, son of Ananus the high priest" (*Ant.* 18.95). Josephus makes no comments regarding the person or conduct of Caiaphas. What inferences, if any, may be made will be considered when the administration of Pontius Pilate is taken into account.

The high priest Caiaphas apparently is not mentioned in rabbinic literature, though the family name may appear.[3] In a discussion concerning the ashes of the red heifer, the Mishnah asks, "Who prepared them (since the time of Ezra)? Simeon the Just and Yohanan the high priest prepared two each, and Elyoʿenai the son of

3. Ilan, *Lexicon of Jewish Names*, 408; D. W. Chapman and E. J. Schnabel, *The Trial and Crucifixion of Jesus: Texts and Commentary* (WUNT 344; Tübingen: Mohr Siebeck, 2015), 10–14.

ha-Qayaf and Hanamel the Egyptian and Ishmael the son of Piabi prepared one each" (*m. Parah* 3:5). This Elyoʿenai the son of ha-Qayaf (הקיף) may have been a son of Joseph Caiaphas.[4] Some manuscripts, however, read ha-Qoph or ha-Quph (הקוף), thus making the identification uncertain. According to the Tosefta, Rabbi Joshua said: "I hereby give testimony concerning the family of the house of ʿAlubaʾi of Bet Shebaʾim and concerning the family of the house of Qayapha [קיפא] of Bet Meqoshesh, that they are children of co-wives, and from them high priests have been chosen, and they offered up sacrifices on the Temple altar" (*t. Yebam.* 1:10). The identification of this "house of Qayapha" with the Caiaphas family is probable. However, we learn nothing from this tradition beyond the simple fact that this family was a high-priestly family that offered sacrifices on the temple altar.

A slightly different version of the Tosefta tradition appears in the Babylonian Talmud: "I testify to you concerning two great families—the house of Zeboʿim of Ben ʿAkmai and the house of Ben Quphai [קופאי] of Ben Meqoshesh—that they were sons of rivals and yet some of them were high priests who ministered upon the altar" (*b. Yebam.* 15b). This tradition adds nothing to what we already know, but the spelling variation in the name Quphai attests to the possibilities of variation, which in turn may have a bearing on the question of the spelling and identification of the name found on the famous ossuary that will be considered shortly. Finally, the Caiaphas family name may also be mentioned in the Jerusalem Talmud, where in *Maʿaś.* 52a we hear of one "Menaḥem, son of Maxima, the brother of Jonathan Caiapha [יונתן קיפא]." Apart from the name itself, there is nothing here that suggests that this Jonathan was related to the high-priestly family of Caiaphas.[5]

The recent discovery of an ossuary on which the name of Caiaphas may be inscribed has generated interest and disagreement.[6] In November 1990, workers in Jerusalem's Peace Forest, about one mile south of the Old City, accidentally uncovered an ancient burial cave in which one dozen ossuaries were found. Six of these ossuaries had lain undisturbed for two millennia; the other six had been ransacked by grave robbers. Two of the untouched ossuaries bear the name קפא. On one of the boxes, two inscriptions read (on one end) יהוסף בר קיפא ("Yehoseph bar Qaipha")[7] and (on one side) יהוסף בר קפא ("Yehoseph bar Qapha"). This ossuary contained the

4. As suggested by M. Stern, "Herod's Policies and Jewish Society at the End of the Second Temple Period," *Tarbiz* 35 (1966): 235–53 (in Hebrew).

5. R. Reich has argued that "Caiaphas" is a nickname and that Josephus' reference to Caiaphas should be translated "Joseph nicknamed 'Caiaphas'" ("Ossuary Inscriptions from the Caiaphas Tomb," *Jerusalem Perspective* 4, nos. 4–5 [1991]: 13–21, at 17–18). The name may have functioned as a nickname, as it seems to in the example from the Jerusalem Talmud. The name on the ossuary, however, seems to read as a patronymic: "son of Qayapha." Could this work as a nickname, that is, as "son of (a man nicknamed) Qayapha"? On p. 19 of his article, Reich allows that Qayapha may have been a family name. This has also been argued more recently in R. Bauckham, "Caiaphas Family," 3–31.

6. For details, see *CIIP* no. 461; Chapman and Schnabel, *Trial and Crucifixion of Jesus*, 13–14.

7. In this chapter, I sometimes transliterate the name קיפא "Qaipha" and at other times I transliterate it "Qayapha." This reflects the fact that it is difficult to know whether the *yod* in the name functions consonantally or as a *mater lectionis*.

bones of a sixty-year-old man (and those of two infants, a toddler, a young boy, and a woman)[8] and could be the ossuary of Caiaphas the high priest, to whom Josephus refers as Joseph Caiaphas (see *Ant.* 18.35, 95, noted above). The sloppy inscription on the side of the ossuary, perhaps made with one of the two iron nails found in the tomb, may be the writing of the relative who placed his bones in the box (to keep a record of whose bones were in which box). *(See figs. 3.1–2.)*

The ornate and well-preserved "Caiaphas" ossuary is housed in the Israel Museum in Jerusalem. The skeletal remains have been interred on the Mount of Olives. In the nearby "Akeldama" field and ravine, the tomb of Annas (Luke 3:2; John 18:13, 24; Acts 4:6; cf. Josephus, *Ant.* 20.197–198), the high-priestly father-in-law of Caiaphas, may also have been identified.[9] According to Josephus, five of the sons of Annas served turns as high priest (*Ant.* 20.197–198). It is probable, therefore, that the influence of Annas extended well beyond his tenure in office.

Several archaeologists have identified the Yehoseph bar Qaipha of the ossuary with Joseph called Caiaphas of the narratives of Josephus and the New Testament Gospels. These include Zvi Greenhut and Ronny Reich,[10] among others.[11] Spelling agreement with the rabbinic traditions noted above and especially the agreement with Josephus, who alone in the literature tells us that Caiaphas' full name was Joseph Caiaphas, has convinced these scholars that the identification is probable. Although some scholars have expressed reservations, wondering if, instead of Qayapha (or Qaipha), the name should be vocalized Qopha, Qupha, or even Qepha,[12]

8. For analysis of the skeletal remains, see J. Zias, "Human Skeletal Remains from the 'Caiaphas' Tomb," *'Atiqot* 21 (1992): 78–80.

9. Ritmeyer and Ritmeyer, "Akeldama," 22–35, 76. On the possible identification of the family house, see A. Rupprecht, "The House of Annas-Caiaphas," *Archaeology in the Biblical World* 1 (1991): 4–17. On the possible identification of an ossuary in which the remains of a relative of the high priest Annas were interred, see D. Flusser, "Der Hohepriester Hannas und sein Geschlecht," in idem, *Entdeckungen im Neuen Testament*, vol. 2, *Jesus—Qumran—Urchristentum* (ed. M. Majer; Neukirchen-Vluyn: Neukirchener, 1999), 185–92.

10. Greenhut, "Burial Cave of Caiaphas Family," 28–36, 76; R. Reich, "Caiaphas Name Inscribed on Bone Boxes," *BAR* 18, no. 5 (1992): 38–44, 76; idem, "Ossuary Inscriptions from the 'Caiaphas' Tomb" (*'Atiqot*); idem, "Ossuary Inscriptions from the Caiaphas Tomb" (*Jerusalem Perspective*). This ossuary is one of the most impressive ossuaries ever discovered, and its beauty lends a measure of support to the Caiaphas identification.

11. Demerls and Long, "Recently Excavated Tomb of Joseph Bar Caipha," 50–58; Flusser, *Jesus*, 195–206; Crossan and Reed, *Excavating Jesus*, 242.

12. Horbury, "'Caiaphas' Ossuaries and Joseph Caiaphas," 32–48; Puech, "A-t-on redécouvert le tombeau du Caïphe?," 42–47; idem, *La croyance des Esséniens en la vie future*, 1:193–95. Horbury points out problems in the "Qayapha" reading, while Puech remarks that the tomb itself is not really an impressive crypt, as one would expect of a high priest's tomb. Moreover, the tomb is not very close to Akeldama, the site of the more impressive tombs. These objections have been answered in S. Gibson, *The Final Days of Jesus: The Archaeological Evidence* (San Francisco: HarperOne, 2009), 82–83, 159. Gibson plausibly suggests that at one time a prominent monument stood above the Caiaphas crypt. The poor quality of the inscription itself does not tell against the identification with the priestly Caiaphas family. Jodi Magness rightly denies a "correlation between the deceased and the quality of the inscriptions on ossuaries" (*Stone and Dung, Oil and Spit: Jewish Daily Life in the Time of Jesus* [Grand Rapids: Eerdmans, 2011], 248n33).

the discovery of the ossuary bearing an inscription that refers to קיפא as a priest has, in my view, settled the matter in favor of the Caiaphas identification.[13]

It should also be pointed out that Greek forms of Jewish names often expand them, for example, by adding another syllable. The name "Qatros" or "Qadros" may offer a pertinent example, for this high-priestly figure, whose name appears as Qadros (קדרוס) in *t. Menaḥ.* 13:19, 21 and as Qatros (קתרס) on a stone weight in the ruins of the "Burnt House" in the Old City, may very well be the Cantheras (Κανθήρας) mentioned in Josephus (*Ant.* 20.16).[14] If so, we have a relevant example of how a shorter, Semitic form of a name transliterates into a longer form in Greek.

Part of the difficulty is the relative rarity of the Qayapha name, which results in inadequate data for comparative analysis, as is the poor quality of the ossuary inscriptions themselves, making certain identification of the *yod* (so Reich et al.), as opposed to the *waw* (so Horbury and Puech), very difficult.[15] Fortunately, the linguistic and paleographic difficulties notwithstanding, the recently discovered ossuary on which Caiaphas is identified as a priest[16] provides a much firmer foundation for identifying the ossuary name with the well-known high priest mentioned in the New Testament.

One final point may be mentioned briefly. Another box in this crypt contains the bones of a woman bearing the name מרים ברת שמעון ("Mariam, daughter of Simeon"). In this ossuary, a coin minted during the reign of Herod Agrippa I (42/43 CE) was found, in the mouth of the skull, probably reflecting the pagan custom of payment to the Greek god Charon for safe passage across the River Styx.[17] Although

---

13. Zissu and Goren, "Ossuary of 'Miriam Daughter of Yeshua Son of Caiaphas,'" 74–95; D. M. Jacobson, "Mariam Daughter of Yeshua, Son of Caiaphas, Priest of Maʿaziah from Beth ʾImri," *PEQ* 144 (2012): 1–3.

14. Reich, "Ossuary Inscriptions from the Caiaphas Tomb," 18–19.

15. I review the morphological and phonetic issues in Evans, *Jesus and the Ossuaries*, 104–8.

16. This is the ossuary mentioned in note 13 above.

17. See Greenhut, "Burial Cave of the Caiaphas Family," 35; idem, "The 'Caiaphas' Tomb in North Talpiyot, Jerusalem," *'Atiqot* 21 (1992): 63–71, esp. 70; Reich, "Caiaphas Name Inscribed on Bone Boxes," 43; R. Hachlili and A. Killebrew, "Was the Coin-on-Eye Custom a Jewish Burial Practice in the Second Temple Period?," *BA* 46 (1983): 147–53, at 148–49. Knowledge among Jewish priestly aristocrats of Greek afterlife mythology is attested by Josephus (*J.W.* 2.155–156), by at least one epitaph (*IG* no. 1648; *NewDocs* 4:221–29, no. 114; Horbury and Noy, *Jewish Inscriptions of Graeco-Roman Egypt*, 234–35, no. 141: "O pitiless Charon"), and by later rabbinic tradition (*b. Moʿed Qaṭ.* 28b, in a comical lament for the departed: "tumbling aboard the ferry and having to borrow his fare").

Depictions of boats on Jewish ossuaries or crypt walls may also allude to the belief of the deceased ferried across the water to the land of the dead, as in B. Mazar, *Beth Sheʿarim: Report on the Excavations during 1936–1940*, vol. 1, *Catacombs 1–4* (New Brunswick, NJ: Rutgers University Press, 1973), plate XX (= Beth Sheʿarim, Hall P, catacomb no. 1). See also E. R. Goodenough, *Jewish Symbols in the Greco-Roman Period*, vol. 1, *The Archaeological Evidence from Palestine* (Bollingen Series 37; New York: Pantheon, 1953), 97–98; vol. 3, *Illustrations*, nos. 67 and 77, for examples in Palestine; and vol. 2, *The Archaeological Evidence from the Diaspora*, 43, and vol. 3, no. 836, for an example in Rome. Saul Lieberman thinks that the "numerous boats on the Jewish graves in Palestine most probably represent the ferry to the other world, i.e., either the divine bark of the ancient Orientals, or Charon's ferry of

we should not read too much significance into this curious feature, it may testify to the extent of penetration of pagan culture into Jewish life, even within priestly circles of the highest rank.[18]

Pilate in Literature and Archaeology

As in the case of the high priest Caiaphas, so it is in the case of the governor Pontius Pilate that our best literary sources are the New Testament Gospels and Josephus. According to all four Gospels, Jesus is brought before the Roman governor, where evidently he is accused of claiming to be the "king of the Jews" (Mark 15:2). At least that is how Pilate understands the accusation (cf. Matt 27:11; Luke 23:3; John 18:33). Had Jesus indeed accepted the recognition as the Lord's Messiah, soon to be seated at the right hand of God, and as one who, as "Son of Man," would come with the clouds of heaven, then his presentation to Pilate as a royal messianic claimant does seem plausible. Luke adds the accusation that Jesus had taught the people to refuse payment of tribute to Caesar, in view of his own kingship (Luke 23:2). It is unlikely that Jesus taught such things in so transparent and explicit a manner. But the accusation nevertheless may reasonably summarize the implications of Jesus' program and claims.

Beyond the trial narrative itself, which results in Jesus' condemnation to the cross, and the account of the later granting of permission for burial (Mark 15:42–44;

---

the Greeks" ("Some Aspects of After Life in Early Rabbinic Literature," in *Harry Austryn Wolfson: Jubilee Volume on the Occasion of His Seventy-Fifth Birthday* [ed. S. Lieberman et al.; Jerusalem: American Academy for Jewish Research, 1965], 2:495–532, at 512–13). Lieberman is probably correct.

18. Numerous coins have been found in ossuaries (cf. Greenhut, "'Caiaphas' Tomb in North Talpiyot," 70). During conference discussion, Joe Zias remarked that many if not most of these coins had been placed in the mouths of the deceased and that after the bodies' decomposition and reburial in the ossuaries they became loose. L. Y. Rahmani opines, rightly in my judgment, that this practice "may well have been seen, by standards of Jewish law, as an act of idolatry" ("A Note on Charon's Obol," *'Atiqot* 22 [1993]: 149–50, at 150). Nevertheless, we must be cautious in our assumptions about how wide this practice was among the Jewish people. This caution is recommended by Rahmani and Hachlili and Killebrew in the studies mentioned above.

There is a significant amount of archaeological data pertaining to other Jewish high priests in our period besides Annas, Caiaphas, and Qatros. On an ossuary we have: "Yehoḥanah, daughter of Yehohanan, son of Theophilus the high priest"; see Rahmani, *Catalogue of Jewish Ossuaries*, 259, no. 871 + plate 132. Theophilus succeeded his brother Jonathan, who served briefly after the removal of Caiaphas (cf. Josephus, *Ant.* 18.123). On an ostracon found at Masada, we have: "A[nani]as the high priest, ʿAqavia his son" (Masada Ostracon no. 461); see Yadin, Naveh, and Meshorer, *Masada I*, 37 + plate 30. The name on the ossuary may refer to Ananias, son of Nedebaeus, who served as high priest from 47 to 59 CE (*Ant.* 20.103). And, as was noted above in ch. 2, we may also have an ossuary inscription in reference to Simon, son of the high priest Boethos (as in Josephus, *Ant.* 15.320–322); see Rahmani, *Catalogue of Jewish Ossuaries*, 85–86, no. 41 + plate 6. And finally, Joezer, son of Boethos, may be attested on an ossuary (see *CIJ* no. 1354; Josephus, *Ant.* 17.164; 18.3).

cf. Matt 27:58; Luke 23:52; John 19:38), the Gospels tell us almost nothing of Pilate the man or his career. The only exception is the grim reference to the Galileans slain by Pilate (Luke 13:1), an event that will be taken up below. Outside of the Gospels, Pilate is mentioned four times in the New Testament (three times in Acts, at 3:13, 4:27, and 13:28) and once in 1 Timothy (6:13). In all of these occurrences, Pilate is referred to in connection with the death of Jesus.[19]

What has generated most of the debate is the Gospels' portrait of Pilate as wavering, weak, and even seemingly concerned to seek justice on Jesus' behalf. We are told that Pilate found no guilt in Jesus (Luke 23:4, 14–16, 22), that he recognized that Jesus had been handed over out of envy (Mark 15:10; Matt 27:18), that he washed his hands of the matter and told the Jews that he was innocent of the man's blood (Matt 27:24), and that the Jews themselves took full responsibility for Jesus' death (Matt 27:25). Many critics find this portrait incredible and assign it to early Christian apologetics in which Pilate is to some extent exculpated and, in contrast, the Jewish participants are blamed. It is pointed out, for example, that Pilate was vicious, was insensitive to Jewish religious sensibilities, thought nothing of killing Jews who were troublesome, and even indulged in anti-Semitic policies, including the minting of offensive coins, perhaps encouraged, even urged, by his political ally Sejanus.

In my judgment, the truth of the matter probably lies somewhere between the Gospels' portraits of a passive, almost benevolent Pilate, on the one hand, and the portrait of Pilate as insensitive and villainous, on the other, as we have it in the writings of Philo and Josephus. Much of my thinking has been shaped by recent work by Daniel Schwartz and Helen Bond[20] and takes into account recent archaeological findings.

Let us begin with a brief review of the negative assessments of Pilate that we find in Philo and Josephus. Philo of Alexandria describes the governor of Judea as a "man of an inflexible, stubborn, and cruel disposition," adding that "briberies, insults, robberies, outrages, wanton injuries, executions without trial, and endless and supremely grievous cruelty" marked his administration (*Embassy* 301–302). Philo's remarks here are primarily in reference to the incident of the golden shields that Pilate had placed in Herod's palace in Jerusalem, an incident that is probably related in some way to an episode reported by Josephus in which Pilate is said to have attempted to have Roman standards relocated to Jerusalem (cf. *J.W.* 2.169–174; *Ant.* 18.55–59).[21] Schwartz rightly recognizes that Philo's negative depiction of Pilate "is part of his exaltation of Tiberius," in which the late emperor becomes a role model for the vain and reckless Gaius Caligula, whose ambition for divine

---

19. All the relevant material relating to Pilate is surveyed in Chapman and Schnabel, *Trial and Crucifixion of Jesus*, 157–98.

20. D. R. Schwartz, "Pontius Pilate," *ABD* 5:395–401; H. K. Bond, *Pontius Pilate in History and Interpretation* (SNTSMS 100; Cambridge: Cambridge University Press, 1998).

21. For arguments that these events were probably one and the same, see Schwartz, "Pontius Pilate," 399, and idem, "Josephus and Philo on Pontius Pilate," *Jerusalem Cathedra* 3 (1983): 26–45. That they were two incidents, see Chapman and Schnabel, *Trial and Crucifixion of Jesus*, 169–70.

honors could have incited a Jewish rebellion.[22] Likewise, Josephus' largely negative portrayal evaporates under close scrutiny. Pilate had only two serious disagreements with the Jewish people. The first involved the standards, in which he backed down. The second involved dipping into the temple treasury reserved for national sacrifices in order to finish paying for the aqueduct that was being constructed in Jerusalem (*J.W.* 2.175; *Ant.* 18.60–62).[23] This time Pilate did not yield, with the result that hundreds of Jews were killed or injured. As Richard Horsley and others have pointed out,[24] Pilate could not have removed funds from the temple treasury without the approval of Caiaphas and (probably) other ruling priests, such as the Captain of the Treasury. Indeed, it is probable that this is the same incident to which reference is made in Luke 13:1: "There were some present at that very time who told him of the Galileans whose blood Pilate had mingled with their sacrifices." If this is the same incident,[25] then those who opposed Pilate's use of sacred funds were not the residents of Jerusalem, but pilgrims from Galilee, who had perhaps come during a festival. In other words, what Caiaphas and colleagues approved, and the residents of Jerusalem accepted (even if not with enthusiasm), devout Galileans in town for the offering of sacrifices could not tolerate. Parts of this aqueduct in and near Jerusalem are visible to this day.

In both of the incidents related by Josephus, the ruling priests are conspicuous by their silence. This is especially startling in the case of Pilate's taking money from the *qorbanas*, for he could not have done this, nor would he have dared to do this, without permission and assistance from the ruling priests themselves. Evidently, Caiaphas, the high priest, and Pilate, the governor, worked well together. It is not surprising that when Pilate was removed from office, in early 37, after his brutal assault on the Samaritans a few months earlier, Caiaphas was also removed from office shortly after (*Ant.* 18.88–89, 95).[26] Finally, the Samaritan incident itself

---

22. Schwartz, "Pontius Pilate," 399.

23. The account from which the money was taken was the "sacred treasure known as *qorbanas* [κορβωνᾶς]" (*J.W.* 2.175). Josephus is here referring to the dedicated offering known as *qorbān* (קרבן; cf. Mark 7:11, "'qorban' [κορβᾶν], that is, 'gift'"; Matt 27:6, "It is not lawful to put them [i.e., Judas' pieces of silver] into the *qorbanas* [εἰς τὸν κορβανᾶν]"), that is, a gift given to God. To take such consecrated items and put them to a secular use would have given offense.

24. R. A. Horsley, "High Priests and the Politics of Roman Palestine," *JSJ* 17 (1986): 23–55.

25. Schwartz, "Pontius Pilate," 398; so also E. M. Smallwood, *The Jews under Roman Rule: From Pompey to Diocletian. A Study in Political Relations* (SJLA 20; Leiden: Brill, 1981 [orig. 1976]), 163. Bond disputes the identification (*Pontius Pilate*, 194–96).

26. For further discussion of these and other incidents, see Brown, *Death of the Messiah*, 1.698–705; J. S. McLaren, *Power and Politics in Palestine: The Jews and the Governing of Their Land, 100 BC–AD 70* (JSNTSup 63; Sheffield: JSOT Press, 1991), 81–87; Bond, *Pontius Pilate*, 24–93. My suggestion that the almost simultaneous removal of Pilate and Caiaphas was not coincidental but probably the result of the Samaritan incident in which both played a role has been criticized in Metzner, *Kaiaphas, der Hohepriester jenes Jahres*, 168. However, Metzner has misunderstood my argument. I do find plausible his conclusion (p. 171) that Caiaphas was about sixty years old when removed from office. The skeleton of the older man in the Caiaphas ossuary is estimated to have been about sixty at the time of death, which, if correct, lends further support to the Caiaphas identification.

probably offers further important evidence of Pilate's cooperation with his Jewish colleagues, for the surprisingly harsh action he took against the Samaritans was probably encouraged by the ruling priests, who not only despised their northern neighbors (especially for placing bones in the temple during the administration of the Roman governor Coponius, who had succeeded the deposed Archelaus; cf. *Ant.* 18.29–30) but who would have had little sympathy for the refounding of the Samaritan temple at Mount Gerizim.

Let us now consider numismatic and archaeological evidence. It has been claimed from time to time that Pilate minted coins, perhaps at the urging of Sejanus, that would be offensive to the Jewish people, perhaps as part of a larger anti-Jewish program.[27] Of thc coins minted during the administration of Pilate, most date from 29 to 32 CE, and most fall into three basic configurations (with combinations thereof). Following Bond's recent study, these may be laid out as follows:[28]

	Obverse	*Reverse*
1.	symbol: three ears of barley	*simpulum* (cultic wine vessel)
	legend: ΙΟΥΛΙΑ ΚΑΙϹΑΡΟϹ	ΤΙΒΕΡΙΟΥ ΚΑΙϹΑΡΟϹ
		date: 29/30 CE
2.	symbol: *lituus* (augur's wand)	wreath with berries
	legend: ΤΙΒΕΡΙΟΥ ΚΑΙϹΑΡΟϹ	date: 30/31 CE
3.	symbol: *lituus* (augur's wand)	wreath with berries
	legend: ΤΙΒΕΡΙΟΥ ΚΑΙϹΑΡΟϹ	date: 31/32 CE

In her review of Jewish coinage from the time of the Hasmoneans to the time of Herod I and the Roman governors of Judea, Bond finds that there was nothing provocative about the coins Pilate had struck.[29] Although the *simpulum* and the *lituus* may have been offensive to the religiously devout given these symbols' pagan cultic associations, they would hardly have been more offensive than many other images that had been pressed on coins issued in Palestine in the previous century or earlier. What is significant is that Pilate did not strike any coins with the image of the Roman emperor or with offensive legends claiming divine status. This is hard to explain if Pilate had in fact attempted to offend his Jewish subjects. Moreover, Pilate's coins remained in circulation for several years, with no new minting until

27. For example, E. Bammel, "Syrian Coinage and Pilate," *JJS* 2 (1950): 108–10; P. L. Maier, "Sejanus, Pilate and the Date of the Crucifixion," *Church History* 37 (1968): 3–13; H. W. Hoehner, "Pontius Pilate," *DJG* 615–17, esp. 616: "Sejanus, whose anti-Semitic policies he had followed."

28. H. K. Bond, "The Coins of Pontius Pilate: Part of an Attempt to Provoke the People or to Integrate Them into the Empire?," *JSJ* 27 (1996): 241–62.

29. Bond, "Coins of Pontius Pilate." For older, different assessments of these coins, see A. Kindler, "More Dates on the Coins of the Procurators," *IEJ* 6 (1956): 54–57; B. Oestreicher, "A New Interpretation of Dates on the Coins of the Procurators," *IEJ* 9 (1959): 193–95. For additional images, see M. Wacks, *The Handbook of Biblical Numismatics from Abraham to the Crusaders* (Houston: Israel Numismatic Service, 1976), 18 + figs. 57 and 58.

halfway through the brief reign of Agrippa I (41–44 CE). This too is very difficult to explain if Pilate's coins had been widely regarded by Jews as offensive. Why wait ten or more years to replace them?

Brian McGing finds the Gospels' portrait of a cautious, opportunistic Pilate wholly credible.[30] These characteristics explain his lengthy tenure, his lack of conflict with the Jewish leaders, the fact that he did not appoint a single high priest, and, finally, the fact that he was removed from office, in all probability for acting uncritically and incautiously according to the wishes of Caiaphas in the Samaritan affair. It seems clear that the Roman governors of Judea and Samaria were guided by the counsel of the ruling priests, who would have explained the significance of the actions of men like Theudas and the anonymous Jew from Egypt. This would explain why the governors reacted the way they did. In all probability, Caiaphas urged Pilate to quash Samaritan hopes to rebuild the temple at Mount Gerizim, not because such a program would have fomented sedition (with which Rome would have been very concerned), but because the Jewish high priest was not about to allow a rival temple to be rebuilt and a rival priesthood to be reestablished. Thus, Caiaphas' professional jealousies may have clouded his better political judgment.

Perhaps the most dramatic archaeological datum concerning Pilate is the stone found at Caesarea Maritima bearing his name and title (*AE* 1971 477).[31] In the New Testament, the full name "Pontius Pilate" occurs three times (Luke 3:1; Acts 4:27; 1 Tim 6:13), and in most manuscripts it is spelled Πόντιος Π(ε)ιλᾶτος (cf. Josephus, *Ant.* 18.35). Pilate normally resided in Caesarea Maritima (on the Mediterranean), but at Passover and other festivals he took up residence in Jerusalem, either in the Antonia (which is doubtful), which overlooked the temple precincts, or in Herod's palace (cf. *J.W.* 2.301, which says that Gesius Florus, the last governor before the outbreak of war, resided in Herod's palace). The Roman historian Cornelius Tacitus (ca. 56–ca. 118 CE) states that "Christus . . . had suffered the death penalty during the reign of Tiberius, by sentence of the procurator Pontius Pilate [*per procuratorem Pontium Pilatum*]" (*Annals* 15.44). Calling Pilate a "procurator" is anachronistic, as some scholars surmised,[32] for prior to the brief reign of Agrippa I (41–44 CE) the Roman governors of Judea were prefects. This conjecture was confirmed by the inscription found at Caesarea Maritima in 1961. Antonio Frova's reconstruction is as follows *(see fig. 3.3)*:[33]

[CAESARIEN]STIBERIÉVM	[Caesarean]s' Tiberieum
[PON]TIVSPILATVS	[Pon]tius Pilate,
[PRAEF]ECTVSIVDA[EA]E	[Pref]ect of Juda[ea]
[D]É[DIT]	[d]e[dicates]

30. B. C. McGing, "Pontius Pilate and the Sources," *CBQ* 53 (1991): 416–38.

31. See *CIIP* no. 1277.

32. For example, Jones, "Procurators and Prefects in the Early Principate," 117–25.

33. Frova, "L'iscrizione di Ponzio Pilato," 419–34, esp. 424–25. This restoration is frequently cited, though its correctness is much debated. For discussion and bibliography, see L. Boffo, *Iscrizioni greche e latine per lo studio della Bibbia* (Brescia: Paideia, 1994), 217–33.

According to this reconstruction, Pontius Pilate has dedicated a "Tiberieum" to the people of Caesarea (i.e., *Caesarien[ibu]s*).

The immediate value of the inscription is that it finally settles the question of Pilate's rank and titulature. According to the third line of the inscription, Pilate held the rank of prefect (*praefectus*). In the Gospels, Pilate is called a ἡγεμών (cf. Matt 27:2; Luke 3:1), a general term that means leader or governor and that can serve as the Greek equivalent for either prefect or procurator. Although there are variations and inconsistencies in the terminology, "prefect" is usually rendered ἔπαρχος, "procurator" ἐπίτροπος, and "governor" ἡγεμών. Mark does not mention Pilate's rank (though the plural ἡγεμόντες appears in the eschatological discourse in conjunction with kings; see 13:9). The position of prefect was more of a military office (i.e., a military governor), while the procurator had broader civil authority and was concerned to protect the emperor's financial interests.

Pilate's rank, however, is about the only important element in this inscription that commands agreement. The first line of the inscription has been the object of a great deal of debate and speculation. Although Frova's restoration is widely cited, especially in popular literature, it has in fact been challenged by many. A whole host of alternative reconstructions have been offered. E. Weber recommends *[Kal(endis) Iulii]s Tiberiéum [M(arcus) ? Po]ntius Pilatus [praef]ectus Iuda[ea]e [dedicavit]*, "The Tiberieum of July First Marcus (?) Pontius Pilate prefect of Judea has dedicated."[34] A. Degrassi suggests *[Dis Augusti]s Tiberiéum [Pon]tius Pilatus [praef]ectus Iuda[ae]e [fecit, d]e[dicavit]*, "The Tiberieum of the Divine Augusti [i.e., Caesar Augustus and Livia, his wife, the mother of Tiberius]. . . ."[35] S. Bartina offers a simpler solution: *[opu]s Tiberiéum*, "The Tiberieum building."[36] C. Gatti proposes an ethnic restoration: *[Iudaei]s Tiberiéum*, "The Tiberieum of the Jews."[37] V. Burr proposes a cultic restoration: *[nemu]s Tiberiéum*, "The Tiberieum of the [sacred] grove."[38] G. Labbé proposes a municipal reading: *[munu]s Tiberiéum*, "The Municipal Tiberieum."[39] Other reconstructions could be mentioned,[40] but one in particular deserves special attention.

---

34. E. Weber, "Zur Inschrift des Pontius Pilatus," *Bonner Jahrbücher* 171 (1971): 194–200.

35. A. Degrassi, "Sull'iscrizione di Ponzio Pilato," *Rendiconti dell'Accademia Nazionale dei Lincei*, ser. 8, *Classe di scienze morali, storiche e filologiche* 19 (1964): 59–65.

36. S. Bartina, "Poncio Pilato en una inscripción monumentaria palestinense," *CB* 19 (1962): 170–75.

37. C. Gatti, "A proposito di una rilettura dell'epigrafe di Ponzio Pilato," *Aev* 55 (1981): 13–21.

38. V. Burr, "Epigraphischer Beitrag zur neueren Pontius-Pilatus-Forschung," in *Vergangenheit, Gegenwart, Zukunft* (ed. W. Burr; Würzburg: Echter, 1972): 37–41.

39. G. Labbé, "Ponce Pilate et la munificence de Tibère: L'inscription de Césarée," *REA* 93 (1991): 277–97.

40. For additional discussion, see esp. Alföldy, "Pontius Pilatus und das Tiberieum," 85–108; idem, "Nochmals: Pontius Pilatus und das Tiberieum von Caesarea Maritima," *Scripta Classica Israelica* 21 (2002): 133–48; I. Di Stefano Manzella, "Pontius Pilatus nell'iscrizione di Cesarea di Palestina," in *Le iscrizioni dei cristiani in Vaticano: Materiali e contributi scientifici per una mostra epigrafica* (ed. I. Di Stefano Manzella; Inscriptiones sanctae sedis 2; Vatican City: Edizioni Quasar, 1997): 209–15 + plate 3.1.2; Labbé, "Ponce Pilate"; Chapman and Schnabel, *Trial and Crucifixion of Jesus*, 165–67. K. C. Hanson and D. E. Oakman think

Recently, Géza Alföldy has concluded that the inscription concerns a Tiberieum that Pontius Pilate restored for the seamen of Caesarea Maritima.[41] His restoration is as follows:

[NAUTI]STIBERIÉVM	[Seamen']s Tiberieum
[PON]TIVSPILATVS	[Pon]tius Pilate,
[PRAEF]ECTVSIVDA[EA]E	[Pref]ect of Jude[a]
[REF]É[CIT]	[restor]e[s]

Alföldy plausibly suggests that the inscription commemorates a rebuilding of the harbor of Caesarea Maritima (perhaps specifically a lighthouse), an achievement in which Pontius Pilate would have taken some pride. The Caesarea Maritima inscription may hint at what occupied most of Pilate's attention during his tenure in office. Recent archaeological work in Caesarea Maritima, including underwater work in the harbor itself, may lend support to this conjecture.[42]

Finally, there is one more significant issue that needs to be treated. It concerns the length of Pilate's tenure in office. Based on Josephus' comment that Valerius Gratus served eleven years (*Ant.* 18.35), scholars usually assume that Pilate became governor in 25 or 26 CE. Schwartz, however, has offered impressive arguments that Gratus' tenure in office was much shorter, that in all probability he retired to Rome not long after his appointment of Caiaphas as high priest in 18 CE. Schwartz conjectures that Pilate took office in 19 CE.[43] If he is correct, this would mean that Pilate and Caiaphas served in their respective offices for a lengthy and almost identical period of time, some eighteen years in the case of Caiaphas (from 18 to early 37 CE), and some seventeen years in the case of Pilate (from 19 to early 37 CE).

What conclusions may we tentatively draw from our observations? I think we may conclude at least four things:

(1) Relatively speaking, Caiaphas and Pilate enjoyed lengthy and peaceful terms in office. Compared to their predecessors and successors, their tenures were remarkably long. The importance of this observation should not be quickly passed over.

(2) It is very probable that there was little friction between Caiaphas and Pilate. This is not to claim that their working relationship was cordial, or that they liked one another, only that they were able to work together peacefully. There is no hint in our sources, literary or archaeological, of any serious disagreement between the high priest and the governor. The few violent clashes that Pilate had, either with

---

the Tiberieum was the theater in which the stone was eventually unearthed (*Palestine in the Time of Jesus: Social Structures and Social Conflicts* [Minneapolis: Fortress, 1998], 78).

41. Alföldy, "Pontius Pilatus und das Tiberieum," 106–7.

42. See A. Raban and E. Linder, "Caesarea, the Herodian Harbour," *International Journal of Nautical Archaeology and Underwater Exploration* 7 (1978): 238–43; R. L. Hohlfelder, "Caesarea Beneath the Sea," *BAR* 8, no. 3 (1982): 42–47, 56; R. L. Hohlfelder et al., "Sebastos, Herod's Harbor at Caesarea Maritima," *BA* 46 (1983): 133–43; L. Vann, "Herod's Harbor Construction Recovered Underwater," *BAR* 9, no. 3 (1983): 10–14. The harbor is described in Josephus, *J.W.* 1.408–414; *Ant.* 15.331–341.

43. Schwartz, "Pontius Pilate," 396–97.

the Jewish people or with the Samaritan people, were probably undertaken after consultation with the ruling priests, and perhaps even had their support.

(3) It is probable that Pilate occupied himself with major projects, such as the renovation of the harbor at Caesarea Maritima, and left Jewish matters in the hands of Caiaphas and his priestly colleagues. One might say that with reference to power and politics Pilate was westward facing, toward the Mediterranean and Rome, not eastward facing, toward Jerusalem.

(4) Finally, the Gospels' portrait of a cautious Pilate who tests the political winds before reaching a decision as to the fate of the popular preacher from Galilee is consistent with our sources when read critically.[44] Pilate, who had only recently arrived in Jerusalem for the Passover, would understandably have been reluctant to offend the Jewish people during the festival. Contrary to popular conceptions of Pilate, the governor was not ordinarily brutal or anti-Semitic. His long tenure in office and the relatively few incidents that could be construed as negative (by tendentious writers like Philo and Josephus) speak in his favor. Pilate's caution and hesitation in his examination of Jesus became the grounds for later Christian apologetic, but in the end, the Roman governor agreed with Jesus' accusers that he held to messianic pretensions and should be executed.

Our sources suggest that the portraits in Jewish and Christian writings indulge in either overly positive or overly negative assessments of the protagonists and antagonists in their respective narratives. In all probability, Pilate was not as venal as Philo and Josephus would have us believe, nor was he as principled as Christian writers would have us believe. The same is probably true in the case of Caiaphas, who was probably not as harsh and callous as the evangelists depict.

Possible Archaeological Evidence relating to Simon of Cyrene

According to Mark 15:21, "they compelled [ἀγγαρεύουσιν] a passer-by, Simon of Cyrene, who was coming in from the country, the father of Alexander and Rufus, to carry his cross" (cf. Matt 27:32; Luke 23:26). We probably have here an example of the law (in Greek called ἀγγαρεία; in Latin called *angaria*)[45] that permitted officials to compel a local to undertake a task.[46] The verb that the evangelist has used (ἀγγαρεύειν) reflects the name of this law.

A number of inscriptions presuppose or refer to this law. One lengthy inscription (*SEG* XXVI 1392) was found in Pisidia and dates to 18/19 CE.[47] The

---

44. On this point, see Brown, *Death of the Messiah*, 694–95; Bond, *Pontius Pilate*, 119, 205.

45. Latin sources also called the law *angarium*. The law is discussed in *Digesta* 50. It was practiced by the Persians and the Ptolemies. It is mentioned in Josephus, *Ant.* 13.52: "I also make free all those Jews who have been made captives and slaves in my kingdom. I also give order that the beasts of the Jews be not pressed for our service [μηδὲ ἀγγαρεύεσθαι]: and let their Sabbaths, and all their festivals and three days before each of them, be free from any imposition."

46. For current bibliography, see Chapman and Schnabel, *Trial and Crucifixion of Jesus*, 276n443.

47. For Latin text, translation, and commentary, see Chapman and Schnabel, *Trial and Crucifixion of Jesus*, 277–80.

primary purpose of the inscription, which is a decree from emperor Tiberius, is to establish prices relating to the law of *angaria*. The inscription details the number of wagons, costs, room and board, travel time, rank of official making the requisition, and the like. In 42 CE, the Roman prefect of Egypt, Lucius Aemilius Rectus, issued a decree (in Greek) (P.London III 1171) setting limits on the practice of *angaria*, probably in response to reports of abuse of the law. We find a similar decree from another Roman prefect in the early second century CE (*PSI* V 446).[48] The incident described in Mark 15:21 is in all probability an example of the law of *angaria* at work.[49]

One of the ossuaries found in the Kidron Valley in 1941 may bear the name of Simon of Cyrene,[50] the man mentioned in the Synoptic Gospels in connection with the crucifixion of Jesus. Inscriptions on ossuaries 9 and 5 raise the possibility that the ossuaries of children of this man Simon may have been found. They have been transcribed as follows:[51]

Ossuary no. 9 front

ΑΛΕΧΑΝΔΡΟϹ	Alexander
ϹΙΜΩΝ	(son of) Simon

Ossuary no. 9 back

ϹΙΜΩΝ ΑΛΕ	Simon Ale
ΑΛΕΧΑΝΔΡΟϹ	Alexander
ϹΙΜΩΝΟϹ	(son) of Simon

Ossuary no. 9 lid

ΑΛΕΧΑΝΔΡΟΥ	of Alexander
אלכסנדרוס קרנית	Alexander QRNYT

Ossuary no. 5

ϹΑΡΑ ϹΙΜΩΝΟϹ	Sara (daughter) of Simon,
ΠΤΥΛΕΜΑΙΚΗ	of Ptolemais

48. For Greek texts, translations, and commentary on P.London III 1171 and *PSI* V 446, see Chapman and Schnabel, *Trial and Crucifixion of Jesus*, 280–82.

49. For discussion of the law of *angaria* and how it may have applied in the case of Simon of Cyrene in Mark 15:21 (and parallels), see E. A. Judge, "The Regional *kanōn* for Requisitioned Transport," in Judge's collection of studies *The First Christians in the Roman World: Augustan and New Testament Essays* (ed. J. R. Harrison; WUNT 229; Tübingen: Mohr Siebeck, 2008), 348–59.

50. Although discovered in 1941 by E. L. Sukenik, who published a very brief announcement in *BASOR* 88 (1942): 36–38, the inscriptions and a detailed description were not published for another twenty years. See Avigad, "Depository of Inscribed Ossuaries," 1–12 + plates I–IV. See also "Tomb South of the Village of Silwan," in Avigad, "Tombs," *NEAEHL* 2:750–53, at 753; *BE* 1963, 285; *SEG* XX 490; *CIIP* no. 324; J. P. Kane, "The Ossuary Inscriptions of Jerusalem," *JSS* 23 (1978): 268–82.

51. Avigad, "Depository of Inscribed Ossuaries," 4–11.

In the inscriptions on ossuary 9, we read of an Alexander, son of Simon (front and back). The inscriptions are carelessly executed. On the front, the given name Alexander and the surname Simon are both in the nominative. This error is corrected on the back, with Simon in the genitive (CIMWNOC). But the inscription is marred in its first line by starting with Simon, the name of the father, and the first three letters of Alexander's name. The inscriber catches his error and restarts in lines 2 and 3. This time he gets it right. On the lid, the inscriber presents us with Alexander's name in Greek (line 1) and in Hebrew (line 2). The genitive "of Alexander" means that the ossuary and bones within it belong to Alexander. The Hebrew line provides us with either the man's nickname or with a place name. קרנית is thought by some to mean "Cyrenean" (or Cyreanite). If this is true (and it is disputed), then we have a very interesting constellation that suggests that we may actually have the ossuary of the person mentioned in Mark's Gospel.

Ossuary 5 refers to a Sara, daughter of Simon, of Ptolemais. It is *Sara* who is from Ptolemais, not *Simon*. Ptolemais is on the Mediterranean coast, equidistant from Tyre to the north and Caesarea Maritima to the south. J. T. Milik thinks that קרנית is an engraver's error and that קרניה ("[the] Cyrenean") was intended.[52] Avigad doubts this explanation, but he too thinks קרנית is related to Cyrene.[53] The name Sara (CAPA), here probably a reference to Alexander's sister, is common to Cyrenaica.[54] Finally, on one ostracon from Masada הקרני appears, possibly in reference to a village in Judea. But it may also mean "the Cyrenean" or "Cyrene" (see Masada Ostracon no. 424).[55] On an ossuary lid from Bethphage, Milik reads בן קרנו.[56] But given the similarity and frequent confusion of *waw* and *yod*, the inscription may read בן קרני, "son of (the) Cyreanite."

Mark reads clumsily, "Simon of Cyrene, who was coming in from the country, the father of Alexander and Rufus," which may mean that Simon, recently arrived from Cyrene, was on hand for the Passover and happened to be among the onlookers when the crucifixion party chanced by. This Simon is said to be the father of Alexander and Rufus. If it can be shown that קרנית does indeed mean "Cyrenean," then the Simon referred to on the ossuary may be the man mentioned in the Gospels. Martin Hengel and Pieter van der Horst entertain the possibility.[57] To be sure, the names Alexander and Simon are common,[58] but the ossuary under consider-

---

52. Bagatti and Milik, *Gli scavi del "Dominus Flevit,"* 81.

53. Avigad, "Depository of Inscribed Ossuaries," 11. The Hebrew New Testament renders "Cyrene" as קוריני (e.g., Matt 27:32; Acts 2:10; 11:20; 13:1).

54. Avigad, "Despository of Inscribed Ossuaries," 9; cf. *SEG* IX, s.v. Σάρρα in the Index, where a Σάρα Σίμωνος is recorded; D. M. Robinson, "Inscriptions from the Cyrenaica," *AJA* 17 (1913): 166–67, no. 24; Horbury and Noy, *Jewish Inscriptions of Graeco-Roman Egypt*, 330.

55. Yadin, Naveh, and Meshorer, *Masada I*, 26 + plate 24.

56. J. T. Milik, "Le couvercle de Bethpagé," in *Hommages à André Dupont-Sommer* (Paris: Adrien-Maisonneuve, 1971), 75–96, at 78.

57. Hengel, *"Hellenization" of Judaea in the First Century*, 67n39; van der Horst, *Ancient Jewish Epitaphs*, 140–41. Van der Horst remarks that "there is at least a good chance that we have here the ossuary of the son of the man who carried Jesus' cross."

58. As emphasized by D. Lührmann, *Das Markusevangelium* (HNT 3; Tübingen: Mohr Siebeck, 1987), 259. For "Alexander" and "Simon," see Ilan, *Lexicon of Jewish Names*, 218–35 (Simon), 258–60 (Alexander).

ation attests the only known instance of an "Alexander, son of Simon." That and the possibility that father and son were from Cyrene are very suggestive.[59]

There are other supporting factors. The Christian church quickly spread to Cyrene, and converts from there visited Jerusalem (cf. Acts 11:20; 13:1). It is possible that Simon of Cyrene played a role in spreading the new faith in his native country.[60] Moreover, in his epistle to the church at Rome, Paul refers to one Rufus (Rom 16:13). This datum, in combination with the ancient and probably reliable tradition that Mark's Gospel was published in Rome, lends a small measure of additional support to this identification. In other words, the Markan evangelist mentioned that Simon of Cyrene was the father of Alexander and Rufus because these men were known to the Christians of Rome (and, as it turns out, one of them was known to Paul also).

At present, the identification of the Alexander mentioned on the ossuary found in the Kidron Valley remains inconclusive, but the inscriptions are very suggestive. If the ossuary can be shown to belong to the Alexander mentioned by the Markan evangelist, then it may shed important light on the spread of Christianity in its earliest stages. From an apologetic perspective, it may also lend important support to the probability that the passion narrative (as well as Easter?) rests upon eyewitness testimony.

Summing Up

The last remark in the preceding section should not be taken to imply that the most important role played by biblical archaeology is an apologetic one. On the contrary, the importance of archaeology lies primarily in the clarification and contextualization that it provides for the biblical literature itself and the assistance it offers interpreters of this literature. The archaeological materials reviewed in this chapter have provided just this kind of exegetical contextuality.

The ossuary of Joseph of the family of Caiaphas is of the quality we would expect of a man who served for many years as Israel's high priest. The inscription found at Caesarea Maritima is just the sort of inscription we should expect to find relating to a Roman prefect concerned with improving facilities in a city that linked a distant province to the empire. The ossuary of Alexander son of Simon may or may not be related to the man mentioned in the Gospels, but either way it does confirm the Jewish link between Jerusalem and Cyrene. These artifacts do not "prove" anything (e.g., that Caiaphas or Pilate were real people of history after all), but they do expand our knowledge of the world of Jewish late antiquity. Finds

59. The same conclusion is reached in A. Lemaire, "The Ossuary of Simon and Alexander," in *The Tomb of Jesus and His Family? Exploring Ancient Jewish Tombs Near Jerusalem's Walls* (ed. J. H. Charlesworth; Grand Rapids: Eerdmans, 2013), 112–21: "nothing contradicts it. It may only be considered as possible" (p. 121).

60. On the Jewish presence in Cyrene, see Acts 6:9 (which mentions a "synagogue of the . . . Cyrenians"); Josephus, *Ag. Ap.* 2.44; *Ant.* 14.114–118; 16.160. We may rightly wonder if Simon's assistance in carrying Jesus' cross may have put him into contact with Jesus' following, which in turn led to his adoption of the new messianic faith.

such as these clarify aspects of the written record, again illustrating how the written record and archaeological discovery are mutually illuminating.

In the following chapter, we shall consider the question of literacy, which could shed light on how the written records that we have came to be. Although our discussion will speak to the question of the literacy of Jesus and his disciples, its primary focus will be on the extent, nature, and evidence of literacy in the Roman Empire in late antiquity.

CHAPTER FOUR

"Have You Never Read?": Jesus and Literacy

In a recent publication, Pieter Botha restated an argument that had been heard before, namely, that Jesus in all probability could not read.[1] A few months later, an essay by Paul Foster appeared in which the opposite conclusion was reached.[2] Both scholars agree that it is not really possible to settle the issue with any degree of certainty. In much of scholarship concerned with antiquity, conclusions are largely decisions based on probability, and so it is with regard to the question of Jesus' literacy. In my opinion, Foster's conclusion is the more compelling of the two. His assessment of the contextual issues is more nuanced and rightly recognizes that what may have obtained in the case of the average Mediterranean person of late antiquity probably did not obtain for Torah-observant Jewry. However, there are some other important factors that should also be taken into consideration. Among these are important archaeological discoveries, some recent. I begin with early Christian writings.

Literary Evidence of the Literacy of Jesus

Three passages in the Gospels suggest that Jesus was able to read. The first passage is Luke 4:16–30, which describes Jesus reading from the scroll of Isaiah and then preaching a homily. Most scholars hesitate to draw firm conclusions from this passage because of its relationship to the parallel passage in Mark 6:1–6, which says nothing about reading Scripture. The second passage is John 8:6, which says Jesus stooped down and wrote in the dust with his finger. The problem here is that in all probability the larger passage to which this verse belongs (viz., John 7:53–8:11) is inauthentic.[3] Even if John 8:6 is accepted

1. See P. F. Craffert and P. J. J. Botha, "Why Jesus Could Walk on the Sea But He Could Not Read and Write," *Neot* 39 (2005): 5–35. Botha argues for the illiteracy of Jesus in the fourth part of this paper, under the heading "Was Jesus Literate?" (pp. 21–32). It is to this part of the paper that reference will be made in the present discussion.

2. P. Foster, "Educating Jesus: The Search for a Plausible Context," *JSHJ* 4 (2006): 7–33. Foster's study is not in response to Botha.

3. It is either omitted or marked off with asterisks or obeli in the earliest manuscripts (omitted in 𝔓^{66,75} ℵ A^{vid} B C^{vid} L N T W X Y Δ Θ Ψ 33 and many others; marked with asterisks

as preserving a genuine reminiscence of something Jesus did, it tells us nothing certain about Jesus' literacy. He may have been doing nothing more than doodling.[4]

The third passage, John 7:15, directly speaks to the question of Jesus' literacy, at least in the narrative world of the Fourth Evangelist. Some in Jerusalem wonder: "How is it that this man has learning, when he has never studied?" Literally, they have asked how he "knows letters" (γράμματα οἶδεν), "not having studied" or "not having learned" (μὴ μεμαθηκώς). But the reference here is to a lack of formal, scribal training, not to having had no education whatsoever. Jesus has not sat at the feet of a trained, recognized rabbi or sage.[5] We encounter the same language in Acts, which describes the reaction of the religious authorities to the disciples of Jesus: "Now when they saw the boldness of Peter and John, and perceived that they were uneducated [ἀγράμματοι], common men [ἰδιῶται], they wondered; and they recognized that they had been with Jesus" (Acts 4:13). The words ἀγράμματοι and ἰδιῶται should not be rendered "unlearned and ignorant," as in the King James Version (and ASV). To be ἀγράμματος was to lack scribal training (so LSJ), and was in fact the opposite of the γραμματεύς, the professional "scribe."[6] To be ἀγράμματος did not necessarily mean to be unable to read.

To be an ἰδιώτης was to be one outside of the guild, or outside of the group, as in 1 Cor 14:16, 23–24, where Paul refers to the "outsider" (so RSV) or "ungifted" (so NASB) as an ἰδιώτης. In contrast to professional trained scribes and priests, the ἰδιώτης was a layman.[7] In 2 Cor 11:6, Paul says of himself, "Even if I am unskilled [ἰδιώτης] in speaking . . ." (RSV). Paul, of course, could and did preach, and did so effectively. Yet he conceded that he lacked formal training in rhetoric and oratory.[8] Hence, he regarded himself as "unskilled" or outside the guild. The word ἰδιώτης may also refer to a commoner, in contrast to royalty.[9] The ἰδιώτης was the unskilled

---

or obeli in E S Λ Π 1077 1424 1443 1445). In other manuscripts, it appears elsewhere in the Fourth Gospel (after 7:36 in 225; after 7:44 in several Georgian manuscripts; after 21:25 in 565 1076 1570 1582 and several Armenian manuscripts), and in some manuscripts it appears in Luke (after 21:38 in f^{13}; after 24:53 in 1333). See the discussion in B. M. Metzger, *A Textual Commentary on the Greek New Testament* (New York: United Bible Societies, 1971), 219–22. The pericope is clearly an intrusion in its present context. Moreover, it contains several non-Johannine words and phrases. "The evidence for the non-Johannine origin of this pericope," Metzger rightly remarks, "is overwhelming" (p. 219). See also the comments in L. M. McDonald and S. E. Porter, *Early Christianity and Its Sacred Literature* (Peabody, MA: Hendrickson, 2000), 578, 587, 625.

4. The evidence is very helpfully reviewed in Foster, "Educating Jesus," 19–21.

5. See again the helpful review of the options and the scholarly opinions in ibid., 17–19.

6. C. K. Barrett, *The Acts of the Apostles* (2 vols.; ICC; Edinburgh: T&T Clark, 1994–98), 2:233–34.

7. According to LSJ, an ἰδιώτης is a common or private person, one who lacks professional training and education.

8. Evidently, Paul's formal education was limited to proto-rabbinic studies (Phil 3:5–6; Acts 22:3), which for Paul apparently did not include training in oratory (1 Cor 1:17; 2:1, 4, 13). In the letter to the Corinthians, Paul is comparing himself to Apollos (1 Cor 4:6), who in Acts is described as "an eloquent man" (Acts 18:24) and to whom the word ἰδιώτης would not have applied.

9. Cf. LXX Prov 6:8: "the labors of which both kings and subjects [ἰδιῶται] apply themselves." According to Josephus, Moses says to God: "I am at a loss to know how I, a mere

(with reference to any profession or trade) or commoner (in contrast to a ruler). The word was used as a loanword in Hebrew, *hedyôṭ*, as seen in *m. Moʿed Qaṭ.* 1:8 ("He that is not skilled [*hahedyôṭ*] may sew after his usual fashion, but the craftsman may make only irregular stitches") and *m. Sanh.* 10:2 ("Three kings and four commoners [*hedyôṭôt*] have no share in the world to come").

The comments in John 7:15 and Acts 4:13 should not be taken to imply that Jesus and his disciples were illiterate. In fact, the opposite is probably the intended sense, as most commentators rightly interpret.[10] That is, despite not having had formal training, Jesus and his disciples evince remarkable skill in the knowledge of Scripture and the ability to interpret it and defend their views. These texts, more than Luke 4:16–30 and John 8:6, lend some support to the probability that Jesus was literate.[11]

One might also mention the *titulus* placed on or near Jesus' cross (cf. Mark 15:26; Matt 27:37; Luke 23:37). Its placement surely implies that some people observing Jesus could read, among them perhaps his own disciples (for whom the *titulus* served as a warning, in keeping with the Roman policy of public execution as a deterrence). According to the Fourth Gospel, "Many of the Jews read [πολλοὶ ἀνέγνωσαν τῶν Ἰουδαίων] this title, for the place where Jesus was crucified was near the city; and it was written in Hebrew, in Latin, and in Greek" (John 19:20). It is interesting to note that the evangelist could assume that "many" Judeans were able to read the *titulus*.

Although there is no unambiguous evidence for the literacy of Jesus,[12] there is considerable contextual and circumstantial evidence that suggests that in all probability he was literate. At the outset, we should keep in mind the nature of Jewish faith itself. It is centered on Scripture, which narrates Israel's sacred story, a story that the Jewish people are admonished to know and to teach their children. According to the Shema, which all Torah-observant Jews were expected to recite daily, parents were to teach their children Torah (cf. Deut 4:9; 6:7; 11:19; 31:12–13; 2 Chr 17:7–9; Eccl 12:9), even to adorn their doorposts with the Shema (Deut 6:9, "you shall write them [וּכְתַבְתָּם / καὶ γράψετε αὐτὰ] on the doorposts of your house and

commoner [ἰδιώτης], blest with no strength, could either find words to persuade my people . . . or constrain Pharaoh" (*Ant.* 2.271). This nuance is also noted in LSJ.

10. What these two texts describe may have more to do with lack of training in speaking and argument. See J. A. Fitzmyer, *The Acts of the Apostles* (AB 31; New York: Doubleday, 1998), 302–3.

11. Even if one takes the position that the narrative of John 7 does not derive from the *Sitz im Leben* of Jesus but reflects the later *Sitz* of the Johannine community, it may well reflect an accurate memory of Jesus and his earliest followers, viz., that though lacking formal training, they could discuss the Scriptures. For review of more legendary materials, such as Mary's relationship to Elizabeth and Zechariah (Luke 1:5–36), that could suggest exposure to more educated circles, or Jesus as a boy in the temple dialoguing with the teachers (Luke 2:40–52), or Jesus as a schoolboy in the *Infancy Gospel of Thomas*, see Foster, "Educating Jesus," 15–17, 22–25. None of this tradition has probative value for assessing the literacy and education of Jesus.

12. As rightly remarked by J. P. Meier, *A Marginal Jew: Rethinking the Historical Jesus*, vol. 1, *The Roots of the Problem and the Person* (ABRL; New York: Doubleday, 1991), 277: "individual texts from the Gospels prove very little about the literacy of Jesus."

on your gates"; cf. 11:20).[13] One should suppose that scriptural commandments such as these, which stand at the heart of Jewish faith (cf. Mark 12:28–33; Jas 2:19), would have encouraged literacy among the Jewish people.[14]

According to Philo and Josephus, approximate contemporaries of Jesus, Jewish parents taught their children Torah and how to read it. Philo claims: "All men guard their own customs, but this is especially true of the Jewish nation. Holding that the laws are oracles vouchsafed by God and having been trained in this doctrine from their earliest years [τοῦτο ἐκ πρώτης ἡλικίας τὸ μάθημα παιδευθέντες], they carry the likenesses of the commandments enshrined in their souls" (*Embassy* 210). It is improbable that the training of which he speaks here did not include basic literacy. Josephus, however, is more explicit: "Above all we pride ourselves on the education of our children [παιδοτροφίαν], and regard as the most essential task in life the observance of our laws and of the pious practices, based thereupon, which we have inherited" (*Ag. Ap.* 1.60). He says later: "(The Law) orders that (children) shall be taught to read [γράμματα παιδεύειν], and shall learn both the laws and the deeds of their forefathers" (*Ag. Ap.* 2.204). The claim that the Law "orders" children to be taught to read derives from Deut 6:9 and 11:20 (cited above). Both Philo and Josephus claim that every Sabbath, after hearing the Law read, the Jewish people discuss it (Philo, *Moses* 2.216; Josephus, *Ag. Ap.* 2.175).

Josephus goes so far as to say that

> most people, so far from living in accordance with their own laws, hardly know what they are. . . . But, should anyone of our nation be questioned about the laws, he would repeat them all more readily than his own name. The result, then, of our thorough grounding in the laws from the first dawn of intelligence is that we have them, as it were, engraven on our souls. (*Ag. Ap.* 2.176, 178)

This may not be too wide of the truth, for Augustine claims that Seneca made a similar remark: "The Jews, however, are aware of the origin and meaning of their rites. The greater part of (other) people go through a ritual not knowing why they do so" (*City of God* 6.11).[15]

It may be admitted that Philo and Josephus are painting idealistic pictures and that perhaps they have in mind affluent families that can afford the luxury of formal education for their children. But it would be a mistake to assume that the pursuit of education, including above all literacy, was limited to the upper class or to professionals. In the story of the seven martyred sons (cf. 2 Macc 7), we have no reason to imagine an upper-class family. In the version presented in 4 Maccabees, the mother reminds her sons of their father's teaching:

> He, while he was still with you, taught [ἐδίδασκεν] you the Law and the Prophets. He read [ἀνεγίνωσκεν] to you of Abel, slain by Cain, of Isaac, offered as a burnt offering,

13. Consistent with this expectation, the author of the *Testament of Levi* has the great patriarch admonish his sons: "Teach your children letters [γράμματα] also, so that they might have understanding throughout all their lives as they ceaselessly read [ἀναγινώσκοντες ἀδιαλείπτως] the Law of God" (*T. Levi* 13:2).

14. Meier, *Marginal Jew*, 275.

15. It is possible, of course, that Augustine's reference is to Josephus and not to Seneca.

and of Joseph, in prison. He spoke to you of the zeal of Phineas, taught [ἐδίδασκεν] you about Hananiah . . . He reminded you of the scripture of Isaiah which says . . . [Isa 43:2] . . . He sang to you the psalm of David which says . . . [Ps 34:19] . . . He recited the proverb of Solomon which says . . . [Prov 3:18] . . . He affirmed the word of Ezekiel . . . [Ezek 37:3] . . . Nor did he forget the song that Moses taught which says . . . [Deut 32:39]. (4 Macc 18:10–19)

The summary here of the father's instruction of his sons clearly presupposes literacy. The portrait is idealized, to be sure, but for it to have any persuasive value in Jewish society, it would have had to be realistic to some degree.

Popular piety expressed in the earliest rabbinic tradition coheres with the testimonies of Philo and Josephus. The sages enjoin, "provide yourself a teacher" (*m. ʾAbot* 1:16; cf. 1:6). In the saying attributed to Judah ben Tema, literacy is assumed to be the norm: "At five years old [one is fit] for the Scripture, at ten for the Mishnah, at thirteen for [keeping] the commandments [i.e., bar mitzvah]" (*m. ʾAbot* 5:21; cf. *b. Ketub.* 50a: "Do not accept a pupil under the age of six; but accept one from the age of six and stuff him [with knowledge] like an ox"). Elsewhere in the Mishnah, we read that "children . . . should be educated . . . so that they will be familiar with the commandments" (*m. Yoma* 8:4). We find a similar injunction in the Tannaitic midrash on Deuteronomy: "Once an infant begins to talk, his father should converse with him in the holy tongue and should teach him Torah, for if he fails to do so it is the same as if he had buried him" (*Sipre Deut.* §56 [on Deut 11:19]; cf. *t. Qidd.* 1:11, "What is the father's duty towards his son? . . . to teach him Torah").[16] If a son lacks the intelligence to ask his father the proper questions concerning the meaning of Passover, his father is to instruct him (*m. Pesaḥ.* 10:4). There is halakic discussion that clearly presupposes that children can read Scripture (cf. *m. Meg.* 4:5–6; *t. Šabb.* 11:17, "If a minor holds the pen . . ."; *Sop.* 5.9: regulations concerning producing extracts of Scripture for children). One of the first things a new proselyte is to learn is the Hebrew alphabet, forwards and backwards (*b. Šabb.* 31a, in reference to Hillel). The rabbinic tradition contains numerous references to schools, to the effect that every synagogue and village had at least one school.[17] The

16. See also *ʾAbot R. Nat.* 6.2: "Rabbi Aqiba took hold of one end of the tablet and his son the other end of the tablet. The teacher wrote down *aleph beth* for him and he learned it; *aleph taw*, and he learned it; the book of Leviticus, and he learned it. He went on studying until he learned the whole Torah." *Gen. Rab.* 63.10 (on Gen 25:27) states: "Rabbi Eleazar ben Rabbi Simeon said: 'A man is responsible for his son until age thirteen.'" Whatever the probative value of this tradition, the training envisioned here is probably for would-be sages and rabbis, not necessarily for the average person.

17. In *b. B. Bat.* 21a, we find the following statement on the organization of public schools: "At length Joshua ben Gamala came and ordained that teachers of young children should be appointed in each district and each town and that children begin their schooling at the age of six or seven." There are many texts that say similar things (e.g., *b. Sanh.* 17b; *y. Meg.* 3:1, 73d; *y. Ketub.* 13:1, 35c = *b. Giṭ.* 58a; *y. Ḥag.* 1:7; *b. Šabb.* 119b; *y. Ketub.* 8:11, 32c). Other traditions presuppose the education of children in literacy (e.g., *b. Ḥag.* 15a–b; *b. Ḥul.* 95b; *b. Giṭ.* 56a; *Song Rab.* 2:5 §3). Some have argued that the discovery of abecedaries points to the existence of schools; e.g., A. R. Millard, "ʾBGD—Magic Spell or Educational Exercise?," *ErIsr* 18 (1985): 39–42. Abecedaries point to *literacy*, not necessarily to *schools*. For a discussion

idealistic and tendentious nature of this material is often not adequately appreciated.[18] Primarily on the basis of the rabbinic tradition, Shemuel Safrai concludes that "the ability to write was fairly widespread . . . [but] less widespread than that of reading which everyone possessed."[19] Notwithstanding his uncritical use of rabbinic sources,[20] Safrai's conclusion that literacy was widespread among Jews may be more correct than not. Several times in the book of Acts, in reference to the synagogues visited by Paul on his missionary journeys, it is assumed that Scripture was read wherever there was a synagogue (as in Acts 13:15, 27; 15:21; cf. 2 Cor 3:15).

Recognizing the limited value of the late, idealized portrait found in rabbinic literature and the apologetically oriented claims of Philo and Josephus, three general factors favor the probability that Jesus was literate: (1) the injunctions of Scripture to teach and learn Torah, (2) the value placed on Torah, of knowing and obeying its laws, and (3) the advantage of being the firstborn son. In view of these factors, it is probable that Jesus received at least some education in literacy. The probability increases when we take into account features of his later ministry. In these features we have, I believe, far more compelling evidence for the literacy of Jesus.

Jesus is frequently called "Rabbi"[21] or "Rabbo(u)ni,"[22] or their Greek equivalents, "master" (ἐπιστάτης)[23] or "teacher" (διδάσκαλος).[24] Jesus refers to himself in this manner, and is called such by supporters, opponents, and nonpartisans. Although prior to 70 CE the designation "Rabbi" was informal, even vague, and lacked the later connotations of formal training and ordination that obtained some-

---

of this issue, though in reference to earlier periods in Israel's history, see M. Haran, "On the Diffusion of Schools and Literacy," in *Congress Volume, Jerusalem 1986* (ed. J. A. Emerton; VTSup 40; Leiden: Brill, 1988), 81–95. J. T. Townsend cautiously concludes that Jewish schools in any number did not emerge until after the Bar Kokhba war ("Ancient Education in the Time of the Early Roman Empire," in *The Catacombs and the Colosseum* [ed. S. Benko and J. J. O'Rourke; Valley Forge, PA: Judson Press, 1971], 139–63). On the whole, however, there is significant evidence for literacy in ancient Israel and in Israel of late antiquity; see A. R. Millard, "An Assessment of the Evidence for Writing in Ancient Israel," in *Biblical Archaeology Today* (ed. A. Biran; Jerusalem: Israel Exploration Society, 1985), 301–12; idem, *Reading and Writing in the Time of Jesus* (BibSem 69; Sheffield: Sheffield Academic, 2000).

18. As seen, for example, in S. Safrai, "Education and the Study of Torah," in *The Jewish People in the First Century: Historical Geography, Political History, Social, Cultural and Religious Life and Institutions* (ed. S. Safrai and M. Stern; 2 vols.; CRINT 1.1–2; Philadelphia: Fortress, 1974–76), 2:945–70; E. Schürer, *The History of the Jewish People in the Age of Jesus Christ* (rev. by G. Vermes, F. Millar, and M. Black; 3 vols.; Edinburgh: T&T Clark, 1973–87), 2:415–20; J. T. Townsend, "Education (Greco-Roman)," *ABD* 2:312–17, esp. 315–17.

19. Safrai, "Education and the Study of Torah," 952. Safrai remarks further, depending on *y. Meg.* 3:1, 73d (cf. *y. Ketub.* 13:1, 35c), that schools were connected with synagogues and that learning Torah was obligatory for boys but not for girls ("Education and the Study of Torah," 953–55). But do these traditions really tell us anything about Jewish literacy in the first century?

20. Uncritical acceptance of the rabbinic tradition of schools in every village is rightly criticized in Meier, *Marginal Jew*, 271, and Botha, "Was Jesus Literate?," 24–25.

21. Mark 9:5; 11:21; 14:45; etc.

22. Mark 10:51; John 20:16.

23. Luke 5:5; 8:24, 45; 9:33, 49; 17:13.

24. Matt 8:19; 9:11; 12:38; Mark 4:38; 5:35; 9:17; 10:17, 20; 12:14, 19, 32; Luke 19:39; John 1:38; 3:2.

time after the destruction of Jerusalem and the temple, it is very probable that during Jesus' lifetime the term reflected at least a limited literacy.

In keeping with his designation as Rabbi, Jesus and others called his closest followers "disciples," a word whose Greek form (μαθηταί),[25] like the Hebrew (*talmîdîm*),[26] derives from the verb "to learn" (μανθάνειν / *lāmad*).[27] This terminology, whose appearance in the Gospels betrays no hint that it was controversial or in any sense a matter of debate or the product of early Christian tendentiousness, creates a strong presumption in favor of Jesus' literacy. In the Jewish setting, the idea of an *illiterate* rabbi who surrounds himself with disciples and debates Scripture and halakah with other rabbis and scribes is hardly credible. Moreover, the numerous parallels between Jesus' teaching and the rabbinic tradition, as well as the many points of agreement between Jesus' interpretation of Scripture and the rabbinic tradition,[28] only add to this conviction. Jesus' teaching in the synagogues[29] is not easily explained if Jesus was unable to read and had not undertaken study of Scripture that involved at least some training in literacy.

In the style of the sages and rabbis of his day, Jesus "sat down" when he taught (cf. the discussion of when to sit or stand in *b. Meg.* 21a).[30] Moreover, Jesus' contemporaries compared him with scribes, that is, with literate people: "And they were astonished at his teaching, for he taught them as one who had authority, and not as the scribes" (Mark 1:22). Although such comparison in itself does not prove that Jesus was literate, it supports the Gospels' portrait of Jesus as a rabbi or teacher, which in turn should require a presumption in favor of literacy. It is difficult to imagine Jesus enjoying a favorable comparison with rival scribes, if—unlike them—he was illiterate.

On occasion, Jesus himself refers to reading Scripture. He asks Pharisees who criticized his disciples for plucking grain on the Sabbath: "Have you never read [ἀνέγνωτε] what David did, when he was in need and was hungry . . . ?" (Mark 2:25; cf. Matt 12:3). To this pericope Matthew adds: "Or have you not read in the law [ἀνέγνωτε ἐν τῷ νόμῳ] how on the Sabbath the priests in the temple profane the Sabbath, and are guiltless?" (Matt 12:5; cf. 19:4, where Matthew again enriches the Markan source in a similar manner; the same is probably the case in Matt 21:16). In another polemical context, Jesus asks the ruling priests and elders: "Have you not read this scripture [οὐδὲ τὴν γραφὴν ταύτην ἀνέγνωτε]: 'The very stone which the builders rejected has become the head of the corner . . . '?" (Mark 12:10). Later,

25. Mark 2:15–16, 18, 23; 3:7, 9; 4:34; 5:31; and Q: Luke 6:20; 10:23; 12:22; 14:26, 27.

26. *m. ʾAbot* 1:1, 11; 2:8; 5:12; 6:6.

27. "This, in turn, is education in the law [ἡ τοῦ νόμου παιδεία], by which we learn [μανθάνομεν] divine matters reverently and human affairs to our advantage" (4 Macc 1:17).

28. R. Riesner, *Jesus als Lehrer* (WUNT II/7; Tübingen: Mohr Siebeck, 1981); B. D. Chilton and C. A. Evans, "Jesus and Israel's Scriptures," in *Studying the Historical Jesus: Evaluations of the State of Current Research* (ed. B. D. Chilton and C. A. Evans; NTTS 19; Leiden: Brill, 1994), 281–335, at 285–98.

29. Matt 4:23; 9:35; Mark 1:21; 6:2; Luke 4:15; 6:6; 13:10; John 6:59. Botha's interesting suggestion concerning this point will be discussed shortly.

30. Matt 5:1; 26:55; Mark 12:41; Luke 4:20; 5:3; cf. Matt 23:2, where Jesus refers to the scribes and Pharisees who sit on the seat of Moses (ἐπὶ τῆς Μωϋσέως καθέδρας ἐκάθισαν).

he asks the Sadducees, who had raised a question about resurrection: "And as for the dead being raised, have you not read in the book of Moses [οὐκ ἀνέγνωτε ἐν τῇ βίβλῳ Μωϋσέως], in the passage about the bush, how God said to him, 'I am the God of Abraham, and the God of Isaac, and the God of Jacob'?" (Mark 12:26). In a discussion with a legal expert (νομικός τις) who has asked what one must do to inherit eternal life, Jesus asks in turn: "What is written in the Law? How do you read? [ἐν τῷ νόμῳ τί γέγραπται; πῶς ἀναγινώσκεις;]" (Luke 10:26).[31]

We find in rabbinic literature statements like "Similarly you read" (e.g., *b. Šabb.* 97a; *b. Ketub.* 111a–b) or "How would you read this verse?" (e.g., *b. Ketub.* 81b; *b. Qidd.* 22a, 40a, 81b). But Jesus' rhetorical and pointed "Have you not read?" seems to be distinctive of his style and surely would have had little argumentative force if he himself could not read.[32] And, finally, even if we discount Luke 4:16–30 as the evangelist's retelling of Mark 6:1–6, it may nevertheless accurately recall Jesus' habit of reading and expounding Scripture in the synagogues of Galilee: "And he came to Nazareth, where he had been brought up; and he went to the synagogue, *as his custom was*, on the Sabbath day. And he stood up to read [ἀνέστη ἀναγνῶναι]" (Luke 4:16, emphasis added). I shall return to this passage below.

It should be noted, too, that in the Gospel stories reviewed above Jesus' literacy is never an issue. There is no evidence of apologetic tendencies whereby Jesus' literary skills are exaggerated by the evangelist or called into question by his opponents. Jesus' ability to read appears to be a given, not an issue.[33]

Indications of Jesus' literacy may also be seen in his familiarity with and use of Scripture. According to the Synoptic Gospels, Jesus quotes or alludes to twenty-three of the thirty-six books of the Hebrew Bible[34] (counting the books of Samuel, Kings, and Chronicles as three books, not six). Jesus alludes to or quotes all five books of Moses, the three Major Prophets (Isaiah, Jeremiah, and Ezekiel), eight of the twelve Minor Prophets,[35] and five of the "Writings."[36] In other words, Jesus quotes or alludes to *all* of the books of the Law, *most* of the Prophets, and *some* of the Writings. According to the Synoptic Gospels, Jesus quotes or alludes to Deuteronomy some fifteen or sixteen times, Isaiah some forty times, and the Psalms some thirteen times. These appear to be his favorite books, though Daniel and Zechariah seem to have been favorites also. Superficially, then, the "canon" of Jesus was pretty

31. J. A. T. Robinson has called this distinctive feature Jesus' "challenging use" of Scripture ("Did Jesus Have a Distinctive Use of Scripture?," in *Twelve More New Testament Studies* [London: SCM, 1984], 35–43). He rightly regards this feature as deriving from Jesus himself and not the early Christian community.

32. So rightly J. D. G. Dunn, *Jesus Remembered* (Christianity in the Making 1; Grand Rapids: Eerdmans, 2003), 314.

33. This important point is made by Foster, "Educating Jesus," 32.

34. See the helpful tabulation in R. T. France, *Jesus and the Old Testament: His Application of Old Testament Passages to Himself and His Mission* (London: Tyndale, 1971), 259–63.

35. Hosea, Joel, Amos, Jonah, Micah, Zephaniah, Zechariah, and Malachi. Omitted are Obadiah, Nahum, Habakkuk, and Haggai.

36. Psalms, Proverbs, Job, Daniel, and Chronicles. Omitted are Song of Songs, Ruth, Lamentations, Ecclesiastes, Esther, Ezra, and Nehemiah.

much what it was for most religiously observant Jews of his time,[37] including—and especially—the producers of the scrolls at Qumran.[38] Moreover, there is evidence that villages and synagogues in the time of Jesus did in fact possess biblical scrolls (cf. 1 Macc 1:56–57; Josephus, *J.W.* 2.229 [in reference to the efforts of Antiochus IV to find and destroy Torah scrolls]; *Life* 134 [in reference to scrolls in Galilee during the early stages of the revolt against Rome]).

Finally, the frequency and poignancy of Jesus' employment of Aramaic tradition in his allusions to and interpretations of Scripture are suggestive of literacy, regular participation in the synagogue (where the Aramaic paraphrase, or targum, developed), and acquaintance with rabbinic and scribal education itself.[39] The dictional, thematic, and exegetical coherence between the teachings of Jesus and the emerging Aramaic tradition has been well documented and need not be rehearsed here.[40]

The data that have been surveyed are most easily explained in reference to a literate Jesus, a Jesus who could read the Hebrew Scriptures, could paraphrase and interpret them in Aramaic, and could do so in a manner that indicated his familiarity with current interpretive tendencies in both popular circles (as in the synagogues) and in professional, even elite circles (as seen in debates with scribes, ruling priests, and elders). Of course, to conclude that Jesus was literate is not necessarily to conclude that Jesus had received formal scribal training. The data do not suggest this. Jesus' innovative, experiential approach to Scripture and to Jewish faith seems to suggest the contrary.

We do not possess any artifact or any archaeological evidence that bears directly on the question of the literacy of Jesus and of his disciples. But there is archaeological evidence that sheds light on literacy in the Roman Empire in the time of Jesus.

Archaeological Evidence of Literacy in the Roman Empire

We have little archaeological evidence that applies to specific, named persons, but we do have a great deal of evidence that applies to the Roman world in a general sense. This evidence comes in many forms, such as public inscriptions, private

---

37. C. A. Evans, "The Scriptures of Jesus and His Earliest Followers," in *The Canon Debate* (ed. L. M. McDonald and J. A. Sanders; Peabody, MA: Hendrickson, 2002), 185–95.

38. In the nonbiblical scrolls of Qumran and the region of the Dead Sea (here the *pesharim* are being excluded), the book of Deuteronomy is quoted some twenty-two times, Isaiah some thirty-five times, and the Psalter some thirty-one times. See J. C. VanderKam, "Authoritative Literature in the Dead Sea Scrolls," *DSD* 5 (1998): 382–402; idem, "Questions of Canon Viewed through the Dead Sea Scrolls," in *The Canon Debate* (ed. L. M. McDonald and J. A. Sanders; Peabody, MA: Hendrickson, 2002), 91–109.

39. One is reminded of the rabbinic dictum "Scripture leads to Targum, Targum leads to Mishnah, Mishnah leads to Talmud, Talmud leads to performance" (*Sipre Deut.* §161 [on Deut 17:19]). Although this dictum postdates Jesus by centuries, it probably in part mirrors earlier concepts of scribal pedagogy.

40. See B. D. Chilton, *A Galilean Rabbi and His Bible: Jesus' Use of the Interpreted Scripture of His Time* (GNS 8; Wilmington, DE: Glazier, 1984); Chilton and Evans, "Jesus and Israel's Scriptures," 299–309.

inscriptions, correspondence, business papers, school books and practice sheets, literary works, government records, judicial warrants and records, graffiti, and magical texts on papyrus, gems, and metal foils of one sort or another. We find texts written in stone, on wood, on papyrus, on painted or plastered walls, and on vellum. In short, wherever people lived, we find—climate and other relevant factors permitting—substantial evidence of literacy.

In every city from late antiquity, we find dozens, if not hundreds, of public inscriptions. These inscriptions are dedications, lists of names, imperial decrees, statements or reminders of law, quotations of famous men, and even rather pedestrian things, such as directions to this building or that place. Many gravestones and tombs are inscribed with more than the name of the deceased; some have lengthy, even poetic obituaries in their epitaphs. Some contain warnings. The impression one gains is that everybody was expected to be able to read; otherwise, what was the point of all of these expensive inscriptions incised on stone?

Writing in the early third century CE, a Roman official ordered a number of mayors in the Hermopolite district in Egypt to post copies of his letter "in the metropolis and in the well-known places . . . so that no one may be unaware of my pronouncements" (P.Oxy. 2705). One is left with the impression that it was expected that most adults would be able to read the official's letter. The same seems to apply in the well-known letter of Claudius to the people of Alexandria, which the Roman prefect Lucius Aemilius Rectus posted in 41 CE (P.Lond. 212 = *CPJ* 153). In his preface to the emperor's letter, the prefect states: "I have deemed it necessary to display the letter publicly in order that reading it one by one [κατ᾽ ἕκαστον ἀναγεινόσκων αὐτήν] you may admire the majesty of our god Caesar and feel gratitude for his goodwill towards the city" (lines 6–11). Even allowing for rhetorical exaggeration, the expectation implied in this statement seems to assume that more than a tiny percentage of the population could read.

To the inscriptions we must add the enormous number of documents from late antiquity that have been found. One thinks especially of the finds at Oxyrhynchus, which range in date from 300 BCE to 500 CE. Close to half a million pages of text, mostly made of papyrus, have been recovered from the dry sands and rubbish mounds just outside the city limits. Less than 10 percent of this discarded "library" has been published to date. In places the heaps of papyri in the landfills ran as much as thirty feet deep. Most of the papyri recovered were found in the first ten feet or so. Below that depth, the sand was damp from the seepage from the nearby canal, fed by the Nile River. Accordingly, most of the papyri had rotted and so could not be recovered. (And much of this decomposed papyrus and garbage was scooped up by local farmers and used as fertilizer.) In rough terms, this could mean that the half million pages recovered represent only about one-third of the written materials thrown into the dump. One wonders how many millions of other documents circulated in Oxyrhynchus that never were thrown into this city's dump. Oxyrhynchus was but one city and not an especially important one at that.[41]

41. For description and assessment of the Oxyrhynchus finds, see W. A. Johnson, *Bookrolls and Scribes in Oxyrhynchus* (Studies in Book and Print Culture; Toronto: University of

Presumably, other cities in the Mediterranean world were every bit as literate as Oxyrhynchus. One thinks of Alexandria (Egypt) and Ephesus (Asia Minor) with their impressive libraries. The former in its heyday boasted almost a half million volumes (cf. Josephus, *Ant.* 1.10). (The magnificent library was destroyed in the seventh-century Arab conquest.) A nearby temple held another thirty-six thousand books. The Celsus Library at Ephesus had some twelve thousand volumes. These were larger and more influential cities. If we had access to a large chunk of the documents that their residents pitched into the trash, would the amount be any less than what we have recovered from Oxyrhynchus? What about Corinth, Athens, Rhodes, and (by the first century CE) Rome? Recall, too, that Marcus Antonius apparently gave Cleopatra, with whom he was completely besotted, some two hundred thousand books. Pliny the Elder claims that in preparing to write his *Natural History* he read two thousand books (*Natural History*, preface §17). There must have been tens of millions, probably hundreds of millions, of documents written and read in the Mediterranean world from the time of Alexander until the fall of the Roman Empire.[42]

Archaeology has provided us with a great number of relevant artifacts, such as examples of quills (whether feather or reed), styli, inkwells, statues or paintings of scribes (usually seated), and abecedaries (i.e., practice sheets for beginning scribes), as well as thousands of manuscripts. In late antiquity, writing surfaces included various metals (such as bronze, copper, lead, tin, silver, and gold), stone, pottery (i.e., ostraca), papyrus (made from the papyrus plant, native to the marshes and banks of the Nile River), and parchment and vellum (stretched, treated, and rubbed animal skin). Jewish books, especially religious books, tended to be made of parchment and vellum (not conventional tanned leather, which was used for sandals and other tools and implements), rather than papyrus. This was probably so because papyrus was imported from Egypt, which may have made it expensive (this point is debated) and which certainly would have made it ritually suspect, in that it was produced by non-Jews. Homegrown animal hides, which were not ritually suspect and which may have been somewhat cheaper, were preferred, as the evidence of the Dead Sea Scrolls makes clear. Of the nine hundred or so documents recovered from the caves in the vicinity of Qumran, only one hundred are made of papyrus; the other eight hundred or so are made of parchment/vellum (and one is made of copper).[43]

We have some interesting artifactual evidence of literacy in Italy itself, thanks to the eruption of Mount Vesuvius in 79 CE, which buried in hot volcanic ash Pompeii, Herculaneum, and a few other nearby villages. One thinks of the well-known painting of the Pompeii couple, bakery owner Terentius Neo and his wife

---

Toronto Press, 2004); A. K. Bowman et al., eds., *Oxyrhynchus: A City and Its Texts* (Graeco-Roman Memoirs 93; London: Egypt Exploration Society, 2007). For a concise overview of the history of the recovery of ancient papyri, see H. Cuvigny, "The Finds of Papyri: The Archaeology of Papyrology," in *The Oxford Handbook of Papyrology* (ed. R. S. Bagnall; Oxford: Oxford University Press, 2009), 30–58.

42. For a survey of libraries in antiquity, see L. Canfora, *The Vanished Library: A Wonder of the Ancient World* (London: Hutchinson Radius, 1989).

43. On the writing materials at Qumran, see M. Bar-Ilan, "Writing Materials," *EDSS* 2:996–97.

(see fig. 4.2). The painting is dated to fifteen years or so before the eruption of Mount Vesuvius. Terentius is depicted holding a book roll and his wife is depicted holding a stylus in her right hand and, in her left, a diptych of *tabulae ceratae* ("waxed tables"), that is, a notebook with wax-coated wooden leaves.[44] The couple, holding their writing implements in a conspicuous manner, evidently wanted to emphasize their literacy, a literacy that included writing as well as reading. Indeed, the wife rests the tip of her stylus against her lower lip and looks thoughtfully into the distance. Her pose is similar to the one found on a fresco discovered at Murecine, near Pompeii, which depicts Calliope, muse of epic poetry. With her right hand Calliope presses the stylus against her lower lip, she holds a dyptich notebook in her left hand, and she looks thoughtfully into the distance.[45] The wife of Terentius appears to be mimicking this pose, what might be called the "Calliope look," which was fashionable in late antiquity.[46] What is interesting is that this literary couple was not of exalted station, nor were they "academic" people (philosophers, scribes, authors); they were a bakery shop owner and his wife! As it so happens, 125 wooden tablets preserving some two hundred pages of text were discovered in a complex of buildings at Murecine. Most of the tablets are concerned with finance and maritime trade.[47]

The same thing is observed at Vindolanda (just south of Hadrian's Wall in Northumberland, northern England), Roman Britannia, where writing tablets were found in 1973, during an excavation conducted by Robin Birley.[48] More than eight hundred tablets, many in fragments, have been recovered to date.[49] Over seven hundred of them have been transcribed and published. The tablets are made from local British wood, such as alder, birch, and oak. There are also examples of tablets made from non-native species of wood, which indicates that some of the tablets were produced elsewhere and were imported. Most of the tablets are diptychs (typically measuring 20 x 8 cm.) produced by scored and folded wood sheets (0.25–0.30 mm. thick), with carbon-based ink writing on the inside. Most of the tablets are letters and reports related to the fortress and military personnel. Several letters are of a private and personal nature. The tablets from the early period date from 92 to 130

44. The portrait of bakery owner Terentius Neo and wife is housed in the National Archaeological Museum in Naples, Italy. For image, see P. Roberts, *Life and Death in Pompeii and Herculaneum* (Oxford: Oxford University Press, 2013), 106 (fig. 112), with discussion on pp. 106–7.

45. The Murecine portrait of Calliope is housed in the National Archaeological Museum in Naples, Italy.

46. For another portrait from Pompeii, featuring a young female, probably single, mimicking Calliope with stylus and *tabulae ceratae* in hand, see Roberts, *Life and Death in Pompeii and Herculaneum*, 105 (fig. 111).

47. On the Murecine tablets, see J. Harris, *Pompeii Awakened: A Story of Rediscovery* (New York: I. B. Tauris, 2007), 257–58.

48. On the discovery of the wooden writing tablets at Vindolanda, see R. Birley, *Discoveries at Vindolanda* (Newcastle upon Tyne: Frank Graham, 1973); idem, *The Roman Documents from Vindolanda* (Greenhead, UK: Roman Army Museum Publications, 1990); A. K. Bowman, *Life and Letters on the Roman Frontier: Vindolanda and Its People* (New York: Routledge, 1998), esp. 13–19.

49. The number has to be revised upwards almost annually as the ongoing excavations at Vindolanda continue to recover more tablets.

CE, with the majority dating before 102. A prominent correspondent was one Flavius Cerialis, prefect of the ninth cohort of Batavians, as was his wife, Sulpicia Lepidina. Tablet 291 is a letter of invitation addressed to Sulpicia by one Claudia Severa, wife of Aelius Brocchus. Claudia has invited her dear friend to her birthday party: "Oh how much I want you at my birthday party. You will make the day so much more fun. I do hope you can make it. Goodbye, sister, my dearest soul."[50] Most of the letter is written in a professional hand, but the closing greetings and signature are in the hand of Claudia herself, making the letter one of the oldest extant Latin writings by a woman. Claudia Severa seems to have been a woman worthy of the Calliope model.

Claudia's hand is in itself of interest. It has been described by a modern epigrapher and Latinist as "a hesitant, ugly and unpractised hand." Yet her Latin is "very elegant."[51] Claudia was an educated, literate woman. She could read and she could write an elegant Latin, but her penmanship was poor. Her abilities and limitations, however, were not atypical. We see the same in other tablets and in many personal letters among the thousands of papyri documents that have been discovered in Egypt. There are many other examples of professionally written letters closed with a different, usually clumsy, hand and signature. Many Greeks and Romans could read and so should be classified as "literate," but their writing skills were limited. One's literacy should not be judged on the basis of one's penmanship.

The biggest surprise of the Vindolanda Tablets relates to the point just made with regard to Claudia. The tablets provide dramatic evidence of widespread literacy in the Roman army, from equestrian officers, whose literacy is not surprising, to low-ranking soldiers, wives, friends, servants, and others, whose high level of literacy is surprising. The Vindolanda Tablets attest professional, well-practiced hands, as well as non-professional hands, whose penmanship ranges from decent and workman-like in appearance to barely legible scrawl marred by misspellings, corrections, and strikeouts. (Indeed, among the tablets are several first and second drafts.) If many of the common soldiers could read and write, what does this say about the general literacy of the Roman Empire?[52] Alan Bowman reasons, "If a literate military establishment appears on the northern frontier of Britain within a decade or two of its occupation by the Romans, then it must have been universal in the Roman provinces."[53]

The evidence from Masada, located at the eastern edge of the Roman Empire, supports the point that Bowman has made. The Roman army recaptured Masada,

50. For a photo of Claudia's invitation to Sulpicia, see Bowman, *Life and Letters on the Roman Frontier*, 162 (plate VI).

51. For comments on Claudia's poor penmanship, see A. K. Bowman, "The Roman Imperial Army: Letters and Literacy on the Northern Frontier," in *Literacy and Power in the Ancient World* (ed. A. K. Bowman and G. Woolf; Cambridge: Cambridge University Press, 1994), 109–25, with quotations from p. 124.

52. On Vindolanda and the question of literacy, see Bowman, "Roman Imperial Army," 124–25; idem, *Life and Letters on the Roman Frontier*, 82–99. For important qualifications with respect to low estimations of literacy in the Roman Empire, see A. K. Bowman, "Literacy in the Roman Empire: Mass and Mode," in *Literacy in the Roman World* (ed. J. H. Humphrey; *JRA* Supplement Series 3; Ann Arbor, MI: *JRA*, 1991), 119–31.

53. Bowman, *Life and Letters on the Roman Frontier*, 83.

which for a time had been held by Jewish rebels. That at least some of the soldiers stationed at Masada could read is demonstrated by the fragmentary remains of four letters, a page of Virgil's *Aeneid* (P.Mas. 721 = *Aeneid* 4.9), a soldier's statement of payment and expenses, and a few other fragments.[54] In addition to the papyri, the Romans left behind some two dozen Greek and Latin graffiti.

The literary evidence of Vindolanda in the northwest and Masada in the east is consistent with the evidence of Mons Claudianus in Roman Egypt, the southeastern corner of the empire. At the Roman quarry in eastern Egypt, hundreds of Greek and Latin ostraca, as well as inscriptions, have been found. The ostraca provide a great deal of information about finances, wages, food supplies, and daily life at the quarry, whose population may have reached about one thousand at its peak.[55] One again is left with the impression that workers and enlisted men, as well as elites, could read and write.

Interestingly enough, the popularity of Virgil is also attested at Mons Claudianus.[56] Perhaps we should not be surprised. According to Quintillian (ca. 35–95 CE), Virgil was a favorite among those interested in epic. Latinist James Clackson observes that the surviving materials support Quintillian's claim. Virgil's work not only appears at Masada and at Mons Claudianus, it also appears at Vindolanda (T.Vindol. 118 and 452) and at Auja el-Hafr (P.Ness. 1 and 2 = *CPL* 8 and 16), ancient Nessana (or Nitzana), Nabatea.[57]

Besides recovering the Roman literary remains, Masada's excavators found more than seven hundred ostraca, many of them from the time of the occupation by the Jewish rebels (66–73 CE). They are written mostly in Aramaic and Hebrew, though a few of them are in Latin and Greek. The contents of the ostraca include single names, lists of names, designations of ownership, designations of tithes, and lists of goods, and one ostracon is a letter concerned with payment.[58] In addition to the ostraca, there were fragments of several Scripture scrolls (Genesis, Leviticus, Deuteronomy, Ezekiel, some of the psalms), apocryphal scrolls (Jubilees, Ben Sira), a portion of a work also found at Qumran (Songs of the Sabbath Sacrifice), and small fragments of other apocryphal texts.

Let us return to Italy and what has been preserved for us thanks to a volcano. For our concerns, the biggest find was the so-called "Villa of the Papyri" (*Villa dei*

---

54. For texts and critical discussion of the Latin papyri found at Masada, see H. M. Cotton and J. Geiger, *Masada II: The Yigael Yadin Excavations 1963–1965, Final Reports. The Latin and Greek Documents* (Jerusalem: Israel Exploration Society, 1989), 27–80 (nos. 721–38). A few of the Greek papyri probably belonged to the Romans.

55. J. Bingen et al., eds., *Mons Claudianus: Ostraca Graeca et Latina* (4 vols.; Cairo: Institut français d'archéologie orientale du Caire, 1992–2009). Vol. 1 contains nos. 1–190, vol. 2 nos. 191–416, vol. 3 nos. 417–631, and vol. 4 nos. 632–896. The work is not yet complete.

56. On this topic, see W. E. H. Cockle, "Writing and Reading Exercises," in *Mons Claudianus: Ostraca Graeca et Latina* (ed. J. Bingen et al.; 4 vols.; Cairo: Institut français d'archéologie orientale du Caire, 1992–2009), 1:179–90, with special reference to O.Claud. no. 190.

57. J. Clackson, "Classical Latin," in *A Companion to the Latin Language* (ed. J. Clackson; Malden, MA: Wiley-Blackwell, 2011), 236–56, at 241–42. The Nessana papyri date to the Byzantine period. Nitzana today is located in Israel's Negev desert, not far from the border with Egypt.

58. For texts and critical discussion of the ostraca found at Masada, see Cotton and Geiger, *Masada II*, 103–29

Papiri) in Herculaneum. The villa is halfway up the slope of Mount Vesuvius. It was discovered in 1750 by Karl Weber, whose men dug a tunnel, following a mosaic-paved walkway, that led them to the villa. From October 1752 to August 1754, Weber and his workers recovered some eleven hundred scrolls, a few tablets, and broken pieces of scrolls and tablets.[59] The scrolls survived because they had been reduced to black carbon by the intense heat of the volcanic eruption. Initial efforts to unroll, disassemble, or dissect these scrolls resulted in the destruction of dozens of them. Only small portions of a very few scrolls could be read. The bulk of the discovery has been stored away unread. Due to recent technological developments, such as multispectral imaging and CT scans, scholars are now in a position to begin reading these scrolls. (The former technology has been used to good effect in reading what had been unreadable or invisible in some of the Dead Sea Scrolls.) For now, however, we must simply appreciate the discovery of a private home that contained a library of over one thousand books.

Something else should be mentioned. Many frescoes have been uncovered at Pompeii and Herculaneum that "show writing materials or people reading and writing. Large numbers of the raw materials for literacy have been discovered in the cities, such as inkwells (for writing on papyri) and styli (for writing on tablets)."[60] Many tablets, in very poor condition of course, have also been found. These materials constitute important evidence for literacy, at least in an urban setting.

Before leaving Pompeii and Herculaneum, we should inquire into the large number of graffiti and what they may imply about literacy. Usually etched into the plaster or paint on walls, in both public and private locations, the graffiti are sometimes humorous, often vulgar, and on occasion threatening. The sloping, vertical style of handwriting of many of these graffiti matches the handwriting seen in the Vindolanda Tablets.

Perhaps as many as one-third of the Pompeii and Herculaneum graffiti are scatological. One graffito, etched into the wall next to a front door by an exasperated home owner, calls upon Jupiter to judge the man who continues to defecate in front of the door:

> *Cacator cave malum*
> *aut si contempseris habeas*
> *Iove iratum.*
> To the one defecating here beware the curse.
> If you have contempt (for this curse) you will have
> an angry Jupiter.[61] (*CIL* IV 7716)

This graffito is quite remarkable. Who was this person who, as we should assume, had made it a habit of using this home owner's porch as a toilet? We cannot

59. On the scrolls found in the Villa of the Papyri in Herculaneum, see A. Maiuri, *Herculaneum and the Villa of the Papyri* (Novara: Istituto Geografico de Agostini, 1974); Harris, *Pompeii Awakened*, 44–61.

60. Roberts, *Life and Death in Pompeii and Herculaneum*, 108–9.

61. For brief comment, see B. Hobson, *Latrinae et foricae: Toilets in the Roman World* (London: Duckworth, 2009), 143. Hobson translates the graffito a bit differently.

be sure, but the most likely candidate is a homeless person who found this particular location convenient (and perhaps private). This activity was not likely a prank undertaken by an ill-mannered neighbor. Once or twice, perhaps, but with such regularity that the man who owned the house felt it necessary to inscribe such a ridiculous inscription on the wall next to his door? One can only imagine what the home owner's neighbors thought. However we should explain it, the important point is that the home owner expected the (homeless?) defecator *to be able to read* the graffito and to be deterred by it!

Other graffiti constitute or contain curses and threats. Two immediately come to mind: "May you be nailed to the cross!" (*CIL* XIV 2082: *in cruce figarus*). Another reads: "Samius (says) to Cornelius, 'Get hung!'" (*CIL* IV 1864: *Samius Cornelio suspendre*). The well-known Palatine Graffito, which depicts a crucified man with the head of a donkey, attests the literacy of the slave who etched it, as well as of those expected to read and enjoy it. Other insults are less severe but are insults nonetheless. We see this illustrated in a snobbish gourmand who scratches on the wall these words: "With whom I don't dine, he is a barbarian to me" (*CIL* IV 1880: *at quem non ceno, barbarus ille mihi est*).[62]

A great many graffiti are not only crude but also exhibit misspellings and grammatical irregularities. One inscriber attempts to express his wisdom with regard to love. Assuming we have succeeded in making sense of his many solecisms, he seems to have written something like this: "Whoever is in love, may he be well. May he perish who doesn't know to be in love. May he perish twice as much, whoever forbids it to be in love" (*CIL* IV 1173: *quisquis ama valia, peria qui noscit amare, bis tanto pereat quisquis amare votat*).[63]

If Pompeii and Herculaneum are anything to go on, there must have been hundreds of thousands, perhaps millions, of graffiti etched into walls, floors, and tombstones in the Mediterranean world. There are many examples in Israel, too, though these are not nearly as "colorful" as those preserved on the scorched walls of Pompeii and Herculaneum.[64] At the very least, these graffiti and inscriptions attest a crude literacy that reaches all levels of society.

---

62. Our Latin-speaking friend is a bit of a barbarian himself in his pronunciation and spelling. His *at* should be *ad*.

63. The translation assumes that *ama* should be *amat*, *valia* should be *valeat*, *peria* should be *pereat*, *noscit* should be *nescit*, and *votat*, from *votare*, is the equivalent of *vetare*. Many of these misspellings are probably due to eccentricities of pronunciation. For more examples of crude graffiti at Pompeii, of which many exhibit misspellings and grammatical errors, see W. Heracus, *Petronii Cena Trimalchionis nebst Ausgewählten pompejanischen Wandinschriften* (Heidelberg: C. Winter, 1909).

64. On graffiti in Israel, see M. E. Stone, ed., *Rock Inscriptions and Graffiti Project* (3 vols.; SBLRBS 28, 29, 31; Atlanta: Scholars Press, 1992–94). Stone and his colleagues catalogued some eight thousand five hundred inscriptions and graffiti found in southern Israel: the Judean desert, the desert of the Negev, and Sinai. The graffiti are in several languages, including Hebrew, Aramaic, Greek, Latin, Nabatean, Armenian, Georgian, (hieroglyphic) Egyptian, and others. Not many date to late antiquity, because, unlike the graffiti and inscriptions of Pompeii and Herculaneum, the graffiti and inscriptions in the deserts of Israel were exposed to the eroding elements. For inscriptions in Israel, see H. M. Cotton et al., eds., *Corpus In-*

The ubiquity of graffiti in such cities as Pompeii and Herculaneum was not unique to Latin speakers. We find similar evidence in the Greek-speaking, eastern half of the Roman Empire. I refer here to the recent excavations of the agora (or marketplace) of Smyrna, whose ruins mostly date from the second to the fourth centuries CE. In 2003, excavators exposed the lower level of a very large area that had been damaged and partially buried as a result of the earthquake of 178. What is of special interest here was the discovery of thousands of graffiti etched into or written on the plastered walls. Because some of this plaster had fallen off the walls (either over the course of time or, in some cases, through the rough and careless work of the excavators), older layers of plaster, also covered with graffiti, were exposed. Excavators have numbered for purposes of identification some 105 areas, comprising piers, arches, and bays.

In many ways the Greek graffiti of Smyrna are similar to the Latin graffiti of Pompeii and Herculaneum. We find the usual vulgarities in word and illustration, as well as declarations of love and promises from young romantics.[65] Riddles, jokes, sports-related drawings and names, sexual themes, and expressions of appreciation or contempt adorn the walls. One graffito appears to represent either the confession of a murderer or perhaps an accusation against a murderer: "Leontios killed the adulterer." Another graffito thanks a god for healing of the eyes.[66]

One graffito, from Pier 100, incised in the plaster, seems to be Christian. It reads:

ἰσόψηφα
κύριος ω
πίστις ω

Literally, this text means "equal in value: lord, 800; faith, 800." The numerical value of "lord" is 800 (which is the value of the letter *omega*, the last letter in the Greek alphabet), and the value of "faith" is 800. Roger Bagnall believes this graffito "can only indicate a Christian character."[67] The message seems to be an affirmation that

scriptionum Iudaeae/Palaestinae, vol. 1, *Jerusalem*, part 1, *1–704* (Berlin: de Gruyter, 2010); H. M. Cotton et al., eds., *Corpus Inscriptionum Iudaeae/Palaestinae*, vol. 1, *Jerusalem*, part 2, *705–1120* (Berlin: de Gruyter, 2012); W. Ameling et al., eds., *Corpus Inscriptionum Iudaeae/Palaestinae*, vol. 2, *Caesarea and the Middle Coast: 1121–2160* (Berlin: de Gruyter, 2011). To date, this collection (referred to in the present book as *CIIP*) only includes inscriptions from Jerusalem and Caesarea Maritima and the middle coast. Cotton and her colleagues have published more than two thousand inscriptions. When the inscriptions from the north coast, Galilea, Decapolis (esp. Scythopolis / Beth She'an), Samaria, and the south are taken into account, the corpus will be immense.

65. The Greek Romeos of Smyrna sometimes used numbers (presumably reflecting the numerical values of the alphabet) to identify the women whom they admired. Most of these declarations read something like: "I love a woman whose number is —."

66. These examples, as well as those that follow, are taken from R. S. Bagnall, *Everyday Writing in the Graeco-Roman East* (Sather Classical Lectures 69; Berkeley: University of California Press, 2012), 7–26. We must express our gratitude to Bagnall, whose timely intervention at the excavation at Smyrna in 2003 prevented unnecessary damage to many of the graffiti.

67. Ibid., 22.

what matters are the Lord (i.e., Jesus) and faith (i.e., believing in Jesus). These constitute the *omega*, that is, the goal or end (probably in the sense of the goal of life).

This Christian graffito is quite early, for the layer of plaster in which it is incised is partly covered by a later layer of plaster on which another graffito is present, one that provides us with a date of 125/126 CE. From this Bagnall rightly infers that the Christian lord-faith graffito must be somewhat earlier. Acccordingly, it is the oldest Christian graffito discovered thus far. Bagnall also notes that another graffito on the same pier reads θελητὴ ἡ κυρία, "Desired Lady" (or "the lady is desired"), which may refer to Mary the mother of Jesus, while another graffito, in Bay 20, seems to read ὁ δεδω[κὼς] τὸ πνεῦμ[α], "the one who has given the Spirit," which could allude to the giving of the Holy Spirit by the risen Jesus (John 20:22) or on the Day of Pentecost (Acts 2:1–4). Finally, Bagnall wonders if the graffito in Bay 28 that is missing letters to the left and reads –καρπος originally read πολυκαρπος, in reference to Polycarp (Πολύκαρπος), the martyred second-century bishop of Smyrna.[68]

Again, the great number of graffiti, this time on the walls of the lower level of the Smyrna marketplace, which reflect various levels of education and social standing, seems to bear witness to a relatively high rate of literacy among the general population. Are we to think that most of these graffiti were scratched into the walls of a public market by the literary elite, as if they alone were able to write? Not at all. Rather, most of these graffiti were written by the non-elite, by people who were for the most part from the lower classes. Their grammar and spelling were often poor. The subject matter of their graffiti was often crude. But these people could write, even if imperfectly. Surely, the abundance of graffiti implies a higher rate of literacy in late antiquity than has been sometimes allowed.[69]

Before leaving this topic, I would like to say a few things about the physical evidence of the literacy of the inhabitants of Israel in late antiquity. We find in urban centers such as Jerusalem, Caesarea Maritima, Caesarea Philippi, and Scythopolis a large number of public and private inscriptions in stone. And, of course, we find far fewer in the smaller villages, as we should expect. What we find in cities and villages alike are great quantities of ostraca, that is, potsherds on which are names and/or brief written notes. *(See fig. 4.1.)*

Popular literacy is attested by these ostraca, which served several purposes, such as receipts, IOUs, and brief notes or letters. One thinks also of brief notes, sometimes addresses or addressees, on ceramic ware such as wine amphorae. When we find the Latin words *regi herodi iudaico* ("for King Herod, king of the Jews") and the like,[70] who was expected to be able to read this? These broken amphorae were found at

---

68. Ibid., 22–23.

69. Here I respectfully disagree with the views expressed in W. V. Harris, *Ancient Literacy* (Cambridge: Harvard University Press, 1989), 260–70. The graffiti of Pompeii, Herculaneum, Smyrna, and elsewhere attest a crude semi-literacy, to be sure, but a literacy nonetheless. See the nuanced criticism of Harris in Bagnall, *Everyday Writing in the Graeco-Roman East*, 25–26, 148n45. Some of the graffiti, surprisingly, are rather literary, showing acquaintance with the finest literature. See K. Milnor, *Graffiti and the Literary Landscape in Roman Pompeii* (Oxford: Oxford University Press, 2014).

70. For several examples, see Masada Ostraca nos. 804–10, 812–13, and 815–16, all dated to 19 BCE. For texts and critical discussion, see Cotton and Geiger, *Masada II*, 149–58.

Masada, Herod's Dead Sea fortress and palace retreat, so evidently the words were read and understood and the amphorae were delivered to the proper address.

This point should be pursued further. The inked notes that identify contents and/or provide the name of the person to whom the item was to be sent suggest literacy among transporters and handlers, as well as cooks and servants. King Herod was not the only person who imported wine and other goods from Italy and elsewhere. The wealthy of Jerusalem and other cities in Israel imported goods, as archaeology in Jerusalem in fact has shown. Not only was wine imported, but so was glassware and high-quality pottery. The elite were not expected to read the labels and addresses—packers, transporters, handlers, and servants were.[71] Once again, it seems that at least a modicum of literacy among the lower classes was assumed.

Popular literacy is also attested in funeral and burial contexts, such as ossuaries and tomb walls. We find many Aramaic, Hebrew, Greek, and Palmyrene inscriptions at Beth Sheʿarim ("House of the Gates"),[72] thanks to the excellent condition of most of the tombs (despite the violence of grave robbers). Several of the Aramaic inscriptions in Catacomb 12 warn would-be intruders (e.g., Hall A, Room III: "Anyone who shall open this burial upon whomever is inside it shall die of an evil end"). In Catacombs 13, 14, and 20, several Hebrew inscriptions have been found, often simply identifying who is interred (e.g., Catacomb 13, Hall B, Room I: "This is the resting place of Yudan son of Levi forever in peace. May his resting place be set in peace. Of Yudan son of Levi"; Catacomb 14, Hall A, Room I: "This [is the tomb of] Rabbi Gamaliel," which is then followed by Gamaliel's title and name in Greek: ΡΑΒΙ ΓΑΜΑΛΙΗΛ).[73]

In addition to the Aramaic and Hebrew inscriptions, there are some 221 Greek inscriptions in the tombs of Beth Sheʿarim. Although most of the Greek inscriptions are simple, often painted in red and consisting of a name and perhaps a word or two (such as εὐμύρι, "good luck!," θάρσι, "have courage," or שלום, "peace," usually written in Hebrew), a few of them are lengthy, sometimes containing literary allusions (e.g., nos. 127, 130, 131, 162, 183).[74] These lengthier examples, whose lettering tends to be of high quality, no doubt reflect the work of educated, literate people

71. The point is underscored in Millard, *Reading and Writing*, 127–28. Millard plausibly suggests that all of Herod's palaces and fortresses, not just Masada, would have been supplied with imports.

72. In the Talmud, the site is called בית שערים or בית שריין (*b. Sanh.* 32b). Josephus refers to it as Βησάρα (*Life* 118–119). The name could also be spelled Βεσάρα. Although the site was founded in the first century BCE, most of the tombs that make up the Beth Sheʿarim necropolis date to the third and fourth centuries. It is believed that Judah the Prince (ca. 135–219), compiler of the Mishnah, was buried at Beth Sheʿarim. That this site is indeed the location of Beth Sheʿarim from late antiquity is confirmed by one of the burial inscriptions: "I, the son of Leontios, lie dead . . . and my brothers too, alas, in my Beth Sheʿarim [Βεσάροις]" (Greek inscription no. 127). It has been suggested that the original name was *Beth Sheʿarayim*, "House of Two Gates." On this, see M. Sharon, *Corpus Inscriptionum Arabicarum Palaestinae* (3 vols.; HOS 30; Leiden: Brill, 1997–2013), 3:xxxvii. The site today is called Bet Sheʿarim National Park. It borders the modern town of Kiryat Tivon, a few kilometers east of Haifa.

73. For these and additional examples, see N. Avigad, *Beth Sheʿarim: The Excavations 1953–1958*, vol. 3, *Catacombs 12–23* (New Brunswick, NJ: Rutgers University Press, 1976), 230–58.

74. All of these examples are found in Schwabe and Lifshitz, *Beth Sheʿarim*, 2:1–200.

(especially so in the case of no. 127). But this is probably not the case with regard to the great majority of the inscriptions. Among these we find "Good luck, Anna" (no. 2), "Sarah, mother of Yose, have courage" (no. 22), "Magna rests in the ossuary" (no. 78), "Samuel, son of Isaac the poor, son of Anastasios" (no. 99), "Here lies Esther, daughter of Anthos, from Tyre" (no. 147), "A priest from Beirut" (no. 148), and "Good luck in your resurrection" (no. 194).[75]

Some of the Greek inscriptions contain a few Hebrew words (e.g., no. 29: שלום Ιούδας θάρσει φίλατε יהודה הקטן, "Peace, Judah, have courage, most beloved little Judah"; no. 41: רבי יוסף בן יצחק Ριββὶ Ιωσῆ ὅσιος υἱὸς Εἰσακίου θάρσει, "Rabbi Yose son of Isaac, Rabbi Yose the pious, son of Isaac, have courage").

Of greater relevance for Jesus and his following are the many ossuaries that date from the Herodian period (ca. 30 BCE to 68 CE). Approximately one-quarter of the 895 ossuaries in Levi Rahmani's catalogue bear inscriptions,[76] most of them of a very informal quality. Indeed, poor penmanship and idiosyncratic spelling, which are frequently encountered, suggest that many of the inscribers were not members of the literary elite. We observe similar features in the hundreds of other ossuaries that do not appear in Rahmani's catalogue and are not yet published.[77] As is the case with the inscriptions found in the catacombs of Beth Sheʿarim, we also find bilingual inscriptions on some of the ossuaries found in and around Jerusalem. Many ossuary inscriptions consist of only a name and perhaps the name of the father (i.e., "so-and-so" or "so-and-so, son of somebody"). Some provide a nickname or make reference to one's occupation. Inscriptions have also been found in village burial caves, some of them of the most simple variety.

What should we infer from all of this archaeological evidence? I repeat the dictum I expressed above: Wherever people lived, we find—climate and other relevant factors permitting—substantial evidence of literacy. The world in which Jesus grew up and became a public figure was in all probability not nearly as illiterate as some modern scholars believe. The literary and archaeological evidence is simply too great. The evidence is extensive, everywhere present (again, climate and other factors permitting), varied in type and genre, and, most importantly, oftentimes indicative of a broad readership from the less affluent and privileged classes. The position taken by some that literacy was largely restricted to the elite is not supported by the archaeological evidence.

Concluding Remarks

In view of the data reviewed above and what strikes me as the most logical inference from it—namely, that Jesus was literate to some degree—why does Professor Botha

---

75. The Greek reads: εὐτυχῶς τῇ ὑμῶν ἀναστάσι.

76. Rahmani, *Catalogue of Jewish Ossuaries*.

77. I have been able to examine many ossuaries in museums and private collections, among them those that belong to the Church of St. Anne in Jerusalem (located near the Lions' Gate). For the opportunity to view the latter I am grateful to Father Pol Vonck.

reach a very different conclusion? He is of course not alone, for other scholars have expressed doubts that Jesus could read.[78] Their doubts may owe in part to William Harris, who in his influential study of literacy in antiquity concluded that most of the adult population was functionally illiterate.[79] In short, says Botha, "it seems unlikely that a person from the rural and peasant background of Jesus of Nazareth would have learnt to read and or write."[80] Botha has invoked a cultural argument, in contrast to the arguments set forth above, which are based on the evidence of literary remains, tradition, and archaeology. Let us review his argument briefly.

Botha begins with literacy in antiquity. He complains about scholarly conclusions that do not sufficiently recognize the relative paucity and ambiguity of the evidence for literacy in the Mediterranean world of late antiquity. He comments: "In general, references to literacy in antiquity reflect fairly unrealistic understandings of literacy."[81] I respectfully disagree. The problem is not so much "unrealistic understandings" as lack of acquaintance with the evidence, which is extensive and widespread. When the environmental requirements for survival are taken into account (whether the arid climes of Egypt and the Dead Sea region, the anoxic bogs of Britain, or the protected plastered walls of Pompeii, Herculaneum, and the lower level of the market at Smyrna), we should not speak of the *paucity* of the physical evidence of literacy but the *abundance* of it. In my view, scholars are not only insufficiently acquainted with this abundant evidence; they have not understood it critically.

What I think has largely escaped many scholars is the implications of the ubiquity of graffiti, many of which are written by poorly educated people, and of the huge quantity of documentary evidence (comprising mostly papyri and ostraca) reflecting everyday business and life. We find countless examples of sloppy penmanship, atrocious spelling and grammar, and unsophisticated language—all from people whose education, if they had any at all, was obviously very limited. Yet these people could read and write.[82]

A major facet of Botha's argument revolves around his description of "Jesus' peasant world."[83] In this world, the expense of education would have been viewed

78. R. W. Funk and R. W. Hoover, eds., *The Five Gospels: The Search for the Authentic Words of Jesus* (New York: Macmillan, 1993), 27; J. D. Crossan, *Jesus: A Revolutionary Biography* (San Francisco: HarperSanFrancisco, 1994), 25–26; R. W. Funk, *Honest to Jesus: Jesus for a New Millennium* (San Francisco: HarperCollins, 1996), 158.

79. Harris, *Ancient Literacy*.

80. Botha, "Was Jesus Literate?," 32.

81. Ibid., 22. Here Botha especially has in mind the conclusions reached in uncritical appeals to Josephus and rabbinic literature. In this regard, I fully share Botha's concerns.

82. Botha questions the value of the papyri, ostraca, and graffiti in determining levels of literacy. See ibid., 23–24. In my view, his position is weakened by the discovery of great quantities of papyri, many of which were written by untrained hands, that is, by persons who obviously could read but who just as obviously were not trained scribes and probably had no formal education. As I have argued, the thousands of non-professional papyri, along with the thousands of ostraca on which are written receipts, brief lists of goods, names, and the like, as well as the tens of thousands of graffiti, offer important evidence of literacy among larger numbers of people in the Mediterranean than Harris and Botha have allowed.

83. Ibid., 25–26.

as an extravagant, unnecessary risk. Botha reasons that the Jewish peasants of the world of Jesus believed it better to spend time in the field or the shop than in study, from which there would be little economic gain. But I wonder how many people really thought this? Would not peasants, as well as artisans, traders, and transporters, recognize the advantages of basic reading, writing, and math? How could such basic skills be regarded as unnecessary luxuries? Surely most people, even of the lowest levels of society, could see that reading and writing lessened the risks in business and life. As has been argued above, the crude literacy of the lower levels of society is what accounted for a large part of the graffiti in late antiquity.

Botha offers another, very creative, imaginative argument, in which he delineates several forms of literacy and their roles within the peasant culture of Galilee and in which Jesus "performs" a "reading."[84] "The historical Jesus could not read or write," Botha explains, but he may well have made use of a scroll in performing what could be described as a "magical reading."[85] Accordingly, the account in Luke 4:16–30, in which Jesus is said to have read from the scroll of Isaiah, may reflect an actual episode. Jesus takes the scroll, unrolls it, paraphrases a passage (though not actually located and read), rolls it up, hands it back to the attendant, and then proclaims his message. The scroll plays an important role in Jesus' dramatic performance but really provides no evidence that Jesus was literate in the sense that he could read and write. As a Galilean peasant, Botha explains, Jesus "was at best able to recognize a few letters (meaning numbers) and construe a few names and/or inscriptional signs."[86]

Botha's proposal of a dramatic performance, perhaps even a "magical reading," is an intriguing suggestion, even if pure speculation. The proposal is consistent with Jesus as healer and exorcist. It is consistent with his experiential use of Scripture and could also explain his dynamic paraphrasing of Scripture.[87] Some of those watching and hearing him may well have formed an impression not too different from what Botha has proposed.

Nevertheless, I find an illiterate Jesus harder to explain, in the light of the Gospel tradition. Jesus was regarded as a teacher—by friend and foe alike. He argued points of Scripture with scribes, Pharisees, Sadducees, and ruling priests. He specifically challenged their readings of Scripture. He taught disciples ("learners"), who in turn preserved his teaching. The movement that Jesus founded produced a legacy of literature, including four Gospels, a narrative of the early church (i.e., the book of Acts), and a number of letters. The sudden emergence of a prolific literary tradition from an illiterate founder is not impossible, of course, but it is less difficult to explain if Jesus was in fact literate.

I also find aspects of Botha's cultural argument unpersuasive. The conclusions reached by Harris—on which evidently Botha, Crossan, and others rely—do not

---

84. Ibid., 27–31.

85. As is also suggested by Funk: "He could be compared to David and Solomon in the popular culture. . . . His rhetorical skills bordered on the magical—he was a word wizard" (*Honest to Jesus*, 158).

86. Botha, "Was Jesus Literate?," 31.

87. On this point, see Chilton, *Galilean Rabbi and His Bible*, 185–88.

reflect a nuanced understanding of the large number and nature of the graffiti and the implications they have for literacy among lower social classes of people who likely had little or no formal education. In any case, are generalizations with regard to the Mediterranean world in general relevant for assessing the literacy of the *Jewish* people? For his part, Botha makes two problematic assumptions: first, that the typical Galilean peasant was illiterate, and second, that Jesus was no more than a typical Galilean peasant.[88] How does he know this? On the contrary, the status and following that Jesus achieved suggest that Jesus was anything but a typical Galilean. Surely no one would deny that Jesus was regarded as atypical by many of his contemporaries, by friend and foe alike.

In the end, it is a question of probability, not proof. I agree with Foster and with his inferences from the sources, to which the archaeological evidence that has been reviewed lends additional support. The decisive factors in the debate are not found in generalities touching the world of Jesus, but in specific and distinctive features found in Jesus himself.

I urge Botha and other like-minded scholars to take into account these specific features: Jesus was a rabbi who instructed disciples, engaged in theological and scriptural debate with religious authorities, frequented synagogues, appeared to be familiar with certain parts of the Jewish Scriptures, and founded a movement that produced literature, not least a body of writings that came to be called the New Testament. In my judgment, probability favors the conclusion that Jesus was literate—not, of course, in the professional or scribal sense, but in a functional sense. The Jews in late antiquity seem not to have been typical people, especially when it came to literacy. And Jesus himself was by no means typical.

One of the atypical features of Jesus was his success in healing and exorcism. In the chapter that follows, we shall look at Jesus' use of Ps 91, a psalm understood to offer protection against the dangers of evil spirits, a passage that comes into play in the Jesus tradition and beyond.

88. So do Crossan and Funk. According to Crossan, "it must be presumed that Jesus also was illiterate" (*Jesus: A Revolutionary Biography*, 25); and according to Funk, "He was also probably technically illiterate—he may not have been able to read and write" (*Honest to Jesus*, 158). Why must illiteracy be presumed? What evidence compels us to presume this? Funk provides no evidence or argument, beyond the claim that Jesus was a peasant, for assuming that he could not read and write. The assumption of illiteracy is usually tied to Jesus' alleged peasant status. The peasant model that some New Testament scholars have constructed in the last twenty-five years or so is highly problematic. See S. L. Mattila, "Jesus and the 'Middle Peasants'? Problematizing a Social-Scientific Concept," *CBQ* 72 (2010): 291–313.

CHAPTER FIVE

Shout at the Devil: Jesus and Psalm 91 in the Light of Early Jewish Interpretation

Mark, the oldest of the Synoptic Gospels, provides readers with a very brief account of Jesus' temptation in the wilderness. *(See fig. 5.1.)* The evangelist only tells us that Jesus "was in the wilderness forty days, tempted by Satan; and he was with the wild beasts; and the angels ministered to him" (Mark 1:13). In Mark, we hear of no conversation between Jesus and Satan, and no one appeals to Scripture. However, in the Gospels of Matthew and Luke readers are presented with much more. These evangelists augment the Markan account of the temptation with a block of material drawn from Q in which Satan three times tempts Jesus and Jesus three times responds with passages from Deuteronomy (cf. Matt 4:1–11; Luke 4:1–13). In what is the second temptation in Matthew (or third in Luke's ordering), Satan urges Jesus to fling himself from the pinnacle of the temple. Jesus need not fear, for, after all, the Scripture assures:

> τοῖς ἀγγέλοις αὐτοῦ ἐντελεῖται περὶ σοῦ
> καὶ ἐπὶ χειρῶν ἀροῦσίν σε, μήποτε προσκόψῃς πρὸς λίθον τὸν πόδα σου.
> "He will give his angels charge of you,"
> and "On their hands they will bear you up, lest you strike your foot against a stone."
> (Matt 4:6)

Satan has quoted most of Ps 91:11–12, which reads in the Masoretic Text:

> 11. כִּי מַלְאָכָיו יְצַוֶּה־לָּךְ לִשְׁמָרְךָ בְּכָל־דְּרָכֶיךָ׃
> 12. עַל־כַּפַּיִם יִשָּׂאוּנְךָ פֶּן־תִּגֹּף בָּאֶבֶן רַגְלֶךָ׃

> 11. For he will give his angels charge of you to guard you in all your ways.
> 12. On their hands they will bear you up, lest you dash your foot against a stone. (RSV)

And in the Old Greek, which translates the Hebrew quite literally:

> 11. ὅτι τοῖς ἀγγέλοις αὐτοῦ ἐντελεῖται περὶ σοῦ τοῦ διαφυλάξαι σε ἐν πάσαις ταῖς ὁδοῖς σου.
> 12. ἐπὶ χειρῶν ἀροῦσίν σε, μήποτε προσκόψῃς πρὸς λίθον τὸν πόδα σου.

11. For he will give his angels charge of you to guard you in all your ways.
12. On their hands they will bear you up, lest you strike your foot against a stone.

Satan's appeal to Ps 91 no longer occasions surprise. Commentators have long suspected that this psalm was understood as offering assurance against demonic affliction. This is seen in rabbinic interpretation, in the targumic paraphrase, and in an apparent allusion to the text in the Greek *Testament of Levi*. Nevertheless, some interpreters have expressed reservations, arguing that the rabbinic and targumic traditions are too late to be of use in New Testament interpretation and that the apparent allusion to Ps 91 in the *Testament of Levi* is either too vague or may actually be a Christian gloss. However, the discovery at Qumran of Ps 91 in combination with exorcism psalms has pretty well settled the matter once and for all: Ps 91 apparently was understood in the time of Jesus as offering divine assurances of protection against demonic powers.

In what follows, we shall look at 11Q11 (11QapocrPs), in which we find three (?) exorcism psalms and Ps 91, and then assess the interpretation of Ps 91 in early Jewish and Christian literature. At the end of this chapter I shall return to the question of Jesus and Ps 91.

The Exorcism Psalms of Qumran

Sandwiched in a cluster of psalms and hymns found in the Great Psalms Scroll from Cave 11 is a composition, 11Q5 (= 11QPs[a]), that introduces David, son of Jesse and composer of many psalms. Among other things, we are told: "And all the songs that he (David) spoke were four hundred and forty-six. And songs to perform over the possessed: four [ושיר לנגן על הפגועים ארבעה]" (11Q5 XXVII, 9–10).[1] As it turns out, we may have actually recovered the "four" psalms to be sung (or performed) over the possessed to which 11Q5 makes reference.[2]

These exorcism psalms are found in 11Q11 (or 11QapocrPs). This scroll seems to comprise three extracanonical psalms plus Ps 91, for four psalms in all.[3] The extra-

1. F. García Martínez and E. J. C. Tigchelaar, *The Dead Sea Scrolls Study Edition*, vol. 2, *4Q274–11Q31* (Leiden: Brill, 1998), 1178–79. See also J. A. Sanders, *The Psalms Scroll of Qumrân Cave 11* (DJD 4; Oxford: Clarendon, 1965), 48, 92–93.

2. So J. P. M. van der Ploeg, "Un petit rouleau de psaumes apocryphes (11QPsAp[a])," in *Tradition und Glaube: Das frühe Christentum in seiner Umwelt* (ed. G. Jeremias, H.-W. Kuhn, and H. Stegemann; K. G. Kuhn Festschrift; Göttingen: Vandenhoeck & Ruprecht, 1971), 128–39 + plates ii–vii, at 129; and E. Puech, "11QPsAp[a]: Un rituel d'exorcismes. Essai de reconstruction," *RevQ* 14 (1990): 377–408, esp. 399–403; idem, "Les deux derniers psaumes davidiques du rituel d'exorcisme, 11QPsAp[a] IV 4–V 14," in *The Dead Sea Scrolls: Forty Years of Research* (ed. D. Dimant and U. Rappaport; STDJ 10; Leiden: Brill, 1992), 64–89, esp. 78–89.

3. P. W. Flint refers to the collection of psalms as a "Davidic Exorcism Handbook" (*The Dead Sea Psalms Scrolls and the Book of Psalms* [STDJ 17; Leiden: Brill, 1997], 167). That 11Q11 comprises four *Davidic* psalms is a plausible conjecture, but it is not certain, given the fragmentary nature of the scroll. For a recent study of the four exorcistic psalms, see I. Fröhlich, "Magical Healing at Qumran (11Q11) and the Question of the Calendar,"

canonical compositions are clearly exorcism psalms. The nature of the Aramaic paraphrase of Ps 91, later rabbinic understanding of it, and its quotation in the temptation of Jesus strongly suggest that this psalm was understood as an exorcism psalm among many Jews in the time of Jesus, not only by those at Qumran, as is indicated by its appearance in 11Q11. The targumic and rabbinic understandings of Ps 91 as an exorcism psalm may well represent late traditions, but these traditions appear to be based on an ancient interpretation attested in 11Q11, the Q story of the temptation of Jesus, and perhaps also the *Testament of Levi*.

The exorcism psalms of 11Q11 are as follows:[4]

First Exorcism Psalm:

"[. . .] and the one who weeps for him [. . .] the curse [. . .] by the LORD [. . .] dragon [. . .] the ear[th . . .] adjur[ing . . .] to [. . .] this [. . .]the demon[s . . .] he will dwe[ll . . .]." (I, 1–10 [formerly frg. A, lines 2–11])

Second Exorcism Psalm:

[To David. Concerning the words of incantation] in the name of [the LORD . . . the ac]t of Solomon when he invok[ed the name of the LORD . . . the sp]irits and the demons [. . .]these (are) [the de]mons. And the pr[ince of hostil]ity, [he (is) Belial w]ho [rules] over the dep[ths of dark]ness [. . . to] magni[fy the Go]d of [. . .] his people accomplish healing [. . . upon] your name finds support. And invok[e . . . Is]rael. Take strength [. . .] the heavens [. . . w]ho separated [. . . Who are y]ou? [. . .] the deep[s . . .] the earth and a[ll that is in the] earth. Who m[ade . . .] and the port[ents . . .] earth? The LORD (is) the on[e who] made ev[erything . . .] his [. . .] adjuring all the an[gels . . .] all the proge[ny . . .] who stand in service before [him . . . he]avens and [all] the earth [. . .] who send upon [. . . ear]th sin and upon every hu[man . . .] they know his wondr[ous works] which they cannot [. . . the LOR]D. If [they] do not [. . .] from before the LORD [. . .] to kill a soul [. . .] the LORD and they will fear that great [. . . o]ne among you [. . .] a th[ousand . . .] from the servants of the LOR[D . . . g]reat

---

in *Studies on Magic and Divination in the Biblical World* (ed. H. R. Jacobus et al.; Biblical Intersections 11; Piscataway, NJ: Gorgias, 2013), 39–49.

4. For Hebrew text and translation, see J. A. Sanders, "A Liturgy for Healing the Stricken," in *The Dead Sea Scrolls: Hebrew, Aramaic, and Greek Texts with English Translations*, vol. 4A, *Pseudepigraphic and Non-Masoretic Psalms and Prayers* (ed. J. H. Charlesworth; PTSDSSP 4A; Louisville: Westminster John Knox, 1997), 216–33; F. García Martínez, E. J. C. Tigchelaar, and A. S. van der Woude, *Qumran Cave 11.II: 11Q2–18, 11Q20–31* (DJD 23; Oxford: Clarendon, 1998), 181–205 + plates xxii–xxv; García Martínez and Tigchelaar, *Dead Sea Scrolls Study Edition*, vol. 2, *4Q274–11Q31*, 1200–1205; M. G. Abegg, P. W. Flint, and E. Ulrich, *The Dead Sea Scrolls Bible: The Oldest Known Bible Translated for the First Time into English* (San Francisco: HarperSanFrancisco, 1999), 539–42. See also Flint, *Dead Sea Psalms Scrolls and the Book of Psalms*, 246–48. For scholarly discussion of these exorcism psalms, see M. Delcor, "L'utilisation des psaumes contre les mauvais esprits à Qoumran," in *La vie de la Parole: De l'Ancien au Nouveau Testament. Études d'exégèse et d'herméneutique bibliques offertes à Pierre Grelot* (ed. P. Grelot; Paris: Desclée, 1987), 61–70; Puech, "11QPsAp[a]: Un rituel d'exorcismes," 377–408; idem, "Les deux derniers psaumes davidiques," 64–89; idem, "Les psaumes davidiques du rituel d'exorcisme (11Q11)," in *Sapiential, Liturgical and Poetical Texts from Qumran* (ed. D. K. Falk, F. García Martínez, and E. M. Schuller; STDJ 35; Leiden: Brill, 2000), 160–81.

[blow] and [. . . and] great [. . .] adjuring [. . .] and the great by [. . .] a mighty one and he will pur[sue . . .] the whole earth. [. . . the G]od of the heavens then [. . .] the LORD will strike you (with) a [might]y bl[ow] in order to destroy you [. . .]. And by his burning wrath [he will send] against you a mighty angel [. . . all his co]mmands which [. . .] pity against you, wh[o . . .] over all those who [will send] you to the great pit [and to] deepest [Sheol], and (far) from the ab[ode . . .] will lie down, and darkness [. . .] forever, and [. . .] with the curse of Aba[ddon . . . by] the burning wrath of the L[ORD . . .] darkness in all . . . tribulations [. . .] your gift [. . . the mi]ghty b[low . . . ri]ghteousness [. . .] who [. . .] the strick[en . . .] volunteers of [. . . Ra]phael will make them whole [. . .].[5] (II, 1–V, 3 [formerly I, 1–IV, 3])

Third Exorcism Psalm:

A Psalm of David, against [. . .] in the name of the LOR[D . . .] against Resheph [. . .] he will come to you at ni[ght, and] you will say to him, "Who are you? [Withdraw from] humanity and from the ho[ly] race! For your appearance is [nothing], and your horns are horns of a dream. You are darkness, not light, [wicked]ness, not righteousness [. . .] the LORD [. . . in Had]es most deep, [enclosed in doors] of bronze [. . .] light and not [. . . never again to see] the sun that [shines on the] righteous [. . .] and then you shall say [. . .] the righteous to come [. . .] to do harm to him [. . . tr]uth from [. . . righ]teousness to [. . .]."[6] (V, 4–VI, 3 [formerly IV, 4–V, 3])

Fourth Exorcism Psalm:

[1] [One who dwells] in the shelter of [the Most High, in the sha]dow of the Almighty [he lodges.] [2] Whoever says [to the LORD, "My refuge] and [my] fortress, [my God (is) my] security in whom [I trust." [3] For h]e will deliver you from [the snare of the fowl]er, from dea[dly] pestilence. [4] [In] his pinions he will cover [you,] and under his [wing]s you will reside. [His] grace (will be) [fo]r you a shield and his truth a buckler. Selah. [5] You will not be afraid of the terror of the night (or) the arrow that flies (by) day, [6] the plague that rages at noon, (or) the pestilence (which) [in darkn]ess stalks. [7] A thousand may fall at your side, or te[n thousand at] your [ri]ght, (but) y[ou] it will n[ot] touch. [8] Only [look] with your eyes [and you will se]e the retribution of the wick[ed]. [9] You have [inv]oked [your] ref[uge,] you have [ma]de (him) your delight. [10] You will [not] se[e . . . n]or shall [misfortune] touch your [te]nts. [11] For he has commanded [. . .] for you to gua[rd you on] your [ways], [12] upon (their) palms [they will lift] you up lest [. . . your] foot [on a st]one, [13] (and upon) a serpent [. . . you will t]read, you will tramp[le . . .] and sea monster. [14] You have [he]ld fast [. . . [15] . . . [16] . . . he will sh]ow you [his] salvatio[n . . .] And th[ey] shall resp[ond Amen, Amen.] Selah.[7] (VI, 4–14 [formerly V, 4–14] = Ps 91:1–16)

A few brief comments are necessary. Only a few words and phrases of the first exorcism psalm survive. That it was thought to be Davidic is plausible, but this is only an educated guess. However, the exorcistic orientation of the fragmentary

5. Translation based on Sanders, "Liturgy for Healing the Stricken," 221–27.

6. Translation based on E. Cook, "Songs to Disperse Demons," in M. Wise, M. Abegg, and E. Cook, *The Dead Sea Scrolls: A New Translation* (San Francisco: HarperSanFrancisco, 1996), 454.

7. Translation based on Sanders, "Liturgy for Healing the Stricken," 231–33. The superscripted numbers refer to the verse numbers of Ps 91, not to the line numbers of 11Q11 col. 6.

psalm is evident. In line 5 we find the word "sea monster," "serpent," or "dragon" (תנין). The word appears in Ps 91:13, where in the RSV it is translated "serpent." The word "demon" (שד) appears in line 10. In line 7, "adjuring" translates משביע, a word that usually means "swearing" (as in swearing an oath). In the context of exorcism, it probably should be taken in the sense of "adjuring" or "exorcising," as in 11Q11 III, 5 ("adjuring all the angels") and IV, 1 ("adjuring").

The opening words of the second exorcism psalm are missing. Perhaps it was originally attributed to David. The name of David's son Solomon—who was well known for his exorcistic skills—appears in line 2. We also find reference to "demons" (שדים) in lines 3 and 4. The reconstruction "prince of hostility" in line 4 is probable. It may also be translated "the Prince of Mastemah" (שר המשטמה), in reference to a malignant spiritual power often mentioned in the Dead Sea Scrolls. "Belial" (בליעל) is plausibly reconstructed in line 5. As mentioned above, "adjuring" occurs in III, 5 and IV, 1. The "thousand" in III, 12 may allude to Ps 91:7, whereas in the rabbinic and targumic traditions it refers to bands of demons. In IV, 7 we have "great pit," in IV, 10 "curse of Abaddon" (קללת האבדון),[8] and in V, 3 anticipation that "Raphael will make them whole."[9]

The third exorcism psalm is clearly identified as belonging to David. In the name of the Lord one can speak (or sing) "against" various demons, including Resheph, an ancient deity understood to be dangerous and punitive though also benevolent by some. Israelites, however, usually regarded him as a demon (as in Deut 32:24; Ps 78:48).[10] The psalm mocks wicked Resheph, asserting in line 7 that his "horns are horns of a dream" (קרניך קרני חלום). One is reminded of the beast of Dan 7 that possessed ten horns and fought against the saints (Dan 7:7–8, 21). The author of the exorcism psalm does not fear the horns of Resheph (cf. Ps 75:10, "All the horns of the wicked he will cut off"). "Satan" could be reconstructed at the end of line 12. The psalm also warns the evil spirits to "[Withdraw from] humanity and from the ho[ly] race!" (11Q11 IV, 6). We probably have here an allusion to the tradition of the Watchers who had intercourse with women (*1 En.* 6–11).[11]

The fourth exorcism psalm is Ps 91 (in the Masoretic Text, but Ps 90 in the Greek). There is no attribution in the Hebrew, but in the Greek the psalm is linked to David (τῷ Δαυιδ);[12] so also in the Aramaic: "David said, I will say to the Lord, 'My refuge and my fortress'" (v. 2). The content of Ps 91 readily lends itself to an exorcistic function. Verse 3 promises deliverance from the "deadly pestilence," while verses 5–6 promise the faithful person that he will "not be afraid of the terror of the night" or the "plague that rages at noon." The creatures mentioned in verse 13

---

8. See M. Hutter, "Abaddon," *DDD* 1. The root meaning is "destruction" or "place of destruction." In Rev 9:11 the word appears as a proper name.

9. Raphael is an angel of healing (cf. Tobit). See M. Mach, "Raphael," *DDD* 688.

10. See P. Xella, "Resheph," *DDD* 700–703.

11. So Fröhlich, "Magical Healing at Qumran," 43.

12. A. Pietersma renders the opening words αἶνος ᾠδῆς τῷ Δαυιδ as follows: "A Laudation. Of an Ode. Pertaining to David" (*The Psalms: A New English Translation of the Septuagint* [Oxford: Oxford University Press, 2000], 91). Davidic attribution, as we shall see, is challenged in the rabbinic tradition.

("serpent," "sea monster," and the like) were sometimes understood as demonic beings. As already mentioned, the "sea monster" (תַּנִּין) here in verse 13 also appears in line 5 of the first exorcism psalm.[13] The conclusion, "And th[ey] shall resp[ond Amen, Amen]" (VI, 14), indicates antiphonal prayer, consistent with use of the psalm to ward off evil.[14]

Psalm 91 in Greek

The antiquity of the demonological understanding of Ps 91 is attested not only in 11Q11 but also in the Greek tradition (= Ps 90). The Hebrew מִדֶּבֶר בָּאֹפֶל יַהֲלֹךְ מִקֶּטֶב יָשׁוּד צָהֳרָיִם ("nor the pestilence that stalks in darkness, nor the destruction that wastes at noonday") of verse 6 is rendered in the LXX ἀπὸ πράγματος διαπορευομένου ἐν σκότει, ἀπὸ συμπτώματος καὶ δαιμονίου μεσημβρινοῦ ("from a thing that passes by in darkness, from a mishap and a noonday demon").[15]

What likely suggested the introduction of the δαιμόνιον in the Greek was the presence of the verb יָשׁוּד, whose root שׁדד (to "devastate" or "waste") could be interpreted as a reference to שֵׁד ("demon").[16] Other elements in Ps 91 encouraged demonic readings. As already noted, the "adder" (פֶּתֶן) and "serpent" (תַּנִּין) in verse 13 readily suggested evil spirits.

The demonological orientation of the Greek facilitated the developing tradition, as we see in the *Testament of Levi* (at 18:12), where the adder and serpent that will be trodden upon become τὰ πονηρὰ πνεύματα ("the evil spirits"). More will be said about this text below. The appearance of δράκων in Ps 90:13 (LXX) also encouraged the demonological trajectory. Demons are often depicted as dragons in the Greek deuterocanonical and pseudepigraphic literature (Bel 14:23, 25, 27–28; *T. Sol.* 12:1, 6; 14:1; *T. Abr.* A 17:14, 16; 19:5, 7; *3 Bar.* 4:4; 5:2). The dragon of the book of Revelation is explicitly identified as "the Devil and Satan [Διάβολος καὶ ὁ Σατανᾶς]"

---

13. See the important studies by H. Lichtenberger, "Ps 91 und die Exorzismen in 11QPsAp[a]," in *Die Dämonen: Die Dämonologie der israelitischen-jüdischen und frühchristlichen Literatur im Kontext ihrer Umwelt* (ed. A. Lange, H. Lichtenberger, and K. F. D. Römheld; Tübingen: Mohr Siebeck, 2003), 416–21; idem, "Qumran and the New Testament," in *The Changing Face of Judaism, Christianity, and Other Greco-Roman Religions in Antiquity* (ed. I. H. Henderson and G. S. Oegema; JSHRZ 2; Gütersloh: Gütersloher Verlagshaus, 2006), 103–29, esp. 121–26 ("Spirits and Demons in the Dead Sea Scrolls"). For further points of connection between Ps 91 and the other exorcism psalms of 11Q11, see ibid., "Qumran and the New Testament," 123–24.

14. As rightly observed by Fröhlich, "Magical Healing at Qumran," 44.

15. We find a couple of minor variants in P.Oxy. 1928, an amulet that cites the whole of the psalm: ἀπὸ πράγματος ἐν σκότει διαφορευομένου ἀπὸ συμπτώματος καὶ δεμονονίου μεσημβρινοῦ (lines 5–6 = v. 6). Note the reversal of διαφορευομένου and ἐν σκότει. This word order (but not spelling) is seen in P.Oxy. 2065 and in P.Laur. 141. The LXX word order is attested in P.Berol. 3601, an amulet that cites Ps 90:1–6a.

16. The original meaning of the Hebrew is itself a matter of debate. See M. E. Tate, *Psalms 51–100* (WBC 20; Dallas: Word, 1990), 448n6c. In the Vulgate, v. 6b reads: *a morsu insanientis meridie.*

(Rev 20:2; see also Philo, *Agriculture* 96; Papias, frag.11.1; Theophilus, *To Autolycus* 2.28: "the wicked demon, who also is called Satan [ὁ κακοποιὸς δαίμων, ὁ καὶ Σατὰν καλούμενος], who then spoke to her through the serpent, and who works even to this day in those men that are possessed by him, invokes as Eve. And he is called 'demon' and 'dragon' [δαίμων δὲ καὶ δράκων καλεῖται]"). Many Greek amulets and magic texts presuppose this interpretation in making use of Ps 90 (91). These texts will be treated below.

Psalm 91 in Aramaic

The Psalms targum has received relatively little scholarly attention, though in recent years that has begun to change.[17] In my very preliminary study, I suggested a fifth-century date for most of the material for this targum, though allowing for much later glosses, on the one hand, as well as the presence of much older turns of phrase and exegetical traditions, on the other.[18] In his recently published translation, David Stec suggests "fourth to sixth century" and acknowledges that *Targum Psalms* probably "contains material belonging to more than one period."[19] In this I am sure that he is correct. The language of the targum seems to be a form of Palestinian Aramaic,[20] and it gives evidence here and there of very old interpretive tradition. The exorcistic orientation of Ps 91 offers an interesting example of this.

Angelology and demonology is accentuated in the Psalms targum.[21] This theme is not absent in the Hebrew Psalter, but it is enhanced and modernized in the Aramaic.[22] Of special interest for the present study is the targum's paraphrase of verses 5–10. The passage begins with David's words to his son Solomon:

5. לא תדחל מן דלוחא דמזיקי דאזלין בליליא מן גיררא דמלאך מותא דשרי בימָמא:
6. מן מותא די בקיבלא מהלך מסיעת שידין דמחבלין בטיהרא:

17. For brief reports of the history of scholarship, complete with bibliography, see C. A. Evans, "The Aramaic Psalter and the New Testament: Praising the Lord in History and Prophecy," in *From Prophecy to Testament: The Function of the Old Testament in the New* (ed. C. A. Evans; Peabody, MA: Hendrickson, 2004), 44–91, esp. 44–75; D. M. Stec, *The Targum of Psalms: Translated, with a Critical Introduction, Apparatus, and Notes* (ArBib 16; Collegeville, MN: Liturgical Press, 2004), 1–26; and T. Edwards, *Exegesis in the Targum of the Psalms: The Old, the New, and the Rewritten* (GD 28, Biblical Studies 1; Piscataway, NJ: Gorgias, 2007), 1–23. Edwards does not discuss *Tg.* Ps 91.

18. Evans, "Aramaic Psalter and the New Testament," 70–75.

19. Stec, *Targum of Psalms*, 2.

20. Ibid., 18. See also E. M. Cook, "The Psalms Targum. Introduction to a New Translation, with Sample Texts," in *Targum and Scripture: Studies in Aramaic Translations and Interpretations in Memory of Ernest G. Clarke* (ed. P. V. M. Flesher; SAIS 2; Leiden: Brill, 2002), 185–201, esp. 186–89.

21. See Stec, *Targum of Psalms*, 6.

22. For several important studies of the general topic, see A. Lange, H. Lichtenberger, and K. F. D. Römheld, eds., *Die Dämonen: Die Dämonologie der israelitischen-jüdischen und frühchristlichen Literatur im Kontext ihrer Umwelt* (Tübingen: Mohr Siebeck, 2003).

7. תדכר שמא דקודשא יפלון מן סטר שמאלך אלפא וריבבותא מן ימינך לותך לא יקרבון למנזק:
8. לחוד בעיינך תהי מסתכל והיך מיתגמרין רשיעי תחמי:
9. עני שלמה וכן אמר ארום אנת הוא יהוה רוחצני במדור עילאה שויתא בית שכינתך:
10. אתיב מרי עלמא וכן אמר לא תארע לך בישתא ומכתשא ומזיקיא לא יקרבון במשכנייך:

5. "You will not be afraid of the terror of *the demons that go about in* the night, nor of the arrow *of the angel of death that he shoots* in the daytime,
6. nor of the *death* that goes about in the darkness, nor of *the company of demons that destroy* at noon.
7. *You will call to remembrance the Holy Name, and* a thousand will fall at your *left* side, and ten thousand at your right hand; (but) *they* will not come near you *to do harm*.
8. You will only look with your eyes, and you will see *how the wicked are being destroyed*."
9. *Solomon answered, and this is what he said*: "Because you, O Lord, are my refuge, *in the most high dwelling place you have set the house of your Shekinah*."
10. *The Lord of the World responded, and this is what he said: "No evil shall befall you, and no plague or demons shall come near your tent."*[23]

I offer a few comments. Verses 5–8 constitute part of David's instructions to his son Solomon.[24] David's speech begins in verse 2 and includes the assurance in verse 3 that God "will deliver you, Solomon my son, from the trap and the snare, from death and tumult." This assurance anticipates Solomon's response in verse 9 and the Lord's added promise in verses 10–16. The targumic paraphrase reflects a very old tradition of Solomon as healer and exorcist par excellence. This tradition was known to Josephus and was greatly embellished in the pseudepigraphic *Testament of Solomon*, a work that probably originated in first-century Jewish circles and was later expanded and enriched in Christian circles. According to Josephus, exorcists in his time made use of spells, incantations, and a special ring thought to derive from Israel's famous monarch. Amulets and magical papyri from later times attest the popularity of Solomon and his ring. More will be said about Solomon's reputation shortly.

The phrase "the terror of the night" in the Hebrew of verse 5 becomes in the targum "the terror of the demons [מזיקין][25] that go about in the night," while "the arrow that flies by day" becomes "the arrow of the angel of death that he shoots in the day(time)." Demons are explicitly referenced elsewhere in Ps 91 (cf. v. 6: "the company of demons [שידין] that destroy at noon"; v. 10: "no plague or demons

23. Translation based on Stec, *Targum of Psalms*, 175. Words in italics indicate places where the Aramaic differs from the Hebrew.

24. The targum does not say that David wrote the psalm, but the appearance of the king's name in v. 2, which is followed by a speech attributed to him in vv. 2–8, implies in some sense Davidic origin.

25. מזיק, "striker," comes from נזק, "to damage."

[מזיקין] shall come near your tent").[26] Recall that "demons" (שידין) appeared in the first and second exorcism psalms in 11Q11.[27]

In verse 5, the arrow becomes the "angel of death," a malevolent being that appears elsewhere in the Psalms targum:

> What man can live and never see death? Who can deliver his soul from the power of Sheol? (Heb. 89:48 [Eng. 89:49])

> Who is the man *who* will live and not see *the angel of* death, who will deliver his soul from *his* hand, *and not go down to his grave* forever? (Targ.)

> Let not the slanderer be established in the land; let evil hunt down the violent man speedily! (Heb. 140:12 [Eng. 140:11])

> The man who speaks with deceitful tongue—they cannot dwell in the land *of the living; the angel of death* will hunt down the men of evil rapacity, *he will smite him in Gehenna.* (Targ.)

The association of the angel of death with Gehenna is to be noted. The wicked can expect to be struck down in Gehenna by the angel of death. Demons number among the allies of the angel of death. Accordingly, demons also plague the wicked (cf. *Tg.* Ps 89:32 [Eng. 89:33]).

In verse 7, the "thousand" that fall at the left hand and the "ten thousand" that fall at the right are probably to be understood as bands of demons. Not only does the context in the Psalms targum suggest this, but this is how the passage is understood in rabbinic interpretation: "If a thousand demons should come against a man's left, they will fall before it . . . even if ten thousand demons should come against the right, they will fall before it" (*Midr. Pss.* 91.4 [on Ps 91:7]).[28]

At this point, it will help to review the exorcism recounted by Josephus. This wily survivor of the great Jewish rebellion tells of one Eleazar, an exorcist who made use of incantations and various items said to be handed down from Solomon. Josephus says:

> Now so great was the prudence and wisdom that God granted Solomon, that he surpassed the ancients, and even the Egyptians. . . . And God granted him knowledge of the art used against demons for the benefit and healing of people. He also composed incantations, by which illnesses are relieved, and left behind forms of exorcisms [ἐξορκώσεων] with which those possessed by demons drive them out, never to return.

---

26. See Stec, *Targum of Psalms*, 6.

27. For more on demons, see G. J. Riley, "Demon," *DDD* 235–40; M. Mach, "Demons," *EDSS* 1:189–92; W. Foerster, "δαίμων κτλ," *TDNT* 2:1–20, esp. 10–16; *Midr. Pss.* 91.3 (on Ps 91:6). שד, whose root meaning is "destruction," is the more common word for demon in biblical literature. It occurs some fifty times in the Hebrew Bible (cf. Deut 32:17; Ps 106:37), about two dozen times in the Scrolls, and about two dozen times in the targumim. Both שד and מזיק are frequently found in rabbinic literature.

28. Translation based on W. G. Braude, *The Midrash on Psalms* (2 vols; YJS 13; New Haven: Yale University Press, 1959), 2:103. Interpreting the thousands as referring to demons is probably an old tradition; claiming that they fall before the "Commandment of the Tefillin" is a much later one.

> And this kind of cure is of very great power among us to this day, for I have seen a certain Eleazar, a countryman of mine, in the presence of Vespasian, his sons, tribunes, and a number of other soldiers, free men possessed by demons, and this was the manner of the cure: he put to the nose of the possessed man a ring that had under its seal one of the roots prescribed by Solomon, and then, as the man smelled it, drew out the demon through his nostrils, and, when the man at once fell down, adjured the demon never to come back into him, speaking the name of Solomon and reciting the incantations that he had composed.[29] (*Ant.* 8.45–47)

According to Josephus, Israel's famous king and patron of wisdom surpassed even the Egyptians. In context, Josephus probably had in mind the Egyptians' fame for magic and exorcism, a reputation that grew out of passages like Gen 41:8 and Exod 7:11 (cf. Wis 17:7; 18:13) and was exaggerated in later traditions.[30] We are told that the Jewish exorcist Eleazar made use of a ring, under whose seal was a root, and incantations believed to have been composed by Solomon himself. The tradition of Solomon as exorcist and healer begins with 1 Kgs 4:29–34 and was embellished in later traditions such as Wis 7:17–21 and the *Testament of Solomon*. In the latter, we are told that an angel gave Solomon a "ring, which had a seal engraved on precious stone" (*T. Sol.* 1:7). No doubt this ring with a seal is the very ring Eleazar claimed to possess. The tradition of the incantations said to have been composed by Solomon grew out of the story in which the king interrogated a host of demons, learning from them the ills they caused and how the demons could be thwarted (cf. the whole of the *Testament of Solomon*).[31] The root that Eleazar had under the seal of the ring is probably the Baaras root described elsewhere in Josephus. This root is said to be flame colored, to emit a brilliant light, and to kill anyone who mishandled it: "it possesses one virtue for which it is prized; for the so-called demons . . . are promptly expelled by this root, if merely applied to the patients" (*J.W.* 7.180–186).

Solomon's fame was widespread in late antiquity, among non-Jews as well as among Jews. It is attested in scores of incantation texts, usually found inscribed on amulets or bowls.[32] Many of these incantations are written in Aramaic and Syriac by

---

29. Translation based on H. St. J. Thackeray and R. Marcus, trans., *Josephus: Jewish Antiquities*, vol. 3, *Books 7–8* (LCL 281; Cambridge: Harvard University Press, 1934), 595–97. For commentary, see C. T. Begg and P. Spilsbury, *Flavius Josephus: Translation and Commentary*, vol. 5, *Judean Antiquities Books 8–10* (ed. S. Mason; Leiden: Brill, 2005), 14–15; R. Deines, "Josephus, Salomo und die von Gott verliehene τέχνη gegen die Dämonen," in *Die Dämonen: Die Dämonologie der israelitischen-jüdischen und frühchristlichen Literatur im Kontext ihrer Umwelt* (ed. A. Lange, H. Lichtenberger, and K. F. D. Römheld; Tübingen: Mohr Siebeck, 2003), 365–94, esp. 372–92.

30. Examples: *b. Qidd.* 49b, "Ten measures of sorcery descended into the world, Egypt received nine, the rest of the world one"; *b. Šabb.* 104b, "Did not Ben Stada bring spells from Egypt?"; and esp. the *Sepher ha-Razim*. See M. Margalioth, *Book of the Mysteries* (Jerusalem: American Academy for Jewish Research, 1966) (in Hebrew). Margalioth dates *Sepher ha-Razim* to the third century, but that is probably too early. See also D. C. Duling, "Solomon, Exorcism, and the Son of David," *HTR* 68 (1975): 235–52.

31. And also the later *Sepher ha-Razim*; cf. Margalioth, *Book of the Mysteries*, 26.

32. See C. C. McCown, "The Christian Tradition as to the Magical Wisdom of Solomon," *JPOS* 2 (1922): 1–24; L. R. Fisher, "'Can This Be the Son of David?,'" in *Jesus and the Historian:*

Jews, Mandeans, and others,[33] and several refer to Solomon: for example, "Charmed and sealed is all sickness . . . by the seal of King Solomon, son of David";[34] "This is the seal-ring of King Solomon, the son of David. . . . Every demon . . . and all roof howlers, lilis [or liliths], and monsters, and all Satans, and idols, and curses . . . are bound and sealed . . . for all his house and all his dwelling, from this day and forever. Amen, Amen, Selah";[35] "Sealed with the seal-ring of El Shaddai, blessed be He, and with the seal-ring of King Solomon, the son of David, who worked spells on male demons and female liliths."[36]

Psalm 91 in the Aramaic presupposes this Solomonic, exorcistic tradition and the demonology that went with it. There is abundant evidence of interest in the first century in Solomon, son of David, as exorcist par excellence. The interpretive orientation of Ps 91 that we have observed at Qumran and in the targum is attested in rabbinic literature and in a variety of textual artifacts.

Psalm 91 in Rabbinic Literature

The interpretive orientation observed in the targum is attested in the Talmud and in a number of midrashic works, including, as one would expect, the midrash on the Psalms. A number of lessons are drawn from Ps 91, but the demonological interpretation that we have seen at Qumran and in the targum is very much in evidence in the midrashim.

The earliest midrash on Ps 91 is found in the Tannaitic work *Sipre*. In an exegesis of the phrase "and keep you" from Num 6:24, we are told that the Lord will keep, or protect, the faithful "from demons," as it says in Ps 91:11, "For he will give his angels

---

Written in Honor of Ernest Cadman Colwell (ed. F. T. Trotter; Philadelphia: Westminster, 1968), 82–97; J. H. Charlesworth, "Solomon and Jesus: The Son of David in Ante-Markan Traditions (Mk 10:47)," in *Biblical and Humane: A Festschrift for John F. Priest* (ed. L. B. Elder, D. L. Barr, and E. S. Malbon; Atlanta: Scholars Press, 1996), 125–51.

33. For collections of texts, see J. A. Montgomery, *Aramaic Incantation Texts from Nippur* (Philadelphia: University Museum of the University of Pennsylvania, 1913); C. H. Gordon, "Aramaic Magical Bowls in the Istanbul and Baghdad Museums," *ArOr* 6 (1934): 319–34 + plates x–xv; E. M. Yamauchi, "Aramaic Magic Bowls," *JAOS* 85 (1965): 511–23; idem, *Mandaic Incantation Texts* (AOS 49; New Haven: American Oriental Society, 1967), esp. 153–305 (texts and translations).

34. Montgomery, *Aramaic Incantation Texts from Nippur*, 231–32. See also the discussion in Charlesworth, "Solomon and Jesus," 137–38.

35. Gordon, "Aramaic Magical Bowls," 322.

36. Ibid., 324. For early references to Lilith, usually thought of as a female demon, see 4Q510 1, 5 ("all the spirits of the destroying angels, spirits of the bastards, Lilith, howlers and desert dwellers"; the same in 4Q511 X, 1) and *2 Bar.* 10:8 ("I shall call the Sirens from the sea, and you Lilin [or Lilith], come from the desert, and you, demons and dragons from the woods"). The name Lilith also appears on Aramaic incantation bowls; see C. H. Gordon, "Two Magic Bowls in Teheran," *Or* 20 (1951): 306–15, esp. 310; Montgomery, *Aramaic Incantation Texts from Nippur*, 190. Indeed, Qumran's 4Q184, which has been called the "Wiles of the Wicked Woman," is probably in reference not to a mortal woman but to Lilith herself. So J. M. Baumgarten, "On the Nature of the Seductress in 4Q184," *RevQ* 15 (1991): 133–43, esp. 140.

charge of you to guard you in all your ways" (*Sipre Num.* §40 [on Num 6:22–27]). The midrash simply presupposes that the angelic protection Ps 91 promises is protection against evil spirits. We should assume that this presupposition is based on the interpretation of verses 5, 6, and 10 that we have seen above—according to which the "terror of the night," the "pestilence," and the "scourge" are understood as references to demons—though these verses are not cited in the Numbers midrash.

Later in the midrash on Numbers, Ps 91:15 ("I will be with him in trouble") is cited as proof that God feels the pain of his people and empathizes with them (*Sipre Num.* §84 [on Num 10:29–36]). Other texts, like Isa 63:9 ("In all their affliction he was afflicted") and Gen 39:20–21 ("the Lord was with Joseph"), are cited for support and illustration. This interpretation of Ps 91:15 recurs throughout the later midrashim (e.g., *ʾAg. Ber.* §72).

What we find in *Sipre Numbers* we find in much expanded and developed form in *Midrash Rabbah*. In *Num. Rab.* 12.3 (on Num 7:1, "On the day when Moses had finished . . .") we find an extended midrash on Ps 91:1–10. Comments on every verse are offered. We are told that Moses composed Ps 91 as protection against demons, especially when he ascended Mount Sinai. On this occasion Moses said, "By the power of His name I put to flight the harmful demons and the destroying angels." The promise of Ps 91:5a ("You will not fear the terror of the night") is understood in reference to "Igrath,[37] daughter of Maḥalath, and her chariot, and of any of the demons who hold sway at night." The promise of Ps 91:5b ("nor the arrow that flies by day") is said to refer to "a kind of demon who 'flies' through the air like a bird, and darts like an 'arrow'" (see also *Deut. Rab.* 6.6 [on Deut 21:10]). The assurance that "a thousand may fall at your side" (Ps 91:7a) is said to refer to a thousand demons, while the "ten thousand at your right hand" (Ps 91:7b) refers to a "myriad of demons."[38] The promise of Ps 91:10b ("no scourge shall come near your tent") alludes to the erection of the tabernacle (or tent) and the extermination of demons.

Two passages in *Midrash Tanḥuma* interpret Ps 91:5–6, 10 with reference to evil spirits. In a midrash on Adam's seduction by evil spirits, Rabbi Simon refers to 1 Kgs 11:23 ("God also raised up as an adversary [שָׂטָן] to him"), explaining that the "adversary," or Satan, brings a pestilence, which can only refer to demons (מזיקין). For proof of this, Ps 91:10 is cited: "no scourge will come near your tent" (*Midr. Tanḥ.* Gen §1 [on Gen 5:1]).[39] Again, the midrash assumes that Ps 91:10 is speaking of demons, as this verse clearly does in the Aramaic paraphrase, and not simply of illness or some other mundane reversal of fortune.

The second passage in which appeal is made to Ps 91, *Midr. Tanḥ.* Num §2 (on Num 7:1), is every bit as interesting. Commenting on Num 7:1 ("when Moses had finished setting up the tabernacle"), this text asserts that setting up the tabernacle

37. Igrath (אגרת) is a female demon. Her mother, Maḥalath (מחלת), is the queen and mother of demons (see *b. Pesaḥ.* 112b) and perhaps should be identified with Lilith. For more on the matriarch of the demons, see M. Hutter, "Lilith," *DDD* 520–21.

38. Translations of *Numbers Rabbah* are adapted from J. J. Slotki, *Midrash Rabbah: Numbers* (New York: Soncino, 1983), 451–57.

39. The midrash equates pestilence (דֶּבֶר) and scourge (נֶגַע).

annihilated the destructive demons (מזיקין).[40] Indeed, when Moses ascended Mount Sinai, he spoke the words of Ps 91 ("He who dwells in the shelter of the Most High . . .").[41] What follows is a running commentary on verses 5, 6, and 10, in which these verses are understood in reference to demons (מזיקין), very much as we observed in the targum.

As we would expect, and as has already been touched upon, in the midrashim Ps 91 is interpreted very much along the lines that we have seen in the targum and elsewhere. In *Midr. Pss.* 17.8 (on Ps 17:7), Ps 91:7 ("A thousand may fall at your side, ten thousand at your right hand") is cited as proof that God will send his angels to protect the righteous against the demons. The tradition reappears in *Midr. Pss.* 55.3 (on Ps 55:19), only this time appeal is made to Ps 91:11 ("For he will give his angels charge of you to guard you").

In the midrash on Ps 91, commentary is provided on all sixteen verses. Commentary on verses 5, 6, and 10 parallels what we have already seen. Mosaic authorship of the psalm is again affirmed (*Midr. Pss.* 91.1 [on Ps 91:1]). Verse 5 is understood to refer to the demon that flies like an arrow. The "destruction that wastes at noonday" (v. 6) also refers to a demon. Rabbi Yose is credited with a colorful description of this demon, whom he dubs "Bitter Destruction." Verse 7 ("A thousand may fall at your side, ten thousand at your right hand") is interpreted differently. The "thousand" and the "ten thousand" do not refer to the demons who "fall"; rather, they refer to the angels who "fall in" alongside a person to protect him (*Midr. Pss.* 91.4 [on Ps 91:7]). The midrash on verse 10 ("no scourge will come near your tent") is applied to the erection of the tabernacle and the defeat of the demons (*Midr. Pss.* 91.5 [on Ps 91:10]), much as we have already seen.

The talmudic literature adds very little to the rabbinic tradition. What we find here is concern with the genre and purpose of Ps 91: see *y. Šabb.* 6:8b; *y. ʿErub.* 10:26c; *b. Šebu.* 15b: "the song against evil occurrences, and some call it against plagues." The identification of Ps 91 in these three passages as, with minor verbal variation, a "song against evil occurrences" (שיר של פגעים) recalls the language in 11Q5 XXVII, 10, considered above.

Interpretation of Ps 91 is fairly consistent throughout the targum and the rabbinic traditions. We shall now see that these interpretive traditions are also reflected in amulets and magic texts of approximately the same period.

Psalm 91 in Amulets and Other Magic Texts

Portions of Ps 91 are quoted in several amulets, magic bowls, and other magic texts, mostly as attempts to ward off evil, especially demonic evil. The incipit of Ps 91 is

40. This midrash is repeated in later works (see *Pesiq. Rab.* 5.10; *Pesiq. Rab Kah.* 1.5).

41. In a number of passages in the midrashim, the point is made that it was *Moses*, not Solomon, who composed Ps 91 (e.g., *Num. Rab.* 12.3 [on Num 7:1]). I suspect that it was the midrash on the tabernacle and the demons that encouraged this understanding of the authorship of Ps 91.

cited dozens of times, especially in amulets.[42] When the incipit is quoted, we should probably assume the whole of the book is in mind. In the case of Ps 91, therefore, the quotation of verse 1 ("He who dwells in the shelter of the Most High . . .") is likely meant to bring to mind the promises of protection found especially in verses 5 ("You will not fear the terror of the night, nor the arrow that flies by day"), 6 ("nor the pestilence that stalks in darkness, nor the destruction that wastes at noonday"), 11 ("For he will give his angels charge of you to guard you in all your ways"), and 13 ("You will tread on the lion and the adder, the young lion and the serpent you will trample under foot"), verses that were routinely interpreted as promises of protection from evil spirits.

The amulets and magic texts that we want to survey here are the non-Christian ones, though it must be admitted that sometimes it is not possible to distinguish a Jewish artifact from a Christian artifact.[43] Both Jews and Christians appealed to Ps 91 and, judging by the surviving evidence, they did so frequently. Christians were especially fond of the psalm, invoking it often, along with Gospel incipits or other overtly Christian elements, for protection against evil powers.[44]

There are two texts from the Cairo Genizah that should be mentioned. Both are part of the Taylor-Schechter (TS) collection. The first is TS k1.18,30, a Hebrew amulet written on two sheets (i.e., k1.18 and k1.30).[45] Part of the text reads: "In the name of HYH, HWH, and YHWH, I have adjured and decreed upon you, O zodiacal sign Leo, to arise with all might and strength . . . to drive away all kinds of demons and demonesses, lilis and liliths, evil diseases, harmful male spirits and harmful female spirits . . . by the power of this holy combination (of letters) . . ." (TS k1.18, lines 1–3, 8–10, 20). In the subsequent lines, 21–25, Ps 91:1 and Deut 6:5 are woven together. The effect is to create *voces magicae*, or "magical words," out of these two biblical texts.

42. "Incipit" refers to the opening words of a book. The Latin verb *incipit* literally means, "it [i.e., the book] begins."

43. As noted by G. Bohak, *Ancient Jewish Magic: A History* (Cambridge: Cambridge University Press, 2008), 212.

44. For a series of recent and learned publications concerned with Christian amulets and related artifacts that make use of Ps 90 (91), see T. J. Kraus, "Septuaginta-Psalm 90 in apotropäischer Verwendung: Vorüberlegungen für eine kritische Edition und (bisheriges) Datenmaterial," *BN* 125 (2005): 39–73; idem, "Psalm 90 der Septuaginta in apotropäischer Verwendung—erste Anmerkungen und Datenmaterial," in *Proceedings of the 24th International Congress of Papyrology, Helsinki, 1–7 August, 2004* (ed. J. Frösén et al.; 2 vols.; Commentationes Humanarum Litterarum 122; Helsinki: Societas Scientiarum Fennica, 2007), 1:497–514; idem, "'He That Dwelleth in the Help of the Highest': Septuagint Psalm 90 and the Iconographic Program on Byzantine Armbands," in *Jewish and Christian Scripture as Artifact and Canon* (ed. C. A. Evans and H. D. Zacharias; LSTS 70; SSEJC 13; London: Continuum, 2009), 137–47. See also J. E. Sanzo, *Scriptural* Incipits *on Amulets from Late Antique Egypt: Text, Typology, and Theory* (STAC 84; Tübingen: Mohr Siebeck, 2014). On the popularity of Ps 90 (91) on Greek amulets in Egypt, see J. Chapa, "Su demoni e angeli: Il Salmo 90 nel suo contesto," in *I papiri letterari cristiani: Atti del convegno internazionale di studi in memoria di Mario Naldini, Firenze, 10–11 giugno 2010* (ed. G. Bastianini and A. Casanova; Florence: Istituto Papirologico "G. Vitelli," 2011), 59–90, at 68–69.

45. For Hebrew text, translation, and critical commentary, see L. H. Schiffman and M. D. Swartz, *Hebrew and Aramaic Incantation Texts from the Cairo Genizah: Selected Texts from Taylor-Schechter Box K1* (Semitic Texts and Studies 1; Sheffield: Sheffield Academic, 1992), 69–82. This text, first published by Cyrus Gordon, was mentioned above in notes 33, 35, and 36.

The first (Ps 91:1, "He who dwells in the shelter of the Most High") is the well-known text that promises protection against evil spirits. The second (Deut 6:5, "you shall love the Lord your God with all your heart") is from the well-known passage, the Shema, that every faithful Jew is to recite daily. Alone, these passages of Scripture are potent; combined in a way that creates a magical chant, they are especially potent.

The second text from the Cairo Genizah is TS k1.127, an Aramaic charm chiefly made up of passages of Scripture and magical words and names.[46] The charm was composed to bring healing to one Bunayna bint Yaman (lines 3, 11, 19) and to protect her from "evil spirits, evil plague, evil diseases, afflictions, chastisements, fever and chills, and any blasts and harmful spirits" (lines 15–17). In line 28, we find an echo of Ps 91:10: ורע שד לא יאונך ("and let no evil demon befall you").

One magic bowl, whose purpose was to bind those who would work black magic against one Brik-Yah-be-Yah son of Marat,[47] concludes with a quotation of Ps 91:7, 10: "It is written: A thousand may fall at your side, ten thousand at your right hand; but it will not come near you. No evil shall befall you, no scourge come near your tent" (line 9). It is possible that this bowl is Christian, for in the list of magical names in line 3 we find Petrus (פתרוס) and Jesus (יאוסס). Their spellings indicate that they are transliterations of the Greek names Πέτρος and Ιησοῦς.[48] Accordingly, it is probable that these are the names associated with the Christian faith. But does the appearance of these names necessarily lead to the conclusion that this Aramaic magic bowl is Christian instead of Jewish? Not at all. We may have here an example of "casting the net wide," in that every potent name that the author of the bowl knows has been included. Indeed, in the list of these names appears Mithras (מתרוס). The appearance of this name hardly requires us to think that the author of the bowl's text or Brik-Yah-be-Yah son of Marat, for whom the bowl was written, was a member of the Mithraic cult. The bowl is probably Jewish, notwithstanding the syncretistic and ecclectic tendencies.

Finally, in a magic bowl whose purpose was to bring healing for one Khusrau son of Izdan-dukh we find quotations of Zech 3:2 ("The LORD rebuke you, O Satan! The LORD who has chosen Jerusalem rebuke you!"), Deut 6:4 ("Hear, O Israel, the LORD our God is one LORD"), and Ps 91:1 ("He who dwells in the shelter of the Most High, who abides in the shadow of the Almighty").[49] The latter two texts, which appear in lines 6–7, are blended together "into a single text by taking one word from one verse followed by one word from the other text."[50]

---

46. For Aramaic text, translation, and critical commentary, see Schiffman and Swartz, *Hebrew and Aramaic Incantation Texts*, 113–22; J. Naveh and S. Shaked, *Amulets and Magic Bowls: Aramaic Incantations of Late Antiquity* (3rd ed.; Jerusalem: Magnes, 1998), 237–38.

47. Isbell, *Corpus of the Aramaic Incantation Bowls*, 118–19 (bowl no. 52).

48. Rightly Gordon, "Aramaic Magical Bowls," 327: "a list of guardian powers, transliterated from a Greek original."

49. For Aramaic text, translation, and critical commentary, see Naveh and Shaked, *Amulets and Magic Bowls*, 184–87. The bowl is housed in the Jewish Historical Museum in Belgrade, catalogued as no. 242/1.

50. Ibid., 187. For further discussion of Ps 91 and other passages of Scripture blended together, see J. Naveh and S. Shaked, *Magic Spells and Formulae: Aramaic Incantations of Late Antiquity* (Jerusalem: Magnes, 1993), 25; C. Müller-Kessler, "The Use of Biblical Quotations in

Jesus and Psalm 91

Having established the antiquity and great longevity of the exorcistic interpretation of Ps 91, we should not be too surprised that this psalm makes an appearance in the temptation narrative. We may now inquire in what ways, if any, this understanding of Ps 91 is reflected in Jesus' teaching, apart from the temptation narrative itself.

There is one passage that recommends itself. According to Luke 10:17–20, the disciples return from their mission, saying, "Lord, even the demons are subject to us in your name!" Jesus replies, saying,

> I saw Satan fall like lightning from heaven [ἐθεώρουν τὸν σατανᾶν ὡς ἀστραπὴν ἐκ τοῦ οὐρανοῦ πεσόντα]. Behold, I have given you authority to tread upon serpents and scorpions [δέδωκα ὑμῖν τὴν ἐξουσίαν τοῦ πατεῖν ἐπάνω ὄφεων καὶ σκορπίων], and over all the power of the enemy [ἐπὶ πᾶσαν τὴν δύναμιν τοῦ ἐχθροῦ]; and nothing shall hurt [οὐ μὴ ἀδικήσῃ] you. (vv. 18–19)

Every significant element in this dominical utterance reflects Jewish demonology. The statement that Satan has fallen from heaven presupposes earlier access to heaven, as in Job 1:6–12; 2:1–7; and Zech 3:1–2. His fall from heaven may allude to Isa 14:12 ("How you are fallen [LXX: ἐκπίπτειν] from heaven, O Day Star, son of Dawn!"), which in *Targum Isaiah* seems to be understood as in reference to Satan. According to the *Life of Adam and Eve*, the devil reproaches Adam as follows: "because of you I am expelled and deprived of my glory, which I had in the heavens in the midst of angels, and because of you I was cast out onto the earth" (12:1). Similarly, in *2 Enoch* we are told that God "hurled (Satan) out from the height, together with his angels" (29:5; cf. 31:4).

Jesus' claim to have given his disciples authority (δέδωκα ὑμῖν τὴν ἐξουσίαν) "to tread upon serpents and scorpions" (τοῦ πατεῖν ἐπάνω ὄφεων καὶ σκορπίων) almost certainly alludes to Ps 91:13, "you will trample down lion and serpent [Old Greek: καταπατήσεις λέοντα καὶ δράκοντα]," a passage that probably underlies the patriarch Levi's pseudepigraphic prophecy of the coming of a faithful priest. It will be a time when "Beliar shall be bound by him. And he shall grant to his children authority to tread [δώσει ἐξουσίαν τοῖς τέκνοις αὐτοῦ τοῦ πατεῖν] on the wicked spirits" (*T. Levi* 18:12). The author of the *Testament of Levi* has substituted the more literal "wicked spirits" (τὰ πονηρὰ πνεύματα) for "lion and serpent" (λέοντα καὶ δράκοντα), the creatures that oftentimes in demonological contexts represent evil spirits. Other parallels should be mentioned: "Then all the spirits of error shall be given over to being trampled underfoot [πάντα τὰ πνεύματα τῆς πλάνης εἰς καταπάτησιν]. And men will have mastery over the evil spirits" (*T. Sim.* 6:6); and "He will liberate every captive of the sons of men from Beliar, and every spirit of error will be trampled down [πᾶν πνεῦμα πλάνης πατηθήσεται]" (*T. Zeb.* 9:8). The closest parallel to Ps 91:13 is *T. Levi* 18:12, where we have "give authority" and "tread on the wicked spirits." It is to this language that Jesus alludes.

Jewish Aramaic Incantation Bowls," in *Studies on Magic and Divination in the Biblical World* (ed. H. R. Jacobus et al.; Biblical Intersections 11; Piscataway, NJ: Gorgias, 2013), 227–45. For references to Ps 91, see pp. 234, 236, and 242.

Joseph Fitzmyer, however, thinks an allusion to Ps 91:13 is "farfetched."[51] He points out that in the Old Greek, ὄφις ("serpent" or "snake"), the word found in Luke 10:19, never renders the Hebrew word תַּנִּין ("dragon" or "sea monster"). It must be admitted that the evangelist Luke probably has made no allusion, at least not consciously. If he had, Jesus' saying would have paralleled the Greek version of the psalm more closely. It is more likely that what lies behind Luke 10:19 is a form of Jesus' saying that reflects not so much the precise wording of Ps 91:13 as an interpretive orientation toward this text.

In any event, several words are used in reference to Satan. In Hebrew, verse 13b reads תִּרְמֹס כְּפִיר וְתַנִּין ("you will tread upon the young lion and the serpent"), which is rendered literally in the Old Greek: καταπατήσεις λέοντα καὶ δράκοντα. The serpent (ὄφις) of Gen 3:1–14 is understood by Paul as a reference to Satan (2 Cor 11:3, "the serpent [ὁ ὄφις] deceived Eve by his cunning"). Elsewhere, Satan (or the devil) is closely associated with the ὄφις (Greek *Life of Adam and Eve* 16:1–4; 17:4; 18:1; 23:4; 25:1; *Rechabites* 20:3; 4 Macc 18:8, "snake of deceit [ἀπάτης ὄφις]"). But Satan is also called a δράκων ("dragon" or "sea monster"), the very word used in Ps 91:13 (= Old Greek Ps 90:13). Indeed, the author of Revelation calls Satan "serpent" (ὄφις) and "dragon" (δράκων): "And the great dragon was thrown down, that ancient serpent, who is called the Devil and Satan [ὁ δράκων ὁ μέγας, ὁ ὄφις ὁ ἀρχαῖος, ὁ καλούμενος Διάβολος καὶ ὁ Σατανᾶς], the deceiver of the whole world—he was thrown down to the earth, and his angels were thrown down with him" (Rev 12:9; cf. 13:4; 20:2).

Satan is also called a "lion": "Be sober, be watchful. Your adversary the devil prowls around like a roaring lion [διάβολος ὡς λέων ὠρυόμενος], seeking someone to devour [καταπιεῖν]" (1 Pet 5:8). The allusion could be to Ps 22:13, "like a ravening and roaring lion" (ὡς λέων ὁ ἁρπάζων καὶ ὠρυόμενος), but 1 Peter may allude to another tradition, one possibly attested in the pseudepigraphic *Joseph and Aseneth*: "For behold, the wild ancient Lion [ὁ λέων ὁ ἄγριος ὁ παλαιὸς] pursues me; and his children are the gods of the Egyptians that I have cast down and destroyed. And their father the devil is trying to devour me [ὁ πατὴρ αὐτῶν ὁ διάβολος καταπιεῖν με πειρᾶται]" (12:9). The "ancient lion" is none other than the devil, father of the Egyptian gods, who is trying to devour the repentant Aseneth. In the *Testament of Solomon*, there are demons who appear as lions (cf. *T. Sol.* 2:3; 11:1).

Jesus also tells his disciples that he has given them authority ἐπὶ πᾶσαν τὴν δύναμιν τοῦ ἐχθροῦ ("over all the power of the enemy"). Elsewhere in the dominical tradition, the devil is called "the enemy" (cf. Matt 13:28–29, "the enemy who sowed them is the devil [ὁ δὲ ἐχθρὸς ὁ σπείρας αὐτά ἐστιν ὁ διάβολος]). One is reminded, too, of what an angry Paul said to Elymas the magician. "You son of the devil, you enemy of all righteousness [υἱὲ διαβόλου, ἐχθρὲ πάσης δικαιοσύνης], full of all deceit and villainy, will you not stop making crooked the straight paths of the Lord?" (Acts 13:10). The devil is called "the enemy" in other Judeo-Christian texts in late antiquity (cf. *Life of Adam and Eve* 2:4; 7:2; 15:1; 25:4; 28:3; *3 Bar.* 13:2; *T. Dan* 6:2–4).

51. J. A. Fitzmyer, *The Gospel according to Luke* (2 vols.; AB 28, 28A; Garden City, NY: Doubleday, 1981–85), 2:863.

Of great interest is the last passage, in which reference is made to the "kingdom of the enemy": "God . . . will stand against the kingdom of the enemy [τῆς βασιλείας τοῦ ἐχθροῦ]. . . . the kingdom of the enemy [ἡ βασιλεία τοῦ ἐχθροῦ] will be brought to an end" (*T. Dan* 6:2, 4). This hope coheres with the following prediction found in the *Testament of Moses*: "Then his (God's) kingdom will appear throughout his whole creation. Then the devil will have an end. . . . For the Heavenly One will arise from his kingly throne" (10:1, 3; cf. Mark 3:26, "And if Satan has risen up against himself and is divided, he cannot stand, but has an end").

Both Jesus' words in Luke 10:19 and the words attributed to the patriarch in *T. Levi* 18:12 allude to Ps 91:13, which promises that the faithful will tread upon the lion and the serpent, and which is part of a larger passage understood as having relevance for exorcism, as we see in 11Q11 and in the Psalms targum and other interpretive traditions.

The appearance of Ps 91 in the Matthean and Lukan versions of the temptation of Jesus is but one indication of many that the demonological orientation of this particular psalm in the Psalms targum derives from early, probably intertestamental tradition. The exorcistic psalms of 11Q11 provide important early attestation of a tradition that comes to expression in interesting ways in the life and teaching of Jesus. The exorcistic interpretation of Ps 91 in the early centuries of the Christian church and rabbinic Judaism bears witness to the ongoing social and religious power of this text.

In the following chapter, we shall look at another powerful text, Deut 21:22–23. This text, which commands the burial of the executed before nightfall, greatly influenced the Jewish people of late antiquity. The influence of this text was such that Roman officials who administered all or parts of Israel in late antiquity evidently yielded to it.

CHAPTER SIX

"Hang Him on a Tree until Dead": Hanging and Crucifixion in Second Temple Israel

The discovery of the skeleton of a crucified man in an ossuary probably dating to the administration of Pontius Pilate, prefect of Judea and Samaria, reopened the question of the practice of crucifixion in Palestine in the late Second Temple period.[1] This significant archaeological discovery also created fresh interest in Dead Sea Scrolls texts that speak of crucifixion and in the process quote or allude to Deut 21:22–23, an important legal text regarding the hanging and burial of executed criminals. In the present chapter, we shall review this evidence, beginning with the passage of Scripture just mentioned.

Deuteronomy 21:22–23 and Hanging in Old Testament Literature

In the Hebrew/Jewish tradition, Deut 21:22–23 is the foundational text on which customs and practices relating to execution were based from the end of the First Temple period on into the first century. The text reads (in the MT and LXX):

> And if a man has committed a crime punishable by death and he is put to death, and you hang him on a tree [וְתָלִיתָ אֹתוֹ עַל־עֵץ / καὶ κρεμάσητε αὐτὸν ἐπὶ ξύλου], his body shall not remain all night upon the tree, but you shall bury him the same day, for a hanged man is accursed by God; you shall not defile your/the land which the Lord your God gives you for an inheritance. (Deut 21:22–23)

The verb "hang" (תלה) occurs some twenty-eight times in the MT and is usually translated κρεμάννυμι in the corresponding passages in the LXX.[2] The first occurrences are found in the story of Joseph and Pharaoh's chief baker. Joseph, the interpreter of dreams, tells the unfortunate baker that "Pharaoh will lift up your head—from you!—and hang you on a tree [וְתָלָה אוֹתְךָ עַל־עֵץ / καὶ κρεμάσει σε ἐπὶ

1. I refer to the discovery near Giv'at ha-Mivtar. This find will be discussed below.

2. For lexical data regarding תלה, see BDB, 1067–68; *TWOT* 2:970–71. For lexical data regarding κρεμάννυμι, see BAG 451; LSJ *ad loc.*; *TDNT* 3:915–21.

ξύλου]; and the birds will eat the flesh from you" (Gen 40:19). And so it happened, the baker was hanged (Gen 40:22; 41:13).[3]

Joshua, the great commander who succeeded Moses and conquered the promised land, hanged some of Israel's enemies. The first was the king of Ai:

> And he hanged the king of Ai on a tree [תָּלָה עַל־הָעֵץ / ἐκρέμασεν ἐπὶ ξύλου] until evening; and at the going down of the sun Joshua commanded, and they took his body down from the tree, and cast it at the entrance of the gate of the city, and raised over it a great heap of stones, which stands there to this day. (Josh 8:29)

Next to be hanged by Joshua were the five kings who attacked Gibeon:

> And afterward Joshua smote them and put them to death, and he hung them on five trees [וַיִּתְלֵם עַל חֲמִשָּׁה עֵצִים / καὶ ἐκρέμασεν αὐτοὺς ἐπὶ πέντε ξύλων]. And they hung upon the trees [וַיִּהְיוּ תְּלוּיִם עַל־הָעֵצִים / καὶ ἦσαν κρεμάμενοι ἐπὶ τῶν ξύλων] until evening; but at the time of the going down of the sun, Joshua commanded, and they took them down from the trees, and threw them into the cave where they had hidden themselves, and they set great stones against the mouth of the cave, which remain to this very day. (Josh 10:26–27)

The hangings recounted in Genesis and Joshua cohere at important points with the law of Deut 21.[4] Pharaoh hangs his chief baker ("on a tree," readers will assume, in the light of the interpretation offered by Joseph). Joshua hangs on trees the king of Ai and the five attacking kings. In the case of the five kings, we are told that they were first put to death (וַיְמִיתֵם / καὶ ἀπέκτεινεν αὐτούς) and then hanged, which corresponds precisely with Deuteronomy ("he is put to death, and you hang him on a tree"). We are not told if the king of Ai was put to death before being hanged; perhaps this was assumed. Moreover, the bodies of the king of Ai and of the five kings who attacked Gibeon were taken down at the end of the day and were buried, as Deut 21 specifically commands. However, in the case of Pharaoh's baker readers may have assumed that the body was left hanging on the tree, for Joseph foretold that the birds would eat his flesh. In any case, readers would not assume that Pharaoh would necessarily have taken down a hanged corpse before nightfall.

The law of Deut 21 appears to focus on the command not to leave the body of the executed criminal hanging on a tree overnight. Admittedly, the Hebrew grammar is somewhat ambiguous, but the translation of the RSV appears to have it right: "And if a man has committed a crime punishable by death and he is put to death, and you hang him on a tree . . ." (v. 22)—that is, if a criminal has been executed according to custom, a custom attested not only in Israel but in surrounding, non-Israelite societies (e.g., Egypt, Persia, and elsewhere). The command is then given

---

3. The imprisonment of the two servants, the eventual release of the cupbearer, and the eventual execution of the baker suggest a case of poisoning, or at least attempted poisoning. One suspect was cleared; the other was convicted.

4. "Joshua scrupulously obeys this law," as noted in R. D. Nelson, *Deuteronomy: A Commentary* (OTL; Louisville: Westminster John Knox, 2002), 262. Of course, in terms of the development of the laws of the Pentateuch/Hexateuch, the precise relationship of the stories of Joshua (and Genesis) to Deut 21 is a bit more complicated. See D. L. Christensen, *Deuteronomy 21:10–34:12* (WBC 6B; Nashville: Nelson, 2002), 487–89. Custom and practice may have influenced the (later) formulation of the law.

in verse 23: "His body shall not remain all night upon the tree, but you shall bury him the same day." The command is not seen in hanging someone on a tree, but in taking the corpse down and burying it on the day of death.[5]

There are other hangings in the Old Testament that should be mentioned. David ordered the hanging of the men who murdered Saul's crippled son Ish-bosheth:

> And David commanded his young men, and they killed them, and cut off their hands and feet, and hanged [וַיִּתְלוּ / καὶ ἐκρέμασαν] them beside the pool at Hebron. (2 Sam 4:12)

David's men recovered the bodies of Saul and his sons, whom the Philistines had hung in the public square in Beth She'an (1 Sam 31:9–13; cf. 2 Sam 21:12).

Hanging is a prominent feature in the book of Esther. Court officials who plotted murder against the Persian king "were both hanged on a tree [וַיִּתָּלוּ שְׁנֵיהֶם עַל־עֵץ / καὶ ἐκρέμασεν αὐτούς]" (Esth 2:23).[6] This event only adumbrates the deadly struggle between Haman and Mordecai, a struggle that ends with the death of one. The former builds gallows on which he hopes to hang the latter (Esth 5:14; 6:4). In the end, however, it is Haman who is hanged: "the gallows which Haman has prepared for Mordecai . . . is standing in Haman's house . . . 'Hang him on it [תְּלֻהוּ עָלָיו / σταυρωθήτω ἐπ' αὐτοῦ].' So they hanged Haman on the tree [וַיִּתְלוּ אֶת־הָמָן עַל־הָעֵץ / καὶ ἐκρεμάσθη Αμαν ἐπὶ τοῦ ξύλου]" (Esth 7:9–10; cf. 8:7). Even the ten sons of Haman are hanged (Esth 9:13–15), which is an expression of severe judgment, in that it indicates that Haman's name and line have been brought to an end.

It is intriguing to note that the Greek translation renders the king's command, תְּלֻהוּ, ("Hang him"), with σταυρωθήτω ("Let him be crucified"), instead of with a form of κρεμάννυμι.[7] This choice in translation provides an important lexical

5. For a different nuance, see the NEB: "When a man is convicted of a capital offence and is put to death, you shall hang him on a gibbet; but his body shall not remain on the gibbet overnight." The third clause is taken in an imperatival sense, "you shall hang him on a gibbet." However, the consecutive construction of the Hebrew favors a continuation of the conditional sense with which the verse begins: "And if a man has committed a crime . . . and (if) he is put to death, and (if) you hang him on a tree . . . ." The prohibition of v. 23, "his body shall not remain [לֹא־תָלִין] all night upon the tree," introduces the command proper. The original purpose of the hanging is uncertain. Some commentators think the public hanging of the person who had been executed (which in Israel usually meant death by stoning, cf. Lev 20:2, 27; 24:14, 16, 23; etc.) was for deterrence. On this interpretation, see S. R. Driver, *A Critical and Exegetical Commentary on Deuteronomy* (ICC; Edinburgh: T&T Clark, 1895), 248–49; P. C. Craigie, *Deuteronomy* (NICOT; Grand Rapids: Eerdmans, 1976), 285; Christensen, *Deuteronomy 21:10–34:12*, 490; Nelson, *Deuteronomy*, 262. Others think it originally had to do with appeasing the deity, to show that the person who broke the divine law had been punished. On this interpretation, see A. Phillips, *Deuteronomy* (CBC; Cambridge: Cambridge University Press, 1973), 143–44. This interpretation may have some support, at least in respect to later times and in the west, in the report that the Gauls "crucify [ἀνασκολοπίζουσι] to the gods . . . malefactors" and offer them up, along with other sacrifices (Diodorus Siculus, *Historical Library* 5.32.6).

6. The Greek does not supply the expected ἐπὶ ξύλου, which is probably understood.

7. In the Greek "Additions to Esther," see also the reference to Haman, who "has been hanged [ἐσταυρῶσθαι] at the gates of Susa, with all his household" (16:18 = 8:12r). On σταυρός and (ἀνα)σταυρόω, see *TDNT* 7:572–84.

clue, suggesting that "hanging" in the first or second century BCE was sometimes understood to refer to crucifixion. In fact, it may suggest that by the first century this was the *normal* understanding of the word "hanging."

First-Century Interpretation of the Texts on Hanging

The interpretation of Gen 40 (the hanging of Pharaoh's baker), 1 Sam 31 (the hanging of Saul and sons), Esth 7 (the hanging of Haman), and Deut 21 (the law of hanging and burial) that we see in the first century BCE and the first century CE is quite instructive, especially as found in Philo, Josephus, and the Dead Sea Scrolls, which will now be considered.[8]

Interpretation of Genesis 40: The Hanging of Pharaoh's Baker

In his allegorical interpretation of the life of the patriarch Joseph, Philo of Alexandria probes the deeper meaning of the dreams of Pharaoh's cupbearer and chief baker. He does this primarily by an imaginative and expansive paraphrase of the story. After hearing the chief baker's dream, Joseph explains: "The three baskets are symbols of three days. When these have passed, the king will order you to be impaled and beheaded, and the birds will feast upon your flesh until you are entirely devoured" (*Joseph* 96). As foretold, three days later Pharaoh remembered his imprisoned servants, "ordering one to be impaled and beheaded and the other to be restored to his former office" (*Joseph* 98).[9]

In the interpretation of the dream, Philo has Joseph predict: "the king will command you to be crucified, and your head to be cut off" (ἀνασκολοπισθῆναι σε καὶ τὴν κεφαλὴν ἀποτμηθῆναι). Accordingly, in narrating the execution Philo says that the chief baker was ordered "impaled and beheaded" (ἀνασκολοπισθῆναι τὴν κεφαλὴν ἀποτμηθέντα). Philo has used the verb ἀνασκολοπίζω instead of κρεμάννυμι, which is the word used in the Greek version of Gen 40–41, a word that literally means "hang." Σκολοπίζω means "impale," while ἀνασκολοπίζω usually means "fix on a stake."[10] When we compare Philo's account with Gen 40:19, we notice the reversal of the sequence of the verbs of execution. This reversal may have significance. The impaled-beheaded sequence of the interpretation of the dream (*Joseph* 96) and execution narrative (*Joseph* 98) stands in contrast to the sequence

8. For much fuller treatments of these passages, see D. W. Chapman, *Ancient Jewish and Christian Perceptions of Crucifixion* (WUNT II/244; Tübingen: Mohr Siebeck, 2008); G. Samuelsson, *Crucifixion in Antiquity* (2nd ed.; WUNT II/310; Tübingen: Mohr Siebeck, 2013); J. G. Cook, *Crucifixion in the Mediterranean World* (WUNT 327; Tübingen: Mohr Siebeck, 2014).

9. Translations of Philo in this chapter are based on F. H. Colson et al., trans., *Philo* (12 vols.; LCL; Cambridge: Harvard University Press, 1929–53).

10. Cf. LSJ *ad loc.* Σκολοπίζω and ἀνασκολοπίζω do not occur in the New Testament writings (but the cognate noun σκόλοψ, "thorn," does, in 2 Cor 12:7). Σκόλοψ can also mean "stake," and, as such, is synonymous with σταυρός.

in Gen 40:19 ("lift up your head" [beheaded] . . . "hang you on a tree" [impaled]). The reversal may reflect the influence of Deut 21:22 (in which "put to death" is followed by "hanged on a tree").

Later in his treatise on Joseph, Philo returns to the cupbearer and the chief baker in order to find additional allegorical meaning. Because of the gravity of his offense, the chief baker "is properly put to death by hanging [θνῄσκει κρεμασθείς], suffering what he has made others to suffer, for indeed he has hanged [ἀνεκρέμασε] and racked the starving man with hunger" (*Joseph* 156). In this instance, Philo's use of κρεμάννυμι/ἀνακρεμάννυμι may reflect the language of LXX Gen 40–41 and perhaps also that of Deut 21.[11]

The patriarch Joseph was of special interest to his namesake Josephus, who claimed likewise to have the power to interpret dreams and portents (*J.W.* 3.351–352), as well as to prophesy (*J.W.* 3.399–408). Josephus also relates the story of the unhappy chief baker. According to Josephus, the patriarch Joseph told the baker "that on the third day he should be crucified [ἀνασταυρωθέντα]." And so it happened that, when "the king solemnized his birthday, he crucified [ἀνεσταύρωσε] the chief baker, but set the cupbearer free from his bonds, and restored him to his former service" (*Ant.* 2.73; cf. 2.77: "the chief baker was crucified [σταυρωθείη] on the very same day"). It is interesting to note that Josephus has employed the verb ἀνασταυρόω instead of κρεμάννυμι.[12]

Interpretation of 1 Samuel 31: The Hanging of Saul

According to LXX 1 Sam 31:10, the Philistines "fastened (Saul's) body on the wall [τὸ σῶμα αὐτοῦ κατέπηξαν ἐν τῷ τείχει] of Beth She'an." The Greek verb καταπήγνυμι translates תקע. The Hebrew means to "thrust" or "drive," in the sense of driving pegs or stakes into the ground, or, in 1 Sam 31:10, fastening the body

11. Chapman, *Ancient Jewish and Christian Perceptions of Crucifixion*, 105; Cook, *Crucifixion in the Mediterranean World*, 235–36. The Hebrew text's "hang on a tree [עֵץ]" becomes "hang on the pole [צליבא]" in *Tg. Neof.* Gen 40:19 and 41:13. This Aramaic language may connote crucifixion. See M. McNamara, *Targum Neofiti 1: Genesis* (ArBib 1A; Collegeville, MN: Liturgical Press, 1992), 184n12.

12. There are some forty-five examples of κρεμάννυμι, σταυρός, σταυρόω, and ἀνασταυρόω in Josephus, the last being the most common. Several examples will be discussed below. Others include *Ant.* 11.17, 103; 12.256 (by order of Antiochus IV, Jews who refused to abandon their faith "were crucified [ἀνεσταυροῦντο] while they were still alive and breathed"); 17.295 (by order of the Roman general Varus, two thousand "were crucified [σταυρωθέντες] on account" of revolt); 18.79; 19.94; 20.102, 129 (Quadratus "crucified [ἀνεσταύρωσεν]" Jewish troublemakers "whom Cumanus had taken captive"); as well as parallels and further examples in *J.W.* 2.75 (Varus), 241 (Quadratus), 253 (by order of Felix, a large number of robbers "were crucified [ἀνασταυρωθέντων]"), 306 (Florus "first chastised with stripes [μάστιξιν προαικισάμενος], and then crucified [ἀνεσταύρωσεν]" many of the "quiet people"), 308 (Florus had "men of the equestrian order whipped, and nailed to the cross [σταυρῷ προσηλῶσαι] before his tribunal"); 3.321; 5.289 (Titus), 449–451 (by order of Titus, those fleeing "were first whipped [μαστιγούμενοι], and . . . were then crucified [ἀνεσταυροῦντο] before the wall of the city"); 7.202; *Life* 420.

of Saul to the wall.[13] The Greek means to "stick in the ground" or "plant firmly,"[14] and so has essentially the same meaning as the Hebrew. In his telling of the story, Josephus says the Philistines "pinned [ἀνεσταύρωσαν] the bodies (of Saul and of his sons) to the walls [πρὸς τὰ τείχη] of the city Beth She'an" (*Ant.* 6.374).[15] We could also say that they were "staked up," or even "crucified," at the walls of the city. It is again interesting to note Josephus' use of the word ἀνασταυρόω. It should also be noted that, according to Josephus, the men of Jabesh-Gilead "were horrified at the thought of leaving (the bodies of Saul and his sons) unburied" (*Ant.* 6.375).

The horror felt concerning an unburied corpse is illustrated in Tobit and in Philo's moving account of Jacob's lament over the death of his son Joseph. Of all Tobit's virtues, it was his burying the dead that was his greatest (1:18–20; 2:3–8; 4:3–4; 6:15; 14:10–13).[16] Some of the persons whose bodies Tobit buried evidently had been executed by state authority, and not simply murdered (cf. 1:18, "I also buried any whom King Sennacherib put to death").[17] Josephus' perspective is consistent with that expressed in Tobit. Explaining Jewish ethical obligations, Josephus states: "We must furnish fire, water, [and] food to all who ask for them, point out the road, not leave a corpse unburied, [and] show consideration even to declared enemies" (*Ag. Ap.* 2.211; cf. 2.205).

Philo gives eloquent expression to Jewish sensitivities on this question in his imaginative recounting of Jacob's grief over the report that his son Joseph has been killed and devoured by wild animals. The patriarch laments: "Child, it is not your death that grieves me, but the manner of it. If you had been buried in your own land, I should have been comforted and watched and nursed your sick-bed, exchanged the last farewells as you died, closed your eyes, wept over your body as it lay there, given it a costly funeral and left none of the customary rites undone" (*Joseph* 22–23).

Interpretation of Esther 7: The Hanging of Haman

In the course of his narration of Jewish history, Josephus recounts the story of Esther and Mordecai. In LXX Esth 2:23, the Persian king is said to have "hanged"

13. BDB 1075; *TWOT* 2:979; S. R. Driver, *Notes on the Hebrew Text and the Topography of the Books of Samuel* (rev. ed.; Oxford: Clarendon, 1913), 230–31. The public display of Saul's body was "brutal evidence of victory" (R. W. Klein, *1 Samuel* [WBC 10; Dallas: Word, 1983], 289). See also the comments in H. W. Hertzberg, *I and II Samuel* (OTL; Philadelphia: Westminster, 1964), 232–33.

14. LSJ *ad loc.* The word occurs two other times in the LXX (Hos 5:2; 9:8).

15. In his account, Josephus has followed 1 Sam 31 rather than the parallel account in 1 Chr 10. See the notes by C. T. Begg in *Flavius Josephus: Translation and Commentary*, vol. 4, *Judean Antiquities Books 5–7* (ed. S. Mason; Leiden: Brill, 2005), 202–3; Chapman, *Ancient Jewish and Christian Perceptions of Crucifixion*, 151–52; Cook, *Crucifixion in the Mediterranean World*, 237.

16. C. A. Moore, *Tobit* (AB 40A; New York: Doubleday, 1996), 120: "To bury someone is *the* most important 'charitable act' in Tobit."

17. F. Zimmermann, *The Book of Tobit: An English Translation with Introduction and Commentary* (Dropsie College Edition: Jewish Apocryphal Literature; New York: Harper & Brothers, 1958), 51: "In other words, the bodies were known to be of marked men executed, not nameless war casualties." The king sought the bodies in order to hang them up.

(ἐκρέμασεν) the two court officials who plotted against him. Josephus, however, says the king "crucified" (ἀνεσταύρωσεν) the officials (*Ant.* 11.208). We see a similar modification in the story of Haman's plot to have Mordecai executed. Because of his jealousy, Haman's wife advises him to have a tall tree (ξύλον) cut down and then request the king "to crucify [ἀνασταυρῶσαι] Mordecai" (*Ant.* 11.246). In due course, the Persian king discovers Haman's plot and orders the villain executed on the very tree, now a "cross" (σταυρός), that he has prepared for Mordecai (*Ant.* 11.266). According to Josephus, the king "ordered that at once (Haman) be hung upon the very cross until he died [ἐκείνου τοῦ σταυροῦ κρεμασθέντα ἀποθανεῖν]" (*Ant.* 11.267). The king later announces by letter: "I have crucified [ἀνεσταύρωσα] the one who devised" the plot against the Jews (*Ant.* 11.280). Indeed, the "ten sons of Haman" are also ordered to be "crucified [ἀνασταυρῶσαι]" (*Ant.* 11.289).

In LXX Esther, the verb that appears most is κρεμάννυμι. Σταυρόω occurs once (in Esth 7:9). Its appearance no doubt encouraged Josephus to make liberal use of σταυρός and ἀνασταυρόω in his retelling of the story. Even if the verb σταυρόω had not appeared in LXX Esther, however, Josephus probably would have spoken of "cross" and "crucify" in his account, just as he did in his paraphrasing of the other stories of Scripture.

Interpretation of Deuteronomy 21: The Law of Hanging

Philo quotes and alludes to Deut 21:22–23 on a few occasions, sometimes with allegorical interpretations. One such interpretation is that of the phrase "hangs on a tree," which Philo considers to be indeed the occasion for a curse because, he says, one ought to "hang" upon God (*Posterity* 26). Accordingly, the cursed one is bound to the body and does not depend on God. In another instance, Philo interprets Deut 21:22–23 literally. The reference is allusive but unmistakable: For men who are particularly wicked, Moses, not able to condemn the felons to a deserved "ten thousand deaths," prescribed a special "punishment for them, commanding those who had slain a man to be hanged" (*Spec. Laws* 3.151), meaning they were crucified.[18] Nevertheless, this severe punishment was not without an element of mercy, Philo reasons, for the lawgiver "pronounced, 'Let not the sun set upon persons hanging [ἀνεσκολοπισμένοις] [on a tree]'; but let them be buried under the earth and be concealed from sight before sunset" (*Spec. Laws* 3.152).

In this passage, Philo twice uses the verb ἀνασκολοπίζω, rather than the LXX's κρεμάννυμι. The paraphrase in *Spec. Laws* 3.152 is distinctive: μὴ ἐπιδυέτω ὁ ἥλιος ἀνεσκολοπισμένοις. There is little doubt that Deut 21:22–23 is in view, but the language of the paraphrase reflects Deut 24:15 ("the sun shall not go down upon" [οὐκ ἐπιδύσεται ὁ ἥλιος ἐπ᾽] the payment of a man's daily wage) and perhaps Josh 8:29 ("and when the sun went down" [καὶ ἐπιδύνοντος τοῦ ἡλίου], Joshua gave instructions" that the king of Ai's body be removed from the tree). The interpretation, however, is in keeping with Philo's allegorical approach:

18. Cook, *Crucifixion in the Mediterranean World*, 236: "It is clear that . . . 'suspension' is death by crucifixion."

> For it was necessary to raise up on high all those who were enemies to every part of the world, so as to show most evidently to the sun, and to the heaven, and to the air, and to the water, and to the earth, that they had been chastised; and after that it was proper to remove them into the region of the dead, and to bury them, in order to prevent their polluting the things upon the earth. (*Spec. Laws* 3.152)

The raising up of executed criminals is "to show most evidently" to all of the created order that "they have been chastised." Showing the created order, or God, that the criminal has been executed demonstrates that the divine law is taken seriously and has been enforced.[19] Philo goes on to say that dead criminals are buried "in order to prevent their polluting the things upon the earth." Here Philo alludes to Deut 21:23 ("you shall not defile your land"). We do not know if the criminal has been first executed and then hanged, or if he was hanged alive and subsequently died.

Two more passages should be mentioned. In both, Philo indulges in his allegorical approach. In the first, he speaks of "souls that love the body" and are caught up in external things. Such souls, "like persons who are crucified [οἱ ἀνασκολοπισθέντες], are attached to corruptible matter till the day of their death" (*Posterity* 61). The linkage of "crucified" with "till the day of their death" (ἄχρι θανάτου) suggests that what Philo has in mind this time is the criminal who is hanged alive and who subsequently succumbs.

In the second passage, Philo again compares crucifixion to the mind that is disconnected from the wisdom of God:

> Therefore, the mind, being deprived of those things which it had made for itself, having, as it were, its neck cut through, will be found headless and lifeless, and like the one nailed [προσηλωμένος], just as those who are crucified to the tree [οἱ ἀνασκολοπισθέντες τῷ ξύλῳ] of hopeless and helpless ignorance. (*Dreams* 2.213)

Although there is no obvious allusion to Deut 21:22–23 here, Philo's use of the verb ἀνασκολοπίζω, which he has used elsewhere when citing or paraphrasing Deut 21:22–23, as well as his reference to "the tree" (τό ξύλον), a word that occurs in Deut 21:22–23, suggests that the Mosaic law of hanging is indeed in view. This passage from Philo is especially important because he speaks of those "nailed" (προσηλόω), an unmistakable reference to crucifixion. Accordingly, we have here a link between the hanging of Deut 21:22–23 and crucifixion as practiced in the Mediterranean world of late antiquity.

Josephus twice alludes to Deut 21:22–23. The first passage is found in the general context of a survey of Mosaic law. After stating that Israel is not to have an altar or temple in any city other than Jerusalem, Josephus pronounces this law:

> He that blasphemes God, let him be stoned, and let him hang all day [κρεμάσθω δι᾽ ἡμέρας], and then let him be buried in an ignominious and obscure manner. (*Ant.* 4.202)

It is probable that Josephus has conflated Deut 21:22–23 with Lev 24:14–16 ("He who blasphemes the name of the LORD shall be put to death . . . all the congregation

19. Reference again should be made to what Diodorus Siculus reports concerning the practice of the Gauls in crucifying malefactors "to the gods" (see note 5 above).

shall stone him"). The references to "hang" (κρεμάννυμι), "all day" (δι' ἡμέρας), and "buried" (θάπτω) recall the language of Deut 21:22–23 (κρεμάσητε αὐτὸν . . . ταφῇ θάψετε αὐτὸν ἐν τῇ ἡμέρᾳ ἐκείνῃ). The actions of "blaspheme" and "stone" reflect Lev 24:14–16. Reference to burial in an "ignominious and obscure manner" likely reflects the practice of the time of Josephus whereby the executed were denied burial in a place of honor (cf. *m. Sanh.* 6:5–6; *Sem.* 13.7).[20]

In the second passage, Josephus expresses indignation over the murder of ruling priests during the Jewish rebellion of 66–70. Not only did the rebels kill the priests, they did not bury them:

> They proceeded to that degree of impiety, as to cast away their dead bodies without burial, although the Jews used to take so much care of the burial of men, that they took down those that were condemned and crucified [ἀνεσταυρωμένους], and buried them before the going down of the sun. (*J.W.* 4.317)

Implicit is the principle of the argument from the minor to the major: If the condemned and crucified are buried, then surely ruling priests are to be buried. The statement "took (them) down and buried (them) before the going down of the sun" (πρὸ δύντος ἡλίου καθελεῖν τε καὶ θάπτειν) once again recalls Deut 21:22–23, along with language borrowed from Deut 24:15, as we saw above in the case of Philo (*Spec. Laws* 3.152). Accordingly, we have another important example of the linkage of Deut 21:22–23 with crucifixion.[21]

What we find in Philo and Josephus is a tendency to apply Deut 21:22–23 to contemporary forms of execution, notably crucifixion. Although in Greek Deut 21:22–23 employs the verb κρεμάννυμι, we also find ἀνασκολοπίζω and σταυρόω in quotations and allusions to this passage. Indeed, these verbs seem to have been used interchangeably.[22] A passage in which Philo complains of the Roman official Flaccus, prefect of Alexandria and Egypt (appointed ca. AD 32), illustrates this point:

> I have known instances before now of men who had been crucified [τῶν ἀνεσκολοπισμένων] when this festival and holiday was at hand, being taken down and given up to their relations, in order to receive the honors of sepulture, and to enjoy such observances as are due to the dead; for it used to be considered, that even the dead ought to derive some enjoyment from the birthday of a good emperor, and also that the sacred character of the festival ought to be regarded. But this man did not order men who had already perished on crosses [ἐπὶ σταυρῶν] to be taken down, but he commanded living men to be crucified [ζῶντας δ' ἀνασκολοπίζεσθαι], men to whom the very time itself gave, if not entire forgiveness, still, at all events, a brief and temporary respite from punishment; and he did this after they had been beaten by blows in

20. See the rich notes by L. H. Feldman in *Flavius Josephus: Translation and Commentary*, vol. 3, *Judean Antiquities Books 1–4* (ed. S. Mason; Leiden: Brill, 2000), 400–402; Chapman, *Ancient Jewish and Christian Perspectives of Crucifixion*, 136–37; Samuelsson, *Crucifixion in Antiquity*, 104, esp. note 246.

21. J. G. Cook, "Crucifixion and Burial," *NTS* 57 (2011): 193–213; idem, *Crucifixion in the Mediterranean World*, 239.

22. By the second century CE, at least, there was "no longer any distinction between the two verbs" (ἀνα)σταυρόω and (ἀνα)σκολοπίζω (*TDNT* 7:410).

> the middle of the theatre; and after he had tortured them with fire and sword; and the spectacle of their sufferings was divided; for the first part of the exhibition lasted from the morning to the third or fourth hour, in which the Jews were scourged, were hung up [μαστιγούμενοι, κρεμάμενοι], were tortured on the wheel, were condemned, and were dragged to execution through the middle of the orchestra; and after this beautiful exhibition came the dancers, and the buffoons, and the flute-players, and all the other diversions of the theatrical contests. (*Flaccus* 83–85)[23]

We encounter the obvious language of crucifixion in the references to individuals being scourged (μαστιγούμενοι) and placed on crosses (ἐπὶ σταυρῶν) while still living (ζῶντας).[24] We also encounter the language of Deut 21:22–23 (κρεμάμενοι) and the verb (ἀνα)σκολοπίζω, a synonym of (ἀνα)σταυρόω. That the law of Deuteronomy may in fact have been in Philo's mind is seen in his bitter complaint about the refusal to allow burial for those executed. Philo notes that on the occasion of the birthday celebration of the emperor (*Flaccus* 81, 83), if not forgiven and released, prisoners were at least given "a brief and temporary respite from punishment" (*Flaccus* 84). Instead, under the administration of Flaccus they were cruelly tortured in various ways and some were crucified.[25]

Qumran has provided important evidence that Deut 21:22–23 could be understood in reference to crucifixion. We see this in the *Temple Scroll*, in which God himself, speaking in the first person, articulates this law for Israel:

> If a man is a traitor against his people and gives them up to a foreign nation, so doing evil to his people, *you are to hang* [ותליתמה] *him on a tree until dead.* On the testimony of two or three witnesses he will be put to death, and they themselves shall hang him on the tree. If a man is convicted of a capital crime and flees to the nations, cursing his people and the children of Israel, *you are to hang* [ותליתמה] *him, also, upon a tree until dead.* But you must not let their bodies remain on the tree overnight; you shall most certainly bury them that very day. Indeed, anyone hung [תלוי] on a tree is accursed of God and men, but you are not to defile the land that I am about to give you as an inheritance.[26] (11QT[a] LXIV, 7–13 = 4Q524 14, 2–4)

---

23. See also *Flaccus* 72: ". . . were scourged [ἐμαστιγοῦντο], were tortured, and after all the ill treatment which their living bodies could endure, found the cross [σταυρός] the end of all, and the punishment from which they could not escape."

24. On a second-century epitaph, the deceased declares that his murderer, a slave, was "crucified alive [ζωὸν ἀνεκρέμασαν] for the wild beasts and birds" (*NewDocs* 8:1).

25. Both Philo and Josephus state that Roman officials normally made allowance for Jewish customs, including burial of the dead, even of executed criminals. Josephus asserts that "Jews are so careful about funeral rites that even malefactors who have been sentenced to crucifixion are taken down and buried before sunset" (*J. W.* 4.317). See also the remarks in Philo, *Embassy* 300 (Jewish "customs . . . safeguarded"); Josephus, *Ag. Ap.* 2.73 (Romans do not require "their subjects to violate their national laws"); *J. W.* 2.220 ("by abstaining from all interference with the customs of the country [the Roman procurators who succeeded Agrippa I] kept the nation at peace"). In the sixth-century compilation of Roman law known as the *Digesta*, burial of the executed is permitted (*Dig.* 48.24.1–3). The law is traced back to emperor Augustus (d. 14 CE).

26. Translation based on M. Wise, M. Abegg, and E. Cook, *The Dead Sea Scrolls: A New Translation* (San Francisco: HarperSanFrancisco, 1996), 490; emphasis added.

Whereas Deut 21:22–23 speaks of one put to death and then hanged, the *Temple Scroll* speaks of one hanged "until dead."[27] Most think crucifixion is in view in the latter text,[28] as also in 4QpNah 3–4, I, 6–8: "[. . . 'He fills] his cave [with prey], his den with game' (Nah 2:12b). This refers to the Lion of Wrath [. . . ven]geance against the Flattery-Seekers, whom he will hang up alive. [And they will become a curse, as it was with traitors] in Israel of old times. For one hanged alive [לתלוי חי] on [a stake is ca]lled {'accursed of God'}."[29]

Many believe that the Lion of Wrath who crucified the Flattery-Seekers was Alexander Jannaeus,[30] whose crucifixion of eight hundred Pharisees is recounted by Josephus:

> His rage was grown so extravagant, that his barbarity proceeded to a degree of impiety; for when he had ordered eight hundred to be hung upon crosses in the midst of the city [ἀνασταυρώσας ἐν μέσῃ τῇ πόλει], he had the throats of their wives and children cut before their eyes; and these executions he saw as he was drinking and lying down with his concubines. (*J.W.* 1.97; cf. *Ant.* 13.380)

One wonders if part of the reason this constituted such a scandal for Josephus (in *Ant.* 13.380 he calls the executions "cruel" and "inhuman") was that the crucified Pharisees were strung up "in the midst of the city," thus showing no regard for the sanctity of the city itself.

27. The reversal of clauses is also seen in some Peshitta manuscripts. On this, see Chapman, *Ancient Jewish and Christian Perceptions of Crucifixion*, 124–25.

28. Among others, see Y. Yadin, "Pesher Nahum (4QpNahum) Reconsidered," *IEJ* 21 (1971): 1–12; M. Hengel, *Crucifixion in the Ancient World and the Folly of the Message of the Cross* (Philadelphia: Fortress, 1977), 84–85; J. Maier, *The Temple Scroll: An Introduction, Translation and Commentary* (JSOTSup 34; Sheffield: JSOT Press, 1985), 132–34; and J. A. Fitzmyer, "Crucifixion in Ancient Palestine, Qumran Literature, and the New Testament," in *To Advance the Gospel: New Testament Studies* (2nd ed.; Biblical Resource Series; Grand Rapids: Eerdmans, 1998), 125–46, esp. 131–35. For a challenge to this line of interpretation, see J. M. Baumgarten, "Does *TLH* in the Temple Scroll Refer to Crucifixion?," *JBL* 91 (1972): 472–81. Baumgarten has been faulted for reading the Qumran materials through a later rabbinic lens. See also Y. Yadin, *The Temple Scroll* (3 vols.; Jerusalem: Israel Exploration Society, 1977–1983), 1:373–79; and E. Puech, "Notes sur 11Q19 LXIV 6–13 et 4Q524 14,2–4: À propos de la crucifixion dans le Rouleau du Temple et dans le judaïsme ancien," *RevQ* 18 (1997): 109–24. See also Chapman, *Ancient Jewish and Christian Perceptions of Crucifixion*, 125–32; Cook, *Crucifixion in the Mediterranean World*, 319–21.

29. On this reconstruction, see the detailed discussion in G. L. Doudna, *4Q Pesher Nahum: A Critical Edition* (JSPSup 35; CIS 8; London: Sheffield Academic, 2001), 389–433, esp. 409–30. Doudna supplies the words "cursed of God," arguing, with good evidence, that they were omitted because of religious sensitivity on the part of the Qumran scribe.

30. S. L. Berrin, *The Pesher Nahum Scroll from Qumran: An Exegetical Study of 4Q169* (STDJ 43; Leiden: Brill, 2004), 167; Chapman, *Ancient Jewish and Christian Perceptions of Crucifixion*, 61. Important caveats are raised in Doudna, *4Q Pesher Nahum*, 431–33. The "Lion of Wrath" may be Jannaeus, but he may have been understood as a foreign conqueror. See also P.-E. Guillet, "Les 800 'Crucifiés' d'Alexandre Jannée," *Cahiers du Cercle Ernest Renan* 100 (1977): 11–16; F. García Martínez, "4QpNah y la crucifixión: Nueva hipótesis de reconstrucción de 4Q169 3–4 I 4–8," *EstBib* 38 (1979): 221–35.

Besides the *Temple Scroll* and 4QpNah, there may be a third Qumran text that refers to crucifixion. In J. A. Fitzmyer's critical edition, the text is identified as 4Q282i (cf. PAM 43.400).[31] According to Greg Doudna, the first three lines should read: ". . . the leaders-astray of . . . by him when he was hung up . . . he will be called [. . .] by them."[32] Doudna suspects the fragment parallels 4QpNah 3–4, II, 8, which speaks of the "leaders-astray of Ephraim." If so, we may also have reference to being hung, or crucified, and called "accursed" (of God).[33] It is important to mention that in all three Qumran texts in which we have reference to crucifixion (assuming that the suggested interpretation of 4Q282i is correct), the context concerns treason (political and/or religious).[34]

As a final comment, the almost formulaic use of phrases from Deut 21:22–23 such as "hang on a tree" and "cursed of God" in reference to crucifixion clarifies the background in which Paul's argument in Gal 3:13 should be understood: "Christ redeemed us from the curse of the law, having become a curse for us—for it is written, 'Cursed be every one who hangs on a tree [ἐπικατάρατος πᾶς ὁ κρεμάμενος ἐπὶ ξύλου].'" The curse of the law, of course, entails a death penalty. Crucifixion, linked to Deut 21:22–23 in Jewish thinking of late antiquity (cf. Deut 27:26, "Cursed be he who does not confirm the words of this law by doing them"), can be seen as a "curse," thus facilitating Paul's theology of substitutionary atonement.[35]

Archaeological Evidence of Crucifixion

There is also important archaeological evidence that bears directly on the question of crucifixion in the late Second Temple period. This evidence includes the skeletal remains found in an ossuary, the Palatine Graffito, curse graffiti, and Christian graffiti and art.

The Skeletal Remains of Yehoḥanan

The important discovery, in 1968, of an ossuary (ossuary no. 4 in Tomb I at Givʿat ha-Mivtar) of a Jewish man named Yehoḥanan who had obviously been crucified provides archaeological evidence that corresponds with, if not corroborates, the

31. J. A. Fitzmyer, "282a–t. 4QUnidentified Fragments B, a–t," in S. J. Pfann, *Qumran Cave 4.XXVI: Cryptic Texts*, and P. Alexander et al., in consultation with J. C. VanderKam and M. Brady, *Miscellanea, Part 1* (DJD 36; Oxford: Clarendon, 2000), 216–27, at 222.

32. Doudna, *4Q Pesher Nahum*, 409.

33. Ibid., 409–11.

34. For further discussion of this topic, see J. M. Baumgarten, "Hanging and Treason in Qumran and Roman Law," *ErIsr* 16 (1982): 7–16.

35. For important qualifications, see K. S. O'Brien, "The Curse of the Law (Galatians 3.13): Crucifixion, Persecution, and Deuteronomy 21.22–23," *JSNT* 29 (2006): 55–76; Chapman, *Ancient Jewish and Christian Perceptions of Crucifixion*, 241–51.

literature that has been reviewed above.[36] The archaeological evidence also provides insight into how Jesus of Nazareth himself may have been crucified.

The ossuary and its contents date to the late 20s CE, that is, during the administration of Pilate, the very Roman prefect who condemned Jesus to the cross. The remains of an iron spike (11.5 cm. in length) are plainly seen still imbedded in the right heel bone (or *calcaneum*) of Yehoḥanan. Those who took down the body of this man apparently were unable to remove the spike, with the result that a piece of wood (perhaps oak, not olive wood or acacia, as commonly thought) remained affixed to the spike. Later, the skeletal remains of the body—spike, fragment of wood, and all—were placed in the ossuary. Forensic examination of the rest of the skeletal remains supports the view that Yehoḥanan was crucified with arms apart, hung from a horizontal beam or tree branch. However, there is no evidence that his arms or wrists were nailed to this cross beam, or *patibulum*. *(See fig. 6.1.)*

The lack of nails or spikes in the hands or wrists of Yehoḥanan is consistent with a passage in Pliny the Elder (23–79 CE), who refers to rope being used in crucifixion (cf. *Natural History* 28.4). Nevertheless, it is recorded by others that many victims of crucifixion did have their hands or wrists nailed to the *patibulum*. Writing in the second century BCE, Plautus refers to the crucifixion victim with "his arms and legs . . . double-nailed" (*Mostellaria* 359–361). Plutarch asks, "Will you nail him to a cross or impale him on a stake?" (*Moralia* 499d). In Pseudo-Plutarch, we are told of an impudent rascal whom Augustus "ordered to be nailed [προσηλωθῆναι] to a ship's mast" (*Regum et imperatorum apophthegmata* 207b). A third-century CE author described it this way: "Punished with limbs outstretched . . . they are fastened (and) nailed to the stake in the most bitter torment, evil food for birds of prey and grim picking for dogs" (*Apotelesmatica* 4.198–200).[37] *(See fig. 6.2.)*

The Skeletal Remains of Antigonus

The nails, skeletal materials, and inscription from the so-called Abba Cave (or Tomb) in Jerusalem, also in the neighborhood of Givʿat ha-Mivtar, have been recently reassessed. The cave was discovered in 1970, and on the inside wall was found a remarkable inscription, in Paleo-Hebrew script (i.e., Hebrew written in very old forms of letters), that identifies the occupant of an ornate ossuary as one "Mattathias son of Judah." In 1974, J. M. Grintz published a brief study in which he

36. Tzaferis, "Jewish Tombs at and near Givʿat ha-Mivtar," 18–32 + plates 1–28; Haas, "Anthropological Observations on the Skeletal Remains from Givʿat ha-Mivtar," 38–59; Zias and Sekeles, "The Crucified Man from Givʿat ha-Mivtar: A Reappraisal," 22–27. The study by Zias and Sekeles offers important corrections to the earlier study by Haas. See the more recent review of the primary evidence and the scholarly discussion in Zias and Charlesworth, "Crucifixion: Archaeology, Jesus, and the Dead Sea Scrolls," 273–89.

37. See the old study by J. W. Hewitt, "The Use of Nails in the Crucifixion," *HTR* 25 (1932): 29–45. Hewitt guessed correctly that crucifixion victims were sometimes tied to the cross with ropes (p. 32), but he erred in expressing doubt that the feet were nailed (pp. 43–45). Hewitt's study is valuable for its survey of the depiction of crucifixion in art, particularly with reference to the nails.

concluded that the inscription referred to none other than Antigonus son of Aristobulus II, whose Hebrew name was Mattathias son of Judah, the last Hasmonean ruler, the man defeated by Herod the Great in 37 BCE.[38] Grintz's interpretation was supported by Nicu Haas later in the year that it was published. Haas described the skeletal remains as belonging to a tall man in his mid-twenties, which would have been the age of Antigonus son of Aristobulus II at the time of his death. A recent study by Yoel Elitzur has confirmed the views of Grintz and Haas.[39] In all likelihood, the ossuary and skeletal remains of the last Hasmonean prince have been discovered.

What makes this case interesting is that Mattathias/Antigonus suffered both crucifixion and beheading. According to Josephus, Marcus Antonius *beheaded* Antigonus in Antioch (Josephus, *Ant.* 15.8–10; cf. Plutarch, *Ant.* 36.4). Dio Cassius seemingly contradicts Josephus when he specifically refers to *crucifixion*, but his full statement can be harmonized with what Josephus says. The Roman historian says: "Antony bound Antigonus to a cross and flogged him—a punishment no other king had suffered at the hands of the Romans—and afterwards he slew him" (*Roman History* 22.6). The slaying "afterwards" probably refers to beheading, which is what Josephus relates.

This is what Haas thought happened to the man whose skeletal remains were recovered from the Abba Cave: He was nailed to a cross (three nails, still bearing traces of human calcium, were recovered from the ossuary)[40] and then (after passing out?) was beheaded, either with a sword or a very sharp ax.[41]

Crucifixion Depicted in Art and Graffiti

On a tomb dating to either the third or the second century BCE is a fresco depicting a crucified man. The tomb was excavated by Antonio Arieti in 1875 and was

---

38. J. M. Grintz, "The Inscription from Givʿat ha-Mivtar: A Historical Interpretation," *Sinai* 75 (1974): 20–23 (in Hebrew); see also idem, "The Last Way of the Last Hasmonean," *Ha-ʾUmmah* 43 (1975): 256–69 (in Hebrew).

39. I say "confirmed" because years ago Patricia Smith called into question the Antigonus identification. She described the skeleton as belonging to a small, elderly woman (not a tall young man) and said the nails had nothing to do with crucifixion. See P. Smith, "The Human Skeletal Remains from the Abba Cave," *IEJ* 27 (1977): 121–24. It is now believed that Smith, who was asked to examine the Abba Cave finds after Haas was injured and no longer able to work, examined the wrong box of bones and artifacts. On the curious history of this important find and the eventual confirmation that the bones really do belong to Antigonus, see Y. Elitzur, "The Abba Cave: Unpublished Findings and a New Proposal Regarding Abba's Identity," *IEJ* 63 (2013): 83–102. Elitzur not only discusses the Antigonus identification, he probes the identity of Abba the priest, the man who at considerable personal risk and suffering arranged to have the remains of Antigonus interred in the burial cave in Jerusalem.

40. I thank Professor Israel Hershkovitz of the Sackler Medical Center of the University of Tel Aviv for allowing me to view the nails recovered from the ornate ossuary found in the Abba Cave.

41. The cut marks in the vertebrae and in the lower mandible are plainly visible. I again thank Professor Hershkovitz for allowing me to examine these important skeletal materials.

subsequently destroyed by modern building. The fresco itself was also damaged. Although the right arm and some of the right portion of the body of the crucified man have not survived, the outstretched left arm is clearly fettered (and nailed?) at the wrist and the horizontal *patibulum* is plain to see.[42]

The well-known Palatine Graffito illustrates a victim of crucifixion in a graphic manner. This graffito was found etched on a plastered wall in what is believed to have been slaves' quarters, perhaps in the *domus Gelotiana*, on the Palatine Hill in Rome.[43] Found in 1857, the graffito has been dated to the first half of the third century.[44] Initially taken to the Kircherian Museum at the Collegio Romano, it is now housed in the Palatine Museum.

The graffito depicts a crucified figure with the head of a donkey. The figure's hands and arms are outstretched, evidently nailed to the cross beam,[45] or *patibulum*. The figure is wearing a short-sleeved *colobium*, or undershirt (typical dress of slaves), that extends from the shoulders to the waist. The feet rest on a short, horizontal plank. To the left (i.e., to the crucified figure's right) is another figure, standing, with one arm upraised. The crucified figure is looking at this man. The upraised hand and arm are either a salute or, as one scholar has suggested, the act of throwing a kiss.[46] Between and beneath the two figures, written in four lines, are the words Αλεξάμενος σέβετε θεόν. Taken at face value, these words mean "Alexamenos, worship God!" But the imperative is unlikely. Most interpreters think σέβετε is probably a misspelling of the indicative form σέβεται. Accordingly, the words are descriptive: "Alexamenos worships (his) God."[47]

---

42. See J. G. Cook, "John 19:17 and the Man on the Patibulum in the Arieti Tomb," *Early Christianity* 4 (2013): 427–53 (with image on p. 430); idem, *Crucifixion in the Mediterranean World*, 454, figs. 1 and 2.

43. For an early report and description, see R. Lanciani, *Ancient Rome in the Light of Recent Discoveries* (Boston: Houghton Mifflin, 1898): 121–22 + plate; E. Staedler, "Das 'Spottkruzifix' vom Palatin: Ein Votivbild?," *Theologische Quartalschrift* 117 (1936): 253–60. For more recent discussion, see H. Solin and M. Itkonen-Kaila, *Graffiti del Palatino* (Acta Instituti Romani Finlandiae 3; Helsinki: Helsingfors, 1966), 211 no. 246; B. H. McLean, *An Introduction to Greek Epigraphy of the Hellenistic and Roman Periods* (Ann Arbor: University of Michigan Press, 2002), 208 ("discovered in the subterranean chambers of the Roman Palatine Hill"); D. L. Balch and C. Osiek, *Early Christian Families in Context: An Interdisciplinary Dialogue* (Grand Rapids: Eerdmans, 2003), 103–4; J. G. Cook, "Envisioning Crucifixion: Light from Several Inscriptions and the Palatine Graffito," *NovT* 50 (2008), 262–85, esp. 282–85.

The original locus of the graffito is disputed. According to G. F. Snyder, the graffito was "found in the servants' quarters of the Imperial Palace" (*Ante Pacem: Archaeological Evidence of Church Life before Constantine* [Macon, GA: Mercer University Press, 1985], 27–28). According to E. Ferguson, the graffito was "scratched on a stone in a guard room on Palatine Hill near the Circus Maximus" (*Backgrounds of Early Christianity* [2nd ed.; Grand Rapids: Eerdmans, 1993], 559–61).

44. M. A. Tomei, *Museo Palatino* (Rome: Electa, 1997), 104–5. An image of the graffito is provided on p. 104. See also Cook, *Crucifixion in the Mediterranean World*, 459 fig. 10.

45. In the manner described in the *Anthologia Latina*: "The criminal, outstretched on the infamous stake, hopes for escape from his place on the cross" (415.23).

46. Cook, "Envisioning Crucifixion," 283n91.

47. Αλεξάμενος may in fact be a form of Alexander.

The crucified figure "is probably a mock representation of Christ or of Anubis, the jackal-headed god of Egypt."[48] Indeed, G. M. A. Hanfmann has called attention to the recounting of the execution of the Seleucid pretender Achaios at Alexandria in 214 BCE. According to Polybius, Achaios was killed and degraded by "cutting off his head and sewing (him) into the hide of a donkey to crucify his body [ἀνασταυρῶσαι τὸ σῶμα]" (*Histories* 8:21). Hanfmann wonders if the Palatine Graffito's depiction of Jesus as a crucified donkey may reflect a tradition of execution and insult visited upon royal pretenders.[49] His depiction in slave's attire and as being admired by a slave is consistent with the Roman view of crucifixion as *servile supplicium*, "slave's punishment," and culturally clarifies the statement in Paul's letter to the Philippian Christians that Christ Jesus "emptied himself, taking the form of a servant . . . humbled himself and became obedient unto death, even death on a cross" (Phil 2:7–8).[50]

Hanfmann has also discussed an *ampulla* (bottle or flask) found at Sardis, dating to the Byzantine period, which on one side depicts a donkey carrying a cross and on the other depicts a donkey carrying a sphere over which is a cross. He suggests that these depictions are mocking illustrations of Jesus' entry into Jerusalem (Matt 21:1–7).[51] I should think, rather, that what is in view is Jesus' carrying the cross to the place of execution (Matt 27:31–32), as well as his teaching that his followers must also be willing to take up the cross (cf. Matt 16:24).

The Puteoli Graffito, discovered in Puzzuoli, Italy, in 1959, offers yet another depiction of a crucified person. It probably dates to the second century, though earlier and later dates have been proposed. It depicts a *tau*-shaped cross on which a severely flagellated naked man hangs.[52] His arms are outstretched on a *patibulum*, to which apparently his wrists have been nailed. His feet appear to be nailed to the vertical pole, and his buttocks apparently are resting on a *sedile*. It is assumed that the crucifixion victim is a man, but a Greek inscription above and to the left reads ΑΛΚΙΜΙΛΑ, which is a woman's name. John Granger Cook plausibly suggests that the person who etched the graffito into the wall had in mind a crucified man,

48. McLean, *Introduction to Greek Epigraphy*, 208. Pagans sometimes mocked Jews, depicting their God as a donkey. The Jewish roots of the Christian movement may well explain the similar mockery of Jesus. From Tertullian (*To the Heathen* 1.14.1–4) we know that Christians were accused of worshipping a deity whose head was that of a donkey. See Cook, "Envisioning Crucifixion," 283–84. At least one scholar has challenged the widely accepted interpretation of the graffito, however: see P. Maser, "Das sogenannte Spottkruzifix vom Palatin: Ein 'frühchristliches' Denkmal im Widersteit der Meinungen," *Das Altertum* 18 (1972): 248–54. For rebuttal, see Balch and Osiek, *Early Christian Families in Context*, 103–4.

49. G. M. A. Hanfmann, "The Crucified Donkey Man: Achaios and Jesus," in *Studies in Classical Art and Archaeology: A Tribute to Peter Heinrich von Blanckenhagen* (ed. G. Kopcke and M. B. Moore; Locust Valley, NJ: Augustin, 1979), 205–7 + plates 55.1–2; Cook, *Crucifixion in the Mediterranean World*, 230n52.

50. Chapman, *Ancient Jewish and Christian Perceptions of Crucifixion*, 252.

51. G. M. A. Hanfmann, "The Donkey and the King," *HTR* 78 (1985): 421–30 + figs. 1 (the donkey carrying the cross) and 2 (the donkey carrying the sphere). See also the discussion in *NewDocs* 4:137.

52. For images, see Cook, *Crucifixion in the Mediterranean World*, 456–57 figs. 5 and 6.

but the person who inscribed the name intended the image to refer to a woman.[53] Unlike the Palatine Graffito, there is no reason to think the Puteoli Graffito depicts the crucified Jesus.

Curse Graffiti

Crucifixion has also been described in crude curse graffiti. One Latin inscription found in the Stabian baths of Pompeii reads *in cruce figarus*, "Get nailed to a cross!" (*CIL* IV.2082).[54] The phrase *in cruce* means "to a/the cross," and the verb *figarus* (= *figaris*) is the second-person singular passive subjunctive of *figere* and means "be fixed," "be fastened," or, in reference to a cross, "get nailed."[55] One scholar suggests the curse is the equivalent of saying, "Go to hell!"[56] In fact, we are told by Plautus (*Pseudolus* 335) that a pimp said to a slave *í in malem crucem* ("Go to an evil cross!"), which, again, is probably the equivalent of "Go to hell!"[57]

Another Latin curse inscription, found on the wall of a basilica in Pompeii, reads *Samius Cornelio suspendre*, "Samius (says) to Cornelius, get hung!" (*CIL* IV.1864).[58] *Suspendre* should be *suspendere*; the former is an infinitive used as an imperative. *Dicit* ("he says") is assumed. Getting hung on a cross is what is implied. That a cross is in view is supported by the observation that *suspendere* is used in Seneca in reference to crucifixion (*Dialogues* 6.20.3).[59]

Christian Graffiti and Art

Early Christian art also sheds some light on the practice of crucifixion in late antiquity. One item of concern for Christians was the fact that the normal practice was to crucify the victim in the nude. This seems to have been so in the case of Jesus,

---

53. J. G. Cook, "Crucifixion as Spectacle in Roman Campania," *NovT* 54 (2012): 68–100, at 92–98, with figs. 4, 5, and 6 on pp. 94–96. On the inscription, see M. Guarducci, "Iscrizione greche e latine in una *taberna* a Pozzuoli," in *Acta of the Fifth International Congress of Greek and Latin Epigraphy, Cambridge, 1967* (Oxford: Blackwell, 1971), 219–23, at 222.

54. Long ago noted in *The Antiquary* 34 (1898): 149. For image, see Cook, *Crucifixion in the Mediterranean World*, 455 fig. 4.

55. J. N. Adams, *The Regional Diversification of Latin, 200 BC–AD 600* (Cambridge: Cambridge University Press, 2007), 448; R. Wallace, *An Introduction to Wall Inscriptions from Pompeii and Herculaneum* (Wauconda, IL: Bolchazy-Carducci, 2005), 51.

56. Cook, "Envisioning Crucifixion," 277; idem, *Crucifixion in the Mediterranean World*, 122.

57. Cook, "Envisioning Crucifixion," 277n68.

58. Cited long ago in J. A. Overbeck, *Pompeji in seinen Gebäuden, Alterthümern und Kunstwerken. Für Kunst- und Alterthumsfreunde* (3rd ed.; Leipzig: Engelmann, 1875), 432, and more recently in Wallace, *Introduction to Wall Inscriptions from Pompeii and Herculaneum*, 51.

59. Cook, "Envisioning Crucifixion," 277n68. Other curses have been found at Pompeii; for example, *vae tibi* ("Woe to you!") and *vei tabescas* ("Go to rot!"), both etched in the amphitheater; and, in a basilica, *ut pereat rogo* ("I ask that he perish"). Cf. Overbeck, *Pompeji in seinen Gebäuden*, 432.

whose clothing was obtained by the guards (John 19:23).[60] However, in Christian art Jesus is depicted as wearing a loincloth or *colobium* (undershirt). A very early example of the former is seen in the wood carving on the door of the Church of Saint Sabina, Rome, which dates to ca. 430. Jesus clad in a *colobium* is seen in an eighth-century icon in the Monastery of Saint Catherine, Mount Sinai. The *colobium* in this icon extends from the shoulders to the feet, in contrast to the *colobium* depicted in the third-century Palatine Graffito, which, as noted above, extends from the shoulders to the waist.[61]

There are also a few "crucifixion gems" that should be mentioned. In these amulets, we again have depicted individuals crucified on *tau*-shaped crosses. One, housed in the British Museum, dates to the late second or early third century and bears the vocative ΙΗϹΟΥ ΧΡΙϹΤΕ in the second line.[62] The wrists appear to be tied, not nailed, to the *patibulum*.

In the Lucina Catacomb of Rome, we find a Greek epitaph that reads "Rufina, peace," beneath which is inscribed an equilateral, or Greek, cross. In the Catacomb of Callixtus, we find the name of the deceased, Irene, this time in Latin, with an elevated cross between the first *e* and the *n*. The Lucina and Callixtus catacombs, along with those of Domitilla and Priscilla, originated in the middle of the second century. Both the Rufina and Irene inscriptions are early and could date to the second half of the second century.[63]

Early Christians also depicted the symbol of the cross in a hidden or disguised manner known as *crux dissimulata*. A favorite design was the anchor, probably suggested by the remark in Heb 6:19 that "We have this as a sure and steadfast anchor [ἄγκυραν]" and by the similarity of the sound of the word ἄγκυρα ("anchor") and the phrase ἐν κυρίῳ ("in the Lord"). The anchor symbol was more or less like an upside-down cross whose horizontal beam was curved and perhaps hooked, as was the fashion of anchors in antiquity. Sometimes the anchor cross included a fish, another well-known hidden symbol of the Christian confession.

These symbols are common in the catacombs near Rome. On the epitaph of Atimetus in the Catacombs of Saint Sebastian, on the Via Appia, Rome, we see the anchor cross on the left and a fish on the right. On a wall in the Catacomb of Priscilla, there is a well-executed anchor, right side up and with an eye at the top, through which the chain or rope would pass. Beneath the eye is a wide horizontal bar (the equivalent of the cross's *patibulum*), and at the bottom of the vertical shaft

---

60. According to John 19:23, the guards gambled for his garments (τὰ ἱμάτια), including his tunic (ὁ χιτών).

61. See D. R. Cartlidge and J. K. Elliott, *Art and the Christian Apocrypha* (New York: Routledge, 2001), 123–27 + figs. 4.31 and 4.32.

62. For images and brief discussion, see F. Harley and J. Spier, "Magical Amulet with Crucifixion," in *Picturing the Bible: The Earliest Christian Art* (ed. J. Spier; New Haven: Yale University Press, 2007), 227–28; Cook, *Crucifixion in the Mediterranean World*, 185, 461 fig. 14.

63. J. Finegan, *The Archeology of the New Testament* (Princeton: Princeton University Press, 1969), 251. For many examples of cross diagrams, including several anchor crosses, see G. Wilpert, "La croce nei monumenti delle catacombe," *Nuovo Bullettino di Archeologia Cristiana* 8 (1902): 5–14.

are the curving, pointed anchor grips. The anchor cross is flanked by fish in vertical pose, with heads up and tails down.[64] Other anchor crosses—sometimes very simple or even crude in execution—appear on catacomb floors and walls. Examples have also been found on seals.

Another important image of the cross is found in the staurogram and its cousin the christogram. These are found etched and painted on various surfaces, some public, some private. Among some of the most interesting, and most ancient, are those found in early Christian books, usually books of Scripture.[65] In recent years, Larry Hurtado has published significant studies of the staurogram in which important corrections and clarifications have been made.[66]

Hurtado calls our attention to the presence of the *tau-rho* (⳨) compendium in three of our oldest Greek New Testament manuscripts, $\mathfrak{P}^{45}$, $\mathfrak{P}^{66}$, and $\mathfrak{P}^{75}$.[67] These manuscripts date to no later than the very beginning of the third century. Three times in $\mathfrak{P}^{66}$, in John 19:19, 25, and 31, the noun σταυρός appears in abbreviated form with the *tau-rho* compendium within it, twice in the genitive, as C⳨OY, and once in the dative (partially restored), as [C̄]⳨̣ω̣. In $\mathfrak{P}^{45}$ and $\mathfrak{P}^{75}$, the same phenomenon occurs (at Luke 14:27 in both, and also in other passages). In due course, the *chi-rho* and other compendia and monograms appeared in Christian manuscripts and art.[68] Hurtado rightly reasons that the appearance of the *tau-rho* at the beginning of the

64. See R. M. Jensen, *Understanding Early Christian Art* (New York: Routledge, 2000), 18; J. L. Reed, *The HarperCollins Visual Guide to the New Testament: What Archaeology Reveals about the First Christians* (San Francisco: HarperOne, 2007), 144–45.

65. K. Aland, "Bemerkungen zum Alter und Entstehung des Christogramms anhand von Beobachtungen bei $\mathfrak{P}^{66}$ und $\mathfrak{P}^{75}$," in *Studien zur Überlieferung des Neuen Testaments und seines Textes* (ANTF 2; Berlin: de Gruyter, 1967), 173–79; M. Black, "The Chi-Rho Sign—Christogram and/or Staurogram?," in *Apostolic History and the Gospel* (ed. W. W. Gasque and R. P. Martin; Grand Rapids: Eerdmans, 1970), 319–27; W. Wischmeyer, "Christogramm und Staurogramm in den lateinischen Inschriften altkirchlicher Zeit," in *Theologia Crucis–Signum Crucis: Festschrift für Erich Dinkler zum 70. Geburtstag* (ed. C. Andresen and G. Klein; Tübingen: Mohr Siebeck, 1979), 539–50; E. Dinkler-von Schubert, "CTAYPOC: Vom 'Wort vom Kreuz' (1 Cor. 1,18) zum Kreuz-Symbol," in *Byzantine East, Latin West: Art-Historical Studies in Honor of Kurt Weitzmann* (ed. D. Mourika et al.; Princeton: Princeton University Press, 1995), 29–39.

66. L. W. Hurtado, *The Earliest Christian Artifacts: Manuscripts and Christian Origins* (Grand Rapids: Eerdmans, 2006), 135–54 + plates 4–6; idem, "The Staurogram in Early Christian Manuscripts: The Earliest Visual Reference to the Crucified Jesus?," in *New Testament Manuscripts: Their Text and Their World* (ed. T. J. Kraus and T. Nicklas; TENTS 2; Leiden: Brill, 2006), 207–26.

67. Hurtado, *Earliest Christian Artifacts*, 141–43.

68. The *chi-rho* compendium antedates Christianity. It was used as an abbreviation for a military tribune (χιλιάρχης), "time" (χρόνος), and "useful" (χρήσιμον or χρηστός). On this, see M. Avi-Yonah, *Abbreviations in Greek Inscriptions (The Near East, 200 B.C.–A.D. 1100)* (London: Oxford University Press, 1940), 112. The *chi-rho* monogram appeared on Roman standards and *vexilla* (flags, standards), to which Justin Martyr makes reference (in *1 Apol.* 55). As a Christian symbol, its earliest artifactual attestation may be in the inscriptions on two funeral stelae, dating to about 200, found in Phrygia. See W. H. Buckler, W. M. Calder, and C. W. M. Cox, "Monuments from Central Phrygia," *JRS* 16 (1926): 61–74, esp. 61–64 + fig. 183; and for more examples, Finegan, *Archeology of the New Testament*, 233–34.

third century in three unrelated manuscripts suggests that the symbol emerged in the second century. This supposition seems confirmed by the discussion in Justin Martyr's *First Apology* (ca. 155) in which Justin suggests that Plato's comment that "he placed him crosswise [ἐχίασεν] in the universe" adumbrates the cross of Christ (*1 Apol.* 60.1–5). Given Justin's earlier discussion of cross-shaped objects (cf. *1 Apol.* 55: "this shows no other form than that of the cross [τὸ σχῆμα τοῦ σταυροῦ]"), Hurtado sees evidence here of a consciousness among mid-second-century Christians of cross sigla, that is, among those who lived at least a generation or more before the copying of the Greek manuscripts that have been discussed.[69] Later manuscripts, of course, elaborate on this theme, sometimes in ingenious ways.[70]

The Herculaneum Cross

Finally, we should consider the cross-shaped impression found in the so-called "Bicentenary House" at Herculaneum during excavations in 1938. This impression was found at eye level in the stucco of an upstairs apartment, perhaps leased, in the words of the archaeologist who excavated the house, "to some modest family of craftsmen or merchants."[71] Amedeo Maiuri concluded that the impression held a cross, which may have been removed during the eruption of Mount Vesuvius.[72] A number of scholars objected to Maiuri's interpretation, suggesting instead that the impression accommodated a bracket for a shelf, or something to that effect.[73]

In a recent study, Leslie Barnard has found the arguments against the cross interpretation to be quite weak.[74] Considered altogether, the evidence supports the

69. Hurtado, *Earliest Christian Artifacts*, 147–48. Hurtado also faults G. F. Snyder for continuing to make the erroneous claim that with regard to Jesus iconography there "is no place in the third century for a crucified Christ, or a symbol of divine death." See Snyder, *Ante Pacem*, 29. This error is not corrected in the 2003 edition.

70. One thinks of the "cruciform" Scripture texts and lectionaries in which the handwritten text on each page is shaped in the form of a cross (i.e., the first dozen lines or so form a narrow column, while the next ten lines or so are wide, forming a horizontal bar, and the last dozen lines or so are once again formed as a narrow column). For an example of a cruciform text, see the plate of codex 047 (eighth century) in B. M. Metzger, *Manuscripts of the Greek Bible: An Introduction to Palaeography* (Oxford: Oxford University Press, 1981), 98–99 + plate 23.

71. A. Maiuri, *Herculaneum and the Villa of the Papyri: Archaeological Guide of the Town* (Novara: Istituto Geografico de Agostini, 1962), 25–26.

72. A. Maiuri, "La croce de Ercolano," *Rendiconti della Pontificia Accademia Romana di Archeologia* 15 (1939): 193–218.

73. G. de Jerphanion, "La croix d'Herculaneum?," *OCP* 7 (1941): 5–35; L. de Bruyne, "La 'crux interpretum' di Ercolano," *Rivista di Archeologia Cristiana* 21 (1945): 281–309; D. Atkinson, "The Origin and Date of the 'Sator' Word-Square," *JEH* 2 (1951): 1–18; E. Dinkler, "Zur Geschichte des Kreuzsymbols," *ZTK* 48 (1951): 148–72 (repr. in idem, *Signum Crucis: Aufsätze zum Neuen Testament und zur christlichen Archäologie* [Tübingen: Mohr Siebeck, 1967], 1–25).

74. L. W. Barnard, "The 'Cross of Herculaneum' Reconsidered," in *The New Testament Age: Essays in Honor of Bo Reicke* (ed. W. C. Weinrich; 2 vols.; Macon, GA: Mercer University Press, 1984), 1:15–27.

cross identification. By the 40s, Christians lived in Rome, as is clear from Paul's letter to them, which was written around the year 55. When in 62 CE Paul arrived in Puteoli, on his way to Rome, he was greeted by Christians (Acts 28:13–15). Puteoli (present-day Pozzuoli) is only thirty kilometers from Herculaneum.

Barnard calls attention to the graffito scratched on the wall of a house in nearby Pompeii. The letters *viv* rest atop a cross and the letter *v* appears on the right, below the *patibulum*. Matteo della Corte interprets the abbreviations thus: *viv(at) crux v(ivat)*,[75] which would mean something like "the cross lives, he lives!" Barnard believes the only plausible interpretation of this graffito is that it is Christian.[76]

Concluding Remarks

Although the forms of crosses used for crucifixion varied in late antiquity,[77] a rather consistent pattern is seen in the way the cross of Jesus of Nazareth was represented in early Christian art and literature. Visual depictions of the crucifixion and cross of Jesus are consistently those of tradition, with only minor variations. These depictions consist of a vertical pole or stake and a horizontal beam or *patibulum*. The vertical pole may extend above the horizontal beam; the horizontal beam may be roughly centered vertically on the vertical pole; or the horizontal beam may rest atop the vertical pole, forming a *tau*-shaped figure.

Literary references to outstretched arms or hands, sometimes nailed, cohere with the visual depictions, especially as seen in the Palatine Graffito and the Puteoli Graffito. The skeletal remains of the early first-century Jewish man Yehoḥanan, whose right heel was found transfixed by an iron spike, have provided archaeological confirmation of both art and literature. Early Christian statements such as we see in Col 2:14 ("the bond which stood against us . . . he set aside, nailing it to the cross [προσηλώσας αὐτὸ τῷ σταυρῷ]"), in Acts 2:23 ("this Jesus . . . having fastened (to the cross) you killed [προσπήξαντες ἀνείλατε]"), and in John 20:25 ("Unless I see in his hands the print of the nails [ἐν ταῖς χερσὶν αὐτοῦ τὸν τύπον τῶν ἥλων]") reflect the grim reality of Roman practice, not rhetorical fancy. Even the crude curse graffiti, such as "Get fastened (or nailed) to a cross" or "Get hung," accurately reflect this reality.

The pseudepigraphic letter of *Barnabas* provides important supporting evidence that the *tau* shaped cross was standard in the Christian movement prior to the middle of the second century. The author states: "the cross, which is shaped like the *tau* [ὁ σταυρὸς ἐν τῷ T], was destined to convey grace" (*Barn.* 9.8) Although

75. M. Della Corte, "Le iscrizione scoperte nel quinquennio 1951–1956," *Notizo degli scavi di antichità* ser. 8, vol. 10 (1958): 77–184, at 113, 183 plate 5 no. 181.

76. Barnard, "'Cross of Herculaneum' Reconsidered," 26.

77. As Seneca remarked: "Yonder I see crosses, not indeed of a single kind, but differently contrived by different peoples; some hang their victims with head toward the ground, some impale their private parts, others stretch out their arms on a fork-shaped gibbet" (*Dialogues* 6.20.3). Josephus similarly records that a variety of crucifixion positions were employed during the siege of Jerusalem in 70 CE (*J.W.* 5.451).

we have no direct or certain knowledge regarding the shape of the cross on which Jesus was hung, all of our early literary and archaeological evidence supports the traditional † (or *tau*) shape.

In Christian books and funerary art, the cross symbol, especially as seen in the *tau-rho* compendium, emerged in the second century and became more or less standard in the third century and beyond. Even when disguised (i.e., the *crux dissimulata*), the traditional form of the cross is evident (as in the anchor crosses, which may have first appeared in the late second century). The depictions of the crucified Jesus variously wearing a loincloth or *colobium* represent attempts to provide a measure of modesty. When the author of Hebrews says Jesus "endured the cross, despising its shame [ὑπέμεινεν σταυρὸν αἰσχύνης καταφρονήσας]" (Heb 12:2), the nakedness of the victim of crucifixion would have been understood as at least part of this shame.

Two (or possibly three) scrolls from Qumran (11QT[a], 4QpNah, and 4Q282i) shed very important light on Deut 21:22–23, clarifying the use of this passage in Philo, in Josephus, and especially in Paul's letter to the churches of Galatia. There can now be no question that the application of Deut 21:22–23 to crucifixion as practiced in the Roman era predated the Christian movement and its application of this text to the crucifixion of Jesus. We should also interpret other passages in this light. These include Acts 5:30; 10:39; 13:29; and 1 Pet 2:24, which speak of Jesus being hung on or taken down from a "tree." All of these passages allude to Deut 21:22–23, a text that, again, we now know was interpreted in Jewish late antiquity as having to do with crucifixion. Even Paul's understandable omission of "by God" (ὑπὸ θεοῦ) in his partial quotation of Deut 21:23 in Gal 3:13 is approximately paralleled in 4QpNah, whose copyist omitted the entire offending phrase "accursed of God." Indeed, the expanded form of Deut 21:22–23 that we find in 11QT[a], which reads "accursed of God and men," coheres with the mockery of passersby that Jesus endured while hanging on the cross (Matt 27:39–43; Mark 15:29–32).

In short, what we see in the Dead Sea Scrolls, archaeology, art, and symbols is a remarkable convergence and coherence with first-century Judeo-Christian literature in which reference to crucifixion is made, whether in passing or in strongly worded and highly emotional language. Most important is the observation of the shift in the understanding of Deut 21:22–23 from that of death followed by the deceased's being hung to being hung or hanging until death has occurred. This Old Testament passage had a long, unsavory, and evolving history of interpretation before the followers of Jesus applied it to their crucified master.

The following chapter will explore further the theme of execution and burial. The archaeological evidence on this subject is particularly rich, and we shall see that once again it sheds important light on the world of Jesus.

CHAPTER SEVEN

The Family Buried Together Stays Together: On the Burial of the Executed in Family Tombs

The Jewish people buried their dead, then later gathered the bones and placed them in containers called ossuaries or in a vault, pit, or niche set aside for this purpose. The practice of gathering the bones of the deceased is called ossilegium or secondary burial (cf. *y. Moʿed Qaṭ.* 1:5, 80c: "At first they would bury them in ditches, and when the flesh had decayed, they would gather the bones and bury them in ossuaries").[1] How far back this practice may be traced and where the practice originated are major questions that lie at the heart of the debate surrounding the significance of the numerous ossuaries found in and around Jerusalem dating to the Herodian period (ca. 35 BCE–70 CE).[2]

The question before us concerns the fate of the remains of those executed. In the Roman world, the executed, especially the crucified, were often left unburied. In the Jewish world, the executed were buried, but not in the family tomb, at least not initially. Jewish literature suggests that after one year the skeletal remains of the executed, that is, of those who had died dishonorably, could be relocated and reburied in the family tomb. But is the literature supported by archaeological finds? And what of the remains of the executed who may have murdered members of their own families? As it so happens, archaeology may shed light on this intriguing question.

Jewish Burial Customs in Late Antique Palestine

In the Jewish world, burial took place on the day of death, or, if death occurred at the end of the day or during the night, burial took place on the following day. Knowing this lends a great deal of pathos to some otherwise familiar Gospel stories.

1. On ossilegium in the time of Jesus and the early church, see Evans, *Jesus and the Ossuaries*.

2. On the origins of ossilegium, see E. M. Meyers, *Jewish Ossuaries: Reburial and Rebirth* (BibOr 24; Rome: Pontifical Biblical Institute, 1971).

We think of the story of the widow from the city of Nain: "As he approached the gate of the town, a man who had died was being carried out. He was his mother's only son, and she was a widow; and with her was a large crowd from the town" (Luke 7:12). Her only son had died that day (or the evening before). Her sorrow is at its rawest when Jesus encounters her. We also think of the desperate father who hurries Jesus to his home, hoping he will arrive in time to heal his dying daughter: "When Jesus came to the leader's house [he] saw the flute players and the crowd making a commotion" (Matt 9:23). As it turns out, before they arrived the girl had died, and the funeral process, complete with music and weeping, was already under way.[3]

Following death, the body was washed and wrapped. We find this custom mentioned in several episodes in the Gospels, and elsewhere. We see it in the story of Lazarus, who is bound and wrapped with cloths (John 11:44). The body of Jesus is wrapped in a clean linen shroud (Matt 27:59; Luke 23:53; John 19:40). The body of Ananias is wrapped and buried (Acts 5:6); so also Dorcas, who "became ill and died. When they had washed her, they laid her in a room upstairs" (Acts 9:37). Moreover, the corpse was usually perfumed (Josephus, *Ant.* 15.61; for spices, see *Ant.* 17.196–199; John 19:39–40).

The day of burial was the first of seven days of mourning (*Sem.* 12.1). This is clearly stated by the first-century Jewish historian Josephus, in reference to the death, burial, and funeral of Herod the Great (d. 4 BCE): "Now Archelaus [Herod's oldest surviving son] continued to mourn for seven days out of respect for his father—the custom of the country prescribes this number of days—and then, after feasting the crowds and making an end of the mourning, he went up to the temple" (Josephus, *Ant.* 17.200). The custom of seven days of mourning originated in Scripture: Joseph "observed a time of mourning for his father seven days" (Gen 50:10), and, in reference to the remains of king Saul and his sons, Israelite men "took their bones and buried them under the tamarisk tree in Jabesh, and fasted seven days" (1 Sam 31:13).

Mourning normally took place at the tomb's entrance or within the tomb itself. This is why archaeologists sometimes find a portion of the floor carved out more deeply, which allowed mourners to pray standing upright, according to the Jewish custom.[4] Of course, the practice of mourners' standing inside the tomb was why corpses were perfumed. Many perfume bottles and jars have been found in tombs and burial caves. One can only imagine how unpleasant the tomb would have become by the sixth and seventh days. Lamps and lamp niches have also been found in tombs, because of the need for light. *(See figs. 7.1–2.)*

One year after death, it was customary to gather the bones and place them in a bone niche or in an ossuary. This is sometimes called secondary burial. This is readily observed in the archaeological excavations of Jewish tombs from the time

3. Life expectancy was short at this time. More than half died before age thirty. For a recent survey of this subject, see Y. Nagar and H. Torgeë, "Biological Characteristics of Jewish Burial in the Hellenistic and Early Roman Periods," *IEJ* 53 (2003): 164–71.

4. An example of a section of floor that has been more deeply carved can be seen in the partially opened tomb on the Mount of Olives at Dominus Flevit. On standing while praying, see Luke 18:11 ("the Pharisee stood and prayed"). The best known synagogue prayer is called the Amidah, or "Standing" Prayer.

of Jesus. Thousands of ossuaries have been recovered (whether properly or looted) from tombs in the vicinity of Jerusalem.[5] The practice of ossilegium is also attested in later rabbinic literature: "When the flesh had wasted away they gathered together the bones and buried them in their own place" (*m. Sanh.* 6:6); "My son, bury me at first in a niche. In the course of time, collect my bones and put them in an ossuary but do not gather them with your own hands" (*Sem.* 12.9; cf. *Sem.* 3.2). The custom of the interval of twelve months from primary burial to secondary burial is also attested in rabbinic literature (cf. *b. Qidd.* 31b). *(See figs. 7.3–4.)*

For executed criminals, however, the rules were different. Criminals were to be buried properly, but not in places of honor, such as the family tomb. This is clearly taught in the earliest writings of the rabbis: "They did not bury (the executed criminal) in the burying-place of his fathers. But two burying-places were kept in readiness by the Sanhedrin, one for them that were beheaded or strangled, and one for them that were stoned or burnt" (*m. Sanh.* 6:5); "Neither a corpse nor the bones of a corpse may be transferred from a wretched place to an honored place, nor, needless to say, from an honored placed to a wretched place; but if to the family tomb, even from an honored place to a wretched place, it is permitted" (*Sem.* 13.7). Not only was the body of a criminal not to be buried in a place of honor, no public mourning for executed criminals was permitted: "they used not to make [open] lamentation . . . for mourning has place in the heart alone" (*m. Sanh.* 6:6).

These are the burial customs of the Jewish people. But did the Jewish people always bury the dead? Was burial important to them? Were they willing to leave people unburied, such as executed criminals? These questions must be asked, because in Roman-controlled Palestine execution normally was at the discretion of Roman authority. Sometimes the executed were crucified and often the crucified were left unburied. Was this the peacetime practice in first-century Palestine?[6]

Jewish Beliefs and the Necessity of Burial

In the Mediterranean world of late antiquity, proper burial of the dead was regarded as a sacred duty, especially in the culture and religion of the Jewish people. The first

5. See Rahmani, *Catalogue of Jewish Ossuaries*. Rahmani catalogues some 895 ossuaries. About 30 percent of them are inscribed, usually with the names (or nicknames) of the deceased. It is estimated that to date about two thousand ossuaries have been catalogued and/or published. Of these, about 650 have inscriptions, of which about six hundred involve names.

6. The archaeological examples that will be considered are all from Jerusalem and its immediate vicinity. The Galilean examples mentioned in the Gospels are nevertheless relevant, for the burial customs of Jews in Galilee and Jews in Judea were not significantly different. The differences in sepulture in and around Jerusalem were mostly due to urbanization, higher density of population, and greater affluence. The customs and practices themselves are essentially identical. For more on this topic, see M. Aviam, "Regionalism of Tombs and Burial Customs in the Galilee During the Hellenistic, Roman and Byzantine Periods," in *Jews, Pagans and Christians in the Galilee: 25 years of Archaeological Excavations and Surveys. Hellenistic to Byzantine Periods* (Land of Galilee 1; Rochester, NY: University of Rochester Press, 2004), 257–313; E. Regev, "Family Burial, Family Structure, and the Urbanization of Herodian Jerusalem," *PEQ* 136 (2004): 109–31.

reason for providing proper burial was for the sake of the dead themselves. The importance of care for the dead and their proper burial is well attested in Scripture, from the amount of attention given to the story of Abraham's purchase of a cave for the burial of Sarah (Gen 23:4–19) to the burial accounts of the patriarchs and monarchs of Israel. Of special interest is the story of Jacob's body being taken to the land of Canaan to be buried in a tomb that he had hewn (Gen 50:4–14). So also Joseph: though buried in Egypt, his bones were exhumed and taken with the Israelites at the time of the exodus, to be eventually buried in Canaan (Gen 50:22–26; Josh 24:32). The bones of the slain Saul and his sons were buried in Jabesh (1 Sam 31:12–13). David later commended the men who did this (2 Sam 2:5, "May you be blessed by the Lord, because you showed this loyalty to Saul your lord, and buried him!"). Saul's bones were later taken to the land of Benjamin (2 Sam 21:12–14).

The wicked and divinely judged were buried, too, such as those in the wilderness who were greedy for meat (Num 11:33–34), or individual criminals who were executed (Deut 21:22–23). Israel's enemies who were slain in battle were buried (1 Kgs 11:15). Even the eschatological enemy hosts of Gog were to be buried (Ezek 39:11–16). To leave the dead, even enemy dead, lying about unburied was to bring a curse on the land (Deut 21:22–23). Explaining Jewish ethical obligations, Josephus states: "We must furnish fire, water, [and] food to all who ask for them, point out the road, not leave a corpse unburied [ἄταφον], [and] show consideration even to declared enemies" (*Ag. Ap.* 2.211; cf. 2.205). In an imaginative retelling of Jacob's grief upon hearing (falsely) that his son Joseph had been killed by wild animals and that nothing of him remained for burial, Philo has the patriarch affirm that had his son died in some other manner, and had his corpse been found lying beside the road, even the "cruelest of men" would have taken pity and "deemed the custom of burial to be its due" (*Joseph* 22–27).

A second reason for burying the dead is to avoid defilement of the land of Israel. This requirement is grounded in the Mosaic law: "When someone is convicted of a crime punishable by death and is executed, and you hang him on a tree, his corpse must not remain all night upon the tree; you shall bury him that same day, for anyone hung on a tree is under God's curse. You must not defile the land that the Lord your God is giving you for possession" (Deut 21:22–23). It is also expressed in Ezekiel: "They will set apart men to pass through the land regularly and bury any invaders who remain on the face of the land, so as to cleanse it. . . . Thus they shall cleanse the land" (Ezek 39:14, 16). The requirement for burial of the criminal is emphasized because of the temptation to neglect the burial of a murderer or traitor. A law would hardly be necessary for the burial of others, whose family members would have needed no encouragement to see to proper and honorable burial of the deceased.

Deuteronomy's law regarding the execution and burial of the condemned remained current at the turn of the era, though not without some important modification, as seen in its elaboration in the *Temple Scroll*, one of the Dead Sea Scrolls, where we read:

> If a man is a traitor against his people and gives them up to a foreign nation, so doing evil to his people, *you are to hang him on a tree until dead*. On the testimony of two or three witnesses he will be put to death, and they themselves shall hang him on the tree.

> If a man is convicted of a capital crime and flees to the nations, cursing his people and the children of Israel, *you are to hang him, also, upon a tree until dead*. But you must not let their bodies remain on the tree overnight; you shall most certainly bury them that very day. Indeed, anyone hung on a tree is accursed of God and men, but you are not to defile the land that I am about to give you as an inheritance [Deut 21:22–23]. (11QT[a] LXIV, 7–13a = 4Q524 14, 2–4; emphasis added)

Whereas Deut 21:22–23 speaks of one put to death and then hung, the *Temple Scroll* speaks of one hanged "until dead." That is, death is understood to follow hanging on the tree, not to precede it. As was discussed in the preceding chapter, most think crucifixion is in view in this passage from the *Temple Scroll* (as also in 4QpNah 3–4, I, 6–8, and perhaps also in 4Q282i, which refers to the hanging up of those who lead the people astray).[7] It is also important to note that this form of execution is linked to treason.

It should also be observed that the requirement to bury the executed person *on the day of his death* is emphasized. The reason given for taking the bodies down and burying them on the day (or evening) of death is to avoid defiling the land, for the executed person is "cursed of God." This is probably the rationale that lies behind the concern regarding the burial of slain enemy soldiers, as in 1 Kgs 11:15 and Ezek 39:11–16, and also in 4Q285, where Israel and the Messiah (the "Branch of David and "Prince of the Congregation") have slain the Roman legions and their emperor and the priests give oversight to the burial of the enemy.

What is important here is that even in the case of the executed criminal, proper burial was anticipated. Various restrictions may have applied, such as the deceased's being forbidden burial in the family tomb—at least until the flesh had decomposed—or those still living not being allowed to mourn publicly, but burial was to take place, in keeping with the scriptural command of Deut 21:22–23 and the Jewish customs that had grown up alongside it.

Archaeological Evidence of Burial in the Roman Era

In the previous chapter, I discussed the discovery of an ossuary (ossuary no. 4 in Tomb I, at Givʿat ha-Mivtar) that contained the bones of a man named Yehoḥanan, who was killed by crucifixion. I have already discussed the details of Yehoḥanan's crucifixion; here I would like to discuss his burial. Yehoḥanan's leg bones were broken, but there is disagreement over how and when they were broken (i.e., while still on the cross, or after being taken down). Some think that the breaks in the lower leg bones of Yehoḥanan, including the cut to the talus bone of the foot, are due to *crurifragium*, the breaking of a victim's bones to hasten his death. Others do not think the talus suffered such an injury. Indeed, the talus in question may actually belong to one of the other two individuals whose skeletal remains were placed in

7. For detailed discussion of these texts from Qumran, see Doudna, *4Q Pesher Nahum*, 389–433; Yadin, *Temple Scroll*, 2:288–91. These texts and others are treated in much greater detail in ch. 6 above.

the ossuary. Accordingly, the conclusion that Yehoḥanan's leg bones were broken before death and decarnation is disputed. Because of the age and degraded condition of the skeletal materials, a measure of uncertainty remains.[8]

If Yehoḥanan's legs were broken before death, this would mean not only that he was taken down and buried (as indicated by the discovery of his remains in an ossuary) but also that his death was intentionally hastened. The most likely and most compelling reason for hastening death in this manner was so that his corpse could be taken down from the cross and placed in a tomb before nightfall, as Scripture commands (Deut 21:22–23) and as Jewish custom required. The Romans had no reason of their own to expedite death by crucifixion; in fact, they would have preferred just the opposite.

We may have the skeletal remains of another person who, like Yehoḥanan, was executed and whose remains eventually were placed in a family tomb. These remains were found in a cluster of tombs on Mount Scopus, north of Jerusalem.[9] The skeletal remains of a woman (aged fifty to sixty) found in Tomb C give clear evidence of her having been attacked. Her right elbow suffered a deep cut that severed the end of the humerus (elbow). Because there is no sign of regrowth or infection, it is surmised that she died from the attack.

In Tomb D, which contains the remains of persons related to those interred in Tomb C, were the remains of a man (aged fifty) who was decapitated. It is plausible to speculate that this man was executed, quite possibly for having murdered the female relative in Tomb C. However, physical anthropologist Joe Zias doubts that the man was executed, because his neck had been struck twice. Being struck twice, he reasons, suggests an act of violence rather than a judicial execution.[10] Zias could be correct, of course, but we should not assume that judicial beheadings were always neatly done and did not require more than one stroke of the sword or ax. One only needs to be reminded of the several badly aimed strokes that finally took off the head of James, Duke of Monmouth, in 1685.[11] Apparently, the executioner was intoxicated. His first stroke buried the axe in the Duke's shoulder! Mary, Queen of Scots, fared no better a century earlier, when, in 1586, her cousin, Elizabeth I, had her executed for treason. It took the executioner three strokes to take off her head.

Multiple cuts do not in fact argue against interpreting beheadings as judicial executions. I have reviewed the evidence of hundreds of Roman-era skeletons that

8. On the problem of determining whether bone was damaged before or after death, see N. J. Sauer, "The Timing of Injuries and Manner of Death: Distinguishing among Antemortem, Perimortem and Postmortem Trauma," in *Forensic Osteology: Advances in the Identification of Human Remains* (ed. K. R. Richards; 2nd ed.; Springfield, IL: Charles C. Thomas, 1998), 321–32.

9. The Mount Scopus tomb was excavated in 1979 by Gershon Edelstein of Israel's Department of Antiquities (now the Israel Antiquities Authority).

10. J. Zias, "Anthropological Evidence of Interpersonal Violence in First-Century AD Jerusalem," *Current Anthropology* 24 (1983): 123–34.

11. The official number is five, but other versions place the number of strokes as high as seven or eight.

have been excavated (mostly in Britain, though some in North Africa and elsewhere in the Roman Empire) and have been found to have suffered decapitation. In about one half of the cases, two or more strokes of the sword or axe were required before the head was separated from the body.[12]

Of special interest for this topic is the discovery of the mass grave left behind in the aftermath of the bloody Battle of Towton, which occurred in Britain in the fifteenth century.[13] Although dating from a much later period than the time of the Romans, the skeletal remains are nevertheless quite instructive because the weapons employed in the battle and the manner of fighting were essentially the same as those used in the Roman period. Approximately one half of the several hundred slain suffered fatal head wounds, and the other half suffered fatal sword or spear thrusts through the body. Only one victim suffered decapitation, and it may have been a postmortem insult, not the actual cause of death.[14] The point is this: If no one—or at most only one—was decapitated in pitched battle, where combatants were armed with axes and swords, what is the probability that someone suffered decapitation in a domestic altercation? I think it is rather slim.

Accordingly, the man in Givʿat ha-Mivtar Tomb D is probably another individual who suffered the death penalty—even if it took two strokes to finish the job—and whose skeletal remains were placed, in due course, in the family tomb. With all due respect to Zias, I believe this means that we apparently have found three executed persons—one by crucifixion and two by beheading—who were buried according to the Jewish customs of the time of Jesus. This means that they were given primary burial (most likely in a place of dishonor, that is, in one of the tombs reserved for executed criminals) and that subsequently their skeletal remains were gathered and placed in ossuaries, which in turn were placed in their family burial vaults—all according to the laws and customs related in ancient Jewish literature. Archaeology, so far as it goes, corroborates what is claimed in the literary remains

12. I recommend J. L. McKinley, "A Decapitation from the Romano-British Cemetery at Baldock, Hertfordshire," *International Journal of Osteoarchaeology* 3 (1993): 41–44; A. Boylston, "Evidence of Weapon-Related Trauma in British Archaeological Samples," in *Human Osteology in Archaeology and Forensic Science* (ed. M. Cox and S. Mays; London: Greenwich Medical Media, 2000), 357–80, esp. 367–68. McKinley and Boylston review a number of cases involving decapitation and observe that multiple strokes were the norm. See also M. Harmon, T. I. Molleson, and J. L. Price, "Burials, Bodies and Beheadings in Romano-British and Anglo-Saxon Cemeteries," *Bulletin of the British Museum of Natural History: Geology* 35 (1981): 145–88; R. J. Watt, "Evidence for Decapitation," in *The Roman Cemetery at Lankhills* (ed. G. Clarke; Winchester Studies 3: Pre-Roman and Roman Winchester; Oxford: Clarendon, 1979), 342–44 + plate XVII. I should also mention the ongoing excavation at Ridgeway, in Dorset, United Kingdom, where a mass burial was discovered in 2009. Oxford Archaeology staff are conducting the excavation. The remains of some fifty beheaded men, probably Viking raiders (ca. 910–1030 CE), have been unearthed. Senior osteologist Angela Boyle reports that most of the skeletons "exhibit evidence of multiple blows to the vertebrae" caused by "a large, very sharp weapon such as a sword" (as reported on the Oxford Archaeology website).

13. The battle took place in 1461 and confirmed the crown for Edward IV (d. 1483).

14. V. Fiorato, A. Boylston, and C. Knüsel, eds., *Blood Red Roses: The Archaeology of a Mass Grave from the Battle of Towton AD 1461* (Oxford: Oxbow, 2000).

from this period. The Gospel accounts of the women going to Jesus' tomb early Sunday morning to perfume his body and mourn privately are completely in step with the literature and archaeology of death and burial.[15]

What I find especially intriguing about the Mount Scopus tomb is not that an executed man was buried in his family tomb (for we have seen this in at least two other cases), but that this man may have been executed for the murder of a family member (i.e., the woman with the injured elbow). It seems that the Jewish custom of permitting criminals proper burial in the family tomb even extended to those who murdered members of their own families. The lapse of one year, the wasting away of the flesh, and the theological belief that in this passage of time and physical decomposition the "sins of the flesh" had in some sense been atoned for made possible a family "reunion" of sorts. Once family, always family, apparently—and so even the blackest of sheep were to slumber amidst the remains of kith and kin.[16] This observation lends further support to studies that have shown just how cohesive the Jewish family was in late antiquity.

The nails that have been recovered from tombs, some within ossuaries, also constitute important evidence of the burial of the crucified. According to Rachel Hachlili's reckoning, some 138 iron nails have been reported.[17] She believes most of these nails were placed in the tombs and/or ossuaries for a purpose. Prominent discoveries of nails in Jerusalem include those found in Jason's Tomb,[18] the Caiaphas Tomb,[19] and the Tomb of Nicanor.[20] Hachlili notes that in a tomb on Mount Scopus five nails were found in one chamber and one nail in another chamber; and nine nail fragments were recovered from Akeldama, in Cave 1, Chamber A.[21] She further notes that several nails were found in some of the tombs of Jericho, includ-

---

15. See J. Magness, "Jesus' Tomb: What Did It Look Like?," in *Where Christianity Was Born* (ed. H. Shanks; Washington, DC: Biblical Archaeology Society, 2006), 212–26. I will comment on this further in the chapter that follows.

16. The strong familial bond, along with the practice of ossilegium, is probably what lies behind Jesus' surprising exhortation to the would-be disciple who requests time to "bury (his) father": "Follow me," Jesus tells the man, "and let the dead bury their own dead" (Matt 8:22). Viewed in the light of ossilegium and how the dead were understood, Jesus has told this man to allow the family members already interred in the family tomb to see to the reburial of his father's bones. For support of this interpretation, see B. R. McCane, "'Let the Dead Bury Their Own Dead': Secondary Burial and Matt 8:21–22," *HTR* 83 (1990): 31–43. On the idea of life (even if greatly diminished) still present in the bones, see Meyers, *Jewish Ossuaries*, 12–16. This idea provided a major part of the motivation to have one's bones buried in Israel, in one's family tomb. A number of those interred in tombs at Beth Sheʿarim, Galilee, had at first been buried outside the land of Israel. The bones of some had been transported from as far away as Rome.

17. R. Hachlili, *Jewish Funerary Customs, Practices, and Rites in the Second Temple Period* (JSJSup 94; Leiden: Brill, 2005), 401–34.

18. L. Y. Rahmani, "Jason's Tomb," *IEJ* 17 (1967): 61–100, at 91.

19. Greenhut, "'Caiaphas' Tomb in North Talpiyot," 63–71.

20. N. Avigad, "Jewish Rock-Cut Tombs in Jerusalem and in the Judean Hill Country," *ErIsr* 8 (1967): 119–42, at 124 (in Hebrew).

21. Hachlili, *Jewish Funerary Customs*, 511.

ing the well-known Goliath Tomb.[22] The older suggestion that the nails were part of wooden coffins has been rejected, and although it is acknowledged that some of these nails might have been used in scratching the names of the deceased into the limestone ossuaries, it is suspected that the true purpose of their presence in the tombs and ossuaries lies elsewhere. *(See fig. 7.5.)*

Archaeologists and anthropologists believe that nails and sometimes other pieces of iron were placed in tombs and ossuaries to ward off evil spirits or to provide protection of one sort or another for the departed. The evidence of the cemeteries at Olynthus (Macedonia) seems to bear this out. Among the six hundred graves excavated in the 1930s, David Robinson and his team found many iron nails, often arranged in distinct patterns, along with grave furniture of one sort or another. In one grave, dating to the fifth century BCE, a man held in his hand six nails and his coin for Charon.[23] Similar findings have been made elsewhere in the lands surrounding the Mediterranean. Coins, as well as iron nails, have been found in some of the Jewish ossuaries, though they are not common. Not many of these coins, if any, were to be used as "payment" to Charon for the deceased to be ferried over the River Styx and on into the next life. There are a few examples where this may have been the case,[24] but Hachlili rightly notes that they hardly support the notion that pagan practices were widespread among Jews in Israel in late antiquity.[25] Jewish superstition regarding iron, however, seems to have been another matter.

In Jewish as well as pagan literature, we are told that crucifixion nails could promote healing and ward off evil.[26] In a discussion concerning what one may carry on the Sabbath, Rabbi Meir (or Rabbi Yose, in other versions) opines that people "may go out with a locust's egg, a fox's (or jackal's) tooth, and a nail from one who has been crucified [וּבְמַסְמֵר מִן הַצָּלוּב] for the sake of healing" (*m. Šabb.* 6:10).[27] But

22. For image, see R. Hachlili, *Jericho: The Jewish Cemetery of the Second Temple Period* (IAA Reports 7; Jerusalem: Israel Antiquities Authority, 1999), fig. III-84.4–6.

23. D. M. Robinson, *Excavations at Olynthus*, part 11, *Necrolynthia, a Study in Greek Burial Customs and Anthropology* (Baltimore: Johns Hopkins Press, 1942), 159–60; cited by Hachlili, *Jewish Funerary Customs*, 511–12.

24. Coins were found in two skulls in tombs in Jericho from our period, in one case a coin from Herod Archelaus (4 BCE–6 CE), and in the other case a coin, bearing the image of a ship, from Herod Agrippa I (41–44 CE). See R. Hachlili, "A Second Temple Period Jewish Necropolis in Jericho," *BA* 43 (1980): 235–40, at 238. But the fact that these coins were found in only two of hundreds of skulls strongly suggests that the practice was not common among Jews. See Hachlili and Killebrew, "Was the Coin-on-Eye Custom a Jewish Burial Practice in the Second Temple Period?," 147–53; Rahmani, "Note on Charon's *Obol*," 149–50.

25. See her discussion in Hachlili, *Jewish Funerary Customs*, 437–43, esp. 441–42. Hachlili also corrects the notion (sometimes expressed in discussions of the image in the Shroud of Turin) that it was customary for Jews to place coins over the eyes of the deceased. It was not.

26. As in *b. Šabb.* 67a, where a crucifixion nail is said to be a remedy for infection or inflammation. A number of magical utterances are discussed in this passage. More will be said below about this text.

27. It was believed that the locust's egg could cure earache, the fox's tooth (or jackal's tooth) could remedy sleep problems, and the nail used in crucifixion could cure infection or fever (see the elaboration in *b. Šabb.* 67a).

the sages strongly disagree, saying that Jews should never carry such items, not even on weekdays, for to do so is to adopt the "ways of the Amorites."[28] On a page from a book of magic recipes found among the thousands of texts recovered from the genizah of the Ben Ezra synagogue in Cairo, we read: "For love. A seal, again. Take a nail from the wood of someone crucified [מסמ"ר מן כשבה מצלוב], and make of it a seal" (TS Arabic 44.44 col. 2, lines 17–18).[29] In this case, the crucifixion nail is expected to empower the seal for the purpose of generating love.

In pagan sources, we find similar value attached to crucifixion nails, cords for binding, crosses, or the corpses of those who have been executed or who died in some other violent way. Pliny the Elder describes the use of a crucifixion nail to cure quartan fever: "These also wrap up in wool and tie round the neck of quartan patients a piece of a nail taken from a cross [*fragmentum clavi a cruce*], or else a cord[30] taken from a crucifixion [*spartum e cruce*], and after the patient's neck has been freed they hide it in a hole where the sunlight cannot reach" (Pliny the Elder, *Natural History* 28.11.46).[31]

Nails were frequently used to "seal" charms and spells written on lead tablets, foils and lamellae (thin plates) made of other metals (such as gold, silver, or tin). These tablets were usually folded (normally twice) or rolled up and then pierced by a nail and hidden. Sometimes the charm was nailed to a specific location, almost always a hidden one (so the intended victim would be unaware of its close proximity). Iron nails and small iron pins were sometimes thrust into effigies or images of the victim (into the eyes, mouth, heart, genitals), more or less as with the modern voodoo doll. Sometimes the nails or pins were thrust into the hands and feet, as a simulation of crucifixion.[32] The magical purpose of the nail was "to fasten, to fix,

28. Again, see *b. Šabb.* 67a. For further notes and commentary, see Chapman, *Ancient Jewish and Christian Perceptions of Crucifixion*, 182–83. In the parallel passage in the Tosefta, in which the "ways of the Amorites"—which are to be avoided—are being discussed, warnings are given against the practice of tying a piece of iron to the leg of the bed of a woman in childbirth (*t. Šabb.* 6:4), throwing a piece of iron into a burial place (6:12), or placing a staff of wood or iron under one's head (6:13). Iron nails or pegs (מסמר או יתד) in the wall of a house in which lay a dead person were regarded as unclean (as stated in CD XII, 17–18 = 4Q266 9 II, 4–5). Hachlili wonders if these items would be removed to the tomb in which the deceased was placed (*Jewish Funerary Customs*, 512). If so, this might account for the presence of some of the iron nails found in tombs and ossuaries.

29. For further notes and commentary, see Naveh and Shaked, *Magic Spells and Formulae*, 220–22; Chapman, *Ancient Jewish and Christian Perceptions of Crucifixion*, 183. The *aleph* in the first word is penned small and placed above the second *mem*.

30. The *spartum* is a rope or cord made from esparto grass employed, among other uses, in lieu of nails to bind the arms of the crucifixion victim to the *patibulum*, or horizontal beam, of the cross.

31. Latin text and translation from W. H. S. Jones, trans., in H. Rackham et al., trans., *Pliny, Natural History* (10 vols.; LCL; Cambridge: Harvard University Press, 1938–62), 8:34–35; cited and discussed in Chapman, *Ancient Jewish and Christian Perceptions of Crucifixion*, 183.

32. As in the experience of one Sophronius, according to *Narratio miraculorum sanctorum Cyri et Joannis* (= *PG* 87:3, col. 3625). This example comes from C. A. Faraone, "The Agonistic Context of Early Greek Binding Spells," in *Magika Hiera: Ancient Greek Magic and*

to tie down, and thus to bind."[33] Indeed, the power of the iron nail was to "add pain and death to the spell."[34]

Several binding spells have been found with nails or nail holes (in cases where the nails have gone missing). Most of these spells range in date from the fourth century BCE to the second century CE and have been been found in Rome and Greece. On the Via Appia, near the Porta San Sebastiano (Rome), fifty-six lead tablets were recovered, most of which were rolled up and pierced by a nail; the tablets were found in small sarcophagi placed in a tomb.[35] In the same location, a lead tablet was found that depicts a figure being bound with chains as well as a bust with pins or nails.[36]

In a grave (the specific location of which is now unknown) in Piraeus, Greece, was recovered a lead tablet rolled up and pierced by a nail.[37] Another lead tablet, folded and fixed with a nail, was also recovered from Piraeus; the original locus of this tablet is unknown, but it was probably a grave.[38] A lead tablet folded and pierced by a nail was found in Attica, Greece (the original *in situ* location is now unknown).[39] A lead tablet was recovered from Athens, Greece; it contains two holes, which were presumably made by nails, though the nails were not found.[40] Another tablet, with one hole and the nail still in place, was found in Athens.[41] A lead tablet, folded and with nail hole, was found near the town of Arkesinê on the Greek island of Amorgos.[42]

It is clear from these examples that superstitions in late antiquity regarding the power of iron nails, especially those used in crucifixion, were not unique to the Jewish people. These beliefs were widespread in the eastern half of the

---

Religion (ed. C. A. Faraone and D. Obbink; Oxford: Oxford University Press, 1991), 3–32, at 9, 27n42. When the nails were removed from the effigy, the paralyzing spell was broken.

33. Accordingly, these curses and charms are called "binding spells." The ancient terminology is seen in the Greek word κατάδεσμος (from καταδέω, "to bind down, bind fast") and its Latin equivalent *defixio* (plural: *defixiones*; from *defigo*, "to define, fix, transfix, restrain"). The quotation is from J. G. Gager, *Curse Tablets and Binding Spells from the Ancient World* (Oxford: Oxford University Press, 1992), 18. For an image of a folded binding spell transfixed by iron nail, see p. 19 fig. 4. See also Faraone, "Agonistic Context of Early Greek Binding Spells," 21n3. Faraone provides additional information about the meaning of κατάδεσμος and *defixio* and their use in magic.

34. Gager, *Curse Tablets and Binding Spells*, 18.

35. For discussion, see ibid., 67–71 (no. 13) + fig. 9.

36. For discussion, see ibid., 71–72 (no. 14) + fig. 10. For another example of a lead tablet rolled up and pierced by a nail that has been recovered from Rome, see pp. 169–70 (no. 78) + fig. 19. And from Mentana, east of Rome, has been recovered a lead tablet with two nail holes; see p. 172 (no. 80).

37. For discussion, see ibid., 124–25 (no. 37).

38. For discussion, see ibid., 124–25 (no. 38).

39. For discussion, see ibid., 126 (no. 40). For more examples of folded lead tablets pierced by a nail from Attica, see pp. 156–57 (no. 62), 164 (no. 73).

40. For discussion, see ibid., 127–29 (no. 41) + fig. 17.

41. For discussion, see ibid., 145 (no. 55). For more examples of lead tablets pierced by a nail from Athens, see pp. 157 (no. 63), 163 (no. 71).

42. For discussion, see ibid., 165 (no. 75).

Mediterranean world. In Greek and Latin settings, nails were sometimes used to simulate crucifixion and were often found in tombs and sarcophagi. Jewish beliefs and practices were very much part of this larger magical tradition.

In pagan magical texts we find that corpses, body parts, and clothing of executed criminals and others who died violently were prized by necromancers, witches, magicians, and producers of charms and incantations (e.g., *PGM* I.247–248: "Take an eye of an ape or of a corpse that has died a violent death"; cf. II.49: "wrap it in a piece of clothing of one who has died violently"; IV.2038–2040: "Go quickly to where someone lies buried"; IV.2164–2170: "Attach to a criminal who has been executed, speak the verses in his ear, and he will tell you everything"). It was believed that the grim relic possessed power and increased the potency of the spell.

It is to traditions such as these that Lucan of Cordoba (first century CE) makes mocking yet poetic reference, when he describes the grisly specimens that the witch collects from the gallows for her use in magic: "She breaks with her teeth the fatal noose, and mangles the carcass that dangles on the gallows, and scrapes the cross of the criminal [*cruces percussaque*]; she tears away the rain-beaten flesh and the bones calcined by exposure to the sun. She purloins the nails that pierced the hands [*insertum manibus chalybem*[43]], the clotted filth, and the black humor of corruption that oozes over all the limbs; and when a muscle resists her teeth, she hangs her weight upon it" (*Civil War* 6.543–549).[44] Lucian of Samosata (second century CE) tells his readers that an "Arab gave me the ring made of iron from crosses [τὸν δακτύλιον . . . σιδήρου τοῦ ἐκ τῶν σταυρῶν πεποιημένον] and taught me the spell of many names" (*The Lover of Lies* 17).[45]

The presence of human calcium on some of the nails recovered from tombs and ossuaries in and around Jerusalem suggests that the nails in question—and perhaps many of the nails found in these locations—were used in crucifixions. The nails recovered from the Abba Tomb were probably the nails used to crucify Mattathias son of Judah (a.k.a., Antigonus son of Aristobulus). Bone fragments cling to them.[46] And, of course, the nail that remains imbedded in the heel of Yehoḥanan is clear evidence of crucifixion. But what of the many other loose nails recovered from ossuaries and tombs?

The two nails found in or near the ossuary bearing the two inscriptions referring to "Yehoseph bar Qayapha" (thought to be a reference to the high priest Joseph

---

43. Lit., "the steel set into the hands."

44. Latin text and translation are taken from J. D. Duff, trans., *Lucan* (LCL; Cambridge: Harvard University Press, 1928), 342–45; cited and discussed in Chapman, *Ancient Jewish and Christian Perceptions of Crucifixion*, 184.

45. Greek text and translation are taken from A. M. Harmon et al., trans., *Lucian* (8 vols.; LCL; Cambridge: Harvard University Press, 1928), 3:346–47; cited and discussed in Chapman, *Ancient Jewish and Christian Perceptions of Crucifixion*, 184.

46. See the report in V. Tzaferis, "The 'Abba' Burial Cave in Jerusalem," *'Atiqot* 7 (1974): 61–64 (in Hebrew) + plates 18–20, with English summary on p. 9*. See now Elitzur, "The Abba Cave: Unpublished Findings and a New Proposal," 83–102, as well as the discussion in ch. 6 above.

called Caiaphas) are of special interest.[47] One nail is straight but has been broken, apparently at some point after recovery from the Caiaphas tomb. The other nail is bent, almost at ninety degrees. There are traces of human calcium on the broken nail and there are traces along the length of the bent nail as well as a substantial amount of calcium affixed to its head.

The presence of this calcium could be explained as the result of the incidental contact of these nails with the bones contained in the ossuary in which the nails were placed. But the presence of substantial amounts of calcium on the bent Caiaphas nail suggests that the nail had been in much more intimate contact with a human bone, and for a lengthy period of time. The presence of similar "rings" of calcium on other nails suggests that they were used in crucifixion and that after the passage of time they were recovered and put to new use. Accordingly, it is probable that both nails recovered from the Caiaphas ossuary or tomb had been used in crucifixion.

It is, of course, most unlikely that the Caiaphas nails were used in the crucifixion of one of the members of the Caiaphas family, given their powerful and illustrious status. Rather, these nails were used to crucify someone else and were later obtained and placed in the Caiaphas tomb because of their alleged protective powers. The same thinking likely lay behind the placing of a coin in the mouth of the Caiaphas relative Mariam, whose remains were found in another ossuary in the Caiaphas tomb.[48]

Although we cannot be certain until many, if not all, of the 138 iron nails recovered from Jewish tombs and ossuaries have been carefully studied, it is possible that many of them were used in crucifixion. Some of them were found in tombs and ossuaries because they were still part of the remains of the crucifixion victim (as in the cases of Yehoḥanan and Mattathias). Others were placed in tombs and ossuaries in the belief that they would offer some sort of benefit and protection for those whose remains had been interred.

If it turns out that many of these nails are in fact crucifixion nails—with many exhibiting the presence of human calcium (suggesting that these nails remained in the bones of the victims even after they were buried)—we would have evidence of the burial of many, not just two, crucified Jews. Such evidence would support the view that burial of the executed, including the crucified, was not unusual in the vicinity of Jerusalem during peacetime in late antiquity.

47. On the Caiaphas tomb and ossuary, see Greenhut, "'Caiaphas' Tomb in North Talpiyot"; Reich, "Ossuary Inscriptions from the Caiaphas Tomb" (*Jerusalem Perspective*), 13–21 + plates and facsimiles; idem, "Ossuary Inscriptions from the 'Caiaphas' Tomb" (*'Atiqot*), 72–77 + figs. 5 and 6. I thank Dr. Israel Hershkovitz of the Sackler Medical Center of the University of Tel Aviv for permitting me to examine the Caiaphas nails and a number of other nails recovered from Jewish tombs. In due course a study of these nails and related skeletal materials will be published by Hershkovitz and other colleagues.

48. Hachlili and Killebrew, "Was the Coin-on-Eye Custom a Jewish Burial Practice in the Second Temple Period?," 147–53; D. Bivin, "A Sadducee Who Believed in an Afterlife?," *Jerusalem Perspective* 4, nos. 4–5 (1991): 7; Greenhut, "'Caiaphas' Tomb in North Talpiyot," 70. On the custom of placing a coin in the mouth of the dead for payment to Charon, see Lucian, *Funerals* 1–10.

Summing Up

Thus far, we have found the buried remains of only three or four Jews confirmed as executed in pre–70 CE Israel. We know that many more than these were executed. And if other executed persons were buried properly, as I have argued would have been the case, why have we not found many more skeletons of executed persons? It has been argued by some that, in light of the fact that thousands of Jews were crucified in the vicinity of Jerusalem in the first century, the discovery of only one properly buried crucifixion victim is proof that the normal Roman practice of not permitting burial for such victims must have obtained even in Jewish Palestine. On the basis of this logic, perhaps one should conclude that Jesus was not buried either.[49]

There are at least four objections that must be raised against this inference. First, almost all of the bones recovered from the time of Jesus are poorly preserved, especially the smaller bones of the feet and hands, which will normally provide evidence, if any, of crucifixion. It was the presence of the nail in the right heel of Yehoḥanan, for example, that made it clear that he had been crucified. However, the presence of the nail was a fluke. It was due to the sharp end being bent back (like a fishhook), perhaps because the nail struck a knot in the upright beam or struck the nail driven in from the opposite side. When Yehoḥanan was taken down from the cross, the nail could not be extracted. Many may not be aware of the fact that the heel of Yehoḥanan was badly degraded and had to be reconstructed. Again, it was only because the iron nail was still present in the heel of Yehoḥanan that archaeologists know he was crucified. Accordingly, no statistics should be inferred from this unusual find.

Second, many crucifixion victims were scourged, beaten, and then tied—not nailed—to the cross. In such cases, skeletal remains would leave no trace of the trauma of crucifixion. Accordingly, we do not know that Yehoḥanan and Mattathias are the only crucifixion victims discovered in a tomb. For all we know, several other crucifixion victims may have been found without our knowing it.

Third, the best-preserved skeletons are found in the better-constructed tombs, in bone pits, or in ossuaries. These tombs were mostly those of the rich or the "middle class," not the poor. The poor were usually buried in smaller natural caves, if in Jerusalem, or in the ground, if elsewhere. Not many of their skeletons have been found, and, when found, the small bones are poorly preserved, if preserved at all. The significance of this point is that it is the poor who are most likely to be crucified, not the wealthy and powerful. Accordingly, the skeletons most likely to provide evidence of crucifixion are those that are least likely to survive, whereas the best-preserved skeletons are the ones least likely to have belonged to those who were crucified.

49. This argument has been advanced by J. D. Crossan, "The Dogs beneath the Cross," in *Jesus: A Revolutionary Biography* (San Francisco: HarperSanFrancisco, 1994), 123–58, and idem, *Who Killed Jesus? Exposing the Roots of Anti-Semitism in the Gospel Story of the Death of Jesus* (San Francisco: HarperSanFrancisco, 1995), and recently accepted by B. D. Ehrman, *How Jesus Became God: The Exaltation of a Jewish Preacher from Galilee* (San Francisco: HarperOne, 2014), 157, 377n8. I am not aware of any archaeologist who agrees with it.

Fourth, the vast majority of the thousands of Jews crucified and left unburied in the vicinity of Jerusalem in the first century died during the rebellion of 66–70 CE. The reason they were not buried is that Rome was at war with the Jewish people and had no wish to accommodate Jewish sensitivities, as Rome normally did during peacetime. It was during peacetime—indeed, during the administration of Pontius Pilate—that both Yehoḥanan and Jesus of Nazareth were crucified. That both were buried according to Jewish customs should hardly occasion surprise. Jewish priestly authorities were expected to defend the purity of Jerusalem (or at least to give the appearance of doing so), while Roman authorities acquiesced to Jewish customs and sensitivities, as Philo and Josephus relate.[50]

The archaeological evidence suggests that Jesus and other Jews executed in peacetime Israel were buried, not in honor, but properly, in accordance with Jewish laws and customs. In the case of Jesus of Nazareth, the expectation would have been to collect his skeletal remains approximately one year after death and transfer them from the place of dishonor to a place of honor, such as his family tomb or burial place. Burial customs and laws permitted this and the strong social and family ties of the Jewish people of late antiquity made it necessary. However Jesus of Nazareth may have been viewed by his family and acquaintances in the immediate aftermath of his execution, it is more than probable that it would have been anticipated that his bones would be gathered and reburied in the family tomb.

In the chapter that follows, we shall focus on the crucifixion and burial of Jesus. We shall ask what light archaeology sheds on these grim subjects, especially given the skeptical idea expressed in some quarters that Jesus might not have been buried at all.

---

50. According to Philo, the Romans' normal policy was "not to disturb the customs which throughout all the preceding ages had been safeguarded without disturbance by kings and by emperors" (*Embassy* 300). Similarly, Josephus states that the Romans do not require "their subjects to violate their national laws" (*Ag. Ap.* 273).

CHAPTER EIGHT

Death Becomes Him: On the Execution and Burial of Jesus

No serious historian, of any religious or nonreligious stripe, doubts that Jesus of Nazareth really lived in the first century and was executed under the authority of Pontius Pilate, the governor of Judea and Samaria.[1] Though this may be common knowledge among scholars,[2] the public may well not be aware of this. Objections, though, still persist, as though reports of Jesus' death have been greatly exaggerated. A recent book has recycled the odd notion that Jesus was not really executed but actually faked his death, with the assistance of the Roman governor and a few others, and then fled to Egypt. Proof of this, it is claimed, is found in two letters said to be written in Aramaic and alleged to have been found under a house in Jerusalem more than fifty years ago. We are assured that these writings are carefully preserved by a collector whose name cannot be revealed and who lives in a city whose identity cannot be disclosed.[3] Of course, neither the author of this fantasy nor the owner of these letters can read Aramaic or possesses the requisite expertise to verify the authenticity of ancient writings. Regrettably, the utter silliness of this scenario escapes many in today's reading public.

The death of Jesus is not only affirmed (or at least presupposed) in every writing of the New Testament and early Christianity, it is attested by early Jewish and Roman writers as well. Josephus, a first-century Jewish historian, apologist, and

---

1. Not surprisingly, the pseudo-scholarship of those who claim that Jesus is a mythical, unhistorical figure, or that there was no village of Nazareth in late antiquity, is not taken seriously by archaeologists and historians. For a recent popular rebuttal of the claims of the "mythicists," see B. D. Ehrman, *Did Jesus Exist? The Historical Argument for Jesus of Nazareth* (New York: HarperCollins, 2012).

2. For exemplary studies, see J. B. Green, *The Death of Jesus: Tradition and Interpretation in the Passion Narrative* (WUNT II/33; Tübingen: Mohr Siebeck, 1988); Brown, *Death of the Messiah*; J. T. Carrol and J. B. Green, with R. E. Van Voorst, J. Marcus, and D. Senior, *The Death of Jesus in Early Christianity* (Peabody, MA: Hendrickson, 1995).

3. M. Baigent, *The Jesus Papers: Exposing the Greatest Cover-Up in History* (San Francisco: HarperSanFrancisco, 2006). This book is one of the worst examples of pseudo-scholarship ever published.

survivor of the catastrophic rebellion against Rome (66–73 CE), states that Jesus, having been accused by the Jewish leaders, was condemned to the cross by Pilate (*Ant.* 18.63–64). According to the Roman historian Tacitus, "Christ . . . suffered the death penalty during the reign of Tiberius, by sentence of the procurator Pontius Pilate" (*Annals* 15.44). Although Tacitus errs slightly in upgrading Pilate's rank (he was a prefect, not a procurator),[4] his terse summary agrees with what we find in Josephus and in the Gospels. Lucian of Samosata, in a mocking reference to Peregrinus and the Christians with whom for a time he associated, refers to Jesus as "the man who was crucified in Palestine" (*Passing of Peregrinus* §11; cf. §13: "that crucified sophist"). And finally, Mar bar Serapion, a Syrian, in a letter written to his son perhaps toward the end of the first century, makes reference to the death of Jesus, the Jewish "wise king."[5]

The reality of the death of Jesus also finds confirmation in the simple fact that it was not anticipated by his followers. When Jesus spoke of his impending suffering and death, Peter, spokesman for the disciples, took his master aside and rebuked him (Mark 8:31–33), a sure sign of Peter's lack of this expectation. What, then, did they expect? They expected to sit at Jesus' right and left, that is, to form Israel's new government (Matt 19:28; Mark 10:35–40; Luke 22:28–30). The kingdom (or rule) of God had dawned and the rule of Satan was coming to an end (Mark 1:15; 3:11, 22–27; Luke 10:17–19; 11:20). How, then, did the martyrdom of God's chosen one fit into this picture?

The death of Jesus actually was a source of embarrassment for Jesus' early followers. It is to this embarrassment that Paul alludes when he declares that he is "not ashamed of the gospel" (Rom 1:16). His assertion that he is not ashamed clearly implies that there is something shameful about the Christian message. What that was in Paul's time is not hard to imagine. In the thinking of the Roman world, sons of God, heroes, and saviors did not die on crosses. In that time, there was no sentimentality attached to Jesus' death and certainly not to the cross, a horrifying symbol in Roman antiquity. In what way any of this could be termed "good news" (the meaning of the word "gospel") would be far from clear to Jews and Gentiles alike. Had Jesus not been executed, had Jesus not been crucified, why make up such a preposterous story?

No, the death of Jesus is no fiction. It is a grim historical reality. It was known to non-Christians, and it was a demoralizing event for Jesus' followers—at least initially—and an ongoing embarrassment as the church proclaimed Jesus as Savior and Son of God throughout the Roman Empire. There can be no doubt that Jesus was executed. But why?

---

4. As discussed above in ch. 3, the inscribed stone discovered in Caesarea Maritima in 1961 settled the question of Pilate's rank. See Boffo, *Iscrizioni greche e latine*, 217–33. Part of the inscription reads: "Pontius Pilatus, praefectus Iudaeae" (with some restoration).

5. All of these texts and others are critically sifted in R. E. Van Voorst, *Jesus Outside the New Testament: An Introduction to the Ancient Evidence* (Studying the Historical Jesus; Grand Rapids: Eerdmans, 2000).

The Reasons for the Death of Jesus

Many people, including Christians, do not know why Jesus was executed, why he encountered deadly opposition. I have heard people say that Jesus was put to death because he was a good man or because hypocritical Pharisees feared him. This really, though, is the stuff of nonsense. The New Testament Gospels reveal several historical factors, all near the end of Jesus' life, that led to his execution; his goodness and his quarrels with Pharisees were not among them.

The first reason Jesus aroused opposition was the manner of his entry into Jerusalem at the beginning of the final week of his ministry. He entered the Holy City mounted on a donkey, amidst shouts of "Hosanna! Blessed is the coming kingdom of our ancestor David!" (Mark 11:1–10, here vv. 9–10, NRSV, modified). Entering the city in this way deliberately mimicked Solomon, David's son, who one thousand years earlier rode the royal mule as part of his declaration of kingship (1 Kgs 1:32–40).[6] Such an entry also answered the ancient prophecy of the anticipated humble king (Zech 9:9).[7] Not only did Jesus' act recall hopes of a coming son of David, but the crowd's response reflected the same popular interpretation of it. Their "hosannas," as an allusion to Ps 118, were a pronouncement that this one who comes to the temple "in the name of the Lord" is none other than David, the one destined to be Israel's king and ruler (see Ps 118:19–27, according to the Aramaic paraphrase).[8] Such an event suggested in unmistakable terms that Israel's king was Jesus, not Caesar. Thus, from the very moment of his entry into Jerusalem, Jesus was set on a collision course with Roman authority.

Jesus' actions in the temple precincts, or grounds, constituted the second reason he aroused opposition. His well-known action here disrupted sacrificial trade and traffic and challenged the ruling priests with very troubling words (Mark 11:15–18): "Is it not written, 'My house shall be called a house of prayer for all the nations'? But you have made it a 'cave of robbers' " (v. 17, NRSV, modified).[9] The first part of these words is a quotation of Isa 56:7, which is part of an oracle that looks forward to the day when all peoples, Gentiles and Jews from afar, will come to Jerusalem and will be welcome. All peoples will worship the God of Israel; their gifts will be received and their prayers will be heard. This oracle expressed nothing new for Jews at that time; it reflects the original purpose for the temple, as also reflected in

---

6. Jesus' entry into Jerusalem was also similar to the entries of other kings and deliverers in the more recent history of Israel leading up to his own day.

7. C. A. Evans, "Jesus and Zechariah's Messianic Hope," in *Authenticating the Activities of Jesus* (ed. C. A. Evans and B. Chilton; NTTS 28.2; Leiden: Brill, 1998), 373–88.

8. On the role of Aramaic Ps 118 in the entry of Jesus into Jerusalem, see C. A. Evans, *Mark 8:27–16:20* (WBC 34B; Nashville: Nelson, 2001), 140, 144–45. Only the Aramaic version inserts the name "David" into Ps 118.

9. The specific grounds of Jesus' complaint are elusive. Accusations of corruption and violence are variegated and ubiquitous in the (mostly Jewish) literature of late antiquity. For an assessment of Jesus' complaint, see C. A. Evans, "Jesus' Action in the Temple and Evidence of Corruption in the First-Century Temple," in *Society of Biblical Literature 1989 Seminar Papers* (ed. David J. Lull; SBLSP 28; Atlanta: Scholars Press, 1989), 522–39.

Solomon's ancient prayer of dedication (1 Kgs 8:41–43). Jesus' action and his questioning appeal to Isaiah's oracle implied that the temple authorities had failed to live up to their calling. The temple had not become a place of prayer for the nations. Rather, it had become a "cave of robbers." Here, in the second part of his utterance, Jesus alludes to Jeremiah's scathing criticism of the temple establishment of his day (Jer 7:11), warning that God would destroy the temple.[10] The ruling priests, scribes, and elders would have been deeply offended by Jesus' critical and offensive words. Threats against temples in the Roman world were taken very seriously.

That preaching angry sermons based on Jer 7 could get one into trouble is attested in Josephus. Josephus tells us of one Jesus ben Ananias, who beginning in 63 CE began prophesying the doom of the city of Jerusalem and her famous temple. Like Jesus of Nazareth, Jesus ben Ananias alluded to Jer 7 while in the vicinity of the temple (Josephus, *J.W.* 6.300–305; cf. Jer 7:34).[11] This Jesus was lucky. Unlike Jesus of Nazareth, Jesus ben Ananias was not executed (despite calls from religious leaders that he be put to death), but was released. However, his luck ran out seven years later when, during the siege of Jerusalem, he was killed by a Roman catapult stone that came hurtling over the walls. *(See fig. 8.1.)*

The third reason Jesus aroused opposition was his telling of the parable of the vineyard (Mark 12:1–12). He narrated this parable as an indirect answer to the question put to him by the ruling priests and their supporters, who demanded to know by what authority Jesus did what he had done in the temple precincts (Mark 11:27–33). It was bad enough that Jesus based his parable on Isaiah's parable of the vineyard, which warned Israel of impending judgment because of its failure to pursue justice (Isa 5:1–7). What made Jesus' parable particularly annoying to the ruling priests was that Isaiah's parable had come to be understood as primarily directed against the temple establishment. We see this perspective in the Aramaic paraphrase of Isa 5, in later rabbinic interpretation, and in a scroll from Qumran that dates to the first century BCE (i.e., 4Q500).[12] Jesus' point was hard to miss:

10. C. A. Evans, "From 'House of Prayer' to 'Cave of Robbers': Jesus' Prophetic Criticism of the Temple Establishment," in *The Quest for Context and Meaning: Studies in Biblical Intertextuality in Honor of James A. Sanders* (ed. C. A. Evans and S. Talmon; BibInt 28; Leiden: Brill, 1997), 417–42.

11. For discussion of Jesus ben Ananias and the parallels with Jesus of Nazareth, see C. A. Evans, "Jesus and the 'Cave of Robbers': Toward a Jewish Context for the Temple Action," *BBR* 3 (1993): 93–110. In a later study, I suggest that ben Ananias may have been part of the Jesus movement and that he took up his proclamation in Jerusalem in response to the murder of James the brother of Jesus of Nazareth. See C. A. Evans, *From Jesus to the Church: The First Christian Generation* (Louisville: Westminster John Knox, 2014), 14–16, 111–15.

12. On the role of Isa 5 and Ps 118 in Jesus' parable of the vineyard, see G. J. Brooke, "4Q500 1 and the Use of Scripture in the Parable of the Vineyard," *DSD* 2 (1995): 268–94; Evans, *Mark 8:27–16:20*, 215–39, esp. 224–31; K. R. Snodgrass, *Stories with Intent: A Comprehensive Guide to the Parables of Jesus* (Grand Rapids: Eerdmans, 2007), 276–99. John Kloppenborg and I disagree over the antiquity and independence of the vineyard parable in the *Gospel of Thomas* §§65–66. I contend that the allusions to Isa 5:1–7 and the concluding quotation of Ps 118:22–23 are original and that the *Thomas* form of the parable is secondary, reflecting the shorter form of the parable found in Luke 20:9–19 and second-century Syrian Christian asceticism. See C. A. Evans, "How Septuagintal is Isa. 5:1–7 in Mark 12:1–9?," *NovT*

Because of their rebellion against God, especially as seen in their plotting to murder his own Son, the ruling priests faced judgment. This threat, together with the implied threat Jesus made earlier when he appealed to Jer 7, prompted the ruling priests to seek Jesus' life.

The fourth reason Jesus aroused opposition was his anointing by the unnamed woman (Mark 14:3–9). For years, commentators were reluctant to interpret this act as a messianic anointing on the part of the woman, suggesting instead that it was a Passover holiday anointing. This scholarly reluctance was probably due to the faulty assumption by some that Jesus did not understand himself in messianic terms. This odd notion has been seriously challenged of late, not least because of the discovery of a scroll from Qumran (4Q521) that speaks of the works of healing that will take place when the Messiah makes his appearance, works that parallel closely those listed in the summary Jesus gives of his ministry in his reply to the imprisoned and discouraged John the Baptist (Matt 11:2–6; Luke 7:18–23).[13] On the basis of this important discovery, scholars are now more open to affirming what the Gospels have said all along—that Jesus understood himself as Israel's Messiah. How to account for the ubiquity of the identification of Jesus as the Messiah had Jesus never thought of himself in these terms was a question that apparently had not sufficiently impressed itself upon these skeptical scholars.

The important point concerning the woman's anointing of Jesus is that immediately after this event takes place, Judas Iscariot departs to betray his master (Mark 14:10–11). The contrast between the named disciple who commits an act of treachery and the unnamed woman who commits an act of devotion has been commented upon.[14] It is a piece of literary artistry, to be sure. But what is sometimes overlooked is that this woman's actions very likely would have been reported to the ruling priests with whom Judas struck his bargain. Not only would Judas earn his pay by directing the officers and thugs of the ruling priests to the place of Jesus' private prayer, he would have offered them testimony as to what Jesus taught and how his followers regarded him. The woman's anointing of Jesus would have been too important to miss. It would have provided all the more reason to destroy Jesus.

---

15 (2003): 105–10; J. S. Kloppenborg, "Egyptian Viticultural Practices and the Citation of Isa 5:1–7 in Mark 12:1–9," *NovT* 44 (2002): 134–59; idem, "Isa 5:1–7 LXX and Mark 12:1, 9, Again," *NovT* 46 (2004): 12–19. Recent major studies have, rightly in my view, concluded that *Thomas* is secondary to the Synoptic Gospels. See S. J. Gathercole, *The Composition of the Gospel of Thomas: Original Language and Influences* (SNTSMS 151; Cambridge: Cambridge University Press, 2012); idem, *The Gospel of Thomas: Introduction and Commentary* (TENTS 11; Leiden: Brill, 2014); M. S. Goodacre, *Thomas and the Gospels: The Case for Thomas's Familiarity with the Synoptics* (Grand Rapids: Eerdmans, 2012).

13. On this important text, see C. A. Evans, "Jesus and the Dead Sea Scrolls," in *The Dead Sea Scrolls after Fifty Years: A Comprehensive Assessment* (ed. Peter W. Flint and James C. VanderKam; Leiden: Brill, 1999), 2:573–98, at 585–88.

14. See, e.g., J. R. Donahue and D. J. Harrington, *The Gospel of Mark* (Sacra Pagina 2; Collegeville, MN: Liturgical Press, 2002), 389, 391; J. R. Edwards, *The Gospel according to Mark* (PNTC; Grand Rapids: Eerdmans, 2002), 411–13; C. Focant, *The Gospel according to Mark: A Commentary* (trans. L. R. Keylock; Eugene, OR: Pickwick, 2012), 561–64.

In the end, the Jewish authorities sought to kill Jesus not because he was a good man, but because Jesus was perceived as a very serious political threat. His message of God's rule threatened the status quo, which the ruling priests did not want overturned. Jesus entered Jerusalem as the anointed son of David, he assumed authority in the temple precincts as though possessed of messianic authority, he appealed to the purpose of the temple in a way that recalled Solomon's dedication of the first temple and in a way that implied that he was Israel's king, and he was in fact anointed by at least one follower, an anointing that in all probability was interpreted as having messianic significance (however Jesus himself may have regarded it). It is hardly surprising that an angry high priest would directly ask Jesus, "Are you the Messiah, the Son of God?," and that the Roman governor would place a placard near the cross that read: "This is Jesus, king of the Jews."

Did Jesus Anticipate His Death?

Before considering the trial and execution of Jesus, we must ask if Jesus anticipated his death. Some critics insist that he did not—that it took him by surprise or that he simply got caught up in a riot and was arrested along with others. I find this quite unlikely as a historical reading of the Gospels, for several reasons.

The obvious place to begin is with Jesus' formal predictions of his suffering and death (e.g., Mark 8:31; 9:31; 10:32–34, among others). Of course, many critical scholars claim these passion predictions are prophecies after the fact, or what are sometimes called *vaticinia ex eventu* ("prophecies from the event"). It must be admitted that these predictions have a formulaic appearance and contain details (such as being mocked, spit upon, and scourged) that suggest knowledge of what in the end actually happened to Jesus. But even if it is acknowledged that the passion predictions have been edited or further stylized in the light of what actually happened to Jesus, that does not necessarily mean that he did not anticipate his death, even death specifically by crucifixion. What is the evidence outside the formal passion predictions that would suggest that Jesus really did anticipate suffering and death?[15]

First, I think it is probable that Jesus anticipated his death, for the violent fate of John the Baptist surely impressed itself on him (Matt 11:2–15; Mark 6:14–29; 9:13). It would be strange to think that it never occurred to Jesus that what had happened to his ally John might happen to him. In fact, Jesus may well have drawn this comparison and conclusion himself and spoken of it. In a saying whose wording

15. I set forth the evidence in C. A. Evans, "Did Jesus Predict His Death and Resurrection?," in *Resurrection* (ed. S. E. Porter, M. A. Hayes, and D. Tombs; JSNTSup 186; RILP 5; Sheffield: Sheffield Academic, 1999), 82–97; idem, "The Last Days of Jesus' Life: Did Jesus Anticipate the Cross?," in *The Gospels: History and Christology: The Search of Joseph Ratzinger–Benedict XVI—I Vangeli: Storia e Cristologia: La ricerca di Joseph Ratzinger–Benedetto XVI* (ed. B. Estrada, E. Manicardi, and A. Puig i Tàrrech; Vatican City: Libreria Editrice Vaticana, 2013), 511–27. See also H. F. Bayer, *Jesus' Predictions of Vindication and Resurrection: The Provenance, Meaning and Correlation of the Synoptic Predictions* (WUNT II/20; Tübingen: Mohr Siebeck, 1986).

and context admittedly are not easy to interpret, Jesus spoke of John the Baptist as Elijah, who "had come" but was not treated with respect. Jesus, who had already directly linked his own ministry with John's, suggested that, by analogy, the same fate also awaited him. He too would "suffer many things and be treated with contempt" (Mark 9:11–13). Accordingly, the execution of John very likely suggested to Jesus that the same fate might well overtake him.

Second, and what I think is impressive evidence that Jesus anticipated his death, is the scene in Gethsemane. Here we see the frightened Jesus fall on his face, begging God to take away the cup of suffering (Mark 14:33–36). This is not the stuff of pious fiction or theological dogma. Indeed, it stands in stark contrast to the serene Jesus portrayed in John 17, where he communed with God in peace, prayed for his disciples, and added a prayer for all those who later would follow after him.

What makes the Gethsemane scene compelling evidence is that Jesus' words and frightened behavior stand in tension with his earlier teaching in which he exhorted his disciples to "take up the cross" and follow him (Mark 8:34). In view of a teaching such as this, it is hard to see how a story such as the Gethsemane prayer could circulate and find its way into the Gospel tradition if it were not based on solid, credible eyewitness testimony. It would simply be too harmful for Jesus' identity if it was not true.

Third, if Jesus anticipated his death, we should expect that he attempted to find meaning in it during his life. And, in fact, that is the case. The widely attested "Words of Institution" (Mark 14:22–25; 1 Cor 11:23–25; *Did.* 9.1–5) provide further evidence that Jesus anticipated his death and sought to understand it. His words allude to several important scriptures (Exod 24:8; Jer 31:31; Zech 9:11). In the shedding of his blood, Jesus found guarantee of the covenant and the kingdom of God. Luke's addition of "new" in the phrase "the new covenant" (Luke 22:20) may well reflect Christian editing for clarification, but in all probability it correctly captures the sense of Jesus' words.[16] The "new covenant" harkens back to the promise of the prophet long ago: "The days are surely coming, says the Lord, when I will make a new covenant with the house of Israel and the house of Judah" (Jer 31:31). The new covenant cannot be established until the blood of God's Son, Israel's Messiah, is shed.

The idea of the saving benefit of a righteous man's death was hardly unusual in the Jewish world, or in the Mediterranean world in general, for that matter. Several texts express the belief that the death of the righteous will benefit, or even save, God's people (e.g., 1 Macc 6:44; 4 Macc 1:11; 17:21–22; 18:3–4; *T. Mos.* 9–10; Ps.-Philo, *Biblical Antiquities* 18:5).[17] Among the most important are traditions associated with

16. On the other hand, the appearance of "new" (καινή) in the earlier version in 1 Cor 11:25 argues for the originality of the adjective.

17. M. Hengel, *The Atonement: The Origins of the Doctrine in the New Testament* (Philadelphia: Fortress, 1981); W. Horbury and B. McNeil, eds., *Suffering and Martyrdom in the New Testament: Studies Presented to G. M. Styler by the Cambridge New Testament Seminar* (Cambridge: Cambridge University Press, 1981); J. W. van Henten and F. Avemarie, *Martyrdom and Noble Death: Selected Texts from Graeco-Roman, Jewish and Christian Antiquity* (London: Routledge, 2002).

the torture and death of the Maccabean martyrs, who in the second century BCE bravely opposed the Syrian tyrant Antiochus IV:

> And if our living Lord is angry for a little while, to rebuke and discipline us, he will again be reconciled with his own servants. . . . I, like my brothers, give up body and life for the laws of our ancestors, appealing to God to show mercy soon to our nation . . . and *through me and my brothers* to bring to an end the wrath of the Almighty that has justly fallen on our whole nation. (2 Macc 7:33, 37–38, NRSV, with emphasis added)

Similarly, Jesus believed that God was angry with his people for having rejected his message. We see this in Jesus' weeping over the city (Luke 19:41–44; Matt 23:37–39 = Luke 13:34–35) and in his ominous allusion to the shepherd in Zech 13:7, whom God will strike down.

If Jesus did anticipate his death, then one might also ask, did he anticipate his resurrection as well? It would have been very strange if he had not anticipated being raised after death, for many pious Jews very much believed in the resurrection (Dan 12:1–3; *1 En.* 22–27; 92–105; *Jub.* 23:11–31; 4 Macc 7:3; 4 Ezra 7:26–42; *2 Bar.* 21:23; 30:2–5; Josephus, *J.W.* 2.154, 165–166; *Ant.* 18.14, 16, 18). One is reminded of the seven martyred sons and their mother, several of whom expressed their firmest conviction of the resurrection (2 Macc 7:14, 23, 29; cf. 4 Macc 8–17).[18] Would Jesus have faced death and then, having earlier affirmed his belief in the resurrection (Mark 12:18–27), have expressed no faith in his own vindication? Surely not. It seems probable that Jesus would have reassured his disciples (and himself) with a confident prediction of his resurrection.

The words of Jesus "after three days rise again" (Mark 8:31) and—in the other Gospels—"on the third day" (Matt 16:21; Luke 9:22; cf. 1 Cor 15:4) probably allude to the oracle of Hosea that promised the renewal of Israel: "After two days he will revive us; on the third day he will raise us up, that we may live before him" (6:2). This is refracted, however, through the Aramaic tradition: "He will revive us *in the days of consolations that will come; on the day of the resurrection of the dead* he will raise us up and we shall live before him" (Hos 6:2, according to the targum, with italicized portion indicating the distinctive reading of the Aramaic). Not only has the text been paraphrased to give expression to the resurrection (which was not exactly the original meaning of the underlying Hebrew), it has also taken on a messianic nuance with the words "in the days of consolations" (cf. 2 Sam 23:1 in the Aramaic). The coherence of Jesus' words with the Aramaic tradition is striking.[19] Jesus' confidence that God would raise him up provides additional evidence that Jesus in all probability did anticipate his death.

---

18. For discussion of these texts in reference to the hope of resurrection, see G. W. E. Nickelsburg, *Resurrection, Immortality and Eternal Life in Intertestamental Judaism* (HTS 26; Cambridge: Harvard University Press, 1972), esp. 106–8; J. W. van Henten, *The Maccabean Martyrs as Saviours of the Jewish People: A Study of 2 and 4 Maccabees* (JSJSup 57; Leiden: Brill, 1997), 172–84; N. T. Wright, "Jesus' Resurrection and Christian Origins," *Greg* 83 (2002): 615–35.

19. For details, see Evans, *Mark 8:27–16:20*, 16–18.

The Trial of Jesus

Since the nineteenth century, the trial of Jesus has been hotly debated, often with reference to Christian anti-Semitism. Some scholars have argued that the trial of Jesus was entirely a Roman affair, while others have asserted that it was mostly a Jewish affair. Today, most scholars rightly recognize the involvement of both Jewish and Roman authorities.[20]

All four New Testament Gospels relate appearances of Jesus before Jewish and Roman authorities, who to one degree or another work in concert. According to Mark, Jesus is arrested by people acting under the authority of the ruling priests, scribes, and elders (14:43–50). Jesus is taken to the high priest (14:53). Jewish authorities then gather at "the courtyard of the high priest" (14:54), which may imply that the proceedings took place at the home of Caiaphas, though that is only an inference. The ruling priests and council seek testimony against Jesus (14:55–56). Various accusations are made, including Jesus' threat against the temple (14:57–58; cf. 13:1–2). When Jesus confesses that he is indeed the Messiah, the Son of God, who will be seated at the right hand of Power, he is accused of blasphemy and condemned as deserving death (14:61–64).[21] The following morning, the Jewish authorities deliver Jesus to Pilate, the Roman prefect of Judea and Samaria (15:1). Pilate questions Jesus ("Are you king of the Jews?") and offers to release him, as part of the governor's traditional "Passover Pardon" (15:2–14). The crowd requests the release of Barabbas and calls for Jesus' death, whereupon Pilate gives Jesus up to be crucified (15:15).

There are distinctive elements in the other Gospels that further flesh out these events. The noticeable addition in Matthew is seen in the reference to the disturbing dream Pilate's wife had, warning the governor to "have nothing to do with that innocent man" (27:19). The Matthean version of the trial before Pilate ends with the governor washing his hands and declaring that he is "innocent of this man's blood" (27:24), to which the crowd responds with the fateful words, "His blood be on us and on our children!" (27:25). Luke's version of the trial before Pilate exhibits a few more distinctive features. Jesus is accused of forbidding the payment of tribute or taxes to Caesar (23:2) and of stirring up the people (23:5). The evangelist also adds the interesting account of Herod Antipas meeting Jesus and of Pilate and Herod's newfound friendship (23:6–12). Luke also strongly emphasizes the innocence of Jesus (23:20–25). The innocent Jesus stands in stark contrast to the murderer Barabbas, whose release the crowd demands.

---

20. A. N. Sherwin-White, *The Trial of Christ: Historicity and Chronology in the Gospels* (London: SPCK, 1965); B. D. Chilton, "The Trial of Jesus Reconsidered," in B. D. Chilton and C. A. Evans, *Jesus in Context: Temple, Purity, and Restoration* (AGJU 39; Leiden: Brill, 1997), 481–500.

21. The accusation of blasphemy—a charge not likely invented by Christians who passed on the Jesus story—is very significant. See C. A. Evans, "In What Sense 'Blasphemy'? Jesus before Caiaphas in Mark 14:61–64," in *Society of Biblical Literature 1991 Seminar Papers* (ed. E. H. Lovering Jr.; SBLSP 30; Atlanta: Scholars Press, 1991), 215–34; D. L. Bock, *Blasphemy and Exaltation in Judaism and the Final Examination of Jesus: A Philological-Historical Study of the Key Jewish Themes Impacting Mark 14:61–64* (WUNT II/106; Tübingen: Mohr Siebeck, 1998).

The trial of Jesus, especially before Pilate, is quite distinctive in the Fourth Gospel.[22] When arrested, Jesus is taken to Annas, a former high priest and father-in-law of Caiaphas, the current high priest (18:12–13). While being questioned, Jesus is struck (18:22–23). Thereafter, Jesus is sent to Caiaphas (18:24) and from there to the Roman Praetorium (18:28). Here the Fourth Gospel differs noticeably from the Synoptic Gospels, in that nothing is said of any interrogation or exchange between Caiaphas and Jesus. But the most distinctive feature of the trial of Jesus in the Gospel of John is the dialogue between Pilate and Jesus (18:29–38), in which Jesus declares that his kingdom "is not from this world" (18:36) and Pilate asks, "What is truth?" (18:38). From a theological point of view, perhaps the most important feature is the emphasis on the legal point that the Jewish authorities were not allowed to execute anyone (18:31–32). This meant that the Romans would execute Jesus, which given the charge of claiming kingship also meant crucifixion (and, therefore, Jesus would be "lifted up"; cf. 12:32). A theological interpretation of being "lifted up" on the cross may have served an apologetic purpose, mitigating the embarrassment of execution at the hands of the Roman authorities.

The trial of Jesus is mentioned in passing elsewhere in the New Testament. In the Pentecost sermon, Peter refers to Jesus as "a man attested to you by God with deeds of power, wonders, and signs that God did through him among you, as you yourselves know—this man, handed over to you according to the definite plan and foreknowledge of God, you crucified and killed by the hands of those outside the law" (Acts 2:22–23). Peter's "you" refers to the Jewish people (cf. Acts 2:14), while "those outside the law" doubtless refers to the Roman authorities. The point is made again in the Temple sermon, where Peter this time accuses fellow Jews: "God . . . has glorified his servant Jesus, whom you handed over and rejected in the presence of Pilate . . . and you killed the Author of life" (Acts 3:13–15). Peter's accusations presuppose (rightly) the collaboration between Jewish and Roman authorities in examining and condemning Jesus. We hear this again in Acts as part of an interpretation of Ps 2, which asks why the nations plot against the Lord and his Anointed. The apostles in prayer declare that "in this city, in fact, both Herod and Pontius Pilate, with the Gentiles and the peoples of Israel, gathered together against your holy servant Jesus, whom you anointed" (Acts 4:27). This theme is echoed in a sermon attributed to Paul: "Even though they found no cause for a sentence of death, they asked Pilate to have him killed" (Acts 13:27). Also, in one of the Pastoral Letters, the author charges his readers "in the presence of God, who gives life to all things, and of Christ Jesus, who in his testimony before Pontius Pilate made the good confession" (1 Tim 6:13).

According to the Gospels, Jesus was arrested at night, more or less in private, while in prayer at a place on the Mount of Olives called Gethsemane. Mark describes the arresting group as "a crowd with swords and clubs, from the chief

---

22. For a probing of historical material in John's passion narrative, see C. H. Dodd, *Historical Tradition in the Fourth Gospel* (Cambridge: Cambridge University Press, 1963), 21–151, as well as several essays in part 3 of P. N. Anderson, F. Just, and T. Thatcher, eds., *John, Jesus, and History*, vol. 2, *Aspects of Historicity in the Fourth Gospel* (SBL ECL 2; Atlanta: SBL Press, 2009).

priests, the scribes, and the elders" (14:43).[23] This group knew where to find Jesus because of information received from Judas Iscariot and because Judas himself had led them to Jesus (Mark 14:10–11, 43–45). Both of these details—men sent by the ruling priests armed with weapons and priests offering bribes—are in a general sense corroborated by Josephus, who tells of similar actions taken by the most powerful of the ruling priests in the first century.[24]

Exactly where Jesus was taken the evening of his arrest is not clear. Mark says he was taken to the high priest (14:53; followed by Luke 22:54), but this priest is not named. Matthew identifies him as Caiaphas (26:57).[25] The Fourth Evangelist complicates things by saying that "first they took him to Annas, who was the father-in-law of Caiaphas" (John 18:13a). Annas is called "high priest" (18:19), even though it was his son-in-law who was actually in office "that year," that is, the year of Jesus' execution (18:13b). According to the Fourth Gospel, Annas interrogated Jesus and then sent him to Caiaphas (18:24). Either the Synoptics did not know of this visit to Annas, or they chose to omit it.[26]

The ensuing examination of Jesus before the Jewish authorities focused on two points: The allegation of a threat against the temple and the identity of Jesus. First, the testimony of the witnesses who said "We heard him say, 'I will destroy this temple that is made with hands, and in three days I will build another, not made with hands'" (Mark 14:58) alludes to Jesus' prophecy of coming judgment on Jerusalem and her temple. He implied this idea in his temple action (Mark 11:17) and in his vineyard parable (12:1–12), and he asserted it plainly in his prophecy (13:1–2). Accordingly, the testimony of these witnesses was not entirely false; Jesus said something to this effect (see also John 2:19). What makes their testimony false, though, is that Jesus warned of judgment *at God's hands, not at his.* Jesus had no plans to destroy and rebuild Jerusalem's temple. But he warned that God would destroy it if his people, especially the ruling priesthood, did not repent.

What brings the hearing before the Jewish council to a dramatic conclusion is Jesus' confession. The high priest asks him: "Are you the Messiah, the Son of the Blessed One?" (Mark 14:61). As we have seen, he has every reason to ask this question. Jesus' entry into the city, the shouts of the crowd, his audacious behavior in the temple precincts, and the report of his anointing all point to a messianic self-understanding. Even his ministry of healing and exorcism could be understood as paralleling the remarkable stories about the famous King Solomon. To the high

23. According to the Fourth Gospel, Jesus was approached by "a detachment of soldiers together with police from the chief priests and the Pharisees" (John 18.3).

24. Josephus uses colorful language to describe the ruling priests and their thuggish servants (*Ant.* 20.205–207: "servants who were utter rascals"; 213: "using his wealth to attract those who were willing to receive bribes"). What Josephus says is echoed in the rabbinic tradition (*t. Menaḥ.* 13:18–19, 21, "their servants come and beat us with clubs").

25. For helpful background, context, and interpretation of the relevant texts, see Bond, *Caiaphas: Friend of Rome and Judge of Jesus?*

26. The large mansions that have been excavated in Jerusalem indicate that large, extended families lived together. It is probable that Annas and Caiaphas lived in the same complex.

priest's question Jesus replies boldly: "I am; and 'you will see the Son of man seated at the right hand of the Power,' and 'coming with the clouds of heaven'" (14:62). Jesus' reply combines two Old Testament passages, both concerned with judgment. The words "Son of man" and "coming with the clouds of heaven" are taken from Dan 7:13, while the words "seated at the right hand" are drawn from Ps 110:1. Both Dan 7 and Ps 110 envision scenes in which God's enemies will be judged. Though our contemporary ears may not rightly hear the audacity of Jesus' claim, the high priest clearly does and he condemns Jesus for it, not only for his daring claim to be God's anointed Son, but also for implying that he will sit in judgment on the high priest, as though the latter were an enemy of God. Indeed, the language of Jesus hints at his divinity.[27] It is hardly surprising that Jesus' bold reply is met with shouts of blasphemy and calls for his death (14:63–65).

The same morning, the Jewish authorities confer and decide to send Jesus to Pilate, the Roman governor. The ball is now in Pilate's court. The Jewish rulers have decided. From this point on, all they can do is cheer or jeer from the sidelines.

But before we turn to Jesus' trial before Pilate, one thing needs to be made crystal clear: The Jewish people should never be blamed for the condemnation and death of Jesus. Not only is such an accusation bad theology, it is bad history. Historically speaking, Jesus was condemned by a very small number of influential Jewish men. He was not condemned by the people as a whole. Even those who cried out for his crucifixion later in the day were but a relatively small number. Theologically speaking, Jesus died for the sins of the whole human race. In that sense, we all sent him to the cross. No one particular people should be blamed. Now on to Pilate.

According to all four Gospels, the focus of Pilate's examination of Jesus was on the allegation that Jesus had presented himself as the king of the Jews (Mark 15:2; Matt 27:11; Luke 23:3; John 18:33). This appears to be confirmed by Jesus' crucifixion as "king of the Jews" (Mark 15:18, 26, with parallels in the other Gospels). It has been persuasively argued that such an epithet was no Christian creation, confessional or otherwise. Christians regarded Jesus as the Messiah (or Christ), Son of God, Lord, and Savior, but not "king of the Jews," a title the Roman Senate granted to Herod the Great (cf. Josephus, *J.W.* 1.282; *Ant.* 14.36; 15.373, 409; 16.291).

I doubt that under normal circumstances Pilate would have had much hesitation in executing a troublemaker. But the occasion of Jesus' execution was the eve of Passover, the holiest of the Jewish holidays. Worse yet, Passover celebrated God's deliverance of his people from foreign bondage. Pilate would certainly have made this connection in knowing the workings of the people he ruled over. Though he did not lack in desire to demonstrate his and Rome's power, sustaining his position as governor of this region and keeping the *pax romana* ("Roman peace") at times required greater precision and acumen. Did he really want to put to death a popular prophet and healer on the eve of the Passover, just outside the walls of Jerusalem? Perhaps a beating or imprisonment would suffice. Let the people decide.

---

27. C. A. Evans, "Jesus' Self-Designation 'The Son of Man' and the Origins of His Deification," in *The Trinity: An Interdisciplinary Symposium on the Trinity* (ed. S. T. Davis, D. Kendall, and G. F. O'Collins; Oxford: Oxford University Press, 1999), 29–47.

The Offer of a Passover Pardon

All four New Testament Gospel writers know of Pilate's so-called Passover Pardon (Mark 15:6–15; Matt 27:15–23; Luke 23:18–25; John 19:10–12). Although some critical scholars have cast doubts on the historicity of this tradition, it is improbable that inauthentic tradition, whose falsity could so readily be exposed, would be utilized by all four evangelists. Besides, there are other accounts, which are not questioned, of Roman and other officials releasing prisoners on the occasions of special days. For example, the Roman historian Livy (ca. 25 BCE) speaks of special cases in which prisoners were released (*History of Rome* 5.13.8). Josephus reports that Herod's son Archelaus, as the newly appointed ethnarch of Judea and Samaria (4 BCE), acquiesced to popular demands to release many prisoners (Josephus, *Ant.* 17.204). Josephus also says that Albinus, procurator of the whole of Herod's former kingdom (62–64 CE), released many prisoners as he prepared to leave office, something akin to a "last-minute" presidential pardon. One official document dating from the year 85 CE reads: "You were worthy of scourging . . . but I give you to the crowds" (P.Florence 61). Here, a Roman official foregoes scourging a criminal, which was often a prelude to crucifixion, and releases the offender. In a slightly different scenario, Pliny the Younger, governor of Bithynia and Pontus (in Asia Minor) in the days of the emperor Trajan (ca. 110 CE), refers to pardons for criminals whereby "these people were released upon their petition to the proconsuls, or their lieutenants" (*Epistles* 10.31). Finally, in the Mishnah (ca. 200 CE), the edited and published collection of Jewish oral law, it is said that "they may slaughter [the Passover lamb] for one . . . whom they have promised to bring out of prison" on the Passover (*m. Pesaḥ.* 8:6).[28]

The evidence as a whole suggests that Roman rulers, as well as at least one Herodian prince, on occasion released prisoners (and so, apparently, did other rulers in the eastern Mediterranean).[29] This was done for purely political reasons, to satisfy the demands of the crowds and to curry their favor. The Passover Pardon, therefore, reflected Pilate's shrewd political instincts, not political weakness or human kindness. The Passover Pardon was intended to show Roman respect for the great Jewish holiday, in effect to say, "In keeping with your celebration of freedom from bondage we shall set free anyone of your choosing." The tradition of the Passover Pardon gave Pilate the opportunity to pass responsibility for the fate of Jesus onto the shoulders of his accusers. "If they so badly want him dead," Pilate reasoned, "then let them take responsibility for passing judgment." Pilate was neither cowardly nor principled. He was a politician and he was clever.[30]

28. For further discussion of the Passover Pardon, see E. Bammel, "The Trial before Pilate," in *Jesus and the Politics of His Day* (ed. E. Bammel and C. F. D. Moule; Cambridge: Cambridge University Press, 1984), 415–51, esp. 425–28; Evans, *Mark 8:27–16:20*, 479–82.

29. For additional background with respect to the Roman world and the Middle East, see R. L. Merritt, "Jesus Barabbas and the Paschal Pardon," *JBL* 104 (1985): 57–68. I do not, however, agree with Merritt's interpretation of Pilate's offer of pardon in the Gospel of Mark.

30. Bond, *Pontius Pilate in History and Interpretation.*

Another factor that supports the historicity of the Passover Pardon is the improbability that the existence of such a custom would have been asserted if there had in fact been none. If Pilate had not released prisoners on the Passover or on other holidays, or at least on one occasion, the evangelists' claim that he did so could have quickly and easily been shown to be false and would therefore have occasioned embarrassment for, or even have discredited altogether, the early church. That all three of the later evangelists took over the story (and the Fourth Evangelist probably did so independently of the Synoptic Gospels) argues that no such embarrassment clung to the story.

Knowing, then, that Jesus had been handed over to him on account of envy and fear, Pilate trod carefully.[31] Before condemning Jesus to death, he sought, in essence, a plebiscite, a decree from the people. Did the people really want Jesus executed, or was it only the few ruling priests who brought the charges and demanded his death? There was no interest in justice here; only politics were at work. Pilate probably knew that Jesus was popular. He was not about to risk offending the populace, especially at Passover season, and so instigate a riot. This was the very thing he wished to avoid. Some might challenge this interpretation by pointing to incidents in which Pilate seemed more than willing to use violence against his subjects. But in these cases, Pilate was defending his own actions. In the case of Jesus, Pilate had nothing at stake other than maintaining the peace.

As the scene unfolds, the ruling priests urge the crowd to call for the release of Jesus bar Abba—not Jesus of Nazareth (Mark 15:11–15). They have vigorously lobbied the governor; now they vigorously lobby the crowd. From their point of view, the danger that Jesus of Nazareth would be released is a very real one. After all, Jesus is known as a popular teacher and healer, and leads no army. He is therefore not an obvious threat to Rome. At most, he is guilty of speaking of a coming kingdom of God and of having a key role in it—things not too different from visions and dreams of others. Perhaps it would be politically more expedient to release him than make a martyr of him. Hence, the ruling priests encouraged the crowd to call for the release of bar Abba, or Barabbas.[32] *(See fig. 8.2.)*

If Jesus of Nazareth is not to be released, then what shall the governor do with him? The alternatives are fairly obvious—either execution or imprisonment. But Pilate forces the crowd to make the decision. This way, he can "wash his hands" (literally in Matt 27:24) of the matter. Politically, Pilate has acted shrewdly and entirely in keeping with his character as we know it from unsympathetic sources (e.g., Philo and Josephus). Once again "they," that is the crowd (cf. Mark 15:11), as well as the ruling priests themselves, shout their demands to Pilate. They shout for the release of Barabbas, but in reference to Jesus they shout "Crucify him!" They do not want prison for Jesus; they want the ultimate penalty: crucifixion. The death of Jesus will hopefully end his movement and fatally discourage his closest followers.

31. See McGing, "Pontius Pilate and the Sources," 416–38; Bond, *Pontius Pilate in History and Interpretation*, 196–202.

32. On noisy crowds clamoring before a Roman authority, see Acts 24:1; Josephus, *Ant.* 18.264–273.

In asking "Why, what evil has he done?" (Mark 15:14), Pilate commits no "tactical blunder," as one commentator suggests,[33] nor is his answer "feeble," as another has supposed.[34] The governor is happy to accommodate the ruling priests' recommendation that Jesus be put to death—as long as in doing so he involves no political risks. His only concern is that his condemnation of Jesus not provoke the Jewish people or be seen as yet another example of Roman brutality. Pilate is not about to create a problem for himself. He wishes only to extricate himself from responsibility (as also does the Roman proconsul Gallio in Corinth, who judges the controversy set before him as a Jewish dispute and not one that falls under his jurisdiction; cf. Acts 18:12–17).[35] If the crowd insists that Jesus be crucified, Pilate would like to know why and he would like for them to announce it publicly.

Not wishing to provoke the crowd, Pilate ultimately releases Barabbas (Mark 15:15). Again, this maneuver does not show weakness. Indeed, in this case Pilate wishes not to offend his *allies* the ruling priests. In his other controversies, the Roman governor came into conflict with the "rabble" or commoners, not the ruling priests. What he has done here is to accede to the wishes of the ruling priests, but not until he is satisfied that to do so is not a mistake. Having released Barabbas to the people, Pilate hands Jesus over to the Roman troops who will carry out the crucifixion.

The Gospels' portrait of Pilate as wavering, wishing to release Jesus but finally acquiescing to the demands of Jerusalem's influential elite, has often been questioned. Many assume that this portrait grew out of apologetic interests, in a desire to present Jesus and early Christianity on the side of Rome. It was the Jewish leaders, after all, not the Roman governor, who desired Jesus' death—so goes the argument. That the evangelists literarily exploited the story of the wavering, uncertain Pilate is quite probable, but their wholesale invention of this portrait is quite doubtful. When we remember the political and social setting of Jewish Palestine in the time of Pilate, we should not be surprised that Pilate was reluctant to execute in such a public and provocative manner a popular prophet from Galilee, whose many followers were present in Jerusalem. Nailing Jesus to a cross could very well have instigated a riot, the very thing Pilate hoped to avoid. If Jesus had no military intentions, then he was little more than a pest. A beating and some jail time would have sufficed (as actually happened in the case of Jesus ben Ananias in Jerusalem in the early 60s; cf. *J.W.* 6.300–309). But no, the ruling priests wanted him dead. Pilate obliged, but only when it had been made clear that the decision to have Jesus executed was not really his.

The Mockery of Jesus

Oftentimes crucifixion victims were mocked, before and during execution. In the case of Jesus, his mockery began with the Jewish council. His face was covered and he was ordered to "prophesy" (Mark 14:65). After all, if he had truly been a prophet,

33. W. L. Lane, *The Gospel of Mark* (NICNT; Grand Rapids: Eerdmans, 1974), 556.
34. V. Taylor, *The Gospel According to St. Mark* (London: Macmillan, 1952), 583.
35. See Fitzmyer, *The Acts of the Apostles*, 629–30.

he would have possessed clairvoyance and, without benefit of sight, could have identified those who struck him. No doubt the officers and thugs employed by the ruling priests found it all quite amusing.

The soldiers under the command of Governor Pilate also mocked Jesus, this time reflecting the Roman fashion: "And they clothed him in a purple cloak; and after twisting some thorns into a crown, they put it on him. And they began saluting him, 'Hail, King of the Jews!' They struck his head with a reed, spat upon him, and knelt down in homage to him" (Mark 15:17–19). The soldiers' mockery was modeled after the homage paid to Caesar. The crown of thorns, meant to resemble a wreath of laurel worn by Caesar, was part of the mockery of Jesus, as were a purple cloak, a reed (symbolizing the scepter), and Jesus' being addressed as a king (Mark 15:18–19). The offer of spiced vinegar to the dying Jesus was also probably part of the ongoing mockery (Mark 15:23; Luke 23:36), in that this drink mimicked spiced wine, which was often served to kings. Sources from late antiquity describe others mocked in a similar fashion.

The mockery of Jesus as a Jewish king finds an approximate parallel in Philo, an older contemporary. The mockery in question occured on the occasion of King Agrippa's visit to Alexandria, when the people seized a lunatic named Carabas, a street person who was often made sport of (*Flaccus* 36–39). According to Philo, they

> drove the poor fellow into the gymnasium and set him up high to be seen by all and put on his head a sheet of byblus spread out wide for a diadem, clothed the rest of his body with a rug for a royal robe, while someone who had noticed a piece of the native papyrus thrown away in the road gave it to him for his scepter. And when as in some theatrical farce he had received the insignia of kingship and had been tricked out as a king, young men carrying rods on their shoulders as spearmen stood on either side of him in imitation of a bodyguard. Then others approached him, some pretending to salute him, others to sue for justice, others to consult him on state affairs. Then from the multitudes there rang out a tremendous shout hailing him as *Mari* [Aramaic: "my lord"], which is said to be the name for "lord" with the Syrians.

The mockery of Carabas (though Agrippa I was the real object) is quite significant, since it illustrates well the kind of mockery to which Jesus was subjected. It does not, however, require us to conclude that Mark and the other evangelists were dependent in some way on this incident or on Philo's work itself. Other incidents approximate the mockery of Jesus. One thinks of the harsh and humiliating treatment of Vitellius (69 CE) at the hands of Roman soldiers, who mockingly made this deposed emperor revisit various stations where at one time he was held in honor (cf. Dio Cassius, *Roman History* 64.20–21); now the honor was turned to shame and mockery.

The mockery of Jesus also mimics aspects of the Roman triumph, whereby Caesar was hailed as emperor and received homage. The purple cloak, the crown of thorns (resembling the crown of ivy), the reed with which Jesus was struck on the head, and the bowing in mock homage were all components of the apparel worn and homage received by the Roman emperor, who at the triumph wore a purple robe and laurel wreath and held a scepter (e.g., Dio Cassius, *Roman History* 6.23;

44.11 [Julius Caesar]; Appian, *Civil Wars* 5.130 [Augustus]; Dio Cassius, *Roman History* 59.25.3 [Gaius Caligula]). Being dressed in purple would have also recalled the attire of Hellenistic kings of an earlier period (cf. 1 Macc 10:20 ["purple robe and golden crown"], 62 ["clothe him in purple"]; 11:58 ["to dress in purple"]; 14:43–44 ["clothed in purple"]; cf. Luke 16:19 ["dressed in purple"]).[36]

We think too of the savage and humiliating treatment of the Maccabean martyr Eleazar, who was stripped, scourged, tortured, and then in his dying breath prayed for the salvation of Israel (4 Macc 6:1–30). One is also reminded of the deposition recording the words of the new emperor Hadrian and a Jewish embassy with reference to the Jewish revolt that occurred toward the end of Trajan's reign (115–117 CE). In this fragmentary document, mention is made of the mockery of a would-be monarch: "Paulus (spoke) about the king, how they brought him forth and (mocked him); and Theon read the edict of Lupus ordering them to lead him forth for Lupus to make fun of the king" (P.Louvre 68 1.1–7). Writing in the early second century CE, Plutarch relates a story in which pirates mocked a prisoner who had claimed the rights of Roman citizenship (*Pompey* 24.7–8). They dressed him up ("threw a toga on him"), extended to him various honors (including falling to their knees), then, finally, made him walk the plank.

Everything we are told about Jesus' arrest, trial(s), and mockery is consistent with what we know of Roman practice in the first century and with the political and social establishment of Judea in the time of Jesus. Although hyper-critics have called into question this and that detail, there is every reason to regard the Gospel accounts of the juridical process that overtook Jesus of Nazareth as essentially reliable. Most of the noted objections, then, amount to something other than valid historical reasoning.

The Crucifixion of Jesus

Jesus was put to death by crucifixion, a form of execution practiced in late antiquity whereby a person was tied or nailed to a pole or cross. To be crucified is, literally, to be "staked." Crucifixion was practiced in the eastern Mediterranean long before the Romans adopted the practice. It was practiced by the Persians (cf. Herodotus, *Histories* 1.128.2; 3.125.3) and other peoples, such as the Assyrians, Scythians, and Thracians. Alexander the Great is said to have crucified thousands (cf. Curtius Rufus, *History of Alexander* 4.4.17), and his successors continued the practice. It is not surprising, then, that in time the Romans adopted this form of execution. It was primarily reserved for murderous or rebellious slaves (and for this reason was known as "slaves' punishment"; Latin: *servile supplicium*). Its primary purpose was to deter rebellion and keep slaves in line.[37]

---

36. For more on Roman aspects of the mockery of Jesus, see T. E. Schmidt, "Mark 15.16–32: The Crucifixion Narrative and the Roman Triumphal Procession," *NTS* 41 (1995): 1–18.

37. Chapman, *Ancient Jewish and Christian Perceptions of Crucifixion*; Cook, *Crucifixion in the Mediterranean World*. Though his work is dated, it is still worth consulting Hengel, *Crucifixion in the Ancient World*.

Some readers may not be aware that Jewish authorities before the Roman period also practiced crucifixion. Most notorious was Alexander Jannaeus (ruled 102–76 BCE), who, Josephus tells us, on one occasion crucified a large number of Pharisees who had opposed him and had allied themselves to a foreign enemy (*J.W.* 1.97–98; cf. *Ant.* 13.380). Josephus' testimony helps explain a reference in the Dead Sea Scrolls, specifically, in one of the *pesharim*, to the "Lion of Wrath" (understood to be Alexander Jannaeus) who "used to hang men alive" (4Q169 3–4, I, 7). This may well be in reference to the incident mentioned by Josephus. Indeed, the practice of crucifixion in Israel in late antiquity, whether by Jewish authorities or Roman authorities, influenced the understanding of Deut 21:22–23. As shown in ch. 6 above, the passage originally meant that the body of the executed man was to be hung on the tree, then taken down and buried before nightfall. But by the time of Jesus, the passage was understood to apply also to those hung while still alive, a practical alteration that reflects the common practice of crucifixion.

As a prelude to his crucifixion, Jesus was scourged (Mark 15:15). Scourging was apparently standard pre-crucifixion procedure in Roman times (cf. *Digesta* 48.19.8.3; Josephus, *J.W.* 2.306). It was done with a whip made of several leather straps, to which were attached sharp, abrasive items, such as nails, glass, or rocks. Scourging resulted in severe laceration of the skin and damage to the flesh beneath. Jesus son of Ananias should be mentioned again. His prophecies of Jerusalem's doom resulted in his being brought before the Roman governor. Although in the end this man was not executed (as the ruling priests wished), he was "flayed to the bone with scourges" (*J.W.* 6.304), the same word used in reference to Jesus of Nazareth. Indeed, Jesus himself warned his followers that they too faced the danger of scourging (cf. Matt 10:17; 23:34).

Supporting the weakened state that Jesus would have been in (most immediately from the scourging), Mark 15:21 relates that the Romans "compelled a passer-by, who was coming in from the country, to carry his cross; it was Simon of Cyrene, the father of Alexander and Rufus."[38] The authenticity of this scene is supported by the observation that Jesus had earlier instructed his disciples to be ready and willing to take up the cross and come after him (Mark 8:34); that is, it is not likely that the early Christians would have invented a story about Jesus being unable to follow his own instruction to the letter.

Mark's reference to the names of Simon's sons, Alexander and Rufus, may suggest that these men were known to Mark's church. What we have here in Mark's narrative may well be eyewitness testimony, in which it was remembered that Jesus was beaten so severely he could not carry his cross, even though in earlier and happier times he had exhorted his own followers to be prepared to do so. Perhaps Simon and eventually his sons also became followers of the man whose cross Simon carried.

---

38. On the possibility that the ossuary of Simon's son Alexander has been found, see ch. 3 above.

Jesus eventually arrived at the place of execution and was crucified. The Gospels say that a *titulus*, or placard, was placed on the cross of Jesus (cf. John 19:19; Matt 27:37; Mark 15:26; Luke 23:38) and that the text on it, which described Jesus as "king of the Jews," was written in more than one language. The epithet "king of the Jews" is Roman and was originally applied to Herod the Great (cf. Josephus, *Ant.* 15.409: "the king of the Jews, Herod"). As mentioned already, this epithet did not originate in Christian circles, for Christians referred to Jesus with different titles. The significance of the *titulus* is that it confirms the messianic self-understanding of Jesus. Jesus had encouraged his disciples to regard him as Israel's anointed king, or, in the language of Rome, the "king of the Jews."

As a matter of custom, Roman authorities placed crosses along well-traveled highways, on the tops of hills, and at city gates. The condemned man usually carried the cross-beam, or *patibulum* (cf. Plautus, *Carbonaria* 2; *Miles gloriosus* 2.4.6–7 §359–360; Plutarch, *Moralia* 554A–B), sometimes with a *titulus* around his neck, declaring his name and punishment, later to be affixed to the upright cross (cf. Suetonius, *Caligula* 32.2; Dio Cassius, *Roman History* 54.3.6–7). This cruel punishment later also befell Christians. The fourth-century church historian and apologist Eusebius tells of a Christian named Attalus, who "was led around the amphitheatre and a placard was carried before him on which was written in Latin, 'This is Attalus, the Christian'" (*Ecclesiastical History* 5.1.44).

Normally crucifixion victims were left to die, however long that took (sometimes several days). The delay of death for victims of crucifixion is evident in that on occasion friends and relatives were allowed to feed their loved one (cf. Matt 27:34; Mark 15:23; John 19:28–29). It was typical protocol for guards to be stationed by the cross until the victim expired, in part due to possible attempts by friends or relatives to rescue the victim. The bodies of the crucified were usually left unburied, to rot and to be picked apart by birds and animals (though Roman law did permit bodies to be taken down and buried; cf. *Digesta* 48.24.1, 3; Josephus, *Life* 420–421).

According to Cicero (*Against Verres* 2.5.168) and Josephus (*J. W.* 7.203), crucifixion was the worst form of death (see also the disturbing comments in Juvenal, *Satires* 14.77–78; Suetonius, *Augustus* 13.1–2; Horace, *Epistles* 1.16.48; Seneca, *Dialogue* 3.2.2; 6.20.3; Isidore of Seville, *Etymologia* 5.27.34; *Mek.* on Exod 15:18 [*Shirata* §10]). Indeed, the words "cross" and "crucify" actually derive from the Latin word meaning "to torture," *cruciare*. The primary political and social purpose of crucifixion was deterrence: "Whenever we crucify the condemned, the most crowded roads are chosen, where the most people can see and be moved by this terror. For penalties relate not so much to retribution as to their exemplary effect" (Ps.-Quintilian, *Declamations* 274; cf. Aristophanes, *Thesmophoriazusae* 1029 and Ps.-Manetho, *Apotelesmatica* 4.198–200; Josephus, *J. W.* 5.450–451).

In the Gospels, the soldiers who crucify Jesus divide his garments among themselves (Matt 27:35; Mark 15:24; Luke 23:34; John 19:23–24). This is consistent with Roman practice (cf. *Digesta* 48.20.1). Tacitus, for example, tells us that "people sentenced to death forfeited their property" (*Annals* 6.29).

The Death of Jesus: History Seen through the Lens of Faith

The death of Jesus came suddenly and dramatically. According to the Synoptic Gospels (Matt 27:46a; Mark 15:34a; Luke 23:44), at about three in the afternoon Jesus suddenly cried out: "Eloi, Eloi, lama sabachthani?" (Mark 15:34b; cf. Matt 27:46b).[39] These Aramaic words, taken from Ps 22:1, mean "My God, my God, why have you forsaken me?" Interpreters are perplexed. How are these words to be understood?

The details of Ps 22 are echoed in various places in the passion narrative. Here, though, we have an explicit quotation, one that is on the lips of Jesus. Some wonder if Jesus had the whole psalm in mind, especially the concluding part that relates vindication and restoration:

> I will tell of your name to my brothers and sisters;
> in the midst of the congregation I will praise you. . . .
> For he did not despise or abhor the affliction of the afflicted;
> he did not hide his face from him,
> but heard when he cried to him. . . .
> Posterity will serve him;
> future generations will be told about the Lord,
> and proclaim his deliverance to a people yet unborn,
> saying that he has done it.
> (vv. 22, 24, 30–31, NRSV, modified according to the Hebrew)

Perhaps Jesus did have the whole of the psalm in mind, including the optimistic conclusion, but the reality of his sense of abandonment must not be minimized. Jesus had not lost his faith in God, as the twofold address "My God, my God" implies. However, he clearly felt utterly abandoned. It is not surprising that the later evangelists choose different concluding utterances: "Father, into your hands I commend my spirit!" (Luke 23:46); "It is finished" (John 19:30). The seemingly faith- and identity-denying words that Jesus uttered may well have been capitalized on by some seeking to discredit him and even avoided by those who followed after him. Again, except that they be historically true, these words are much too scandalous to report.

As he was staked to the cross, bystanders thought Jesus had called for Elijah (ἐλωΐ ["my God"], approximating the sound of Ελία [the vocative of Ελίας, "Elijah"]).[40] We are told that "someone ran, filled a sponge with sour wine, put it on a stick, and gave it to him to drink" (Mark 15:36). If this act was one of mockery, not of sympathy, the soldiers probably would not have hindered this person. "Let us see if Elijah comes" may have been part of the mockery and, if so, it parallels what the ruling priests said earlier: "Let the Messiah, the King of Israel [ὁ χριστὸς ὁ βασιλεὺς Ἰσραήλ], come down from the cross now, so that we may see and believe" (Mark 15:32).

---

39. Mark's Greek ἐλωΐ ἐλωΐ λεμὰ σαβαχθάνι appears to transliterate אלוהי אלוהי למא שבקתני. Matthew's transliteration, ἠλὶ ἠλὶ λεμὰ σαβάχθανι, may be a mix of Aramaic and Hebrew.

40. Matthew's ἠλί would more closely resemble Elijah's name.

It is possible that a sympathetic bystander raced up to Jesus to give him a stimulant to help keep him conscious long enough to see if Elijah would indeed appear, either in his eschatological role (as Jesus, it would have been assumed, hoped) or in his occasional role as assistant of the troubled and stricken. It is more probable, however, that the gesture was part of the mockery that had been going on since the conclusion of the hearing before the ruling priests (Mark 14:65). While on the cross, Jesus had been mocked as the one who threatened to destroy and rebuild the temple in three days (15:29), he had been invited to come down from the cross and so convince skeptics that he really was Israel's King Messiah (15:32), and now the mockers wished to "see if Elijah comes" in answer to Jesus' anguished cry.

The bystanders did not have long to wait. "Then Jesus gave a loud cry and breathed his last" (Mark 15:37). The act of shouting was itself the death. That is, Jesus did not shout out and then, a moment later, die. His death manifested itself *as a shout*. By telling it this way, the evangelist Mark, if not the tradition before him, shows that Jesus' very death displayed his power; the release of his spirit (as implied in the verb ἐξέπνευσεν) was awesome. The death of Jesus has been viewed through the lens of faith. It is not likely that others understood his death that way.

Stunned by what he had witnessed, the centurion declared, "Truly this man was God's Son!" (Mark 15:39). Impressed by the manner of Jesus' death and the signs that attended it, the Roman centurion confessed of Jesus what he should only confess of the Roman emperor: Jesus the crucified Messiah—not Caesar—is the "son of God." The mockery was now over. In calling Jesus the Son of God, the centurion switched his allegiance from Caesar, the official "son of God," to Jesus, the real Son of God. The centurion now ascribed to Jesus what he had earlier ascribed to Caesar: Caesar is not *divi filius* ("son of God," alluding to the Latin title of the great emperor Augustus), Jesus is.[41] At least this is what the words "Son of God" meant for the evangelist and other followers of Jesus.

The Burial of Jesus: Faith through the Lens of History

Critical discussion of the Gospel resurrection narratives suffers, in my estimation, from a lack of adequate acquaintance with Jewish traditions of death and burial, especially with respect to the burial of executed persons or persons who in some way died dishonorable deaths. It sometimes suffers too from wrong inferences from archaeological evidence and historical records. In a controversial book published two decades ago, a scholar suggested that Jesus' body—in keeping with Roman practice—probably was not taken down from the cross and given customary Jewish burial. It was suggested that Jesus' corpse was either left hanging on the cross, or,

41. On the meaning of the centurion's declaration, see W. T. Shiner, "The Ambiguous Pronouncement of the Centurion and the Shrouding of Meaning in Mark," *JSNT* 78 (2000): 3–22; T. H. Kim, "The Anarthrous υἱὸς θεοῦ in Mark 15,39 and the Roman Imperial Cult," *Bib* 79 (1998): 221–41.

at best, was cast into a ditch and covered with lime. In either case, his corpse was left exposed to birds and animals.[42] Jesus was not properly buried; the story of the empty tomb is no more than theology and apologetic legend.

The question of the empty tomb is important for critical assessment of the resurrection stories. If Jesus' earliest followers actually knew that Jesus had been buried and that his tomb was later found empty, it makes their proclamation that Jesus was *resurrected* (and not just a spirit) more intelligible. After all, there must have been compelling reason to speak of resurrection, instead of simply speaking of apparitions (which, given the culture, would have been believed more easily). Jews who believed in resurrection thought in terms of a general, eschatological resurrection, not the resurrection of an individual. The claim that Jesus was resurrected would have been viewed as problematic, even for his own followers.

That burial was extremely important to the Jewish people is not at issue; no one denies this. The evidence for it is seen in Israel's ancient Scriptures and in the more recent writings of late antiquity.[43] Explaining Jewish ethical obligations, Josephus states: "We must furnish fire, water, [and] food to all who ask for them, point out the road, not leave a corpse unburied [ἄταφον], [and] show consideration even to declared enemies" (*Ag. Ap.* 2.211; cf. 2.205).

Jews were concerned that the dead be properly buried out of compassion for both the deceased and their family and friends. But the most important motivation for proper burial of the dead was to avoid defilement of the land of Israel. This requirement is grounded in the Mosaic law: "And if a man has committed a crime punishable by death and he is put to death, and you hang him on a tree, his body shall not remain all night upon the tree, but you shall bury him the same day, for a hanged man is accursed by God; you shall not defile your land which the LORD your God gives you for an inheritance" (Deut 21:22–23). It is also expressed in Ezekiel: "They will set apart men to pass through the land continually and bury those remaining upon the face of the land, so as to cleanse it. . . . Thus shall they cleanse the land" (Ezek 39:14, 16).

This commitment to the purity of the land meant that even the executed, *including the crucified*, were to be buried properly. That this was the practice in Israel in the first century, during peacetime, is explicity stated by Josephus: "Jews are so careful about funeral rites that even malefactors who have been sentenced to crucifixion [καὶ τοὺς ἐκ καταδίκης ἀνεσταυρωμένους] are taken down and buried before sunset" (*J.W.* 4.317). The implications of this important statement need to be carefully considered.

Josephus is speaking of his own time (37 CE–ca. 100 CE), not some other period. In his time, only Rome had the authority to execute malefactors. Only Rome

42. Crossan, *Who Killed Jesus? Exposing the Roots of Anti-Semitism in the Gospel Story*, 160–88. The position that Crossan takes is restated, with a little more archaeological and historical nuance, in Crossan and Reed, *Excavating Jesus*, 230–70. More recently, it has been followed in Ehrman, *How Jesus Became God*, 157, 377n8.

43. For a fuller discussion of the relevant materials, see ch. 6 above. Some of this material will be briefly recapitulated here.

crucified people in Judea and Samaria in the time of Jesus.[44] Josephus himself knows this perfectly well. He tells us that after the removal of Herod's son Archelaus, ethnarc of Judea and Samaria, in 6 CE, "Coponius, one of the equestrian order among the Romans, was sent as a governor, having the authority to kill put into his hands by Caesar [τοῦ κτείνειν λαβὼν παρὰ Καίσαρος ἐξουσίαν]" (*J.W.* 2.117).[45] The authority to execute malefactors was no longer in local hands (i.e., Archelaus) but in the hands of the Roman governors. Coponius was the first of seven governors who served in the rank of prefect from 6 to 41 CE.[46]

Accordingly, when Josephus speaks of crucified malefactors being buried before sunset (that is, being buried the day of their crucifixion), he is speaking of malefactors crucified *by Romans*. Yet, these malefactors were buried, which implies that the Roman governor permitted them to be buried according to Jewish law and practice. Permission to bury the executed, including the crucified, is in keeping with what both Philo and Josephus state with regard to Roman respect for Jewish law and sensitivities. The former states that the Romans had not disturbed "the customs which throughout all the preceding ages had been safeguarded with disturbance by kings and by emperors" (*Embassy* 300). The latter agrees, adding that the Romans do not require "their subjects to violate their national laws" (*Ag. Ap.* 2.73) and that "by abstaining from all interference with the customs of the country [they] kept the nation at peace" (*J.W.* 2.220). Of course, one of the most important of these customs was the proper burial of a corpse (*J.W.* 2.11). Therefore, although Rome and Rome alone possessed capital power, the Jewish custom of burying the dead, even the executed, on the very day of death was respected.

Of course, there was one exception. An infraction within the Jerusalem temple precincts could lead to immediate execution. In this place and this place alone did Jewish rulers possess capital authority. Philo states that "death is inexorably pronounced against all those who enter into the inner circuit of the sacred precincts" (*Embassy* 212). Josephus also refers to this legal reality, in reference to the barriers and inscriptions warning Gentiles against trespass (Josephus, *J.W.* 5.193–194:

44. A. N. Sherwin-White, *Roman Society and Roman Law in the New Testament: The Sarum Lectures 1960–61* (Oxford: Oxford University Press, 1963), 36: "capital power was the most jealously guarded of all the attributes of government, not even entrusted to the principal assistants of the governors." Sherwin-White adds: "though the local city councils and sanhedrins could arrest and punish robbers and brigands with imprisonment, execution for these offences depended on the procurator" (p. 43).

45. The political reality of the first century is echoed in a later Talmudic tradition. In *b. Šabb.* 108a reference is made to the authority of "the Kingdom [מלכות]," i.e., Rome, to put someone to death. In this tradition, mention is made of "a certain Boethusian," meaning a member of the pre–70 CE aristocratic family of ruling priests, whose patriarch was a high priest named Boethos. In rabbinic literature, Boethusians are sometimes equated with Sadducees.

46. The prefects were Coponius (6–9 CE), Marcus Ambibulus (9–12 CE), Annius Rufus (12–15 CE), Valerius Gratus (15–26 or 15–19 CE), Pontius Pilate (26–36 or 19–36 CE), Marcellus (36–37 CE), and Marullus (37–41 CE). In 41 CE, Agrippa I (a.k.a. Herod Agrippa) was appointed "king of the Jews" and ruled over all of Israel (Galilee, Samaria, Judea, and other territories). After his death in 44 CE (cf. Acts 12:20–23; Josephus, *J.W.* 2.219; *Ant.* 19.343–350), Roman procurators were appointed who administered Israel alongside Agrippa II.

"slabs giving warning, some in Greek, some in Latin . . . that no foreigner was permitted to enter the holy place"; 6.124–126: "none may pass the barrier"; *Ant.* 15.417: "an inscription prohibiting the entrance of a foreigner under threat of the penalty of death").[47]

Annas the younger violated Roman capital authority when he condemned to death James the brother of Jesus and a few others. The Roman governor Festus had died and his replacement Albinus had not yet arrived. Annas was reprimanded by Agrippa II and was deposed (*Ant.* 20.200–203). It is possible that Annas believed his actions were within his jurisdiction: one recalls that according to widely held Christian tradition, James frequented the temple precincts and even entered the sanctuary (Hegesippus, *apud* Eusebius, *Ecclesiastical History* 2.23.6). In fact, according to tradition, it was in the precincts themselves that James was accused of blasphemy (ibid., 2.23.10–15) and was then flung from the "pinnacle of the temple" (however that is to be understood) into the ravine below (ibid., 2.23.16–18).[48] Whatever the case, the angry inhabitants of Jerusalem (mostly Christians?), King Agrippa II, and the newly arrived Roman governor Albinus believed that Annas had overstepped his authority and he was therefore removed from office (ibid., 2.23.21–24 [quoting Josephus]; Josephus, *Ant.* 20.200–203).

The incident involving James and Annas dramatically confirms that after the removal of Archelaus in 6 CE Rome alone possessed the "power to kill" in Judea. The Jewish high priest possessed this power only in the temple precincts and, evidently, only under carefully defined conditions. Outside of the precincts themselves, the high priest and the Jewish council (or Sanhedrin) did not possess capital authority. The action taken against James was deemed unlawful.

This is why the Jewish authorities say to Pontius Pilate, "It is not lawful for us to put any man to death" (John 18:31). Pilate had told the Jewish rulers to judge Jesus according to their law (much as Gallio would say to Jewish religious leaders in Corinth). This they did, but they could not execute Jesus; only Roman authority could.

We observe the same dynamics at work in the case of Jesus ben Ananias (*J.W.* 6.300–309). His prophecies regarding the impending doom of Jerusalem and her temple outraged the Jewish aristocracy. According to Josephus, the Jewish magistrates brought ben Ananias before Albinus the Roman governor (presumably

47. The descriptions of these warnings provided by Philo and Josephus have been confirmed by the discovery of two stone inscriptions (*OGIS* 598; *CIJ* 1400; *SEG* VIII 169; *CIIP* 2), one complete (housed in Istanbul) and one partial (housed in Jerusalem). For text, translation, and discussion, see Boffo, *Iscrizioni greche e latine*, 343–48; Evans, *Jesus and the Ossuaries*, 31–35; *CIIP* 2 (for text, image, discussion, and bibliography).

48. What is in mind is probably what Josephus was talking about when he describes the precincts' Royal Portico, which extended from the eastern ravine (the Kidron Valley) to the western ravine (the Tyropoeon Valley): "For while the depth of the [western] ravine was great, and no one who bent over to look into it from above could bear to look down to the bottom, the height of the portico standing over it was so very great that if anyone looked down from its rooftop, combining the two elevants, he would become dizzy and his vision would be unable to reach the end of so measureless a depth" (*Ant.* 15.412).

demanding that the man be put to death), but the governor found him harmless and released him.

Rome possessed capital power, but in all other matters Jewish laws and customs were observed. This included the burial of all dead, including the corpses of those put to death, even those put to death by crucifixion.

The objection raised against the Gospels' story of the burial of Jesus rests primarily on the mistaken belief that victims of Roman crucifixion were not permitted to be buried. Rather, it is suggested, their corpses were left hanging on the cross, to be picked apart by birds and animals. That this often happened is not in dispute here. However, I have argued that Roman authority in Jewish Palestine, especially in the vicinity of the city of Jerusalem itself, did in fact permit the burial of the executed. I will now argue that, with some exceptions, Roman law in fact permitted the burial of the executed throughout the empire.

We find important and relevant material on this subject in book 48 of the *Digesta*, compiled by the Roman emperor Justinian in the sixth century (530–533 CE). All three of the paragraphs that make up chapter 24, the final chapter, are helpful. The chapter is entitled *De cadaveribus punitorum* ("On the bodies of the punished").[49] The first and third paragraphs, which directly relate to burial, are as follows:

> Ulpian, *Duties of Proconsul*, book 9: The bodies of those who are condemned to death should not be refused their relatives; and the Divine Augustus, in the Tenth Book of his *Life*, said that this rule had been observed. At present, the bodies of those who have been punished are only buried when this has been requested and permission granted; and sometimes it is not permitted, especially where persons have been convicted of high treason. (48.24.1)

> Paulus, *Views*, book 1: The bodies of persons who have been punished should be given to whoever requests them for the purpose of burial. (48.24.3)

The *Digesta* refers to requests to take down bodies of the crucified. Josephus himself made this request of Titus and it was granted (*Life* 420–421). In general, the Romans often did not permit the crucified to be buried, request or no request. Non-burial was part of the horror—and the deterrent—of crucifixion. But crucifixion during peacetime just outside the walls of Jerusalem was another matter. Burial would have been expected, even demanded. Given that Rome did permit burial of the executed, and given the testimony of Philo and Josephus

49. For Latin text, see T. Mommsen, ed., *Iustiniani Digesta* (Corpus Iuris Civilis; Editio stereotypa quinta; vol. 1; Berlin: Weidmann, 1889). My English translation is based on Olivia Robinson, trans., "Book Forty-Eight," in *The Digest of Justinian* (ed. T. Mommsen and P. Krueger; ed. and trans. A. Watson; 4 vols.; Philadelphia: University of Pennsylvania Press, 1985; repr. 1998), 4:863–64. For critical discussion of the *Digesta*, its sources, and its meaning, see T. Honoré, *Justinian's Digest: Character and Compilation* (Oxford: Oxford University Press, 2010); D. W. Chapman and E. J. Schnabel, *The Trial and Crucifixion of Jesus: Texts and Commentary* (WUNT 344; Tübingen: Mohr Siebeck, 2015), 233–35. The material quoted from the *Digesta* is old, ranging from the first, second, and early third centuries.

to the effect that Roman authority respected Jewish laws and customs, it is very probable that the bodies of Jesus and the men crucified with him would have been properly buried.[50]

However, one might argue that because Jesus was crucified as "king of the Jews" (Mark 15:26), he was guilty of high treason and so might very well have been denied burial, as *Digesta* 48.24.1 states. It seems most unlikely, however, that Jesus was condemned for "high treason," given the discussion of treason (*maiestas*) in *Digesta* 48.4.1–11. Cited authorities include Ulpian, Marcian, and Scaevola. Almost all of the examples discussed in *Digesta* 48.4 involve serious violence against the state, "against the Roman people or against their safety," including plotting the death of the emperor, plotting or attempting to assassinate a Roman official, raising an army, failing to relinquish command of an army, siding with an enemy of the empire, fomenting armed rebellion, and turning an ally against Rome. None of this applies to Jesus and his following.[51]

Another important point needs to be made. The process that led to the execution of Jesus, and perhaps also to the execution of the two men crucified with him, was *initiated by the Jewish Council*. According to law and custom, when the Jewish Council (or Sanhedrin) condemned someone to death, by whatever means, it fell to the Council to have that person buried. This was the role played by Joseph of Arimathea, a member of the Jewish Council (Mark 15:43). The executed were to be buried properly, but not in places of honor, such as the family tomb. This is clearly taught in the earliest writings of the rabbis: "They did not bury (the executed criminal) in the burying-place of his fathers. But two burying-places were kept in readiness *by the Sanhedrin*, one for them that were beheaded or strangled,[52] and one for them that were stoned or burnt" (*m. Sanh.* 6:5, emphasis added). The place reserved for burial of criminals was sometimes referred to as a "wretched place": "Neither a corpse nor the bones of a corpse may be transferred from a wretched place to an honored place, nor, needless to say, from an honored place to a wretched place; but if to the family tomb, even from an honored place to a wretched place, it is permitted" (*Sem.* 13.7). Not only was the body of a criminal not to be buried in a place of honor, no public mourning for executed criminals was permitted: "they used not to make [open] lamentation . . . for mourning has place in the heart alone"

50. The Romans were open to permitting the bodies of the executed to be buried because of their fear of ghosts and restless spirits. It was commonly believed that the spirits of those not properly buried would roam the earth, haunting and harming the living. On this fear, see D. Felton, *Haunted Greece and Rome: Ghost Stories from Classical Antiquity* (Austin: University of Texas Press, 1999), 8–12. I pursue this topic further at the end of ch. 10 below.

51. This is why the "militant revolutionist" theories of S. G. F. Brandon and others have not persuaded historians. I refer to S. G. F. Brandon, *Jesus and the Zealots: A Study of the Political Factor in Primitive Christianity* (New York: Scribner's Sons, 1967). For critique, see M. Hengel, *Was Jesus a Revolutionist?* (trans. W. Klassen; FBBS 28; Philadelphia: Fortress, 1971); orig. *War Jesus Revolutionär?* (CH 110; Stuttgart: Calwer, 1970). Note also what is said in E. P. Sanders, *Jesus and Judaism* (London: SCM Press, 1985), 68: "Brandon's view, in fact, will get no full airing at all, since I consider that it has been sufficiently refuted; it cannot in any case be said to have influenced many."

52. "Strangled" would include those hanged and those crucified (who often suffocated).

(*m. Sanh.* 6:6). None of this law would make any sense if executed criminals were not in fact buried. There would have been no need to set aside tombs for executed criminals. There would simply be no remains to transfer from a "wretched place" to an "honored place."

The Jewish Council was responsible to oversee the proper burial of the executed because the bodies of the executed were normally not surrendered to family and friends. The burial of the executed in "wretched places," that is, in tombs set aside for criminals, was part of the punishment. No public mourning and lamentation were permitted. The remains of the executed could not be transferred from these dishonorable tombs for one year. After one year (see *b. Qidd.* 31b), the remains could be taken by family members to the family tomb or to some other place of honor. *(See fig. 8.3.)*

In view of all that has been considered above, we can concur with Jodi Magness, a Jewish archaeologist who serves on the faculty of the University of North Carolina at Chapel Hill, that the

> Gospel accounts of Jesus' burial are largely consistent with the archaeological evidence. Although archaeology does not prove there was a follower of Jesus named Joseph of Arimathea or that Pontius Pilate granted his request for Jesus' body, the Gospel accounts describing Jesus' removal from the cross and burial are consistent with archaeological evidence and with Jewish law.[53]

Finally, one more point needs to be made. The Fourth Gospel emphasizes the fact that whereas the legs of the men crucified with Jesus were broken, the legs of Jesus were not (John 19:31–33). John's point, of course, is to prove that in shedding his blood on the eve of Passover but not having his legs broken, Jesus qualifies as the Passover lamb (see John 19:36, where Exod 12:46 is quoted as "fulfilled"). Had there been no reason to hasten the deaths of the crucified men (because no burial was anticipated), no legs would have been broken. The evangelist writes as though breaking the legs to hasten death was a given and his readers would be familiar with the practice. It was therefore required of the evangelist to note that in the case of Jesus this was not necessary and that therefore he died as the "lamb of God" (John 1:29, 36).

Summing Up

The evidence strongly encourages us to conclude that in all probability Jesus was buried and that his corpse and those of the two men crucified with him would not have been left hanging overnight, and perhaps indefinitely (or, at most, cast into

53. Magness, "Jesus' Tomb: What Did It Look Like?," 212–26, with quotation from p. 224. Magness rightly contradicts Crossan's claim that the burial of Yehoḥanan was unusual and that Jesus of Nazareth probably was not buried. One should also consult J. G. Cook, "Crucifixion and Burial," 193–213. Cook concludes that the story of Joseph of Arimathea and the burial of Jesus is consistent with archaeology and with Jewish laws of burial, including burial of the condemned and executed.

a ditch or shallow grave, exposed to animals).[54] Quite apart from any concerns with the deceased men or their families, the major concern would have had to do with the defilement of the land and the holy city. Politically, too, it seems unlikely that on the eve of Passover, a holiday that celebrates Israel's liberation from foreign domination, Pilate would have wanted to provoke the Jewish population. Moreover, it is equally improbable that the ruling priests, who had called for Jesus' death, would have wanted to appear completely indifferent to Jewish sensitivities, either with respect to the dead or with respect to corpse impurity and defilement of the land. It seems most probable that the priests would have raised no objections to the burial of the three men. Indeed, they probably would have arranged to have them buried, before nightfall, in tombs reserved for executed criminals, as Jewish law, customs, and sensitivities demanded.

The terse, almost matter-of-fact burial narrative we find in Mark 15, which is followed in large part by Matthew and Luke, exhibits realism at every point. The narrative agrees with what is known of the relevant Jewish and Roman literature and archaeological data, both with respect to Palestine and elsewhere in the empire. That the body of Jesus was taken down from the cross and placed in a known tomb, under the direction of someone acting on behalf of the Jewish Council, should be accepted as historical.

If it is agreed that Jesus was indeed buried, we may ask where he was buried. A filmmaker has recently claimed that he thinks he knows where. In the following chapter, we shall consider this claim and take the opportunity to place the question into a fuller and more historical and archaeologically sensitive context.

54. In a recent study, Mark Smith has reached the same conclusion. See M. D. Smith, "Capital Punishment and Burial in the Roman Empire," in *Bethsaida in Archaeology, History and Ancient Culture: A Festschrift in Honor of John T. Greene* (ed. J. H. Ellens; Newcastle upon Tyne: Cambridge Scholars, 2014), 395–436.

CHAPTER NINE

Keeping Up Appearances: The Talpiot Tomb Façade in Context

Many Jewish tombs of late antiquity present artistic and architectural themes that reflect Herod's impressive temple. In a recent publication, Peter Richardson remarks: "There are suggestive connections between Jerusalem tombs and Herod's architecture. . . . In many respects the tombs and the temple are mutually reinforcing. The temple sheds light on the tombs and the tombs on the temple."[1] These artistic and architectural themes include pilasters, doors, gates, columns, and cornices and involve decorated ossuaries, gabled ossuary lids, rosettes or circular *patera*, and the like. Richardson is quite correct. His observation will be pursued further in this chapter.

The symbolism of Jewish art and architecture is vital for understanding the significance of the pointed gable and circle excised over the entrance of the East Talpiot tomb, a tomb that has generated a great deal of popular interest recently. It has been asserted that this artistic pattern reflects early Jewish Christianity and that its presence on the façade of the East Talpiot tomb may well indicate that this was the tomb of Jesus and his family. Assessment of such a startling claim can only be made by comparing this tomb with pre–70 CE Jerusalem tombs and ossuaries.

Decorated and Monumental Tombs

It is estimated that the necropolis surrounding Jerusalem (which is found mostly to the north, east, and south of the city) is made up of some 800 tombs,[2] some two

1. P. Richardson, *Building Jewish in the Roman East* (Waco, TX: Baylor University Press, 2004), 299–307, with quotations from pp. 305 and 307.

2. Jewish law required burial outside the city wall (e.g., *m. B. Bat.* 2:9, "Carrion, tombs, and tanning yards must be kept fifty cubits from a town"). As Jerusalem's boundaries expanded during the Second Temple period, it became necessary to relocate human remains. Exceptions were made in the cases of tombs of kings and prophets (cf. *t. B. Bat.* 1:9). Few tombs are found to the west of the city; burying in this area was probably avoided in order to prevent odor from being carried by winds from the west.

dozen of which can be classified as monumental tombs and mausolea.[3] Several impressive examples of such tombs run the length of the Kidron Valley, at the base of Mount Scopus, northeast of the Old City, and at the base of the Mount of Olives, opposite the eastern side of the Temple Mount.[4]

Our survey begins with the so-called Tomb of Simon the Just, located about one kilometer north of the Old City, a short distance from the Nablus Road. The tomb is named after Simon the high priest (d. 196 BCE), who is celebrated in the Wisdom of Yeshua ben Sira (cf. Sir 50:1–21; *m. ʾAbot* 1:2). However, the tomb actually belonged to one Julia Sabine, from the beginnings of the Common Era, as indicated by an inscription. Although this tomb is of little architectural significance, the ancient tradition of Jewish pilgrimage to it is important and will occasion comment later.[5] As one walks south through the Kidron Valley, one can view the so-called Tomb (or Pillar) of Absalom,[6] an unusual mausoleum that dates to the first century CE and stands some twenty meters high, eclectically ornamented with Ionic columns, a Doric frieze, and an Egyptian cornice. The structure is crowned with a concave conical roof, its most distinctive feature. It gains the name "Pillar of Absalom" from 2 Sam 18:18: "Now Absalom in his lifetime had taken and set up for himself the pillar which is in the King's Valley, for he said, 'I have no son to keep my name in remembrance'; he called the pillar after his own name, and it is called 'Absalom's pillar' to this day."[7] Tucked behind and to the northeast of the Tomb of Absalom is the Tomb (or Cave) of Jehoshaphat,[8] which is also misnamed. The latter comprises eight chambers and its entrance is supported by two square pillars. Built later (perhaps early in the first century CE), the Tomb of Jehoshaphat

3. Following J. Fedak, *Monumental Tombs of the Hellenistic Age: A Study of Selected Tombs from the Pre-Classical to the Early Imperial Era* (Toronto: University of Toronto Press, 1990), 140–57, 410–56 (notes). On these pages the monumental tombs of Jerusalem and Petra are discussed.

4. Avigad, "Tombs," *NEAEHL* 2:750–53; H. Geva, "Tombs," *NEAEHL* 2:747–49, 753–56; Finegan, *Archeology of the New Testament*, 181–202; J. Magness, *The Archaeology of the Holy Land: From the Destruction of Solomon's Temple to the Muslim Conquest* (Cambridge: Cambridge University Press, 2012), 230–39.

5. A. Kloner, "The 'Caves of Simeon the Just' and 'The Minor Sanhedrin': Two Burial Complexes from the Second Temple Period in Jerusalem," in *What Athens Has to Do with Jerusalem: Essays on Classical, Jewish, and Early Christian Art and Archaeology in Honor of Gideon Foerster* (ed. L. V. Rutgers; Interdisciplinary Studies in Ancient Culture and Religion 1; Leuven: Peeters, 2002), 125–49, at 125–33.

6. Finegan, *Archeology of the New Testament*, 195–96; Fedak, *Monumental Tombs of the Hellenistic Age*, 143–44; E. Puech and J. Zias, "Le tombeau de Zacharie et Siméon au monument funéraire dit d'Absalom dans la Vallée de Josaphat," *RB* 110 (2003): 321–35; J. Zias, "The Tomb of Absalom Reconsidered," *NEA* 68 (2005): 148–65; Hachlili, *Jewish Funerary Customs*, 32–34, 132–33; Magness, *Archaeology of the Holy Land*, 236.

7. Apparently, the identification of this monument as "Absalom's Pillar" was first suggested by Benjamin of Tudela in 1170. Local Palestinians sometimes call this tomb "Pharaoh's Hat."

8. Finegan, *Archeology of the New Testament*, 195–96; Fedak, *Monumental Tombs of the Hellenistic Age*, 144; Hachlili, *Jewish Funerary Customs*, 33–34. Of Jehoshaphat, king of Judah, it is said: "And Jehoshaphat slept with his fathers, and was buried with his fathers in the city of David his father; and Jehoram his son reigned in his stead" (1 Kgs 22:50; cf. 2 Chr 21:1).

belonged to the same family that owned the Tomb of Absalom. Its gabled façade will be discussed below.

Moving south, one next encounters the Tomb of the Sons of Hezir, a priestly family,[9] whose entrance is adorned with two Doric columns and which dates to the first or second century BCE. After the Hezir tomb comes the so-called Tomb of Zechariah, with its Ionic pilasters and pyramid-shaped top.[10] The tomb is covered with small, neatly incised Hebrew inscriptions, and probably dates to the first century BCE. Next comes the so-called Tomb of Pharaoh's Daughter.[11] The tomb is east of Ophel and north of the Silwan Village and is one of several very early tombs. It is monolithic and at one time it too was adorned by a pyramid top. It contains a burial chamber and a gabled ceiling. Immediately south is a second monolithic tomb, sometimes called the Tomb of the Royal Steward. The façade was removed by Charles Clermont-Ganneau in 1870 and is now in the British Museum. Part of a fragmentary inscription reads "[. . .]yahu who is over the house." Adjacent are the remains of another monolithic tomb.[12]

Where the Kidron and Hinnom valleys intersect, one finds the Akeldama tombs. Several of these tombs are of the highest quality, judging by the interior architecture, artistic touches, and adorned ossuaries. One of these tombs may have belonged to the family of Annas, the high priest between 9 and 15 CE (cf. Josephus, *Ant.* 20.198; Luke 3:2; John 18:13; Acts 4:6). It is palatial in size, design, and ornamentation, and at one time was adorned with an impressive superstructure. The quality of this tomb complex and its location (remnants of the siege wall mentioned by Josephus are nearby; cf. *J.W.* 5.506) support the identification.[13]

Moving west and then north along the Hinnom Valley, one approaches the area in which is found the Tomb of Herod's Family. This tomb, discovered in 1892, is about one-third of a kilometer due west of the southwest corner of the wall of the

9. Finegan, *Archeology of the New Testament*, 192–93; Fedak, *Monumental Tombs of the Hellenistic Age*, 142; D. Barag, "The 2000–2001 Exploration of the Tombs of Benei Hezir and Zechariah," *IEJ* 53 (2003): 78–110; Hachlili, *Jewish Funerary Customs*, 31. The name Hezir appears in the list of priestly courses (1 Chr 24:15; cf. Neh 10:20).

10. H. E. Stutchbury, "Excavations in the Kidron Valley," *PEQ* 93 (1961): 101–13; Finegan, *Archeology of the New Testament*, 192–94; Fedak, *Monumental Tombs of the Hellenistic Age*, 142–43; Puech and Zias, "Le tombeau de Zacharie et Siméon," 563–77 + plates II–IV; Hachlili, *Jewish Funerary Customs*, 32 + fig. II-3a; Magness, *Archaeology of the Holy Land*, 235–36.

11. Fedak, *Monumental Tombs of the Hellenistic Age*, 140; Hachlili, *Jewish Funerary Customs*, 132.

12. The Silwan tombs were surveyed and partially excavated in the 1960s and 1970s, with the results published, in Hebrew, in 1983. For an English translation of this work, see D. Ussishkin, *The Village of Silwan: The Necropolis from the Period of the Judean Kingdom* (Jerusalem: Israel Exploration Society, 1993)

13. G. Avni, "Christian Secondary Use of Jewish Burial Caves in Jerusalem in the Light of New Excavations at the Aceldama Tombs," in *Early Christianity in Context: Monuments and Documents* (ed. F. Manns and E. Alliata; SBFCMa 38; Jerusalem: Franciscan Printing Press, 1993), 265–76; Avni, Greenhut, and Ilan, "Three New Burial Caves of the Second Temple Period in Aceldama (Kidron Valley)," 206–18; Ritmeyer and Ritmeyer, "Akeldama: Potter's Field or High Priest's Tomb?," 22–35, 76, 78; Avni, Greenhut, et al., *The Akeldama Tombs: Three Burial Caves in the Kidron Valley*; Hachlili, *Jewish Funerary Customs*, 274–80 + figs. VI-26, 27, 28, 29.

Old City, not far from the modern King David Hotel, on the site of the Nicophoria Monastery.[14] The tomb's superstructure is long gone, but the crypt is beautifully decorated and contained several decorated sarcophagi. Its distinctive feature is the large wheel-shaped stone that served as the door to the vault.[15]

Another half kilometer west, one comes to the Tomb of Jason, which was discovered in 1956 in Rehavia (or Rehov), western Jerusalem. The tomb is supported by a single pillar, instead of the traditional two pillars, and is topped with a pyramid.[16] Along with a Greek inscription and several Aramaic inscriptions, charcoal drawings of ships were found scrawled on the walls of the crypt. Coins and pottery found in the crypt date the earliest use of the tomb to the beginning of the first century BCE. The tomb remained in use until the first century CE.

Due north of the Old City, one comes to the Tomb of Queen Helena of Adiabene, daughter of Izates the proselyte (Josephus, *J.W.* 5.147).[17] (The tomb is also called, mistakenly, the Tombs of the Kings.) It is by far the largest and most impressive tomb in Jerusalem. A monumental staircase leads down through an arch and into an expansive garden area. The broad opening included a façade twenty-seven meters wide, supported by two large pillars. The queen and two members of her family were interred in this tomb sometime after 50 CE. When excavated, the tomb contained several decorated sarcophagi. On one of them were inscribed the words צדן מלכתה, "Queen Saddan." According to Josephus (*Ant.* 20.95), Helena's tomb was adorned with three pyramids (though the location of these pyramids and their relation to the tomb are disputed), possibly one for herself and one for each of her two sons. Supposedly, in 1865 Louis Félicien de Saulcy entered the tomb and found an inscription in Aramaic (Palmyrene?) that included the title and name "Helena the Queen." There is no trace of this inscription today.

14. C. Schick, "Recent Discoveries at the 'Nicophorieh,'" PEFQS 24 (1892): 115–20; R. A. S. Macalister, "The Nicophorieh Tomb," PEFQS 33 (1901): 397–402; Abel, "Exils et tombeaux des Herodes," 56–74; Finegan, *Archeology of the New Testament*, 192–94; Fedak, *Monumental Tombs of the Hellenistic Age*, 147, 198; Hachlili, *Jewish Funerary Customs*, 37–41, 116–17.

15. It is not certain that what is traditionally called "Herod's Family Tomb" is in reality the tomb of Herod's family. For a recent assessment of Herod's building projects, see E. Netzer, *The Architecture of Herod, the Great Builder* (TSAJ 117; Tübingen: Mohr Siebeck, 2006). Netzer, of course, has recently gained notoriety for discovering what he believes is Herod's tomb, at the Herodium. For preliminary comments, see R. Wenning, "Das Grab Herodes des Großen: Israel–Herodium," *WUB* 45 (2007): 68–69; D. M. Jacobson, "Has Herod's Place of Burial Been Found?," *PEQ* 139 (2007): 147–48. The Herodium is situated about eight miles (twelve kilometers) south of modern-day Jerusalem.

16. N. Avigad, "Aramaic Inscriptions in the Tomb of Jason," *IEJ* 17 (1967): 101–11; P. Benoit, "L'inscription grecque du tombeau de Jason," *IEJ* 17 (1967): 112–13; Rahmani, "Jason's Tomb," 61–100; Fedak, *Monumental Tombs of the Hellenistic Age*, 140–41; Puech, "Inscriptions funéraires palestiniennes: Tombeau de Jason et ossuaires," 481–583; Hachlili, *Jewish Funerary Customs*, 34–36 + fig. II-5.

17. L.-H. Vincent and P. M.-A. Steve, *Jérusalem de l'Ancien Testament: Recherches d'archéologie et d'histoire* (Paris: Gabalda, 1954), 346–62; Finegan, *Archeology of the New Testament*, 199–202 + fig. 229; Fedak, *Monumental Tombs of the Hellenistic Age*, 146–47; Hachlili, *Jewish Funerary Customs*, 36–37 + fig. II-6; Magness, *Archaeology of the Holy Land*, 236–39.

The Frieze Tomb, located one and a half kilometers north of the Old City, is marked with an ornate façade with a Doric frieze (hence the tomb's name) supported by two pillars. The frieze, topped by a decorated Corinthian cornice, boasts four artistic rosettes.[18] Two hundred and fifty meters to the northwest, one comes to the so-called Two-Storied Tomb, or Pilaster Tomb, first excavated by K. Galling.[19] As its name implies, this tomb consists of two stories, originally presenting either a gabled or flat roofline. Parts of the upper story have survived, along with a Doric frieze. Hachlili draws attention to the artistic and architectural links between this tomb and some of the Petra tombs.[20]

Another three hundred meters or so to the northwest, one comes upon the Tomb of Pillars, or Two-Columned Tomb. It originally boasted two columns (though one is now lost), a porch, a central chamber, and three rooms. It is similar to the Two-Storied Tomb.[21] Immediately to the north, one comes to the so-called Tombs of the Sanhedrin. These comprise a cluster of ornate tombs, one of which boasts a beautiful gabled façade, a large central hall, and several burial chambers with staircases leading to various levels.[22]

About one hundred meters to the east of the Sanhedrin Tombs complex is the so-called Tomb of the Grapes,[23] which derives its name from the sculpted grape clusters that adorn the tympanum above the entrance. Centered in the tympanum, just below the point of the gabled top, is an ornate rosette. About one-half of a kilometer north, one comes to the Tomb of Umm el-ʿAmmed (in Naḥal Zofim). The Cave of Umm el-ʿAmmed (named after the wadi in which it is located) was decorated with a façade and possessed two chambers with burial niches. The ornate cornice is supported by two columns and two pilasters.[24]

A short distance south of The Hebrew University, on Mount Scopus, one comes to the Tomb of the Hermit and the Tomb of Nicanor. The Tomb of Nicanor was

---

18. N. Avigad, "The Rock-Carved Façades of the Jerusalem Necropolis," *IEJ* 1 (1950–51): 96–106, at 100 + fig. 5; Hachlili, *Jewish Funerary Customs*, 46 + fig. II-13a.

19. K. Galling, "Ein Etagen-Pilaster-Grab in Norden von Jerusalem," *ZDPV* 59 (1936): 111–23, at 118 + fig. 5.

20. Hachlili, *Jewish Funerary Customs*, 50–52 + fig. II-16a. See also Avigad, "Rock-Carved Façades of the Jerusalem Necropolis," 105–6; Fedak, *Monumental Tombs of the Hellenistic Age*, 147.

21. Fedak, *Monumental Tombs of the Hellenistic Age*, 147–48; Hachlili, *Jewish Funerary Customs*, 71.

22. J. Jotham-Rothschild, "The Tombs of Sanhedria," *PEQ* 84 (1952): 23–38; 86 (1954): 16–22; Fedak, *Monumental Tombs of the Hellenistic Age*, 147–48; Hachlili, *Jewish Funerary Customs*, 43–45, 124–26 + fig. II-14b; Kloner, "'Caves of Simeon the Just' and 'The Minor Sanhedrin,'" 134–44; Magness, *Archaeology of the Holy Land*, 238. This tomb complex evidently gained its name because it accommodated approximately seventy persons, the traditional number of members in the old Sanhedrin. Members of the Sanhedrin, as everyone else, would have been buried in family tombs, however, not together in a special tomb set aside for them.

23. R. A. S. Macalister, "On a Rock Tomb North of Jerusalem," PEFQS 33 (1900): 54–61; Hachlili, *Jewish Funerary Customs*, 46–48 + fig. II-14a.

24. Avigad, "Rock-Carved Façades of the Jerusalem Necropolis," 103 + fig. 7; Fedak, *Monumental Tombs of the Hellenistic Age*, 144–45 + fig. 208; Hachlili, *Jewish Funerary Customs*, 30, 128–29.

discovered on Mount Scopus in 1902.[25] This large tomb, dating to the first century CE and possessing four branches of burial chambers, contained several decorated ossuaries, one of which includes an important inscription that reads: "The bones of the (sons) of Nicanor the Alexandrian who made the doors. Nicanor Alexa."

Since the discovery of this ossuary, it has been speculated that this person Nicanor is none other than the person after whom the "Nicanor Gate" is named in rabbinic tradition. According to the Talmudic tractate *Yoma*, "there were seven gates in the temple court, three to the north, three to the south, and one to the east. . . . to the east the Nicanor Gate . . ." (*b. Yoma* 19a). The same tractate later states that Nicanor fetched the gates from Alexandria of Egypt and that they were made of "Corinthian bronze" (*b. Yoma* 38a). This is precisely what Josephus says: "Of the gates nine were completely overlaid with gold and silver, as were also their doorposts and lintels; but one, that outside the sanctuary, was of Corinthian bronze, and far exceeded in value those plated with silver and gold" (*J.W.* 5.201; cf. *m. Mid.* 2:3: "All the gates that were there had been changed with gold, save only the doors of the Nicanor Gate").

The agreement between the ossuary inscription and these literary traditions is so striking that many scholars believe the ossuary did indeed contain the remains of the man after whom the gate was named. At least one scholar, however, has challenged the identification.[26] But the rarity of the name Nicanor[27] and the precision of the agreement in the essential details strongly argue for the identification. Commentators have also wondered if the "Beautiful Gate" mentioned in Acts (3:2, τὴν θύραν τοῦ ἱεροῦ τὴν λεγομένην Ὡραίαν; 3:10, τῇ ὡραίᾳ πύλῃ) is in fact the Nicanor Gate.[28]

Observation of the monumental tombs, especially those that run along the Kidron Valley, clarifies Jesus' scathing remarks against his critics: "You are like white-washed tombs" and "You build the tombs of the prophets!" (Matt 23:27, 29). At the approach of major festivals, these tombs were whitewashed, and sometimes the inscriptions were highlighted with bright colors.[29] Jesus' graphic comparisons

25. C. S. Clermont-Ganneau, "The 'Gate of Nicanor' in the Temple of Jerusalem," PEFQS (1903): 93, 125–31; G. Dickson, "The Tomb of Nicanor of Alexandria," PEFQS (1903): 326–32; S. Corbett, "Some Observations on the Gateways to the Herodian Temple in Jerusalem," *PEQ* 84 (1952–53): 7–14 + plates I–V; Finegan, *Archeology of the New Testament*, 237–38; E. Bammel, "Nicanor and His Gate," in *Judaica: Kleine Schriften I* (WUNT 37; Tübingen: Mohr Siebeck, 1986), 39–41; J. Schwartz, "Once More on the Nicanor Gate," *HUCA* 62 (1991): 245–83; Hachlili, *Jewish Funerary Customs*, 42–43; Magness, *Archaeology of the Holy Land*, 239.

26. P. Roussel, "Nikanor d'Alexandrie et la porte du temple de Jérusalem," *REG* 37 (1924): 79–82.

27. Tal Ilan can identify only three other real persons who bore this name. See Ilan, *Lexicon of Jewish Names in Late Antiquity*, 297–98.

28. Several commentators accept the identification; see Peterson, *The Acts of the Apostles* (PNTC), 168n12. Others think the Nicanor Gate and the Beautiful Gate are two different gates. For scholarly literature and succinct discussion, see Fitzmyer, *The Acts of the Apostles* (AB 31), 277–78.

29. Traces of red paint can still be found in part of the inscription on the Tomb of the Sons of Hezir. See Hachlili, *Jewish Funerary Customs*, 168 + fig. V-3. The interiors of some

would have readily conjured up familiar images in the minds of his hearers. The point is that the followers of Jesus would have been very aware of the artistic and architectural motifs of these tombs. They would been familiar with the faux gables beneath which rosettes or circular *patera* were often found. Knowing that the gable and rosette often adorned the monumental tombs of the Jerusalem elite, including aristocratic priestly families, why would the family and followers of Jesus choose the same architectural motif for the tomb of their master?

The East Talpiot Tomb

Our survey of the decorated and monumental tombs will assist us in placing the East Talpiot tomb into its proper context. We must inquire into the quality of the tomb, its location, and the social class of people most likely to have owned and occupied this tomb. When these questions are answered in the fuller context of the Jerusalem necropolis, we shall be in a much better position to assess the East Talpiot tomb. *(See fig. 9.1.)*

In February 2007, Simcha Jacobovici, host and producer of the Canadian television program "The Naked Archaeologist," announced, along with writer Charles Pellegrino and movie producer and director James Cameron, that a tomb in East Talpiot, south Jerusalem, may well have been the tomb of Jesus of Nazareth and his family.[30] However, there are several problems with the hypothesis that the East Talpiot tomb excavated by Yosef Gat and Amos Kloner in 1980[31] is none other

---

tombs were also painted. Geometric designs in the Akeldama Tomb (Cave 3, Chamber C) are highlighted in red. The Goliath family tomb of Jericho is adorned with painted floral patterns. For further examples, see A. Siegelman and Y. Neeman, "A Painted Tomb Near Caesarea," *'Atiqot* 21 (1992): 56–62; A. Kloner, "The Cave of the Birds—A Painted Tomb on the Mount of Olives," in *Ancient Jerusalem Revealed* (ed. H. Geva; Jerusalem: Israel Exploration Society, 1994), 306–10; A. Barbet, "Un tombeau peint inscrit de Sidon," *Syr* 74 (1997): 141–60.

30. See S. Jacobovici and C. Pellegrino, *The Jesus Family Tomb: The Discovery, the Investigation, and the Evidence That Could Change History* (San Francisco: HarperCollins, 2007). The release of this book coincided with a television documentary that aired on Discovery Channel and other cable outlets. Neither author is an archaeologist, historian, or biblical scholar. The possibility that the East Talpiot tomb may have been connected to Jesus and his family was previously explored in a *London Times* story and a BBC documentary that aired in 1996. It has also been explored in J. D. Tabor, *The Jesus Dynasty* (New York: Simon & Schuster, 2006), 22–33, 56–57. The book by Jacobovici and Pellegrino has been severely criticized by archaeologist Jonathan Reed in the *Review of Biblical Literature* (in a review posted in June 2007). Reed states that "there is plenty of deceit" in *The Jesus Family Tomb*. Many would say that the documentary was even more egregious.

31. The tomb was accidentally uncovered in March of 1980 during construction in the Jerusalem neighborhood of East Talpiot, in close proximity to what is now 273 Dov Gruner Street. The tomb is now beneath street level and the entrance to it is sealed. A brief report of the discovery and excavation was published the year after the excavation. See Y. Gat, "East Talpiot," *Hadashot Arkeologiyot* 76 (1981): 24–25 (in Hebrew). Gat died before publishing a longer, more detailed report. Sixteen years after the excavation, Amos Kloner published an English report. See A. Kloner, "A Tomb with Inscribed Ossuaries in East Talpiyot, Jerusalem,"

than the tomb of Jesus of Nazareth and his family. To reach this conclusion, Jacobovici and Pellegrino make several claims, most of which have serious problems. The present essay treats two of these problematic claims, both having to do with questions of symbolism. They are: (1) the claim that the X-mark at the beginning of the ossuary inscription "Yeshua, son of Yehosef" signifies a cross and as such is a Christian symbol; and (2) the claim that the gable-and-circle excision above the tomb's entrance is a Jewish-Christian symbol. Both of these claims are quite dubious, if not demonstrably false.

Dubious Claim 1: The X-mark on the "Yeshua, son of Yehosef" ossuary

Ten ossuaries were recovered from the East Talpiot tomb in 1980. Nine of the ten have been warehoused.[32] (The tenth ossuary, not placed in the IAA warehouse, is described in the Gat and Kloner reports as uninscribed and unadorned;[33] it is not the so-called James Ossuary, which was found a number of years before the discovery of the East Talpiot tomb and its ten ossuaries.[34]) One of the unadorned ossuaries bears the inscription "Yeshua [or Jesus], son of Yehosef [or Joseph]." The inventory number of this ossuary is 80.503.[35] Incised to the right of the inscription (that is, at the beginning of the inscription, since Hebrew and Aramaic are written from right to left), on one end of this ossuary, is an X-mark. Because a few Christian marks have been found on ossuaries in and around Jerusalem (such as the *chi-rho* symbol), it is theoretically possible that the X-mark on the East Talpiot tomb ossuary is a Christian mark. Indeed, a few archaeologists and scholars have in the past argued that some of the X-marks on ossuaries are Christian symbols of the cross,[36] though others have vigorously challenged this interpretation.[37]

'Atiqot 29 (1996): 15–22 (with sketches by S. Gibson). We now have an updated report in A. Kloner and S. Gibson, "The Talpiot Tomb Reconsidered: The Archaeological Facts," in *The Tomb of Jesus and His Family? Exploring Ancient Jewish Tombs Near Jerusalem's Walls* (ed. J. H. Charlesworth; Grand Rapids: Eerdmans, 2013), 29–75.

32. Rahmani, *Catalogue of Jewish Ossuaries*, 222–24 (nos. 701–709).

33. See Kloner, "Tomb with Inscribed Ossuaries in East Talpiyot, Jerusalem," 21, where the tenth ossuary is described as "plain," that is, lacking adornment and inscription.

34. *Pace* Tabor, *Jesus Dynasty*, 20–22, 32–33. It is now speculated (by James Tabor in private communication) that the James Ossuary was an eleventh ossuary and that it had been taken from the Talpiot tomb a great many years before the discovery and excavation of the tomb in 1980.

35. It appears in Rahmani, *Catalogue of Jewish Ossuaries*, 223, as no. 704.

36. As first suggested by pioneer archaeologist Charles S. Clermont-Ganneau. His suggestion has been defended and developed further in Bagatti and Milik, *Gli scavi del "Dominus Flevit,"* 63–69; J. Daniélou, *Primitive Christian Symbols* (Baltimore: Helicon, 1964), 139–45.

37. The suggestion that some of these marks are Christian has been challenged, for example, by C. H. Kraeling, "Christian Burial Urns?," *BA* 9 (1946): 16–20. E. R. Goodenough agrees with Kraeling, concluding that the X-marks, as well as +-marks found on ossuaries, have nothing to do with Christianity. See G. E. Wright, "New Information Regarding the Supposed 'Christian' Ossuaries," *BA* 9 (1946): 43; Goodenough, *Jewish Symbols in the Greco-Roman Period*, vols. 1–3 and specifically 1:130–31 (for discussion) and figs. 227, 228, and 229 in vol. 3 (for photographs); R. H. Smith, "The Cross Marks on Jewish Ossuaries," *PEQ* 106

It is far more probable that the X-mark on ossuary 80.503 is the mark of the stonemason who made the ossuary, or a position-directioning mark made by the person who incised the inscription. The typical function of the X-mark was to align the lid with the ossuary, so that those making use of the ossuary would readily know which end of the lid should go with which end of the ossuary. This function is clearly seen in several ossuaries.[38] In the case of ossuary 80.503, Rahmani notes that a mark resembling an asterisk appears on the narrow end of the lid.[39] This mark corresponds with the X-mark to the right of the inscription, "Yeshua, son of Yehosef," which appears on the narrow end of the ossuary, beneath the asterisk mark on the lid. In view of the function of the stonemason's marks on other ossuaries, and in view of the correspondence of the asterisk mark and X-mark on ossuary 80.503, it seems highly probable that what we have here is another instance of a stonemason's mark intended to indicate which way the lid should be placed. Consequently, it is highly improbable that the X-mark to the right of the inscription symbolizes a cross or anything with a religious meaning. More will be said on this point in the next section of this chapter, where mention will be made of one of the Dominus Flevit ossuaries.

One more issue needs to be raised concerning ossuary 80.503. The name Yeshua in the inscription is barely discernible. Nevertheless, comparison with three other ossuary inscriptions in which the name Yeshua occurs,[40] as well as the fact

---

(1974): 53–66. Smith sensibly concludes that the "crude cross marks on ossuaries are non-religious in nature" (p. 66). He wonders, moreover, why Christians would incise crude cross signs that cannot be distinguished from marks "placed there as guides for the matching of lids to receptacles" (p. 65). See also P. C. Hammond, "'Mason's Marks' and Other Archaeological Signs," *PEQ* 132 (2000): 123–30. Hammond subdivides the general category "masons' marks" into "building instructions" and "positioning directions." The X-marks on ossuaries fall into the second subcategory. Marks providing building instructions and positioning directions have been found elsewhere in the antique Middle East. See J. W. Crowfoot and G. M. Crowfoot, *Early Ivories from Samaria* (London: Palestine Exploration Fund, 1938), 6–9; G. R. Driver, *Semitic Writing: From Pictograph to Alphabet* (Schweich Lectures of the British Academy, 1944; Oxford: Oxford University Press, 1948), 115–16; and P. C. Hammond, *The Excavation of the Main Theater at Petra, 1961–1962* (London: B. Quaritch, 1965), 70–71 + plates 33 (nos. 3 and 4) and 47–50. In his description (*Catalogue of Jewish Ossuaries*, 223), Rahmani mentions both the X-mark on the ossuary and the corresponding asterisk on the lid. Jacobovici's misinterpretation of the X-mark on ossuary 80.503 is egregious and his misleading comments unfortunate.

38. See Figueras, *Decorated Jewish Ossuaries*, plates 7 and 8, for examples of the stonemason's mark. Nos. 63, 64, 468, 577, 638, and 658 are clear examples of X-marks and other types of marks that indicate proper alignment of lid with ossuary. See also Rahmani, *Catalogue of Jewish Ossuaries*, 166 (no. 392 + plate 56). Corresponding X-marks also appear on the end of the Nicanor ossuary and its lid; cf. Finegan, *Archeology of the New Testament*, 237–38. In my examination of the ossuaries in the IAA's storage facility at Beth Shemesh, I observed a number of examples. An interesting one is ossuary 81.518, which has a +-mark on one side and a corresponding +-mark on the lid above. I thank Miki Sebanne, head of the IAA Beth Shemesh Storage and Research Facility, for permitting me this opportunity.

39. Rahmani, *Catalogue of Jewish Ossuaries*, 223.

40. See ibid., 77 (no. 9), 108 (no. 121), and 113 (no. 140). Of the three, the last has a form of the name that comes closest to the form of the name in ossuary 80.503.

that the inscription of another ossuary in the East Talpiot tomb (80.501) reads "Yehudah, son of Yeshua,"[41] indicates that Yeshua is probably the correct reading of ossuary 80.503. But the matter remains complicated, for some epigraphers believe the name Yeshua may have been incised over another name, perhaps Yudan or Hanun.[42] If so, this is quite unusual and raises yet more unanswered questions. The inscription of ossuary 80.503, as well as its stonemason's marks, needs further study.[43]

Dubious Claim 2: The gable-and-circle excision above the tomb's entrance is a Jewish-Christian symbol

Perhaps the most dubious element in the East Talpiot tomb hypothesis is the claim that the pointed gable and circle over the tomb's entrance constitute an early Jewish-Christian symbol. The gable over a circle (or rosette, *patera*, or another centered design) is not mysterious, and it is not Christian. On the contrary, it is a Jewish adaptation of classical architecture, and it is pre-Christian. Here Peter Richardson's observation about the influence of the Herodian temple on tombs and ossuaries is quite pertinent.[44]

The pointed gable, below which a circle, rosette, or *patera* often appears, is a common feature in Roman architecture, including that of sepulture.[45] The Jewish

41. See ibid., 223 (no. 702). Rahmani comments that the "reading ישוע [on 80.503] is corroborated by the inscription on no. 702 referring to Yeshuaʿ, the father of Yehudah."

42. The name Yudan has been suggested by Stephen Pfann. See S. Pfann, "Demythologizing the Talpiot Tomb: The Tomb of Another Jesus, Mary, and Joseph," in *The Tomb of Jesus and His Family? Exploring Ancient Jewish Tombs Near Jerusalem's Walls* (ed. J. H. Charlesworth; Grand Rapids: Eerdmans, 2013), 165–205, at 178.

43. For now, see R. Hachlili, "What's in a Name?," in *The Tomb of Jesus and His Family? Exploring Ancient Jewish Tombs Near Jerusalem's Walls* (ed. J. H. Charlesworth; Grand Rapids: Eerdmans, 2013), 125–49. Hachlili finds the proposed identification of the name on ossuary 80.503 with Jesus of Nazareth very unlikely. See also Pfann, "Demythologizing the Talpiot Tomb." In Pfann's learned study, he raises serious objections to the suggested identifications with Jesus and various members of his family. Although the focus of the present study is not the various names on the ossuaries of the Talpiot tomb, it should be noted that there is a troubling tendency toward misleading exaggeration with regard to this matter in *The Tomb of Jesus and His Family?* On the back cover of the book, it is claimed that the names on the ossuaries include those of "James" and "Mary Magdalene." This is simply false. The James Ossuary was not found in the Talpiot tomb and the name "Mary Magdalene" does not appear on any of the ossuaries.

44. The principal weakness of *The Tomb of Jesus and His Family?* is that no essay in this collection addresses the question of the meaning of the excised symbol over the entrance to the East Talpiot tomb. However, this is the single most important issue. When this symbol is properly interpreted, the hypothesis that it was a symbol of the early Christian movement collapses.

45. For examples of the pointed gable and circle or *patera* in Roman sepulture (ranging from the second century BCE to the second century CE, and none of which is Christian or Jewish), see J. M. C. Toynbee, *Death and Burial in the Roman World* (Ithaca, NY: Cornell University Press, 1971), 22–24 (+ plate 6), 247 (+ plates 77 and 78); M. Carroll and J. Rempel, eds., *Living through the Dead: Burial and Commemoration in the Classical World* (Studies in Funerary Archaeology 5; Oxford: Oxbow, 2011), 55 (+ plate 3.4), 61 (+ plate 3.8).

elite adopted this architectural feature during the Roman era, specifically in the first century BCE. It was probably a feature of the buildings of the temple precincts, if not of the sanctuary itself. Accordingly, the gable-circle symbol not only predated Jesus, it was classical.[46] After its adoption in the first century BCE, it became a standard feature among the cosmopolitan Jewish elite.

The pointed gable over a circle or rosette is seen in many tombs and ossuaries, some of which predate the Christian era and none of which is believed to have anything to do with Jesus and his movement. We see this artistic design in the outer and inner façades of the so-called "Sanhedrin Tombs" in Jerusalem. Over the inner entrance of this tomb complex, one can see a pointed gable over a rosette comprising acanthus leaves. A gable is also found over the outer entrance, but without a rosette.[47] This pattern is also seen in the Hinnom Valley Tomb, the Tomb of Jehoshaphat, and the so-called Grape Tomb.[48]

In his *Jewish Symbols in the Greco-Roman Period*, Erwin Goodenough provides several photographs and facsimiles that depict the gable and circle/rosette/*patera*. Among these items are ossuaries, a tomb façade, a coin (struck by Philip, tetrarch of Gaulanitis in the time of Jesus), and epitaph art.[49] One of the more common features is the Torah ark (which contains Scripture scrolls), over which appears the pointed gable and circle. Goodenough remarks that "the box with Moses, and all the arks of the synagogue, shows a form extremely old, one chiefly associated with tombstones. . . . It is customary to call this object a temple, but it may well have been a chest which, like the Ark, brought the divine presence." He comments further, with reference to another example of a Torah ark: "The design was almost certainly affected, or made to seem pertinent, by the great stone Temple of Herod."[50] As already noted, Richardson, in his recent study, has come to the same conclusion.

46. The meaning offered in Jacobovici and Pellegrino, *Jesus Family Tomb*, 11–12, 128–30 for the gable-circle design in Jewish sepulture is incomplete, inaccurate, and misleading. See Reed's comments in his *RBL* review of this book, referred to above: "the faux-gabled roof and circular *patera* are also common in Roman domestic shrines . . . The chevron symbol . . . shows Jewish adaptation of Roman architectural or ornamental themes" (p. 4). For further discussion, see Figueras, *Decorated Jewish Ossuaries*, 55 (the gable), 63–65 (the circle).

47. See Jotham-Rothschild, "Tombs of Sanhedria"; N. Avigad, "Sanhedrin Tombs," *NEAEHL* 2:752 (with photograph).

48. Hachlili, *Jewish Funerary Customs*, plate IV-2 (of Tomb of Jehoshaphat; with pointed gable over circular vine and cluster); 45, fig. II-12 (the Hinnom Valley Tomb); 46–49 + fig. II-14; p. 139 + fig. IV-7 (the "Grape Tomb" and the Tomb of Jehoshaphat). See also Goodenough, *Jewish Symbols in the Greco-Roman Period*, vol. 3, figs. 23 (the Sanhedrin Tombs) and 24 (the "Grape Tomb"). For discussion of the "Grape Tomb," see Goodenough, *Jewish Symbols in the Greco-Roman Period*, 1:80.

49. Goodenough, *Jewish Symbols in the Greco-Roman Period*, vol. 3, figs. 142, 143, 239 (ossuaries), 508 (tomb façade), 676 (coin struck by Philip, tetrarch of Gaulanitis), 707 and 710 (epitaph art: Torah arks with gable and circle); for commentary on fig. 710, see 2:6, "I should judge that the circle within the gable would have been a wreath or rosette in a larger drawing." See also M. Avi-Yonah, *Art in Ancient Palestine: Selected Studies* (Jerusalem: Magnes, 1981), plates 12.4, 13.8, 15.4–5, and 16.1.

50. E. R. Goodenough, *Jewish Symbols in the Greco-Roman Period: Abridged Edition* (ed. J. Neusner; Princeton: Princeton University Press, 1988): for Torah arks, adorned with

In a study of the Jews of ancient Rome, Harry Leon provides an image of an epitaph at the bottom of which is a Torah ark containing six Scripture scrolls. Over the ark is a pointed gable.[51] Excavations of the Jewish tombs of Beth Sheᶜarim in Galilee have uncovered the same artistic motifs. Again, we find a Torah ark at the top of which is the gable above a circle (or rosette), painted on a sealing stone. Benjamin Mazar comments: "The subject portrayed on this sealing-stone is one of the most common in ancient Jewish art; it occurs in synagogues in Palestine and abroad, in catacombs, on tombstones, on gold glass from Rome, etc. In all of these instances we frequently find representations of the Holy Ark ('hekhal') or an Ark between two Menorahs."[52]

It has already been mentioned that the symbol of pointed gable over circle or rosette appears on coins minted by Philip the tetrarch, son of Herod the Great.[53] The same symbol appears on coins minted by Agrippa I.[54] The symbol is also found on Hasmonean coins from an earlier period and, with some variation, on Bar Kokhba coins of a later period. The rosette over a temple façade is a standard feature in Bar Kokhba's coins.[55]

The gable-and-circle/rosette pattern is found on several ossuaries, with the circle or rosette on the end of the ossuary over which rests the gabled lid, or on the end of the lid itself, thus forming the very pattern seen over the entrance to the East Talpiot tomb.[56] An ossuary found on Mount Scopus is particularly relevant, for it depicts monumental façades, with temple motifs, on all four sides.[57] Both ends

---

pointed gables (beneath which appear rosettes or similar patterns), see figs. 9, 38, and 47. The first quotation above is taken from p. 205 and is in reference to fig. 47. The second quotation above is taken from p. 197 and is in reference to fig. 38.

51. Leon, *Jews of Ancient Rome,* plate xx, fig. 34, with transcription and translation on p. 325.

52. Mazar, *Beth Sheᶜarim*, vol. 1, *Catacombs 1–4*, 110–13, with quotation from p. 111. See figs. 1 and 2 on p. 113. These images depict exactly what Mazar describes. See also Avigad, *Beth Sheᶜarim*, vol. 3, *Catacombs 12–23*, plate XLIV.1, which depicts a pointed gable over an elaborate rosette or half shell; for discussion, see p. 145; and see Figueras, *Decorated Jewish Ossuaries*, 28–29, for discussion of rosettes/circles.

53. For another example, see Wacks, *Handbook of Biblical Numismatics*, 14 no. 36 (struck 30/31 CE). See also the discussion in M. H. Jensen, *Herod Antipas in Galilee: The Literary and Archaeological Sources on the Reign of Herod Antipas and Its Socio-Economic Impact on Galilee* (WUNT II/215; Tübingen: Mohr Siebeck, 2006), 198–200. Jensen notes that most of Philip's coins presented a temple façade. It is speculated that observant Jews were told that the temple façade was in reference to the Jewish temple in Jerusalem, while pagans and non-observant Jews probably assumed it was in reference to the Roman temple called the Augusteum.

54. Wacks, *Handbook of Biblical Numismatics*, 15 no. 38 (struck 42/43 CE).

55. L. Mildenberg, *The Coinage of the Bar Kokhba War* (Typos: Monographien zur antiken Numismatik 6; Frankfurt am Main: Sauerländer, 1984), 32 (fig. 1). For other figures (by way of comparison), see 34 (figs. 2 and 3), 35 (fig. 4), 41 (fig. 10).

56. See Rahmani, *Catalogue of Jewish Ossuaries*, 143–44 (no. 282 + plate 40), 146 (no. 294 + plate 42), 166 (no. 392 + plate 56), 169–70 (no. 408 + plate 59), 184–85 (no. 482 + plate 72), and 262–63 (no. 893 + plate 134); Hachlili, *Jewish Funerary Customs,* plate III-3 (of a wooden coffin found at Naḥal David; end of gabled lid presents a rosette).

57. A. Kloner, "An Ossuary from Jerusalem Ornamented with Monumental Facades," in *Ancient Jerusalem Revealed* (ed. H. Geva; Jerusalem: Israel Exploration Society, 1994), 235–38. We are concerned with ossuary 14 found in Chamber E (now catalogued as 74.1508).

and one side present pointed gables over entrances. Beneath two of these pointed gables (on one end of the ossuary and on the less finished side of the ossuary) is a circle, in a pattern quite like what we see over the entrance to the East Talpiot tomb.[58] Ossuary 05.401 presents side by side on the front three rectangular architectural designs, each crowned with a gable. Beneath two of the gables are rosettes. Ossuary 69.685 presents on the front side two gabled designs. Beneath the gable, on the right, is a rosette. Ossuary 97.3942 presents a gabled architectural motif on one end. The pattern is formed with a series of small circles. *(See figs. 9.2–4.)*

At this point, comment should be made about the appearance of the pointed gable-and-circle pattern found on one of the ossuaries in the Dominus Flevit burial complex. Jacobovici draws attention to the similarity between this pattern and the gable and circle over the entrance of the East Talpiot tomb. Because some of the ossuaries at Dominus Flevit may have contained the remains of Christians, Jacobovici reasons that the appearance of this pattern lends support to the hypothesis that the East Talpiot tomb belonged to Jesus of Nazareth and his family. The argument here is again specious and misinterprets the archaeological data.[59] Examination of the very ossuary cited by Jacobovici shows that the ^-mark and circle (actually, more of a dot) combination on the end of the ossuary corresponds with an identical mark on the end of the lid.[60] Once again, it is an example of the stonemason's

---

The excavation was carried out in May and June of 1974. See also Rahmani, *Catalogue of Jewish Ossuaries*, 184–85 (no. 482 + plate 72). This ossuary is on display in the Israel Museum.

58. See Kloner, "Ossuary from Jerusalem Ornamented with Monumental Facades," 236, figures on the lower left of the page (end of the ossuary) and lower right of page (less finished side of the ossuary, to the right). One will observe examples of the pointed gable over a circle. Some of the artistic motifs parallel those found in some of the Akeldama tombs, which may have belonged to high-priestly families (including the high priest Annas, mentioned in John 18). See Avni, Greenhut, et al., *The Akeldama Tombs: Three Burial Caves in the Kidron Valley*, color plate 4 and pp. 26–29, depicting Cave 3, Chamber C.

59. One must refer to the television documentary; but also, again, see Jacobovici and Pellegrino, *Jesus Family Tomb*, 128–30. The significance of the pointed gable is interpreted in the light of much later European architecture, Knights Templar legends, and Masonic symbols. Jacobovici wonders if the gable reflects the hope of the founding of a third temple. This is not serious historical scholarship or biblical archaeology; it is the fantasy we see in *The Da Vinci Code*. For (quite negative) preliminary scholarly reaction to the East Talpiot tomb hypothesis, see E. M. Meyers, "The Jesus Tomb Controversy: An Overview," *NEA* 69 (2006). 116–18; S. Gibson, "Is the Talpiot Tomb Really the Family Tomb of Jesus?," *NEA* 69 (2006): 118–24; J. K. Zangenberg, "Yeshua aus Talpiot und Jesus von Nazaret: Bemerkungen zum angeblichen Grab Jesu und seiner Familie," *WUB* 44 (2007): 2–7; R. Riesner, "Ein falsches Jesus-Grab, Maria Magdalena und kein Ende," *ThBeitr* 38 (2007): 296–99. In the television documentary, Shimon Gibson's views are misrepresented. In his published statement, he flatly disagrees with the suggestion that the pointed gable and circle (or rosette or wreath) has anything to do with Jesus or the Christian movement: "There is nothing to commend this tomb as the family tomb of Jesus" ("Is the Talpiot Tomb Really the Family Tomb of Jesus?," 123). He also rightly calls attention to the stonemason's marks, noting that they were detected on three of the ossuaries in the East Talpiot tomb (pp. 122–23). For further discussion, see S. Gibson, *The Final Days of Jesus*, 175–87.

60. I thank Jeff Baxter for making it possible for me to enter the crypt at Dominus Flevit and examine the ossuary.

mark indicating which end of the lid goes with which end of the ossuary.[61] (In the documentary, the lid is not shown, thus obscuring the true purpose of the ^-mark. The pointed gable and circle pattern, like that found over the entrance to the East Talpiot tomb, is suggestive of the Herodian temple and not the Jesus movement.)

Depictions of the Torah ark, complete with gable and circle (or rosette), are found in synagogue art.[62] In the mosaic on the floor in the synagogue at Susiya, we find a pointed gable over a half rosette, flanked by two menorahs.[63] Although partially restored, the synagogue mosaic at Sepphoris presents a gable atop a temple design (with six pillars). Beneath the gable is a half rosette.[64] At Beth She᾿an, we find the pointed gable over a half rosette, resting on four pillars, flanked by two menorahs.[65] Striking examples are found in the art adorning the walls of the Dura Europos synagogue, where the designs are in reference to the Jerusalem temple.[66] Similar patterns have been observed in tomb architecture in nearby Petra (Jordan).[67] Of special interest is the famous Khazneh (or "Treasury"), where beneath a pointed gable one observes a centered design surrounded by vines.[68]

It is intriguing to consider the depiction of Samson carrying the gate of Gaza on his shoulders in the mosaic in the Huqoq synagogue.[69] The gate does not follow the architectural designs we have observed, which in one way or another reflect the Jewish temple. The gate of Gaza, in contrast, is depicted with a rounded arch, beneath which are four squares, forming the door or gate, flanked by supports with a brick-like pattern. There are no pillars, no gable, and no rosette, whether full or

---

61. For additional examples of the stonemason's marks appearing on Dominus Flevit ossuaries, see Bagatti and Milik, *Gli scavi del "Dominus Flevit,"* table 27, photographs 72 and 74. One will observe that in photograph 72 the stonemason's mark is the familiar ^, only its left-hand angle extends beyond the intersection with the right-hand angle. In photograph 74, the ^-mark rests on a horizontal line, thus forming a triangle. Both of these examples are stonemason's marks indicating alignment of lid with ossuary. If these marks have any symbolic significance, it would have to do with the Jewish temple.

62. See J. F. Strange, "The Art and Archaeology of Ancient Judaism," in *Judaism in Late Antiquity*, part 1, *The Literary and Archaeological Sources* (ed. J. Neusner; HOS 16; Leiden: Brill, 1995), 64–114, esp. 73–76, where it is observed that the art and architecture of synagogues often reflected the architecture of the Herodian temple. On p. 77, Strange calls attention to the mosaic on the floor of the synagogue at Hammath Tiberias, which depicts a gabled Torah shrine, with half circle beneath the gable. See also R. Hachlili, *Ancient Synagogues*, figs. V-24, V-28, VI-1a. On p. 101, we also see the facsimile of a similar mosaic on the floor of the Beth Alpha Synagogue. See also Hachlili, *Ancient Synagogues*, figs. IV-53a and b, V-29, VI-3a.

63. See Hachlili, *Ancient Synagogues*, figs. IV-47, IV-55c, V-46a, VI-1c.

64. See ibid., fig. VI-1b.

65. See ibid., fig. VI-3b.

66. See J. Gutman, *The Dura-Europos Synagogue: A Re-evaluation (1932–1992)* (USFSHJ 25; Atlanta: Scholars Press, 1992), 149. On the north half of the west wall, one can see several examples of the pointed gable over a rosette (p. 215 [fig. 5]).

67. See the plates in F. Bourbon, *Petra: Jordan's Extraordinary Ancient City* (New York: Barnes & Noble Books, 2004), 47, 51; J. McKenzie, *The Architecture of Petra* (British Academic Monographs in Archaeology 1; Oxford: British Academy, 1990), 2–9 + table 1.

68. Fedak, *Monumental Tombs of the Hellenistic Age*, 151–53 + fig. 225.

69. I thank Jodi Magness for allowing me and my graduate students the opportunity to view the synagogue at Huqoq and for discussing the significance of the Samson mosaic.

half circle.[70] The differences in the depiction of the gate of Gaza highlight the distinctive features of Jewish depictions of Torah arks and/or the Jerusalem temple itself. When a different referent is in view, such as the gate of Gaza, the familiar patterns and motifs do not appear, thus demonstrating a conscious and clear distinction between Jewish religious architecture, on the one hand, and non-Jewish architecture, on the other.

The evidence is overwhelming. The pointed gable and circle over the entrance to the East Talpiot tomb is Jewish, illustrative of Jewish religious symbols, and has nothing to do with Jesus and the early Christians. Indeed, the symbol is probably in reference to the Jewish temple. Given the fact that aristocratic and high-priestly families were buried in the greater Talpiot area and the fact that every name in the East Talpiot tomb is Hasmonean,[71] it is probable that this tomb belonged to a relatively well-to-do Jerusalem family with ties to the temple.[72] Indeed, some of the members of the family buried in the East Talpiot tomb may have been priests. The suggestion that the gable and circle constituted an early Christian symbol—and a secret one at that—has no foundation and ignores a mountain of evidence that points to the contrary.

I conclude this section with one final observation. There is no historical evidence of Christian interest in the East Talpiot tomb, no veneration, no tradition whatsoever.[73] This stands in contrast to Jewish interest in the tombs of the righteous, such as the Tomb of Simon the Just, and Christian interest in the tomb over which the Church of the Holy Sepulchre is built and Peter's house in Capernaum, to mention only a few of the many venerated sites. That first-century Jews were interested in holy places, including the tombs of prophets, kings, and other worthies, is attested in various sources (such as Josephus and the *Lives of the Prophets*). It is difficult to imagine how the tomb of Jesus and his family, complete with a symbol excised in plain view over its entrance that supposedly represents his movement, could have been completely forgotten, leaving behind not one shred of evidence indicating interest in the tomb.

A Second Tomb in East Talpiot

Simcha Jacobovici and James Tabor have identified a second tomb at Talpiot that they think is linked to the Christian movement.[74] This tomb is about sixty meters from the first Talpiot tomb. The tomb has not been excavated because it is now

70. See Hachlili, *Ancient Synagogues*, fig. VIII-13b.

71. On the popularity of Hasmonean names, especially among the upper class, see the discussion in Ilan, *Lexicon of Jewish Names*, 6–8; and Avni, Greenhut, et al., *Akeldama Tombs*, 69–70.

72. However, the East Talpiot tomb is not on the level that we see in some of the monumental tombs surveyed at the beginning of this essay.

73. In his negative review of *The Jesus Family Tomb*, Reed makes a similar point in reference to Paul, who knew Jerusalem and the Jerusalem church, yet "did not have the faintest clue about this tomb. His and other early Christians' silence on a matter that would gut their central theological claim is inconceivable" (p. 4).

74. J. D. Tabor and S. Jacobovici, *The Jesus Discovery: The New Archaeological Find That Reveals the Birth of Christianity* (New York: Simon & Schuster, 2012).

located beneath a condominium. In 2010, Jacobovici and his team guided a robotic camera through a pipe and were able to take several photographs of the tomb and its contents, including several ossuaries. One of these ossuaries contains an image that Jacobovici and Tabor think depicts the prophet Jonah being vomited from the mouth of a fish. Another ossuary contains a Greek inscription. Jacobovici and Tabor think this second Talpiot tomb, sometimes called "Talpiot Tomb II" or the "Patio Tomb," contains the remains of some of the followers of Jesus. If so, this could lend support to the hypothesis that the first Talpiot tomb contained the remains of Jesus and members of his family. However, almost no one agrees with Jacobovici and Tabor's interpretation of the second Talpiot tomb.

In the paragraphs that follow, I will review Jacobovici and Tabor's claims regarding the two ossuaries—one containing an image (ossuary 6) and the other (ossuary 5) a Greek inscription.[75] As in the case of the first Talpiot tomb, we shall see that the major claims on which the identification of this second tomb with either Jesus or his movement is based are seriously problematic.

Dubious Claim 1: The image on ossuary 6 is that of a fish vomiting Jonah, which is in reference to the resurrection of Jesus

In his review of the debate, James Charlesworth delineates three possible interpretations of the image on the first ossuary (i.e., ossuary 6), namely, that the image is either of (1) a *nefesh*, (2) an amphora, or (3) a fish.[76] It is the last interpretation that is preferred by Jacobovici and Tabor, and Charlesworth, with some hesitation, also accepts the fish-Jonah interpretation. This delineation of the options is based on a problematic understanding of ossuary artwork, especially as it relates to the variegated depictions of the *nefesh*.

It is probable that the image on ossuary 6 is a *nefesh*.[77] When one reviews all of the ossuaries (some one thousand) in the IAA Storage and Research Facility in Beth Shemesh, as well as the hundreds that are found in other collections, one will observe variations in the artwork used to portray the *nefesh* symbol. One will see pillars, usually with pedestals or pediments, which may or may not be part of a larger architectural theme likely designed to bring to mind the temple. Some pillar-shaped examples of the *nefesh* have floral patterns. Burial urns are sometimes depicted, usually with

75. For a list and brief descriptions of the ossuaries from the second Talpiot tomb, see J. H. Charlesworth, "What Is the Message of 'the Patio Tomb' in Talpiot, Jerusalem?," in *The Tomb of Jesus and His Family? Exploring Ancient Jewish Tombs Near Jerusalem's Walls* (Grand Rapids: Eerdmans, 2013), 555–75, at 574. For a schematic of the tomb, including its contents, see Tabor and Jacobovici, *Jesus Discovery*, 60 (fig. 15). The tomb is made up of a central chamber and nine niches (three on the west side, three on east side, and three on north side). The original entrance is on the south side. Ossuary 1 is located in niche 1, ossuaries 2–4 in niche 2, ossuaries 5 and 6 in niche 3, skeletal remains in niches 4 and 5, skeletal remains and ossuary 7 in niche 6, and skeletal remains in niches 7 and 8. The contents of niche 9, if any, are unknown.

76. Charlesworth, "What Is the Message of 'the Patio Tomb'?," 559–60.

77. The *nefesh* (lit., "soul" or "life," in Hebrew) represents the life of the person whose remains are within the ossuary.

handles, sometimes resting on a pedestal, pediment, or circle. One often finds amphorae or amphora-like designs. The amphorae often have handles; they may or may not flare out at either the top or bottom. Sometimes they are augmented with either a circle or a triangle, at the top or at the bottom. The amphora-like designs may rest on a pedestal or pediment. In my view, the image on ossuary 6, which some think is a fish, is a *nefesh* that shares some of the features seen in other examples of the *nefesh*.

Here is a tabulation of what I think are the most important ossuaries that have a bearing on the interpretation of ossuary 6 in niche 3 of the second Talpiot tomb. All of the ossuaries described here are housed in the IAA Storage and Research Facility in Beth Shemesh:

Ossuary 70.192: pillar with floral design, flanked by rosettes

Ossuary 70.185: centered rosette, flanked by two amphorae, with fish-like fins at top and bottom

Ossuary 69.664/1: burial urn, with prominent handles, resting on pediment

Ossuary 69.193: pointed, triangular pillar, narrow in the middle (to accommodate the two flanking rosettes), resting on a broad base

Ossuary 68.674: burial urn, with prominent handles, resting on rounded foot

Ossuary 68.269: fluted pillar with pyramid top, resting on stepped pediment; circular "handles" are presented at point where pyramid rests on pillar; flanked by rosettes

Ossuary 56.1931: dagger, with point up and ball at the end of the handle; flanked by rosettes

Ossuary 81.517: fluted pillar with capital and circular "handles" at the top, resting on pediment; flanked by rosettes

Ossuary 74.1543: fluted pillar with capital and circular "handles" at the top, resting on pediment; flanked by rosettes

Ossuary 71.664: plain pillar with symmetrical capital and pedestal, enclosed in an oval, with triangular foot

Ossuary 71.431: pillar with floral design, flanked by rosettes

Ossuary 71.408: pillar with floral design, flanked by rosettes; pillar may be resting on two tablets (Ten Commandments?)

Ossuary 02.1238: pointed, triangular pillar, narrow in the middle (to accommodate the two flanking rosettes), resting on a broad base

Ossuary 01.1520: pointed, triangular pillar, narrow in the middle (to accommodate the two flanking rosettes), resting on a broad base

Ossuary 99.1360: pointed, triangular pillar, narrow in the middle (to accommodate the two flanking rosettes), resting on a broad base

Ossuary 94.2079: fluted pillar with floral design on top; resting on stepped brick pediment; flanked by rosettes

Ossuary 93.1706: pillar with floral design, flanked by rosettes

Ossuary 93.498: ornate pillar, resting on stepped pediment; semicircular design rests atop the pillar

Ossuary 92.192: fluted pillar with capital and circular "handles" at the top, resting on pediment; flanked by rosettes

Ossuary 91.464: fluted pillar with ornate capital, resting on stepped pediment; flanked by rosettes

Ossuary 89.2817: pointed, triangular pillar, narrow in the middle (to accommodate the two flanking rosettes), resting on a broad base

Ossuary 89.2815: pillar with floral design, flanked by rosettes

Ossuary 07.275: rectangle with border, resting on stepped pediment; flanked by rosettes

Ossuary 05.400: "knitting needle," sharp end up, resting on small circle

Most, if not all, of the designs found in the examples above are also attested in other collections of ossuaries, such as those housed in the Albright Institute of Archaeological Research, the Armenian Patriarchate, the Pontifical Biblical Institute, Hebrew University, Holy Cross Monastery, Gallicantu Convent, Dominus Flevit, the Flagellation Museum, the museum of the Church of St. Anne, and others, all in Jerusalem. Other important collections are found in the British Museum (London) and the Musée du Louvre (Paris). The most pertinent examples have been catalogued by Pau Figueras.[78] These include fluted pillars, with or without circular "handles," usually resting on stepped pediments;[79] pillars with floral designs;[80] daggers or spear-points, some with a circular end of handle;[81] and burial urns, some of which rest on a small triangle or circle, while others are in the shape of a vase or amphora.[82] The *nefesh* on ossuary 6 in the second Talpiot tomb could be an urn or an amphora, with small handles, resting on a circle. If it is an urn, this would more easily explain the horizontal lines and geometric patterns (which are quite un-fish-like) on the image. Also against the fish interpretation is the vertical orientation of the image. This orientation supports the urn interpretation; in contrast, one would expect a fish moving through the water to be represented in a horizontal fashion and, moreover, to be in a horizontal position when it spews out something or someone onto the shore. Charlesworth counters this objection, suggesting that any other angle than downward "would mean that 'Jonah' was launched into the air."[83] But that is precisely how Jonah is depicted in art. In both paintings of Jonah being spewed from the mouth

78. Figueras, *Decorated Jewish Ossuaries* (see above, note 38).

79. Ibid., plates 21 and 22.

80. Ibid., plates 11, 12, and 13.

81. Ibid., plate 14. For dagger with circle at end of handle, see ossuary 7. Compare it to IAA ossuary 56.1931.

82. Ibid., plate 30. Ossuary 356 (from the Church of St. Anne) is especially interesting. The urns on ossuaries 84 and 324 resemble amphorae.

83. Charlesworth, "What Is the Message of 'the Patio Tomb'?," 561.

of the fish on the walls of the San Sebastiano and Priscilla catacombs in Rome, the fish is in a horizontal pose and Jonah is *launched into the air*.[84]

But for the sake of argument, let us suppose that the image on ossuary 6 is not a *nefesh* but a fish, a fish spewing out the prophet Jonah (see Jonah 2:11 [Eng. 2:10]). And let us suppose that the name Jonah (יונה) is actually present in the squiggle of lines and markings at the bottom of the image, in what is imagined to be the head or mouth of the fish, and that the circle or ball on which the image rests is a depiction of the prophet wrapped in seaweed.[85] Let us further suppose that the whole point of the image is to express hope in life beyond the grave.[86] But why does any of this require a Christian interpretation? Or a reference to Jesus?

Jonah, after all, was a famous prophet. In the first-century pseudepigraphon *Lives of the Prophets*, Jonah is said to have given "portents" (τέρας) regarding the fate of Jerusalem (*Liv. Pro.* 10:8). Accordingly, there may well have been in circulation in first-century Jewish Palestine eschatological ideas linked to Jonah. A pious Jew may well have depicted the prophet spewed from the fish as portending life after death. A similar thought may have occurred to Jesus or to one of his followers. As a matter of fact, a similar thought seems to have occurred to some Jewish interpreters.

In rabbinic tradition, it was believed that the lad raised up by Elijah was none other than Jonah, whose raising adumbrated the future resurrection (*y. Sukkah* 5.1, 55a; *Pirqe R. El.* §33). Because of his faithfulness in proclaiming God's message, he was delivered from Sheol and was granted entry into Paradise (*Midr. Jonah* §2; *Midr. Pss.* 26.7 [on Ps 26:9]). In this rabbinic tradition, the prophet Jonah was twice dead and twice raised up. The first time he died and was raised up was when he was a boy. The second time was when he found himself in the belly of the great fish and after three days was spewed out. The rabbis likened Jonah's experience with the fish to death (so also the targum[87]) and his escape from the fish to entry into the next life. The rabbinic typology is similar to what we find in Matt 12:40.

But did the comparison between the death and resurrection of Jesus and the near death and miraculous escape of Jonah originate with Jesus or with a pre–70 CE follower? Did this idea enter Christian exegesis and theology prior to 70? Perhaps, perhaps not. The comparison appears in tradition that is *distinctive to Matthew*, in the context of material drawn from Q and influenced by Mark. The Matthean evangelist has added, "For as Jonah was three days and three nights in the belly of the whale, so will the Son of man be three days and three nights in the heart

84. The images can be found in Jacobovici and Tabor, *Jesus Discovery*, 81–92 (figs. 22, 23).

85. Supporters of the Jonah interpretation suggest that the squiggle of lines represents the seaweed in which the prophet was entangled (see Jonah 2:6 [Eng. 2:5]; "weeds were wrapped about my head"). For arguments that the name Jonah is present in the "mouth" of the fish image and that the ball at the bottom of the image represents a stick figure of Jonah wrapped in seaweed, see Charlesworth, "What Is the Message of 'the Patio Tomb'?," 561, 563–69.

86. See the arguments in Charlesworth, "What Is the Message of 'the Patio Tomb'?," 560–63.

87. Whereas at Jonah 2:6 the Hebrew reads "the waters closed in over my soul," the Aramaic reads "the waters closed in over me *unto death*."

of the earth" (Matt 12:40 RSV). This saying, which is taken from LXX Jonah 2:1, is not found in the Markan and Lukan parallels (Mark 8:11–13; Luke 11:29–30).[88] The saying could be a Matthean gloss, not an original part of Q.[89] Indeed, the saying in Matt 12:40 could be a post-Matthean gloss, for Justin Martyr quotes Matt 12:39 verbatim but does not quote 12:40. The apologist argues that Jesus' "obscure" (παρακεκαλυμμένα) sign of Jonah would have been "understood by the audience [to mean] that after his crucifixion he should rise again on the third day" (*Dialogue with Trypho* 107). Justin's argument would be strange, had Matt 12:40 been part of the text. The audience would not have had to infer anything, for in this verse Jesus' resurrection typology is explicit, not hidden or obscure. We have good reason, then, to wonder if the analogy between Jonah and the resurrection of Jesus was even known in the first century.

Accordingly, there really is no firm evidence that the comparison between Jonah's escape from the fish and Jesus' resurrection from the dead was in circulation *prior* to 69 CE, when Jewish ossilegium, so far as we know, ceased in Jerusalem because of the arrival of the Roman army. The assumption that a depiction of Jonah on a pre-69 ossuary must necessarily have been produced by a member of the Jesus movement is highly questionable. If there was clear evidence of something Christian in the Patio Tomb, then the proposed Jonah interpretation perhaps would gain a modicum of support. Some think there is additional Christian evidence in the Patio Tomb, which brings us to the second dubious claim.

Dubious Claim 2: The Greek inscription on ossuary 5 refers to the resurrection of Jesus

On ossuary 5 in niche 3 of the Patio Tomb, we find a Greek inscription. Jacobovici and Tabor think it reads as follows:

ΔΙΟϹ
ΙΔΙΟ
ΥΨΩ
ΑΓΒ

88. In Mark 8:12, Jesus refuses to give a sign: "I say to you, no sign shall be given to this generation." In Luke 11:29, Jesus says that "no sign shall be given to it except the sign of Jonah." Matthew follows this Q tradition verbatim (at Matt 12:39), but adds v. 40 to clarify what the "sign of Jonah" is. For commentary, see Allison and Davies, *Critical and Exegetical Commentary on the Gospel according to Saint Matthew*, 2:355–56.

89. See R. Bultmann, *The History of the Synoptic Tradition* (Oxford: Blackwell, 1972), 118: "the interpretation of the sign of Jonah in terms of the death and resurrection of Jesus is a quite secondary formulation of the Church"; U. Luz, *Matthew 8–20* (Hermeneia; Minneapolis: Fortress, 2001), 217: "[it is] Matthew's explanation"; J. Nolland, *The Gospel of Matthew* (NIGTC; Grand Rapids: Eerdmans, 2005), 509: "[it is] an interpretive element" of Luke 11:30. In Jacobovici and Tabor, *Jesus Discovery*, 85, Matt 12:40 is assumed to represent Q tradition and as such to derive from the historical Jesus. This is very problematic. As stated, the verse is better understood as either a Matthean gloss some years after 70 CE or a post-Matthean scribal gloss that dates to sometime in the second century.

They take this to be, in some way, a reference to the hope of resurrection, a hope based on the resurrection of Jesus. This expression of resurrection faith, they believe, confirms their interpretation of the image on ossuary 6; that is, both ossuaries in niche 3 bear witness to the hope of resurrection that the believer has because of the resurrection of Jesus.

The problem here is that we have circular reasoning. The doubtful interpretation of the image on ossuary 6 encourages a very speculative interpretation of the Greek inscription on ossuary 5. The speculative interpretation of one "confirms" the speculative interpretation of the other. On top of that, the conclusion that ossuaries 5 and 6 are somehow linked to the Jesus movement is then seen to confirm the Jesus family interpretation of the first Talpiot tomb some sixty meters away. And, of course, what encourages us to see a reference to Jesus and resurrection in the Patio Tomb? The tomb's proximity to the first Talpiot tomb. The argument is quite circular.[90]

Jacobovici and Tabor believe that their Jesus/resurrection interpretation of ossuaries 5 and 6 is further confirmed by other ossuaries, found elsewhere in Jerusalem, on which the name Jesus appears. They appeal to ossuaries discovered by Eleazar Sukenik in 1945, which the great scholar believed were Christian. Sukenik interpreted one of these inscriptions as reading "Jesus, woe!" and another as reading "Jesus, bring me up!"[91] Scholars have not, however, followed Sukenik's interpretation.[92] Appeal to disputed evidence hardly provides support for a circular argument that is for the most part based on special pleading.

The problem with the interpretation that Jacobovici and Tabor recommend for the inscription on ossuary 5 in the Patio Tomb is that it is not at all clear that it is speaking of "lifting up" in the sense of *resurrection*. Indeed, exactly how the inscription reads is not clear. How many words (given the possibilities of awkward word breaks and abbreviations) are present in this inscription is not certain. A number of readings and translations have been proposed, including warnings about not distubing the remains in the ossuary. *If* the inscription is theological, it is far more likely that words such as "divine," "Yahweh," and "lift up" refer to lifting up or *exalting God*, not exalting, lifting up, or resurrecting the person whose remains are in the ossuary.

The word ΔΙΟϹ could be the genitive of Ζεύς ("Zeus"), but that hardly makes grammatical sense and is most unlikely in a Jewish context. But ΔΙΟϹ could also be the adjective δῖος, meaning "divine." If so, then the most likely meaning of the

90. See the reasoning in Jacobovici and Tabor, *Jesus Discovery*, 93–94. After admitting to uncertainty with regard to the meaning of the Greek inscription on ossuary 5, they state: "Given the context provided by the image of the 'sign of Jonah,' it seems more likely to us that it refers both to Jesus as a celebratory declaration of faith in his resurrection as well as to the resurrection of those in the tomb who have faith in him." Accordingly, the much disputed "fish" image confirms the meaning of the very uncertain Greek inscription, all of which is encouraged by the widely rejected theory of the first Talpiot tomb.

91. E. L. Sukenik, "The Earliest Records of Christianity," *AJA* 51 (1947): 351–65.

92. J. P. Kane, "By No Means 'The Earliest Records of Christianity'—with an Emended Reading of the Talpioth Inscription ΙΗϹΟΥϹ ΙΟΥ," *PEQ* 103 (1971): 103–8. For additional bibliography, see Evans, *Jesus and the Ossuaries*, 91.

inscription is "May divine Yahweh be lifted up." This reading understands the verb ΥΨΩ as an abbreviation for ΥΨΩΘΗΤΩ, the latter of which is found, for example, in Ps 17:47 (Heb. 18:47): ὑψωθήτω ὁ θεός, "May God be exalted." The fourth word of the inscription, which Jacobovici and Tabor read as ΑΓΒ, could be read as ΑΓΙΩ, in which case the inscription would mean something like "May the Lord God be exalted in (his) holy (place)." One thinks of Ps 107:8 (Heb. 108:8): "God spoke in his holy place [ἁγίῳ], 'I will be exalted [ὑψωθήσομαι] . . .'"; or Tob 13:9: "My God I exalt [τὸν θεόν μου ὑψῶ]." The language of exalting God (or the Lord), where in the Greek version of the Old Testament the word ὑψοῦν is used, is commonplace.[93] If we read ΑΓΒ, then the inscription might read, "May divine Yahweh be lifted up, Agab(us)," or "O divine Yahweh, I Agab(us) exalt (you)."

In view of the use of the language that we find in the Greek inscription of ossuary 5, it is much more likely that the inscription speaks of the exaltation of God than of resurrection. In any event, there is nothing about this inscription that compels us to think of Jesus or the Messiah.[94] Moreover, there is nothing about the image of ossuary 6, which is probably a *nefesh* (whether or not it bears the characteristics of a fish), that compels us to think the reference is to Jesus or to the faith of one of his followers.

Ossuary Temple Motifs

In the first part of this chapter, I emphasized the importance of temple motifs in the architecture and artwork of many of the tombs that surround Jerusalem. Now I would like to review the evidence as it relates to the ossuaries themselves. This brief survey is intended primarily as a supplement to the point that has been made regarding the significance of the gable and rosette/*patera* motif over the entrance to the first Talpiot tomb. The evidence strongly suggests that the gable symbolized the Jerusalem temple. The present survey will identify several other temple motifs in ossuary art. These motifs complement the temple symbol represented by the gable and rosette seen on many tombs and ossuaries.

---

93. Among others, see the following passages in the LXX where θεός or κύριος is combined with ὑψοῦν: Exod 15:2; Num 14:17; 2 Sam 22:47; Neh 9:5; Jdt 16:1; Tob 12:6; 13:4, 7; Ps 7:7; 9:33; 17:47; 20:14; 29:2; 33:4; 45:11; 56:6, 12; 63:8; 98:5, 9; 107:6; 117:28; 144:1; 148:13; Sir 43:30; Isa 2:2, 11, 17; 5:16; 12:4; 30:18; 33:10. In *Jesus Discovery*, 93, Jacobovici and Tabor refer to Ps 9:14, which speaks of lifting up the righteous. They also appeal to John 12:32, where Jesus speaks of being lifted up from the earth (i.e., on the cross); Acts 2:32–33, where Peter speaks of Jesus having been lifted up to God's right hand; Acts 5:31, where Peter again declares that God has lifted up Jesus to his right hand; and Phil 2:9, where Paul speaks of God having lifted up Jesus to the highest. John dates to the end of the first century, while Acts dates to the 60s, or, as some scholars think, to the 80s or later, and Philippians dates to the early 60s. It is better to explain the language on ossuary 5 in reference to the numerous passages in Scripture that we know were available and known to Palestinian Jews, than in reference to Christian theology, which is expressed in later New Testament texts.

94. In *Jesus Discovery*, 60 (fig. 15), Jacobovici and Tabor misleadingly refer to ossuary 5 as bearing a "Messianic Inscription." Nothing in the inscription suggests a messianic theme.

Josephus describes at length the enormous size, grandeur, and beauty of the temple sanctuary and precincts that Herod the Great enlarged and rebuilt in 20–19 BCE and beyond (*J. W.* 1.401; *Ant.* 15.380–425). The temple was "built of hard, white stones" (*Ant.* 15.392). Included were "entrance doors," which, along with their lintels, were "adorned with multicoloured hangings . . . with interwoven designs of pillars" (15.393). Under "the cornice spread a golden vine with grape clusters" (15.394). Herod "surrounded the temple with very large porticoes," which were supported "by a great wall . . . the greatest ever heard of" (15.395–396). The "great stones" were prominent and plainly in view (15.399). Josephus speaks of the "doors of the temple" (15.401), "four gates" in the western court and "many steps" linking the precincts with the city (15.410). He speaks of the "Royal Portico, which had three aisles" (15.411). Josephus tells us that the columns of the portico "stood in four rows" and were quite wide (15.413). He speaks of the ornamented ceilings of the porticoes (15.416). In other contexts, he speaks of the seven-branched candelabrum, or menorah (*J. W.* 3.144, 147), which the Romans seized as a prize when the temple was destroyed (*J. W.* 7.148). And finally, Josephus speaks of the architraves, or lintels, and their supporting columns (*Ant.* 15.416). "These structures," says Josephus, "seemed incredible to those who had not seen them, and were beheld with amazement by those who set eyes on them" (*Ant.* 15.416). In the much briefer description in *Jewish Wars*, Josephus asserts that the unsurpassing greatness of Herod's temple is seen in its "great colonnades around the temple courts" (*J. W.* 1.401).

We should infer from what Josephus says that the prominent features of the temple and its precincts were not only plainly visible but were distinctive features of which the inhabitants of Jerusalem were aware and of which many would have been very proud. In the time of Josephus, the temple and its magnificent precincts constituted a very tangible expression of Jewish religious devotion and faith. For this reason, it is not surprising that most, if not all, of the prominent and distinctive features of the great Jewish temple and its precincts are presented in one way or another on many of the monumental tombs and ornamented ossuaries of Jerusalem.

Enough has been said above about the monumental tombs. Here I want to list a number of ossuaries that exhibit the prominent and distinctive features of the temple and its precincts, which included supporting walls, steps, colonnades, and various buildings. Also included among these features are the already much-discussed pointed gable and rosette, as well as many other architectural and artistic motifs. (Unless otherwise stated, the ossuaries discussed below are housed in the IAA Storage and Research Facility in Beth Shemesh.)

Besides rosettes, the most common features of Jewish ossuaries from Jerusalem and its vicinity are columns, pillars, and pilasters.[95] Some of these, as suggested above, probably were meant to depict the *nefesh* of the deceased. But the pillar design itself was likely intended to recall the many magnificent pillars and colonnades that were prominent features of the Herodian temple and its precincts. Typical are ossuaries that depict on the long front side two pillars in the center, flanked by rosettes, bordered by stone blocks (e.g., ossuary 69.668; ossuary 69.188;

95. For discussion, see Figueras, *Decorated Jewish Ossuaries*, 59–62.

ossuary 69.194; ossuary 69.200). There are a number of variations on this theme. We find examples of three pillars flanked by rosettes, bordered by stone blocks (e.g., ossuary 70.165), or five pillars in the center, flanked by rosettes, bordered by stone blocks (ossuary 69.114). On another ossuary we have four plain pillars (ossuary 74.1502).

There are many ossuaries that depict a single ornate, fluted pillar, usually crowned with an ornate capital and resting on a stepped pediment made of stone blocks and flanked by rosettes (e.g., ossuary 74.1543; ossuary 81.517; ossuary 91.464; ossuary 92.192; ossuary 94.2079). In one example, we find depicted a wide, fluted pillar sitting on a foundation, crowned with capital and artistic design, flanked by two rosettes (ossuary 69.673). In another, we have an ornate pillar resting on a stepped pediment (resembling blocks of stone), crowned with an ornate capital comprising three complex circles whose intention was possibly to reflect the ceiling design of the porticoes in the temple precincts. The pillar is flanked by rosettes. Across the top of the ossuary are several more of the complex circles (ossuary 69.126). Another depicts a fluted pillar crowned with a pyramid of stone blocks, resting on a stepped pediment, flanked by rosettes (ossuary 68.269; recall the Tomb of Zechariah, with its pyramid top). Finally, one ossuary presents an ornate pillar with a semicircular capital, resting on a stepped pediment made of stone blocks (ossuary 93.498). There are additional examples in other collections.[96]

Many of the ossuaries that depict pillars usually depict them resting on stepped pedestals or pediments presented as stone blocks. The steps themselves recall the steps and stairs that enabled access to the temple precincts (Josephus, *Ant.* 15.410; Acts 21:35, 40). In some ossuaries, stone blocks comprise the main feature.[97] The long front side of one ossuary is designed as stone blocks (though the work is not complete) adorned with two ornate rosettes (ossuary 62.336). At least two ossuaries are adorned with stone blocks resembling those of the retaining walls of the Temple Mount (ossuary 74.1507; ossuary 74.1513). Another ossuary possesses a gable lid adorned with stone blocks (ossuary 70.193). There are more examples of ossuaries depicting "stone work."[98] It is very likely that these examples of stonework were meant to recall the great stones of the temple and the Temple Mount (Josephus, *Ant.* 15.392, 399: "the great size of the stones was seen along the front surface"; Mark 13:1, "Look, Teacher, what wonderful stones and what wonderful buildings!"; Luke 21:5, "some spoke of the temple, how it was adorned with noble stones").

Another common feature in ossuary art is the depiction of arches and porticoes, again reflecting the temple and its precincts.[99] We find examples of twin arched porticoes supported by ornate pillars (ossuary 95.1339, on display in the Israel Museum), or divided and flanked by pillars, flanked by rosettes, and bordered by stone blocks (ossuary 62.337). One ossuary depicts a gabled portico flanked by pillars, which are flanked by rosettes and bordered by stone blocks (ossuary

---

96. Ibid., plate 19 (ossuaries 8, 137, 192, 203).
97. For discussion, see ibid., 53–55.
98. Ibid., plate 18.
99. For discussion, see ibid., 55–59.

89.2825). In another we find an arched portico, flanked by rosettes, bordered by stone blocks (ossuary 69.105). Another depicts excised twin arched porticoes, separated by a floral pattern (ossuary 61.543). There are additional examples in other museums and collections.[100] On the recently recovered decorative stone from the first-century synagogue of Magdala, one observes a series of arched porticoes and pillars on the front and side. The back, other side, and top of this interesting stone contain art that at this time we think is related to the temple.[101]

Another featured architectural motif is the door or gate.[102] In one ossuary we find a door with ornate border resting on a stepped pediment made of stone blocks, flanked by very ornate rosettes, with floral accessories (ossuary 07.275). Another example is seen in an ossuary that depicts three gabled gates (or porticoes), with rosettes in the outside gates (ossuary 05.401). There are additional examples of doors and gates in other collections.[103] We also find depicted on one ossuary two gabled structures, with a rosette centered in the structure on the right, separated and flanked by two ornate pillars (ossuary 69.685).

Another feature worth considering is the small complex circles that resemble buttons. These are probably representations of ceiling patterns and decoration, as we see, for example, in the curved ceiling of the Arch of Titus, which stands in the Roman Forum. The front of one ossuary is covered with these complex circles (ossuary 62.328). In the center of another ossuary we find two rows of complex circles, flanked by rosettes (ossuary 76.26). Figueras presents two more examples. In one, the "ceiling" pattern adorns the front side of the ossuary; in the other, the pattern adorns the top of a flat lid.[104]

Among the furnishings of the temple sanctuary, the most important items were the menorah and the altar. Both of these, especially the former, are depicted in ossuary art (and on the inside of the Arch of Titus). One ossuary depicts three rosettes with the center rosette flanked by menorahs (ossuary 70.148). Another ossuary, painted red, presents a stylized menorah flanked by rosettes (ossuary 75.709, on display in the Israel Museum). Figueras provides several more examples of the menorah in ossuary art.[105] Michael Avi-Yonah identifies on another ossuary what he thinks is an altar.[106] It is necessary again to mention the decorative stone found in the first-century synagogue of Magdala, on which are several temple-related

100. Ibid., plates 18 (ossuary 367) and 19 (ossuaries 135, 136, 137, 192, 366, 432, 578).

101. For descriptions and discussion, see Hachlili, *Ancient Synagogues*, 40–41; Aviam, "Decorated Stone from the Synagogue at Migdal," 205–20; Bauckham, "Migdal Synagogue Stone," 113–35, Bauckham and De Luca, "Magdala as We Now Know It," 91–118, esp. 106–10.

102. For discussion, see Figueras, *Decorated Jewish Ossuaries*, 55–59.

103. Ibid., plate 20 (esp. ossuaries 58, 140, 344, 360).

104. Ibid., plates 24 (ossuary 332) and 23 (ossuary 383), respectively.

105. Ibid., plate 11 (ossuaries 128, 173, 262, 263, 561, 627). For discussion, see ibid., pp. 43–45.

106. See M. Avi-Yonah, "Oriental Elements in the Art of Palestine in the Roman and Byzantine Periods," *QDAP* 10 (1942): 105–51, at 148 + plate 29 no. 6; repr. in *Art in Ancient Palestine: Selected Studies* (Jerusalem: Magnes, 1981), 44 + plate 8 no. 6. This example is discussed in Goodenough, *Jewish Symbols in the Greco-Roman Period*, 1:129 + note 168; vol. 3, fig. 224; and is followed in Figueras, *Decorated Jewish Ossuaries*, 75 + plate 31 (ossuary 138).

symbols, including the menorah. On this stone, the menorah is flanked by two vases and seems to be enclosed in a structure supported by pillars.

On several ossuaries we find depicted ceremonial vases,[107] vines, branches, and other artistic designs. All of these designs are related to the temple and its precincts. On one ossuary, we observe two rosettes flanking a floral pattern with complex circles in four corners (ossuary 07.278). On another are depicted three rosettes flanking two floral patterns with complex circles in four corners (ossuary 07.274). Another interesting ossuary depicts a rosette flanked by fish-like vases or amphorae with some floral patterns (ossuary 70.185). I should also mention the sarcophagus recovered from the Goliath family tomb in Jericho, which, with traces of pigment, boasts a beautiful presentation of grapevines, leaves, and clusters (sarcophagus K 29244, on display in the Israel Museum). Ceremonial vases and other symbols are present on the synagogue stone from Magdala.[108]

Perhaps the best example of an ossuary with temple motifs is on display in the Israel Museum (ossuary 74.1508). All four sides depict elegant building façades decorated with floral motifs. This ossuary is, in effect, a miniature temple. On the front, we see a gate (or door) beneath a pointed gable. This door is flanked by four arched porticoes. On the left end, we observe a door beneath an ornate lintel. Above the lintel is a pointed gable. Beneath the point of the gable is a circle. This artwork closely resembles that found on the entrance to the first Talpiot tomb.

Summing Up

The artistic motifs found on many tombs in Jerusalem and on many ossuaries recovered from these tombs reflect various features of the temple's architecture and its various furnishings and ornamentation. Not only does the supposed evidence in favor of identifying the two Talpiot tombs as having something to do with Jesus and his movement fail to convince, the architectural and artistic features of Jerusalem's ossuaries and tombs, including the entrance of the first Talpiot tomb, strongly argue against linking the Talpiot tombs to Jesus and his movement.[109] In short, the architectural and artistic evidence has either been ignored or egregiously misrepresented by those who advocate the linkage of the Talpiot tombs to Jesus and his movement.

107. For discussion, see Figueras, *Decorated Jewish Ossuaries*, 72–74.

108. Another decorated stone has been recovered quite recently from the fourth-century Horvat Kur synagogue. The stone appears to date to before 70 CE. See Zangenberg, "Ein Dorf auf dem Hügel," 131–44, at 140–43.

109. The only way the first Talpiot tomb could have had anything to do with Jesus is if it had been the tomb of Joseph of Arimathea, which out of mercy was made available for the burial of Jesus. The tomb's quality and ornamentation are consistent with what we would expect of a family with ties to the Sanhedrin. Nevertheless, I find it inconceivable that Jesus and members of his family, including his mother, and perhaps his brother James, who led the Christians in Jerusalem for some twenty years, could have been buried in the Talpiot tomb without a trace of this having been left behind in history or in the form of archaeological evidence.

It is vexatious, but the dramatic and often inaccurate claims in the media are what we have come to expect. The Talpiot tombs are interesting, as are all other tombs in Jerusalem and elsewhere, and they should be studied carefully. But their value is hardly enhanced by mishandling or ignoring evidence and leaping to unwarranted and sensational conclusions.[110]

In the chapter that follows, we shall look at what is written on tombs and how these epitaphs and the artwork that sometimes accompanies them inform us about fears and beliefs in late antiquity.

---

110. Some of these issues are discussed in E. M. Meyers and C. Meyers, eds., *Archaeology, Bible, Politics, and the Media: Proceedings of the Duke University Conference, April 23–24, 2009* (Winona Lake, IN: Eisenbrauns, 2012). The 2009 Duke conference was prompted by Jacobovici's claims in 2007 regarding the first Talpiot tomb and by the Jerusalem conference in 2008 that was convened in response to those claims. Many of the papers presented at the latter conference were published in Charlesworth, ed., *The Tomb of Jesus and His Family?* With regard to the Jerusalem conference, the comments of archaeologist Jodi Magness are especially apropos. She participated in this conference, thinking "this was the best way to refute publicly the claimed [Jesus] identification" of the Talpiot tomb. "Nevertheless," she writes, "I came away from the conference discouraged because, although *all of the archaeologists who attended reject Jacobovici's claim*, this is not how things were presented to or by the media" (emphasis added). See J. Magness, "Confessions of an Archaeologist: Lessons I Learned from the Talpiyot Tomb Fiasco and Other Media Encounters," in Meyers and Meyers, eds., *Archaeology, Bible, Politics, and the Media*, 89–95, with quotations from 93. Magness chose not to publish a paper in *The Tomb of Jesus and His Family?*

CHAPTER TEN

The Talking Dead: Postmortem Beliefs in Pagan, Jewish, and Christian Epitaphs

Burial inscriptions constitute an important category of the remains of human culture. These inscriptions sometimes offer hope or advice, either in reference to the deceased or in reference to grieving family members or passersby. Sometimes inscriptions offer warnings, even threats and curses, designed to discourage vandals and grave robbers. Samples of all of these themes are found in Jewish and non-Jewish inscriptions alike.[1] Grave inscriptions also cohere with philosophical literature in which the nature of life, mortality, and the possibility of an afterlife are discussed. Grave inscriptions provide a very down-to-earth perspective, as it were, of what philosophers and writers sometimes talk about. In a sense, through these inscriptions the dead can talk to the living.[2]

A survey of Greek and Roman epitaphs will help us place in context Jewish ideas about life and death. The non-Jewish epitaphs will help us perceive in what ways Jewish ideas were similar to or different from Greek and Roman ideas, whereas the Jewish epitaphs themselves will potentially clarify the statements about

---

1. Helpful works include A. Deissmann, *Light from the Ancient East* (New York: George H. Doran, 1927); J. E. Sandys, *Latin Epigraphy: An Introduction to the Study of Latin Inscriptions* (2nd ed., rev. by S. G. Campbell; Cambridge: Cambridge University Press, 1927), 60–81; R. A. Lattimore, *Themes in Greek and Latin Epitaphs* (Illinois Studies in Language and Literature 28.1–2; Urbana, IL: University of Illinois Press, 1942); Toynbee, *Death and Burial in the Roman World*; A. E. Gordon, *Illustrated Introduction to Latin Epigraphy* (Berkeley: University of California Press, 1983), B. F. Cook, *Greek Inscriptions* (Reading the Past 5; London: British Museum; 1987); L. J. F. Keppie, *Understanding Roman Inscriptions* (Baltimore: Johns Hopkins University Press, 1991); van der Horst, *Ancient Jewish Epitaphs*; Horbury and Noy, *Jewish Inscriptions of Graeco-Roman Egypt*; Leon, *Jews of Ancient Rome*; P. Shore, *Rest Lightly: An Anthology of Latin and Greek Tomb Inscriptions* (Wauconda, IL: Bolchazy-Carducci, 1997).

2. The idea is well expressed in a funerary inscription from Lyon: "Since the letters on the stone preserve my voice, it will live on through your voice when you read these lines" (*CIL* XIII 2104). This inscription is cited and discussed in M. Carroll, "*Memoria* and *Damnatio Memoriae*: Preserving and Erasing Identities in Roman Funerary Commemoration," in *Living through the Dead: Burial and Commemoration in the Classical World* (ed. M. Carroll and J. Rempel; Studies in Funerary Archaeology 5; Oxford: Oxbow, 2011), 65–90, at 67.

resurrection and afterlife that we encounter in Jewish literature, including the New Testament. They may also clarify aspects of Jesus' teaching.

The epitaphs range in date from as early as the fourth century BCE to as late as the third century CE. Most of those that I discuss below are from the eastern half of the Mediterranean, but I do include a few from the west. The Jewish epitaphs come from the Diaspora as well as from the land of Israel itself. My survey is but a small sampling of a very large corpus of materials. Although I have selected a few epitaphs because of their distinctive features, I have attempted to provide a sampling that fairly represents the typical themes and sentiments we find in these inscriptions. I begin with the Greek and Roman epitaphs.

Themes in Greek and Roman Epitaphs

Coping with death was of great importance in Greece and Rome. The peoples of both of these lands gave this subject a great deal of thought and developed a series of beliefs and practices surrounding it.[3] These beliefs are discussed in the literature of late antiquity. Some of them are expressed in these peoples' epitaphs, and some of these epitaphs are accompanied by supporting visual imagery.

According to the great lexicographer Hesychius of Alexandria (fifth century CE), death (θάνατος) is the "separation of the soul from the body" (χωρισμὸς τῆς ψυχῆς ἀπὸ τοῦ σώματος).[4] Similarly, Iamblichus opines that the soul "goes forth from the body, and upon going forth is separated and scattered" (*apud* Stobaeus, *Eclogues* 1). Some likened the body to a house in which the soul is imprisoned (e.g., Plato, *Cratylus* 400c; *Phaedo* 81d). Death, then, could be seen as an escape. Even so, proper burial and attendant rites were important in order to ensure safe passage into the next world.[5]

Of course, not everyone believed this. In the epitaphs, as well as the literature, we find expressions of skepticism and denial with respect to life after death. But these expressions, which often come from Epicureans and Stoics, are the exception.[6] Most Greeks and Romans believed in some form of afterlife for the soul,[7] but did

3. For general introductions, see R. Garland, *The Greek Way of Death* (London: Duckworth, 1985); C. Edwards, *Death in Ancient Rome* (New Haven: Yale University Press, 2007).

4. Lattimore, *Themes in Greek and Latin Epitaphs*, 21n1.

5. Toynbee, *Death and Burial in the Roman World*, 34–35; M. Erasmo, *Death: Antiquity and Its Legacy* (Oxford: Oxford University Press, 2012), 5–6.

6. We hear statements such as "When life ends, all things perish and turn to nothing" (*CLE* I 420: *omni cum vita pereunt et inania fiunt*); "We are and were nothing. Look, reader, how swiftly we mortals pass from nothing to nothing" (*CLE* II 1495: *nil sumus et fuimus. mortales, respice, lector, in nihil a nihilo quam cito recidimus*); or the commonplace "I was not, I was, I am not, I care not" (*non fui, fui, non sum, non curo*). These examples are cited and discussed in Toynbee, *Death and Burial in the Roman World*, 34. Another example reads: "Nothing of my life endures" (*CIL* II 1088: *non mihi vita supe(r)stat*). For full text of the latter, as well as brief comment, see Shore, *Rest Lightly*, 52–53.

7. Toynbee, *Death and Burial in the Roman World*, 33–39. In the following foolish epitaph from Asia Minor, we seem to have a soldier's version of Epicurean philosophy: "I was

they hope for the *resurrection of the body*? The evidence is at best ambiguous. On the face of it, it would seem not. According to Aeschylus (fifth century BCE), the god Apollo explicitly denies that humans experience resurrection:

> When the dust has soaked up a man's blood,
> Once he is dead, there is no resurrection [ἀνάστασις].[8]
> (Aeschylus, *Eumenides* 647–648)

Apollo's position seems clear enough. In the following lines of *Eumenides*, the son of Zeus explains why resurrection is not possible:

> This is a thing for which my father [Zeus] never made
> Curative spells. All other states, without effort
> Of hard breath, he can completely rearrange.[9]
> (*Eumenides* 649–651)

There is no resurrection for a human, says Apollo, for Zeus "never made curative spells" that can restore life. Any other state or condition Zeus can alter (with no more effort than merely speaking the word); but he cannot undo death. It is in this light that we should probably interpret many Greek and Roman epitaphs. From statements like these, many scholars have assumed that the ancient Greeks and Romans did not entertain ideas about resurrection.

In a recent study, Stanley Porter has challenged this widely held view, contending that the "Greeks did have a significant tradition of bodily resurrection."[10] Porter appeals to a number of texts and authors who, in various ways, give expression to the belief that the human soul survived the death of the body, often with the souls of the righteous entering a blessed realm and the souls of the wicked entering tartarus (or hell). On the specific hope of resurrection, Porter cites Diodorus Siculus (first century BCE), who says of the goddess Isis:

> [S]he discovered also the drug which gives immortality, by means of which she not only raised [ἀναστῆσαι] from the dead her son Horus, who had been the object of plots on the part of the Titans and had been found dead under the water, giving him his soul again, but also made him immortal.[11]
> (Diodorus Siculus, *Historical Library* 1.25.6)

Has Isis (often identified by the Greeks as Demeter) come to possess the "cure," which had not been provided by Zeus? To be sure, this is an important text, but it

---

T(itus) Cissonius brother of Q(uintus?), veteran of the fifth Gallic Legion. While I lived I drank freely [*bibi libenter*] You who still live, drink!" (*CIL* III 293). For full Latin text and brief comment, see Shore, *Rest Lightly*, 50.

8. The text is cited and discussed by F. F. Bruce, *Paul: Apostle of the Heart Set Free* (Grand Rapids: Eerdmans, 1977), 246–47; and S. E. Porter, "Resurrection, the Greeks and the New Testament," in *Resurrection* (ed. S. E. Porter, M. A. Hayes, and D. Tombs; JSNTSup 186; RILP 5; Sheffield: Sheffield Academic, 1999), 52–81, at 52.

9. The translation here is based on R. Lattimore, *Aeschylus I* (New York: Washington Square Press, 1967), 172.

10. Porter, "Resurrection, the Greeks and the New Testament," 53.

11. The passage is cited and discussed in ibid., 76.

is not clear in what sense Horus has been "raised up." That he has regained his life is clear, that he became immortal (lit., "undying") is affirmed, but exactly in what sense he has been *resurrected*, as opposed to being resuscitated, is hard to tell. And in any case, would the resurrection of the mythical Horus tell us anything about Greek hopes for the bodily resurrection of humans?

What makes answering these questions difficult is that Porter cannot adduce additional passages that speak of resurrection. The story of Demeter's rescue of her daughter Persephone from the underworld is not really about resurrection as such. The cult of Demeter/Persephone promised security and bliss in the next life, but not bodily resurrection.[12] I would say the same with regard to the delightful and exciting myth of Hercules' victory over Death that enabled him to recover Alcestis, who had died, and to return her to her husband, Admetus. Is this a story of resurrection? The context of *Eumenides* makes it clear that the rescue of this woman from death was exceptional (and in any event, her restoration to life did not make her immortal, as in resurrection). Its exceptional nature suggests that neither resuscitation nor resurrection was in fact expected.[13] Although Porter's essay sheds light on Greek beliefs about the afterlife and at the same time shows how ambiguous Jewish ideas of afterlife and resurrection were in late antiquity (a topic that will be pursued below), it does not show that Greeks held to ideas of bodily resurrection. And as far as the evidence we have indicates, neither did the Romans.

Most Greeks and Romans did entertain ideas about the survival of the soul at death. Beliefs about what form this survival might take varied. Some of the expressions of this hope are quite faint. Here is a sample of Greek and Roman epitaphs (the dates are often unknown):

> Αἰθὴρ μὲν ψυχὰς ὑπεδέξατο, σώ[ματα δὲ χθών.]
> Air has taken their souls, but earth their bodies.[14]
> (*EG* 21b)

> [ψ]υχὴν αἰθέρι δοὺς σῶμα ἐκάλυψε [κόνει.]
> The soul given to the air, the body concealed in dust.[15]
> (*IG* IX 2.641.6)

12. On the cult of Demeter, see Pausanias, *Description of Greece* 2.12.5; 2.34.10; 2.35.4–8; 2.36.7; Callimachus, *Hecale* frag. 31. In the *Homeric Hymn to Demeter* (sixth century BCE), we are told, in anticipation of later traditions, that the goddess possessed the power to grant immortality to a mortal.

13. The rescue of Alcestis is discussed or alluded to in Plato (*Phaedrus* 179b) and Aeschylus (*Eumenides* 723–724), and in both cases the event is viewed as exceptional. Moreover, there is nothing eschatological about it. In my view, these passages, which are discussed in Porter, "Resurrection, the Greeks and the New Testament," 77–80, tell us nothing about Greek beliefs in bodily resurrection.

14. The epitaph quotes Thucydides, *History* 1.63. For brief discussion, see Lattimore, *Themes in Greek and Latin Epitaphs*, 31. The translations of epitaphs in this chapter are normally my own, though in some cases I have been influenced by or have adapted the translations of Lattimore, *Themes in Greek and Latin Epitaphs*, and Shore, *Rest Lightly*.

15. For brief discussion, see Lattimore, *Themes in Greek and Latin Epitaphs*, 31–32.

τὸ δὲ σῶμα καλύπτει
γαῖα, λαβοῦσα γέρας τοῦθ᾽ ὃ δέδωκε πάλαι.
Earth hides your body,
taking back the gift that she gave long ago.[16]
(*EG* 288.2–3)

ὀστέα μὲν καὶ σάρκας ἔχει χθὼν παῖδα τὸν ἡδύν,
ψυξὴ δ᾽ εὐσεβέων οἴχεται εἰς θάλαμον.
Earth keeps the bones and flesh of the dear child,
but his soul has gone to the house of the blessed.[17]
(*EG* 90)

μήτηρ μή με δάκρυε· τίς ἡ χάρας; . . . ἀλλὰ σεβάζου·
ἀστὴρ γὰρ γενόμην θεοῖς ἀκρεσπέριος.
Mother, do not weep for me. What is the use? . . . Instead, revere me.
For I have become an evening star, among the gods.[18]
(*IG* XII 7123.5–6)

Αἰλιανῶι τόδε [σῆμα] πατὴρ ἀγαθῶι πι[νυτῶι τε,]
θ[νη]τὸν κηδ[εύσα]ς σῶμα· τὸ δ᾽ ἀθάνατ[ον]
ἐς μακά[ρ]ων ἀνόρο[υσ]ε κέαρ· ψυχὴ γὰρ ἀείζ[ως,]
ἣ τὸ ζῆν παρέχει [κ]αὶ θεόφιν κατέβη.
ἴσχεο [σὺ] στοναχῶν, πά[τε]ρ, ἴσχε δέ, μῆτερ, ἀδελφούς·
σῶ[μα] χ[ι]τῶν ψυχῆς· τ[ὸ]ν δὲ θεὸν σέβε μου.
(His) father built this tomb for Aelianus, the good and wise,
Out of concern for his son's mortal body. But the immortal heart
soared up to the abode of the blessed. For everliving is the soul
that offers life and comes down from God. Though you mourn,
restrain yourself, (my) father; mother, restrain my brothers.
The body is but the garment of the soul. Reverence my God.[19]
(*EG* 651)

Μίκκης οὔνομα μοῦνον ἔχει τάφος, εὐσεβέες δὲ
ψυξὴν καὶ πεδίων τέρμονες Ἠλυσίων.
The tomb keeps only the name of Micca; with the pious
is her soul, even among the Elysian fields.[20]
(*EG* 338.1–2)

A! DOLOR ET GEMITUS INLUSAQ(UE) VOTA TUORUM!
NON TAMEN AD MANES, SED CAELI AD SIDERA PERGIS.

---

16. For brief discussion, see ibid., 32.

17. For brief discussion, see ibid., 33. This example and the ones that precede reflect a dualism according to which the body belongs to the earth and the soul belongs to ether, the winds, or the heavens (ibid., 31).

18. For brief discussion, see ibid., 35.

19. For brief discussion, see Shore, *Rest Lightly*, 56–57.

20. For brief discussion, see Lattimore, *Themes in Greek and Latin Epitaphs*, 36. Note the irregular spellings of ὄνομα ("name") and μόνος ("only"). These spellings appear in other epitaphs as well.

Ah, sorrow and mourning and your parents' hopes reduced
to a mockery! But not to the shades of the departed but
rather to the stars of heaven you are journeying.[21]
(*CIL* VIII 8567, last part of inscription)

.... UTQUE ERAT INFANS
FLEBILIS ET MISERE RAPTUS AD INFERIAS.
.... while still a child he was
borne with tears and sorrow to the netherworld.[22]
(*CIL* VI 14786, last part of inscription)

ὕπνος ἔχει σε, μάκαρ, πολυήρατε δῖε Σαβῖνε,
καὶ ζῇς ὡς ἥρως καὶ νέκυς οὐκ ἐγένου·
εὕδεις δ' ὡς ἔτι ζῶν ὑπὸ δένδρεσι σοῖς ἐνὶ τύμβοις·
ψυχαὶ γὰρ ζῶσιν τῶν ἄγαν εὐσεβέων.
Sleep holds you fast, blessed and much loved, noble Sabinus.
And you live on as a hero and have not become a corpse.
You sleep as if yet living, beneath the trees among the tombs of your people.
For the souls of the truly pious live.[23]
(*EG* 433)

It is interesting to note that the dualism of several of the above epitaphs coheres with Israel's ancient account of the creation of humankind: "Then the LORD God formed man of dust from the ground, and breathed into his nostrils the breath of life; and man became a living being [ψυχὴν ζῶσαν]" (Gen 2:7). Many in the ancient world and the world of late antiquity understood human ontology in dichotomized terms, with the physical reality shed at death and the nonphysical (the soul, spirit, ether, and the like) released. What was distinctive to the Jewish people, at least to some groups of the Jewish people, was belief in the resurrection of the *body* (as in Dan 12:2; Mark 12:18–27; John 5:29; 11:24; but flatly rejected by the Sadducees; cf. Mark 12:18; Josephus, *J.W.* 2.165).

According to Josephus, the Essenes believed something similar to the Greek idea of the soul separating from the body and passing into the air, heavenward. His comments are occasioned by mention of the Essenes' courage in the face of death. Josephus has this to say of the Essenes who were captured and tortured by the Romans during the great Jewish rebellion (66–73 CE):

> Smiling in their agonies and mildly deriding their tormentors, they cheerfully resigned their souls, confident that they would receive them back again [προσφερόντων εὔθυμοι τὰς ψυχὰς ἠφίεσαν ὡς πάλιν κομιούμενοι]. For it is a fixed belief of theirs that bodies [τὰ σώματα] are corruptible and their constituent matter impermanent, but that souls

21. For brief discussion, see Shore, *Rest Lightly*, 64–65. The expression "stars of heaven" is not necessarily Christian. Shore comments that "as far back as the Orion myth, pagan mortals were envisioned as ascending into the sky."

22. Translation adapted from Shore, *Rest Lightly*. For brief discussion, see ibid., 71. The epitaph is from Rome.

23. For brief discussion, see ibid., 48. The epitaph is from Syria and dates to the second century CE.

> are immortal and imperishable [τὰς δὲ ψυχὰς ἀθανάτους ἀεὶ διαμένειν]. Emanating from the finest ether, these souls become entangled, as it were, in the prison-house of the body, to which all are dragged down by a sort of natural spell; but when once they are released from the bonds of the flesh, then, as though liberated from a long servitude, they rejoice and are borne aloft. Sharing the belief of the sons of Greece, they maintain that for virtuous souls there is reserved an abode beyond the ocean. . . . The Greeks, I imagine, had the same conception when they set apart the Isles of the Blessed [τὰς μακάρων νήσους] for their brave men. . . . (*J.W.* 2.153–156)

Josephus' description of the Essenes' beliefs sounds suspiciously similar to Greek beliefs, some of which are attested in the epitaphs cited above. Of course, Josephus does not hide the similarity; he asserts it: "Sharing the belief of the sons of Greece, they maintain that for virtuous souls there is reserved an abode beyond the ocean" (2.155). The reference to "an abode beyond the ocean" is to the Isles of the Blessed (μακάρων νῆσοι), a theme that appears in Greek literature and epitaphs.[24] The language of Josephus is throughout quite similar to what we find in Greek literature and epitaphs. Especially noticeable are statements such as these: "the prison-house of the body," "released from the bonds of the flesh," "liberated from a long servitude," and "they rejoice and are borne aloft."

Some scholars think Josephus is either misinformed or being disingenuous. I suspect that the latter is the case, for Josephus knows perfectly well what he is doing. He has taken pains to describe the "philosophies" of the Pharisees and Essenes in terms meant to parallel the most influential of the Greek philosophies.[25] This should hardly occasion surprise, given how Josephus takes pains to show that the theology taught by Moses influenced the greatest of the Greek philosophers, including Pythagoras, Anaxagoras, Plato, and the Stoic philosophers.[26] The claim that the beliefs of the Essenes regarding the afterlife are essentially the same as those of the Greeks is pure Josephus.

Nevertheless, at the beginning of his description of the Essenes Josephus lets slip language that more accurately reflects their views. When he says that the Essenes "cheerfully resigned their souls, confident that they would receive them back

24. Hesiod, *Works and Days* 156–169; Pindar, *Olympian Ode* 2, 57–73; Euripides, *Bacchae* 1338–1339; Plutarch, *Life of Sertorius* 8.2–3.

25. In *Ant.* 18.12–13, Josephus describes the views of the Pharisees in a way that is meant to recall the Stoics. In fact, he claims that his training under the hermit Bannus was modeled after Stoicism (*Life* 12).

26. See Josephus, *Ag. Ap.* 1.162–165; 2.165–169. In the first passage, Josephus asserts that "Pythagoras . . . clearly not only knew about our customs but was also especially keen in his emulation of them" (1.162) and that some of this great philosopher's teaching in fact reflected Mosaic law (1.164). In the second passage, Josephus states that Pythagoras, Anaxagoras, Plato, and the Stoic philosophers "practically all seem to have thought in this way about the nature of God" (2.168). That is, according to Josephus the greatest of the Greek philosophers embraced at least some of Moses' teaching about God. For discussion of these passages, see J. M. G. Barclay, *Flavius Josephus: Translation and Commentary*, vol. 10, *Against Apion* (ed. S. Mason; Leiden: Brill, 2007), 91–98, 261–67. Barclay notes that Josephus especially appeals to the fame of Pythagoras "to claim a general congruence between Pythagorean and Judean theology" (p. 96).

again [πάλιν κομιούμενοι]," Josephus has echoed the language of the martyred brothers and their mother in the gruesome account in 2 Maccabees. Regarding the third son we are told: "When it was demanded, he quickly put out his tongue and courageously stretched forth his hands and said nobly, 'I got these from Heaven, and because of his laws I disdain them, and from him I hope to get them back again [πάλιν ἐλπίζω κομίσασθαι]'" (2 Macc 7:10–11). The faithful mother encourages her seventh, youngest son to face martyrdom bravely: "Do not fear this hangman, but prove worthy of your brothers and accept death so that in his mercy I may get you back again along with your brothers [σὺν τοῖς ἀδελφοῖς σου κομίσωμαί σε]" (2 Macc 7:29). The Essenes' confidence "to get back again" (πάλιν κομίζειν) their lives (or souls) comes from this well-known account of the martyrdom of the mother and her seven sons. This is the language of resurrection, in which one expects to receive back a living body; such language—rather than the Greek philosophy and terminology that Josephus attributes to them—likely expresses the true expectations of the Essenes.[27]

It must be admitted that on the basis of what has survived of the Essene library at Qumran, it does not appear that the idea of the resurrection of the dead was emphasized. The expectation of resurrection is explicitly expressed in at least one writing from Qumran. When the Messiah appears, "whom heaven and earth will obey," the infirm will be healed and "the dead he will make alive [מתים יחיה]" (4Q521 2+4 II, 12). This clause clearly echoes the language of Isaiah: "Your dead shall live [יִחְיוּ מֵתֶיךָ], their bodies shall rise" (Isa 26:19a).

The men of Qumran were fond of the book of Daniel, judging by the number of Daniel scrolls they possessed. Bedouin and archaeologists recovered two Daniel scrolls from Cave 1, five from Cave 4, and one from Cave 6. In addition to the Daniel scrolls, the Qumran community also possessed a number of scrolls related to Daniel, such as the Prayer of Nabonidus (4Q242), the Vision of Daniel (4Q243, 4Q244, 4Q245), the Son of God scroll (4Q246), and the Four Kingdoms texts (4Q552, 4Q553).[28] Although overshadowed by the Major Prophets (Isaiah, Jeremiah, and Ezekiel), Daniel is nevertheless formally quoted a number of times in other scrolls.

I underscore the popularity of Daniel at Qumran because this book affirms the resurrection: "And many of those who sleep in the dust of the earth shall awake, some to everlasting life, and some to shame and everlasting contempt" (Dan 12:2). The language of awakening from sleep is a metaphor for resurrection. We know this because sleep is a common euphemism for death in biblical literature (see John 11:11; Acts 7:60; 1 Cor 15:51; 1 Thess 4:13; 5:10), and also because Dan 12:2 alludes to

27. Josephus knew the doctrine of the resurrection, even if he obfuscated it somewhat to make it sound more like Greco-Roman beliefs. See *J.W.* 2.163; 3.374; *Ag. Ap.* 2.218. It should be noted that Josephus was not the only Jew to portray the law of Moses and other Jewish teachings in terms of Greco-Roman traditions. The Greek myth of the "Isles of the Blessed" is presented in a Jewish pseudepigraphic work known as the *History of the Rechabites*. One also thinks of a number of other Jewish writings from late antiquity, some pseudepigraphic, that imitate Homer and other Greek historians and playwrights.

28. 4Q242, 4Q243, 4Q244, 4Q246, 4Q552, and 4Q553 are written in Aramaic and clearly parallel and elaborate on themes in the book of Daniel.

Isa 26:19b: "O dwellers in the dust, awake and sing for joy." Just as Isaiah's "dwellers in the dust" will awake and be made alive again, so Daniel's "those who sleep in the dust" will awake, in the sense of being resurrected. The Greek version understands the passage rightly and so makes this explicit: "And many of those who sleep in the flat of the earth will arise [ἀναστήσονται], some to everlasting life. . . ."

Hope of resurrection is expressed in the Pseudo-Ezekiel texts (4Q385, 4Q386), which are based on Ezekiel's vision of the dry bones (Ezek 37). Whereas in Ezekiel the vision is a metaphor of national restoration, in the Qumran scrolls the vision is interpreted as a prophecy of the resurrection of the righteous. The aforementioned Vision of Daniel may have included a prophecy of resurrection (see 4Q245 2 4–5: "[. . . th]ese then shall arise [. . .] the holy ones will return"). Resurrection seems to be envisioned in the *Hodayot* as well: ". . . bodies, covered with worms of the dead, might rise up from the dust to an et[ernal] council" (1QH[a] XIX, 15).

These scrolls support the description of the Essenes' understanding of resurrection that we find in Hippolytus (flourished early third century CE). He states that the Essenes "confess that the flesh will rise again [τὴν σάρκα ἀναστήσεσθαι], and that it will be immortal [ἔσεσθαι ἀθάνατον], in the same manner as the soul is already imperishable" (*Refutation* 9.22). Evidently drawing on the same material known to Josephus (but apparently not on Josephus himself), Hippolytus goes on to speak of the Essenes' belief that the souls of the righteous, awaiting judgment, rest in a place of light, which the Greeks call the "Isles of the Blessed." It seems that Hippolytus has summarized the whole of the tradition regarding the Essenes, unlike Josephus, who omitted reference to the resurrection, knowing that this would have puzzled, if not repelled, his Greco-Roman readers. In my opinion, the testimony of Hippolytus, even if briefer, is truer to the Essenes' understanding of the postmortem state than is the testimony of Josephus.[29] Here again we have an instance where Josephus has presented the theology of his countrymen in very Greco-Roman philosophical terms. His description of the views of the Essenes on the afterlife should not be taken at face value.

There simply is no compelling evidence that Greeks and Romans entertained ideas of bodily resurrection or, if they did, that these ideas influenced Jewish eschatology in late antiquity. The hope of bodily resurrection was a Jewish hope, not a Greek one. How this hope was expressed in Jewish and Christian epitaphs will be considered below. But first we shall consider visual aspects of Greco-Roman ideas about the afterlife.

Imagery in Greek and Roman Epitaphs and Art

The art, architecture, and other forms of imagery on tombs and epitaphs can also be very informative. The sepulture of late antiquity was intended to remind the living of the dead, to convey messages and sentiments of the dead, to show respect for

29. So Puech, *La croyance des Esséniens en la vie future*, 703–69. There is no indication here in Hippolytus that he is trying to make the Essenes sound either like Greeks or like Christians.

the dead, to aid the dead in their passage to the "other world," and to protect the living from the dead. In a word, sepulture in late antiquity was intended to "bring closure," both for the dead and the living.

The primary purpose of almost every aspect of sepulture was memory, that is, to keep alive the memory of the departed. Included in the language of sepulture (whether in literature or in epitaphs) are μνήμη (and μνημοσύνη) and *memoria*, the Greek and Latin words for "memory." Their respective verbal cognates are μνημονεύειν and *monere* ("to remember"). Also related to these words are μνῆμα (and μνημόσυνον) and *monumentum*, from which we derive our English word "monument."[30] A monument is a structure whose purpose is to bring to remembrance the life and achievements of the person (or family) whose remains are housed within it.

Memory of the dead was very important in Greek, Roman, and Jewish culture. As one scholar recently put it: "[I]n the Ancient World the dead were not marginalised and forgotten but remained very much part and parcel of everyday life."[31] There is substantial documentation, both on paper and on metal and stone, to support this conclusion.

For the Greeks, tombs were built and epitaphs inscribed, as one epitaph explains, "for the sake of consolation and memory [παραμυθίας ἕνεκα καὶ μνήμης]" (*IG* XII 1.1064). Another epitaph explains:

> When I lived the living praised me; but now I am dead.
> This stone speaks for me. On behalf of me,
> a dead man, it guards my voice and
> publishes it forever to the living.
> (*SP* 145a)

This fascinating epitaph gives expression to an important theme relating to memory. Although the deceased individual in question can no longer speak, his stone monument will speak for him.

Many Greek epitaphs give expression to this purpose:

> But even so they honored me with a formal burial when I died,
> and they engraved the tomb for the sake of memory [μνημοσύνης ἕνεκεν].
> (*EG* 313b)

> Your body in its bosom, Callisto, earth has hidden,
> but memory of your virtue [σῆς δ' ἀρετῆς μνήμην] you have left to your friends.
> (*EG* 56)

---

30. It should be noted that there are spelling variations in the Greek and Latin inscriptions.

31. J. Drinkwater, "Preface," in *Living through the Dead: Burial and Commemoration in the Classical World* (ed. M. Carroll and J. Rempel; Studies in Funerary Archaeology 5; Oxford: Oxbow, 2011), viii–xii, with quotation from p. viii. See also the comments in E.-J. Graham, "From Fragments to Ancestors: Re-defining the Role of *os resectum* in Rituals of Purification and Commemoration in Republican Rome," in Carroll and Rempel, eds., *Living through the Dead*, 91–109, at 91.

Aristarchus third son of Numenius, of Patara, to Euphranasse
daughter of Olympus, of Patara, his wife, in remembrance and love
[μνήμης ἕνεκα καὶ φιλοστοργίας].
(*CIG* 4285)

A monument for your virtue,
your father Theocles set up, and with ever memorable praise [ἀειμνήστοισι δὲ ἐπαίνους] your city glorified you, even after you died and passed beneath the earth.
(*EG* 209)

It is not just reward for the character of Atthis the much-lamented,
nor what her virtue deserves, yet we have set up a
monument [μνάμαν] to bear her name forever.
(*EG* 204)

In one epitaph, the deceased expresses no confidence that his offspring will live up to his expectations, especially with respect to the duties of sepulture. It reads:

Nothing human is sure of privacy. Only he who builds
his own tomb [τάφον] for himself while alive gets what is rightfully due him.
Forgetfulness falls upon children when their father is dead.
(*MAMA* IV 212)

In the Roman world, the monument "was designed to preserve memory, and it was designed to reflect and be appropriate to the essence and standing (*substantia et dignitas*) of an individual or family."[32] Pliny the Younger (ca. 61–112), shocked and saddened by the report of the death of his friend Fannius, who had labored long on a history only to die before its completion, describes him as one of "those who think of posterity and seek to be remembered in works [*memoriam sui operibus extendunt*]" (*Epistles* 5.5). Elsewhere, Pliny elaborates on this theme: "Everyone who has done some great and memorable deed [*omnes . . . qui magnum aliquid memorandumque fecerunt*] should, I think, not only be excused but even praised if he wishes to ensure the immortality he has earned, and by the very words of his epitaph seeks to perpetuate the undying glory of his name" (*Epistles* 9.19.3).

Of course, not everyone wanted a monument. Pliny quotes his friend Frontinus, who expressly forbade that a monument be erected for him: "A monument is money wasted; our memory will endure [*memoria nostri durabit*] if our life has deserved it" (9.19.6).

Pliny perceptively recognized that Frontinus, like others, wished to be remembered, but not by monument or epitaph (9.19.8). Nevertheless, as we know from elsewhere in his correspondence, Pliny did not share his friend's optimism that he would be remembered if he did not have a monument and an epitaph inscribed in stone. One might profess that memory of a great man's deeds might live on in the

32. Carroll, "*Memoria* and *Damnatio Memoriae*," 65–90, with quotation from p. 66. Carroll cites *Digesta* 77.7.2.6; 35.1.27. Here and throughout the discussion of memory in the classical world I depend on Carroll's study.

memory of the public, but if there is no monument and no epitaph, the memory may fade. Pliny says this with respect to the monument dedicated to the consul Verginius Rufus, whose heirs failed to have his name and an epitaph inscribed on it (6.10.1–4). For this reason, Pliny advises the recipient of his letter: "Loyalty in friendship is so rare and the dead so easily forgotten that we ought to set up our own monuments and anticipate all the duties of our heirs" (6.10.5).

Unlike devout Jews, who rarely depicted the human form (because of Exod 20:4, "You shall not make for yourself a graven image, or any likeness of anything that is in heaven above, or that is in the earth beneath, or that is in the water under the earth"), affluent Greeks and Romans sometimes commissioned sculpted reliefs portraying the deceased seated, bidding loved ones farewell, or busts below which the deceased's life and virtues are summarized, perhaps with a word of advice for the passerby *(see fig. 10.1)*. Here are a few:

> And I have built you a great tomb in a conspicuous place
> for all to see, and put splendid doors on it and added
> a portrait statue [εἴδωλον] altogether like you.[33]
> (*EG* 590, lines 3–5)

> The man (who was) wise in all things and eminent among the citizens, reaching the end of a long life, the black bosom of gloomy Hades welcomed (him) and laid (him) on the hallowed couch of the pious. His son, together with his wedded wife, set up this memorial [μνῆμα] of (one who) perished along a rough path. Stranger, having bidden farewell to Democles, (son) of Democles, may you travel with safe footsteps.[34]
> (*CIG* 3256)

> Who can say, having looked at a fleshless corpse,
> whether it was Hylas or Thersites, passerby?[35]
> (*IG* XIV 2131)

> Recognize Rhoummas when you look at him in a portrait carved in marble,
> a man who performed great (deeds of) faith through prayer;
> dying he did not indeed die, for he came by a good repute.[36]
> (*SEG* XII 561)

---

33. The translation is from Lattimore, *Themes in Greek and Latin Epitaphs*, 227.

34. This text is inscribed on a stone relief depicting the deceased seated. Cook, *Greek Inscriptions*, 26–27 + plate 17. The monument dates to the second or first century BCE.

35. This text is found on a stone relief depicting the deceased, with a somewhat skeletal, cadaverous appearance, lying on his back. No doubt the gruesome image represents the epitaph's "fleshless corpse" (σκῆνος λιπόσαρκον). The question asked in the epitaph is rhetorical. Hylas refers to a beautiful young man seized by the nymphs (Apollodorus 1.9.19), while Thersites was regarded as the ugliest man who ever lived (Homer, *Iliad* 2.216). The point is that in death there is no difference. See Cook, *Greek Inscriptions*, 26, 28 + plate 19. The monument probably dates to the second century CE.

36. This text is on a marble bust of excellent quality dating to the early second century CE. The details of this sculpted bust are quite fine. The left eye lacks a pupil, suggesting that in life Rhoummas was partially blind. See Cook, *Greek Inscriptions*, 26–27 + plate 18.

POTITUS VALERIUS, MARCI FILIUS . . . MESSALLA . . . TRIB[UNUS]
MILIT[UM], Q[UAESTOR], PR[AETOR] URB[ANUS], C[ONSUL],
PROCO[NSUL] PROVINC[IAE] ASIAE BIS, LEG[ATUS] IMP[ERATORIS]
CAESARIS AUGUSTI IN SYRIA.
Potitus Valerius Messalla, son of Marcus . . . military tribune,
quaestor, urban praetor, consul, proconsul of the province
of Asia twice, legate of the Emperor Augustus in Syria.[37]
(*CIL* VI 37075 = *ILS* 8964)

QUID SUMUS AUTO LOQUIMUR, VITA EST QUID DENI[QUE NOSTRA(?)]
VEL MODO NOBISCUM VIXIT HOMO, NUNC HOMO NO[N EST.]
STAT LAPIS ET NOMEN TANTUM, VESTIGIA NULLA.
QUID QUASI IAM VITA EST? NON EST QUOD QUAERERE CU[RES.]
What are we or what do we say at last this life is?
Just that a man has lived among us and now is no more.
Just the stone and the inscription remain, and no other traces.
Now what is life? It is nothing that you should trouble yourself to inquire about.[38]
(*CE* 801)

D.M. CERELIAE FORTUNATAE CONIUGI CARISSIMAE, CUM QUA V(IXI)
ANN(IS) XI S(INE) U(LLA) Q(UERELLA) . . .
Μή μου παρέλθῃς τὸ ἐπίγραμμα, ὁδοιπόρε,
ἀλλὰ σταθεὶς ἄκουε καὶ μαθὼν ἄπι·
οὐκ ἔστι ἐν ᾅδου πλοῖον, οὐ πορθμεὺς Χάρων,
οὐκ Αἴακος κλειδοῦχος, οὐχὶ Κέρβερος κύων·
ἡμεῖς δὲ πάντες οἱ κάτω τεθνηκότες
ὀστέα, τέφρα γεγόναμεν, ἄλλο δὲ οὐδὲ ἕν.
εἴρηκα σοι ὀρθῶς· ὕπαγε, ὁδοιπόρε,
μὴ καὶ τεθνακὼς ἀδ[ό]λεσχός σοι φανῶ.
To the shade of Cerelia Fortunata, my most precious wife, with whom I lived
for eleven years without a single quarrel . . .
Do not pass by my epitaph, Wayfarer,
But when you have stopped, listen and learn, then depart.
There is no boat to carry you to Hades, no ferryman Charon,
No judge Aeacus, no dog Cerberus.
All of us below who are dead
Have become bones and ashes. I have not one more thing (to say).
I have spoken to you truthfully. Depart, Wayfarer,
Lest though dead I seem to you a teller of tales.[39]
(*EG* 646)

[NUNC EREPT]A DOMU CARA SUEIS TEGITUR.
[OMNE DECUS VOLT]US ET EO LAUDATA FIGURA
[UMBRA LEVIS NUN]C EST ET PARVOS ET OSSA CINIS.

37. Gordon, *Illustrated Introduction to Latin Epigraphy*, 106–7.

38. Shore, *Rest Lightly*, 32. The inscription, of uncertain date, is from Rome.

39. This bilingual epitaph takes pains to debunk most of the Greco-Roman afterlife myths. It probably dates toward the end of the third century CE. See ibid., 72–73.

Now she who was so dear to her family
Has been carried off from her home and is covered by earth.
Her fair face and figure praised as fair
Now are an insubstantial shadow,
Her bones but a bit of ash.[40]
(*CIL* I,2 1222, second half of epitaph)

Αβεῖτα ζήσασα ἔτη ι
μῆνας δύω
χαίρετε
Avita, having lived 10 years
two months.
Farewell.[41]
(*CIG* 6866)

Greeks, Romans, Egyptians, and other peoples sometimes made death masks and death portraits. Some of these masks and portraits remained in the tomb, but sometimes they were kept in the homes of the living, as reminders of the appearance of the deceased. A great many such artifacts have been recovered, including mummy masks made of cartonnage (pieces of used papyrus glued together) and beautiful painted portraits, usually executed on thin sheets of wood, busts made of stone, wood, or wax (i.e., wax *imagines*). Whereas the mummy masks are stylized and artificial, the painted portraits on wood offer very realistic likenesses of the departed.[42]

I conclude this section with reference to the tomb of Marceius Vergileus Eurysaces, near the Porta Maggiore in Rome. It is a tall structure resting on a series of round and square pillars. The top section of this structure presents twelve horizontal cylinders (actually, only eleven, for the top left corner of the façade has crumbled, taking the twelfth cylinder with it). At the very top, sheltered by an overhang, is a frieze detailing the activities of baking. We see men working

40. There are some odd spellings in this epitaph (in what is provided above, as well as in the first part, which is not cited). For *sueis* in line 1, read *suis*. See ibid., 34. The theme of being covered by the earth (in line 2) is commonplace in Greek and Roman epitaphs.

41. The brief epitaph is for a girl named Avita (as it would be spelled in Latin), who lived only ten years and two months. For children, precise chronology in epitaphs is common. The epitaph is inscribed on stone. Avita is depicted seated with a book roll in her lap. A reading stand is in front of her, perhaps supporting a second book roll. A dog sits behind her. At the top of the grave stone is a faux gable. Beneath the peak of the gable is a *patera*. Small leaves divide the words. Leaves and flowers decorate the margins. See Cook, *Greek Inscriptions*, 28–29 + plate 20.

42. For further discussion of images of the deceased, see M. L. Bierbrier, ed., *Portraits and Masks: Burial Customs in Roman Egypt* (London: British Museum, 1997); M.-F. Aubert and R. Cortopassi, eds., *Portraits funéraires de l'Egypte romain* (Paris: Réunion des musées nationaux, 2004); J. Pollini, "Ritualizing Death in Republican Rome: Memory, Religion, Class Struggle, and the Wax Ancestral Mask Tradition's Origin and Influence on Veristic Portraiture," in *Performing Death: Social Analyses of Funerary Traditions in the Ancient Near East and Mediterranean* (ed. N. Laneri; OIS 3; Chicago: Oriental Institute of the University of Chicago, 2007), 237–85; Carroll, "*Memoria* and *Damnatio Memoriae*," 68–69.

with grain, kneading dough, and inserting loaves into an oven. The baking theme could suggest that the cylinders were intended to represent corn-measures. All of this detail illustrates the work of the late Marceius, who in extant portions of his epitaph is described as *pistor et redemptor* ("master-baker and contractor")[43] The costly monument serves as a reminder of this baker's success in life and business.

The Importance of Memory in Jewish Tradition

The Jewish people were as anxious that the dead be remembered as were the Greeks and Romans. As in Greco-Roman memorials, Jewish epitaphs often recalled the piety of the deceased. Sometimes zeal for the Law of Moses is highlighted.

Before turning to the epitaphs, it will be helpful to cite a few passages from Jewish literature that appeared at the turn of the era. I begin with an important passage from Jesus ben Sirach (ca. 180 BCE):

> And there are some who have no memorial [μνημόσυνον], who have perished as though they had not lived; they have become as though they had not been born, and so have their children after them. But these were men of mercy, whose righteous deeds have not been forgotten; their prosperity will remain with their descendants, and their inheritance to their children's children. Their descendants stand by the covenants; their children also, for their sake. Their posterity will continue for ever, and their glory will not be blotted out. Their bodies were buried in peace, and their name lives to all generations. Peoples will declare their wisdom, and the congregation proclaims their praise. (Sir 44:9–14)

The beginning of this text speaks of those "who have no memorial, who have perished as though they had not lived" as though "they had not been born." These may be the impious, who have been forgotten and leave nothing behind. But they may be anonymous righteous persons, who are not remembered and celebrated as the well-known "famous men" about to be recalled and praised in Sir 44–49. The persons mentioned here in verse 9 may be examples of the righteous described in Isa 57:1–2.[44]

If the forgotten of verse 9 are not the forgotten impious but the forgotten righteous, as the context seems to suggest, then we should understand the balance of the passage (vv. 10–15) as praise for them. They may be forgotten (by name), but they were "men of mercy" whose deeds, paradoxically, will in fact be remembered and will result in an inheritance for their descendants. Their descendants will stand firm in the covenants, and they will have posterity. Therefore, their "bodies were buried in peace, and their name lives to all generations." All people will "declare their wisdom" and the congregation of Israel "proclaims their praise."

43. For discussion and plates, see Toynbee, *Death and Burial in the Roman World*, 128 + plates 34 and 35.

44. This is the perspective favored in P. W. Skehan and A. A. Di Lella, *The Wisdom of Ben Sira* (AB 39; Garden City, NY: Doubleday, 1987), 501.

This passage in Sirach sums up the concerns that lie behind many of the Jewish epitaphs. We hear the same concern for remembrance, though more briefly, in the Wisdom of Solomon (first century BCE):

> Because of her I shall have immortality, and leave an everlasting remembrance [μνήμην αἰώνιον] to those who come after me. (Wis 8:13)

Because of God's Wisdom ("her"), the righteous man who is speaking (ostensibly Solomon) will have immortality, in that he will be remembered forever (not in the sense that he will never physically die).[45] Philo also links the pursuit of wisdom with finding "everlasting life instead of death [ἀντὶ θανάτου ζωὴν ἀίδιον]" (*Flight* 97). But again, it is doubtful that some sort of afterlife is in view.

Leaving behind a memory worthy of emulation is well expressed in the account in 2 Maccabees of the martyrdom of Eleazar, the righteous elder who refused to comply with the demands of Antiochus IV and his lieutenants. After Eleazar's torture and death, it is said of him:

> So in this way he died, leaving in his death an example of nobility and a memorial of courage [ὑπόδειγμα γενναιότητος καὶ μνημόσυνον ἀρετῆς], not only to the young but to the great body of his nation. (2 Macc 6:31)

Hearing these words, especially the word "memorial" (μνημόσυνον), most Greeks and Romans would think of their own funerary traditions.[46] But in the Jewish tradition, μνημόσυνον (= the Heb. nouns זֵכֶר and זִכָּרוֹן) was also used in reference to the name of God (Exod 3:15)[47] and to the Passover (Exod 12:14; 13:9), as well as to other events, such as the placing of the memorial of stones at the Jordan (Josh 4:7).[48] To be sure, the language of 2 Macc 6:31 reflects Jewish traditions of sepulture, but the scriptural antecedents infuse it with significant theological meaning as well.

The death of Jonathan (ca. 143/142 BCE), one of the great Hasmonean leaders, occasioned the building of a great monument:

> And Simon sent and took the bones of Jonathan his brother and buried him in Modein, the city of his fathers. And all Israel mourned for him with great mourning and grieved for him many days. And Simon built upon the grave [τάφον] of his father and of his brothers and made it highly visible with hewn stone on the back and on the front. He also set up seven pyramids, each one opposite another, for his father and his mother and

45. So E. G. Clarke, *The Wisdom of Solomon* (CBC; Cambridge: Cambridge University Press, 1973), 59; A. T. S. Goodrick, ed., *The Book of Wisdom* (London: Rivingtons, 1913), 209: the text speaks of "undying fame."

46. Daniel Schwartz calls our attention to what is said of the philosopher Zeno, who encouraged the young man to seek "virtue and moderation . . . setting his own life as an example for all [ἀρετὴν καὶ σωφροσύνην . . . παράδειγμα τὸν ἴδιον βίον ἐκθεὶς ἅπασιν]" (Diogenes Laertius, *Lives of Eminent Philosophers* 7.10). See D. R. Schwartz, *2 Maccabees* (CEJL; Berlin: de Gruyter, 2008), 294.

47. Part of the verse reads: "This is My name forever, and this is My memorial-name to all generations" (Exod 3:15b NASB). The Greek version reads: "This is an everlasting name of mine and a memorial of generations to generations [μνημόσυνον γενεῶν γενεαῖς]."

48. For discussion of these and other passages, see R. Doran, *2 Maccabees: A Critical Commentary* (Hermeneia; Minneapolis: Fortress, 2012), 155.

> his four brothers. For them he devised mechanisms, setting large pillars around them, and he placed suits of armor on the pillars for an everlasting name [ὄνομα αἰώνιον] and beside the suits of armor carved ships to be seen by all those who sail the sea. This tomb [τάφος], which he made in Modein, remains to this day. (1 Macc 13:25–30 NETS)

Jewish burial customs are reflected in this story. Although Jonathan was killed in Baskama (northeast Galilee?), his bones were collected and returned to Modein (about thirty kilometers northwest of Jerusalem), where he was raised and where his father and other family members were buried. Simon took the opportunity to enlarge and enhance the Hasmonean family tomb. We are told that "he made it highly visible with hewn stone on the back and on the front." What is rendered "he made it highly visible" is literally "he lifted it up in (plain) view" (ὕψωσεν αὐτὸν τῇ ὁράσει). The seven pyramids, one each for Simon's brothers and parents, are the tomb's most distinctive feature. Pyramids or pyramid-shaped roofs would remain fashionable in and around Jerusalem for the next two centuries. The tomb was also ornamented with "suits of armor" and "carved ships," which were meant to bring to mind Jonathan's military achivements in the Jewish struggle for freedom.

It is in this latter feature that we observe Hellenistic tradition. The tomb is said to boast large pillars (v. 29). The passage speaks of "mechanisms" (μηχανήματα) that were set up as part of the tomb. In the parallel passage in *Jewish Antiquities*, which depends on 1 Maccabees, Josephus says there were porticoes surrounding the tomb (στοὰς περὶ αὐτό), which again reflects Greek sepulture at its finest (*Ant.* 13.211). To commemorate victory in battle, the Greeks would build a τρόπαιον (lit., "trophy"), which would include a suit of armor taken from the enemy and put on prominent display. The τρόπαιον could be set up at the site of the battle or in a temple. Because the Seleucids had erected τρόπαια in their realm, of which Israel had been a part, the Jewish people would have known what they were and what they signified.[49] It is interesting to observe that although the Hasmonean revolt was occasioned in part by the threat of Hellenization, those who led the revolt adopted Hellenistic names, pedagogy, and architecture.[50]

I conclude this section with a Jewish-Christian reflection on burial found in a pseudepigraphon. In one of the Christian interpolations in *4 Baruch* (9:14–32),[51] we find an interesting tradition concerning the burial of the prophet Jeremiah:

> And having come, Baruch and Abimelech buried him, and taking the stone, they placed (it) upon his tomb [μνῆμα], having inscribed on it thus: "This is the stone that was the helper of Jeremiah." (*4 Bar.* 9:32)

49. For further discussion, see J. Goldstein, *I Maccabees* (AB 41; Garden City, NY: Doubleday, 1976), 474–75. The exact location of the Hasmonean city of Modein (or Modi'in) is debated. It is believed that the Hasmonean tomb built by Simon is at Ras Medieh. If this is the location of the tomb, little remains.

50. For a concise and informative assessment of this point, see Hengel, *"Hellenization" of Judaea in the First Century*.

51. *Fourth Baruch*, also known as the *Omissions of Jeremiah*, was probably composed in the first century CE, perhaps in Palestine. A second-century Christian scribe extended the work by adding most or all of 8:12–9:32. The Christian elements are especially evident in 9:14–32.

In this imaginative recounting of the martyrdom of Jeremiah, the author tells his readers that the stone placed upon the tomb of the prophet was the stone that had initially deceived those who desired to kill Jeremiah. The purpose of the stone, which resembled Jeremiah, was to confuse and delay until the prophet had concluded his prophecy (9:24–29). When Jeremiah finished, the stone spoke to the prophet's tormentors, identifying the real Jeremiah (9:30–31). Placed on the tomb of the prophet, the stone is inscribed with the words, "This is the stone that was the helper [ὁ λίθος ὁ βοηθός] of Jeremiah," probably an allusion to the old Ebenezer tradition: "Then Samuel took a stone and set it up between Mizpah and Jeshanah, and called its name Ebenezer [אֶבֶן הָעָזֶר / ἀβενεζερ, λίθος τοῦ βοηθοῦ]; for he said, 'Hitherto the Lord has helped us [עֲזָרָנוּ / ἐβοήθησεν ἡμῖν]'" (1 Sam 7:12; cf. 4:1; 5:1). In any event, we have here in this curious tradition a memorial stone that literally speaks.

The value placed on being remembered is witnessed in the Last Supper, when Jesus speaks the Words of Institution (Matt 26:26–29; Mark 14:22–25; Luke 22:14–20; 1 Cor 11:23–25). In tradition shared by Paul and the author of Luke, memory is explicitly mentioned: "This is my body which is given for you. Do this in remembrance of me [τοῦτο ποιεῖτε εἰς τὴν ἐμὴν ἀνάμνησιν]" (Luke 22:19; 1 Cor 11:24; cf. v. 25; Justin Martyr, *1 Apol.* 66.3).[52] The deed that Jesus wishes his disciples to remember is his sacrifice, the giving of his body and the shedding of his blood. In uttering these words, Jesus has placed himself in the company of Israel's pious martyrs, whose sacrifice benefited Israel (Josephus, *J. W.* 2.201; *Ant.* 13.6). Jesus is not to be remembered by a monument or epitaph on a tomb; he is to be remembered by his disciples when they eat together.

It is in the same setting that the unnamed woman anoints the head of Jesus. When the disciples reproach the woman for "wasting" the costly ointment, Jesus defends her: "Let her alone; why do you trouble her? She has done a beautiful thing to me. . . . She has done what she could; she has anointed my body beforehand for burying. And truly, I say to you, wherever the gospel is preached in the whole world, what she has done will be told in memory of her [ὃ ἐποίησεν αὕτη λαληθήσεται εἰς μνημόσυνον αὐτῆς]" (Mark 14:6–9). We again have the language of memorial common to epitaphs. But again, her good deed will not be inscribed on a tomb; it will be told by those who proclaim Jesus' good news of the kingdom.

In the case of both the Words of Institution and the words to the woman, Jesus has used the funerial language of memorial.[53] But for Jesus the primary reference is to the language of Passover: "This day shall be for you a memorial day [וְהָיָה הַיּוֹם הַזֶּה לָכֶם לְזִכָּרוֹן / καὶ ἔσται ἡ ἡμέρα ὑμῖν αὕτη μνημόσυνον], and you shall keep it as a feast to the Lord; throughout your generations you shall observe it as an ordinance

52. Justin reads: "Do this in remembrance of me; this is my body [τοῦτο ποιεῖτε εἰς τὴν ἀνάμνησίν μου· τουτέστι τὸ σῶμά μου]." The reversal of the order of the two clauses is curious.

53. The Greeks ate meals in memory of the dead (Cicero, *On Ends* 2.101; Diogenes Laertius, *Lives of Eminent Philosophers* 10.18, where Epicurus makes provision in his will for funeral offerings and celebrations for his birthday and other notable dates).

for ever" (Exod 12:14; cf. 13:9; Deut 16:3).[54] When Jesus commands his disciples "Do this in remembrance of me" (Luke 22:19; 1 Cor 11:24b, 25b), he has reinterpreted the μνημόσυνον of the Passover tradition. In effect, Jesus has become the new object of the Passover memorial.[55]

Themes in Jewish Epitaphs

The themes in Jewish epitaphs are for the most part similar to those observed in Greek and Roman epitaphs. There are major differences, of course. Greek and Roman mythology rarely appears. Instead, we often find affirmation of one God, the God of Israel. The word "peace" often appears, usually in Hebrew, even in Greek and Latin inscriptions. Consolation, praise, record of deeds, laments, and warnings against violation of sepulture are the most common themes in Jewish burial inscriptions.

I begin with inscriptions from three of the tombs in and around Jerusalem. On the Tomb of Jason we read, in Aramaic (line 1): "Make a powerful lament for Jason . . . (you) who have built yourself a tomb [קבור], Elder, rest in peace [הוה שלם]!"[56] The remarkable inscription in the Abba Cave (or Tomb) is inscribed in beautiful paleo-Hebrew script. It refers to "Mattathias son of Judah" (מתתי בר יהוד), who is probably none other than Antigonus son of Aristobulus, defeated by Herod in 37 BCE.[57] The inscription on the prominent façade of the Benei Hezir Tomb in the Kidron reads: "This is the tomb and the *nefesh* [הקבר והנפש] of Eleazar, Ḥanian, Yoʿezer, Yehudah, Shimʿon, Yoḥanan sons of Yosef son of Oved; Yosef and Eleazar, sons of Ḥaniah, priests from the Sons of Ḥezir [כהנים מבני חזיר]."[58]

Finally, two Byzantine-era Greek inscriptions were inscribed on the south side of the so-called Tomb of Absalom (also known as "Absalom's Pillar"). Two horizontal lines above the robber's hole read (with restorations): τόδε μνεμεῖον Ζακκαρίας μάρτυρος πρεσβητέρου θεοσεβεστάτου παππέας Ιοάννου ("Here is the tomb of Zachariah, witness, old, very pious, father of John").[59] To the right of the robber's hole, written sideways, a six-line inscription reads (with restorations): ὁ θάφος Συμεὼν ὁ ἦν δικαιότατος ἄνθρώπος καὶ γῆρας ἡ εὐσηβήστατος καὶ παράκλησιν

54. J. T. Carrol, *Luke. A Commentary* (NTL; Louisville: Westminster John Knox, 2012), 435: "The Passover meal's call to remembrance of God's liberation of the people from slavery in Egypt . . . is merged with memory of Jesus."

55. Fitzmyer, *The Gospel according to Luke*, 2:1401; idem, *First Corinthians* (AB 32; New Haven: Yale University Press, 2008), 440–41; R. Ciampa and B. S. Rosner, *The First Letter to the Corinthians* (PNTC; Grand Rapids: Eerdmans, 2010), 551.

56. Hachlili, *Jewish Funerary Customs*, 163–66 + fig. V-1.

57. Elitzur, "The Abba Cave: Unpublished Findings and a New Proposal," 83–102. See the comments in ch. 7 above.

58. Hachlili, *Jewish Funerary Customs*, 167–68 + fig. V-3.

59. The epitaph alludes to Luke 1:5–23, 57–80. I have translated μάρτυρος as "witness," rather than "martyr," because the author of the "epitaph" on the Tomb of Absalom was probably thinking of Zechariah's testimony in Luke 1:67–79.

λαοῦ προσδεχόμενος ("The tomb of Simeon who was a very just man and a very devoted old one, and for the consolation of the people was waiting").[60]

Several tombs and ossuaries have inscribed on them warnings against theft and violation. The warnings in Jewish sepulture are somewhat milder than those in Greek and Roman epitaphs, though threats, and even curses, are sometimes found. We begin with a few warnings in Hebrew and Aramaic. *(See fig. 10.2.)*

On an ossuary from Jerusalem we read (on the side) "father Dostas" and (on the lid) "Dostas, our father, and not to be opened [דוסתס אבונה ולא למפתח]."[61] More ominous are the warnings found in the necropolis of Beth Sheʿarim, in Galilee. Some of these warnings predict certain and unpleasant death: "Anyone who shall open this burial upon him who is inside it shall die of an evil end [ימות בסוף ביש]";[62] "He who is buried here is Simeon, son of Yoḥanan; and on oath whoever shall open upon him shall die of an evil end [ובשבועה דכל דיפתח עלוי יהי מאית בסוף ביש]."[63]

Here are a few Greek examples of Jewish epitaphs in which appeal to God is explicit or implied: "I, Hesychios, lie here with my wife; whoever dares to open upon us shall not have a share in eternal life [μὴ ἔχῃ μέρος εἰς τὸν βίον ἀόνιον]";[64] "Nobody shall open, in accordance with the divine and secular law";[65] "Anyone who changes this lady's place, He who promised to make alive the dead [ζωποιῆσε τοῦς νεκρούς] will Himself judge (him)."[66] Other significant warnings are found on the Uzziah plaque and on the "qorban" ossuary.[67]

Outside of the land of Israel, Jewish warnings against violation of sepulture sometimes become more threatening.[68] Several epitaphs, all of them written in Greek, threaten fines and divine judgment: "If someone does something against these things, he will face the judgment of God [ἕξῃ κρίσιν πρὸς τὸν θεόν]";[69] "No

60. Once again the epitaph alludes to a passage in Luke's infancy narrative; this time it is Luke 2:25–35, especially v. 25, where it is said of Simeon: ὁ ἄνθρωπος οὗτος δίκαιος καὶ εὐλαβὴς προσδεχόμενος παράκλησιν τοῦ Ἰσραήλ ("this man was righteous and devout, looking for the consolation of Israel").

61. Rahmani, *Catalogue of Jewish Ossuaries*, 94 (no. 70); *CIIP* no. 375.

62. Avigad, *Beth Sheʿarim*, vol. 3, *Catacombs 12–23*, 233–34 (no. 1) + fig. 104.

63. Ibid., 234–35 (no. 2) + fig. 105. See also 235 (no. 3) + fig. 106, which is only partially preserved: "Anyone who shall open . . . ."

64. Schwabe and Lifshitz, *Beth Sheʿarim*, vol. 2, *The Greek Inscriptions*, 112–14 (no. 129): ἀόνιον = ἀώνιον.

65. Ibid., 123–24 (no. 134).

66. Ibid., 139–40 (no. 162): ζωποιῆσε = ζωποιῆσει.

67. On the King Uzziah inscription, see *CIIP* no. 602; on the ossuary with the qorban inscription, see Evans, *Jesus and the Ossuaries*, 96–98; *CIIP* no. 287. For a learned assessment of this inscription and its relevance for Jesus, see Fitzmyer, "Aramaic Qorbân Inscription from Jebel Hallet et-Tûrî and Mk 7:11/Mt 15:5," 60–65; repr. in idem, *Essays on the Semitic Background of the New Testament*, 93–100. For discussion and plate of the Uzziah inscription, see Hachlili, *Jewish Funerary Customs*, 497–98 + fig. XI-10. For additional examples of grave warnings, some reaching back to the First Temple era, see *Jewish Funerary Customs*, 496–507.

68. J. H. M. Strubbe, "Curses against Violation of the Grave in Jewish Epitaphs from Asia Minor," in *Studies in Early Jewish Epigraphy* (ed. J. W. van Henten and P. W. van der Horst; AGJU 21; Leiden: Brill, 1994), 70–128.

69. *TAM* IV.1 (no. 375); Strubbe, "Curses against Violation of the Grave," 107–8 (no. 2).

one else may be put in it; but if someone will bury (another corpse here), he knows the law of the Jews [ἰς ὃ ἕτερος οὐ τεθῇ· εἰ δέ τις ἐπιτηδεύσι, τὸν νόμον οἶδεν τῶν Εἰουδέων]";[70] "But whoever will attempt to place another (corpse) in it, will receive eternal scourge from the immortal God [ὅς δ᾽ ἂν ἐπιχειρήσει ἕτερον ἐπεισενενκεῖν, λήψεται παρὰ τοῦ ἀθανάτου θεοῦ μάστειγα αἰώνιον]";[71] "But if one of them is not afraid of these curses, may the sickle of curse enter their houses and leave no one behind [ἐὰν δέ τις αὐτῶν μὴ φοβηθῇ τούτων τῶν καταρῶν, τὸ ἀρᾶς δρέπανον εἰσέλθοιτο εἰς τὰς οἰκήσις αὐτῶν καὶ μηδίναν ἐνκαταλείψετο]";[72] "If anyone will bury another corpse or commit injustice (to the tomb) by way of purchase, he will get the curses that are written in Deuteronomy [εἴ τις θάψει ἕτερον νεκρὸν ἢ ἀδικήσει λόγῳ ἀγορασίας, ἔσται αὐτῷ αἱ ἀραὶ ἡ γεγραμμέναι ἐν τῷ Δευτερονομίῳ]";[73] "Whoever will disturb (the tomb), may an iron broom mangle (his) house and (the same) for the man who has given advice [ὅς ἂν ἀνορύσει, σάρον σιδαροῦν τὸν οἰκῶνα σάναιτο καὶ τῷ συμβουλεύσαντι]";[74] "Whoever breaks open (this grave) and puts in another corpse, or purchases the grave or defiles the inscription, the wrath of God will destroy his whole family [ὅς ἂν ἀνορύξξι καὶ βαλῖ ἄλλον νεκρὸν ἢ τύνβον πρίατε ἢ γράμμα μιάνι, ἐξολέσι ἐκίνου σύνπαν γένος ἡ θεοῦ ὀργή]";[75] "He has erected the stele upon the tomb. If someone will harm this (stele), may he obtain the wrath of the immortal God [τύμβῳ ἔπι στήλην τήνδ᾽ εἵδρυσεν· εἰ δέ τις αὐτὴν σείνετε, ἀθανάτοιο θεοῦ μήνιμα λάβοιτο]";[76] and finally, "But if someone either buys this grave or erases the inscription, the wrath of God will destroy his whole family [εἰ δέ τις ἢ τύνβον πρίατα ἢ γράμμα μιώσῃ, ἐξολέσι κίνου σύνπαν γένος ἡ θεοῦ ὀργή]."[77] *(See fig. 10.3.)*

One epitaph from Rheneia, a small island near Delos, calls upon God to take revenge against murderers:

---

70. *CIJ* II 774; Strubbe, "Curses against Violation of the Grave," 108 (no. 3).

71. *CIG* III 3891; Strubbe, "Curses against Violation of the Grave," 109–10 (no. 4).

72. *CIJ* II 768; *MAMA* VI 316; Strubbe, "Curses against Violation of the Grave," 111–14 (no. 6).

73. *CIJ* II 760; *MAMA* VI 335A; Strubbe, "Curses against Violation of the Grave," 115–17 (no. 7). The curses of Deuteronomy are also referenced in *MAMA* VI 335; Strubbe, "Curses against Violation of the Grave," 117–18 (no. 8).

74. *CIG* III 3861B; *CIJ* II 762; Strubbe, "Curses against Violation of the Grave," 121–22 (no. 10). οἰκῶνα ("house") is partially restored. εἰκῶνα ("image," "likeness") has also been suggested. The tomb and curse may be pagan, not Jewish. The threat of the iron broom that mangles appears in *SEG* VI 172; Strubbe, "Curses against Violation of the Grave," 122–23 (no. 11). Pagan elements sometimes do appear in Jewish (and Christian) epitaphs. Lamenting the death of his young daughter Theodosia, her father asks, "But O pitiless Charon [ὦ νηλεόθυμε Χάρον], why did she in her gentleness so much delight you, leaving to her father grief unbounded?" See *NewDocs*, vol. 4, no. 114; Horbury and Noy, *Jewish Inscriptions*, 234–35 (no. 141).

75. *MAMA* VI 325; Strubbe, "Curses against Violation of the Grave," 123–25 (no. 12).

76. *SEG* I 452; *MAMA* I 267; Strubbe, "Curses against Violation of the Grave," 125–26 (no. 13).

77. Inv. No. 72932 of the Museo Nazionale Romano at Rome; Strubbe, "Curses against Violation of the Grave," 126–27 (no. 14).

> I call upon and pray to God the Most High, the Lord of the spirits and of all flesh, against those who have treacherously murdered or poisoned the poor Heraclea, who died untimely, and who have unjustly shed her innocent blood. May the same happen to them who have murdered or poisoned her and to their children, Lord, you who see everything, and you, angels of God, for whom every soul humiliates itself on this day with supplications, that you revenge her innocent blood and settle your account with them as soon as possible.[78] (*CIJ* II 725)

Many inscriptions in Israel contain dolorous elements, such as ". . . having gone to Hades [ἐλθὼν εἰς Αδην], I, Justus, lie here"[79] and the common exclamation of "woe [חבל]!"[80] Consider also the following inscription, interpreted by Frank Cross to read: "No man can go up [לאית לאנש למעלה] (from the grave), nor (can) Eleazar or Shappirah."[81] This inscription, which appears to deny any hope of resurrection, is found on an ossuary found on Mount Scopus.[82]

The wish for "peace" (שלום) is quite common in Jewish epitaphs. The benediction is usually written in Hebrew, even when the inscription itself is in Greek or Latin; for example, one Greek inscription reads: "Jacob from Caesarea, the head of the synagogue [ἀρχισυνάγωγος], of Pamphylia. Peace [שלום]."[83] We find the word sometimes in transliteration, as in "Farewell [σαλλόμ], Athan, son of Doron."[84] Naturally, the blessing appears often in Hebrew inscriptions, sometimes asyndetically, other times as part of a sentence; for example, "Rabbi Joshua, son of Rabbi Hillel, son of Ation. (May his) resting place be in peace";[85] "This is the coffin of the lady Mega, the wife of Rabbi Joshua son of Levi. Peace";[86] "Peace on Yeshurun forever [Hebrew]; (Tomb) of Abraham son of the blessed Robel (son) of Pharbaithos [Greek]."[87] Sometimes the afterlife is in view, as in "Peace on her resting place. May her soul have eternal life [נשמתה לחיי עולם]."[88] An example of the Hebrew wish for peace occurring in a Latin epitaph is: "Peace [שלום]. Here lies in peace [*in pace*]

78. For discussion, see van der Horst, *Ancient Jewish Epitaphs*, 148–49 (no. 6).

79. Schwabe and Lifshitz, *Beth Sheʿarim*, 97–110 (no. 127). For further discussion, see van der Horst, *Ancient Jewish Epitaphs*, 151–52 (no. 8). An inscription from Leontopolis expresses the same gloomy sentiment: "When he had already achieved the span of 53 years, he who tames all himself snatched him off to Hades [αὐτὸς ὁ πανδαμάτωρ ἥρπασεν εἰς Αίδην]" (*CPJ* 1530A). For discussion, see van der Horst, *Ancient Jewish Epitaphs*, 156–57.

80. Mazar, *Beth Sheʿarim*, vol. 1, *Catacombs 1–4*, 201–2 (no. 67), 207 (nos. 130 and 132); Schwabe and Lifshitz, *Beth Sheʿarim*, 115–16 (nos. 117 and 119).

81. F. M. Cross, "A Note on a Burial Inscription from Mount Scopus," *IEJ* 33 (1983): 245–46.

82. The inscription was first published by L. Y. Rahmani and J. Naveh, "A Jewish Rock-Cut Tomb on Mt. Scopus," *ʿAtiqot* 14 (1980): 49–54.

83. Schwabe and Lifshitz, *Beth Sheʿarim*, 190 (no. 203).

84. Ibid., 66 (no. 91). The transliterated σαλλόμ could be rendered either "farewell" or "peace."

85. Avigad, *Beth Sheʿarim*, 243 (no. 16, Hebrew) + fig. 116; cf. 245 (no. 19, Hebrew) + fig. 118.

86. Ibid., 248–49 (no. 23, Hebrew) + fig. 122.

87. *CIJ* II 1175; Horbury and Noy, *Jewish Inscriptions*, 243 (no. 152).

88. *CIJ* II 1536; Horbury and Noy, *Jewish Inscriptions*, 223–25 (no. 133); from a second-century CE mummy label.

Joses the Alexandrian, of good memory, who lived more or less . . . years."[89] Several of the Jewish epitaphs found in Rome, mostly written in Greek, often adorned with a menorah, include reference to peace, either in Hebrew or in Greek.[90]

We find hope for resurrection, eternal life, or heaven expressed in some Jewish epitaphs: "May their resurrection [עמידן] (be with the righteous)";[91] "This is the grave of dear father Yehudah known as Gurk. May his resting place be with the righteous, his resurrection with the worthy [עמידתו הכשרים]";[92] "May your portion be good, my lord father and my lady mother, and may your soul(s) be bound (in the bond) of immortal life [ἀθανάτου βίου]";[93] "Good luck in your resurrection [εὐτυχῶς τῇ ὑμῶν ἀναστάσι]!";[94] "Now this grave hides in its bosom my chastely nurtured body, but my soul has flown to the holy ones [ψυχὴ δ᾽ εἰς ὁσίους ἔπετε]";[95] and "This tomb contains the dwindling remains of noble Karteria . . . (your daughter) erected this monument so that even after the end of life's term you may both enjoy again new indestructible riches [ἀσκύλευτον . . . πλοῦτον]."[96] One is reminded of Jesus' advice to his followers: "Lay up for yourselves treasures in heaven, where neither moth nor rust consumes and where thieves do not break in and steal" (Matt 6:20).

Some expressions of hope seem fainter: "Be of good courage [θάρσι], lady Calliope from Byblos; no one is immortal [οὐδὶς ἀθάνατος]";[97] "May your lot be good

---

89. *CIJ* I 644; Horbury and Noy, *Jewish Inscriptions*, 235–36 (no. 142). The number indicating how many years Joses lived is no longer extant.

90. I have perused the first two hundred inscriptions gathered in *CIJ*. Reference to *peace* is found in nos. 16, 18, 20, 24, 32, 35, 37, 41, 44 (with menorah), 50 (with menorah), 55 (with menorah), 62 (with menorah), 63, 69, 81, 84, 85, 86 (with menorah), 88, 89 (with menorah), 92, 93, 99 (with menorah), 100 (with menorah), 101, 102, 103, 105 (with menorah), 106, 109, 110 (with menorah), 111 (with menorah), 117, 121, 124, 126, 129, 131, 133, 136 (with menorah), 137, 138 (with menorah), 140, 145, 146, 147, 148 (with menorah), 149, 151 (with menorah), 152 (with menorah), 154, 156, 157, 158, 159 (with menorah), 167, 168, 169, 171 (with menorah), 172, 180, 185 (with menorah), 192, and 195. Traces of menorahs appear in poorly preserved inscriptions, which means the percentage of inscriptions in which a reference to peace is accompanied by the depiction of the menorah is probably even higher than the foregoing list implies. For a convenient assemblage of the *CIJ* inscriptions, see Leon, *Jews of Ancient Rome*, 264–346. Laurence Kant estimates that the "menorah appears in at least 144 out of 534 inscriptions in Rome." See L. H. Kant, "Jewish Inscriptions in Greek and Latin," *ANRW* II.20, no. 2 (1987): 671–713, with quotation from p. 702.

91. Avigad, *Beth Sheʿarim*, 241–43 (no. 15) + fig. 115. The epitaph is in Hebrew.

92. Ibid., 242 (an Aramaic epitaph near Tiflis in the Caucasus).

93. Schwabe and Lifshitz, *Beth Sheʿarim*, 114–16 (no. 130).

94. Ibid., 180–81 (no. 194) + fig. 20. Note that this wish for "good luck" in the resurrection is in the plural. The wish apparently applies to the whole family.

95. *CIJ* II 1510; Horbury and Noy, *Jewish Inscriptions*, 69–74 (no. 33). The epitaph is preserved on a second- or first-century BCE stela from Leontopolis (Egypt). The term ὅσιοι ("holy ones") usually refers to the righteous (LXX Ps 29:5; 36:28), sometimes to martyrs (Wis 18:5; 1 Macc 7:17).

96. Schwabe and Lifshitz, *Beth Sheʿarim*, 157–67 (no. 183). The epitaph is inscribed on a marble slab.

97. Ibid., 124 (no. 136); cf. 35–36 (no. 59) + fig. 1, 97–107 (no. 127), 186 (no. 187), and 179–80 (no. 193) + fig. 19.

[εὐμοίρει], Aristeas!";[98] "Lady Esther, Esther, have courage [θάρσι], Esther";[99] "Lord, remember your servant";[100] and "The tomb of Calliope the elder, the freedwoman of Procopios, of blessed memory";[101] "Childless I went to the house of Hades [ἄτεκνος ἔβαν εἰς Ἀΐδαο δόμους]."[102]

I conclude with the following epitaph, which seems to hold out little hope for a pleasant afterlife. The epitaph is from Leontopolis (Egypt) and is of uncertain date (probably turn of the era):

> I am Jesus, my father was Phameis, passer-by;
> and at the age of sixty I went down to Hades.
> All of you weep together for him who suddenly passed
> to the deep place of the ages, to dwell in darkness
> [εἰς μυχὸν αἰώνων ἐν σκοτίᾳ διάγειν].
> And you, Dositheus, bewail me; for it is laid upon you
> to pour forth most bitter tears over my tomb.
> You are my child, for I departed childless.
> Weep, all together, for the hapless Jesus.[103]
> (*CIJ* II 1511)

Themes in Christian Epitaphs

Christian epitaphs often refer to belief in the resurrection and/or faith in Christ. However, traces of pre-Christian conventions often remain. Here are a few examples:

> τοῖς γλυκυτάτοις γονεῦσιν ἕως ἀναστάσεως.
> To my sweet parents, until their resurrection.[104]
> (*CIG* 9439)

> Discreet Maritima, you have not left the sweet light.
> For you have with you Christ [fish symbol, instead of actual name "Christ"]
> who is immortal through all things [παναθάνατον κατὰ πάντα]. For it
> is ever piety that leads you on.[105]
> (*CIG* 9687)

---

98. Ibid., 144 (no. 171), 145 (no. 173); cf. 32 (no. 52), 33–34 (no. 57), 44–45 (no. 69), and 95 (no. 124).

99. Ibid., 23–24 (no. 39); cf. 24–25 (no. 40), 25 (no. 41), 26 (no. 43), 63–64 (no. 87), 64 (no. 88), 65 (no. 89), and 81 (no. 102).

100. Ibid., 167–68 (no. 184).

101. Ibid., 185–86 (no. 200).

102. *CIJ* II 1530; Horbury and Noy, *Jewish Inscriptions*, 90–94 (no. 38) + plate XII. The epitaph is preserved on a stela from Leontopolis from the turn of the era. For further discussion of Jewish afterlife ideas, see Lieberman, "Aspects of After Life in Early Rabbinic Literature," 2:495–532.

103. Horbury and Noy, *Jewish Inscriptions*, 74–78 (no. 34). For further discussion, see van der Horst, *Ancient Jewish Epitaphs*, 155–56 (no. 12). The Jewish name Jesus, variously spelled in Greek, appears in several inscriptions in Israel and Egypt. Contrast 1 Thess 4:13.

104. Lattimore, *Themes in Greek and Latin Epitaphs*, 306.

105. Ibid., 302.

> ψυχὴ χαίρει ἀώνιος.
> The immortal soul rejoices.[106]
> (*IG* XIV 134)
>
> He has died and lives and looks on the light, which is really imperishable [ἄφθιτον];
> he lives for the living, and has died for those who are in truth dead.[107]
> (*EG* 726, lines 8–9)
>
> ψυχὴ δ' αὐτοῖο ἶν' ἀθάνατος θεὸς ἔστιν·
> Ἀβραμίοις κόλποις ἀναπαύετε ὥ μακάρων τις.
> His soul is where immortal God is.
> He rests in Abraham's bosom, like one of the blessed ones.[108]
> (*SEG* VI 295, lines 5–6)
>
> Here lies Artemia, a child bright and sweet, fair visage, and most charming in her speech. Having lived four years, in her fifth year she departed to Christ, an innocent who passed over without warning into the heavenly kingdom [*ad caelestia regna transivit*].[109]
> (*RGM* 489)
>
> Here lies Martianus
> Who lost the joys of youth
> and left behind only tears
> for his parents.
> He lived 26 years, less 16 days.
> He has gone to God [*in deo ivit*].[110]
> (*RGM* 497)

In some Christian epitaphs, the pagan themes are more clearly pronounced. This is especially seen in warnings:

> And the angels of God, to whom on this day
> every soul is humbled to suppliance [ταπεινοῦται μεθ' ἱκετείας], that
> He may avenge this innocent blood, and that with all speed.[111]
> (*CIG* 9292)
>
> Lest the dreaded fiery judgment of Gehenna [πυρόεσσα κρίσις δεινήευσα Γεέννης] overtake you, and great agony of the soul from cold Tartarus [Ταρτάρου ἐκ κρυεροῦ].[112]
> (*IG* VII 583, lines 4–5)

---

106. Ibid.

107. Ibid.

108. Ibid. The language of the epitaph recalls the parable of the rich man and Lazarus (Luke 16:19–30), in which the rich man, in agony in Hades, sees "Abraham far off and Lazarus in his bosom [ἐν τοῖς κόλποις αὐτοῦ]" (v. 23).

109. Shore, *Rest Lightly*, 24. The inscription is from ancient Cologne.

110. Ibid. The inscription is from ancient Cologne.

111. Lattimore, *Themes in Greek and Latin Epitaphs*, 307. The inscription dates to the second century CE and may refer to those who murdered a young girl.

112. Ibid., 308.

May he find no pity in any god; may Satan [Σατανᾶς] come into their house
and destroy them utterly.[113]
(*Corinth* VIII.1 136)

ἐχέτω τὴν μερίδα τοῦ Ἰούδα τοῦ προδότου.
May he share the lot of Judas the betrayer.[114]
(*BCH* II 319)

ἕξει πρὸς τὸν θεόν.
He shall be answerable to God.[115]

One epitaph is especially interesting, in that it belongs to a certain Petrus (i.e., Peter) of Jewish background who became a Christian. It is dated to the sixth century and is from Aquileia, Italy:

Here rests
Petrus, who (is also called) Papario,
son of Olympius the Jew,
and who alone
of his family
has deserved to attain the grace of Christ [*ad XRI meruit gratiam*]
and was becomingly
buried in this holy
aula on
the 14th day of
July in the 4th indiction.[116]
(*CIJ* II 643A)

The Importance of Pacifying the Dead

One of the major concerns in burial and sepulture was pacifying the dead. Greeks, Romans, and Jews feared the restless departed.[117] One of the major reasons for

113. Ibid.

114. Ibid.

115. Ibid. The epitaph was originally published in W. M. Ramsay, *The Cities and Bishoprics of Phrygia* (2 vols.; Oxford: Clarendon, 1895–97), 514–16.

116. For discussion of this epitaph, see van der Horst, *Ancient Jewish Epitaphs*, 158–59 (no. 15); Kant, "Jewish Inscriptions in Greek and Latin," 686n97. Kant calls our attention to an inscription from Smyrna (ca. 125 CE) that refers to donations made by οἱ πότε Ἰουδαῖοι (*CIJ* II 742). It is not clear if "the former Jews" in question have become Christians or have simply ceased identifying themselves as practicing Jews. In another inscription, we read of one Μόσσατες δὲ Ἰυδεῖς, which perhaps should be rendered "Mossates from the Jews," which may imply that Mossates was no longer with the Jews. For comment, see Kant, 707 supplemental note 8. The example comes from Y. Le Bohec, "Inscriptions juives et judaïsantes de l'Afrique romaine" and "Juifs et judaïsants dans l'Afrique romaine: Remarques onomastiques," *Antiquités africaines* 17 (1981): 165–207 and 209–29, respectively. The inscription in question is no. 75 in Le Bohec's collection.

117. For a succinct summary of the evidence, see Toynbee, *Death and Burial in the Roman World*, 34–39.

proper burial (in a vault or beneath the earth), often including various rites, was to quiet the spirit of the deceased. Greeks, Romans, and Jews feared ghosts, believing that lack of burial or improper burial could result in restless, even vindictive, spirits roaming the earth, haunting, and in some cases inflicting harm on, the living. There are some remarkable accounts. One immediately thinks of the story of the ghost of Temesa (in Magna Graecia, southern Italy, on the shore of the Tyrrhenian Sea). According to Pausanias:

> Here (in Temesa) one of his (Odysseus') sailors got drunk and violated a maiden, for which offense he was stoned to death by the natives. Now Odysseus, it is said, cared nothing about his loss and sailed away. But the ghost [τὸν δαίμονα] of the stoned man never ceased killing without distinction the people of Temesa, attacking both old and young, until, when the inhabitants had resolved to flee from Italy for good, the Pythian priestess forbad them to leave Temesa, and ordered them to propitiate [ἱλάσκεσθαι] the Hero, setting him a sanctuary apart and building a temple, and to give him every year as wife the fairest maiden in Temesa. So they performed the commands of the god and suffered no more terrors from the ghost [ἀπὸ τοῦ δαίμονος].[118]
> (*Description of Greece* 6.6.7–9)

What makes this story extraordinary is that the man who was stoned to death—whose corpse we may assume was either not buried at all or was buried but without ceremony (which seems implied by the remark that Odysseus "cared nothing about" the man's death)—became a terror against the people of Temesa, even though, according to their norms, they were justified in the manner in which they punished him for his crime (rape in antiquity was often punished with death). Even though the dead man deserved no pity, his corpse nevertheless had to be treated with dignity. Because it was not so treated, the man's ghost not only haunted the people of Temesa, it "never ceased killing without distinction." To placate the angry ghost (called a δαίμων), it was necessary to build a temple in its honor and to supply it annually with a fair maiden who in some sense was the ghost's wife.[119]

We have another example from the tales of Homer. The ashes of Achilles were mixed with those of another recently cremated man. When the Greeks prepared to depart from Troy, the ghost of Achilles appeared, demanding sacrifice. The fearful Greeks obliged, cutting the throat of one Polyxena and spilling her blood over the grave of Achilles. Their action satisfied the ghost of Achilles, making it possible for the Greeks to go home untroubled.[120]

The Homeric stories are, of course, myths. The stories of the ghosts of the sailor and Achilles are the stuff of fiction. But there are tales that claim to be factual. One of the most interesting concerns the hated emperor Caligula, who in 41 CE was

118. Translation based on W. H. S. Jones, trans., *Pausanias: Description of Greece*, vol. 3 (LCL 272; Cambridge: Harvard University Press, 1988), 39, 41. The story is discussed in Felton, *Haunted Greece and Rome*, 10.

119. Readers will be glad to learn that a brave warrior, greatly moved by the fate of one particular fair maiden, challenged the ghost to battle and defeated it. The ghost then departed and sank into the sea, never to be seen again.

120. There are several versions of this story. I am dependent on Felton, *Haunted Greece and Rome*, 10, 103n55.

brutally assassinated: "As Gaius looked around, (Sabinus) split (Caligula's) jawbone with a blow of his sword. As he lay upon the ground and with writhing limbs called out that he still lived and others dispatched him with thirty wounds . . . Some even thrust their swords through his privates" (Suetonius, *Caligula* 58.3).

For political reasons, Caligula's body was hastily and partially cremated and then buried in secret. There was to be no pomp and circumstance and no public mourning. Suetonius tells us:

> His body was conveyed secretly to the gardens of the Lamian family, where it was partly consumed on a hastily erected pyre and buried beneath a light covering of turf; later his sisters on their return from exile dug it up, cremated it, and consigned it to the tomb. Before this was done, it is well known that the caretakers of the gardens were disturbed by ghosts [*umbris*[121] *inquietatos*], and that in the house where he was slain not a night passed without some fearsome apparition [*terrore*], until at last the house itself was destroyed by fire.[122] (*Caligula* 59)

This story reflects the fears of the people of the Mediterranean world in late antiquity. Although Caligula was an evil man and committed many foul crimes, his murder and then the careless and disrespectful burial of his remains set the stage for the haunting of the gardens of the Lamian family. After all, Caligula was a member of an illustrious family, some of whose members had been divinized. Not until the emperor's body was properly cremated and then placed in a respectable tomb did the hauntings cease.

Similar stories circulated about Nero, another hated emperor and the last of the Julio-Claudian line. Declared an enemy of the state in 68 CE, Nero committed suicide. His body was treated with dignity, then cremated. His ashes were placed in the family tomb of the Domitii on the summit of the Hill of the Gardens (Suetonius, *Nero* 49.2–4; 50). Despite his remains' having been treated better than they deserved, Nero apparently did not rest lightly in his grave.

Among other things, devotees adorned Nero's tomb with flowers, notes, and the emperor's decrees, as though he were still living. Rumors floated about that he was in fact alive and that he would soon return and take revenge on those who had condemned him. Caught up in these rumors, a young man who somewhat resembled the dead emperor claimed to be Nero *redivivus* (all of this is described in Suetonius, *Nero* 57). But perhaps the most intriguing story comes from Pliny the Younger, who tells us of his friend Fannius, who died before he was able to complete his history of Nero:

> Fannius had in fact had a premonition long ago of what has now happened. He dreamed in his sleep one night that he was lying on his couch, dressed and ready for work, and with his desk in front of him, just as usual; then he fancied that Nero appeared, sat down on the end of the bed, took up the first volume Fannius had pub-

121. The word *umbra* literally means "shade" or "shadow," but it was often used in reference to ghostly apparitions.

122. Translation based on J. C. Rolfe, trans., *Suetonius*, vol. 1 (rev. ed.; LCL 31; Cambridge: Harvard University Press, 1998), 505, 507. It was believed that destruction by fire was the only certain way to get rid of a ghost. I again depend on Felton, *Haunted Greece and Rome*, 10, 103n56.

> lished about his crimes, and read it through to the end; then he did the same to the second and third volumes, after which he departed. Fannius was horrified, and inferred that his writing would end at the point where Nero stopped reading; and so it did.[123] (Pliny the Younger, *Epistles* 5.5.5–6)

Fannius may well have had such a dream and relayed it to his friend Pliny. Writing about Nero's many crimes likely created the psychological framework in which Fannius would experience a terrifying dream, which he interpreted as portending his death soon to come. Fannius' fear of the restless, evil dead, a fear that many of his contemporaries shared, no doubt played a part in his thinking.[124]

In telling the story of Temesa above, the word Pausanias used in reference to the ghost of the sailor who was stoned to death was δαίμων. This word (and its cognate δαιμόνιον), routinely understood in Jewish and Christian literature in reference to an evil spirit, was used in Greco-Roman literature to refer to divinities and spirits of the departed. If human souls (ψυχαί) really do survive death, says Sextus Empericus, "the same (souls) become *daimons* [δαίμοσι αἱ αὐταὶ γίνονται]" (*Against the Mathematicians* 9.71). Plutarch tells his readers of a conjured spirit who says to one Euthynoüs: "(I am) the *daimon* of your son [δαίμων τοῦ υἱέος σου]" (*Moralia* 109d). Elsewhere, Plutarch speaks of "mean and malignant demons [τὰ φαῦλα δαιμόνια καὶ βάσκανα]" (*Dion* 2). In magic texts, we hear of the "*daimons* of men who once gazed on the light [δαίμονες ἀνθρώπων οἱ πρὶν φάος εἰσορόωντες]" (*PGM* I.317).[125]

Violation of a tomb caused one to run the risk of arousing an angry demon, according to the wise sayings in Pseudo-Phocylides:

> μὴ τύμβον φθιμένων ἀνορύξῃς μηδ᾽ ἀθέατα
> δείξῃς ἠελίῳ καὶ δαιμόνιον χόλον ὄρσῃς
> καὶ τάχα δ᾽ ἐκ γαίης ἐλπίζομεν ἐς φάος ἐλθεῖν
> λείψαν᾽ ἀποιχομένων· ὀπίσω δὲ θεοὶ τελέθονται.
> Do not dig up the grave of the deceased, nor expose to the sun something unseen and stir up demonic wrath [δαιμόνιον χόλον].
> We hope that perhaps the remains of the departed will come to the light (again) out of the earth; and afterward they will become gods [θεοὶ τελέθονται].

Josephus explicitly identifies δαιμόνια with the spirits of the wicked. In reference to a dangerous and difficult-to-obtain plant that was used in exorcism, Josephus says:

> [I]t is only valuable on account of one virtue it has, that if it be only brought to sick persons, it quickly drives away those called demons, which are no other than the spirits

123. Translation based on B. Radice, trans., *Pliny the Younger: Letters*, vol. 1, *Books 1–7* (LCL 55; Cambridge: Harvard University Press, 1969), 357.

124. See the discussion of Pliny and Nero in Felton, *Haunted Greece and Rome*, 63–76.

125. It is surmised that this line was originally placed between lines 317 and 318. See H. D. Betz, ed., *The Greek Magical Papyri in Translation, Including the Demotic Spells*, vol. 1, *Texts* (2nd ed.; Chicago: University of Chicago Press, 1992), 11 + note 59. For Greek text, see *PGM* 2:239, where the missing line appears as line 9 in Hymn 4.

> of wicked humans [τὰ ... καλούμενα δαιμόνια, ταῦτα δὲ πονηρῶν ἐστιν ἀνθρώπων πνεύματα], that enter into men that are alive, and kill them [τοῖς ζῶσιν εἰσδυόμενα καὶ κτείνοντα τούς], unless they can obtain some help against them.[126] (*J.W.* 7.185)

Josephus equates δαιμόνια with the spirits of wicked humans without qualification or debate. He simply takes this identification for granted. Similarly, a half century earlier Philo, almost in passing and likewise without defense or explanation, could refer to Caligula's "dismissing all thought of his dead wife's *daimons* [τοῖς δαίμοσι τῆς ἀποθανούσης γυναικός]" (*Embassy* 65). We may infer from statements such as these that this view, in which demons were believed to be the spirits of humans, was widely held in the first century CE by Greeks, Romans, and Jews, at all levels of society.

After surveying the above evidence and more, Peter Bolt concludes that in the New Testament era it was generally believed that δαιμόνια were malevolent spirits active in this world and that their primary purpose was to harm humans, especially with regard to the afterlife, with the aim of reducing them to the same fate as themselves.[127] Bolt believes, rightly in my view, that Jesus and his contemporaries held to the same belief. A few passages will make this clear.

The panic of the desperate father whose son is afflicted with an evil spirit reflects the fear that demons can kill. He tells Jesus: "[The evil spirit] has often cast him into the fire and into the water, to destroy him" (Mark 9:22). This is an example of what Josephus was talking about above. The goal of evil demons was to harm, even to kill, humans.

When the "unclean spirit" (τὸ πνεῦμα τὸ ἀκάθαρτον)[128] in the Capernaum synagogue is confronted, he demands to know of Jesus: "What have you to do with us, Jesus of Nazareth? Have you come to destroy us? I know who you are, the Holy One of God" (Mark 1:24). The implication of these questions is that Jesus has come to destroy evil spirits, to bring their malevolent work to an end. These questions are addressed to Jesus because the evil spirit knows that he is no ordinary exorcist; he is "the Holy One of God." The demon's declaration that he recognizes Jesus is probably a threat.

The Capernaum demon's fear of destruction becomes a reality for the demonic host that has taken possession of the outcast in the vicinity of Gerasa (Mark 5:1–20). That this man lives "among the tombs" (Mark 5:5) suggests that the demons who possess him are indeed the evil spirits of the dead who lie buried in these tombs.[129]

---

126. This translation is a slightly modified version of the one found in *The Works of Josephus: Complete and Unabridged* (new ed.; trans. W. Whiston; Peabody, MA: Hendrickson, 1987), 759.

127. P. G. Bolt, "Jesus, the Daimons and the Dead," in *The Unseen World: Christian Reflections on Angels, Demons and the Heavenly Realm* (ed. A. N. S. Lane; Grand Rapids: Baker, 1996), 75–102, at 84–86. My brief discussion draws heavily on Bolt's learned study.

128. The parallel at Luke 4:33 reads πνεῦμα δαιμονίου ἀκαθάρτου ("a spirit of an unclean demon").

129. The belief that the spirits of the departed linger near their tombs and mortal remains is an ancient one. Socrates is remembered to have said that ghosts are the "souls that *have not been purely released*, but still participate in the realm of the visible, and for that

That the people who live nearby find it necessary to bind the possessed man "with fetters and chains" strongly implies that the man attacks humans. These efforts, however, apparently do little good, for "the chains he wrenched apart, and the fetters he broke in pieces" (Mark 5:3–4), a demonstration of strength that would have worryingly brought to mind the great strength of Samson (Judg 16:9, 12). The evil spirits may also have attacked the man himself, as could be implied by the statement that he "was always crying out and bruising himself with stones" (Mark 5:5).

We are told that the name of this demonic host is "Legion [Λεγιών], for we are many" (Mark 5:9). This name would have readily brought to mind a Roman legion. The story's location on the east side of the Sea of Galilee, where the population was mostly Gentile, supports such an interpretation. Like the Capernaum demon, Legion recognizes that Jesus is no ordinary professional exorcist and so asks him: "What have you to do with me, Jesus, Son of the Most High God? I adjure you by God, do not torment me" (Mark 5:7). Fearing destruction, the demonic host bargains with Jesus, proposing that it be sent into the nearby herd of swine.[130] Jesus permits the demons to enter the swine, but the herd stampedes into and perishes in the lake, presumably destroying the demons.[131]

Given the widespread belief that restless spirits of the dead sometimes became malevolent demons, it is not surprising that the people of late antiquity sought in various ways to mitigate the dangers. One way, as we have seen in the examples reviewed above, was to comply with the conventions of burial and sepulture, even to go beyond the conventions in offerings, sacrifices, and dedicated buildings. The Jewish people took great care in burial of the dead primarily out of their concern with the purity of the land (as explicitly commanded in Deut 21:22–23). But they, too, had a healthy fear of the dead and so, among other things, avoided cemeteries, especially at night.[132]

---

reason are seen" (Plato, *Phaedo* 81c–d, emphasis added). Ghosts "not purely released" include those who die before their time, who die violently, who die before marriage, and who have not been buried.

130. If the Roman legion Legio Fretensis X, which we know was present in Israel later in the first century, was either present during the time of Jesus or perhaps earlier, then the demonic host Legion's recalling the Roman army would be almost a certainty, for the mascot of Legio Fretensis X was the head of a boar. For archaeological evidence of the presence of Legio Fretensis X in Israel, see *CIIP* nos. 1235, 1353, and 1354.

131. The dynamics of this story are not easy to sort out. The point that is clear, however, is that Legion, as powerful as this demonic collective was, was no match for Jesus. In meeting Jesus, they met their doom. The similarities of the stories involving the Capernaum spirit and the Gerasene host were not lost on the author of the recently published P.Oxy. 5072. In this text, we find a creative blend of details from the two stories. In the account recorded in this fragmentary papyrus, the frightened demon asks Jesus, "Son of God . . . Have you come before the time to st[rike] us?" (recto, line 4). See J. Chapa in OP LXXVI no. 5072. We hear an echo of the gloss in Matt 8:29, the parallel of Mark 5:7.

132. The fear of cemeteries, especially at night, is expressed in rabbinic tradition: "Who is an imbecile? One who goes out alone at night, and who sleeps in a graveyard, and who rips his clothing, and who loses what is given him" (*t. Ter.* 1:3); "But if he spent the night in a cemetery . . . he did it in order that the spirit of impurity [*or* unclean spirit] might rest upon him" (*b. Ḥag.* 3b). In Paris Codex Gr. 2419, folio 247b, we have a Greek fragment of the

Another way to protect oneself from demons was to wear phylacteries and amulets. The latter were very popular with Greeks, Romans, Jews, and Christians. Jewish phylacteries and amulets contained verses of Scripture, usually Deut 6:4–5 (the Shema) and verses from Ps 91, a psalm understood to offer protection from evil spirits.[133] Jews also made use of binding spells and magical bowls.[134] Many Christians made use of these devices also.

One of the more curious ways of protecting oneself and one's family from restless spirits was through a process that involved bone-cutting—a practice known as *os resectum* ("severed bone")—whereby one of the fingers of the deceased was cut off and retained. Greeks and especially Romans engaged in this practice, evidently believing that it could pacify the spirit of the deceased so that it would not haunt or harm anyone.

The practice of *os resectum* is alluded to here and there in the literature.[135] In discussing burial procedures, Varro (116–27 BCE) explains that "if a bone of the dead man has been kept out for the ceremony of purifying the household, the household remains in mourning . . . until in the purification the bone is covered with soil" (*On the Latin Language* 5.23). Cicero (106–43 BCE) remarks in passing that it is unnecessary for him to explain "in what manner the severed bone [*os resectum*] is buried in the earth" (*Laws* 2.22.55). Lexicographer Sextus Pompeius Festus (second century CE) refers to *os resectum*, stating that cremation should not take place until the finger of the corpse has been removed (*On the Meaning of Words* 62). These statements are helpful, to be sure, but they leave many questions unanswered.

Given the vagueness of our sources, it is not surprising that the exact nature of the procedure of *os resectum* is debated.[136] Nevertheless, it is widely agreed that the practice was intended to purify the family of the deceased,[137] on the one hand, and to enable the spirit of the deceased to move into the afterlife, on the other. A number of archaeological discoveries have clarified to some degree the brief comments that survive in the literature.[138] In any event, proper burial of the deceased,

---

Testament of Adam, a Jewish work (second century) that was expanded by Christians (third century). At 1:4 we are told that at a certain hour "demons pass through among the tombs [διέρχονται δαίμονες ἐν τοῖς μνήμασιν], and going there (one) will be harmed." For text, see M. R. James, "A Fragment of the Apocalypse of Adam in Greek," in *Apocrypha Anecdota II* (TS 2.3; Cambridge: Cambridge University Press, 1893), 138–45, at 142. The story is told that Hanina ben Dosa (first century CE) was walking alone *at night* when he met the "queen of the demons." She claimed that had he not enjoyed Heaven's protection, she would have harmed him. Hanina then banned her from passing through inhabited places (cf. *b. Pesaḥ.* 112b).

133. See ch. 5 above.

134. On these materials, see Naveh and Shaked, *Magic Spells and Formulae*; idem and idem, *Amulets and Magic Bowls*; Bohak, *Ancient Jewish Magic: A History*.

135. My discussion of *os resectum* relies on Graham, "From Fragments to Ancestors" (see note 30 above).

136. The debate centers on whether cremation or the removal of the bone occurred first.

137. In the case of the death of a member of the household, a Jewish family would enter a state of ritual impurity for one week. Washing on the third and seventh days restored purity (Num 19:11–12).

138. These include the earthenware vessels recovered from San Cesareo; the skeletal remains recovered in Lincoln, England (from the Roman period); and the bones recovered

which included the practice of *os resectum*, was deemed necessary to insure that the spirit of the deceased would rest in peace and not disturb the living.[139]

In cases in which an enemy had been slain, either in single combat or in battle, there were ways to protect oneself from the vengeful ghost. One way was to mutilate the corpse in what was called "armpitting" (μασχαλίσμος), a procedure in which the extremeties were cut off and hung around the armpits of the corpse (Apollonius Rhodius, *Argonautica* 4.447; Sophocles, *Electra* 442–46). It was believed that if the ghost should make an unwelcome appearance, the corpse's having undergone this procedure would make the ghost too weak to inflict harm.

Of course, magic and exorcism offered other ways of dealing with demons who, for whatever reason, had failed to cross over to the other side. Greeks and Romans called upon the services of magicians and sorcerors, who through various spells and gimmicks could, it was hoped, drive away the ghosts and evil spirits. In cases in which a ghost or demon was sent out against someone, a sorceror could perchance redirect the spirit, perhaps returning it to attack its sender.[140]

Jewish exorcists and healers were especially well regarded in late antiquity, not only by Jews but also by Greeks and Romans. Probably the most successful was Jesus of Nazareth, whose exorcistic and healing powers apparently did not involve the usual supporting paraphernalia, such as spells, magical items (like "Solomon's ring"), *voces magicae*, and the invocation of the names of worthies (e.g., Solomon, Elijah, and the like).

What apparently impressed Jesus' contemporaries were the simplicity and the power of his healings and exorcisms. We are told that witnesses of his acts of healing and exorcism said things like "What is this? A new teaching! With authority he commands even the unclean spirits, and they obey him" (Mark 1:27); "We never saw anything like this!" (Mark 2:12). Consistent with these remarks are the questions and challenges from the frightened demons themselves (as in Mark 1:24, "Have you come to destroy us?"; or 5:7, "I adjure you by God, do not torment me"). Consistent, too, is the invocation of the name of Jesus by at least one professional exorcist in the time of Jesus (Mark 9:38) and by others in the time of the early church (Acts 19:13) and beyond (*PGM* IV.3019, where appeal is made to Jesus, "the God of the Hebrews").

Jesus makes comments about demons that more or less cohere with the beliefs and stories that have been reviewed above. He tells his disciples, "When the unclean spirit has gone out of a man, he passes through waterless places seeking rest; and finding none he says, 'I will return to my house from which I came' " (Luke 11:24; cf. Matt 12:43–44). Reference to the search for "waterless places" reflects the belief that demons feared water, a theme attested in the first-century *Testament of Solomon*, where one Asmodeus, an especially dangerous demon, pleads, "I beg you,

---

from the *columbarium* of Pomponius Hylas near the Via Appia in Rome. See Graham, "From Fragments to Ancestors," 95–100 (+ fig. 5.3), 104–5 (+ fig. 5.7), 106.

139. Ibid., 105–6.

140. For further examples, see D. Ogden, *Magic, Witchcraft, and Ghosts in the Greek and Roman Worlds: A Sourcebook* (2nd ed.; Oxford: Oxford University Press, 2009), 146–78.

King Solomon, do not condemn me to water" (*T. Sol.* 5:11; cf. 5:12; 18:15, 41; 25:7). Viewing the human as a "house" where the demon might take up residence is also consistent with the views of late antiquity.

On another occasion, Jesus concedes that some demons are not easily cast out: "This kind cannot be driven out by anything but prayer" (Mark 9:29). A later Christian scribe added "and fasting" (witnessed in 𝔓⁴⁵ א^b A C D et al.; cf. Matt 17:21, itself a gloss), probably on the basis of the association of prayer and fasting in other texts (Luke 2:37; Acts 14:23; *Did.* 1.3; Polycarp, *Phil.* 7.2; Irenaeus, *Against Heresies* 2.31.2), but perhaps on the basis of actual practice in the early church.[141]

Summing Up

Burial inscriptions, artwork, and architecture provide us with important information about ancient beliefs regarding death and the afterlife. The archaeological aspects of sepulture and epitaphs clarify stories recorded and ideas expressed in ancient literature and help us perceive how the beliefs and practices of the Jewish people were like or unlike the beliefs and practices of their Greek and Roman neighbors. In some ways, the remains of sepulture are the most important remains of human culture. This is especially so in the case of the world of Jesus of Nazareth, much of whose teaching was founded on beliefs about God and life that transcend the mortal and temporal realm.

141. The archaeology of exorcism is itself an interesting topic, though it cannot be pursued here. I have treated some aspects of it in C. A. Evans, "Jesus, Healer and Exorcist: The Non-Christian Archaeological Evidence," in *A City Set on a Hill: Essays in Honor of James F. Strange* (ed. D. A. Warner and D. D. Binder; Fayetteville, AR: BorderStone Press, 2014), 55–77.

Bibliography

Abegg, M. G., P. W. Flint, and E. Ulrich. *The Dead Sea Scrolls Bible: The Oldest Known Bible Translated for the First Time into English.* San Francisco: HarperSanFrancisco, 1999.

Abel, F.-M. "Exils et tombeaux des Herodes." *RB* 53 (1946): 56–74.

Adams, J. N. *The Regional Diversification of Latin, 200 BC–AD 600.* Cambridge: Cambridge University Press, 2007.

Adan-Bayewitz, D. "Dating the Pottery from the Galilee Boat Excavation." *BAR* 14, no. 5 (1988): 24–29.

Aland, K. "Bemerkungen zum Alter und Entstehung des Christogramms anhand von Beobachtungen bei 𝔓[66] und 𝔓[75]." Pages 173–79 in *Studien zur Überlieferung des Neuen Testaments und seines Textes.* ANTF 2; Berlin: de Gruyter, 1967.

Alföldy, G. "Nochmals: Pontius Pilatus und das Tiberieum von Caesarea Maritima." *Scripta Classica Israelica* 21 (2002): 133–48.

———. "Pontius Pilatus und das Tiberieum von Caesarea Maritima." *Scripta Classica Israelica* 18 (1999): 85–108.

Allison, D. C., Jr., and W. D. Davies. *A Critical and Exegetical Commentary on the Gospel according to Saint Matthew.* Vol. 2, *Commentary on Matthew VIII–XVIII.* ICC. Edinburgh: T&T Clark, 1991.

Ameling, W., et al., eds. *Corpus Inscriptionum Iudaeae/Palaestinae.* Vol. 2, *Caesarea and the Middle Coast: 1121–2160.* Berlin: de Gruyter, 2011.

Anderson, P. N., F. Just, and T. Thatcher, eds. *John, Jesus, and History.* Vol. 2, *Aspects of Historicity in the Fourth Gospel.* SBL ECL 2. Atlanta: SBL Press, 2009.

Appold, M. "The Mighty Works of Bethsaida: Witness of the New Testament and Related Traditions." Pages 229–42 in vol. 1 of *Bethsaida: A City by the North Shore of the Sea of Galilee.* Edited by R. Arav and R. A. Freund. Kirksville, MO: Truman State University Press, 1995.

Arav, R. "The Archaeology of Bethsaida and the Historical Jesus Quest." Pages 317–31 in *The Archaeology of Difference: Gender, Ethnicity, Class and the "Other" in Antiquity: Studies in Honor of Eric M. Meyers.* Edited by D. R. Edwards and C. T. McCollough. Boston: ASOR, 2007.

———. "Bethsaida." Pages 145–66 in *Jesus and Archaeology.* Edited by J. H. Charlesworth. Grand Rapids: Eerdmans, 2006.

———. "Bethsaida, 2000." *IEJ* 51 (2001): 239–46.

———. "Bethsaida—A Response to Steven Notley." *NEA* 74 (2011): 92–100.

Arav, R. "Bethsaida Rediscovered." *BAR* 26, no. 1 (2000): 44–56.

———. "Betsaida—Geschichte und materielle Kultur einer Stadt im Königreich Geschirr." Pages 52–65 in *Leben am See Gennesaret: Kulturgeschichtliche Entdeckungen in einer biblischen Region*. Edited by G. Fassbeck. Mainz: von Zabern, 2003.

———. "New Testament Archaeology and the Case of Bethsaida." Pages 75–99 in *Das Ende der Tage und die Gegenwart des Heils: Begegnungen mit dem Neuen Testament und seiner Umwelt: Festschrift für Heinz-Wolfgang Kuhn zum 65. Geburtstag*. Edited by M. Becker and W. Fenske. AGJU 44. Leiden: Brill, 1999.

———. "A Response to Notley's Reply." *NEA* 74 (2011): 103–4.

Arav, R., and R. A. Freund, eds. *Bethsaida: A City by the North Shore of the Sea of Galilee*. 4 vols. Kirksville, MO: Truman State University Press, 1995–2009.

Atkinson, D. "The Origin and Date of the 'Sator' Word-Square." *JEH* 2 (1951): 1–18.

Atkinson, K. "On Further Defining the First-Century C.E. Synagogue: Fact or Fiction?" A Rejoinder to H. C. Kee." *NTS* 43 (1997): 491–502.

Aubert, M.-F., and R. Cortopassi, eds. *Portraits funéraires de l'Egypte romain*. Paris: Réunion des musées nationaux, 2004.

Aviam, M. "The Decorated Stone from the Synagogue at Migdal." *NovT* 55 (2013): 205–20.

———. *Jews, Pagans and Christians in the Galilee: 25 Years of Archaeological Excavations and Surveys: Hellenistic to Byzantine Periods*. Land of Galilee 1. Rochester, NY: University of Rochester Press, 2004.

———. "Regionalism of Tombs and Burial Customs in the Galilee During the Hellenistic, Roman and Byzantine Periods." Pages 257–313 in *Jews, Pagans and Christians in the Galilee: 25 Years of Archaeological Excavations and Surveys: Hellenistic to Byzantine Periods*. Land of Galilee 1. Rochester, NY: University of Rochester Press, 2004.

Aviam, M., R. Bauckham, and S. De Luca, eds. *Magdala, Jewish City of Fish*. Waco, TX: Baylor University Press, forthcoming.

Avigad, N. "Aramaic Inscriptions in the Tomb of Jason." *IEJ* 17 (1967): 101–11.

———. *Beth Sheʿarim: The Excavations 1953–1958*. Vol. 3, *Catacombs 12–23*. New Brunswick, NJ: Rutgers University Press, 1976.

———. "A Depository of Inscribed Ossuaries in the Kidron Valley." *IEJ* 12 (1962): 1–12.

———. "Excavations in the Jewish Quarter of the Old City of Jerusalem." *IEJ* 20 (1970): 1–8.

———. "Jewish Rock-Cut Tombs in Jerusalem and in the Judean Hill Country." *ErIsr* 8 (1967): 119–42 (Hebrew).

———. "Palatial Mansion." *NEAEHL* 2:733–35.

———. "The Rock-Carved Façades of the Jerusalem Necropolis." *IEJ* 1 (1950–51): 96–106.

———. "Sanhedrin Tombs." *NEAEHL* 2:752.

———. "Tombs." *NEAEHL* 2:750–53.

Avi-Yonah, M. *Abbreviations in Greek Inscriptions (The Near East, 200 BC–AD 1100)*. London: Oxford University Press, 1940.

———. *Art in Ancient Palestine: Selected Studies*. Jerusalem: Magnes, 1981.

———. "Oriental Elements in the Art of Palestine in the Roman and Byzantine Periods." *QDAP* 10 (1942): 105–51.

———. "A Priestly List of Courses from Caesarea." *IEJ* 12 (1962): 137–9.

Avni, G. "Christian Secondary Use of Jewish Burial Caves in Jerusalem in the Light of New Excavations at the Aceldama Tombs." Pages 265–76 in *Early Christianity in Context: Monuments and Documents.* Edited by F. Manns and E. Alliata. SBFCMa 38. Jerusalem: Franciscan Printing Press, 1993.

Avni, G., Z. Greenhut, and T. Ilan. "Three New Burial Caves of the Second Temple Period in Aceldama (Kidron Valley)." Pages 206–18 in *Ancient Jerusalem Revealed.* Edited by H. Geva. Jerusalem: Israel Exploration Society, 1994.

Avni, G., Z. Greenhut, et al. *The Akeldama Tombs: Three Burial Caves in the Kidron Valley, Jerusalem.* IAA Reports 1. Jerusalem: Israel Antiquities Authority, 1996.

Bagatti, B. *The Church from the Circumcision.* Jerusalem: Franciscan Printing Press, 1971.

———. *Gli scavi di Nazaret.* Vol. 1, *Dalle origini al secolo XII.* SBFCMa 17. Jerusalem: Franciscan Printing Press, 1967. Translated as *Excavations in Nazareth.* Vol. 1, *From the Beginning till the XII Century.* Translated by E. Hoade. Jerusalem: Franciscan Printing Press, 1969–2001.

Bagatti, B., and J. T. Milik. *Gli scavi del "Dominus Flevit": Monte Oliveto-Gerusalemme.* Vol. 1, *La necropoli del periodo Romano.* SBFCMa 13. Jerusalem: Franciscan Printing Press, 1958.

Bagnall, R. S. *Everyday Writing in the Graeco-Roman East.* Sather Classical Lectures 69. Berkeley: University of California Press, 2012.

Baigent, M. *The Jesus Papers: Exposing the Greatest Cover-Up in History.* San Francisco: HarperSanFrancisco, 2006.

Balch, D. L., and C. Osiek. *Early Christian Families in Context: An Interdisciplinary Dialogue.* Grand Rapids: Eerdmans, 2003.

Bammel, E. "Nicanor and His Gate." Pages 39–41 in *Judaica: Kleine Schriften I.* WUNT 37. Tübingen: Mohr Siebeck, 1986.

———. "Syrian Coinage and Pilate." *JJS* 2 (1950): 108–10.

———. "The Trial before Pilate." Pages 415–51 in *Jesus and the Politics of His Day.* Edited by E. Bammel and C. F. D. Moule. Cambridge: Cambridge University Press, 1984.

Barag, D. "The 2000–2001 Exploration of the Tombs of Benei Hezir and Zechariah." *IEJ* 53 (2003): 78–110.

Barag, D., and D. Flusser. "The Ossuary of Yehoḥanah Granddaughter of the High Priest Theophilus." *IEJ* 36 (1986): 39–44.

Barbet, A. "Un tombeau peint inscrit de Sidon." *Syr* 74 (1997): 141–60.

Barclay, J. M. G. *Flavius Josephus: Translation and Commentary.* Vol. 10, *Against Apion.* Edited by S. Mason. Leiden: Brill, 2007.

Bar-Ilan, M. "Writing Materials." *EDSS* 2:996–7.

Barnard, L. W. "The 'Cross of Herculaneum' Reconsidered." Pages 15–27 in vol. 1 of *The New Testament Age: Essays in Honor of Bo Reicke.* Edited by W. C. Weinrich. Macon, GA: Mercer University Press, 1984.

Barrett, C. K. *The Acts of the Apostles.* 2 vols. ICC. Edinburgh: T&T Clark, 1994–98.

Bartina, S. "Poncio Pilato en una inscripción monumentaria palestinense." *CB* 19 (1962): 170–75.

Bartlett, J. R., ed. *Archaeology and Biblical Interpretation.* New York: Routledge, 1997.

Bauckham, R. "The Caiaphas Family." *JSHJ* 10 (2012): 3–31.

———. "Further Thoughts on the Migdal Synagogue Stone." *NovT* 57 (2015): 113–35.

———. "Magdala in Rabbinic Literaure." In *Magdala, Jewish City of Fish.* Edited by M. Aviam, R. Bauckham, and S. De Luca. Waco, TX: Baylor University Press, forthcoming.

Bauckham, R., and S. De Luca. "Magdala as We Now Know It." *Early Christianity* 6 (2015): 91–118.

Baumgarten, J. M. "Does *TLH* in the Temple Scroll Refer to Crucifixion?" *JBL* 91 (1972): 472–81.

———. "Hanging and Treason in Qumran and Roman Law." *ErIsr* 16 (1982): 7–16.

———. "On the Nature of the Seductress in 4Q184." *RevQ* 15 (1991): 133–43.

Bayer, H. F. *Jesus' Predictions of Vindication and Resurrection: The Provenance, Meaning and Correlation of the Synoptic Predictions.* WUNT II/20. Tübingen: Mohr Siebeck, 1986.

Begg, C. T. *Flavius Josephus: Translation and Commentary.* Vol. 4, *Judean Antiquities Books 5–7.* Edited by S. Mason. Leiden: Brill, 2005.

Begg, C. T., and P. Spilsbury. *Flavius Josephus: Translation and Commentary.* Vol. 5, *Judean Antiquities Books 8–10.* Edited by S. Mason. Leiden: Brill, 2005.

Benoit, P. "L'inscription grecque du tombeau de Jason." *IEJ* 17 (1967): 112–13.

Berlin, A. M., and J. A. Overman, eds. *The First Jewish Revolt: Archaeology, History, and Ideology.* New York: Routledge, 2002.

Berrin, S. L. *The Pesher Nahum Scroll from Qumran: An Exegetical Study of 4Q169.* STDJ 43. Leiden: Brill, 2004.

Betz, H. D., ed. *The Greek Magical Papyri in Translation, Including the Demotic Spells.* Vol. 1, *Texts.* 2nd ed. Chicago: University of Chicago Press, 1992.

Bierbrier, M. L., ed. *Portraits and Masks: Burial Customs in Roman Egypt.* London: British Museum Press, 1997.

Binder, D. D. *Into the Temple Courts: The Place of Synagogues in the Second Temple Period.* SBLDS 169. Atlanta: SBL Press, 1999.

———. "The Mystery of the Magdala Stone." Pages 17–48 in *A City Set on a Hill: Essays in Honor of James F. Strange.* Edited by D. A. Warner and D. D. Binder. Fayetteville, AR: BorderStone Press, 2014.

Bingen, J., et al., eds. *Mons Claudianus: Ostraca Graeca et Latina.* 4 vols. Cairo: Institut français d'archéologie orientale du Caire, 1992–2009.

Biran, A., and J. Aviram, eds. *Biblical Archaeology Today, 1990: Proceedings of the Second International Congress on Biblical Archaeology.* Jerusalem: Israel Exploration Society, 1993.

Birley, R. *Discoveries at Vindolanda.* Newcastle upon Tyne: Frank Graham, 1973.

———. *The Roman Documents from Vindolanda.* Greenhead, UK: Roman Army Museum Publications, 1990.

Bivin, D. "A Sadducee Who Believed in an Afterlife?" *Jerusalem Perspective* 4, nos. 4–5 (1991): 7.

Black, M. "The Chi-Rho Sign—Christogram and/or Staurogram?" Pages 319–27 in *Apostolic History and the Gospel*. Edited by W. W. Gasque and R. P. Martin. Grand Rapids: Eerdmans, 1970.

Blaiklock, E. M. *The Archaeology of the New Testament*. 2nd ed. Nashville: Nelson, 1984.

Bock, D. L. *Blasphemy and Exaltation in Judaism and the Final Examination of Jesus: A Philological-Historical Study of the Key Jewish Themes Impacting Mark 14:61–64*. WUNT II/106. Tübingen: Mohr Siebeck, 1998.

Bockmuehl, M. N. A. "Simon Peter and Bethsaida." Pages 53–90 in *The Missions of James, Peter, and Paul: Tensions in Early Christianity*. Edited by B. D. Chilton and C. A. Evans. NovTSup 115. Leiden: Brill, 2005.

Boffo, L. *Iscrizioni greche e latine per lo studio della Bibbia*. Brescia: Paideia, 1994.

———. "L'ordine imperiale di Nazaret (?) sulla violazione dei sepolcri." Pages 319–33 in *Iscrizioni greche e latine per lo studio della Bibbia*. Brescia: Paideia, 1994.

Bohak, G. *Ancient Jewish Magic: A History*. Cambridge: Cambridge University Press, 2008.

Bolt, P. G. "Jesus, the Daimons and the Dead." Pages 75–102 in *The Unseen World: Christian Reflections on Angels, Demons and the Heavenly Realm*. Edited by A. N. S. Lane. Grand Rapids: Baker, 1996.

Bond, H. K. *Caiaphas: Friend of Rome and Judge of Jesus?* Louisville: Westminster John Knox, 2004.

———. "The Coins of Pontius Pilate: Part of an Attempt to Provoke the People or to Integrate Them into the Empire?" *JSJ* 27 (1996): 241–62.

———. *Pontius Pilate in History and Interpretation*. SNTSMS 100. Cambridge: Cambridge University Press, 1998.

Bonnie, R., and J. Richard. "Building D1 at Magdala Revisited in the Light of Public Fountain Architecture in the Late-Hellenistic East." *IEJ* 62 (2012): 71–88.

Bottini, G. C., L. Di Segni, and E. Alliata, eds. *Christian Archaeology in the Holy Land, New Discoveries: Essays in Honour of Virgilio C. Corbo, OFM*. SBFCMa 36. Jerusalem: Franciscan Printing Press, 1990.

Bourbon, F. *Petra: Jordan's Extraordinary Ancient City*. New York: Barnes & Noble Books, 2004.

Bowman, A. K. *Life and Letters on the Roman Frontier: Vindolanda and Its People*. New York: Routledge, 1998.

———. "Literacy in the Roman Empire: Mass and Mode." Pages 119–31 in *Literacy in the Roman World*. Edited by J. H. Humphrey. *JRA* Supplement Series 3. Ann Arbor: *JRA*, 1991.

———. "The Roman Imperial Army: Letters and Literacy on the Northern Frontier." Pages 109–25 in *Literacy and Power in the Ancient World*. Edited by A. K. Bowman and G. Woolf. Cambridge: Cambridge University Press, 1994.

Bowman, A. K., and J. D. Thomas. *The Vindolanda Writing Tablets*. Newcastle upon Tyne: Frank Graham, 1974.

Bowman, A. K., et al., eds. *Oxyrhynchus: A City and Its Texts.* Graeco-Roman Memoirs 93. London: Egypt Exploration Society, 2007.

Boylston, A. "Evidence of Weapon-Related Trauma in British Archaeological Samples." Pages 357–80 in *Human Osteology in Archaeology and Forensic Science.* Edited by M. Cox and S. Mays. London: Greenwich Medical Media, 2000.

Brandon, S. G. F. *Jesus and the Zealots: A Study of the Political Factor in Primitive Christianity.* New York: Scribner's Sons, 1967.

Braude, W. G. *The Midrash on Psalms.* 2 vols. YJS 13. New Haven: Yale University Press, 1959.

Breytenbach, C. "Mark and Galilee: Text World and Historical World." Pages 75–85 in *Galilee through the Centuries: Confluence of Cultures.* Edited by E. M. Meyers. Duke Judaic Studies 1. Winona Lake, IN: Eisenbrauns, 1999.

Brooke, G. J. "4Q500 1 and the Use of Scripture in the Parable of the Vineyard." *DSD* 2 (1995): 268–94.

Brown, R. E. *The Death of the Messiah: From Gethsemane to the Grave: A Commentary on the Passion Narratives in the Four Gospels.* 2 vols. ABRL. New York: Doubleday, 1994.

Bruce, F. F. *Paul: Apostle of the Heart Set Free.* Grand Rapids: Eerdmans, 1977.

Bruyne, L. de. "La 'crux interpretum' di Ercolano." *Rivista di Archeologia Christiana* 21 (1945): 281–309.

Buckler, W. H., W. M. Calder, and C. W. M. Cox. "Monuments from Central Phrygia." *JRS* 16 (1926): 61–74.

Bultmann, R. *The History of the Synoptic Tradition.* Oxford: Blackwell, 1972.

Burr, V. "Epigraphischer Beitrag zur neueren Pontius-Pilatus-Forschung." Pages 37–41 in *Vergangenheit, Gegenwart, Zukunft.* Edited by W. Burr. Würzburg: Echter, 1972.

Canfora, L. *The Vanished Library: A Wonder of the Ancient World.* London: Hutchinson Radius, 1989.

Carmi, I. "How Old Is the Galilee Boat?" *BAR* 14, no. 5 (1988): 30–33.

———. "Radiocarbon Dating of the Boat." Pages 127–8 in *The Excavations of an Ancient Boat in the Sea of Galilee (Lake Kinneret).* Edited by S. Wachsmann, J. R. Steffy, et al. *'Atiqot* 19. Jerusalem: Israel Antiquities Authority, 1990.

Carrol, J. T. *Luke: A Commentary.* NTL. Louisville: Westminster John Knox, 2012.

Carrol, J. T., and J. B. Green, with R. E. Van Voorst, J. Marcus, and D. Senior. *The Death of Jesus in Early Christianity.* Peabody, MA: Hendrickson, 1995.

Carroll, M. "*Memoria* and *Damnatio Memoriae*: Preserving and Erasing Identities in Roman Funerary Commemoration." Pages 65–90 in *Living through the Dead: Burial and Commemoration in the Classical World.* Edited by M. Carroll and J. Rempel. Studies in Funerary Archaeology 5. Oxford: Oxbow, 2011.

Carroll, M., and J. Rempel, eds. *Living through the Dead: Burial and Commemoration in the Classical World.* Studies in Funerary Archaeology 5. Oxford: Oxbow, 2011.

Cartlidge, D. R., and J. K. Elliott. *Art and the Christian Apocrypha.* New York: Routledge, 2001.

Casey, M. *Aramaic Sources of Mark's Gospel.* SNTSMS 102. Cambridge: Cambridge University Press, 1998.

Chancey, M. A. *Greco-Roman Culture and the Galilee of Jesus.* SNTSMS 134. Cambridge: Cambridge University Press, 2005.

———. *The Myth of a Gentile Galilee.* SNTSMS 118. Cambridge: Cambridge University Press, 2002.

Chapa, J. "Su demoni e angeli: Il Salmo 90 nel suo contesto." Pages 59–90 in *I papiri letterari cristiani: Atti del convegno internazionale di studi in memoria di Mario Naldini, Firenze, 10–11 giugno 2010.* Edited by G. Bastianini and A. Casanova. Florence: Istituto Papirologico "G. Vitelli," 2011.

Chapman, D. W. *Ancient Jewish and Christian Perceptions of Crucifixion.* WUNT II/244. Tübingen: Mohr Siebeck, 2008.

Chapman, D. W., and E. J. Schnabel. *The Trial and Crucifixion of Jesus: Texts and Commentary.* WUNT 344. Tübingen: Mohr Siebeck, 2015.

Charlesworth, J. H., ed. *Jesus and Archaeology.* Grand Rapids: Eerdmans, 2006.

———. "Solomon and Jesus: The Son of David in Ante-Markan Traditions (Mk 10:47)." Pages 125–51 in *Biblical and Humane: A Festschrift for John F. Priest.* Edited by L. B. Elder, D. L. Barr, and E. S. Malbon. Atlanta: Scholars Press, 1996.

———. "What Is the Message of 'the Patio Tomb' in Talpiot, Jerusalem?" Pages 555–75 in *The Tomb of Jesus and His Family? Exploring Ancient Jewish Tombs Near Jerusalem's Walls.* Grand Rapids: Eerdmans, 2013.

Chilton, B. D. "Caiaphas." *ABD* 1:803–6.

———. *A Galilean Rabbi and His Bible: Jesus' Use of the Interpreted Scripture of His Time.* GNS 8. Wilmington, DE: Glazier, 1984.

———. "The Trial of Jesus Reconsidered." Pages 481–500 in *Jesus in Context: Temple, Purity, and Restoration.* B. D. Chilton and C. A. Evans. AGJU 39. Leiden: Brill, 1997.

Chilton, B. D., and C. A. Evans. "Jesus and Israel's Scriptures." Pages 281–335 in *Studying the Historical Jesus: Evaluations of the State of Current Research.* Edited by B. D. Chilton and C. A. Evans. NTTS 19. Leiden: Brill, 1994.

Christensen, D. L. *Deuteronomy 21:10–34:12.* WBC 6B. Nashville: Nelson, 2002.

Ciampa, R., and B. S. Rosner. *The First Letter to the Corinthians.* PNTC. Grand Rapids: Eerdmans, 2010.

Clackson, J. "Classical Latin." Pages 236–56 in *A Companion to the Latin Language.* Edited by J. Clackson. Malden, MA: Wiley-Blackwell, 2011.

Clarke, E. G. *The Wisdom of Solomon.* CBC. Cambridge: Cambridge University Press, 1973.

Clermont-Ganneau, C. S. "The 'Gate of Nicanor' in the Temple of Jerusalem." PEFQS (1903): 93, 125–31.

———. "Une stèle du temple de Jérusalem." *RA* 28 (1872): 214–34, 290–6.

Cline, E. H. *Biblical Archaeology: A Very Short Introduction.* Oxford: Oxford University Press, 2009.

Cockle, W. E. H. "Writing and Reading Exercises." Pages 179–90 in vol. 1 of *Mons Claudianus: Ostraca Graeca et Latina.* Edited by J. Bingen et al. Cairo: Institut français d'archéologie orientale du Caire, 1992–2009.

Cohen, O. "Conservation of the Boat." Pages 15–22 in *The Excavations of an Ancient Boat in the Sea of Galilee (Lake Kinneret)*. Edited by S. Wachsmann, J. R. Steffy, et al. *'Atiqot* 19. Jerusalem: Israel Antiquities Authority, 1990.

Cook, B. F. *Greek Inscriptions*. Reading the Past 5. London: British Museum, 1987.

Cook, E. M. "The Psalms Targum: Introduction to a New Translation, with Sample Texts." Pages 185–201 in *Targum and Scripture: Studies in Aramaic Translations and Interpretations in Memory of Ernest G. Clarke*. Edited by P. V. M. Flesher. SAIS 2. Leiden: Brill, 2002.

Cook, J. G. "Crucifixion and Burial." *NTS* 57 (2011): 193–213.

———. "Crucifixion as Spectacle in Roman Campania." *NovT* 54 (2012): 68–100.

———. *Crucifixion in the Mediterranean World*. WUNT 327. Tübingen: Mohr Siebeck, 2014.

———. "Envisioning Crucifixion: Light from Several Inscriptions and the Palatine Graffito," *NovT* 50 (2008): 262–85.

———. "John 19:17 and the Man on the Patibulum in the Arieti Tomb." *Early Christianity* 4 (2013): 427–53.

Corbett, J. "New Synagogue Excavations in Israel and Beyond." *BAR* 37, no. 4 (2011): 52–59.

Corbett, S. "Some Observations on the Gateways to the Herodian Temple in Jerusalem." *PEQ* 84 (1952–53): 7–14.

Corbo, V. C. "La città romana di Magdala: Rapporto preliminare dopo la quarta campagna di scavo, 1975." Pages 355–78 in vol. 1 of *Studia Hierosolymitana in onore del P. Bellarmino Bagatti*. Edited by E. Testa, I. Mancini, and M. Piccirillo. SBFCMa 22. Jerusalem: Franciscan Printing Press, 1976.

———. *The House of St. Peter at Capharnaum: A Preliminary Report of the First Two Campaigns of Excavations, April 16–June 19, Sept. 12–Nov. 26, 1968*. Translated by S. Saller. SBFCMi 5. Jerusalem: Franciscan Printing Press, 1969.

———. "Scavi archeologici a Magdala." *LASBF* 24 (1974): 5–37.

Corbo, V. C., S. Loffreda, and A. Spijkerman. *La Sinagoga de Cafarnao, dopo gli scavi del 1969*. SBFCMi 9. Jerusalem: Franciscan Printing Press, 1970.

Cotton, H. M., and J. Geiger. *Masada II: The Yigael Yadin Excavations 1963–1965, Final Reports; The Latin and Greek Documents*. Jerusalem: Israel Exploration Society, 1989.

Cotton, H. M., et al., eds. *Corpus Inscriptionum Iudaeae/Palaestinae*. Vol. 1, *Jerusalem*, part 1, *1–704*. Berlin: de Gruyter, 2010.

———, eds. *Corpus Inscriptionum Iudaeae/Palaestinae*. Vol. 1, *Jerusalem*, part 2, *705–1120*. Berlin: de Gruyter, 2012.

Craffert, P. F., and P. J. J. Botha. "Why Jesus Could Walk on the Sea But He Could Not Read and Write." *Neot* 39 (2005): 5–35.

Craigie, P. C. *Deuteronomy*. NICOT. Grand Rapids: Eerdmans, 1976.

Cross, F. M. "A Note on a Burial Inscription from Mount Scopus." *IEJ* 33 (1983): 245–46.

Crossan, J. D. "The Dogs beneath the Cross." Pages 123–58 in *Jesus: A Revolutionary Biography*. San Francisco: HarperSanFrancisco, 1994.

———. *Jesus: A Revolutionary Biography*. San Francisco: HarperSanFrancisco, 1994.

———. *Who Killed Jesus? Exposing the Roots of Anti-Semitism in the Gospel Story of the Death of Jesus*. San Francisco: HarperSanFrancisco, 1995.

Crossan, J. D., and J. L. Reed. *Excavating Jesus: Beneath the Stones, Behind the Texts.* San Francisco: HarperSanFrancisco, 2001.

Crowfoot, J. W., and G. M. Crowfoot. *Early Ivories from Samaria.* London: Palestine Exploration Fund, 1938.

Cullmann, O. *Peter: Disciple, Apostle, Martyr: A Historical and Theological Study.* Translated by F. V. Filson. 2nd ed. London: SCM, 1962. Translation of *Petrus: Jünger, Apostel, Märtyrer: das historische und das theologische Petrusproblem.* 1st ed. Zurich: Zwingli-Verlag, 1952.

Cumont, F. "Un rescrit impérial sur la violation de sépulture." *Revue historique* 163 (1930): 241–66.

Currie, R., and S. G. Hyslop. *The Letter and the Scroll: What Archaeology Tells Us about the Bible.* Washington, DC: National Geographic, 2009.

Cuvigny, H. "The Finds of Papyri: The Archaeology of Papyrology." Pages 30–58 in *The Oxford Handbook of Papyrology.* Edited by R. S. Bagnall. Oxford: Oxford University Press, 2009.

Daniélou, J. *Primitive Christian Symbols.* Baltimore: Helicon, 1964.

Dark, K. R. "Archaeological Evidence for a Previously Unrecognized Roman Town near the Sea of Galilee." *PEQ* 145 (2013): 185–202.

———. "Early Roman-Period Nazareth and the Sisters of Nazareth Convent." *AJ* 92 (2012): 1–28.

———. "Has Jesus' Nazareth House Been Found?" *BAR* 41, no. 2 (2015): 54–63, 72.

———. "The Roman-period and Byzantine Landscape between Sepphoris and Nazareth." *PEQ* 140 (2008): 87–107.

Darvill, T. *The Concise Oxford Dictionary of Archaeology.* 2nd ed. Oxford: Oxford University Press, 2008.

De Luca, S. "La città ellenistico-romana di Magdala/Taricheae: Gli scavi del Magdala Project 2007 e 2008: Relazione preliminare e prospettive di indagine." *LASBF* 59 (2009): 343–62.

———. "Urban Development of the City of Magdala/Tarichaeae in the Light of the New Excavations: Remains, Problems and Perspectives." Paper presented at the symposium *Greco-Roman Galilee* at Kinneret College. Kinneret, Israel, 21 June 2009. Published as "La città ellenistico-romana di Magdala/Taricheae. Gli scavi del Magdala Project 2007 e 2008: Relazione preliminare e prospettive di indagine." *LA* 59 (2009): 343–62.

De Luca, S., and A. Lena. "Magdala." In *The Archaeological Record of Galilean Cities, Towns, and Villages.* Vol. 2 of *Galilee in the Late Second Temple and Mishnaic Periods, 100 BCE–200 CE.* Edited by D. Fiensy and J. R. Strange. Minneapolis: Fortress, forthcoming.

Degrassi, A. "Sull'iscrizione di Ponzio Pilato." *Rendiconti dell'Accademia Nazionale dei Lincei*, ser. 8, *Classe di scienze morali, storiche e filologiche* 19 (1964): 59–65.

Deines, R. "Josephus, Salomo und die von Gott verliehene τέχνη gegen die Dämonen." Pages 365–94 in *Die Dämonen: Die Dämonologie der israelitischen-jüdischen und frühchristlichen Literatur im Kontext ihrer Umwelt.* Edited by A. Lange, H. Lichtenberger, and K. F. D. Römheld. Tübingen: Mohr Siebeck, 2003.

Deissmann, G. A. *Light from the Ancient East.* New York: George H. Doran, 1927.
Delcor, M. "L'utilisation des psaumes contre les mauvais esprits à Qoumran." Pages 61–70 in *La vie de la Parole: De l'Ancien au Nouveau Testament; Études d'exégèse et d'herméneutique bibliques offertes à Pierre Grelot.* Edited by P. Grelot. Paris: Desclée, 1987.
Della Corte, M. "Le iscrizione scoperte nel quinquennio 1951–1956." *Notizo degli scavi di antichità* ser. 8, vol. 10 (1958): 77–184.
Derenbourg, J. "Une stèle du temple d'Hérode." *JA* 20 (1872): 178–95.
Di Stefano Manzella, I. "Pontius Pilatus nell'iscrizione di Cesarea di Palestina." Pages 209–15 in *Le iscrizioni dei cristiani in Vaticano: Materiali e contributi scientifici per una mostra epigrafica.* Edited by I. Di Stefano Manzella. Inscriptiones sanctae sedis 2. Vatican City: Edizioni Quasar, 1997.
Dickson, G. "The Tomb of Nicanor of Alexandria." PEFQS (1903): 326–32.
Dinkler, E. "Zur Geschichte des Kreuzsymbols." *ZTK* 48 (1951): 148–72. Reprinted in idem, *Signum Crucis: Aufsätze zum Neuen Testament und zur christlichen Archäologie.* Tübingen: Mohr Siebeck, 1967, 1–25.
Dinkler-von Schubert, E. "stauros: Vom 'Wort vom Kreuz' (1 Cor. 1,18) zum Kreuz-Symbol." Pages 29–39 in *Byzantine East, Latin West: Art-Historical Studies in Honor of Kurt Weitzmann.* Edited by D. Mourika et al. Princeton: Princeton University Press, 1995.
Dodd, C. H. *Historical Tradition in the Fourth Gospel.* Cambridge: Cambridge University Press, 1963.
Domeris, W. R., and S. M. Long. "The Recently Excavated Tomb of Joseph Bar Caipha and the Biblical Caiaphas." *JTSA* 89 (1994): 50–58.
Donahue, J. R., and D. J. Harrington. *The Gospel of Mark.* Sacra Pagina 1. Collegeville, MN: Liturgical Press, 2002.
Doran, R. *2 Maccabees: A Critical Commentary.* Hermeneia. Minneapolis: Fortress, 2012.
Doudna, G. L. *4Q Pesher Nahum: A Critical Edition.* JSPSup 35; CIS 8. London: Sheffield Academic, 2001.
Drinkwater, J. Preface to *Living through the Dead: Burial and Commemoration in the Classical World.* Edited by M. Carroll and J. Rempel. Studies in Funerary Archaeology 5. Oxford: Oxbow, 2011.
Driver, G. R. *Semitic Writing: From Pictograph to Alphabet.* Schweich Lectures of the British Academy, 1944. Oxford: Oxford University Press, 1948.
Driver, S. R. *A Critical and Exegetical Commentary on Deuteronomy.* ICC. Edinburgh: T&T Clark, 1895.
———. *Notes on the Hebrew Text and the Topography of the Books of Samuel.* Rev. ed. Oxford: Clarendon, 1913.
Duday, H. *The Archaeology of the Dead: Lectures in Archaeothanatology.* Studies in Funerary Archaeology 3. Oxford: Oxbow, 2009.
Duling, D. C. "Solomon, Exorcism, and the Son of David." *HTR* 68 (1975): 235–52.
Dunn, J. D. G. *Jesus Remembered.* Christianity in the Making 1. Grand Rapids: Eerdmans, 2003.

Edwards, C. *Death in Ancient Rome*. New Haven: Yale University Press, 2007.
Edwards, D. R., and C. T. McCollough, eds. *Archaeology and the Galilee: Texts and Contexts in the Graeco-Roman and Byzantine Periods*. SFSHJ 143. Atlanta: Scholars Press, 1997.
Edwards, J. R. *The Gospel according to Mark*. PNTC. Grand Rapids: Eerdmans, 2002.
Edwards, T. *Exegesis in the Targum of the Psalms: The Old, the New, and the Rewritten*. GD 28: Biblical Studies 1. Piscataway, NJ: Gorgias, 2007.
Ehrman, B. D. "Cephas and Peter." *JBL* 109 (1990): 463–74.
———. *Did Jesus Exist? The Historical Argument for Jesus of Nazareth*. New York: HarperCollins, 2012.
———. *How Jesus Became God: The Exaltation of a Jewish Preacher from Galilee*. San Francisco: HarperOne, 2014.
Elitzur, Y. "The Abba Cave: Unpublished Findings and a New Proposal Regarding Abba's Identity," *IEJ* 63 (2013) 83–102.
Ellens, J. H., ed. *Bethsaida in Archaeology, History and Ancient Culture: A Festschrift in Honor of John T. Greene*. Newcastle upon Tyne: Cambridge Scholars, 2014.
Erasmo, M. *Death: Antiquity and Its Legacy*. Oxford: Oxford University Press, 2012.
Evans, C. A. "The Aramaic Psalter and the New Testament: Praising the Lord in History and Prophecy." Pages 44–91 in *From Prophecy to Testament: The Function of the Old Testament in the New*. Edited by C. A. Evans. Peabody, MA: Hendrickson, 2004.
———. "Did Jesus Predict His Death and Resurrection?" Pages 82–97 in *Resurrection*. Edited by S. E. Porter, M. A. Hayes, and D. Tombs. JSNTSup 186. RILP 5. Sheffield: Sheffield Academic, 1999.
———. "From 'House of Prayer' to 'Cave of Robbers': Jesus' Prophetic Criticism of the Temple Establishment." Pages 417–42 in *The Quest for Context and Meaning: Studies in Biblical Intertextuality in Honor of James A. Sanders*. Edited by C. A. Evans and S. Talmon. BibInt 28. Leiden: Brill, 1997.
———. *From Jesus to the Church: The First Christian Generation*. Louisville: Westminster John Knox, 2014.
———. "How Septuagintal is Isa. 5:1–7 in Mark 12:1–9?" *NovT* 45 (2003): 105–10.
———. "In What Sense 'Blasphemy'? Jesus before Caiaphas in Mark 14:61–64." Pages 215–34 in *Society of Biblical Literature 1991 Seminar Papers*. Edited by E. H. Lovering Jr. SBLSP 30. Atlanta: Scholars Press, 1991.
———. "Jesus' Action in the Temple and Evidence of Corruption in the First-Century Temple." Pages 522–39 in *Society of Biblical Literature 1989 Seminar Papers*. Edited by David J. Lull. SBLSP 28. Atlanta: Scholars Press, 1989.
———. *Jesus and His World: The Archaeological Evidence*. Louisville: Westminster John Knox, 2012.
———. "Jesus and the 'Cave of Robbers': Toward a Jewish Context for the Temple Action." *BBR* 3 (1993): 93–110.
———. "Jesus and the Dead Sea Scrolls." Pages 573–98 in vol. 2 of *The Dead Sea Scrolls after Fifty Years: A Comprehensive Assessment*. Edited by Peter W. Flint and James C. VanderKam. Leiden: Brill, 1999.

———. “Jesus and the Ossuaries.” *BBR* 13 (2003): 21–46.
———. *Jesus and the Ossuaries: What Jewish Burial Practices Reveal about the Beginning of Christianity.* Waco, TX: Baylor University Press, 2003.
———. “Jesus and Zechariah’s Messianic Hope.” Pages 373–88 in *Authenticating the Activities of Jesus.* Edited by C. A. Evans and B. Chilton. NTTS 28.2. Leiden: Brill, 1998.
———. “Jesus, Healer and Exorcist: The Non-Christian Archaeological Evidence.” Pages 55–77 in *A City Set on a Hill: Essays in Honor of James F. Strange.* Edited by D. A. Warner and D. D. Binder. Fayetteville, AR: BorderStone Press, 2014.
———. “Jesus’ Self-Designation ‘The Son of Man’ and the Origins of His Deification.” Pages 29–47 in *The Trinity: An Interdisciplinary Symposium on the Trinity.* Edited by S. T. Davis, D. Kendall, and G. F. O’Collins. Oxford: Oxford University Press, 1999.
———. “The Last Days of Jesus’ Life: Did Jesus Anticipate the Cross?” Pages 511–27 in *The Gospels: History and Christology. The Search of Joseph Ratzinger–Benedict XVI—I Vangeli: Storia e Cristologia: La ricerca di Joseph Ratzinger–Benedetto XVI.* Edited by B. Estrada, E. Manicardi, and A. Puig i Tàrrech. Vatican City: Libreria Editrice Vaticana, 2013.
———. *Mark 8:27–16:20.* WBC 34B. Nashville: Nelson, 2001.
———. “On the Recently Discovered James Ossuary,” *DavarLogos* 2 (2003): 65–72.
———. “The Scriptures of Jesus and His Earliest Followers.” Pages 185–95 in *The Canon Debate.* Edited by L. M. McDonald and J. A. Sanders. Peabody, MA: Hendrickson, 2002.
Fagan, B. M., ed. *The Oxford Companion to Archaeology.* Oxford: Oxford University Press, 1996.
Fant, C., and M. G. Reddish. *Lost Treasures of the Bible: Understanding the Bible through Archaeological Artifacts in World Museums.* Grand Rapids: Eerdmans, 2008.
Faraone, C. A. “The Agonistic Context of Early Greek Binding Spells.” Pages 3–32 in *Magika Hiera: Ancient Greek Magic and Religion.* Edited by C. A. Faraone and D. Obbink. Oxford: Oxford University Press, 1991.
Faraone, C. A., and D. Obbink, eds. *Magika Hiera: Ancient Greek Magic and Religion.* Oxford: Oxford University Press, 1991.
Fedak, J. *Monumental Tombs of the Hellenistic Age: A Study of Selected Tombs from the Pre-Classical to the Early Imperial Era.* Toronto: University of Toronto Press, 1990.
Feldman, L. H. *Flavius Josephus: Translation and Commentary.* Vol. 3, *Judean Antiquities Books 1–4.* Edited by S. Mason. Leiden: Brill, 2000.
Felton, D. *Haunted Greece and Rome: Ghost Stories from Classical Antiquity.* Austin: University of Texas Press, 1999.
Ferguson, E. *Backgrounds of Early Christianity.* 2nd ed. Grand Rapids: Eerdmans, 1993.
Figueras, P. *Decorated Jewish Ossuaries.* DMOA 20. Leiden: Brill, 1983.
Finegan, J. *The Archeology of the New Testament.* Princeton: Princeton University Press, 1969.

———. *Light from the Ancient Past: The Archaeological Background of Judaism and Christianity.* 2nd ed. Princeton: Princeton University Press, 1969.

Fiorato, V., A. Boylston, and C. Knüsel, eds. *Blood Red Roses: The Archaeology of a Mass Grave from the Battle of Towton AD 1461.* Oxford: Oxbow, 2000.

Fisher, L. R. "'Can This Be the Son of David?'" Pages 82–97 in *Jesus and the Historian: Written in Honor of Ernest Cadman Colwell.* Edited by F. T. Trotter. Philadelphia: Westminster, 1968.

Fisher, T. "Faunal Analysis: Zooarchaeology in Syro-Palestinian/Israeli Archaeology." Pages 84–121 in *Bethsaida in Archaeology, History and Ancient Culture: A Festschrift in Honor of John T. Greene.* Edited by J. H. Ellens. Newcastle upon Tyne: Cambridge Scholars, 2014.

———. "A Zooarchaeological Analysis of Change in Animal Utilization at Bethsaida from Iron Age II through the Early Roman Period." PhD diss., The University of Tennessee, 2005.

Fitzmyer, J. A. "282a-t. 4QUnidentified Fragments B, a-t." In *Qumran Cave 4.XXVI: Cryptic Texts and Miscellanea, Part 1.* Edited by S. J. Pfann et al. DJD 36. Oxford: Clarendon, 2000.

———. *The Acts of the Apostles.* AB 31. New York: Doubleday, 1998.

———. "Aramaic Kepha' and Peter's Name in the New Testament." Pages 121–32 in *Text and Interpretation: Studies in the New Testament Presented to Matthew Black.* Edited by E. Best and R. M. Wilson. Cambridge: Cambridge University Press, 1979.

———. "The Aramaic Qorbân Inscription from Jebel Hallet et-Tûrî and Mk 7:11/Mt 15:5." *JBL* 78 (1959): 60–65. Reprinted in pages 93–100 of *Essays on the Semitic Background of the New Testament.* SBLSBS 5. Missoula: Scholars Press, 1974,

———. "Crucifixion in Ancient Palestine, Qumran Literature, and the New Testament." Pages 125–46 in *To Advance the Gospel: New Testament Studies.* 2nd ed. Biblical Resource Series. Grand Rapids: Eerdmans, 1998.

———. *Essays on the Semitic Background of the New Testament.* London: Geoffrey Chapman, 1971; reprinted as SBLSBS 5; Missoula: Scholars Press, 1974.

———. *First Corinthians.* AB 32. New Haven: Yale University Press, 2008.

———. *The Gospel according to Luke.* 2 vols. AB 28, 28a. Garden City, NY: Doubleday, 1981–85.

———. "The Name Simon." *HTR* 56 (1963): 1–5. Reprinted in pages 105–10 of *Essays on the Semitic Background of the New Testament.* London: Geoffrey Chapman, 1971; reprinted as SBLSBS 5; Atlanta: Scholars Press, 1974.

———. *To Advance the Gospel: New Testament Studies.* New York: Crossroad, 1981.

Fitzmyer, J. A., and D. J. Harrington. *A Manual of Palestinian Aramaic Texts (Second Century BC–Second Century AD).* BibOr 34. Rome: Pontifical Biblical Institute, 1978.

Flint, P. W. *The Dead Sea Psalms Scrolls and the Book of Psalms.* STDJ 17. Leiden: Brill, 1997.

Flusser, D. "Der Hohepriester Hannas und sein Geschlecht." Pages 185–92 in *Entdeckungen im Neuen Testament.* Vol. 2, *Jesus—Qumran—Urchristentum.* Edited by M. Majer. Neukirchen-Vluyn: Neukirchener Verlag, 1999.

———. *Jesus*. Rev. ed. In collaboration with R. S. Notley. Jerusalem: Magnes, 1997.
Focant, C. *The Gospel according to Mark: A Commentary*. Translated by L. R. Keylock. Eugene, OR: Pickwick, 2012.
Foerster, G. "The Synagogues at Masada and Herodium." Pages 24–29 in *Ancient Synagogues Revealed*. Edited by L. I. Levine. Jerusalem: Israel Exploration Society, 1981. Originally published in *ErIsr* 11 (1973): 224–28 (Hebrew).
Fortner, S. "The Fishing Implements and Maritime Activities of Bethsaida-Julias (et-Tell)." Pages 269–82 in vol. 2 of *Bethsaida*. Edited by R. Arav and R. Freund. Kirksville, MO: Truman State University Press, 1995.
Foster, P. "Educating Jesus: The Search for a Plausible Context." *JSHJ* 4 (2006): 7–33.
France, R. T. *The Gospel of Matthew*. NICNT. Grand Rapids: Eerdmans, 2007.
———. *Jesus and the Old Testament: His Application of Old Testament Passages to Himself and His Mission*. London: Tyndale, 1971.
Fröhlich, I. "Magical Healing at Qumran (11Q11) and the Question of the Calendar." Pages 39–49 in *Studies on Magic and Divination in the Biblical World*. Edited by H. R. Jacobus et al. Biblical Intersections 11. Piscataway, NJ: Gorgias, 2013.
Frova, A. "L'iscrizione di Ponzio Pilato a Cesarea." *Rendiconti dell'Istituto Lombardo* 95 (1961): 419–34.
Funk, R. W. *Honest to Jesus: Jesus for a New Millennium*. San Francisco: HarperCollins, 1996.
Funk, R. W., and R. W. Hoover, eds. *The Five Gospels: The Search for the Authentic Words of Jesus*. New York: Macmillan, 1993.
Gager, J. G. *Curse Tablets and Binding Spells from the Ancient World*. Oxford: Oxford University Press, 1992.
Galling, K. "Ein Etagen-Pilaster-Grab in Norden von Jerusalem." *ZDPV* 59 (1936): 111–23.
Galor, K. *Archaeology of Jerusalem: From the Origins to the Ottomans*. New Haven: Yale University Press, 2013.
García Martínez, F. "4QpNah y la Crucifixión: Nueva hipótesis de reconstrucción de 4Q169 3–4 I 4–8." *EstBib* 38 (1979): 221–35.
García Martínez, F., and E. J. C. Tigchelaar. *The Dead Sea Scrolls Study Edition*. Vol. 2, *4Q274–11Q31*. Leiden: Brill, 1998.
García Martínez, F., E. J. C. Tigchelaar, and A. S. van der Woude. *Qumran Cave 11.II: 11Q2–18, 11Q20–31*. DJD 23. Oxford: Clarendon, 1998.
Garland, R. *The Greek Way of Death*. London: Duckworth, 1985.
Gat, Y. "East Talpiot." *Hadashot Arkeologiyot* [*Archaeological News*] 76 (1981): 24–25 (Hebrew).
Gathercole, S. J. *The Composition of the Gospel of Thomas: Original Language and Influences*. SNTSMS 151. Cambridge: Cambridge University Press, 2012.
———. *The Gospel of Thomas: Introduction and Commentary*. TENTS 11. Leiden: Brill, 2014.
Gatti, C. "A proposito di una rilettura dell'epigrafe di Ponzio Pilato." *Aev* 55 (1981): 13–21.
Geva, H. "Tombs." *NEAEHL* 2:747–49.

Gibson, S. *The Final Days of Jesus: The Archaeological Evidence.* San Francisco: HarperOne, 2009.

———. "Is the Talpiot Tomb Really the Family Tomb of Jesus?" *NEA* 69 (2006): 118–24.

Goldstein, J. *I Maccabees.* AB 41; Garden City, NY: Doubleday, 1976.

Goodacre, M. S. *Thomas and the Gospels: The Case for Thomas's Familiarity with the Synoptics.* Grand Rapids: Eerdmans, 2012.

Goodenough, E. R. *Jewish Symbols in the Greco-Roman Period.* Vol. 1, *The Archaeological Evidence from Palestine.* Bollingen Series 37. New York: Pantheon, 1953.

———. *Jewish Symbols in the Greco-Roman Period.* Vol. 2, *The Archaeological Evidence from the Diaspora.* Bollingen Series 37. New York: Pantheon, 1953.

———. *Jewish Symbols in the Greco-Roman Period.* Vol. 3, *Illustrations.* Bollingen Series 37. New York: Pantheon, 1953.

———. *Jewish Symbols in the Greco-Roman Period: Abridged Edition.* Edited by J. Neusner. Princeton: Princeton University Press, 1988.

Goodrick, A. T. S., ed. *The Book of Wisdom.* London: Rivington, 1913.

Gordon, A. E. *Illustrated Introduction to Latin Epigraphy.* Berkeley: University of California Press, 1983.

Gordon, C. H. "Aramaic Magical Bowls in the Istanbul and Baghdad Museums." *ArOr* 6 (1934): 319–34.

———. "Two Magic Bowls in Teheran." *Or* 20 (1951): 306–15.

Gowland, R., and C. Knüsel, eds. *Social Archaeology of Funerary Remains.* Studies in Funerary Archaeology 1. Oxford: Oxbow, 2006.

Grabbe, L. L. "Synagogue and Sanhedrin in the First Century." Pages 1723–45 in vol. 2 of *Handbook for the Study of the Historical Jesus.* Edited by T. Holmén and S. E. Porter. Leiden: Brill, 2011.

Graf, F. *Magic in the Ancient World.* Revealing Antiquity 10. Cambridge: Harvard University Press, 1997.

Graham, E.-J. "From Fragments to Ancestors: Re-defining the Role of *os resectum* in Rituals of Purification and Commemoration in Republican Rome." Pages 91–109 in *Living through the Dead: Burial and Commemoration in the Classical World.* Edited by M. Carroll and J. Rempel. Studies in Funerary Archaeology 5. Oxford: Oxbow, 2011.

Green, J. B. *The Death of Jesus: Tradition and Interpretation in the Passion Narrative.* WUNT II/33. Tübingen: Mohr Siebeck, 1988.

Greenhut, Z. "Burial Cave of the Caiaphas Family." *BAR* 18, no. 5 (1992): 28–36, 76.

———. "The 'Caiaphas' Tomb in North Talpiyot, Jerusalem." *'Atiqot* 21 (1992): 63–71.

Grintz, J. M. "The Inscription from Giv'at ha-Mivtar: A Historical Interpretation." *Sinai* 75 (1974): 20–23 (Hebrew).

———. "The Last Way of the Last Hasmonean," *Ha-ʾUmmah* 43 (1975) 256–69 (Hebrew).

Groh, D. E. "The Stratigraphic Chronology of the Galilean Synagogue from the Early Roman Period through the Early Byzantine Period (ca. 420 CE)." Pages

51–69 in vol. 1 of *Ancient Synagogues: Historical Analysis and Archaeological Discovery.* Edited by D. Urman and P. V. M. Flesher. StPB 47. Leiden: Brill, 1995.

Guarducci, M. "Iscrizione greche e latine in una *taberna* a Pozzuoli." Pages 219–23 in *Acta of the Fifth International Congress of Greek and Latin Epigraphy, Cambridge, 1967.* Oxford: Blackwell, 1971.

Guillet, P.-E. "Les 800 'Crucifiés' d'Alexandre Jannée." *Cahiers du Cercle Ernest Renan* 100 (1977): 11–16.

Gutman, J. *The Dura-Europos Synagogue: A Re-evaluation (1932–1992).* USFSHJ 25. Atlanta: Scholars Press, 1992.

Haas, N. "Anthropological Observations on the Skeletal Remains from Giv'at ha-Mivtar." *IEJ* 20 (1970): 38–59.

Hachlili, R. *Ancient Synagogues—Archaeology and Art: New Discoveries and Current Research.* HOS. Section 1: Ancient Near East 105. Leiden: Brill, 2013.

———. *Jericho: The Jewish Cemetery of the Second Temple Period.* IAA Reports 7. Jerusalem: Israel Antiquities Authority, 1999.

———. *Jewish Funerary Customs, Practices, and Rites in the Second Temple Period.* JSJSup 94. Leiden: Brill, 2005.

———. "A Second Temple Period Jewish Necropolis in Jericho." *BA* 43 (1980): 235–40.

———. "What's in a Name?" Pages 125–49 in *The Tomb of Jesus and His Family? Exploring Ancient Jewish Tombs Near Jerusalem's Walls.* Edited by J. H. Charlesworth. Grand Rapids: Eerdmans, 2013.

Hachlili, R., and A. Killebrew. "Was the Coin-on-Eye Custom a Jewish Burial Practice in the Second Temple Period?" *BA* 46 (1983): 147–53.

Hammond, P. C. *The Excavation of the Main Theater at Petra, 1961–1962.* London: B. Quaritch, 1965.

———. "'Mason's Marks' and Other Archaeological Signs." *PEQ* 132 (2000): 123–30.

Hanfmann, G. M. A. "The Crucified Donkey Man: Achaios and Jesus." Pages 205–7 in *Studies in Classical Art and Archaeology: A Tribute to Peter Heinrich von Blanckenhagen.* Edited by G. Kopcke and M. B. Moore. Locust Valley, NJ: Augustin, 1979.

———. "The Donkey and the King." *HTR* 78 (1985): 421–30.

Hanson, K. C., and D. E. Oakman. *Palestine in the Time of Jesus: Social Structures and Social Conflicts.* Minneapolis: Fortress, 1998.

Haran, M. "On the Diffusion of Schools and Literacy." Pages 81–95 in *Congress Volume, Jerusalem 1986.* Edited by J. A. Emerton. VTSup 40. Leiden: Brill, 1988.

Harley, F., and J. Spier. "Magical Amulet with Crucifixion." Pages 227–28 in *Picturing the Bible: The Earliest Christian Art.* Edited by J. Spier. New Haven: Yale University Press, 2007.

Harmon, M., T. I. Molleson, and J. L. Price. "Burials, Bodies and Beheadings in Romano-British and Anglo-Saxon Cemeteries." *Bulletin of the British Museum of Natural History: Geology* 35 (1981): 145–88.

Harrell, J. A. "Final Blow to IAA Report: Flawed Geochemistry Used to Condemn James Inscription." *BAR* 30, no. 1 (2004): 38–41.

Harris, J. *Pompeii Awakened: A Story of Rediscovery.* New York: I. B. Tauris, 2007.

Harris, W. V. *Ancient Literacy.* Cambridge: Harvard University Press, 1989.
Hendel, R. S. "Giants at Jericho." *BAR* 35, no. 2 (2009): 20, 66.
Hengel, M. *The Atonement: The Origins of the Doctrine in the New Testament.* Philadelphia: Fortress, 1981.
———. *Crucifixion in the Ancient World and the Folly of the Message of the Cross.* Philadelphia: Fortress, 1977.
———. *The "Hellenization" of Judaea in the First Century after Christ.* Philadelphia: Trinity Press International, 1989.
———. *Was Jesus a Revolutionist?* Translated by W. Klassen. FBBS 28. Philadelphia: Fortress, 1971. Translation of *War Jesus Revolutionär?* CH 110. Stuttgart: Calwer, 1970.
Henten, J. W van. *The Maccabean Martyrs as Saviours of the Jewish People: A Study of 2 and 4 Maccabees.* JSJSup 57. Leiden: Brill, 1997.
Henten, J. W. van, and F. Avemarie. *Martyrdom and Noble Death: Selected Texts from Graeco-Roman, Jewish and Christian Antiquity.* London: Routledge, 2002.
Heracus, W. *Petronii Cena Trimalchionis nebst Ausgewählten pompejanischen Wandinschriften.* Heidelberg: C. Winter, 1909.
Hertzberg, H. W. *I and II Samuel.* OTL. Philadelphia: Westminster, 1964.
Hewitt, J. W. "The Use of Nails in the Crucifixion." *HTR* 25 (1932): 29–45.
Hobson, B. *Latrinae et foricae: Toilets in the Roman World.* London: Duckworth, 2009.
Hoehner, H. W. "Pontius Pilate." *DJG* 615–17.
Hohlfelder, R. L. "Caesarea Beneath the Sea." *BAR* 8, no. 3 (1982): 42–47, 56.
Hohlfelder, R. L., et al. "Sebastos, Herod's Harbor at Caesarea Maritima." *BA* 46 (1983): 133–43.
Hölscher, G. "Zur jüdischen Namenkunde." Pages 148–57 in *Vom Alten Testament: Karl Marti zum siebzigsten Geburtstage gewidmet.* Edited by K. Budde. BZAW 41. Giessen: Töpelmann, 1925.
Honoré, T. *Justinian's Digest: Character and Compilation.* Oxford: Oxford University Press, 2010.
Horbury, W. "The 'Caiaphas' Ossuaries and Joseph Caiaphas." *PEQ* 126 (1994): 32–48.
Horbury, W., and B. McNeil, eds. *Suffering and Martyrdom in the New Testament: Studies Presented to G. M. Styler by the Cambridge New Testament Seminar.* Cambridge: Cambridge University Press, 1981.
Horbury, W., and D. Noy. *Jewish Inscriptions of Graeco-Roman Egypt.* Cambridge: Cambridge University Press, 1992.
Horsley, G. H. R., ed. *New Documents Illustrating Early Christianity.* Vol. 4. North Ryde: Macquarie University, 1987.
Horsley, R. A. *Archaeology, History, and Society in Galilee: The Social Context of Jesus and the Rabbis.* Valley Forge: Trinity Press International, 1996.
———. "High Priests and the Politics of Roman Palestine." *JSJ* 17 (1986): 23–55.
———. "Synagogues in Galilee and the Gospels." Pages 46–69 in *The Evolution of the Synagogue: Problems and Progress.* Edited by H. C. Kee and L. H. Cohick. Harrisburg, PA: Trinity Press International, 1999.

Horst, P. W. van der. *Ancient Jewish Epitaphs: An Introductory Survey of a Millennium of Jewish Funerary Epigraphy (300 BCE–700 CE)*. Kampen: Kok Pharos, 1991.

Hurtado, L. W. *The Earliest Christian Artifacts: Manuscripts and Christian Origins*. Grand Rapids: Eerdmans, 2006.

———. "The Staurogram in Early Christian Manuscripts: The Earliest Visual Reference to the Crucified Jesus?" Pages 207–26 in *New Testament Manuscripts: Their Text and Their World*. Edited by T. J. Kraus and T. Nicklas. TENTS 2. Leiden: Brill, 2006.

Hutter, M. "Lilith." *DDD* 520–21.

Ilan, T. *Lexicon of Jewish Names in Late Antiquity*. Part 1, *Palestine 300 BCE–200 CE*. TSAJ 91. Tübingen: Mohr Siebeck, 2002.

Iliffe, J. H. "The θάνατος Inscription from Herod's Temple: Fragment of a Second Copy." *QDAP* 6 (1936): 1–3.

Isbell, C. *Corpus of the Aramaic Incantation Bowls*. SBLDS 17. Missoula: Scholars Press, 1975.

Jacobovici, S., and C. Pellegrino. *The Jesus Family Tomb: The Discovery, the Investigation, and the Evidence That Could Change History*. San Francisco: HarperCollins, 2007.

Jacobson, D. M. "Has Herod's Place of Burial Been Found?" *PEQ* 139 (2007): 147–48.

———. "Mariam Daughter of Yeshua, Son of Caiaphas, Priest of Maʿaziah from Beth ʾImri." *PEQ* 144 (2012): 1–3.

James, M. R. "A Fragment of the Apocalypse of Adam in Greek." Pages 138–45 in *Apocrypha Anecdota II*. TS 2.3. Cambridge: Cambridge University Press, 1893.

Jensen, M. H. *Herod Antipas in Galilee: The Literary and Archaeological Sources on the Reign of Herod Antipas and Its Socio-Economic Impact on Galilee*. WUNT II/215. Tübingen: Mohr Siebeck, 2006.

———. "Magdala/Taricheae and the Jewish Revolt." In *Magdala, Jewish City of Fish*. Edited by M. Aviam, R. Bauckham, and S. De Luca. Waco, TX: Baylor University Press, forthcoming.

Jensen, R. M. *Understanding Early Christian Art*. New York: Routledge, 2000.

Jerphanion, G. de. "La croix d'Herculaneum?" *OCP* 7 (1941): 5–35.

Johnson, S. E. *Jesus and His Towns*. GNS 29. Wilmington, DE: Glazier, 1989.

Johnson, W. A. *Bookrolls and Scribes in Oxyrhynchus*. Studies in Book and Print Culture. Toronto: University of Toronto Press, 2004.

Jones, A. H. M. "Procurators and Prefects in the Early Principate." Pages 117–25 in *Studies in Roman Government and Law*. Oxford: Blackwell, 1960.

———. *Studies in Roman Government and Law*. Oxford: Blackwell, 1960.

Josephus. Translated by H. St. J. Thackeray and R. Marcus. 13 vols. LCL. Cambridge: Harvard University Press, 1934.

The Works of Josephus: Complete and Unabridged. Translated by W. Whiston. New ed. Peabody, MA: Hendrickson, 1987.

Jotham-Rothschild, J. "Tombs of the Sanhedria." *PEQ* 84 (1952): 23–38; 86 (1954): 16–22.

Judge, E. A. "The Regional *kanōn* for Requisitioned Transport." Pages 348–59 in *The First Christians in the Roman World: Augustan and New Testament Essays.* Edited by J. R. Harrison. WUNT 229. Tübingen: Mohr Siebeck, 2008.

Kane, J. P. "By No Means 'The Earliest Records of Christianity'—with an Emended Reading of the Talpioth Inscription ΙΗCΟΥC ΙΟΥ." *PEQ* 103 (1971): 103–8.

———. "The Ossuary Inscriptions of Jerusalem." *JSS* 23 (1978): 268–82.

Kant, L. H. "Jewish Inscriptions in Greek and Latin." *ANRW* II.20, no. 2 (1987): 671–713.

Katzev, S. W. "The Ancient Ship of Kyrenia, Beneath Cyprus Seas." Pages 286–99 in *Great Moments in Greek Archaeology.* Edited by P. Valavanis and D. Hardy. Oxford: Oxford University Press, 2007.

Keall, E. J. "Brother of Jesus Ossuary: New Tests Bolster Case for Authenticity." *BAR* 29, no. 4 (2003): 52–55, 70.

Kee, H. C. "The Changing Meaning of Synagogue: A Response to Richard Oster." *NTS* 40 (1994): 281–83.

———. "Defining the First-Century CE Synagogue: Problems and Progress." *NTS* 41 (1995): 481–500. Reprinted in pages 7–26 of *The Evolution of the Synagogue: Problems and Progress.* Edited by H. C. Kee and L. H. Cohick. Harrisburg, PA: Trinity Press International, 1999.

———. "The Transformation of the Synagogue after 70 C.E.: Its Import for Early Christianity." *NTS* 36 (1990): 481–500.

Kee, H. C., and L. H. Cohick, eds. *The Evolution of the Synagogue: Problems and Progress.* Harrisburg, PA: Trinity Press International, 1999.

Kelso, J. *An Archaeologist Looks at the Gospels.* Waco, TX: Word, 1969.

Keppie, L. J. F. *Understanding Roman Inscriptions.* Baltimore: Johns Hopkins University Press, 1991).

Kim, T. H. "The Anarthrous υἱὸς θεοῦ in Mark 15,39 and the Roman Imperial Cult." *Bib* 79 (1998): 221–41.

Kindler, A. "More Dates on the Coins of the Procurators." *IEJ* 6 (1956): 54–57.

Klein, R. W. *1 Samuel.* WBC 10. Dallas: Word, 1983.

Klein, S. *Jüdisch-Palästinisches Corpus Inscriptionum (Ossuar-, Grab- und Synagogeninschriften).* Vienna: Löwit, 1920.

Kloner, A. "A Burial Cave of the Second Temple Period at Giv'at Ha-Mivtar." Pages 191–224 in *Jerusalem in the Second Temple Period: Abraham Schalit Memorial Volume.* Edited by A. Oppenheimer, U. Rappaport, and M. Stern. Jerusalem: Yad Izhak Ben-Zvi, 1980 (Hebrew).

———. "A Burial Cave of the Second Temple Period at Giv'at Ha-Mivtar, Jerusalem." *Qadmoniot* 19–20 (1972): 108–9 (Hebrew).

———. "The Cave of the Birds—A Painted Tomb on the Mount of Olives." Pages 306–10 in *Ancient Jerusalem Revealed.* Edited by H. Geva. Jerusalem: Israel Exploration Society, 1994.

———. "The 'Caves of Simeon the Just' and 'The Minor Sanhedrin': Two Burial Complexes from the Second Temple Period in Jerusalem." Pages 125–49 in *What Athens Has to Do with Jerusalem: Essays on Classical, Jewish, and Early Christian Art and Archaeology in Honor of Gideon Foerster.* Edited by L. V.

Rutgers. Interdisciplinary Studies in Ancient Culture and Religion 1. Leuven: Peeters, 2002.

———. "An Ossuary from Jerusalem Ornamented with Monumental Facades." Pages 235–38 in *Ancient Jerusalem Revealed*. Edited by H. Geva. Jerusalem: Israel Exploration Society, 1994.

———. "A Tomb with Inscribed Ossuaries in East Talpiyot, Jerusalem," *'Atiqot* 29 (1996) 15–22.

Kloner, A., and S. Gibson. "The Talpiot Tomb Reconsidered: The Archaeological Facts." Pages 29–75 in *The Tomb of Jesus and His Family? Exploring Ancient Jewish Tombs Near Jerusalem's Walls*. Edited by J. H. Charlesworth. Grand Rapids: Eerdmans, 2013.

Kloppenborg, J. S. "Egyptian Viticultural Practices and the Citation of Isa 5:1–7 in Mark 12:1–9." *NovT* 44 (2002): 134–59.

———. "Isa 5:1–7 LXX and Mark 12:1, 9, Again." *NovT* 46 (2004): 12–19.

———. "The Theodotos Synagogue Inscription and the Problem of First-Century Synagogue Buildings." Pages 236–82 in *Jesus and Archaeology*. Edited by J. H. Charlesworth. Grand Rapids: Eerdmans, 2006.

Kloppenborg Verbin, J. S. "Dating Theodotos (*CIJ* 1404)." *JJS* 51 (2000): 243–80.

Kokkinos, N. "The Foundation of Bethsaida-Julias by Philip the Tetrarch." *JJS* 59 (2008): 236–51.

Kraeling, C. H. "Christian Burial Urns?" *BA* 9 (1946): 16–20.

Kraus, T. J. "'He That Dwelleth in the Help of the Highest': Septuagint Psalm 90 and the Iconographic Program on Byzantine Armbands." Pages 137–47 in *Jewish and Christian Scripture as Artifact and Canon*. Edited by C. A. Evans and H. D. Zacharias. LSTS 70; SSEJC 13. London: Continuum, 2009.

———. "Psalm 90 der Septuaginta in apotropäischer Verwendung—erste Anmerkungen und Datenmaterial." Pages 497–514 in vol. 1 of *Proceedings of the 24th International Congress of Papyrology, Helsinki, 1–7 August, 2004*. Edited by J. Frösén et al. Commentationes Humanarum Litterarum 122. Helsinki: Societas Scientiarum Fennica, 2007.

———. "Septuaginta-Psalm 90 in apotropäischer Verwendung: Vorüberlegungen für eine kritische Edition und (bisheriges) Datenmaterial." *BN* 125 (2005): 39–73.

Kuhn, H.-W. "Bethsaida in the Gospel of Mark." Pages 115–31 vol. 3 of *Bethsaida: A City by the North Shore of the Sea of Galilee*. Edited by R. Arav and R. Freund. Kirksville, MO: Truman State University Press, 1995, 1999, 2004, 2009.

———, ed. *Betsaida/Bethsaida—Julias (et-Tell): Die ersten 25 Jahre der Ausgrabung (1987–2011)—The First Twenty-Five Years of Excavation (1987–2011)*. NTOA: Series Archaeologica 4. Göttingen: Vandenhoeck & Ruprecht, 2014.

———. "Der Gekreuzigte von Giv'at ha-Mivtar: Bilanz einer Entdeckung." Pages 303–34 in *Theologia Crucis–Signum Crucis: Festschrift für Erich Dinkler zum 70. Geburtstag*. Edited by C. Andresen and G. Klein, eds. Tübingen: Mohr Siebeck, 1979.

———. "Did Jesus Stay at Bethsaida? Arguments from Ancient Texts and Archaeology for Bethsaida and Et-Tell." Pages 2973–3021 in vol. 4 of *Handbook for the Study of the Historical Jesus*. Edited by T. Holmén and S. E. Porter. Leiden: Brill, 2011.

———. "Jesu Hinwendung zu den Heiden im Markusevangelium im Verhältnis zu Jesu historischen Wiren in Betsaida, mit einem Zwischenbericht zur Ausgrabung eines vermuteten heidnischen Tempels auf et-Tell (Betsaida)." Pages 204–40 in *Die Weite des Mysteriums: Christliche Identität im Dialog: für Horst Buerkle*. Edited by K. Kraemer and A. Paus. Freiburg im Breisgau: Herder, 2000.

Kuhn, H.-W., and R. Arav. "The Bethsaida Excavations: Historical and Archaeological Approaches." Pages 77–106 in *The Future of Early Christianity: Essays in Honor of Helmut Koester*. Edited by B. A. Pearson. Minneapolis: Fortress, 1991.

Labbé, G. "Ponce Pilate et la munificence de Tibère: L'inscription de Césarée." *REA* 93 (1991): 277–97.

Lagrange, M.-J. "Epigraphie sémitique." *RB* 2 (1893): 220–22.

Lanciani, R. *Ancient Rome in the Light of Recent Discoveries*. Boston: Houghton Mifflin, 1898.

Lane, W. L. *The Gospel of Mark*. NICNT. Grand Rapids: Eerdmans, 1974.

Lange, A., H. Lichtenberger, and K. F. D. Römheld, eds. *Die Dämonen: Die Dämonologie der israelitischen-jüdischen und frühchristlichen Literatur im Kontext ihrer Umwelt*. Tübingen: Mohr Siebeck, 2003.

Lattimore, R. A. *Aeschylus I*. New York: Washington Square, 1967.

———. *Themes in Greek and Latin Epitaphs*. Illinois Studies in Language and Literature 28/1–2. Urbana, IL: University of Illinois Press, 1942.

Le Bohec, Y. "Inscriptions juives et judaïsantes de l'Afrique romaine." *Antiquités africaines* 17 (1981): 165–207.

———. "Juifs et judaïsants dans l'Afrique romaine: Remarques onomastiques." *Antiquités africaines* 17 (1981): 209–229.

Lemaire, A. "Burial Box of James the Brother of Jesus." *BAR* 28, no. 6 (2002): 24–33, 70.

———. "Critical Evaluation of the IAA Committee Reports Regarding the Ossuary Inscription." *Polish Journal of Biblical Research* 2, no. 2 (2003): 29–60.

———. "L'ossuaire de 'Jacques fils de Joseph, le frère de Jésus." *Polish Journal of Biblical Research* 2, no. 2 (2003): 81–87.

———. "The Ossuary of Simon and Alexander." Pages 112–21 in *The Tomb of Jesus and His Family? Exploring Ancient Jewish Tombs Near Jerusalem's Walls*. Edited by J. H. Charlesworth. Grand Rapids: Eerdmans, 2013.

Leon, H. J. *The Jews of Ancient Rome*. Morris Loeb Series. Philadelphia: Jewish Publication Society of America, 1960; rev., Peabody, MA: Hendrickson, 1995.

Levine, L. I. *The Ancient Synagogue: The First Thousand Years*. 2nd ed. New Haven: Yale University Press, 2005.

———. "The Nature and Origin of the Palestine Synagogue Reconsidered." *JBL* 115 (1996): 425–48.

Lichtenberger, H. "Ps 91 und die Exorzismen in 11QPsAp[a]." Pages 416–21 in *Die Dämonen: Die Dämonologie der israelitischen-jüdischen und frühchristlichen Literatur im Kontext ihrer Umwelt*. Edited by A. Lange, H. Lichtenberger, and K. F. D. Römheld. Tübingen: Mohr Siebeck, 2003.

———. "Qumran and the New Testament." Pages 103–29 in *The Changing Face of Judaism, Christianity, and Other Greco-Roman Religions in Antiquity*. Edited by I. H. Henderson and Gerbern S. Oegema. JSHRZ 2. Gütersloh: Gütersloher Verlagshaus, 2006.

Lieberman, S. "Some Aspects of After Life in Early Rabbinic Literature." Pages 495–532 in vol. 2 of *Harry Austryn Wolfson: Jubilee Volume on the Occasion of His Seventy-Fifth Birthday.* Edited by S. Lieberman et al. Jerusalem: American Academy for Jewish Research, 1965.

Lifshitz, B. *Donateurs et fondateurs dans les synagogues juives: Répertoire des dédicaces grecques relatives à la construction et à la réfection des synagogues.* CahRB 7. Paris: Gabalda, 1967.

Loffreda, S., and V. Tzaferis. "Capernaum." *NEAEHL* 1:291–6.

Lucan. Translated by J. D. Duff. LCL. Cambridge: Harvard University Press, 1928.

Lucian. Translated by A. M. Harmon et al. 8 vols. LCL. Cambridge: Harvard University Press, 1928.

Lührmann, D. *Das Markusevangelium.* HNT 3. Tübingen: Mohr Siebeck, 1987.

Luz, U. *Matthew 8–20.* Hermeneia. Minneapolis: Fortress, 2001.

Macalister, R. A. S. "On a Rock Tomb North of Jerusalem." PEFQS 33 (1900): 54–61.

Macalister, R. A. S. "The Nicophorieh Tomb." PEFQS 33 (1901): 397–402.

Mach, M. "Demons." *EDSS* 1:189–92.

Magness, J. *The Archaeology of the Holy Land: From the Destruction of Solomon's Temple to the Muslim Conquest.* Cambridge: Cambridge University Press, 2012.

———. *The Archaeology of Qumran and the Dead Sea Scrolls.* Studies in the Dead Sea Scrolls and Related Literature. Grand Rapids: Eerdmans, 2002.

———. "Confessions of an Archaeologist: Lessons I Learned from the Talpiyot Tomb Fiasco and Other Media Encounters." Pages 89–95 in *Archaeology, Bible, Politics, and the Media: Proceedings of the Duke University Conference, April 23–24, 2009.* Edited by E. M. Meyers and C. Meyers. Winona Lake, IN: Eisenbrauns, 2012.

———. "Jesus' Tomb: What Did It Look Like?" Pages 212–26 in *Where Christianity Was Born.* Edited by H. Shanks. Washington, DC: Biblical Archaeology Society, 2006.

———. "Ossuaries and the Burials of Jesus and James." *JBL* 124 (2005): 121–54.

———. *Stone and Dung, Oil and Spit: Jewish Daily Life in the Time of Jesus.* Grand Rapids: Eerdmans, 2011.

Maier, J. *The Temple Scroll: An Introduction, Translation and Commentary.* JSOTSup 34. Sheffield: JSOT Press, 1985.

Maier, P. L. "Sejanus, Pilate and the Date of the Crucifixion." *Church History* 37 (1968): 3–13.

Maiuri, A. "La croce di Ercolano." *Rendiconti della Pontificia Accademia Romana di Archeologia* 15 (1939): 193–218.

———. *Herculaneum and the Villa of the Papyri: Archaeological Guide of the Town.* Novara: Istituto Geografico de Agostini, 1962.

———. *Herculaneum and the Villa of the Papyri.* Novara: Istituto Geografico de Agostini, 1974.

Margalioth, M. *Book of the Mysteries.* Jerusalem: American Academy for Jewish Research, 1966 (Hebrew).

Maser, P. "Das sogenannte Spottkruzifix vom Palatin: Ein 'frühchristliches' Denkmal im Widersteit der Meinungen." *Das Altertum* 18 (1972): 248–54.

Mattila, S. L. "Jesus and the 'Middle Peasants'? Problematizing a Social-Scientific Concept." *CBQ* 72 (2010): 291–313.

Mazar, B. *Beth She'arim: Report on the Excavations during 1936–1940*. Vol. 1, *Catacombs 1–4*. New Brunswick, NJ: Rutgers University Press, 1973.

McCane, B. R. "'Let the Dead Bury Their Own Dead': Secondary Burial and Matt 8:21–22." *HTR* 83 (1990): 31–43.

McCown, C. C. "The Christian Tradition as to the Magical Wisdom of Solomon." *JPOS* 2 (1922): 1–24.

McDonald, L. M., and S. E. Porter. *Early Christianity and Its Sacred Literature*. Peabody, MA: Hendrickson, 2000.

McGing, B. C. "Pontius Pilate and the Sources." *CBQ* 53 (1991): 416–38.

McKenzie, J. *The Architecture of Petra*. British Academic Monographs in Archaeology 1. Oxford: British Academy, 1990.

McKinley, J. L. "A Decapitation from the Romano-British Cemetery at Baldock, Hertfordshire." *International Journal of Osteoarchaeology* 3 (1993): 41–44.

McLaren, J. S. *Power and Politics in Palestine: The Jews and the Governing of Their Land, 100 BC–AD 70*. JSNTSup 63. Sheffield: JSOT Press, 1991.

McLean, B. H. *An Introduction to Greek Epigraphy of the Hellenistic and Roman Periods*. Ann Arbor: University of Michigan Press, 2002.

McNamara, M. *Targum Neofiti 1: Genesis*. ArBib 1A; Collegeville, MN: Liturgical Press, 1992.

McNamer, E. "Philip, Julia, and the Imperial Cult." Pages 242–51 in *Bethsaida in Archaeology, History and Ancient Culture: A Festschrift in Honor of John T. Greene*. Edited by J. H. Ellens. Newcastle upon Tyne: Cambridge Scholars, 2014.

McRay, J. *Archaeology and the New Testament*. Grand Rapids: Baker, 1991.

Meier, J. P. *A Marginal Jew: Rethinking the Historical Jesus*. Vol. 1, *The Roots of the Problem and the Person*. ABRL. New York: Doubleday, 1991.

Merritt, R. L. "Jesus Barabbas and the Paschal Pardon." *JBL* 104 (1985): 57–68.

Metzger, B. M. *Manuscripts of the Greek Bible: An Introduction to Palaeography*. Oxford: Oxford University Press, 1981.

———. "The Nazareth Inscription Once Again." Pages 75–92 in *New Testament Studies. Philological, Versional, and Patristic*. NTTS 10. Leiden: Brill, 1980.

———. *New Testament Studies: Philological, Versional, and Patristic*. NTTS 10; Leiden: Brill, 1980.

———. *A Textual Commentary on the Greek New Testament*. New York: United Bible Societies, 1971.

Metzner, R. *Kaiaphas, der Hohepriester jenes Jahres: Geschichte und Deutung*. AJEC 75. Leiden: Brill, 2010.

Meyer, B. F. *The Aims of Jesus*. London: SCM, 1979.

Meyers, E. M., ed. *Galilee through the Centuries: Confluence of Cultures*. Duke Judaic Studies 1. Winona Lake, IN: Eisenbrauns, 1999.

———. "The Jesus Tomb Controversy: An Overview." *NEA* 69 (2006): 116–18.

———. *Jewish Ossuaries: Reburial and Rebirth*. BibOr 24. Rome: Pontifical Biblical Institute, 1971.

———, ed. *The Oxford Encyclopedia of Archaeology in the Near East*. 5 vols. New York: Oxford University Press, 1997.

Meyers, E. M., and C. Meyers, eds. *Archaeology, Bible, Politics, and the Media: Proceedings of the Duke University Conference, April 23–24, 2009*. Winona Lake, IN: Eisenbrauns, 2012.

Meyers, E. M., and J. F. Strange. *Archaeology, the Rabbis and Early Christianity*. London: SCM, 1981.

Meyers, E. M., and M. A. Chancey, eds. *Alexander to Constantine: Archaeology of the Land of the Bible*. Vol. 3. New Haven: Yale University Press, 2012.

Mildenberg, L. *The Coinage of the Bar Kokhba War*. Typos: Monographien zur antiken Numismatik 6; Frankfurt am Main: Sauerländer, 1984.

Milik, J. T. "Le couvercle de Bethpagé." Pages 75–96 in *Hommages à André Dupont-Sommer*. Paris: Adrien-Maisonneuve, 1971.

———. "Trois tombeaux juifs récemment découverts au Sud-Est de Jérusalem." *LASBF* 7 (1956–57): 232–39.

Millard, A. R. "An Assessment of the Evidence for Writing in Ancient Israel." Pages 301–12 in *Biblical Archaeology Today*. Edited by A. Biran. Jerusalem: Israel Exploration Society, 1985.

———. "*'BGD*—Magic Spell or Educational Exercise?" *ErIsr* 18 (1985): 39–42.

———. *Reading and Writing in the Time of Jesus*. BibSem 69. Sheffield: Sheffield Academic, 2000.

Milnor, K. *Graffiti and the Literary Landscape in Roman Pompeii*. Oxford: Oxford University Press, 2014.

Mitchell, M. M. "Does the 'James Ossuary' Bring Us Closer to Jesus?" *RSN: SBL Edition* 4, no. 2 (2003): 9–10.

Mommsen, T., ed. *Iustiniani Digesta*. Corpus Iuris Civilis: Editio stereotypa quinta, vol. 1. Berlin: Weidmann, 1889.

Montgomery, J. A. *Aramaic Incantation Texts from Nippur*. Philadelphia: University Museum of the University of Pennsylvania, 1913.

Moore, C. A. *Tobit*. AB 40A. New York: Doubleday, 1996.

Müller-Kessler, C. "The Use of Biblical Quotations in Jewish Aramaic Incantation Bowls." Pages 227–45 in *Studies on Magic and Divination in the Biblical World*. Edited by H. R. Jacobus et al. Biblical Intersections 11. Piscataway, NJ: Gorgias, 2013.

Murphy-O'Connor, J. *The Holy Land: An Oxford Archaeological Guide from Earliest Times to 1700*. 5th ed. Oxford and New York: Oxford University Press, 2008.

———. "Where Was James Buried?" *BRev* 19, no. 3 (2003): 34–42.

Nagar, Y., and H. Torgeë. "Biological Characteristics of Jewish Burial in the Hellenistic and Early Roman Periods." *IEJ* 53 (2003): 164–71.

Naveh, J. "The Ossuary Inscriptions from Giv'at ha-Mivtar, Jerusalem." *IEJ* 20 (1970): 33–37.

Naveh, J., and S. Shaked. *Amulets and Magic Bowls: Aramaic Incantations of Late Antiquity*. 3rd ed. Jerusalem: Magnes, 1998.

———. *Magic Spells and Formulae: Aramaic Incantations of Late Antiquity.* Jerusalem: Magnes, 1993.

Nelson, R. D. *Deuteronomy: A Commentary.* OTL. Louisville: Westminster John Knox, 2002.

Netzer, E. *The Architecture of Herod, the Great Builder.* TSAJ 117. Tübingen: Mohr Siebeck, 2006.

———. "Did the Magdala Springhouse Serve as a Synagogue?" Pages 165–72 in *Synagogues in Antiquity.* Edited by A. Kasher, A. Oppenheimer, and U. Rappaport. Jerusalem: Yad Izhak Ben Zvi, 1987 (Hebrew).

———. "A Synagogue from the Hasmonean Period Recently Exposed in the Western Plain of Jericho." *IEJ* 49 (1999): 203–21.

Nickelsburg, G. W. E. *Resurrection, Immortality and Eternal Life in Intertestamental Judaism.* HTS 26. Cambridge: Harvard University Press, 1972.

Nolland, J. *The Gospel of Matthew.* NIGTC. Grand Rapids: Eerdmans, 2005.

Notley, R. S. "Et-Tell Is Not Bethsaida." *NEA* 70 (2007): 220–30.

———. "Reply to Arav," *NEA* 74 (2011): 101–3.

Nun, M. "Ports of Galilee: Modern Drought Reveals Harbors from Jesus' Time." *BAR* 25, no. 4 (1999): 19–31, 64.

O'Brien, K. S. "The Curse of the Law (Galatians 3.13): Crucifixion, Persecution, and Deuteronomy 21.22–23." *JSNT* 29 (2006): 55–76.

Oestreicher, B. "A New Interpretation of Dates on the Coins of the Procurators." *IEJ* 9 (1959): 193–95.

Ogden, D. *Magic, Witchcraft, and Ghosts in the Greek and Roman Worlds: A Sourcebook.* 2nd ed. Oxford: Oxford University Press, 2009.

Oster, R. E., Jr., "Supposed Anachronism in Luke–Acts' Use of ΣΥΝΑΓΩΓΗ: A Rejoinder to H. C. Kee." *NTS* 39 (1993): 178–208.

Overbeck, J. A. *Pompeji in seinen Gebäuden, Alterthümern und Kunstwerken. Für Kunst- und Alterthumsfreunde.* 3rd ed. Leipzig: Engelmann, 1875.

Pausanias. *Description of Greece.* Vol. 3, *Books 6–8.21.* Translated by W. H. S. Jones. LCL 272. Cambridge: Harvard University Press, 1988.

Parker Pearson, M. *The Archaeology of Death and Burial.* Texas A&M University Anthropology 3. College Station, TX: Texas A&M University Press, 2000.

Parrot, A. *Golgotha and the Church of the Holy Sepulchre.* SBA 6. London: SCM, 1957

Peachey, C. "Model Building in Nautical Archaeology: The Kinneret Boat." *BA* 53 (1990): 46–53

Peterson, D. G. *The Acts of the Apostles.* PNTC. Grand Rapids: Eerdmans, 2009.

Pfann, S. "Demythologizing the Talpiot Tomb: The Tomb of Another Jesus, Mary, and Joseph." Pages 165–205 in *The Tomb of Jesus and His Family? Exploring Ancient Jewish Tombs Near Jerusalem's Walls.* Edited by J. H. Charlesworth. Grand Rapids: Eerdmans, 2013.

Phillips, A. *Deuteronomy.* CBC. Cambridge: Cambridge University Press, 1973.

Philo. Translated by F. H. Colson et al. 12 vols. LCL. Cambridge: Harvard University Press, 1929–53.

Pietersma, A. *The Psalms: A New English Translation of the Septuagint.* Oxford: Oxford University Press, 2000.

Pixner, B. *Paths of the Messiah and Sites of the Early Church from Galilee to Jerusalem: Jesus and Jewish Christianity in Light of Archaeological Discoveries.* Edited by R. Riesner. San Francisco: Ignatius Press, 2010.

Pliny. *Natural History.* Translated by H. Rackham, W. H. S. Jones, et al. 10 vols. LCL. Cambridge: Harvard University Press, 1938–62.

Pliny the Younger. *Letters.* Vol. 1, *Books 1–7.* Translated by B. Radice. LCL 55. Cambridge: Harvard University Press, 1969.

Ploeg, J. P. M. van der. "Un petit rouleau de psaumes apocryphes (11QPsAp[a])." Pages 128–39 in *Tradition und Glaube: Das frühe Christentum in seiner Umwelt.* Edited by G. Jeremias, H.-W. Kuhn, and H. Stegemann. K. G. Kuhn Festschrift. Göttingen: Vandenhoeck & Ruprecht, 1971.

Pollini, J. "Ritualizing Death in Republican Rome: Memory, Religion, Class Struggle, and the Wax Ancestral Mask Tradition's Origin and Influence on Veristic Portraiture." Pages 237–85 in *Performing Death: Social Analyses of Funerary Traditions in the Ancient Near East and Mediterranean.* Edited by N. Laneri. OIS 3. Chicago: Oriental Institute of the University of Chicago, 2007.

Porten, B., and A. Yardeni. *Textbook of Aramaic Documents from Ancient Egypt.* Vol. 1, *Letters.* Winona Lake, IN: Eisenbrauns, 1986.

Porter, S. E. "Resurrection, the Greeks and the New Testament." Pages 52–81 in *Resurrection.* Edited by S. E. Porter, M. A. Hayes, and D. Tombs. JSNTSup 186. RILP 5. Sheffield: Sheffield Academic, 1999.

Preisendanz, K., ed. *Papyri Graecae Magicae: Die Griechischen Zauberpapyri.* 2 vols. Leipzig: Teubner, 1928–31.

Puech, E. "11QPsAp[a]: Un rituel d'exorcismes; Essai de reconstruction." *RevQ* 14 (1990): 377–408.

———. "À propos de l'ossuaire de Jacques le frère de Jésus." *Polish Journal of Biblical Research* 2, no. 1 (2002): 7–23.

———. "A-t-on redécouvert le tombeau du grand-prêtre Caïphe?" *MdB* 80 (1993): 42–47.

———. "Inscriptions funéraires palestiniennes: Tombeau de Jason et ossuaires." *RB* 90 (1983): 481–583.

———. *La croyance des Esséniens en la vie future: Immortalité, résurrection, vie éternelle? Histoire d'une croyance dans le judaïsme ancien.* 2 vols. EBib 21–22. Paris: Gabalda, 1993.

———. "Le tombeau de Siméon et Zacharie dans la vallée de Josaphat." *RB* 111 (2004): 563–77.

———. "Les deux derniers psaumes davidiques du rituel d'exorcisme, 11QPsAp[a] IV 4–V 14." Pages 64–89 in *The Dead Sea Scrolls: Forty Years of Research.* Edited by D. Dimant and U. Rappaport. STDJ 10. Leiden: Brill, 1992.

———. "Les psaumes davidiques du rituel d'exorcisme (11Q11)." Pages 160–81 in *Sapiential, Liturgical and Poetical Texts from Qumran.* Edited by D. K. Falk, F. García Martínez, and E. M. Schuller. STDJ 35. Leiden: Brill, 2000.

———. "Notes sur 11Q19 LXIV 6–13 et 4Q524 14,2–4: À propos de la crucifixion dans le Rouleau du Temple et dans le judaïsme ancien." *RevQ* 18 (1997): 109–24.

Puech, E., and J. Zias. "Le tombeau de Zacharie et Siméon au monument funéraire dit d'Absalom dans la Vallée de Josaphat." *RB* 110 (2003): 321–35.
Raban, A. "The Boat from Migdal Nunia and the Anchorages of the Sea of Galilee from the Time of Jesus." *International Journal of Nautical Archaeology and Underwater Exploration* 17 (1988): 311–29.
Raban, A., and E. Linder. "Caesarea, the Herodian Harbour." *International Journal of Nautical Archaeology and Underwater Exploration* 7 (1978): 238–43.
Rahmani, L. Y. *A Catalogue of Jewish Ossuaries in the Collections of the State of Israel.* Jerusalem: Israel Antiquities Authority, 1994.
———. "Jason's Tomb." *IEJ* 17 (1967): 61–100.
———. "A Note on Charon's *Obol*." *'Atiqot* 22 (1993): 149–50.
Rahmani, L. Y., and J. Naveh. "A Jewish Rock-Cut Tomb on Mt. Scopus." *'Atiqot* 14 (1980): 49–54.
Ramsay, W. M. *The Cities and Bishoprics of Phrygia.* 2 vols. Oxford: Clarendon, 1895–1897.
Rapuano, Y. "The Hasmonean Period 'Synagogue' at Jericho and the 'Council Chamber' Building at Qumran." *IEJ* 51 (2001): 48–56.
Reed, J. L. *Archaeology and the Galilean Jesus: A Re-examination of the Evidence.* Harrisburg, PA: Trinity Press International, 2000.
———. *The HarperCollins Visual Guide to the New Testament: What Archaeology Reveals about the First Christians.* San Francisco: HarperOne, 2007.
Regev, E. "Family Burial, Family Structure, and the Urbanization of Herodian Jerusalem." *PEQ* 136 (2004): 109–31.
Reich, R. "Caiaphas Name Inscribed on Bone Boxes." *BAR* 18, no. 5 (1992): 38–44, 76.
———. "Ossuary Inscriptions from the 'Caiaphas' Tomb." *'Atiqot* 21 (1992): 72–77.
———. "Ossuary Inscriptions from the Caiaphas Tomb." *Jerusalem Perspective* 4, nos. 4–5 (1991): 13–21.
Reich, R., and M. Zapata Meza. "A Preliminary Report on the *Miqwa'ot* of Migdal." *IEJ* 64 (2014): 63–71.
Richardson, P. *Building Jewish in the Roman East.* Waco, TX: Baylor University Press, 2004.
Riesner, R. "Das Boot vom See Gennesaret," *BK* 41 (1986): 135–38.
———. "Ein falsches Jesus Grab, Maria Magdalena und kein Ende." *ThBeitr* 38 (2007): 296–99.
———. *Jesus als Lehrer.* WUNT II/7. Tübingen: Mohr Siebeck, 1981.
———. "Synagogues in Jerusalem." Pages 179–211 in *The Book of Acts in Its Palestinian Setting.* Edited by R. Bauckham. Grand Rapids: Eerdmans, 1995.
Riley, G. J. "Demon." *DDD* 235–40.
Ritmeyer, L., and K. Ritmeyer. "Akeldama: Potter's Field or High Priest's Tomb?" *BAR* 20, no. 6 (1994): 22–35, 76, 78.
Robinson, D. M. *Excavations at Olynthus.* Part 11, *Necrolynthia, a Study in Greek Burial Customs and Anthropology.* Baltimore: Johns Hopkins Press, 1942.
———. "Inscriptions from the Cyrenaica." *AJA* 17 (1913): 166–67.
Roberts, P. *Life and Death in Pompeii and Herculaneum.* Oxford: Oxford University Press, 2013.

Robinson, J. A. T. "Did Jesus Have a Distinctive Use of Scripture?" Pages 35–43 in *Twelve More New Testament Studies*. London: SCM, 1984.

Rousseau, J. J. "The Impact of the Bethsaida Finds on Our Knowledge of the Historical Jesus." Pages 187–207 in *Society of Biblical Literature 1995 Seminar Papers*. Edited by E. H. Lovering Jr. SBLSP 34. Atlanta: Scholars Press, 1995.

Rousseau, J. J., and R. Arav. *Jesus and His World: An Archaeological and Cultural Dictionary*. Minneapolis: Fortress, 1995.

Roussel, P. "Nikanor d'Alexandrie et la porte du temple de Jérusalem." *REG* 37 (1924): 79–82.

Runesson, A. "Architecture, Conflict, and Identity Formation: Jews and Christians in Capernaum from the First to the Sixth Century." Pages 231–57 in *Religion, Ethnicity, and Identity in Ancient Galilee: A Region in Transition*. Edited by J. K. Zangenberg, H. W. Attridge, and D. B. Martin. WUNT 210; Tübingen: Mohr Siebeck, 2007.

Runesson, A., D. D. Binder, and B. Olsson. *The Ancient Synagogue from Its Origins to 200 C.E.: A Source Book*. Leiden: Brill, 2010.

Rupprecht, A. "The House of Annas-Caiaphas." *ABW* 1 (1991): 4–17.

Rutgers, L. V., ed. *What Athens Has to Do with Jerusalem: Essays on Classical, Jewish, and Early Christian Art and Archaeology in Honor of Gideon Foerster*. Interdisciplinary Studies in Ancient Culture and Religion 1. Leuven: Peeters, 2002.

Safrai, S. "Education and the Study of Torah." Pages 945–70 in vol. 2 of *The Jewish People in the First Century: Historical Geography, Political History, Social, Cultural and Religious Life and Institutions*. Edited by S. Safrai and M. Stern. CRINT 1.2. Philadelphia: Fortress, 1976.

Samuelsson, G. *Crucifixion in Antiquity*. 2nd ed.; WUNT II/310. Tübingen: Mohr Siebeck, 2013.

Sanders, E. P. *The Historical Figure of Jesus*. New York: Penguin, 1993.

———. *Jesus and Judaism*. London: SCM, 1985.

Sanders, J. A. "A Liturgy for Healing the Stricken." Pages 216–33 in *The Dead Sea Scrolls: Hebrew, Aramaic, and Greek Texts with English Translations*. Vol. 4A, *Pseudepigraphic and Non-Masoretic Psalms and Prayers*. Edited by J. H. Charlesworth. PTSDSSP 4A. Louisville: Westminster John Knox, 1997.

———. *The Psalms Scroll of Qumrân Cave 11*. DJD 4. Oxford: Clarendon, 1965.

Sandys, J. E. *Latin Epigraphy: An Introduction to the Study of Latin Inscriptions*. 2nd ed., revised by S. G. Campbell. Cambridge: Cambridge University Press, 1927.

Sanzo, J. E. *Scriptural* Incipits *on Amulets from Late Antique Egypt: Text, Typology, and Theory*. STAC 84. Tübingen: Mohr Siebeck, 2014.

Sauer, N. J. "The Timing of Injuries and Manner of Death: Distinguishing among Antemortem, Perimortem and Postmortem Trauma." Pages 321–32 in *Forensic Osteology: Advances in the Identification of Human Remains*. Edited by K. R. Richards. 2nd ed. Springfield, IL: Charles C. Thomas, 1998.

Savage, C. E. *Biblical Bethsaida: An Archaeological Study of the First Century*. Lanham, MD: Lexington Books, 2011.

———. "Supporting Evidence for a First-Century Bethsaida." Pages 193–206 in *Religion, Ethnicity, and Identity in Ancient Galilee: A Region in Transition*. Edited by J. Zangenberg, H. W. Attridge, and D. B. Martin. WUNT 210. Tübingen: Mohr Siebeck, 2007.

Schick, C. "Recent Discoveries at the 'Nicophorieh.'" PEFQS 24 (1892): 115–20.

Schiffman, L. H., and M. D. Swartz. *Hebrew and Aramaic Incantation Texts from the Cairo Genizah: Selected Texts from Taylor-Schechter Box K1*. Semitic Texts and Studies 1. Sheffield: Sheffield Academic, 1992.

Schmidt, T. E. "Mark 15.16–32: The Crucifixion Narrative and the Roman Triumphal Procession." *NTS* 41 (1995): 1–18.

Schürer, E. *The History of the Jewish People in the Age of Jesus Christ*. 3 vols. Revised by G. Vermes, F. Millar, and M. Black. Edinburgh: T&T Clark, 1973–87.

Schwabe, M., and B. Lifshitz. *Beth She'arim*. Vol. 2, *The Greek Inscriptions*. New Brunswick, NJ: Rutgers University Press, 1974.

Schwartz, D. R. *2 Maccabees*. CEJL. Berlin: de Gruyter, 2008.

———. "Josephus and Philo on Pontius Pilate." *Jerusalem Cathedra* 3 (1983): 26–45.

———. "Pontius Pilate." *ABD* 5:395–401.

Schwartz, J. "Once More on the Nicanor Gate." *HUCA* 62 (1991): 245–83.

Shanks, H. "Between Authenticity and Forgery." *RSN: SBL Edition* 4, no. 2 (2003): 6–8.

———. "Cracks in James Bone Box Repaired." *BAR* 29, no. 1 (2003): 20–25.

———. *James Brother of Jesus: The Forgery Trial of the Century*. Washington, DC: Biblical Archaeology Society, 2012.

———. *Jerusalem Forgery Conference: Biblical Archaeology Society Special Report*. Washington, DC: Biblical Archaeology Society, 2007.

———. *Jerusalem's Temple Mount: From Solomon to the Golden Dome*. New York: Continuum, 2007.

———, ed. *Where Christianity Was Born*. Washington, DC: Biblical Archaeology Society, 2008.

Shanks, H., and B. Witherington III. *The Brother of Jesus*. San Francisco: HarperCollins, 2003.

Sharon, M. *Corpus Inscriptionum Arabicarum Palaestinae*. 3 vols., HOS 30. Leiden: Brill, 1997–2013.

Sherwin-White, A. N. *Roman Society and Roman Law in the New Testament: The Sarum Lectures 1960–61*. Oxford: Oxford University Press, 1963.

———. *The Trial of Christ: Historicity and Chronology in the Gospels*. London: SPCK, 1965.

Shiner, W. T. "The Ambiguous Pronouncement of the Centurion and the Shrouding of Meaning in Mark." *JSNT* 78 (2000): 3–22.

Shore, P. *Rest Lightly: An Anthology of Latin and Greek Tomb Inscriptions*. Wauconda, IL: Bolchazy-Carducci, 1997.

Shroder, J. F., Jr., and M. Inbar. "Geological and Geographic Background to the Bethsaida Excavations." Pages 65–98 in vol. 1 of *Bethsaida: A City by the North Shore of the Sea of Galilee*. Edited by R. Arav and R. A. Freund. Kirksville, MO: Truman State University Press, 1995.

Shroder, J. F., Jr., M. P. Bishop, K. J. Cornwell, and M. Inbar. "Catastrophic Geomorphic Process and Bethsaida Archaeology, Israel." Pages 115–73 in vol. 2 of *Bethsaida: A City by the North Shore of the Sea of Galilee*. Edited by R. Arav and R. A. Freund. Kirksville, MO: Truman State University Press, 1995.

Siegelman, A., and Y. Neeman. "A Painted Tomb Near Caesarea." *'Atiqot* 21 (1992): 56–62.

Skehan, P. W., and A. A. Di Lella. *The Wisdom of Ben Sira*. AB 39. Garden City, NY: Doubleday, 1987.

Slotki, J. J. *Midrash Rabbah: Numbers*. New York: Soncino, 1983.

Smallwood, E. M. *The Jews under Roman Rule: From Pompey to Diocletian: A Study in Political Relations*. SJLA 20. Leiden: Brill, 1981.

Smith, M. D. "Capital Punishment and Burial in the Roman Empire." Pages 395–436 in *Bethsaida in Archaeology, History and Ancient Culture: A Festschrift in Honor of John T. Greene*. Edited by J. H. Ellens. Newcastle upon Tyne: Cambridge Scholars, 2014.

Smith, P. "The Human Skeletal Remains from the Abba Cave." *IEJ* 27 (1977): 121–24.

Smith, R. H. "The Cross Marks on Jewish Ossuaries." *PEQ* 106 (1974): 53–66.

Snodgrass, K. R. *Stories with Intent: A Comprehensive Guide to the Parables of Jesus*. Grand Rapids: Eerdmans, 2007.

Snyder, G. F. *Ante Pacem: Archaeological Evidence of Church Life before Constantine*. Macon, GA: Mercer University Press, 1985.

Solin, H., and M. Itkonen-Kaila. *Graffiti del Palatino*. Acta Instituti Romani Finlandiae 3. Helsinki: Helsingfors, 1966.

Staedler, E. "Das 'Spottkruzifix' vom Palatin: Ein Votivbild?" *Theologische Quartalschrift* 117 (1936): 253–60.

Stec, D. M. *The Targum of Psalms: Translated, with a Critical Introduction, Apparatus, and Notes*. ArBib 16. Collegeville, MN: Liturgical Press, 2004.

Steffy, J. R. "The Kyrenia Ship: An Interim Report on Its Hull Construction." *AJA* 38 (1985): 71–101.

Stern, E., ed. *The New Encyclopedia of Archaeological Excavations in the Holy Land*. 4 vols. New York: Simon & Schuster, 1993.

———, ed. *The New Encyclopedia of Archaeological Excavations in the Holy Land*. Vol. 5, *Supplementary Volume*. New York: Simon & Schuster, 2008.

Stern, M. "Herod's Policies and Jewish Society at the End of the Second Temple Period." *Tarbiz* 35 (1966): 235–53 (Hebrew).

Steudel, A. "The Houses of Prostration CD XI, 21–XII, 1—Duplicates of the Temple." *RevQ* 16 (1993): 49–68.

Stone, M. E., ed. *Rock Inscriptions and Graffiti Project*. 3 vols. SBLRBS 28, 29, 31. Atlanta: Scholars Press, 1992–94.

Strange, J. F. "The Art and Archaeology of Ancient Judaism." Pages 64–114 in *Judaism in Late Antiquity*. Part 1, *The Literary and Archaeological Sources*. Edited by J. Neusner. HOS 16. Leiden: Brill, 1995.

———. "Beth-Saida." *ABD* 1:692–93.

———. "The Capernaum and Herodium Publications, Part 2." *BASOR* 233 (1979): 68–69.

———. "Magdala." *ABD* 4:463–64.

Strange, J. F., and H. Shanks. "Has the House Where Jesus Stayed in Capernaum Been Found?" *BAR* 8, no. 6 (1982): 26–37.

———. "Synagogue Where Jesus Preached Found at Capernaum." *BAR* 9, no. 6 (1983): 24–31.

Strubbe, J. H. M. "Curses against Violation of the Grave in Jewish Epitaphs from Asia Minor." Pages 70–128 in *Studies in Early Jewish Epigraphy.* Edited by J. W. van Henten and P. W. van der Horst. AGJU 21. Leiden: Brill, 1994.

Stutchbury, H. E. "Excavations in the Kidron Valley." *PEQ* 93 (1961): 101–13.

Suetonius. *Lives of the Caesars.* Translated by J. C. Rolfe. Vol. 1. Revised edition. LCL 31. Cambridge: Harvard University Press, 1998.

Sukenik, E. L. *Ancient Synagogues in Palestine and Greece.* The Schweich Lectures on Biblical Archaeology, 1930. London: British Academy, 1934.

———. "The Earliest Records of Christianity." *AJA* 51 (1947): 351–65.

———. "A Jewish Tomb Cave on the Slope of Mount Scopus." *Qovetz* 3 (1934): 62–73 (Hebrew).

———. *Jüdische Gräber Jerusalems um Christi Geburt.* Jerusalem: Azriel, 1931.

Tabor, J. D. *The Jesus Dynasty.* New York: Simon & Schuster, 2006.

Tabor, J. D., and S. Jacobovici. *The Jesus Discovery: The New Archaeological Find That Reveals the Birth of Christianity.* New York: Simon & Schuster, 2012.

Tal, D., M. Haramatic, and S. Gibson. *Flights into Biblical Archaeology.* 3rd ed. Jerusalem: Israel Antiquities Authority, 2007.

Tate, M. E. *Psalms 51–100.* WBC 20. Dallas: Word, 1990.

Taylor, J. E. "Missing Magdala and the Name of Mary 'Magdalene.'" *PEQ* 146 (2014): 205–23.

Taylor, V. *The Gospel According to St. Mark.* London: Macmillan, 1952.

Tomei, M. A. *Museo Palatino.* Rome: Electa, 1997.

Townsend, J. T. "Ancient Education in the Time of the Early Roman Empire." Pages 139–63 in *The Catacombs and the Colosseum.* Edited by S. Benko and J. J. O'Rourke. Valley Forge: Judson Press, 1971.

———. "Education (Greco-Roman)." *ABD* 2:312–17.

Toynbee, J. M. C. *Death and Burial in the Roman World.* Ithaca, NY: Cornell University Press, 1971.

Tzaferis, V. "The 'Abba' Burial Cave in Jerusalem." *'Atiqot* 7 (1974): 61–64 (Hebrew).

———. "Crucifixion: The Archaeological Evidence." *BAR* 11, no. 1 (1985): 44–53.

——— "Jewish Tombs at and near Giv'at ha-Mivtar." *IEJ* 20 (1970): 18–32.

Tzaferis, V., et al. *Excavations at Capernaum 1, 1978–1982.* Winona Lake, IN: Eisenbrauns, 1989.

Ussishkin, D. *The Village of Silwan: The Necropolis from the Period of the Judean Kingdom.* Jerusalem: Israel Exploration Society, 1993.

Van Voorst, R. E. *Jesus Outside the New Testament: An Introduction to the Ancient Evidence.* Studying the Historical Jesus. Grand Rapids: Eerdmans, 2000.

VanderKam, J. C. "Authoritative Literature in the Dead Sea Scrolls." *DSD* 5 (1998): 382–402.

———. "Questions of Canon Viewed through the Dead Sea Scrolls." Pages 91–109 in *The Canon Debate*. Edited by L. M. McDonald and J. A. Sanders. Peabody, MA: Hendrickson, 2002.

Vann, L. "Herod's Harbor Construction Recovered Underwater." *BAR* 9, no. 3 (1983): 10–14.

Vincent, L.-H., and P. M.-A. Steve. *Jérusalem de l'Ancien Testament: Recherches d'archéologie et d'histoire*. Paris: Gabalda, 1954.

Wachsmann, S. "The Date of the Boat." Pages 129–30 in *The Excavations of an Ancient Boat in the Sea of Galilee (Lake Kinneret)*. Edited by S. Wachsmann, J. R. Steffy, et al. *'Atiqot* 19. Jerusalem: Israel Antiquities Authority, 1990.

———. "The Excavation of the Kinneret Boat," *BAIAS* 6 (1986–87): 50–52.

———. "The Galilee Boat: 2,000-Year-Old Hull Recovered Intact." *BAR* 14, no. 5 (1988): 18–23.

———. *The Sea of Galilee Boat: A 2000 Year Old Discovery from the Sea of Legends*. Cambridge, MA: Perseus, 2000.

Wachsmann, S., and K. Raveh. "The Discovery." Pages 1–7 in *The Excavations of an Ancient Boat in the Sea of Galilee (Lake Kinneret)*. Edited by S. Wachsmann, J. R. Steffy, et al. *'Atiqot* 19; Jerusalem: Israel Antiquities Authority, 1990.

Wacks, M. *The Handbook of Biblical Numismatics from Abraham to the Crusaders*. Houston: Israel Numismatic Service, 1976.

Wallace, R. *An Introduction to Wall Inscriptions from Pompeii and Herculaneum*. Wauconda, IL: Bolchazy-Carducci, 2005.

Warner, D. A., and D. D. Binder, eds. *A City Set on a Hill: Essays in Honor of James F. Strange*. Fayetteville, AR: BorderStone Press, 2015.

Watt, R. J. "Evidence for Decapitation." Pages 342–44 in *The Roman Cemetery at Lankhills*. Edited by G. Clarke. Winchester Studies 3: Pre-Roman and Roman Winchester. Oxford: Clarendon, 1979.

Weber, E. "Zur Inschrift des Pontius Pilatus." *Bonner Jahrbücher* 171 (1971): 194–200.

Wenning, R. "Das Grab Herodes des Großen. Israel–Herodium." *WUB* 45 (2007): 68–69.

———. "Israel, Magdala: Die wirkliche Synagoge? Und die älteste?" *WUB* 55 (2010): 65.

Wilburn, A. T. *Materia Magica: The Archaeology of Magic in Roman Egypt, Cyprus, and Spain*. New Texts from Ancient Cultures. Ann Arbor: University of Michigan Press, 2012.

Wilpert, G. "La croce nei monumenti delle catacombe." *Nuovo Bullettino di Archeologia Cristiana* 8 (1902): 5–14.

Wilson, M. R. "Bones and Objects of Bone." *DDL* 1:199–207.

Wischmeyer, W. "Christogramm und Staurogramm in den lateinischen Inschriften altkirchlicher Zeit." Pages 539–50 in *Theologia Crucis–Signum Crucis: Festschrift für Erich Dinkler zum 70. Geburtstag*. Edited by C. Andresen and G. Klein. Tübingen: Mohr Siebeck, 1979.

Wise, M., M. Abegg, and E. Cook. *The Dead Sea Scrolls: A New Translation*. San Francisco: HarperSanFrancisco, 1996.

Wright, G. E. "New Information Regarding the Supposed 'Christian' Ossuaries." *BA* 9 (1946): 43.

Wright, N. T. "Jesus' Resurrection and Christian Origins." *Greg* 83 (2002): 615–35.

Wyssmann, P. "Israel, Horvat Kur: Ein Münzdeposit aus einer spätantiken Synagoge in Galiläa." *WUB* 68 (2013): 60–61.

Yadin, Y. "Epigraphy and Crucifixion." *IEJ* 23 (1973): 18–22.

———. "Pesher Nahum (4QpNahum) Reconsidered." *IEJ* 21 (1971): 1–12.

———. *Masada: Herod's Fortress and the Zealots' Last Stand.* New York: Random House, 1966.

———. "Synagogue at Masada." Pages 19–23 in *Ancient Synagogues Revealed.* Edited by L. I. Levine. Jerusalem: Israel Exploration Society, 1981.

———. *The Temple Scroll.* 3 vols. Jerusalem: Israel Exploration Society, 1977–1983.

Yadin, Y., J. Naveh, and Y. Meshorer. *Masada I: The Yigael Yadin Excavations 1963–1965, Final Reports; The Aramaic and Hebrew Ostraca and Jar Inscriptions / The Coins of Masada.* Jerusalem: Israel Exploration Society, 1989.

Yamauchi, E. M. "Aramaic Magic Bowls." *JAOS* 85 (1965): 511–23.

———. *Mandaic Incantation Texts.* AOS 49. New Haven: American Oriental Society, 1967.

Yavor, Z. "The Synagogue and Miqveh Complex." Pages 40–61 in *Gamla II: The Architecture: The Shmarya Gutmann Excavations, 1976–1989.* Edited by D. Syon and Z. Yavor. IAA Reports 44. Jerusalem: Israel Antiquities Authority, 2010.

Zangenberg, J. K. "Archaeological News from the Galilee: Tiberias, Magdala and Rural Galilee." *Early Christianity* 1 (2010): 471–84.

———. "Bethsaida: Reassessing the Bethsaida Identification." *BAR* 26, no. 3 (2000): 10–12.

———. "Ein Dorf auf dem Hügel: Neue Entdeckungen des Kinneret Regional Project in der Synagoge von Horvat Kur." Pages 131–44 in *Bauern, Fischer und Propheten: Galiläer zur Zeit Jesu.* Edited by J. K. Zangenberg and J. Schröter. Darmstadt: von Zabern, 2012.

———. "Israel, Horvat Kur: Antike jüdische Synagoge weiter ausgegraben." *WUB* 67 (2013): 58–69.

———. "Israel, Horvat Kur: Erneut antike Synagoge am See Gennesaret entdeckt." *WUB* 58 (2010): 62–63.

———. "Magdala—Auferstehung aus Ruinen." Pages 182–83 in *Judäa und Jerusalem: Leben in römischer Zeit.* Edited by J. Schefzyk and W. Zwickel. Stuttgart: Katholisches Bibelwerk, 2010.

———. "Yeshua aus Talpiot und Jesus von Nazaret: Bemerkungen zum angeblichen Grab Jesu und seiner Familie." *WUB* 44 (2007): 2–7.

Zapata Meza, M. "Magdala Archaeological Project (2010–2012): Preliminary Report." *'Atiqot,* forthcoming.

Zias, J. "Anthropological Evidence of Interpersonal Violence in First-Century AD Jerusalem." *Current Anthropology* 24 (1983): 233–34.

———. "Human Skeletal Remains from the 'Caiaphas' Tomb. *'Atiqot* 21 (1992): 78–80.

———. "The Tomb of Absalom Reconsidered." *NEA* 68 (2005): 148–65.

Zias, J., and J. H. Charlesworth. "Crucifixion: Archaeology, Jesus, and the Dead Sea Scrolls." Pages 273–89 in *Jesus and the Dead Sea Scrolls.* Edited by J. H. Charlesworth. ABRL. New York: Doubleday, 1992.

Zias, J., and E. Sekeles. "The Crucified Man from Giv'at ha-Mivtar: A Reappraisal." *IEJ* 35 (1985): 22–27.

Zimmermann, F. *The Book of Tobit: An English Translation with Introduction and Commentary.* Dropsie College Edition: Jewish Apocryphal Literature. New York: Harper & Brothers, 1958.

Zissu, B., and Y. Goren. "The Ossuary of 'Miriam Daughter of Yeshua Son of Caiaphas, Priests [of] Ma'aziah from Beth 'Imri.'" *IEJ* 61 (2011): 74–95.

Zulueta, F. de. "Violation of Sepulture in Palestine at the Beginning of the Christian Era." *JRS* 22 (1932): 184–97.

Index of Modern Authors

Index of Ancient Sources

Old Testament

Genesis

Exodus

Leviticus

Numbers

Deuteronomy

Joshua

Judges

1 Samuel

2 Samuel

1 Kings

1 Chronicles

2 Chronicles

Nehemiah

Esther

New Testament

Apocrypha and Pseudepigrapha

Figure 1.1: Bethsaida. Excavated area near the highest point of Bethsaida. Archaeologists: Rami Arav and Richard Freund. Photo courtesy of Greg Monette. [*see* p. 13]

Figure 1.2: Stone Anchor from Bethsaida. Currently in storage at the Yigal Allon Centre in Ginosar. Courtesy of the Yigal Allon Centre and the Israel Antiquities Authority / Photo: Greg Monette. [*see* p. 16]

Figure 1.3: Magdala *miqwê*. One of three *miqwāʾôt* excavated at the site currently identified as "Magdala" (Migdal I). Archaeologists: Arfan Najar, Dina Avshalom-Gorni, and Marcela Zapata Meza. The sump pump is required to lower the level of the water, which continues to be fed by a spring. Photo courtesy of Greg Monette. [*see* p. 20]

Figure 1.4: Magdala Synagogue. Synagogue, with (replica of) decorated stone, exposed at the site currently identified as Magdala. [*see* p. 25]

Figure 2.1: Inscribed Ossuary, Simon, Builder of the Sanctuary, Giv^{c}at ha-Mivtar, 1st cent. CE. Inscriptions on this first-century ossuary from Giv^{c}at ha-Mivtar twice identify the deceased as "Simon, builder of the temple." On the face this is written in Hebrew; on the end it is written in Aramaic. The neatly executed inscriptions were written by the same hand. Photo © The Israel Museum, Jerusalem. [*see* p. 34]

Figure 2.2: Foundation of Capernaum Synagogue. The fourth-century limestone synagogue rests on an older basalt foundation that is neither square nor level. Many think this part of the foundation belonged to a first-century synagogue. Photo © Israelarchive Alexander Schick / www.bibelausstellung.de. [*see* p. 35]

Figure 2.3: Kinneret (Sea of Galilee) Boat. First-century BCE boat, housed and conserved in the Yigal Allon Centre in Ginosar. Courtesy of the Yigal Allon Centre and the Israel Antiquities Authority / Photo: Jerome Hall and Greg Monette. [*see* p. 37]

Figure 2.4: First-Century Nazareth House. A first-century BCE/CE house in Nazareth that early Byzantine Christians believed was inhabited by Jesus and his family. We thank the Sisters of Nazareth. [*see* p. 46]

Figure 3.1: Ossuary of Caiaphas, Jerusalem, 1st cent. CE (side). The inscription "Joseph bar Caiaphas" appears on the back and on the end (pictured) of this ornate limestone ossuary. Photo © The Israel Museum, Jerusalem. [*see* p. 53]

Figure 3.2: Ossuary of Caiaphas, Jerusalem, 1st cent. CE (front). Front view of the ossuary believed to have contained the remains of high priest Joseph bar Caiaphas. Courtesy of the Israel Museum, Jerusalem / Photo: Greg Monette. [*see* p. 53]

Figure 3.3: Pontius Pilate Inscription, Caesarea, 1st cent. CE. Dedicatory inscription in which Pontius Pilate, prefect of Judea, is mentioned; found at Caesarea in 1961. Photo © The Israel Museum, Jerusalem. [*see* p. 59]

Figure 4.1: Prohibition of Entry of Gentiles into the Temple. According to Philo and Josephus, several inscriptions were posted in the temple precincts warning Gentiles not to get too close to the holy sanctuary. This offers further evidence of the expectation of general literacy. A complete inscription with this warning is housed in Istanbul. The fragment pictured here is housed in the Israel Museum in Jerusalem. Photo © The Israel Museum, Jerusalem. [*see* p. 84]

Figure 4.2: A Literate Baker and His Wife. Fresco portrait of bakery shop owner Terentius Neo and his wife holding a bookroll, stylus, and waxed tablets. Originally uncovered in the atrium of a villa in Pompeii; displayed in the Museo Archaeologico Nazionale, Naples, Italy. Photo courtesy of www.HolyLandPhotos.org. [*see* p. 78]

Figure 5.1: Judean Wilderness—Wadi Qilt. In antiquity, the wilderness was viewed as a place haunted by evil spirits. [*see* p. 91]

Figure 6.1: Yehoḥanan ben Hagkol Ossuary, Jerusalem, 1st cent. CE. Ossuary of one Yehoḥanan (ca. 20 CE) found at Givʿat ha-Mivtar. Photo © The Israel Museum, Jerusalem. [*see* p. 121]

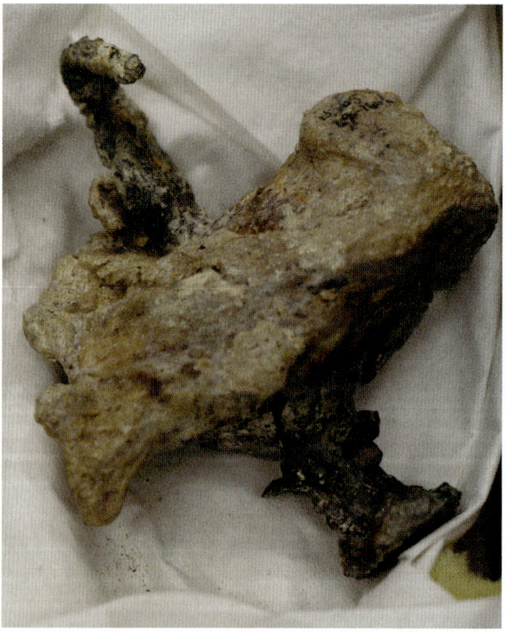

Figure 6.2: Right Heel of Yehoḥanan, the Crucified Man. When the skeletal remains were removed from the ossuary, Yehoḥanan's right heel was found still transfixed by an iron spike, demonstrating that he had been crucified. Photo courtesy of Greg Monette. [*see* p. 121]

Figure 7.1: Family Tomb in Turya, near Nazareth. One of the tombs in the village of Turya, close to Nazareth. Many of these burial niches still contain bones from antiquity. Some of the niches contain the skeletal remains of two or more members of a family. Photo courtesy of Greg Monette. [*see* p. 132]

Figure 7.2: Tomb at Dominus Flevit, Mount of Olives, Jerusalem. Partially reconstructed tomb at Dominus Flevit ("the Lord wept") on the Mount of Olives. Burial niches and several ossuaries are exhibited. Photo courtesy of Greg Monette. [*see* p. 132]

Figure 7.3: Shroud Tomb (Tomb of the Leper), Akeldama, Jerusalem. Entrance to a tomb at Akeldama that was found to contain a full-length skeleton wrapped in a burial shroud and sealed in a niche. The anoxic condition of the sealed niche prevented total decomposition of the tissue, thus allowing a portion of the scalp and hair to survive. A biopsy revealed that the man had died from the complications brought on by leprosy (Hansen's disease), which probably explains why his bones were not disarticulated and placed in an ossuary one year after death. [*see* p. 133]

Figure 7.4: Burial Niche in Shroud Tomb (Tomb of the Leper), Akeldama, Jerusalem. The burial niche in the Shroud Tomb, in which were found the remains of the man who died from Hansen's disease (leprosy). [*see* p. 133]

Figure 7.5: Nails Recovered from Mount Zion. Iron nails, used in construction but similar to nails used in crucifixion, have been recovered from the Mount Zion excavation. Archaeologist: Shimon Gibson. [*see* p. 139]

Figure 8.1: Second Temple Model. Model reconstruction of the Temple Mount (facing the Eastern Gate) and the city of Jerusalem ca. 66 CE, displayed at the Israel Museum. The center structure is the holy sanctuary. Photo © The Israel Museum, Jerusalem. [*see* p. 150]

Figure 8.2: Mount Zion Excavation. Staff and volunteer excavators enjoy a break at the Mount Zion archaeological excavation directed by Shimon Gibson. The upscale first-century home that is being excavated likely belonged to a wealthy family, perhaps priestly, who in all probability would have had misgivings about the message and activities of someone like Jesus of Nazareth. [*see* p. 160]

Figure 8.3: Ossuaries in a Burial Cave on the Mount of Olives. Several ossuaries and niches can be viewed at Dominus Flevit on the Mount of Olives. [*see* p. 173]

Figure 9.1: Talpiot Tomb. The entrance to the controversial tomb exposed in 1980 in East Talpiot, Jerusalem, and excavated by Joseph Gat, Amos Kloner, and Shimon Gibson. Photo courtesy of Amos Kloner. [*see* p. 181]

Figure 9.2: Ossuary with Architectural Decoration, Jerusalem, 1st cent. BCE (front). Ossuary (ca. first century BCE) found at Mt. Scopus, adorned on all four sides to resemble Herod's temple. Currently on display in the Israel Museum. Courtesy of the Israel Museum, Jerusalem / Photo: Greg Monette. [*see* p. 187]

Figure 9.3: Ossuary with Architectural Decoration, Jerusalem, 1st cent. BCE (side). The left side of the so-called "Temple Ossuary" closely resembles the architecture and design of the Talpiot Tomb. Seen side by side, the similarities of the entrance to the Talpiot Tomb and the Temple Ossuary are obvious. The inference that should be drawn is that the pointed gable and *patera* of the Talpiot Tomb are intended to resemble the Jerusalem temple. Photo © The Israel Museum, Jerusalem. [*see* p. 187]

Figure 9.4: The Author Seated on the Lid That Seals the Talpiot Tomb. The Talpiot Tomb is now sealed underground in close proximity to 273 Dov Gruner Street, Jerusalem. About fifty meters from where the author is seated is Talpiot Tomb II, or the "Patio Tomb." Photo courtesy of Jeff Baxter. [*see* p. 187]

Figure 10.1: Funerary Stele, Athens, 4th cent. BCE. Greek and Roman funerary stelae commonly depict the deceased seated, either shaking hands with surviving family members or holding their last will and testament. This fourth-century BCE funerary stele shows a woman bidding her family farewell. Photo © The Israel Museum, Jerusalem. [*see* p. 214]

Figure 10.2: Tomb of Rabbi Judah the Prince, Beth Sheʿarim. It is believed that this beautiful façade and entrance belong to the tomb of Rabbi Judah ha-Nasi ("the Prince"), who at the beginning of the third century CE supervised the compilation and publication of the work that became known as the Mishnah. Photo courtesy of Dwight Crowell. [*see* p. 222]

Figure 10.3: Niches in Beth Sheʿarim Tomb. Many burial niches in the Beth Sheʿarim tombs are designed as trenches. Many warnings are directed against those who would place another corpse atop one already in the grave. Photo courtesy of Dwight Crowell. [*see* p. 223]